CIMA

OPERATIONAL

PAPER P1

PERFORMANCE OPERATIONS

STUDY TEXT

Our text is designed to help you study **effectively** and **efficiently**.

In this edition we:

- **Highlight** the **most important elements** in the syllabus and the **key skills** you will need
- **Signpost** how each chapter links to the syllabus and the learning outcomes
- **Provide** lots of **exam alerts** explaining how what you're learning may be tested
- **Include examples** and **questions** to help you apply what you've learnt
- **Emphasise key points** in **section summaries**
- **Test your knowledge** of what you've studied in **quick quizzes**
- **Examine your understanding** in our **exam question bank**
- **Reference all the important topics** in the **full index**

FOR EXAMS IN NOVEMBER 2011 AND MAY 2012

LEARNING MEDIA

First edition 2009
Third edition June 2011

ISBN 9780 7517 9481 6
(Previous ISBN 9780 7517 8463 3)

e-ISBN 9780 7517 9605 6

British Library Cataloguing-in-Publication Data
A catalogue record for this book
is available from the British Library

Published by

BPP Learning Media Ltd
BPP House, Aldine Place
London W12 8AA

www.bpp.com/learningmedia

Printed in the United Kingdom

Your learning materials, published by BPP
Learning Media Ltd, are printed on paper sourced
from sustainable, managed forests.

We are grateful to the Chartered Institute of
Management Accountants for permission to
reproduce past examination questions. The
suggested solutions in the exam answer bank have
been prepared by BPP Learning Media Ltd.

Contents

How our Study Text can help you pass

Streamlined studying	• We show you the best ways to study efficiently
	• Our Text has been designed to ensure you can easily and quickly navigate through it
	• The different features in our Text emphasise important knowledge and techniques
Exam expertise	• **Studying P1** on page xiv introduces the key themes of the syllabus and summarises how to pass
	• We highlight throughout our Text how topics may be tested and what you'll have to do in the exam
	• We help you see the complete picture of the syllabus, so that you can answer questions that range across the whole syllabus
	• Our Text covers the syllabus content – no more, no less
Regular review	• We frequently summarise the key knowledge you need
	• We test what you've learnt by providing questions and quizzes throughout our Text

Our other products

BPP Learning Media also offers these products for the P1 exam:

Practice and Revision Kit	Providing lots more question practice and helpful guidance on how to pass the exam
Passcards	Summarising what you should know in visual, easy to remember, form
Success CDs	Covering the vital elements of the P1 syllabus in less than 90 minutes and also containing exam hints to help you fine tune your strategy
i-Pass	Providing computer-based testing in a variety of formats, ideal for self-assessment
Interactive Passcards	Allowing you to learn actively with a clear visual format summarising what you must know
Strategic case study kit	Providing question practice with specially written questions, based on the preseen issued by CIMA

You can purchase these products by visiting http://www.bpp.com/mybpp

CIMA Distance Learning

BPP's distance learning packages provide flexibility and convenience, allowing you to study effectively, at a pace that suits you, where and when you choose. There are four great distance learning packages available.

Online classroom	Bringing the classroom experience to you via the web and offering you great flexibility, with the quality for which BPP classroom courses are renowned
Basics Plus	Combining the paper-based and e-learning approaches of our Basics and Basics Online distance learning packages
Basics	Consisting of high quality BPP Learning Media study materials and access to BPP Professional Education subject experts
Basics Online	Including the best online learning and practice

You can find out more about these packages by visiting http://www.bpp.com/courses/examination-courses/accounting--finance/cima-2011/ways-to-study.aspx

Features in our Study Text

 Section Introductions explain how the section fits into the chapter

 Key Terms are the core vocabulary you need to learn

KEY TERM

 Key Points are points that you have to know, ideas or calculations that will be the foundations of your answers

KEY POINT

 Exam Alerts show you how subjects are likely to be tested

 Exam Skills are the key skills you will need to demonstrate in the exam, linked to question requirements

 Formulae To Learn are formulae you must remember in the exam

LEARN

 Exam Formulae are formulae you will be given in the exam

EXAM

 Examples show how theory is put into practice

 Questions give you the practice you need to test your understanding of what you've learnt

 Case Studies link what you've learnt with the real-world business environment

CASE STUDY

 Links show how the syllabus overlaps with other parts of the qualification, including Knowledge Brought Forward that you need to remember from previous exams

 Website References link to material that will enhance your understanding of what you're studying

 Further Reading will give you a wider perspective on the subjects you're covering

 Section Summaries allow you to review each section

BPP
LEARNING MEDIA

Streamlined studying

What you should do	In order to
Read the Chapter and Section Introductions	See why topics need to be studied and map your way through the chapter
Go quickly through the explanations	Gain the depth of knowledge and understanding that you'll need
Highlight the Key Points, Key Terms and Formulae To Learn	Make sure you know the basics that you can't do without in the exam
Focus on the Exam Skills and Exam Alerts	Know how you'll be tested and what you'll have to do
Work through the Examples and Case Studies	See how what you've learnt applies in practice
Prepare Answers to the Questions	See if you can apply what you've learnt in practice
Revisit the Section Summaries in the Chapter Roundup	Remind you of, and reinforce, what you've learnt
Answer the Quick Quiz	Find out if there are any gaps in your knowledge
Answer the Question(s) in the Exam Question Bank	Practise what you've learnt in depth

Should I take notes?

Brief notes may help you remember what you're learning. You should use the notes format that's most helpful to you (lists, diagrams, mindmaps).

Further help

BPP Learning Media's *Learning to Learn Accountancy* provides lots more helpful guidance on studying. It is designed to be used both at the outset of your CIMA studies and throughout the process of learning accountancy. It can help you **focus your studies on the subject and exam**, enabling you to **acquire knowledge, practise and revise efficiently and effectively**.

Syllabus and learning outcomes

Paper P1 Performance Operations

The syllabus comprises:

Topic and Study Weighting

A	Cost Accounting Systems	30%
B	Forecasting and Budgeting Techniques	10%
C	Project Appraisal	25%
D	Dealing with Uncertainty in Analysis	15%
E	Managing Short-Term Finance	20%

Learning Outcomes

Lead	Component	Syllabus content
A Cost accounting systems		
1 Discuss costing methods and their results	(a) compare and contrast marginal (or variable), throughput and absorption accounting methods in respect of profit reporting and stock valuation; (b) discuss a report which reconciles budget and actual profit using absorption and/or marginal costing principles; (c) discuss activity-based costing as compared with traditional marginal and absorption costing methods, including its relative advantages and disadvantages as a system of cost accounting; (d) apply standard costing methods, within costing systems, including the reconciliation of budgeted and actual profit margins; (e) explain why and how standards are set in manufacturing and in service industries with particular reference to the maximisation of efficiency and minimisation of waste; (f) interpret material, labour, variable overhead, fixed overhead and sales	(i) Marginal (or variable), throughput and absorption accounting systems of profit reporting and stock valuation. (ii) Activity-based costing as a system of profit reporting and stock valuation. (iii) Criticisms of standard costing in general and in advanced manufacturing environments in particular. (iv) Integration of standard costing with marginal cost accounting, absorption cost accounting and throughput accounting. (v) Manufacturing standards for material, labour, variable overhead and fixed overhead. (vi) Price/rate and usage/efficiency variances for materials, labour and variable overhead. (vii) Further subdivision of total usage/efficiency variances into mix and yield components. (Note: The calculation of mix variances on both individual and average valuation bases is required.) (viii) Fixed overhead expenditure and volume variances. (Note: the subdivision of fixed overhead volume variance into capacity and efficiency elements will not be examined.)

			variances, distinguishing between planning and operational variances;	(ix)	Planning and operational variances.
		(g)	prepare reports using a range of internal and external benchmarks and interpret the results;	(x)	Standards and variances in service industries (including the phenomenon of 'McDonaldization'), public services (e.g. Health), (including the use of 'diagnostic related' or 'reference' groups), and the professions (e.g. labour mix variances in audit work).
		(h)	explain the impact of just-in-time manufacturing methods on cost accounting and the use of 'back-flush accounting' when work in progress stock is minimal.	(xi)	Sales price and sales revenue/margin volume variances (calculation of the latter on a unit basis related to revenue, gross margin and contribution margin). Application of these variances to all sectors, including professional services and retail analysis.
				(xii)	Interpretation of variances: interrelationship, significance.
				(xiii)	Benchmarking.
				(xiv)	Back-flush accounting in just-in-time production environments. The benefits of just-in-time production, total quality management and theory of constraints and the possible impacts of these methods on cost accounting and performance measurement.
2	Explain the role of MRP and ERP systems	(a)	explain the role of MRP and ERP systems in supporting standard costing systems, calculating variances and facilitating the posting of ledger entries.	(i)	MRP and ERP systems for resource planning and the integration of accounting functions with other systems, such as purchase ordering and production planning.
3	Apply principles of environmental costing	(a)	apply principles of environmental costing in identifying relevant internalised costs and externalised environmental impacts of the organisation's activities.	(i)	Types of internalised costs relating to the environment (e.g. emissions permits, taxes, waste disposal costs) and key externalized environmental impacts, especially carbon, energy and water usage. Principles for associating such costs and impacts with activities and output.

B	Forecasting and budgeting techniques				
1	Explain the purposes of forecasts, plans and budgets.	(a)	explain why organisations prepare forecasts and plans;	(i)	The role of forecasts and plans in resource allocation, performance evaluation and control.
		(b)	explain the purposes of budgets, including planning, communication, co-ordination, motivation, authorisation, control and evaluation, and how these may conflict.	(ii)	The purposes of budgets and the budgeting process, and conflicts that can arise (e.g. between budgets for realistic planning and budgets based on 'hard to achieve' targets for motivation).
2	Prepare forecasts of financial results.	(a)	calculate projected product/service volumes employing appropriate forecasting techniques;	(i)	Time series analysis including moving totals and averages, treatment of seasonality, trend analysis using regression analysis and the application of these techniques in forecasting product and service volumes.
		(b)	calculate projected revenues and costs based on product/service volumes, pricing strategies and cost structures.	(ii)	Fixed, variable, semi-variable and activity based categorisations of cost and their application in projecting financial results.
3	Prepare budgets based on forecasts.	(a)	prepare a budget for any account in the master budget, based on projections/forecasts and managerial targets;	(i)	Mechanics of budget construction: limiting factors, component budgets and the master budget, and their interaction.
		(b)	apply alternative approaches to budgeting.	(ii)	Alternative approaches to budget creation, including incremental approaches, zero-based budgeting and activity-based budgets.
C	Project appraisal				
1	Prepare information to support project appraisal	(a)	explain the processes involved in making long-term decisions;	(i)	The process of investment decision making, including origination of proposals, creation of capital budgets, go/no go decisions on individual projects (where judgements on qualitative issues interact with financial analysis), and post audit of completed projects.
		(b)	apply the principles of relevant cash flow analysis to long-run projects that continue for several years;		
		(c)	calculate project cash flows, accounting for tax and inflation, and apply perpetuities to derive 'end of project' value where appropriate;	(ii)	Identification and calculation of relevant project cash flows taking account of inflation, tax, and 'final' project value where appropriate.
				(iii)	Activity-based costing to derive approximate 'long-run' costs appropriate for use in strategic decision making.

		(d)	apply activity-based costing techniques to derive approximate 'long-run' product or service costs appropriate for use in strategic decision making;	(iv)	Need for and method of discounting.
		(e)	explain the financial consequences of dealing with long-run projects, in particular the importance of accounting for the 'time value of money';	(v)	Sensitivity analysis to identify the input variables that most affect the chosen measure of project worth (payback, ARR, NPV or IRR).
				(vi)	Identifying and integrating non-financial factors in long-term decisions.
		(f)	apply sensitivity analysis to cash flow parameters to identify those to which net present value is particularly sensitive;	(vii)	Methods of dealing with particular problems: the use of annuities in comparing projects with unequal lives and the profitability index in capital rationing situations.
		(g)	prepare decision support information for management, integrating financial and non-financial considerations.		
2	Evaluate project proposals	(a)	evaluate project proposals using the techniques of investment appraisal;	(i)	The techniques of investment appraisal: payback, discounted payback, accounting rate of return, net present value and internal rate of return.
		(b)	compare and contrast the alternative techniques of investment appraisal;	(ii)	Application of the techniques of investment appraisal to project cash flows and evaluation of the strengths and weaknesses of the techniques.
		(c)	prioritise projects that are mutually exclusive, involve unequal lives and/or are subject to capital rationing.		

D	Dealing with uncertainty in analysis				
1	Analyse information to assess the impact on decisions of variables with uncertain values	(a)	analyse the impact of uncertainty and risk on decision models that may be based on relevant cash flows, learning curves, discounting techniques etc;	(i)	The nature of risk and uncertainty.
				(ii)	Sensitivity analysis in decision modeling and the use of computer software for "what if" analysis.
				(iii)	Assignment of probabilities to key variables in decision models.
		(b)	apply sensitivity analysis to both short and long-run decision models to identify variables that might have significant impacts on project outcomes;	(iv)	Analysis of probabilistic models and interpretation of distributions of project outcomes.
				(v)	Expected value tables and the value of information.
				(vi)	Decision trees for multi-stage decision problems.

(c) analyse risk and uncertainty by calculating expected values and standard deviations together with probability tables and histograms;

(d) prepare expected value tables;

(e) calculate the value of information;

(f) prepare and apply decision trees.

E   Managing short-term finance

| 1 | Analyse the working capital position and identify areas for improvement | (a) explain the importance of cash flow and working capital management;

(b) interpret working capital ratios for business sectors;

(c) analyse cash-flow forecasts over a twelve-month period;

(d) discuss measures to improve a cash forecast situation;

(e) analyse trade debtor and creditor information;

(f) analyse the impacts of alternative debtor and creditor policies;

(g) analyse the impacts of alternative policies for stock management | (i) The link between cash, profit and the balance sheet.

(ii) The credit cycle from receipt of customer order to cash receipt and the payment cycle from agreeing the order to making payment.

(iii) Working capital ratios (e.g. debtor days, stock days, creditor days, current ratio, quick ratio) and the working capital cycle.

(iv) Working capital characteristics of different businesses (e.g. supermarkets being heavily funded by creditors) and the importance of industry comparisons.

(v) Cash-flow forecasts, use of spreadsheets to assist in this in terms of changing variables (e.g. interest rates, inflation) and in consolidating forecasts.

(vi) Variables that are most easily changed, delayed or brought forward in a forecast.

(vii) Methods for evaluating payment terms and settlement discounts.

(viii) Preparation and interpretation of age analyses of debtors and creditors.

(ix) Establishing collection targets on an appropriate basis (e.g. motivational issues in managing credit control).

(x) Centralised versus decentralized purchasing. |

				(xi)	The relationship between purchasing and stock control.
				(xii)	Principles of the economic order quantity (EOQ) model and criticisms thereof.
2	Identify short-term funding and investment opportunities	(a)	identify sources of short-term funding;	(i)	Use and abuse of trade creditors as a source of finance.
		(b)	identify alternatives for investment of short-term cash surpluses;	(ii)	Types and features of short-term finance: trade creditors, overdrafts, short-term loans and debt factoring.
		(c)	identify appropriate methods of finance for trading internationally.	(iii)	The principles of investing short term (i.e. maturity, return, security, liquidity and diversification).
				(iv)	Types of investments (e.g. interest-bearing bank accounts, negotiable instruments including certificates of deposit, short-term treasury bills, and securities).
				(v)	The difference between the coupon on debt and the yield to maturity.
				(vi)	Export finance (e.g. documentary credits, bills of exchange, export factoring, forfeiting).

Old and new syllabuses

The syllabus for the P1 *Performance Operations* paper contains most of the topics from the old syllabus paper P1 *Performance Evaluation*, as well as some new ones.

The following topics have been added into the syllabus, with references to the chapter in which they are covered:

- Environmental costing (Chapter 12)
- Project appraisal (Chapters 15, 16, 17 and 18)
- Risk and uncertainty (Chapter 19)
- Working capital (Chapter 1)
- Short-term funding (Chapters 2, 3, 4 and 5)

If you (unfortunately) failed the old syllabus P1 *Performance Evaluation* paper and you are now sitting the new syllabus P1 paper, please note that the following topics have been removed from the new P1 syllabus:

- Behavioural aspects of budgeting and performance evaluation
- Process costing
- Responsibility accounting
- Transfer pricing

Studying P1

1 What's P1 about?

1.1 Current performance evaluation and future projections

P1 looks at how information is obtained, evaluated and used to control and predict business performance. For example, budgets are used along side cost accounting systems to **evaluate business performance**. Cash **projections** are used to **evaluate** individual projects and predict their performance. **Cash flow forecasts** are used to **control working capital**. All of these examples use estimated (and therefore uncertain) information and P1 looks at measuring the **risk** associated with this **uncertainty**.

There is assumed prior knowledge of Certificate level papers, particularly C1 *Fundamentals of Management Accounting* and C3 *Fundamentals of Business Maths*.

1.2 Managing short-term finance

This element of the syllabus concentrates on what's required for the business's **day-to-day operations** and short-term financing requirements including its working capital of inventory, receivables, payables and cash. P1 covers how working capital is measured and managed, how an organisation determines its **short-term financing requirements** and **where it can invest surplus cash**.

1.3 Cost accounting systems

There are **different ways** of carrying out costing. These include traditional management accounting techniques and new alternatives which may be more appropriate for the modern business environment. The various costing **methods impact** upon the business's **inventory valuation** and **profitability**.

1.4 Standard costing

A standard cost is the planned unit of cost of a product or service. Without this, producing a budget would be very difficult. **Standard costing and variance analysis** act as a **control mechanism** by establishing standards and highlighting activities that do not conform to plan.

1.5 Forecasting and budgeting

A budget is a plan of what the organisation is aiming to achieve and what it has set as a target. There are several different techniques used to produce a budget but they are all produced to **ensure** that **objectives are achieved**. It is important that results are measured regularly and compared to budget so that management can try to take **corrective action** if areas of the business are not performing well.

1.6 Project appraisal

You are expected to understand and apply techniques for **evaluating long-term proposals**. This includes identifying relevant cash flows, using investment appraisal techniques (including DCF and ARR) and factoring in inflation and taxation, ranking the projects and applying sensitivity analysis.

1.7 Dealing with uncertainty in analysis

This part of the syllabus looks at techniques for **measuring risk and evaluating uncertainty**. These techniques include expected values, sensitivity analysis and decision trees. You need to be familiar with the techniques and their application across a variety of decision making tools such as relevant cash flows, DCF and CVP analysis.

2 What's required

2.1 Explanation

As well as testing your knowledge and understanding, you are asked to demonstrate the skill of explaining key ideas, techniques or approaches. Explaining means providing simple definitions and covering the reasons **why** these approaches have been developed. You'll gain higher marks if your explanations are clearly focused on the question and you can supplement your explanations with examples. You could try using the PEA approach. Point, Explain, Apply. Make your point in a sentence. Explain that point in another sentence by answering the reader's 'so what?' or 'why?'. Then apply it to the scenario so that your point relates to the organisation or specific situation in the question.

2.2 Interpretation and recommendation

You will probably have to interpret the results of any calculations that you carry out. You must understand that interpretation isn't just saying figures have increased or decreased. It means explaining **why** figures have changed and also the consequences of the changes. You will also have to provide recommendations. For example, you may be given some details or working capital ratios and then asked to explain how **that particular business** could improve its day-to-day working capital management and what sources of short-term finance it will need.

2.3 What the examiner means

The table below has been prepared by CIMA to help you interpret the syllabus and learning outcomes and the meaning of exam questions.

You will see that there are 5 levels of Learning objective, ranging from Knowledge to Evaluation, reflecting the level of skill you will be expected to demonstrate. CIMA Certificate subjects were constrained to levels 1 to 3, but in CIMA's Professional qualification the entire hierarchy will be used.

At the start of each chapter in your study text is a topic list relating the coverage in the chapter to the level of skill you may be called on to demonstrate in the exam.

Learning objectives	Verbs used	Definition
1 Knowledge What are you expected to know	• List • State • Define	• Make a list of • Express, fully or clearly, the details of/facts of • Give the exact meaning of
2 Comprehension What you are expected to understand	• Describe • Distinguish • Explain • Identify • Illustrate	• Communicate the key features of • Highlight the differences between • Make clear or intelligible/state the meaning of • Recognise, establish or select after consideration • Use an example to describe or explain something

3 Application

How you are expected to apply your knowledge	• Apply	• Put to practical use
	• Calculate/ compute	• Ascertain or reckon mathematically
	• Demonstrate	• Prove with certainty or to exhibit by practical means
	• Prepare	• Make or get ready for use
	• Reconcile	• Make or prove consistent/compatible
	• Solve	• Find an answer to
	• Tabulate	• Arrange in a table

4 Analysis

How you are expected to analyse the detail of what you have learned	• Analyse	• Examine in detail the structure of
	• Categorise	• Place into a defined class or division
	• Compare and contrast	• Show the similarities and/or differences between
	• Construct	• Build up or compile
	• Discuss	• Examine in detail by argument
	• Interpret	• Translate into intelligible or familiar terms
	• Prioritise	• Place in order of priority or sequence for action
	• Produce	• Create or bring into existence

5 Evaluation

How you are expected to use your learning to evaluate, make decisions or recommendations	• Advise	• Counsel, inform or notify
	• Evaluate	• Appraise or assess the value of
	• Recommend	• Propose a course of action

3 How to pass

3.1 Study the whole syllabus

You need to be comfortable with **all areas of the syllabus**, as questions, particularly the objective testing questions in Section A, will often span a number of syllabus areas. Remember that all questions in paper P1 are compulsory.

3.2 Lots of question practice

You can **develop application skills** by attempting questions in the Exam Question Bank and later on questions in the BPP Practice and Revision Kit.

3.3 Exam technique

The following points of exam technique are particularly relevant to this paper.

- You should consider in advance how you are going to use the **20 minutes' reading time.** It gives you a great opportunity to read through the paper and consider your answers. You can use it to analyse the Section B question, or read carefully through the Section C questions.

- **Read the question carefully**. You must make sure that you answer the actual question set rather than what you would like the question to say! It is easy to write all that you know about a topic but you must remember to stick to the actual requirement of the question.

- Make sure that you develop **time management skills**. You have 1.8 minutes per mark so Section A, for example, must be completed in 36 minutes. You should not go over on time on any question. If you have not finished the question, move on and come back to it if you have time at the end.

- Practise your writing skills. You need to be able to write short paragraphs which answer the question.

4 Brought forward knowledge

You may be tested on knowledge or techniques you've learnt at lower levels. CIMA C1 *Fundamentals of Management Accounting* and C3 *Fundamentals of Business Maths* are particularly important for this paper.

5 Links with other exams

Some of the topics in the P1 paper will be covered in more detail in later exams so it is important to keep your books and notes. For example, knowledge of budgeting, relevant costing, sensitivity analysis and modern philosophies such as JIT and TQM will all be needed for the P2 exam. Knowledge of project appraisal will be required for the F3 exam.

The exam paper

Format of the paper

		Number of marks
Section A:	A variety of multiple choice and other objective test questions, 2-4 marks each	20
Section B:	6 compulsory questions, 5 marks each	30
Section C:	2 questions, 25 marks each	50
		100

Time allowed: 3 hours, plus 20 minutes reading time

Numerical content

The paper is likely to have a mixture of numerical and written parts and the percentage of numerical questions is likely to vary with each exam sitting. You are probably unlikely to get a Section B or Section C question which is entirely numerical or entirely written. Section A questions will probably contain some multiple choice questions which refer to the meanings of terms. So, you cannot expect Section A to be entirely numerical either.

Breadth of question coverage

Questions may cover more than one syllabus area.

May 2011 exam paper

Section A

1   Eight objective test questions

Section B

2   (a)   Budgets as performance targets
     (b)   Perfect information
     (c)   Optimum replacement cycle
     (d)   Factoring
     (e)   Export finance
     (f)   Yield to maturity

Section C

3   Budgeting and variances

4   NPV, IRR, discounted payback, post completion audit

March 2011 resit exam paper

Section A

1   Eight objective test questions

Section B

2   (a)   Zero-based budgeting
      (b)   Perfect information
      (c)   Attitudes to risk
      (d)   Factoring
      (e)   Investments
      (f)   Coupon rate and yield to maturity

Section C

3   Activity-based costing

4   NPV, IRR and sensitivity analysis

November 2010 exam paper

Section A

1   Eight objective test questions

Section B

2   (a)   Zero-based budgeting
      (b)   Maximin, maximax and minimax regret criteria
      (c)   Attitudes to risk
      (d)   Expected receipts and bad debts
      (e)   Investments
      (f)   Working capital cycle length

Section C

3   Activity-based costing

4   Relevant cash flows, NPV and IRR calculation and comparison

September 2010 resit exam paper

Section A

1 Eight objective test questions

Section B

2 (a) Trade receivables
  (b) EOQ
  (c) Backflush accounting
  (d) ZBB
  (e) ABC, ABB
  (f) Decision tree

Section C

3 Operating statement, planning and operational variances

4 NPV, IRR

May 2010 exam paper

Section A

1 Eight objective test questions

Section B

2 (a) Preparation of age analysis of trade receivables
  (b) EOQ and cost of holding and ordering inventory
  (c) Manufacturing resource planning
  (d) Benefits of an activity based budgeting system
  (e) Production budget preparation
  (f) Decision tree preparation

Section C

3 Operating statement, variances and standard costing

4 NPV calculation, interpretation of expected value, IRR and standard deviation

Specimen exam paper

Section A

1   Seven objective test questions

Section B

2   (a)   Debtor days and debt factoring
     (b)   Non-financial factors of debt factoring
     (c)   Decision trees
     (d)   Regression analysis and forecasting
     (e)   Budgets – motivation vs control
     (f)   Environmental failure costs

Section C

3   NPV and ARR
4   Variance analysis

MANAGING SHORT-TERM FINANCE

Part A

WORKING CAPITAL AND THE OPERATING CYCLE

In this chapter we consider functions of the financial manager relating to the **management of working capital** in general terms, including how much working capital the business requires and the impact on working capital of changes in the business.

topic list	learning outcomes	syllabus references	ability required
1 Working capital	E1(a)	E1(ii)	comprehension
2 Working capital ratios	E1(b), (e)	E1(iii)	analysis
3 Working capital requirements	E1(a)	E1(ii)	comprehension

1 Working capital

1.1 What is working capital?

Introduction

Every business needs adequate **liquid resources** to maintain **day-to-day cash flow**. It needs enough to pay wages and salaries as they fall due and enough to pay suppliers if it is to keep its workforce and ensure its supplies. Maintaining adequate working capital is not just important in the short term. Sufficient liquidity must be maintained in order to ensure the **survival** of the business in the **long term** as well. Even a profitable company may fail if it does not have adequate cash flow to meet its liabilities as they fall due.

KEY TERM

WORKING CAPITAL is the capital available for conducting the day-to-day operations of an organisation; normally the excess of current assets over current liabilities.   *(CIMA Official Terminology)*

1.2 Working capital characteristics of different businesses

Different businesses will have different working capital characteristics. There are three main aspects to these differences.

(a)   Holding inventories (from their purchase from external suppliers, through the production and warehousing of finished goods, up to the time of sale)

(b)   Taking time to pay suppliers and other payables

(c)   Allowing customers (receivables) time to pay

The current assets of a business can be subdivided into **permanent current assets** (the core levels of inventory and receivables) and **fluctuating current assets**, which vary from period to period.

1.3 Examples

(a)   Supermarkets and other retailers receive much of their sales in cash or by credit card or debit card. However, they typically buy from suppliers on credit. They may therefore have the advantage of significant cash holdings, which they may choose to invest.

(b)   A company which supplies to other companies, such as a wholesaler, is likely to be selling and buying mainly on **credit**. Co-ordinating the flow of cash may be quite a problem. Such a company may make use of short-term borrowings (such as an overdraft) to manage its cash.

(c)   Smaller companies with a limited trading record may face particularly severe problems. Lacking a long track record, such companies may find it difficult to obtain credit from suppliers. At the same time, customers will expect to receive the length of credit period that is normal for the particular business concerned. The firm may find itself squeezed in its management of cash.

1.4 What is working capital management?

Ensuring that **sufficient liquid resources** are **maintained** is a matter of working capital management. This involves achieving a balance between the requirement to **minimise** the risk of **insolvency** and the requirement to **maximise** the **return** on assets. Efficient working capital management is vital if the organisation is to stay in business. Profitable businesses can go under very quickly if liquidity is not maintained. The business must decide what level of cash and inventories are to be maintained and how they are to be funded.

A business pursuing an **aggressive** working capital policy will hold **minimal cash** and inventories and use short-term financing to fund both permanent and fluctuating current assets. This policy carries the **highest risk** of insolvency and the highest level of financial return.

A business pursuing a **conservative** policy will hold **large levels** of ready **cash** and safety inventory and use long-term funding for both non-current and most current assets. This is the **least risky** option but results in the **lowest expected return**.

An excessively conservative approach to working capital management resulting in high levels of cash holdings will harm profits because the opportunity to make a return on the assets tied up as cash will have been missed.

A **moderate** policy will match short-term finance to fluctuating current assets and non-fluctuating current (and non-current) assets will be matched by long-term funding.

1.5 The working capital cycle 5/10, 11/10

Working capital cycle is the period of time which elapses between the point at which cash begins to be expended on the production of a product and the collection of cash from a purchaser.

(CIMA Official Terminology)

The connection between investment in working capital and cash flow may be illustrated by means of the **working capital cycle** (also called the **cash cycle, operating cycle** or **trading cycle**).

The working capital cycle in a manufacturing business equals:

The average time that raw materials remain in inventory	X
Less the period of credit taken from suppliers	(X)
Plus the time taken to produce the goods	X
Plus the time finished goods remain in inventory after production is completed	X
Plus the time taken by customers to pay for the goods	X
	X

If the turnover periods for inventories and receivables lengthen, or the payment period to payables shortens, then the operating cycle will lengthen and the investment in working capital will increase.

Example: working capital cycle

Wines Co buys raw materials from suppliers that allow Wines 2.5 months credit. The raw materials remain in inventory for 1 month, and it takes Wines 2 months to produce the goods. The goods are sold within a couple of days of production being completed and customers take on average 1.5 months to pay.

Required

Calculate Wines's working capital cycle.

Solution

We can ignore the time finished goods are in inventory as it is no more than a couple of days.

	Months
The average time that raw materials remain in inventory	1.0
Less: The time taken to pay suppliers	(2.5)
The time taken to produce the goods	2.0
The time taken by customers to pay for the goods	1.5
	2.0

The company's working capital cycle is 2 months. This can be illustrated diagrammatically as follows.

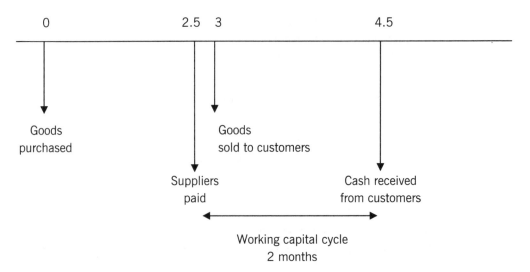

The working capital cycle is the period between the suppliers being paid and the cash being received from the customers.

1.6 Managing the cycle

A **longer** working capital cycle requires **more financial resource**, so management will seek whenever possible to **reduce** the length of the cycle. Their possible options are as follows.

(a) **Reduce** levels of **raw materials inventory**. This may be done by the introduction of some type of just-in-time system, which will necessitate more efficient links with suppliers. Production delays due to running out of inventory must be avoided.

(b) **Reduce work in progress** by reducing production volume or improving techniques and efficiency.

(c) **Reduce finished goods inventory**, perhaps by improving distribution. This may lead to delays in fulfilling customer orders.

(d) **Delay payments to suppliers**. This can lead to loss of discounts and of supplier goodwill.

(e) **Reduce** period of **credit given to customers**. This may mean offering discounts and more aggressive credit control may lead to loss of customers.

1.7 Cash flow planning

Since a company must have adequate cash inflows to survive, management should plan and control cash flows as well as profitability. **Cash budgeting** is an important element in short-term cash flow planning.

The purpose of cash budgets is to make sure that the organisation will have **enough cash inflows** to meet its cash outflows. If a budget reveals that a short-term cash shortage can be expected, steps will be taken to meet the problem and **avoid the cash crisis** (perhaps by arranging a bigger bank overdraft facility).

Cash budgets and cash flow forecasts on their own do not give full protection against a cash shortage and enforced liquidation of the business. There may be unexpected changes in cash flow patterns. When unforeseen events have an adverse effect on cash inflows, a company will only survive if it can maintain adequate cash inflows despite the setbacks.

Question 1.1	Cash flow patterns

Learning outcome E1(a)

Give examples of unforeseen changes which may affect cash flow patterns.

Section summary

The amount tied up in **working capital** is equal to the value of all inventory and receivables less payables. This amount directly affects the liquidity of the organisation.

Working capital cycle is the period of time which elapses between the point at which cash begins to be expended on the production of a product and the collection of cash from a purchaser.

(CIMA Official Terminology)

2 Working capital ratios

Introduction

Working capital ratios may help to indicate whether a company has too much working capital (over-capitalised) or too little (overtrading).

2.1 The current ratio and the quick ratio

The standard test of liquidity is the **current ratio**. It can be obtained from the statement of financial position.

KEY TERM

$$\text{CURRENT RATIO} = \frac{\text{Current assets}}{\text{Current liabilities}}$$

A company should have enough current assets that give a promise of 'cash to come' to **meet its commitments** to **pay its current liabilities**. Obviously, a ratio **in excess of 1** should be expected; an ideal is probably about 2. Otherwise, there would be the prospect that the company might be unable to pay its debts on time. In practice, a ratio comfortably in excess of 1 should be expected, but what is 'comfortable' varies between different types of businesses.

Some manufacturing companies might hold large quantities of raw material inventories, which must be used in production to create finished goods. Finished goods might be warehoused for a long time, or sold on lengthy credit. In such businesses, where **inventory turnover is slow**, most inventories are **not very easy** to **turn into liquid assets**, because the cash cycle is so long. For these reasons, we calculate an additional liquidity ratio, known as the **quick ratio** or acid test ratio.

KEY TERM

$$\text{QUICK RATIO, or ACID TEST RATIO} = \frac{\text{Current assets less inventories}}{\text{Current liabilities}}$$

This ratio should ideally be at least 1 for companies with a slow inventory turnover. For companies with a fast inventory turnover, a quick ratio can be less than 1 without suggesting that the company is in cash flow difficulties.

The current ratio and the quick ratio are known as liquidity ratios.

2.2 The receivables collection period

A rough measure of the average length of time it takes for a company's customers to pay is the '**receivable days**' ratio.

KEY TERM

$$\text{RECEIVABLE DAYS RATIO} = \frac{\text{Average trade receivables}}{\text{Average daily sales on credit terms}}$$

(CIMA Official Terminology)

An equivalent measure is the receivables turnover period.

KEY TERM

$$\text{RECEIVABLES TURNOVER PERIOD} = \frac{\text{Average trade receivables}}{\text{Credit sales for the year}} \times 365 \text{ days}$$

The trade receivables are not the **total** figure for receivables in the statement of financial position, which includes prepayments and non-trade receivables. The trade receivables figure will be itemised in an analysis of the total receivables, in a note to the accounts.

The estimate of receivables days is only approximate.

(a)   The statement of financial position value might be used instead of the average. However, don't forget that the statement of financial position value of receivables might be abnormally high or low compared with the 'normal' level the company usually has.

(b)   Sales revenue in the income statement excludes sales tax, but the receivables figure in the statement of financial position includes sales tax. We are not strictly comparing like with like. If the figures are too distorted by sales tax, adjustment will be needed.

(c)   Average receivables may not be representative of year-end sales if sales are growing rapidly.

2.3 The payables payment period

Similar measures can be used for payables.

The payables payment period indicates the average time taken, in calendar days, to pay for supplies received on credit.

KEY TERM

$$\text{PAYABLES DAYS RATIO} = \frac{\text{Average trade payables}}{\text{Average daily purchases on credit terms}} \qquad \textit{(CIMA Official Terminology)}$$

$$\text{PAYABLES PAYMENT PERIOD, or PAYABLES TURNOVER PERIOD} = \frac{\text{Average trade payables}}{\text{Purchases on credit terms for year}} \times 365 \text{ days}$$

If the credit purchases information is not readily available, cost of sales can be used instead. Don't forget however that some elements of cost of sales (for example, labour costs) are not relevant to trade payables. Note also that credit purchases in the income statement do not include sales tax.

Exam alert

The specimen exam paper contained a payables days calculation question in Section A. The question gave you the previous year's payables days and purchases and required you to work backwards to obtain a year end trade payables balance. You then had to use this balance in the current year's calculation.

2.4 The inventory turnover period

The inventory turnover period shows **how long goods are being kept** in inventory.

Another ratio worth calculating is the inventory turnover period. This is another estimated figure, obtainable from published accounts, which indicates the average number of days that items of inventory are held for. As with the average receivable collection period, it is only an approximate figure; there may be distortions caused by seasonal variations in inventory levels. However it should be reliable enough for finding changes over time.

KEY TERM

$$\text{INVENTORY TURNOVER} = \frac{\text{Inventory}}{\text{Average daily cost of sales in period}} \quad or \quad \frac{\text{Average inventory}}{\text{Cost of sales}}$$

The inventory turnover period can also be calculated:

$$\text{INVENTORY TURNOVER PERIOD} = \frac{\text{Inventory}}{\text{Cost of sales}} \times 365 \text{ days}$$

A lengthening inventory turnover period indicates:

(a)   A slowdown in trading, or

(b)   A build-up in inventory levels, perhaps suggesting that the investment in inventories is becoming excessive

Where a business is manufacturing goods for resale, inventory turnover will have three components:

Raw materials: $\dfrac{\text{average materials inventory}}{\text{purchases of raw materials}} \times 365$

WIP: $\dfrac{\text{average work in progress}}{\text{manufacturing cost}} \times 365$

Finished goods: $\dfrac{\text{average finished goods}}{\text{cost of sales}} \times 365$

Where average values are not available, closing values can be used.

Where no breakdown of inventories is supplied, just use the overall ratio: $\dfrac{\text{average inventory}}{\text{cost of sales}}$

If we add together the inventory days and the receivable days, this should give us an indication of how soon inventory is convertible into cash, thereby giving a further indication of the company's liquidity.

All the ratios calculated above will **vary industry by industry**; hence **comparisons** of ratios calculated with other similar companies in the same industry are important. There are organisations which specialise in **inter-firm comparison**. A company submits its figures to one of these organisations and receives an analysis of the average ratios for its industry. It can then compare its own performance to that of the industry as a whole.

The receivables turnover period, payables turnover period and inventory turnover period are known as **efficiency ratios**.

Exam skills

Remember that exam questions will probably ask you to discuss the results of any ratios that you calculate.

Another term you may come across is **capital employed**. This usually means non-current assets + current assets – current liabilities.

LEARNING MEDIA

Section summary

Working capital ratios may help to indicate whether a company has too much working capital (over-capitalised) or too little (overtrading).

$$\text{Receivable days ratio} = \frac{\text{Average trade receivables}}{\text{Average daily sales on credit terms}} \qquad \textit{(CIMA Official Terminology)}$$

$$\text{Receivables turnover period} = \frac{\text{Average trade receivables}}{\text{Credit sales for the year}} \times 365 \text{ days}$$

$$\text{Payables days ratio} = \frac{\text{Average trade payables}}{\text{Average daily purchases on credit terms}} \qquad \textit{(CIMA Official Terminology)}$$

$$\text{Payables payment period, or payables turnover period} = \frac{\text{Average trade payables}}{\substack{\text{Purchases on credit} \\ \text{terms for year}}} \times 365 \text{ days}$$

$$\text{Inventory turnover} = \frac{\text{Inventory}}{\text{Average daily cost of sales in period}} \quad \text{or} \quad \frac{\text{Average inventory}}{\text{Cost of sales}}$$

3   Working capital requirements

Introduction

Current assets may be financed either by long-term funds or by current liabilities.

Liquidity ratios are a **guide** to the risk of **cash flow problems** and insolvency. If a company suddenly finds that it is unable to renew its short-term liabilities (for example, if the bank suspends its overdraft facilities, or suppliers start to demand earlier payment), there will be a **danger of insolvency** unless the company is able to turn enough of its **current assets** into **cash quickly**.

3.1 The need for funds for investment in current assets

Current liabilities are often a **cheap method of finance** (trade payables do not usually carry an interest cost) and companies may therefore consider that, in the interest of higher profits, it is worth accepting some risk of insolvency by increasing current liabilities, taking the maximum credit possible from suppliers.

3.2 The volume of current assets required

The **volume of current assets** required will depend on the **nature** of the company's business. For example, a manufacturing company may require more inventories than a company in a service industry. As the **volume of output** by a company **increases**, the **volume of current assets** required will **also increase**.

Even assuming efficient inventory holding, receivable collection procedures and cash management, there is still a certain degree of choice in the total volume of current assets required to meet output requirements. Policies of low inventory-holding levels, tight credit and minimum cash holdings may be contrasted with policies of high inventories (to allow for safety or buffer inventories) easier credit and sizeable cash holdings (for precautionary reasons).

3.3 Over-capitalisation and working capital

If there are **excessive** inventories, receivables and cash, and very few payables, there will be an **over-investment** by the company in current assets. **Working capital** will be **excessive** and the company will be in this respect **over-capitalised**. The return on investment will be lower than it should be, and long-term funds will be unnecessarily tied up when they could be invested elsewhere to earn profits.

Over-capitalisation with respect to working capital should not exist if there is good management, but the warning signs of excessive working capital would be unfavourable accounting ratios, including the following.

(a)   **Sales/working capital**

The volume of sales as a multiple of the working capital investment should indicate whether, in comparison with previous years or with similar companies, the total volume of working capital is too high.

(b)   **Liquidity ratios**

A current ratio greatly in excess of 2:1 or a quick ratio much in excess of 1:1 may indicate over-investment in working capital.

(c)   **Turnover periods**

Excessive turnover periods for inventories and receivables, or a short period of credit taken from suppliers, might indicate that the volume of inventories or receivables is unnecessarily high, or the volume of payables too low.

Example: working capital ratios

Calculate liquidity and working capital ratios from the following accounts of a manufacturer of products for the construction industry, and comment on the ratios.

	20X8 $m	20X7 $m
Sales revenue	2,065.0	1,788.7
Cost of sales	1,478.6	1,304.0
Gross profit	586.4	484.7
Current assets		
Inventories	119.0	109.0
Receivables (note 1)	400.9	347.4
Short-term investments	4.2	18.8
Cash at bank and in hand	48.2	48.0
	572.3	523.2
Payables: amounts falling due within one year		
Loans and overdrafts	49.1	35.3
Income taxes	62.0	46.7
Dividend	19.2	14.3
Payables (note 2)	370.7	324.0
	501.0	420.3
Net current assets	71.3	102.9

Notes

		20X8 $m	20X7 $m
1	Trade receivables	329.8	285.4
2	Trade payables	236.2	210.8
3	We are not given a breakdown of inventories		

Solution

	20X8		20X7	
Current ratio	$\dfrac{572.3}{501.0}$ = 1.14		$\dfrac{523.2}{420.3}$ = 1.24	
Quick ratio	$\dfrac{453.3}{501.0}$ = 0.90		$\dfrac{414.2}{420.3}$ = 0.99	
Receivables' turnover period	$\dfrac{329.8}{2,065.0}$ × 365 = 58 days		$\dfrac{285.4}{1,788.7}$ × 365 = 58 days	
Inventory turnover period	$\dfrac{119.0}{1,478.6}$ × 365 = 29 days		$\dfrac{109.0}{1,304.0}$ × 365 = 31 days	
Payables turnover period	$\dfrac{236.2}{1,478.6}$ × 365 = 58 days		$\dfrac{210.8}{1,304.0}$ × 365 = 59 days	

The company is a manufacturing group serving the **construction industry**, and so would be expected to have a **comparatively lengthy receivables turnover period**, because of the relatively **poor cash flow** in the construction industry. It is clear that the company **compensates** for this by ensuring that they do **not pay** for raw **materials** and other costs before they have **sold** their **inventories** of finished goods (hence the similarity of receivables and payables turnover periods).

The company's **current ratio** is a little **lower** than **average** but its **quick ratio** is **better** than average and very little less than the current ratio. This suggests that **inventory** levels are **strictly controlled**, which is reinforced by the low inventory turnover period. It would seem that working capital is **tightly managed**, to avoid the poor liquidity which could be caused by a high receivables turnover period and comparatively high payables.

3.4 Overtrading   5/10

KEY TERM

OVERTRADING is the condition of a business which enters into commitments in excess of its available short-term resources. This can arise even if the company is trading profitably, and is typically caused by financing strains imposed by a lengthy operating cycle or production cycle.   *(CIMA Official Terminology)*

In contrast with over-capitalisation, **overtrading** happens when a business tries to do **too much too quickly** with **too little long-term capital**, so that it is trying to support too large a volume of trade with the capital resources at its disposal.

Even if an overtrading business operates at a **profit**, it could easily run into serious **trouble** because it is **short of money**. Such liquidity troubles stem from the fact that it does not have enough capital to provide the **cash** to pay its **debts** as they fall due.

Example: overtrading

Great Ambition appoints a new managing director who has great plans to expand the company. He wants to increase revenue by 100% within two years, and to do this he employs extra sales staff. He recognises that customers do not want to have to wait for deliveries, and so he decides that the company must build up its inventory levels. There is a substantial increase in the company's inventories. These are held in additional warehouse space which is now rented. The company also buys new cars for its extra sales representatives.

The managing director's policies are immediately successful in boosting sales, which double in just over one year. Inventory levels are now much higher, but the company takes longer credit from its suppliers, even though some suppliers have expressed their annoyance at the length of time they must wait for payment. Credit terms for receivables are unchanged, and so the volume of receivables, like the volume of sales, rises by 100%.

In spite of taking longer credit, the company still needs to increase its overdraft facilities with the bank, which are raised from a limit of $40,000 to one of $80,000. The company is profitable, and retains some profits in the business, but profit margins have fallen. **Gross profit margins** are lower because some prices have been reduced to obtain extra sales. **Net profit margins** are lower because overhead costs are higher. These include sales representatives' wages, car expenses and depreciation on cars, warehouse rent and additional losses from having to write off out-of-date and slow-moving inventory items.

The statement of financial position of the company changed over time from (A) to (B).

	Statement of financial position (A)		Statement of financial position (B)	
	$	$	$	$
Non-current assets		160,000		210,000
Current assets				
Inventory	60,000		150,000	
Receivables	64,000		135,000	
Cash	1,000		–	
		125,000		285,000
Total assets		285,000		495,000
Current liabilities				
Bank	25,000		80,000	
Payables	50,000		200,000	
		75,000		280,000
Share capital	10,000		10,000	
Retained earnings	200,000		205,000	
		210,000		215,000
Total equity/liabilities		285,000		495,000
Sales revenue	$1,000,000		$2,000,000	
Gross profit	$200,000		$300,000	
Net profit	$50,000		$20,000	

In situation (B), the company has reached its overdraft limit and has four times as many payables as in situation (A) but with only twice the sales revenue. Inventory levels are much higher, and inventory turnover is lower.

This is an example of overtrading. If Great Ambition had to pay its next trade payable, or salaries and wages, before it received any income, it could not do so without the bank allowing it to exceed its overdraft limit. The company is profitable, although profit margins have fallen, and it ought to expect a prosperous future. But if it does not sort out its cash flow and liquidity, it will not survive to enjoy future profits.

Solution

Suitable solutions to the problem would be measures to reduce the degree of overtrading. **New capital** from the shareholders could be injected. Short-term finance could be converted to longer-term finance. **Better control** could be applied to inventories and receivables. The company could **abandon ambitious plans** for increased sales and more non-current asset purchases until the business has had time to consolidate its position, and build up its capital base with retained profits. It partly requires the business to take a long-term view of future prospects, and **avoid short-termism**.

SHORT-TERMISM is a bias towards paying particular attention to short-term performance, with a corresponding relative disregard to the long term.   *(CIMA Official Terminology)*

KEY TERM

3.5 Symptoms of overtrading

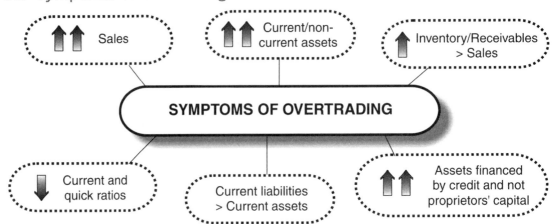

When business seeks to increase its sales too rapidly without an adequate capital base, there is a danger of overtrading. Overtrading may also be caused by the following.

(a)   When a business repays a loan, it often replaces the old loan with a new one. However a business might **repay a loan** without **replacing it**, with the consequence that it has **less long-term capital** to finance its current level of operations.

(b)   A business might be profitable, but in a period of inflation, its **retained profits** might be **insufficient** to pay for replacement non-current assets and inventories, which now cost more because of inflation. The business would then rely increasingly on credit, and find itself eventually unable to support its current volume of trading with a capital base that has fallen in real terms.

3.6 The working capital requirement

Computing the working capital requirement is a matter of calculating the value of current assets less current liabilities, perhaps by taking averages over a one year period.

Example: working capital requirements

The following data relate to Corn Co, a manufacturing company.

Sales for the year	$1,500,000

Costs as percentages of sales

	%
Direct materials	30
Direct labour	25
Variable overheads	10
Fixed overheads	15
Selling and distribution	5

On average:

(a)   Receivables take 2.5 months before payment.

(b)   Raw materials are in inventory for three months.

(c)   Work-in-progress represents two months' worth of half produced goods.

(d)   Finished goods represents one month's production.

(e)   Credit is taken as follows.

       (i)   Direct materials   2 months
       (ii)   Direct labour   1 week
       (iii)   Variable overheads   1 month
       (iv)   Fixed overheads   1 month
       (v)   Selling and distribution   0.5 months

Work-in-progress and finished goods are valued at material, labour and variable expense cost.

Compute the working capital requirement of Corn assuming the labour force is paid for 50 working weeks a year.

Solution

(a)   The annual costs incurred will be as follows.

		$
Direct materials	30% of $1,500,000	450,000
Direct labour	25% of $1,500,000	375,000
Variable overheads	10% of $1,500,000	150,000
Fixed overheads	15% of $1,500,000	225,000
Selling and distribution	5% of $1,500,000	75,000

(b)   The average value of current assets will be as follows.

		$	$
Raw materials	3/12 × $450,000		112,500
Work-in-progress			
Materials (50% complete)	1/12 × $450,000	37,500	
Labour (50% complete)	1/12 × $375,000	31,250	
Variable overheads (50% complete)	1/12 × $150,000	12,500	
			81,250
Finished goods			
Materials	1/12 × $450,000	37,500	
Labour	1/12 × $375,000	31,250	
Variable overheads	1/12 × $150,000	12,500	
			81,250
Receivables	2.5/12 × $1,500,000		312,500
			587,500

(c)   Average value of current liabilities will be as follows.

		$	$
Materials	2/12 × $450,000	75,000	
Labour	1/50 × $375,000	7,500	
Variable overheads	1/12 × $150,000	12,500	
Fixed overheads	1/12 × $225,000	18,750	
Selling and distribution	0.5/12 × $75,000	3,125	
			116,875

(d)   Working capital required is ($(587,500 – 116,875)) = <u>470,625</u>

It has been assumed that all the direct materials are allocated to work-in-progress when production starts.

Question 1.2   Overtrading

Learning outcome E1(a)

Define what is meant by the term 'overtrading' and describe some of the typical symptoms.

Question 1.3   Quick ratio

Learning outcome E1(b)

The figures below have been extracted from the accounts of Premier Co.

	$
Sales revenue	750,000
Cost of sales	500,000
Gross profit	250,000
Current assets	
Inventories	75,000
Trade receivables	100,000
Other receivables	10,000
Cash at bank and in hand	5,000
	190,000
Current liabilities	
Overdraft	30,000
Dividend	40,000
Trade payables	80,000
Other payables	10,000
	160,000
Net current assets	30,000

What is the quick ratio?

A   0.69
B   0.72
C   0.82
D   1.19

Section summary

Over-capitalisation means that the organisation has an excess of working capital.

Overtrading means that the organisation has too little working capital.

Chapter Roundup

✓ The amount tied up in **working capital** is equal to the value of all inventory and receivables less payables. The amount directly affects the liquidity of the organisation.

✓ **Working capital cycle** is the period of time which elapses between the point at which cash begins to be expended on the production of a product and the collection of cash from a purchaser.

(CIMA Official Terminology)

✓ Working capital ratios may help to indicate whether a company has too much working capital (over-capitalised) or too little (overtrading).

$$\text{Receivable days ratio} = \frac{\text{Average trade receivables}}{\text{Average daily sales on credit terms}}$$ *(CIMA Official Terminology)*

$$\text{Receivables turnover period} = \frac{\text{Average trade receivables}}{\text{Credit sales for the year}} \times \textbf{365 days}$$

$$\text{Payables days ratio} = \frac{\text{Average trade payables}}{\text{Average daily purchases on credit terms}}$$ *(CIMA Official Terminology)*

$$\text{Payables payment period, or payables turnover period} = \frac{\text{Average trade payables}}{\substack{\text{Purchases on credit} \\ \text{terms for year}}} \times \textbf{365 days}$$

$$\text{Inventory turnover} = \frac{\text{Inventory}}{\text{Average daily cost of sales in period}} \quad \textbf{or} \quad \frac{\text{Average inventory}}{\text{Cost of sales}}$$

✓ **Over-capitalisation** means that the organisation has an excess of working capital.

✓ **Overtrading** means that the organisation has too little working capital.

Quick Quiz

1   Which of the following is the most likely to be a symptom of overtrading?

A	Static levels of inventory turnover	C	Increase in the level of the current ratio
B	Rapid increase in profits	D	Rapid increase in sales

2   The operating cycle is:

	A The time	
Less	B The time	
Plus	C The time	
Plus	D The time	
Plus	E The time	

Fill in the blanks.

3   Fill in the blanks with the following:

Current liabilities; current assets; inventories; 1.

$$\text{Quick ratio} = \frac{\text{less}}{\rule{4cm}{0.4pt}} \quad \text{(This should be at least ....)}$$

4   Which of the following describes *overcapitalisation* and which describes *overtrading*?

A   A company with excessive investment in working capital
B   A company trying to support too large a volume of trade with the capital resources at its disposal

5   Which of the following statements best defines the current ratio?

A   The ratio of current assets to current liabilities.
     For the majority of businesses it should ideally be about 2.

B   The ratio of current assets to current liabilities.
     For the majority of businesses it should ideally be about 1.

C   The ratio of current assets excluding inventory to current liabilities.
     For the majority of businesses it should ideally be about 1.

D   The ratio of current assets excluding inventory to current liabilities.
     For the majority of businesses it should ideally be about 2.

6   The receivables payment period is a calculation of the time taken to pay by all receivables.

True   ☐

False   ☐

7   What is the working capital requirement of a company with the following average figures over a year?

	$
Inventory	3,750
Trade receivables	1,500
Cash and bank balances	500
Trade payables	1,800

8   WHB Co has the following year end balances.

	$		$
Sales	879,000	Raw material inventory	123,000
Cost of production	690,000	WIP inventory	90,600
Cost of sales	771,000	Finished goods	101,400
Purchases of raw materials	533,400	Receivables	187,800
		Payables	102,000

Using efficiency ratios, calculate the length of the working capital cycle to the nearest day.

Answers to Quick Quiz

1   D   Rapid increase in sales

2   A   The time raw materials remain in inventory
      B   The time period of credit taken from suppliers
      C   The time taken to produce goods
      D   The time finished goods remain in inventory after production is completed
      E   The time taken by customers to pay for goods

3   Quick ratio $= \dfrac{\text{Current assets less inventories}}{\text{Current liabilities}}$ (This should be at least 1)

4   A   Overcapitalisation
      B   Overtrading

5   A   The ratio of current assets to current liabilities: 2

6   False. The calculation normally only includes trade receivables.

7   Working capital requirement = current assets less current liabilities = 3,750 + 1,500 + 500 – 1,800
                                                    = \$3,950

8   188 days

				Days
$\dfrac{\text{Raw materials inventory}}{\text{Raw materials purchases}}$	x 365 =	$\dfrac{123{,}000}{533{,}400}$	x 365 =	84
$\dfrac{\text{Work in progress}}{\text{Manufacturing cost}}$	x 365 =	$\dfrac{90{,}600}{690{,}000}$	x 365 =	48
$\dfrac{\text{Finished goods}}{\text{Cost of sales}}$	x 365 =	$\dfrac{101{,}400}{771{,}000}$	x365 =	48
$\dfrac{\text{Trade receivables}}{\text{Sales}}$	x 365 =	$\dfrac{187{,}800}{879{,}000}$	x 365 =	78
$\dfrac{\text{Trade payables}}{\text{Purchases}}$	x 365 =	$\dfrac{102{,}000}{533{,}400}$	x 365 =	(70)
				188

Answers to Questions

1.1 Cash flow patterns

Your list probably included some of the following.

(a) A **change** in the **general economic environment**. An economic recession will cause a slump in trade.

(b) A **new product**, launched by a competitor, which takes business away from a company's traditional and established product lines.

(c) **New cost-saving product technology**, which forces the company to invest in the new technology to remain competitive.

(d) **Moves by competitors** which have to be countered (for example a price reduction or a sales promotion).

(e) **Changes in consumer preferences**, resulting in a fall in demand.

(f) **Government action** against certain trade practices or against trade with a country that a company has dealings with.

(g) **Strikes** or other industrial action.

(h) **Natural disasters**, such as floods or fire damage, which curtail an organisation's activities.

1.2 Overtrading

'Overtrading' refers to the situation where a company is **over-reliant** on **short-term finance** to support its operations. This is **risky** because short-term finance may be **withdrawn** relatively **quickly** if suppliers lose confidence in the business, or if there is a general tightening of credit in the economy. This may result in a **liquidity crisis** and even bankruptcy, even though the firm is **profitable**. The fundamental **solution** to overtrading is to **replace short term finance** with **longer term finance** such as term loans or equity funds.

The term overtrading is used because the condition commonly arises when a company is **expanding rapidly**. In this situation, because of increasing volumes, more **cash** is needed to pay input costs such as **wages** or **purchases than** is currently being collected **from customers**. The result is that the company runs up its overdraft to the limit and sometimes there is insufficient time to arrange an increase in facilities to pay other payables on the due dates.

These problems are often **compounded** by a general **lack of attention** to **cost control** and **working capital management**, such as receivables collection, because most management time is spent organising selling or production. The result is an unnecessary **drop** in **profit margins**.

When the overdraft limit is reached the company frequently raises funds from **other expensive short term sources**, such as receivables factoring or receivables prompt payment discounts, and delays payment to suppliers, instead of underpinning its financial position with equity funds or a longer term loan. The consequent under-capitalisation delays investment in non-current assets and staff and can **further harm** the quality of the firm's operations.

1.3 Quick ratio

B   The quick ratio is the ratio of current assets excluding inventories to current liabilities.

In this case: $\dfrac{190,000 - 75,000}{160,000} = 0.72$

Now try the question from the Exam Question Bank	Number	Level	Marks	Time
	Q1	Examination	15	27 mins

CASH FLOW FORECASTS

Survival in business depends on the ability to generate cash. **Cash flow information** directs attention towards this critical issue. Cash flow is a more comprehensive concept than 'profit' which is dependent on accounting conventions and concepts.

The **cash budget** is an extremely important mechanism for monitoring cash flows. Various complications about timing of cash flows or lack of particular figures may be included in cash budget exam questions.

At the heart of this chapter is the method for systematically preparing a cash budget. You must be able to set out a budget clearly, supported by appropriate workings.

Section 6 looks at why cash flow problems arise and methods for **easing cash shortages**.

Section 7 concentrates on **float**. Float is the time difference between when a payment is first initiated and when the funds become available for use.

topic list	learning outcomes	syllabus references	ability required
1 Cash flows and profit	E1(c)	E1(i)	analysis
2 The purpose of cash forecasts	E1(c), (d)	E1(v)	analysis
3 Cash budgets in receipts and payments format	E1(c), (d)	E1(v)	analysis
4 Cleared funds cash forecasts	E1(c)	E1(v)	analysis
5 Cash forecasts based on financial statements	E1(c)	E1(vi)	analysis
6 The need for cash management	E1(c)	E1(vi)	analysis
7 Cash management services	E1(c)	E1(vi)	analysis

1 Cash flows and profit

1.1 Types of cash transaction

Introduction

There are many types of cash transaction. They can be distinguished by their **purpose** (ie what they are for), their **form** (how they are implemented), and their frequency.

Sometimes the following distinctions are made.

(a) **Capital** and **revenue** items

    (i)   **Capital** items relate to the **long-term functioning** of the business, such as raising money from shareholders, or acquiring non-current assets.

    (ii)   **Revenue** items relate to **day-to-day operations**, as in the operating cycle, including other matters such as overdraft interest.

(b) **Exceptional** and **unexceptional** items

    (i)   **Exceptional** items are **unusual**. An example would be the costs of closing down part of a business.

    (ii)   **Unexceptional** items include **everything else**. You have to be careful using this distinction, as the phrase 'exceptional item' has a precise meaning in the preparation of a company's financial statements.

(c) **Regular** and **irregular** items

    (i)   **Regular** items occur at **predictable intervals**. Such intervals might be frequent such as the payment of wages every week or month, or relatively infrequent, such as the disbursement of interim and final dividends twice a year. A capital item might be the regular repayment of principal and interest on leased property. Annual disbursements are sums of money paid at yearly intervals.

    (ii)   **Irregular** items **do not occur at regular intervals**.

1.2 Cash flows and profit

Trading profits and **cash flows** are different. A company can make losses but still have a net cash income from trading. A **company** can also make profits but have a net cash deficit on its trading operations.

(a) Cash may be obtained from a transaction which has **nothing** to do with **profit or loss**. For example, an issue of shares or loan stock for cash has no immediate effect on profit but is obviously a source of cash. Similarly, an increase in bank overdraft provides a source of cash for payments, but it is not reported in the income statement.

(b) Cash may be paid for the **purchase of non-current assets**, but the charge in the income statement is depreciation, which is only a part of an asset's cost.

(c) When a non-current asset is sold there is a profit or loss on sale **equal to the difference** between the **sale proceeds** and the '**net book value**' of the asset in the statement of financial position at the time it is sold.

(d) Cash flows also differ from trading profits due to changes in the amount of the company's inventories, receivables and payables.

    (i)   **Profit** is sales minus the cost of sales.

    (ii)   **Operational cash flow** is the difference between cash received and cash paid from trading.

(iii)   Cash received differs from sales because of changes in the amount of receivables.

	$
Customers owing money at the start of the year	X
Sales during the year	X
Total money due from customers	X
Less customers owing money at the end of the year	(X)
Cash receipts from customers during the year	X

(iv)   Cash paid differs from the cost of sales because of changes in the amount of inventories and payables.

	$
Closing inventories at the end of the year	X
Add cost of sales during the year	X
	X
Less opening inventories at the start of the year	(X)
Equals purchases	Y

	$
Payments owing to suppliers at the start of the year	X
Add purchases	Y
	X
Less payments still owing to suppliers at the end of the year	(X)
Equals **cash payments** to suppliers during the year	X

(v)   Operational cash flow therefore differs from profit because of changes in the amount of receivables, inventories and payables between the start and end of a period.

Question 2.1	Profits and cash flow

Learning outcome E1(c)

Assume that Beta achieved sales revenue in a particular year of $200,000 and the cost of sales was $170,000. Inventories were $12,000, payables $11,000 and receivables $15,000 at the start of the year. At the end of the year, inventories were $21,000, payables were $14,000 and receivables $24,000.

Required

Calculate the profits and the operational cash flow resulting from the year's trading.

The difference between profit and cash flow has important implications.

(a)   If a company is profitable but short of cash, one reason could be an increase in the other elements of working capital. Instead of seeking credit from a bank to finance the growth in working capital, management may consider whether **operational cash flows could be improved** by squeezing working capital, and:

(i)   Reducing receivables
(ii)   Reducing inventories
(iii)   Taking more trade credit from suppliers

Better control over working capital could remove the need to borrow.

(b)   If a company is making losses, it could try to maintain a positive operational cash flow by **taking more credit** (ie by increasing its payables and so reducing working capital). (Supplier companies would then consider whether to give the extra credit required, or whether to refuse because the risk would be too great.)

Question 2.2

Profits compared with cash flow

Learning outcome E1(c)

Write brief notes on why the reported profit figure of a business for a period does not normally represent the amount of cash generated in that period.

Section summary

Trading profits and **cash flows** are different. A company can make losses but still have a net cash income from trading. A **company** can also make profits but have a net cash deficit on its trading operations.

2 The purpose of cash forecasts

Introduction

Cash forecasting ensures that sufficient funds will be available when they are needed to sustain the activities of an enterprise. Efficient financial planning also minimises interest payments and maximises the return from any spare cash. Interest rates will differ according to whether money is being lent to, or borrowed from, the bank. The **time value of money** is another important factor. The bank will charge a higher rate of interest on a long-term loan than on a short term loan and will pay a higher rate of interest on an account subject to a longer notice of withdrawal than on an account that requires only 24 hours notice.

All of these factors must be considered when forecasting cash requirements.

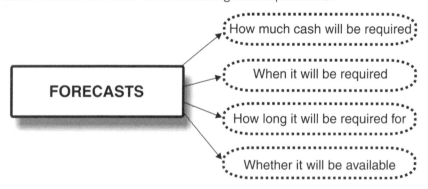

Banks have increasingly insisted that customers provide cash forecasts (or a business plan that includes a cash forecast) as a precondition of lending. A newly established company wishing to open a bank account will also normally be asked to supply a **business plan**. The cash and sales forecasts will also allow the bank to **monitor** the **progress** of the new company, and control its lending more effectively.

2.1 Deficiencies

Any forecast **deficiency** of cash will have to be funded.

(a)   If **borrowing** arrangements are not already secured, a source of funds will have to be found. If a company cannot fund its cash deficits it could be wound up.

(b)   The firm can make arrangements to **sell any short-term financial investments** to raise cash.

(c)   The firm can delay payments to suppliers, or pull in payments from customers. This is sometimes known as **leading and lagging**.

Because cash forecasts cannot be entirely accurate, companies should have **contingency funding**, available from a surplus cash balance and liquid investments, or from a bank facility.

Forecasting gives management time to arrange its funding. Planning in advance, instead of a panic measure to avert a cash crisis, gives a business more choice on **when to borrow**, and will probably mean obtaining a **lower interest rate**.

2.2 Forecasting a cash surplus

If a **cash surplus** is forecast, having an idea of both its **size** and **how long** it will exist could help decide how **best to invest it**.

In some cases, the amount of interest earned from surplus cash could be significant for the company's earnings. The company might then need a forecast of its interest earnings in order to indicate its prospective earnings per share to stock market analysts and institutional investors.

2.3 Types of forecast

KEY TERM

A CASH BUDGET is a detailed budget of estimated cash inflows and outflows, incorporating both revenue and capital items.

(CIMA Official Terminology)

In companies that use cash flow reporting for control purposes, there will probably be:

- A cash budget divided into monthly or quarterly periods
- A statement comparing actual cash flows against the monthly or quarterly budget
- A revised cash forecast
- A statement comparing actual cash flows against a revised forecast

Revised forecasts should be prepared to keep forecasts **relevant** and **up-to-date**. Examples would be a revised three-month forecast every month for the next three-month period, or a revised forecast each month or each quarter up to the end of the annual budget period.

A **rolling forecast** is a forecast that is **continually updated**. When actual results are reported for a given time period (say for one month's results within an annual forecast period) a further forecast period is added and forecasts for intermediate time periods are updated. A rolling forecast can therefore be a 12-month forecast which is updated at the end of every month, with a further month added to the end of the forecast period and with figures for the intervening 11 months revised if necessary.

Cash flow control with budgets and revised forecasts

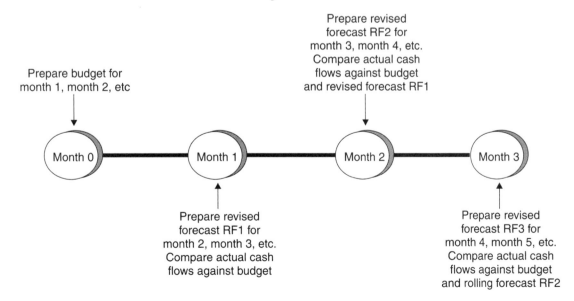

Section summary

Cash flow forecasts provide an early warning of liquidity problems and funding needs. Banks often expect business customers to provide a cash forecast as a condition of lending.

Cash budgets and forecasts can be used for control reporting.

3 Cash budgets in receipts and payments format

Introduction

A cash budget is a detailed forecast of cash receipts, payments and balances over a planning period. It is formally adopted as part of the business plan or master budget for the period.

3.1 Assumptions

For each item of cash inflow or outflow, assumptions must be made about the **quantity** and timing of the flow. The total amount of receipts and payments will be derived from other budgets, such as the company's operating budgets and capital expenditure budget. Assumptions will already have been made for these to prepare the profit or loss budget. Assumptions about the **time to pay** must be introduced for cash forecasting.

The forecasting method can be either one or a combination of the following.

- Identifying a particular cash flow, and scheduling when it will be received or paid
- Projecting future trends and seasonal cycles in business activity and cash flows
- Analysing historical payment patterns of regular repeat payments

3.2 Preparing the cash budget

Cash budgets are prepared by taking **operational budgets** and converting them into forecasts as to when receipts and payments occur. The forecast should indicate the highest and lowest cash balance in a period as well as the balance at the end.

The steps in preparing the cash budget are as follows:

Preparation

1   Set up a proforma cash budget

	Month 1 $	Month 2 $	Month 3 $
Cash receipts			
Receipts from customers	X	X	X
Loan etc	X	X	X
	X	X	X
Cash payments			
Payments to suppliers	X	X	X
Wages etc	X	X	X
	X	X	X
Opening balance	X	X	X
Net cash flow (receipts - payments)	X	X	X
Closing balance	X	X	X

Sort out cash receipts

2   Establish budgeted sales month by month

3   Establish the length of credit period taken by customers

$$\text{Receivables collection period (no. of days credit)} = \frac{\text{average (or year-end) receivables during period}}{\substack{\text{total credit sales} \\ \text{in period}}} \times \text{no. of days in period}$$

4   Determine when budgeted sales revenue will be received as cash (by considering cash receipts from total receivables)

5   Establish when opening receivables will pay

6   Establish when any other cash income will be received

Sort out cash payments

7   Establish production quantities and material usage quantities each month

8   Establish material inventory changes and hence the quantity and cost of materials purchases each month

9   Establish the length of credit period taken from suppliers and calculate when cash payments to suppliers will be made

$$\text{Payables payment period (no. of days credit)} = \frac{\text{average (or year-end) payables during period}}{\substack{\text{total purchases on} \\ \text{credit in period}}} \times \text{no. of days in period}$$

10   Establish when amount due to opening payables will be paid

11   Establish when any other cash payments (excluding non-cash items such as depreciation) will be made

12   Show clearly on the bottom of the budget opening position, net cash flow and closing position

If an overdraft is shown, suggest delaying payments to suppliers, speeding up payments from customers, reducing production volumes or arranging further overdraft facilities

3.3 Cash payments

Assumptions about payments are easier to make than assumptions about income. Assumptions about payments to suppliers can take account of:

(a)   The **credit terms** given by suppliers (or groups of suppliers), company policy on purchase orders and the administration of cheque payments

(b)   Any **specific supply arrangements**, (such as a delivery once every two months, with payment for each delivery at the end of the following month)

(c)   **Past practice** (eg the proportion of invoices (by value) paid in the month of supply and invoice, the proportion paid in the month following, and so on)

(d)   **Predictable dates** for certain payments, such as payments for rent, business rates, telephones, electricity and company tax

As a guideline, assumptions about payments should lean towards caution, ie if in doubt, budget for earlier payments.

3.4 Fixed cost expenditures

Some items of expenditure will be regarded as **fixed costs** in the operating budget. Salaries, office expenses and marketing expenditure are three such items. With some fixed costs, it could be assumed that there will be an **equal monthly expenditure** on each item, with cash payment in the month of expenditure perhaps, or in the month following. Other costs may not be monthly. If annual building rental is payable quarterly in advance, the budget should plan for payments on the specific dates.

3.5 Receipts

Assumptions about receipts might be more difficult to formulate than assumptions about payments.

(a) For a company that depends almost entirely on consumer sales by cash, credit card and debit card, the major uncertainty in the cash flow forecast will be the **volume of sales**. The timing of receipts from a large proportion of those sales will be predictable (payment with sale).

(b) Companies that have a **mixture of cash and credit sales** must attempt to **estimate** the **proportion** of **each** in the total sales figure, and then formulate assumptions for the timing pattern of receipts from credit sales.

(c) There are several ways of estimating when receipts will occur.

    (i) If the company has **specific credit terms**, such as a requirement to pay within 15 days of the invoice date, it could assume that:

        (1) Invoices will be sent out at the time of sale

        (2) A proportion, say 25%, will be paid within 15 days (1/2 month)

        (3) A proportion, say 65%, will be paid between 16 days and 30 days (one month after invoice)

        (4) A proportion (say 9%) will pay in the month following

        (5) There will be some bad debts (say 1%, a proportion that should be consistent with the company's budgeted expectations)

    (ii) If there is a policy of cash discounts for early payment, the **discounts allowed** should be provided for in the forecasts of receipts.

    (iii) The time **customers take to pay** can be estimated from past experience. Care should be taken to allow for seasonal variations and the possibility that payments can be slower at some times of the year than at others (for example, delays during holiday periods).

    (iv) **Payment patterns** can also vary from one country to another. Companies in France and Italy for example will often take several months after the invoice date to pay amounts due.

3.6 Calendar variations

Assumptions could be required to take account of calendar variations.

(a) **Days-in-the-month effect.** It could be assumed that receipts will be the same on every day of the 20th/21st/22nd/23rd etc working day each month. Alternatively, it could be assumed that receipts will be twice as high in the first five days of each month. Assumptions should generally be based on past experience.

(b) **Days-in-the-week effect.** Where appropriate, assumptions should be made about the cash inflows on each particular day of the week, with some days regularly producing higher cash inflows than other days. Such forecasts should be based on historical analysis.

Receipts for some companies, particularly retailers, follow a **regular weekly pattern** (with some variations for holidays and seasons of the year). Companies should be able to estimate total weekly takings in cash (notes and coins), cheques and credit card vouchers, the number of cheques and credit card vouchers handled and the deposit spread (for each day, the percentage of the total takings for the week, eg 10% on Monday, 15% on Tuesday).

3.7 Time periods and overdraft size

Dividing the forecast period into time periods should coincide as closely as possible with significant cash flow events, to provide management with information about the **high or low points for cash balances**. In other words, as well as predicting the **month end surplus or overdraft**, the **maximum overdraft** *during* **the month** should be predicted.

Example: timing of cash flows

Oak Tree Villa operates a retail business. Purchases are sold at cost plus $33\frac{1}{3}$%. Or put another way, purchases are 75% of sales.

(a)

	Budgeted sales	Labour cost	Expenses incurred
	$	$	$
January	40,000	3,000	4,000
February	60,000	3,000	6,000
March	160,000	5,000	7,000
April	120,000	4,000	7,000

(b)   It is management policy to have sufficient inventory in hand at the end of each month to meet sales demand in the next half month.

(c)   Payables for materials and expenses are paid in the month after the purchases are made or the expenses incurred. Labour is paid in full by the end of each month.

(d)   Expenses include a monthly depreciation charge of $2,000.

(e)   (i)   75% of sales are for cash.
        (ii)   25% of sales are on one month's interest-free credit.

(f)   The company will buy equipment for cash costing $18,000 in February and will pay a dividend of $20,000 in March. The opening cash balance at 1 February is $1,000.

Required

(a)   Prepare an income statement for February and March
(b)   Prepare a cash budget for February and March

Solution

(a)   INCOME STATEMENT

	February		March		Total	
	$	$	$	$	$	$
Sales		60,000		160,000		220,000
Cost of purchases (75%)		45,000		120,000		165,000
Gross profit		15,000		40,000		55,000
Less: labour	3,000		5,000		8,000	
expenses	6,000		7,000		13,000	
		9,000		12,000		21,000
		6,000		28,000		34,000

(b)   *Workings*

    (i)   *Receipts:*

		$
in February	75% of Feb sales (75% × $60,000)	45,000
	+ 25% of Jan sales (25% × $40,000)	10,000
		55,000
in March	75% of Mar sales (75% × $160,000)	120,000
	+25% of Feb sales (25% × $60,000)	15,000
		135,000

    (ii)

	Purchases in January $		Purchases in February $
Purchases:			
For Jan sales (50% of $30,000) *	15,000		
For Feb sales (50% of $45,000)	22,500	(50% of $45,000)	22,500
For Mar sales	–	(50% of $120,000)	60,000
	37,500		82,500

These purchases are paid for in February and March.

* Remember that the question says that it is management policy to have sufficient inventory on hand for 50% of next month's sales. You can also use the formula: Purchases = Closing inventory + sales demand – opening inventory. So for January we have (45,000 × 50%) + (40,000 × 75%) – (30,000 × 50%) = 37,500.

    (iii)   *Expenses.* Cash expenses in January ($4,000 – $2,000) and February ($6,000 – $2,000) are paid for in February and March respectively. Depreciation is not a cash item.

CASH BUDGET

	February $	March $	Total $
Receipts from sales	55,000	135,000	190,000
Payments			
Trade payables	37,500	82,500	120,000
Expenses payables	2,000	4,000	6,000
Labour	3,000	5,000	8,000
Equipment purchase	18,000	–	18,000
Dividend	–	20,000	20,000
Total payments	60,500	111,500	172,000
Receipts less payments	(5,500)	23,500	18,000
Opening cash balance b/f	1,000	(4,500)*	1,000
Closing cash balance c/f	(4,500)*	19,000	19,000

* The cash balance at the end of February is carried forward as the opening cash balance for March.

Notes

1   The profit in February and March means that there is sufficient cash to operate the business as planned.

2   Steps should be taken either to ensure that an overdraft facility is available for the cash shortage at the end of February, or to defer certain payments so that the overdraft is avoided.

Exam alert

The specimen exam paper contained a Section A question asking for a calculation of the cash to be paid to suppliers in a 6 month period. It is always useful to remember that

(a)   purchases = usage + closing inventory − opening inventory and

(b)   payments to suppliers = purchases + opening payables − closing payables.

3.8 Cash budgets and opening receivables and payables

One situation which can be problematic is if you are required to analyse an **opening statement of financial position** to decide how many outstanding receivables will pay what they owe in the first few months of the cash budget period, and how many outstanding payables must be paid.

Example: receivables and payables

For example, suppose that a statement of financial position as at 31 December 20X4 shows that a company has the following receivables and payables.

Receivables	$150,000
Trade payables	$ 60,000

You are informed of the following.

(a)   Customers are allowed two months to pay.

(b)   1½ months' credit is taken from trade suppliers.

(c)   Sales and materials purchases were both made at an even monthly rate throughout 20X4.

Required

Determine in which months of 20X5 the customers will eventually pay and the suppliers will be paid.

Solution

(a)   Since customers take two months to pay, the $150,000 of receivables in the statement of financial position represent credit sales in November and December 20X4, who will pay in January and February 20X5 respectively. Since sales in 20X4 were at an equal monthly rate, the cash budget should plan for receipts of $75,000 each month in January and February from the receivables in the opening statement of financial position.

(b)   Similarly, since suppliers are paid after 1½ months, the statement of financial position payables will be paid in January and the first half of February 20X5, which means that budgeted payments will be as follows.

	$
In January (purchases in second half of November and first half of December 20X4)	40,000
In February (purchases in second half of December 20X4)	20,000
Total payables in the statement of financial position	60,000

(The payables in the statement of financial position of $60,000 represent 1½ months' purchases, so that purchases in 20X4 must be $40,000 per month, which is $20,000 per half month.)

Example: a month-by-month cash budget in detail

Now you have some idea as to the underlying principles, let us put these to work. From the following information which relates to George and Zola, prepare a month by month cash budget for the second half of 20X5 and make brief comments as you consider might be helpful to management.

(a)   The company's only product, a leather bag, sells at $40 and has a variable cost of $26 made up as follows.

Material	$20
Labour	$4
Variable overhead	$2

(b)   Fixed costs of $6,000 per month are paid on the 28th of each month.

(c)   *Quantities sold/to be sold on credit*

May	June	July	Aug	Sept	Oct	Nov	Dec
1,000	1,200	1,400	1,600	1,800	2,000	2,200	2,600

(d)   *Production quantities*

May	June	July	Aug	Sept	Oct	Nov	Dec
1,200	1,400	1,600	2,000	2,400	2,600	2,400	2,200

(e)   Cash sales at a discount of 5% are expected to average 100 units a month.

(f)   Customers are expected to settle their accounts by the end of the second month following sale.

(g)   Suppliers of material are paid two months after the material is used in production.

(h)   Wages are paid in the same month as they are incurred.

(i)   70% of the variable overhead is paid in the month of production, the remainder in the following month.

(j)   Company tax of $18,000 is to be paid in October.

(k)   A new delivery vehicle was bought in June, the cost of which, $8,000 is to be paid in August. The old vehicle was sold for $600, the buyer undertaking to pay in July.

(l)   The company is expected to be $3,000 overdrawn at the bank at 30 June 20X5.

(m)   The opening and closing inventories of raw materials, work in progress and finished goods are budgeted to be the same.

Solution

CASH BUDGET FOR 1 JULY TO 31 DECEMBER 20X5

	July $	Aug $	Sept $	Oct $	Nov $	Dec $	Total $
Receipts							
Credit sales	40,000	48,000	56,000	64,000	72,000	80,000	360,000
Cash sales	3,800	3,800	3,800	3,800	3,800	3,800	22,800
Sale of vehicles	600						600
	44,400	51,800	59,800	67,800	75,800	83,800	383,400
Payments							
Materials	24,000	28,000	32,000	40,000	48,000	52,000	224,000
Labour	6,400	8,000	9,600	10,400	9,600	8,800	52,800
Variable overhead (W1)	3,080	3,760	4,560	5,080	4,920	4,520	25,920
Fixed costs	6,000	6,000	6,000	6,000	6,000	6,000	36,000
Company tax				18,000			18,000
Purchase of vehicle		8,000					8,000
	39,480	53,760	52,160	79,480	68,520	71,320	364,720
Excess of receipts over payments	4,920	(1,960)	7,640	(11,680)	7,280	12,480	18,680
Balance b/f	(3,000)	1,920	(40)	7,600	(4,080)	3,200	(3,000)
Balance c/f	1,920	(40)	7,600	(4,080)	3,200	15,680	15,680

Working

Variable overhead

	June $	July $	Aug $	Sept $	Oct $	Nov $	Dec $
Variable overhead production cost	2,800	3,200	4,000	4,800	5,200	4,800	4,400
70% paid in month		2,240	2,800	3,360	3,640	3,360	3,080
30% in following month		840	960	1,200	1,440	1,560	1,440
		3,080	3,760	4,560	5,080	4,920	4,520

Comments

(a) There will be a small overdraft at the end of August but a much larger one at the end of October. It may be possible to delay payments to suppliers for longer than two months or to reduce purchases of materials or reduce the volume of production by running down existing inventory levels.

(b) If none of these courses is possible, the company may need to negotiate overdraft facilities with its bank.

(c) The cash deficit is only temporary and by the end of December there will be a comfortable surplus. The use to which this cash will be put should ideally be planned in advance.

Question 2.3   Cash forecast

Learning outcome E1(c)

Tom Ward has worked for some years as a sales representative, but has recently been made redundant. He intends to start up in business on his own account, using $15,000 which he currently has invested. Tom maintains a bank account showing a small credit balance, and he plans to approach his bank for the necessary additional finance. Tom asks you for advice and provides the following additional information.

(a) Arrangements have been made to purchase non-current assets costing $8,000. These will be paid for at the end of September and are expected to have a five-year life, at the end of which they will possess a nil residual value.

(b)   Inventories costing $5,000 will be acquired on 28 September and subsequent monthly purchases will be at a level sufficient to replace forecast sales for the month.

(c)   Forecast monthly sales are $3,000 for October, $6,000 for November and December, and $10,500 from January 20X7 onwards.

(d)   Selling price is fixed at the cost of inventory plus 50%.

(e)   Two months' credit will be allowed to customers but only 1 month's credit will be received from suppliers of goods.

(f)   Running expenses, including rent, are estimated at $1,600 per month, all paid in cash.

(g)   Tom intends to make monthly cash drawings of $1,000.

Required

Prepare a forecast cash budget for the 6 months October 20X6 to March 20X7.

Question 2.4   Cash budget

Learning outcome E1(a)

You are presented with the following budgeted data for your organisation for the period November 20X1 to June 20X2. It has been extracted from functional budgets that have already been prepared.

	Nov X1 $	Dec X1 $	Jan X2 $	Feb X2 $	Mar X2 $	Apr X2 $	May X2 $	June X2 $
Sales	80,000	100,000	110,000	130,000	140,000	150,000	160,000	180,000
Purchases	40,000	60,000	80,000	90,000	110,000	130,000	140,000	150,000
Wages	10,000	12,000	16,000	20,000	24,000	28,000	32,000	36,000
Overheads	10,000	10,000	15,000	15,000	15,000	20,000	20,000	20,000
Dividends		20,000						40,000
Capital expenditure			30,000			40,000		

You are also told the following.

(a)   Sales are 40% cash, 60% credit. Credit sales are paid two months after the month of sales.
(b)   Purchases are paid the month following purchase.
(c)   75% of wages are paid in the current month and 25% the following month.
(d)   Overheads are paid the month after they are incurred.
(e)   Dividends are paid three months after they are declared.
(f)   Capital expenditure is paid two months after it is incurred.
(g)   The opening cash balance on 1 January 20X2 is $15,000.

The managing director is pleased with the above figures as they show sales will have increased by more than 100% in the period under review. In order to achieve this he has arranged a bank overdraft with a ceiling of $50,000 to accommodate the increased inventory levels and wage bill for overtime worked.

Required

(a)   Prepare a cash budget for the six month period January to June 20X2.

(b)   Comment upon your results in the light of your managing director's comments and offer advice.

(c)   If you have access to a computer spreadsheet package and you know how to use it, try setting up the cash budget on it. Then make a copy of the budget and try making changes to the estimates to see their effect on cash flow.

Section summary

Cash budgets are prepared by taking **operational budgets** and converting them into forecasts as to when receipts and payments occur. The forecast should indicate the highest and lowest cash balance in a period as well as the balance at the end.

4 Cleared funds cash forecasts

4.1 Cleared funds

Introduction

Knowing what **cleared funds** are likely to be has a direct and immediate relevance to cash management in the **short-term**. If a company expects to have insufficient cleared funds in the next few days to meet a payment obligation, it must either borrow funds to meet the obligation or (if possible) defer the payment until there are cash receipts to cover it.

Float refers to the amount of money tied up between the time a payment is initiated and **cleared funds** become available in the recipient's bank account for immediate spending.

A **cleared funds cash forecast** is a short-term cash forecast of the cleared funds available to a company in its bank accounts, or of the funding deficit that must be met by **immediate borrowing**. Cleared funds forecasts should be reviewed and updated regularly, *daily* for companies with large and uncertain cash flows. Uncertainty might be caused by the internal organisation of the recipient.

(a)   The recipient might delay the banking of cheques.

(b)   Cheques do sometimes get held up by bureaucracy.

4.2 Preparing a cleared funds forecast

There should be relatively few items in a cleared funds forecast, and each forecast should generally relate to a **particular bank account** unless balances can be netted against each other.

A cleared funds forecast can be prepared by a combination of three methods.

(a)   **Obtaining information** from the **company's banks**.

(b)   **Forecasting for other receipts and payments** that have occurred but have not yet been lodged with a bank. You should be already familiar with bank reconciliations.

(c)   **Adapting the cash budget**.

(i)   Analyse the cash budget into suitable time periods.

(ii)   Identify cash book payments and receipts.

(iii) Adjust these for float times.

Question 2.5	Types of forecast

Learning outcomes E1(a)

Kim O'Hara runs an import/export retail business, largely on a cash basis. He likes to negotiate the best possible deals from his suppliers and this generally means a strict adherence to any payment terms so as to benefit from any settlement discounts. He also orders his supplies at the last possible moment, as he is a firm believer in 'just-in-time' philosophy. On the other hand Creighton, a listed company, is a large software house, dealing with major clients. Which type of forecast would be most appropriate to each business?

Section summary

Cleared funds are used for short-term planning. They take clearance delays into account.

5 Cash forecasts based on financial statements

Introduction

A statement of financial position based forecast is an estimate of the company's statement of financial position at a future date. It is used to identify either the cash surplus or the funding shortfall in the company's statement of financial position at the **forecast date**.

Exam alert

Exam questions in this area could ask you to calculate cash forecasts from profit forecasts and from statement of financial position forecasts.

5.1 The statement of financial position

The statement of financial position is produced for **financial accounting purposes. It is not an estimate of cash inflows and outflows.** However a number of sequential forecasts can be produced, for example a forecast of the statement of financial position at the end of each year for the next five years.

5.2 Estimating a future statement of financial position

A statement of financial position estimate calls for some prediction of the amount/value of each item in the company's statement of financial position, **excluding cash and short-term investments**, as these are what we are trying to predict. A forecast is prepared by taking each item in the statement of financial position, and estimating what its value might be at the future date. The assumptions used are critical, and the following guidelines are suggested.

(a)   Intangible **non-current assets** (gross book value) and long term investments, if there are any, should be taken at their current value unless there is good reason for another treatment.

(b)   Some estimate of **non-current asset purchases** (and disposals) will be required. Revaluations can be ignored as they are not cash flows.

(c)   **Current assets**. Statement of financial position estimates of inventories and receivables can be based on fairly simple assumptions. The estimated value for inventories and receivables can be made in any of the following ways.

   (i)   **Same as current amounts**. This is unlikely if business has boomed.

   (ii)   **Increase by a certain percentage**, to allow for growth in business volume. For example, the volume of receivables might be expected to increase by a similar amount.

   (iii) **Decrease by a certain percentage**, to allow for tighter management control over working capital.

   (iv)   **Assume to be a certain percentage** of the company's estimated **annual sales revenue** for the year.

   (v)   The firm can assume that the operating cycle will more or less **remain the same**. In other words, if a firm's customers take two months to pay, this relationship can be expected to continue.

(d) **Current liabilities.** Some itemising of current liabilities will be necessary, because no single set of assumptions can accurately estimate them collectively.

    (i) **Trade payables and accruals** can be estimated in a similar way to current assets, as indicated above.

    (ii) Current liabilities include **bank loans** due for repayment within 12 months. These can be identified individually.

    (iii) **Bank overdraft facilities** might be in place. It could be appropriate to assume that there will be no overdraft in the forecast statement of financial position. Any available overdraft facility can be considered later when the company's overall cash requirements are identified.

    (iv) **Taxation.** Any company tax payable should be estimated from anticipated profits and based on an estimated percentage of those profits.

    (v) **Dividends payable.** Any ordinary dividend payable should be estimated from anticipated profits, and any preferred dividend payable can be predicted from the coupon rate of dividend for the company's preferred shares.

    (vi) **Other payables** can be included if required and are of significant value.

(e) **Long-term payables.** Long-term payables are likely to consist of long-term loans, and any other long-term finance debt. Unless the company has already arranged further long-term borrowing, this item should include just existing long-term debts, minus debts that will be repaid before the statement of financial position date.

(f) **Share capital and reserves.** With the exception of the retained earnings, the estimated statement of financial position figures for share capital and other reserves should be the same as their current amount unless it is expected or known that a new issue of shares will take place before the statement of financial position date.

(g) An estimate is required of the change in the company's **accumulated profits** in the period up to the end of the reporting period date. This reserve should be calculated as:

    (i) The existing value of accumulated profits

    (ii) Plus further retained profits anticipated in the period to the statement of financial position date (ie post tax profits minus estimated dividends)

The various estimates should now be brought together into a statement of financial position. The figures on each side of the statement of financial position will not be equal, and there will be one of the following.

(a) A surplus of share capital and reserves over net assets (total assets minus total liabilities). If this occurs, the company will be forecasting a **cash surplus**.

(b) A surplus of net assets over share capital and reserves. If this occurs, the company will be forecasting a **funding deficit**.

Example: Extra funding

Alpha has an existing statement of financial position and an estimated statement of financial position in one year's time before the necessary extra funding is taken into account, as follows. (Note that for the purpose of this exercise liabilities have been deducted from assets.)

	Existing		Forecast after one year	
	$	$	$	$
Non-current assets		100,000		180,000
Current assets	90,000		100,000	
Short-term payables	(60,000)		(90,000)	
Net current assets		30,000		10,000
		130,000		190,000
Long-term payables		(20,000)		(20,000)
Deferred taxation		(10,000)		(10,000)
Total net assets		100,000		160,000
Share capital and reserves				
Ordinary share capital		50,000		50,000
Other reserves		20,000		20,000
Retained earnings		30,000		50,000
		100,000		120,000

The company is expecting to increase its net assets in the next year by $60,000 ($160,000 – $100,000) but expects retained profits for the year to be only $20,000 ($50,000 – $30,000). There is an excess of net assets over share capital and reserves amounting to $40,000 ($160,000 – $120,000), which is a funding deficit. The company must consider ways of obtaining extra cash (eg by borrowing) to cover the deficit. If it cannot, it will need to keep its assets below the forecast amount, or to have higher short-term payables.

A revised projected statement of financial position can then be prepared by introducing these new sources of funds. This should be checked for realism (eg by ratio analysis) to ensure that the proportion of the statement of financial position made up by non-current assets and working capital, etc is sensible.

Main uses of statement of financial position-based forecasts

(a)   As longer-term (strategic) estimates, to assess the scale of funding requirements or cash surpluses the company expects over time

(b)   To act as a check on the realism of cash flow-based forecasts (The estimated statement of financial position should be **roughly** consistent with the net cash change in the cash budget, after allowing for approximations in the statement of financial position forecast assumptions)

5.3 Deriving cash flow from income statement and statement of financial position information

The previous paragraphs concentrated on preparing a forecast statement of financial position, with estimated figures for receivables, payables and inventory. Cash requirements might therefore be presented as the '**balancing figure**'. However, it is possible to derive a forecast figure for cash flows using both the statement of financial position and income statement.

This is examined in the example below, which is based on the first question (Profits and cash flow) in this chapter. For the time being, assume that there is no depreciation to worry about. The task is to get from profit to operational cash flow, by taking into account movements in working capital.

	Profit $	Operational cash flow $
Sales	200,000	200,000
Opening receivables (∴ received in year)		15,000
Closing receivables (outstanding at year end)		(24,000)
Cash in		191,000
Cost of sales	170,000	170,000
Closing inventory (purchased, but not used, in year)		21,000
Opening inventory (used, but not purchased, in year)		(12,000)
Purchases in year		179,000
Opening payables (∴ paid in year)		11,000
Closing payables (outstanding at year end)		(14,000)
Cash out		176,000
Profit/operational cash flow	30,000	15,000

		Profit $	Operational cash flow $
Profit			30,000
(Increase)/Decrease in inventories	Opening	12,000	
	Closing	(21,000)	
			(9,000)
(Increase)/Decrease in receivables	Opening	15,000	
	Closing	(24,000)	
			(9,000)
Increase/(Decrease) in payables	Closing	14,000	
	Opening	(11,000)	
			3,000
Operational cash flow			15,000

In practice, a business will make many other adjustments. The profit figure includes items which **do not involve** the **movement of cash**, such as the annual **depreciation** charge, which will have to be **added back** to arrive at a figure for cash.

Both 'receipts and payments' forecasts and forecasts based on financial statements could be used alongside each other. The cash management section and the financial controller's section should reconcile differences between forecasts on a continuing basis, so that the forecast can be made more accurate as time goes on.

All cash forecasts can now be prepared quickly and easily on **spreadsheets**. This enables revised figures to be calculated whenever assumptions are changed.

Section summary

A cash flow forecast can be prepared by projecting the movement in the statement of financial position or income statement.

6 The need for cash management

6.1 Cash flow problems

Introduction

This section looks at why cash flow problems arise and methods of easing shortages.

We have already used the concept of the **operating cycle**, which connects investment in working capital with cash flows. Cash flow problems can arise in several ways.

CASH FLOW PROBLEMS	
Making losses	Continual losses will eventually mean problems, whose timing depends on the size of losses and whether depreciation is significant; if it is, problems arise on replacement of assets
Inflation	Ever-increasing cash flows required just to replace used-up and worn out assets
Growth	Growth means business needs to support more receivables and inventory
Seasonal business	Cash flow difficulties may occur at certain times when cash inflows are low and outflows high, as inventories are being built up
One-off items of expenditure	Large items such as a loan repayment or the purchase of expensive non-current asset such as freehold land

6.2 Methods of easing cash shortages

6.2.1 Improving the business

Cash deficits can arise out of **basic trading factors** underlying the business such as falling sales or increasing costs. Clearly, the way to deal with these items is to take normal business measures, rectifying the fall in sales by marketing activities or, if this cannot be achieved, by cutting costs.

6.2.2 Controlling the operating cycle: short-term deficiencies

Cash deficits can also arise out of the business's management of the operating cycle and from timing differences. The following are possibilities.

(a)   **Borrowing** from the bank. This is only a short-term measure. It is possible that a bank will convert an overdraft into a long-term loan, or perhaps new overdraft limits can be set up.

(b)   **Raising capital.** This is likely to be expensive and should be generally used for long-term investment, not short term cash management.

(c)   **Different sources of finance** (such as leasing) might be used.

When a company cannot obtain resources from any other source such as a loan or an increased overdraft, it can take the following steps.

(a)   **Postponing capital expenditure**

(i)   It might be imprudent to postpone expenditure on non-current assets which are needed for the **development** and **growth** of the business.

(ii)   On the other hand, some **capital expenditures** might be **postponable** without serious consequences. The routine replacement of motor vehicles is an example. If a company's policy is to replace company cars every two years, it may decide, if cash is short, to replace cars every three years.

(b)   **Accelerating cash inflows which would otherwise be expected in a later period**

The most obvious way of bringing forward cash inflows would be to press receivables for earlier payment (leading and lagging receivables).

(c)   **Reversing past investment decisions by selling assets previously acquired**

Some assets are less crucial to a business than others and so if cash flow problems are severe, the option of selling short-term investments or even property might have to be considered.

(d) **Negotiating a reduction in cash outflows, so as to postpone or even reduce payments**

There are several ways in which this could be done.

(i) **Longer credit** might be taken from suppliers (leading and lagging payables).

(ii) **Loan repayments** could be rescheduled by agreement with a bank.

(iii) A **deferral of the payment of tax** could be agreed with the taxation authorities.

(iv) **Dividend payments** could be **reduced**. Dividend payments are discretionary cash outflows, although a company's directors might be constrained by shareholders' expectations.

(v) **Inventory levels** could decrease to reduce the amount of money tied up in their production cost.

Example: leading and lagging

Assume that Gilbert Gosayne sells Nullas. Each Nulla costs $50 to make and is sold for $100. The bank has refused an overdraft to Gilbert Gosayne. Suppliers are normally paid at the end of Month 1; the Nullas are sold on the 15th of Month 2. Payment is received on the first day of Month 3.

(a) Under this system we have the following forecast.

	Inflows $	Outflows $	Balance $
Month 1 (end)	–	50	(50)
Month 2	–	–	(50)
Month 3 (beginning)	100	–	50

In other words the cash cycle means that the firm is in deficit for all of Month 2. As the bank has refused an overdraft, the suppliers will not be paid.

(b) If, however, Gilbert Gosayne persuades its suppliers to wait for two weeks until the 15th of Month 2 and offers a settlement discount of $5 to customers to induce them to pay on the 15th of Month 2, the situation is transformed.

	Inflows $	Outflows $	Balance $
Month 1	–	–	–
Month 2	95	50	45
Month 3	–	–	45

In practice, it is not that simple.

(a) Suppliers can object to their customers taking extra credit and it can also harm their businesses, thus jeopardising their ability to make future supplies. The customer also loses the possibility of taking advantage of trade discounts.

(b) Customers might refuse to pay early, despite the inducement of a discount.

In fact, a firm's customers and suppliers might be 'leading and lagging' themselves.

A firm might be in a position to choose which of its suppliers should be paid now rather than later. Certain suppliers have to be paid early, if they are powerful. The bank is a powerful supplier: it is worth keeping the bank happy even if the firm loses out on a few trade discounts in the process.

Shortening the operating cycle is helpful in dealing with **short-term deficiencies** and saving interest costs, but it is not necessarily a long term solution to the business's funding problems. This is because a shorter operating cycle time will **reduce the amount of cash** that a company needs to invest in its operating activities.

Section summary

Cash shortages can be eased by postponing capital expenditure, selling assets, taking longer to pay suppliers and pressing customers for earlier payment (leading and lagging).

7 Cash management services

Introduction

This section looks at measures to reduce the amount of time between payment initiation and the availability of the fund.

7.1 Computerised cash management

A relatively recent development in banking services is that of cash management services for corporate customers. A company with many different bank accounts can obtain information about the cash balance in each account through a computer terminal in the company's treasury department linked to the bank's computer. The company can then arrange to move cash from one account to another and so manage its cash position more efficiently.

7.2 Float

As already mentioned, the term 'float' is sometimes used to describe the amount of time between:

(a)   The time when a **payment** is **initiated** (for example when a debtor sends a cheque in payment, probably by post), and

(b)   The time when the **funds** become **available** for use in the recipient's bank account.

REASONS FOR LENGTHY FLOAT	
Transmission delay	Postal delays of a day, maybe longer
Lodgement delay	Delay in banking payments received, payee delaying presentation to bank of cash/cheques received
Clearance delay	Time for bank to clear cheque, payment not available for use by recipient until clearance (2-3 days in UK)

There are several measures that could be taken to reduce the float.

(a)   The payee should ensure that the **lodgement delay** is kept to a minimum. **Cheques** received should be presented to the bank on the day of receipt.

(b)   The payee might, in some cases, arrange to **collect cheques** from the payer's premises. This would only be practicable, however, if the payer is local. The payment would have to be large to make the extra effort worthwhile.

(c)   The payer might be asked to pay through his own branch of a bank. The payer can give his bank detailed payment instructions, and use the credit clearing system of the bank giro. The **bank giro** is a means of making credit transfers for customers of other banks and other branches. The payee may include a bank giro credit slip on the bottom of his invoice, to help with this method of payment.

(d)   **BACS** (Bankers' Automated Clearing Services), a system which provides for the computerised transfer of funds between banks, could be used. BACS is available to corporate customers of banks for making payments. The customer must supply a magnetic tape or disk to BACS, which contains details of payments, and payment will be made in two days.

(e)   For regular payments **standing orders** or **direct debits** might be used.

(f)   **CHAPS** (Clearing House Automated Payments System) is a computerised system for banks to make same-day clearances (that is, immediate payment) between each other. Each member bank of CHAPS can allow its own corporate customers to make immediate transfers of funds through CHAPS. However, there is a large minimum size for payments using CHAPS.

Example: cash management

Ryan Coates owns a chain of seven clothes shops. Takings at each shop are remitted once a week on Thursday evening to the head office, and are then banked at the start of business on Friday morning. As business is expanding, Ryan Coates has hired an accountant to help him. The accountant gave him the following advice.

'Sales revenue at the seven shops totalled $1,950,000 last year, at a constant daily rate, but you were paying bank overdraft charges at a rate of 11%. You could have reduced your overdraft costs by banking the shop takings each day, except for Saturday's takings. Saturday takings could have been banked on Mondays.'

Comment on the significance of this statement, stating your assumptions. The shops are closed on Sundays.

Solution

(a)   A bank overdraft rate of 11% a year is approximately 11/365 = 0.03% a day.

(b)   Annual takings of $1,950,000 would be an average of $1,950,000/312 = $6,250 a day for the seven shops in total, on the assumption that they opened for a 52 week year of six days a week (312 days).

(c)   Using the approximate overdraft cost of 0.03% a day, the cost of holding $6,250 for one day instead of banking it is 0.03% × $6,250 = $1.875.

(d)   Banking all takings up to Thursday evening of each week on Friday morning involves an unnecessary delay in paying cash into the bank. The cost of this delay would be either:

(i)   The opportunity cost of investment capital for the business, or
(ii)   The cost of avoidable bank overdraft charges

It is assumed here that the overdraft cost is higher and is therefore more appropriate to use. It is also assumed that, for interest purposes, funds are credited when banked.

Takings on	Could be banked on	*Number of days delay incurred by Friday banking*
Monday	Tuesday	3
Tuesday	Wednesday	2
Wednesday	Thursday	1
Thursday	Friday	0
Friday	Saturday	6
Saturday	Monday	4
		16

In one week, the total number of days delay incurred by Friday banking is 16. At a cost of $1.875 a day, the weekly cost of Friday banking was $1.875 × 16 = $30.00, and the annual cost of Friday banking was $30.00 × 52 = $1,560.

(e)   *Conclusion*. The company could have saved about $1,560 a year in bank overdraft charges last year. If the overdraft rate remains at 11% and sales continue to increase, the saving from daily banking would be even higher next year.

Section summary

Reasons for a lengthy float include transmission delay, lodgement delay and clearance delay. There are several measures which can be taken to reduce the float.

Chapter Roundup

- ✓   **Trading profits** and cash flows are different. A company can make losses but still have a net cash income from trading. A company can also make profits but have a net cash deficit on its trading operations.

- ✓   **Cash flow forecasts** provide an early warning of liquidity problems and funding needs. Banks often expect business customers to provide a cash forecast as a condition of lending.

- ✓   Cash budgets and forecasts can be used for **control reporting**.

- ✓   Cash budgets are prepared by taking **operational budgets** and converting them into forecasts as to when receipts and payments occur. The forecast should indicate the highest and lowest cash balance in a period as well as the balance at the end.

- ✓   **Cleared funds** are used for short-term planning. They take clearance delays into account.

- ✓   A cash flow forecast can be prepared by projecting the movement in the statement of financial position or income statement.

- ✓   **Cash shortages** can be eased by postponing capital expenditure, selling assets, taking longer to pay suppliers and pressing customers for earlier payment (leading and lagging).

- ✓   Reasons for a lengthy float include transmission delay, lodgement delay and clearance delay. There are several measures which can be taken to reduce the float.

Quick Quiz

1   Operational cash flows of a business could be improved directly by:

- *Reducing/Increasing* receivables
- *Reducing/Increasing* inventories
- *Reducing/Increasing* the credit period for the company's trade payables

Delete the word in italics that does not apply.

2   Explain what a rolling forecast is in not more than 20 words.

3   The 'float' is the time between (A) .... and (B) .... (Fill in the blanks)

4   List the twelve main steps involved in preparing a cash budget.

5   Heavy Metal is preparing its cash flow forecast for the next quarter. Which of the following items should be excluded from the calculations?

A   The receipt of a bank loan that has been raised for the purpose of investment in a new rolling mill

B   Depreciation of the new rolling mill

C   A tax payment that is due to be made, but which relates to profits earned in a previous accounting period

D   Disposal proceeds from the sale of the old rolling mill

6   What are the main uses of forecasts based on the statement of financial position?

7   The cash flow forecast prepared by Heavy Metal suggests that the overdraft limit will be exceeded during the second month of the forecast period due to the timing of the asset purchase. However, by the end of the quarter the overdraft should be back to a level similar to that at the start of the period. Which of the following courses of action would you recommend to overcome this problem?

A   Acquire the asset using a finance lease rather than by outright purchase
B   Seek help from a venture capital company
C   Make a rights issue to raise the additional funds
D   Negotiate with the bank for a short-term loan to cover the deficit

8   Possible reasons for a lengthy float are:

(A) .... delay

(B) .... delay

(C) .... delay

9   Hallas is a small manufacturing business that uses a large number of suppliers, many of which are located outside the UK. The accountant has suggested that Hallas could improve its cash position by sending payments out using surface mail rather than airmail as at present. If Hallas did this, which of the following would it be taking advantage of?

A   Lodgement delay
B   Clearance delay
C   Transmission delay
D   Collection delay

Answers to Quick Quiz

1   Cash flows could be improved by:

- Decreasing receivables
- Decreasing inventories
- Increasing the credit period for the company's trade payables

2   A forecast that is continually updated

3   (A)   Initiation of a payment
    (B)   When cleared funds become available in the recipient's bank account

4   *Step*

1	Set up a proforma cash budget
2	Establish budgeted sales month by month
3	Establish the length of credit period taken by customers
4	Determine when budgeted sales revenue will be received as cash
5	Establish when opening receivables will pay
6	Establish when any other cash income will be received
7	Establish production quantities and material usage quantities each month
8	Establish material inventory changes and quantity and cost of month-by-month materials purchases
9	Establish length of credit period taken from suppliers and calculate when cash payments to suppliers will be made
10	Establish when amount due to opening payables will be paid
11	Establish when any other cash payments will be made
12	Show clearly on the bottom of the budget opening position, net cash flow and closing position

5   B   This is a non-cash item and should therefore be excluded.

6   •   As longer-term estimates, to assess the scale of funding requirements or cash surpluses the company expects over time

    •   To act as a check on the realism of cash flow-based forecasts

7   D   Since the cash flow problems appear to be temporary in nature, it is appropriate to use a short-term solution. Additional long-term capital should not be required.

8   (A)   Transmission delay
    (B)   Lodgement delay
    (C)   Clearance delay

9   C   Transmission delay

Answers to Questions

2.1 Profits and cash flow

	Profit $	Operational cash flow $
Sales	200,000	200,000
Opening receivables (∴ received in year)		15,000
Closing receivables (outstanding at year end)		(24,000)
Cash in		191,000
Cost of sales	170,000	170,000
Closing inventory (bought, but not used, in year)		21,000
Opening inventory (used, but not bought, in year)		(12,000)
Purchases in year		179,000
Opening payables (∴ paid in year)		11,000
Closing payables (outstanding at year end)		(14,000)
Cash out		176,000
Profit/operational cash flow	30,000	15,000

2.2 Profits compared with cash flow

The principal reasons why profit will not equal cash flow are as follows.

(a)   The '**matching concept**' means that costs and revenues do not equal payments and receipts. Revenue is recognised in the income statement when goods are sold, and any revenue not received is recorded as a receivable. Similarly, costs are incurred when a resource is acquired or subsequently used, not when it happens to be paid for.

(b)   **Some items appearing** in the income statement do not **affect cash flow**. For example, depreciation is a 'non-cash' deduction in arriving at profit.

(c)   Similarly, items may **affect cash flow** but not profit. Capital expenditure decisions (apart from depreciation) and inventory level adjustments are prime examples.

2.3 Cash forecast

The opening cash balance at 1 October will consist of Tom's initial $15,000 less the $8,000 expended on non-current assets purchased in September, ie the opening balance is $7,000. Cash receipts from credit customers arise two months after the relevant sales.

Payments to suppliers are a little more tricky. We are told that cost of sales is 100/150 × sales. Thus for October cost of sales is 100/150 × $3,000 = $2,000. These goods will be purchased in October but not paid for until November. Similar calculations can be made for later months. The initial inventory of $5,000 is purchased in September and consequently paid for in October.

The forecast budget can now be constructed.

CASH FORECAST FOR THE SIX MONTHS ENDING 31 MARCH 20X7

	October $	November $	December $	January $	February $	March $
Payments						
Suppliers	5,000	2,000	4,000	4,000	7,000	7,000
Running expenses	1,600	1,600	1,600	1,600	1,600	1,600
Drawings	1,000	1,000	1,000	1,000	1,000	1,000
	7,600	4,600	6,600	6,600	9,600	9,600
Receipts						
Customers	–	–	3,000	6,000	6,000	10,500
Surplus/(shortfall)	(7,600)	(4,600)	(3,600)	(600)	(3,600)	900
Opening balance	7,000	(600)	(5,200)	(8,800)	(9,400)	(13,000)
Closing balance	(600)	(5,200)	(8,800)	(9,400)	(13,000)	(12,100)

2.4 Cash budget

(a)

	January $'000	February $'000	March $'000	April $'000	May $'000	June $'000
Sales revenue						
Cash (40%)	44	52	56	60	64	72
Credit (60%, 2 months)	48	60	66	78	84	90
	92	112	122	138	148	162
Purchases	60	80	90	110	130	140
Wages 75%	12	15	18	21	24	27
25%	3	4	5	6	7	8
Overheads	10	15	15	15	20	20
Dividends			20			
Capital expenditure			30			40
	85	114	178	152	181	235
b/f	15	22	20	(36)	(50)	(83)
Net cash flow	7	(2)	(56)	(14)	(33)	(73)
c/f	22	20	(36)	(50)	(83)	(156)

(b) The overdraft arrangements are quite inadequate to service the cash needs of the business over the six-month period. If the figures are realistic then action should be taken now to avoid difficulties in the near future. The following are possible courses of action.

(i)   **Activities** could be **curtailed**.

(ii)   Other **sources of cash** could be **explored**, for example a long-term loan to finance the capital expenditure and a factoring arrangement to provide cash due from receivables more quickly.

(iii) Efforts to **increase the speed of debt collection** could be made.

(iv)   **Payments to suppliers** could be **delayed**.

(v)   The **dividend payments** could be **postponed** (the figures indicate that this is a small company, possibly owner-managed).

(vi)   Staff might be **persuaded to work at a lower rate** in return for, say, an annual bonus or a profit-sharing agreement.

(vii) **Extra staff** might be taken on to reduce the amount of overtime paid.

(viii) The **inventory holding policy** should be **reviewed**. It may be possible to meet demand from current production and minimise cash tied up in inventories.

2.5 Types of forecast

Kim O'Hara would be best served by a **cleared funds forecast**, Creighton by a **cash book based forecast**.

	Number	Level	Marks	Time
Now try the question from the Exam Question Bank	Q2	Examination	15	27 mins

CASH MANAGEMENT

In this chapter, we discuss **short- and medium-term finance**. This involves looking at the use of **bank loans** and **overdrafts**. The choice between taking out a loan or overdraft is often very important. You should concentrate on understanding **when different forms of borrowing** might be **most appropriate** for a business.

We also look at different methods of **financing foreign trade**.

In the second part of this chapter, we look at the ways in which **cash can be invested** in the short-term, and identify the purpose and main features of various types of short-term investment. The characteristics of different types of instrument may be tested in an MCQ. Alternatively in a longer question you might be asked to explain which types of investment an investor might choose.

3

topic list	learning outcomes	syllabus references	ability required
1 Budgeting for borrowings	E2(a)	E2(ii)	comprehension
2 Overdrafts	E2(a)	E2(ii)	comprehension
3 Loans	E2(a)	E2(ii)	comprehension
4 Trade payables as a source of finance	E2(a)	E2(i)	comprehension
5 Export finance	E2(c)	E2(vi)	comprehension
6 Cash surpluses	E2(b)	E2(iii)	comprehension
7 Cash investments: bank and building society accounts	E2(b)	E2(iv)	comprehension
8 Marketable securities: prices and interest rates	E2(b)	E2(v)	comprehension
9 Other types of investment	E2(b)	E2(iv)	comprehension
10 Risk and exposure	E2(b)	E2(iv)	comprehension

1 Budgeting for borrowings

Introduction

As far as borrowing is concerned, there are three aspects to the **maintenance of liquidity**. These are controlling timing differences, minimising risk and providing against contingencies.

1.1 Maintaining liquidity

(a) The firm needs enough money to function operationally, pay salaries, suppliers and so on. Of course, eventually it will receive funds from customers, but the length of the cash cycle can mean reliance on **overdraft finance** at times.

(b) The firm needs to minimise the **risk** that some of its sources of finance will be removed from it.

(c) The firm also needs to provide against the **contingency** of any sudden movements in cash. Contingency measures can take the form of special arrangements with the bank, insurance policies and so on.

Some of these needs are more pressing than others.

(a) **Working capital**

Working capital is often financed by an overdraft – this is a result of lagged payments and receipts as discussed earlier and the willingness of businesses to offer credit.

(b) **Long-term finance**

This is used for major investments. Capital expenditure is easier to put off than, say, wages in a crisis, but a long-term failure to invest can damage the business and reduce its capacity.

(c) **Overseas finance**

The borrowing might be required to finance **assets overseas**, in which case the **currency** of the borrowing might be important.

KEY TERMS

Bank borrowing can be obtained in the following ways.

(a) OVERDRAFT FACILITY. A company, through its current account, can borrow money on a short-term basis up to a certain amount. Overdrafts are repayable on demand.

(b) TERM LOAN. The customer borrows a fixed amount and pays it back with interest over a period or at the end of it.

(c) COMMITTED FACILITY. The bank undertakes to make a stipulated amount available to a borrower, on demand.

(d) A REVOLVING FACILITY is a facility that is renewed after a set period. Once the customer has repaid the amount, the customer can borrow again.

(e) UNCOMMITTED FACILITY. The bank, if it feels like it, can lend the borrower a specified sum. The bank has no obligation to lend.

Section summary

Maintenance of **liquidity** is an important corporate objective. Organisations may have problems due to **timing differences, risk** and **contingencies**.

2 Overdrafts

Introduction

Where payments from a current account exceed the balance on the account for a temporary period, the bank finances the deficit by means of an **overdraft**.

Overdrafts are a form of short-term lending, technically repayable on demand. Businesses may not need to use the overdraft facilities that they have been granted.

OVERDRAFTS	
Amount	Should not exceed limit, usually based on known income
Margin	Interest charged at base rate plus margin on daily amount overdrawn and charged quarterly. Fee may be charged for large facility
Purpose	Generally to cover short-term deficits
Repayment	Technically repayable on demand
Security	Depends on size of facility
Benefits	Customer has flexible means of short-term borrowing; bank has to accept fluctuation

2.1 Overdraft as short-term borrowing

By providing an overdraft facility to a customer, the bank is committing itself to provide an overdraft to the customer whenever the customer wants it, up to the agreed limit. The bank will earn interest on the lending, but only to the extent that the customer uses the facility and goes into overdraft. If the customer does not go into overdraft, the bank cannot charge interest.

The bank will generally charge a **commitment fee** when a customer is granted an overdraft facility or an increase in the overdraft facility. This is a fee for granting an overdraft facility and agreeing to provide the customer with funds if and whenever needed.

2.2 Overdrafts and the operating cycle

Many businesses require their bank to provide financial assistance for normal trading over the **operating cycle**.

For example, suppose that a business has the following operating cycle.

	$	$
Inventories and receivables		10,000
Bank overdraft	1,000	
Payables	3,000	
		4,000
Working capital		6,000

The business now buys inventories costing $2,500 for cash, using its overdraft. Working capital remains the same, $6,000, although the bank's financial stake has risen from $1,000 to $3,500.

	$	$
Inventories and receivables		12,500
Bank overdraft	3,500	
Payables	3,000	
		6,500
Working capital		6,000

A bank overdraft provides support for normal trading finance. In this example, finance for normal trading rises from $(10,000 – 3,000) = $7,000 to $(12,500 – 3,000) = $9,500 and the bank's contribution rises from $1,000 out of $7,000 to $3,500 out of $9,500.

A feature of bank lending to support normal trading finance is that the amount of the overdraft required at any time will depend on the **cash flows of the business**: the timing of receipts and payments, seasonal variations in trade patterns and so on. An overdraft will increase in size if the customer writes more cheques, but will reduce in size when money is paid into the account.

There should be times when there will be no overdraft at all, and the account is in credit for a while. In other words, the customer's account may well **swing** from overdraft into credit, back again into overdraft and again into credit, and so on. The account would then be a **swinging account**. The purpose of the overdraft is to bridge the gap between cash payments and cash receipts.

When a business customer has an overdraft facility, and the account is always in overdraft, then it has a **solid core** (or **hard core**) instead of swing. For example, suppose that the account of Blunderbuss has the following record for the previous year:

							Debit
	Average balance		Range				turnover
Quarter to	$		$		$		$
31 March 20X5	40,000 debit	70,000 debit	–	20,000 debit			600,000
30 June 20X5	50,000 debit	80,000 debit	–	25,000 debit			500,000
30 September 20X5	75,000 debit	105,000 debit	–	50,000 debit			700,000
31 December 20X5	80,000 debit	110,000 debit	–	60,000 debit			550,000

These figures show that the account has been permanently in overdraft, and the hard core of the overdraft has been rising steeply over the course of the year (from a minimum overdraft of $20,000 in the first quarter to one of $60,000 in the fourth quarter).

If the hard core element of the overdraft appears to be becoming a **long-term feature** of the business, the **bank** might wish, after discussions with the customer, to **convert** the hard core of the overdraft into a **medium-term loan**, thus giving formal recognition to its more permanent nature. Otherwise annual reductions in the hard core of an overdraft would typically be a requirement of the bank.

2.3 The purpose of an advance for day-to-day trading

The purpose of a bank overdraft for normal day-to-day trading is to help with the financing of current assets. However, there are a number of different reasons why a business might need an overdraft facility. Only **some** of these reasons will be sound and acceptable to a bank.

Borrowing by a business will either **increase the assets** of the business or **decrease its liabilities**.

2.4 Increasing business assets

If borrowing is to increase the business assets, a bank will first check whether the purpose is to acquire more **non-current assets** or more **current assets**. A customer might ask for an overdraft facility to help with day to day trading finance, when the *real* cause of his shortage of liquidity is really a decision to purchase a new non-current asset. There is nothing wrong with asking a bank for financial assistance with the purchase of non-current assets. But borrowing to purchase a non-current asset **reduces the liquidity** of the business, and might even make it illiquid.

Exam alert

Factoring (in the next chapter) is of course another means of raising finance. An exam question could ask whether it is more beneficial to an entity to factor its debts or to raise finance by another means, such as an overdraft.

Question 3.1   Bank overdraft

Learning outcome E2(a)

The directors of Wrong Wreason have asked their bank for a $50,000 overdraft which they say will be used for normal trading operations. They present two statements of financial position, one indicating the firm's position before the loan and one after. What do you think the bank's response will be?

WRONG WREASON – STATEMENT OF FINANCIAL POSITION (BEFORE)

	$	$
Non-current assets		200,000
Current assets	120,000	
Current liabilities: trade payables	60,000	
Working capital		60,000
		260,000
Share capital and reserves		260,000

WRONG WREASON – STATEMENT OF FINANCIAL POSITION (AFTER)

	$	$	$
Non-current assets (200,000 + 50,000)			250,000
Current assets		120,000	
Current liabilities: bank overdraft	50,000		
trade payables	60,000		
		110,000	
Working capital			10,000
			260,000
Share capital and reserves			260,000

An overdraft facility for **day-to-day trading** should therefore be either to **increase total current assets**, or to **reduce other current liabilities.**

2.5 Increasing total current assets

A request for an overdraft facility to increase total current assets can be pinpointed more exactly, to a wish by the company:

- To increase its **inventory** levels
- To increase its overall **receivables**
- To increase its overall sales **turnover**

The underlying guide to a bank's attitude to lending (in addition to avoiding risk) is whether the finance will be temporary (and 'swinging') or longer term. There might be a number of reasons for a business **increasing its inventory levels** without increasing its total sales.

REASONS FOR INCREASING INVENTORY LEVELS	
Large order	Overdraft suitable, temporary finance to enable business to fulfil order
Inventory build up anticipating seasonal peak	Overdraft suitable, temporary finance to support cost of inventory
Speculative purchase, eg buying raw materials	Overdraft suitable, provided finance temporary and not unacceptably risky
Permanent increase without increase in sales	Overdraft probably not suitable; need for review of finance facilities; inventory may be unsaleable

Reasons for a business wanting to **increase its total receivables** without increasing its sales turnover might be:

(a)   A loss of efficiency in the credit control, invoicing and debt collection procedures of the business, or

(b)   The inability of existing customers to pay without being allowed more credit

In both cases, the bank will be cautious about agreeing to an increased overdraft facility. Delays in invoicing should be eliminated by the business; however, if more credit must be allowed to maintain sales, a bank might agree to an overdraft facility for this purpose.

When a business **increases its sales turnover**, it will almost certainly have to increase its investment in inventories and receivables. It will probably be able to obtain more credit from trade payables, but the balance of the extra finance required will have to be provided out of extra proprietors' capital or other lending. A danger with business expansion is **overtrading**, and a bank will be wary of requests to support ambitious expansion schemes.

2.6 Using an overdraft to reduce other current liabilities

A bank might be asked to provide an overdraft facility to enable a business to pay its tax bills, or to reduce its volume of trade payables. The payment of tax might be sales tax (generally every quarter) or year end corporation tax. An overdraft facility to help a business to pay tax when it falls due is a 'legitimate' and acceptable purpose for an overdraft, although the bank might wish to know why the business had not set funds aside to pay the tax. A bank should be able to expect that the overdraft would soon be paid off out of profits from future trading.

An **extension** to an overdraft in order to pay trade suppliers must be for the purpose of **reducing the overall average volume of trade payables**, which in turn implies a significant change in the trade payables position of the business, all other things being equal. Why might such a reduction in total trade payables be required?

(a)   **To take advantage of attractive purchase discounts offered by suppliers for early settlement of debts**. This should be an acceptable purpose for an extra overdraft to a bank, because taking the discount would reduce the costs and so increase the profits of the business.

(b)   **To pay suppliers who are pressing for payment**. A bank will deal **cautiously** with such a request. It might be because the supplier is desperate for money. If the business *customer* is getting into difficulties, and is falling behind with paying their debts, a banker would take the view that agreeing to an increased overdraft would simply mean taking over debts that might one day never be paid, and so may not agree to such a proposition.

Section summary

Overdrafts are a form of short-term lending, technically repayable on demand. Businesses may not need to use the overdraft facilities that they have been granted.

3 Loans

Introduction

Bank loans tend to be a **source** of **medium-term finance**, linked with the purchase of specific assets. Interest and repayments will be set in advance.

3.1 When a loan is appropriate

A customer might ask the bank for an overdraft facility when the bank would wish to suggest a loan instead; alternatively, a customer might ask for a loan when an overdraft would be more appropriate.

(a)   In most cases, when a customer wants finance to help with 'day to day' trading and cash flow needs, an **overdraft** would be the **appropriate method** of financing. The customer should not be short of cash all the time, and should expect to be in credit in some days, but in need of an overdraft on others.

(b)   When a customer wants to borrow from a bank for only a **short period of time**, even for the purchase of a major non-current asset such as an item of plant or machinery, an overdraft facility might be more suitable than a loan, because the customer will stop paying interest as soon as the account goes into credit.

(c)   When a customer wants to borrow from a bank, but cannot see their way to repaying the bank except over the course of a few years, the **medium– or long-term nature** of the financing is best catered for by the provision of a loan rather than an overdraft facility.

3.2 Advantages of an overdraft over a loan

(a)   The customer only pays interest when overdrawn.

(b)   The bank has the flexibility to review the customer's overdraft facility periodically, and perhaps agree to additional facilities, or insist on a reduction in the facility.

(c)   An overdraft can do the same job as a loan: a facility can simply be renewed every time it comes up for review.

(d)   Being short-term debt, an overdraft will not affect the calculation of a company's gearing.

Bear in mind, however, that overdrafts are normally **repayable on demand**.

3.3 Advantages of a loan

(a)   Both the customer and the bank **know exactly** what the repayments of the loan will be and how much interest is payable, and when. This makes planning (budgeting) simpler.

(b)   The customer does not have to worry about the bank deciding to reduce or **withdraw** an overdraft facility before being in a position to repay what is owed. There is an element of 'security' or 'peace of mind' in being able to arrange a loan for an agreed term.

(c)   Loans normally carry a **facility letter** setting out the precise terms of the agreement.

For purchases of a non-current asset it is important, however, that the **term of the loan should not exceed** the **economic or useful life** of the asset purchased with the money from the loan. A business will often expect to use the revenues earned by the asset to repay the loan, and obviously, an asset can only do this as long as it is in operational use.

Section summary

Bank loans tend to be a **source** of **medium-term finance**, linked with the purchase of specific assets. Interest and repayments will be set in advance.

There are advantages and disadvantages to having an overdraft instead of a loan.

4 Trade payables as a source of finance

Introduction

Trade credit from suppliers is another possible short-term source of finance.

4.1 Trade payables as a source of short-term finance

Taking credit from suppliers is a normal feature of business and nearly every company has at any time a number of suppliers waiting for payment.

It may be thought that this is a form of interest free borrowing, but:

(a)   Any available settlement discounts will be lost
(b)   It will lead to a loss of supplier goodwill
(c)   If the supplier resorts to legal action, this may affect the organisation's future credit rating.

The organisation must weigh up the cost of lost discounts against the value of the number of days borrowing obtained. It may be more financially worthwhile to pay the supplier early and obtain the discount than to hang onto the funds and invest them for the additional days.

Section summary

Trade credit from suppliers is another possible short-term source of finance, but is has its disadvantages.

5 Export finance   5/11

5.1 Finance for foreign trade

Introduction

Foreign trade raises special **financing problems**.

Foreign trade financing problems include the following.

(a)   When goods are sold abroad, the customer might ask for credit. The period of credit might be 30 days or 60 days, say, after receipt of the goods; or perhaps 90 days after shipment. Exports take time to arrange, and there might be **complex paperwork**. Transporting the goods can be slow, particularly if they are sent by sea. These delays in foreign trade mean that exporters often build up large investments in inventory and receivables.

(b)   The risk of bad debts can be greater with foreign trade than with domestic trade. If a foreign customer refuses to pay a debt, the exporter must pursue the debt in the customer's own country, where procedures will be subject to the laws of that country.

There are various measures available to exporters to overcome these problems. (Apart from credit risks, there are other risks, including the risk of currency (exchange rate) fluctuations and political risks.)

5.2 Reducing the investment in foreign receivables

A company can reduce its **investment in foreign receivables** by insisting on earlier payment for goods. Another approach is for an exporter to **arrange for a bank to give cash for a foreign debt**, sooner than the exporter would receive payment in the normal course of events. There are several ways in which this might be done.

METHODS OF OBTAINING CASH FOR FOREIGN DEBTS	
Advances against collections	Exporter asks bank to handle, and bank makes 80-90% advance against value of collection. Banks expect repayment from proceeds. Used when the bill/cheque is payable in exporter's own country
Documentary credits	Described later in the chapter
Negotiation of bills or cheques	Similar to an advance against collection, used when the bill/cheque is payable outside exporter's country (eg in foreign buyer's country)

5.3 Advantages of using bills of exchange in international trade

(a)　They provide a **convenient method** of **collecting payments** from foreign buyers.

(b)　The exporter can seek **immediate finance**, using term bills of exchange, instead of having to wait until the period of credit expires (ie until the maturity of the bill). At the same time, the foreign buyer is allowed the full period of credit before payment is made.

(c)　On payment, the foreign buyer keeps the bill as **evidence of payment**, so that a bill of exchange also serves as a receipt.

(d)　If a bill of exchange is dishonoured, it may be used by the drawer to **pursue payment** by means of legal action in the drawee's country.

(e)　The buyer's bank might add its name to a term bill, to indicate that it **guarantees payment** at maturity. On the continent of Europe, this procedure is known as **'avalising'** bills of exchange.

5.4 Reducing the bad debt risk

Methods of minimising bad debt risks are broadly similar to those for domestic trade. An exporting company should vet the creditworthiness of each customer, and grant credit terms accordingly. Methods of reducing the risks of bad debts in foreign trade are described below.

5.5 Export factoring

Export factoring relates to export trade and is similar to the factoring of domestic trade debts.

KEY TERM

FACTORING is the sale of debts to a third party (the factor) at a discount, in return for prompt cash. A factoring service may be with recourse, in which case the supplier takes the risk of the debt not being paid, or without recourse when the factor takes the risk. *(CIMA Official Terminology)*

5.6 Main aspects of factoring

(a)　**Administration** of the **client's invoicing**, **sales accounting** and debt collection services are generally involved.

(b)　The arrangement is likely to provide **credit protection** for the client's debts, whereby the factor takes over the risk of loss from bad debts and so 'insures' the client against such losses.

(c)　The factor will **make payments** to the client **in advance** of collecting the debts. This is sometimes referred to as 'factor finance' because the factor is providing cash to the client against outstanding debts.

A factoring service typically offers prepayment of up to 80% against approved invoices. Service charges vary between around 0.75% and 3% of total invoice value, plus finance charges at levels comparable to bank overdraft rates for those taking advantage of prepayment arrangements.

Factoring, as compared with forfaiting (which we discuss below), is widely regarded as an appropriate mechanism for trade finance and collection of receivables for **small to medium-sized exporters**, especially where there is a flow of **small-scale contracts**.

5.7 Forfaiting

KEY TERM

FORFAITING is a method of export finance whereby a bank purchases from a company a number of sales invoices or promissory notes, usually obtaining a guarantee of payment of the invoices or notes.

Forfaiting is the most common method of providing **medium-term** (say, three to five years) export finance. It has normally been used for export sales involving **capital goods** (machinery etc), where payments will be made over a number of years.

Forfaiting works as follows.

(a)   An exporter of capital goods finds an overseas buyer who wants medium-term credit to finance the purchase. The buyer must be willing to pay **some of the cost** (perhaps 15%) at once and to pay the balance in **regular instalments** normally for the next five years.

(b)   The buyer will either issue a **series** of **promissory notes**, or accept a **series of drafts** with a final maturity date, say, **five years ahead** but providing for regular payments over this time. In other words, a series of promissory notes maturing every six months, usually each for the same amount.

(c)   In most cases, however, the buyer will be required to find a bank which is willing to guarantee **(avalise)** the notes or drafts.

(d)   At the same time, the exporter must find a bank that is willing to be a **'forfaiter'**.

(e)   The exporter will deliver the goods and receive the avalised promissory notes or accepted bills. They will then sell them to the forfaiter, who will purchase them **without recourse to the exporter**. The forfaiter must now bear the risk, ie:

(i)   Risks of non-payment
(ii)   Political risks in the buyer's country
(iii)   Transfer risk, the buyer's country not meeting its foreign exchange obligations
(iv)   Foreign exchange risk
(v)   The collection of payment from the avalising bank

The diagram below should help to clarify the procedures.

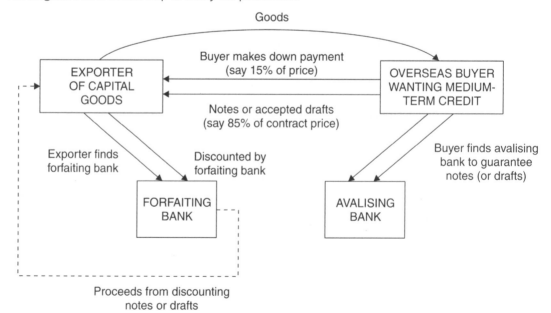

Forfaiting can be an expensive choice, and arranging it takes time. However, it can be a useful way of enabling trade to occur in cases where other methods of ensuring payment and smooth cash flow are not certain, and in cases where trade may not be possible by other means.

5.8 Documentary credits

Documentary credits ('letters of credit') provide a method of payment in international trade which gives the exporter a risk-free method of obtaining payment.

(a) The exporter receives **immediate payment** of the amount due to him, less the discount, instead of having to wait for payment until the end of the credit period allowed to the buyer.

(b) The buyer is able to get a **period of credit** before having to pay for the imports.

The process works as follows:

(a) The buyer and the seller first of all agree a contract for the sale of the goods, which provides for payment through a documentary credit.

(b) The **buyer** then requests a bank in his country to issue a **letter of credit** in favour of the exporter. This bank which issues the letter of credit is known as the **issuing bank.**

(c) The issuing bank, by issuing its letter of credit, guarantees payment to the beneficiary.

Documentary credits are **slow** to arrange, and **administratively cumbersome**; however, they might be considered essential where the **risk of non-payment is high**, or when **dealing** for the **first time** with an **unknown buyer**.

Section summary

It is worth remembering that the exporter can obtain finance from the foreign buyer by insisting on **cash with order** and the importer can obtain finance from the foreign supplier by means of normal trade credit, perhaps evidenced by a term bill of exchange.

Export factoring provides all the advantages of factoring generally and is especially useful in assessing credit risk.

Forfaiting provides medium-term finance for importers of capital goods.

6 Cash surpluses

Introduction

Many companies have temporary cash surpluses which they need to manage so as to earn a return. **Banks** provide one avenue for investment, but larger firms can invest in other forms of financial instrument in the money markets. Generally speaking, the greater the return offered, the riskier the investment.

6.1 Managing cash

Cash is an asset of a business; if it is to be invested, it must be invested profitably, and the investment must be secure.

6.2 Liquidity

We need to consider what we mean by surplus. Take the following example.

Example: liquidity

(a) Drif Co receives money every month from cash sales and from trade receivables for credit sales of $1,000. It makes payments, in the normal course of events of $800 a month. In January, the company uses an overdraft facility to buy a car for $4,000.

	Jan	Feb	March
	$	$	$
Brought forward	–	(3,800)	(3,600)
Receipts	1,000	1,000	1,000
Payments	(800)	(800)	(800)
Car	(4,000)	0	0
Overdrawn balance	(3,800)	(3,600)	(3,400)

The company has been left with a persistent overdraft, even though, in operating terms it makes a monthly surplus of $200.

(b) Guide Co on the other hand has monthly cash receipts of $1,200 and monthly cash payments of $1,050. The company sets up a special loan account: it borrows $5,000 to buy a car. This it pays off at the rate of $80 a month.

	Jan	Feb	March
	$	$	$
Brought forward	–	70	140
Receipts	1,200	1,200	1,200
Payments	(1,050)	(1,050)	(1,050)
Loan repayment	(80)	(80)	(80)
Operating surplus	70	140	210

Which do you consider has the healthier finances? Clearly Drif Co produces an operating surplus (before the motor purchase) of $200 ($1,000 – $800) a month, which is more than Guide ($150, ie $1,200 – $1,050). Furthermore Guide Co has a much higher net debt, the loan for the car being $5,000 as opposed to $4,000.

Yet, in effect the financing arrangements each has chosen has turned the tables. Drif Co is relying on normal overdraft finance which will be **repayable on demand**. Its normal **operating surplus** of receipts from sales and receivables over payments to suppliers has been completely swamped by the long-term financing of a car.

On the other hand, Guide Co, by arranging a separate term loan, which is more secure from Guide Co's point of view, is able to run an **operating surplus** of $70 a month. It has effectively separated an operating surplus arising out of month to month business expenses from its cash requirements for capital investment (in the car), leaving a **financial inflow**.

This shows the following.

(a) A 'surplus' can sometimes be created by the way in which **financial information** is **presented**.
(b) It is often necessary to distinguish **different kinds** of cash transaction (eg capital payments).
(c) Different types of debt have **different risks** for the company attached to them.

Cash surpluses may arise from **seasonal factors**, so that surpluses generated in good months are used to cover shortfalls later. In this case, the management of the business needs to ensure that the surpluses are big enough to cover the later deficits. The mere existence of a surplus in one or two months in a row is no guarantee of liquidity in the long term.

6.3 Safety

Considerations of **safety** are also important. Cash surpluses are rarely hoarded on the company's premises, where they can be stolen: but what should be done with them, in the short term?

(a)   They are assets of the company, and do need to be **looked after** as well as any other asset.

(b)   In time of inflation, money effectively **falls in value**.

(c)   Any surplus must be kept **secure**: as depositors in the collapsed Icelandic banks must be painfully aware, some banks are not as secure as others. Some investments are riskier than others.

Question 3.2	Investing cash

Learning outcome E2(b)

Compare the following two situations. Steve and Andy are both in the car repair business. Both own equipment worth $4,000 and both owe $200 to suppliers. Steve, however, has accumulated $1,000 in cash which is deposited in a non interest bearing current account at his bank. Andy has $100 in petty cash.

| | Steve | Andy |
	$	$
Non-current assets	4,000	4,000
Cash at bank	1,000	100
Payables	(200)	(200)
Net assets	4,800	3,900
Profit for the year	1,200	1,200

Which would you say is the more profitable?

There is the other question about cash surpluses: what do you do with them, to make a profit? They are business assets like any other.

(a)   In the long term, a company with an ever increasing cash balance can:

  (i)   **Invest it in new business opportunities** for profit
  (ii)   **Return it to owners/shareholders** by way of increased drawings/dividends

(b)   In the short term, surplus funds need to be invested so that they can earn a return when they are not being used for any other purpose.

  (i)   A return can be earned perhaps by an earlier payment of business debts. The return is the 'interest' saved.

  (ii)   Otherwise, there is a variety of deposit accounts and financial instruments which can be used to earn a return on the cash surpluses until they are needed. These are discussed in the next section of this chapter.

6.4 Guidelines for investing

Any business will normally have a number of guidelines as to how the funds are invested. A firm will try and maximise the return for an **acceptable** level of risk. What is acceptable depends on the preferences of the firm in question.

To maintain liquidity, it is often company policy that the surplus funds should be **invested** in financial instruments which are **easily converted** into cash; in effect, enough of the surplus funds should be invested to maintain liquidity.

There have been a number of reported incidents where a firm's corporate treasury department took too many risks with the firm's funds, investing them in risky financial instruments to gain a profit. These went sour, and firms have been left with high losses, arising solely out of treasury operations, with little relevance to the firm's main business.

Guidelines can cover issues such as the following examples.

(a)   Surplus funds can only be invested in **specified types of investment** (eg no equity shares).

(b)   All investments must be **convertible into cash** within a set number of days.

(c)   Investments should be **ranked**: surplus funds to be invested in higher risk instruments only when a sufficiency has been invested in lower risk items (so that there is always a cushion of safety).

(d)   If a firm invests in certain financial instruments, a **credit rating** should be obtained. Credit rating agencies, issue gradings according to risk.

6.5 Legal restrictions on investments

The type of investments an organisation can make is restricted by law in certain special cases:

(a)   Where public (ie taxpayers') money is invested by a **public sector** (central or local government) institution

(b)   Where the money is invested by a company on behalf of personal investors in cases such as **pension schemes**

(c)   In the case of **trusts** (as determined by the relevant Act)

Section summary

A company has a variety of opportunities for using its **cash surpluses**, but the choice of obtaining a return is determined by considerations, of **profitability**, **liquidity** and **safety**.

Surplus funds can be deposited in **interest bearing accounts** offered by banks, finance houses or building societies. Generally speaking:

- These are for a fixed period of time
- Early withdrawal may not be permitted, or may result in a penalty
- The principal does not decline in monetary value

7   Cash investments: bank and building society accounts

Introduction

Banks and building societies offer various different facilities for earning interest on cash deposits.

7.1 High street bank deposits

Commercial banks in most countries offer a wide range of different types of interest earning account. The main banks and many building societies may also pay interest on some types of **current account** (for day-to-day transactions). Some of these may be of limited relevance to large corporations, but for sole traders and small businesses, high street bank products are important.

For someone who wishes to invest a small sum for a short period, **deposit account** facilities may be available from the banks.

7.2 High interest deposit accounts and high interest cheque accounts

If you have a larger amount of money to invest, you may be able to place the money in a high interest account. Access is usually still immediate, but the rate of interest offered will be higher.

7.3 Option deposits

These arrangements are offered in many countries for predetermined periods of time ranging from 2 to 7 years with minimum deposits. The interest rates, which may be linked to base rates, reflect the longer term nature of the arrangement and the corresponding lack of withdrawal facilities before the expiry of the agreed term. For businesses, these might be of limited relevance.

7.4 Other facilities

Banks may offer special facilities for very large amounts.

(a)   With very large amounts, it may be possible to get fixed rate quotes for **money market deposits** for varying intervals such as seven days up to eighteen months or longer.

(b)   For still larger amounts it is possible to arrange for the money to be deposited with the bank's finance company at better rates than that available for normal deposits. Alternatively the business can go direct to a finance company itself.

Section summary

Banks offer several different facilities for earning interest on cash deposits.

---

8 Marketable securities: prices and interest rates   11/10, 3/11

Introduction

In the cash investments discussed in the previous section, the investor's initial capital is secure. The investor cannot get back less than they put in. Another common feature is that such investments are not marketable.

8.1 Marketable securities

However, there are also **marketable securities**, such as gilts, bonds and certificates of deposit. Such securities are bought and sold, and they earn interest. What determines their price?

8.2 Prices of fixed interest stocks

The price of marketable securities is affected by the following.

(a)   The **interest rate** (known as the **coupon rate**) on a stock is normally fixed at the outset, but it may become more or less attractive when compared with the interest rates in the money markets as a whole. Let us take an example. Suppose that investors in the market expect a return of 6.47%.

    (i) $2\frac{1}{2}$% Consolidated Stock pays $2.50 interest for every $100 of the stock's nominal value. However, the increased return means that:

$$\frac{\$2.50}{\text{Price of }\$100\text{ nominal}} = 6.47\%$$

therefore, the **expected** price is $\dfrac{\$2.50}{0.0647} = \$38.64$

Where general interest rates rise, the price of stocks will fall.

(ii)   Where general interest rates fall, the price of stocks will rise. For example, if the market required a return of 6%, the price of $100 nominal of a non-redeemable 2½% stock would be:

$\dfrac{\$2.50}{Price} = 6\%$ therefore, the expected price is $41.67.

Both these examples ignore two other features affecting prices of stocks.

(b)   The **risk** associated with the payment of interest and the **eventual repayment of capital**. Some Government securities are considered virtually risk-free but other fixed interest stocks may not be.

(c)   The **length of time to redemption** or **maturity**. Suppose the following market values were quoted on 25 March 20X2.

9% Treasury Stock 20X5 $113.8029
9% Treasury Stock 20X9 $142.6311

The first stock is due to be redeemed in 20X5, whereas the second will not be redeemed until the year 20X9. In both cases, as with all government securities except those that are index-linked, the stocks will be redeemed at their nominal value of $100. The closer a stock gets to its redemption date the closer the price will approach $100. This is known as the **pull to maturity**.

8.3 Yields on fixed interest stocks

The paragraphs below concentrate on gilts (government securities) but the principles involved apply equally to any other fixed interest stocks including, for example company loan stock.

8.4 Interest yield

The yield for a particular gilt is an expression for the return on the stock if it was bought at the price ruling and held for one year.

KEY TERM

INTEREST YIELD (also known as the flat yield or running yield) is the interest or coupon rate expressed as a percentage of the market price.

$$\text{Interest yield} = \frac{\text{Gross interest}}{\text{Market price}} \times 100\%$$

Question 3.3   Interest yield

Learning outcome E2(b)

On 19 March 20X0 the market price of 9% Treasury Stock 20X9 is $134.1742. What is the interest yield?

The interest yield in practice is influenced by two other factors.

(a)   **Accrued interest**

The interest on 10% Treasury Stock 20X3 is paid in two equal instalments on 8 March and 8 September each year. Thus, if an investor were to sell their stock on 1 June 20X0, in the absence of any other rules they would be forgoing a considerable amount of interest which will be received on 8 September 20X0 by the purchaser. **The price paid by the purchaser must reflect this**

amount of accrued interest, and this type of calculation is tested in Question 3.4: Cost of purchase.

(b)   **Cum int** and **Ex int**

For administrative reasons, issuers of securities (eg the government) must close their books some time before the due date for the payment of interest, so that they can prepare and send out the necessary documentation in time for it to reach the registered owners of securities before the due dates. Any person who buys stocks **ex int** will not receive the next interest payment. This will be sent to the former owner.

8.5 Redemption yields   5/11, 5/10

KEY TERM

REDEMPTION YIELD is the rate of interest at which the total of the discounted values of any future payments of interest and capital is equal to the current price of a security.   *(CIMA Official Terminology)*

The interest yield takes no account of the fact that most Government stocks are redeemable (ie that their face value will be repaid) nor of the proximity of the redemption date although we have seen how the pull to maturity can affect the price. A more realistic measure of the overall return available from a stock is the **gross redemption yield**. This takes account of both the **interest payable until redemption** and the **redemption value**.

Example: redemption yield (yield to maturity)

A bond with a coupon rate of 8% is redeemable in 9 years time for $100. Its current market price is $91. What is the percentage yield to maturity?

Solution

This is an internal rate of return calculation. (You should remember this from your CIMA C3 studies. We will look at it again in Chapter 16.) We will take two discount rates and see where the IRR is likely to fall.

Nine annual receipts of $8 and the final receipt in 9 years' time of $100, discounted at the IRR, will give us the current market price of $91.

We will begin by taking 10% as the discount rate.

t = 9, r = 10

($8 × 5.759) + ($100 × 0.424) = $46.07 + $42.40 = $88.47

This is very close to $91. Now we will try 9%.

t = 9, r = 9

($8 × 5.995) + ($100 × 0.46) = $47.96 + $46 = $93.96

We can see that the IRR must be midway between 10% and 9%.

(88.47 + 93.96)/2 = 91.22

So the percentage yield to maturity is 9.5%.

Note: If you are struggling to remember your CIMA C3 knowledge for this question you may want to leave it for now and return to it after you have studied Part D of this Study Text.

Yields are determined by **market prices** which in turn reflect the **demand for particular stocks**. Thus, if a yield is relatively low it can be concluded that the price is relatively high and that the demand for the stock is also relatively high. Conversely, a high yield means that a stock is relatively unpopular.

The major factors affecting choice are these.

(a)   Whether the investor is looking for **income or capital appreciation**

(b)   The investor's **tax position**

(c)   The investor's **attitude to the risk** inherent in gilts resulting from changes in interest rates. (It is important to remember that although the eventual repayment of a gilt is not in doubt, the market price may fluctuate widely between the date of purchase and the eventual redemption)

(d)   **Other aspects** of the **investor's business**. (The banks and building societies tend traditionally to concentrate on holding short-dated stocks (redeemable soon) while the insurance companies and pension funds which have long-term liabilities often match these with long-dated gilts (redeemable further in the future)).

Section summary

The **yield** (profitability) of a money market instrument depends on:

- Its face value
- The interest rate offered
- The period of time before it is redeemed (ie converted into cash) by the issuer

9 Other types of investment

Introduction

This section looks at other types of investment such as treasury bills and certificates of deposit.

9.1 Government securities: example – gilts

KEY TERM

The term GILTS is short for 'gilt-edged securities' and refers to marketable British Government securities. These stocks, although small in number (around 100), dominate the fixed interest market in the UK.

The *Financial Times* classifies gilts according to the length of their lives.

(a)   Shorts – lives up to five years (Stock Exchange up to seven years)

(b)   Mediums – lives from five to fifteen years (Stock Exchange seven to fifteen years)

(c)   Longs – lives of more than fifteen years

(d)   Undated stocks (Issued many years ago these are sometimes known as irredeemable or one-way option stocks. These include *War Loan 3$^1/_2$%, Conversion Loan 3$^1/_2$%, Consolidated Stock 2$^1/_2$%*. Each has certain other peculiarities)

(e)   Index-linked stocks

By 'life' is meant the **number of years** before the issuer repays the principal amount.

9.1.1 Fixed interest gilts

Most gilts are fixed interest, and their prices and yields follow the principles outlined in Section 8 above.

9.1.2 Treasury bills

KEY TERM

A TREASURY BILL is government short-term debt, maturing in less than one year, and generally issued at a discount.

(CIMA Official Terminology)

Treasury bills are issued weekly by the government to finance short-term cash deficiencies in the government's expenditure programme. The holder is paid the full value of the bill on maturity. Since they are negotiable, they can be re-sold, if required, before their maturity date.

Treasury bills do not pay interest, but the purchase price of a Treasury bill is less than its face value, the amount that the government will eventually pay on maturity. There is thus an **implied rate of interest** in the price at which the bills are traded.

9.1.3 Index-linked stocks

There are various **index-linked Treasury stocks** in issue. The first such stock, 2% Treasury Stock 1996, was issued in March 1981. Both the interest and the eventual redemption value are linked to inflation.

These gilts offer a **guaranteed real return** equal to the **coupon rate**. Many investment fund managers would have considered such a return highly satisfactory over the last fifteen years.

9.1.4 Gilt prices in the Financial Times

Gilt prices are to be found in the *Financial Times.* For all categories other than index-linked gilts, the information is presented as follows.

Monday edition

Notes	Price (£)	Wk% +/–	Amount £m	Interest due	Last xd
Treas 10pc 20X3	121.0801	0.4	2,506	Mr 8 Se 8	22.2

Tuesday to Saturday editions

| | Yield | | | | 52 week | |
Notes	Int	Red	Price (£)	+ or –	High	Low
Treas 10pc 20X3	8.27	4.72	120.9273	+0.0600	123.52	115.44

The first (Monday) example above shows that:

(a)   10% Treasury Stock 20X3 was quoted at £121.0801 at the close of business on the previous Friday, a change of +0.4% in the week.

(b)   £2,506 million of the stock was in issue.

(c)   Interest is due on 8 March and 8 September.

(d)   The stock last went **ex-interest** on 22 February. In other words, if you bought the stock after 22 February, you will not receive the interest due on 8 March. This interest will be paid to whoever held the stock up to 22 February.

The second (Tuesday to Saturday) example shows that:

(a)   The current price of the same stock was £120.9273 at the close of business on the previous day, which is £0.06 higher than the price on the day before.

(b)   The highest quoted price in the 52 weeks to date is £123.52; the lowest is £115.44.

(c)   The gross interest yield and the gross redemption yield are given in the first two columns.

9.1.5 Purchase, sale and issue of gilts

| Question 3.4 | Cost of purchase |

Learning outcome E2(b)

Suppose that a client wishes to purchase 13¾% Treasury Stock 2002-05 with a nominal value of £5,000. The transaction is executed by a stockbroker, who charges commission of 0.8%, in March 2001 at a price of £111.5064. Accrued interest is 56 days. What will be the total cost?

Gilts can be dealt in any amount down to 1p. It is therefore quite possible to buy, say, £13,456.83 nominal value of a particular stock. This facility is often useful to investors who wish to round up an existing holding to some convenient figure. Similarly, it is quite possible to spend an exact amount on a particular stock. For example, an investor might ring up his stockbroker and ask him to buy £5,000 worth of the 13¾% Treasury Stock on the day referred to in the Question above. The broker would then buy stock with a nominal value of:

$$£5,000 \times \frac{£100}{£111.5064} = £4,484.05$$

9.2 Local authority stocks

We have already mentioned that it is possible for investors to deposit their money with local authorities. In addition to these investments there are a very large number of marketable local authority securities.

These stocks may, in most respects, be considered as being very similar to British Government Stocks. The main differences are as follows.

(a) The security of a local authority is not considered quite as **good** as that of the central government.

(b) The market in most of the stocks is **much thinner** (ie there are not many transactions) than for gilts, since the amounts involved are smaller and the stocks tend to be held by just a few institutions.

As a result of the points listed above, the yield on local authority stocks tends to be rather higher than on gilts.

9.3 Certificates of deposit

KEY TERM

A CERTIFICATE OF DEPOSIT is a negotiable instrument that provides evidence of a fixed term deposit with a bank. Maturity is normally within 90 days, but can be longer. *(CIMA Official Terminology)*

9.3.1 Issue of CDs

Certificates of deposit (CDs) are issued by an institution (bank or building society), certifying that a specified sum has been deposited with the issuing institution, to be repaid on a specific date. The term may be as short as seven days, or as long as five years. Since CDs are negotiable, if the holder of a CD cannot wait until the end of the term of the deposit and wants cash immediately, the CD can be sold. The appeal of a CD is that it offers an attractive rate of interest, *and* can be easily sold. CDs are sold on the market at a discount which reflects prevailing interest rates.

CDs have one major advantage over a money-market time deposit with the same bank or building society, namely **liquidity**. Unlike a money market deposit which cannot be terminated until it matures, CDs can be liquidated **at any time** at the prevailing market rate. In return for this liquidity, the investor must, however, accept a lower yield than a money market deposit would command.

9.4 Bills of exchange

KEY TERM

A **BILL OF EXCHANGE** is a negotiable instrument, drawn by one party on another, for example by a supplier of goods on a customer, who by accepting (signing) the bill, acknowledges the debt, which may be payable immediately (a sight draft) or at some future date (a time draft). The holder of the bill can, thereafter, use an accepted time draft to pay a debt to a third party, or can discount it to raise cash.

(CIMA Official Terminology)

9.4.1 Definitions

(a)   The **bill** is **drawn** on the company or person who is being ordered to pay.
(b)   The **drawer** orders payment of the money.
(c)   The **drawee** is the party who is to pay, and to whom the bill is addressed.
(d)   The **payee** receives the funds.

Using the example of a cheque. A (the drawer), writes out a cheque to B (the payee). The cheque instructs A's bank (the drawee), to pay B a sum of money. The drawee of a bill of exchange does not have to be a bank, and the payment date does not have to be immediate.

A bill is an unconditional order to pay, and it will always include the word 'pay' and be phrased so as to make it clear that the order is unconditional. The bill must also specify the name of the payee, which might be the drawer ('Pay... to our order') or a third party ('Pay.... to XYZ or order....').

For a term bill with a future payment date, the **drawee** signs their acceptance of the order to pay (**accepts the bill** in other words, agrees to pay) and returns the bill to the drawer or the drawer's bank. When a bill is accepted, it becomes an IOU or promise to pay. If the bill is dishonoured the drawer can take legal action against the drawee.

9.4.2 Discounting bills

As an IOU, an accepted bill of exchange is a form of debt. It is a **negotiable instrument**.

(a)   The holder of the bill can hold on to the bill until maturity, then present it to the specified bank for payment.

(b)   Alternatively, the bill holder can **sell the bill** before **maturity**, for an amount below its payment value (ie at a discount). The **buyer** of a bill expects to make a profit by purchasing the bill at a discount to its face value and then either receiving full payment at maturity on presenting the bill for payment, or reselling the bill before maturity. The buyer could be a bank or a supplier with which the seller has a debt.

The seller obtains immediate cash from the buyer of the bill, but in effect is borrowing short-term funds, with the interest rate for borrowing built into the discount price. The size of the discount will reflect the interest rate that the buyer of the instrument wishes to receive, and the term to the instrument's maturity. To calculate the discounted amount to be paid the following formula is used.

$$\text{Discounted price} = F \times \left[1 - \frac{RT}{Y} \right]$$

Where F = Face value
R = Discount rate
T = Number of days
Y = Number of days in year

For example, a bill of exchange with a face value of $50,000 payable in 60 days where the buyer requires a discount rate of 5%.

$$\text{Discounted price} = \$50,000 \times \left[1 - \frac{60 \times 0.05}{365} \right] = \$49,589$$

Bills of exchange are also used to finance domestic and international trade, because they are tradeable instruments for short-term credit.

Money market instruments are traded on either an interest rate basis or a discount basis.

(a) When an **interest rate** basis applies, a **principal sum** is lent and the borrower repays the **principal plus interest** at maturity. The interest rate is specified and applied to the principal amount for the term of the loan to calculate the amount of interest payable. Bank loans are made on this basis.

(b) When a **discount basis** applies, a **specified sum** is **payable at maturity** to the holder of a money market instrument. If the instrument is purchased before maturity, the price will be less than the amount payable at maturity.

9.5 Other commercial stocks

9.5.1 Bonds

KEY TERMS

A BOND is a debt instrument normally offering a fixed rate of interest (coupon) over a fixed period of time, with a fixed redemption value.

COUPON is the annual interest payable on a bond, expressed as a percentage of the nominal value.

(CIMA Official Terminology)

BOND is a term given to any fixed interest (mostly) security, whether it be issued by the government, a company, a bank or other institution. (Gilts are therefore **UK government bonds**.) Businesses also issue bonds. They are usually for the long term. They may or may not be secured.

Example: Bond selling price

An unquoted bond has a coupon rate of 6%. It will repay its face value of $1,250 at the end of 10 years. The yield to maturity is 12%. What is the selling price of the bond?

Solution

You may need your old CIMA C3 notes to remind you of the net present value (NPV) technique. Alternatively you can come back to this question after studying Part D of this Study Text which covers NPVs.

The selling price of the bond is the **net present value** of the **interest** received every year for 10 years **and the $1,250** which we receive **at the end** of 10 years.

- The **coupon rate** of 6% determines **the amount of** interest received annually

- However, the amounts received are then discounted at the **discount factor** of 12% (the **yield to maturity**)

Interest = $1,250 × 6% = $75 (each year)

As the interest is received **each year**, it is an **annuity**. We need to look at the **cumulative present value tables** (at the back of this book) for 12% for 10 years. This gives us 5.650.

The $1,250 is received after 10 years so we need to look at the **present value tables** for 12% for 10 years. This gives us 0.322.

The net present value is therefore

$(75 × 5.650) + $(1,250 × 0.322) = $826

This is the **selling price** for the bond.

Exam alert

A question like this appeared in Section A of the specimen paper for 4 marks. Coupon rates, yield to maturity and government bonds have appeared in Section A in the May 2010, September 2010 and November 2010 exams and in Section B of the March 2011, November 2011 and May 2011 exams.

9.5.2 Commercial paper

KEY TERM

COMMERCIAL PAPER is unsecured short-term loan notes issued by companies, and generally maturing within three months.

Like a gilt, CP is traded often at a discount reflecting the yield required. It is a type of promissory note, and companies find them useful for short term borrowing (usually 3 months), and is unsecured. It is therefore risky. Although formal **credit ratings** are not required in some countries, they do help investors make rational choices. A firm's CP is therefore given a credit rating by third party agencies to assess its risk.

Loan stocks are issued in return for loans **secured on a particular asset of the business**. The factory, for example, may be offered as **security**. The loan is for the long term. Loan stock holders take priority over other payables when a business is wound-up. They can force a liquidation.

9.6 Money-market accounts

These are similar in principle to a bank deposit account. Here funds are deposited with a bank or other financial institution for a fixed period of time and cannot be accessed until the term has ended. Terms range from overnight to 12 months.

Section summary

Gilts are securities issued by the UK government. Other fixed interest marketable securities include **local authority bonds**, and **corporate debt**.

A **certificate of deposit** is a certificate indicating that a sum of money has been deposited with a bank and will be repaid at a later date. As CDs can be bought and sold, they are a liquid type of investment.

A **bill of exchange** is like a cheque, only it is not drawn on a bank. It orders the drawee to pay money.

Commercial paper and **loan stock** are debt instruments issued by companies: commercial paper is unsecured.

10   Risk and exposure

Introduction

Businesses should have guidelines in place covering **what sort of investments** are **allowed** and how much should be **invested** in **lower risk** securities.

10.1 Risk

Risk can be considered under the following headings:

(a)   **Default risk**. The risk that payments of interest or capital will not be received on schedule.

(b)   **Price risk**. The risk that the value of a fixed interest investment will be adversely affected by a rise in interest rates.

(c)   **Foreign exchange risk**. The risk that value of foreign investment may be adversely affected by movement in exchange rates.

(d)   **Tax and regulation risk**. The risk that legal or tax charges at home or abroad impact upon the value of investments.

10.2 The relationship between risk and return

The return expected by an investor will depend on the level of risk. The higher the risk, the higher the required return. This can be illustrated as in the diagram below.

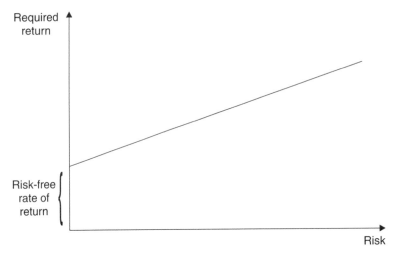

Marketable UK securities can be ranked in order of increasing risk and increasing expected return.

- Government securities
- Local authority stocks
- Other 'public' corporation stocks
- Company loan stocks
- Other secured loans
- Unsecured loans
- Convertible loan stocks
- Preference shares
- Equities

Low risk

High risk

(a) **Government stock**

   The risk of default is negligible and hence this tends to form the base level for returns in the market. The only uncertainty concerns the movement of interest rates over time, and hence longer dated stocks will tend to carry a higher rate of interest.

(b) **Company loan stock**

   Although there is some risk of default on company loan stock (also called corporate bonds), the stock is usually secured against corporate assets.

(c) **CDs and Bills of Exchange**

   The riskiness of CDs and bills of exchange varies with the creditworthiness of the issuers. They are riskier than government (and probably local government) securities, but less risky than shares.

10.3 Diversification and holding a portfolio

Holding more than one investment always carries less risk than holding only one. If only one investment is held, the investor could lose a lot if this one investment fails. The extent to which risk can be reduced will depend on the relationship which exists between the different returns. The process of reducing risk by increasing the number of separate investments in a portfolio is known as **diversification**.

Section summary

Businesses should have guidelines in place covering **what sort of investments** are **allowed** and how much should be **invested** in **lower risk** securities. The relative attractiveness of investing in any of these securities derives from their **return** and the **risk**. **Diversification** across a range of separate investments can reduce risk for the investor.

Chapter Roundup

✓ Maintenance of **liquidity** is an important corporate objective. Organisations may have problems due to **timing differences**, **risk** and **contingencies**.

✓ **Overdrafts** are a form of short-term lending, technically repayable on demand. Businesses may not need to use the overdraft facilities that they have been granted.

✓ Bank loans tend to be a **source** of **medium-term finance**, linked with the purchase of specific assets. Interest and repayments will be set in advance.

✓ There are advantages and disadvantages to having an overdraft instead of a loan.

✓ **Trade credit** from suppliers is another possible short-term source of finance, but it has its disadvantages.

✓ It is worth remembering that the **exporter** can obtain finance from the foreign buyer by insisting on **cash with order** and the **importer** can obtain finance from the foreign supplier by means of normal trade credit, perhaps evidenced by a term bill of exchange.

✓ **Export factoring** provides all the advantages of factoring generally and is useful in assessing credit risk.

✓ **Forfaiting** provides medium-term finance for importers of capital goods.

✓ A company has a variety of opportunities for using its **cash surpluses**, but the choice of obtaining a return is determined by considerations of **profitability**, **liquidity** and **safety**.

✓ Surplus funds can be deposited in **interest bearing accounts** offered by banks, finance houses or building societies. Generally speaking:

- These are for a fixed period of time
- Withdrawal may not be permitted, or may result in a penalty
- The principal does not decline in monetary value

✓ Banks offer several different facilities for earning interest on cash deposits.

✓ The **yield** (profitability) of a money market instrument depends on:

- Its face value
- The interest rate offered
- The period of time before it is redeemed (ie converted into cash) by the issuer

✓ **Gilts** are securities issued by the UK government. Other fixed interest marketable securities include **local authority bonds**, and **corporate debt**.

✓ A **certificate of deposit** is a certificate indicating that a sum of money has been deposited with a bank and will be repaid at a later date. As CDs can be bought and sold, they are a liquid type of investment.

✓ A **bill of exchange** is like a cheque, only it is not drawn on a bank. It orders the drawee to pay money.

✓ **Commercial paper** and **loan stock** are debt instruments issued by companies: commercial paper is unsecured.

✓ Businesses should have guidelines in place covering **what sort of investments** are **allowed** and how much should be **invested** in **lower risk** securities.

✓ The relative attractiveness of investing in any of these securities derives from their **return** and the **risk**. **Diversification** across a range of separate investments can reduce risk for the investor.

Quick Quiz

1   Which of the following is **not** a type of bank borrowing?

    A   Term loan
    B   Certificate of deposit
    C   Revolving facility
    D   Uncommitted facility

2   Match the name of the bank borrowing facilities detailed below with the relevant description.

    Facility   *Description*

    A Overdrift   1   Renewable after a set period.

    B Revolving facility 2   Borrowing of a fixed amount for a fixed period.

    C Term loan   3   Borrowing through the customer's current account up to a certain limit.
                             Repayable on demand.

3   What reasons may make a business ask for an overdraft to reduce trade payables?

4   Which of the following is normally an advantage of an overdraft over a term loan?

    A   No risk of the bank withdrawing the facility
    B   Interest only paid to the extent that funds are required
    C   Better for borrowing to finance purchase of non-current assets
    D   Planning and budgeting are simpler

5   Banks are generally likely to grant an overdraft facility when a business is building up its inventory.

    True   ☐

    False ☐

6   Which of the following methods could *not* be used to reduce the risk of bad debts in foreign trade?

    A   Export factoring
    B   Forfaiting
    C   Advances against collections
    D   Documentary credits

7   Apart from liquidity, what are the other two key considerations which a business should bear in mind in managing cash?

8   .... is an unsecured short-term loan note issued by companies, and generally maturing within three months.

9   Interest yield = $\dfrac{\boxed{}}{\boxed{}}$ × 100%. Fill in the boxes.

10 On a particular day, 9% Treasury Stock 2012 is quoted at a price of $141. What is the coupon rate?

11 The market prices of gilts will generally fall if interest rates rise.

    True   ☐

    False ☐

12   Rank the following in order of risk (1 for the lowest risk).

	Preferred shares
	Government securities
	Company loan stock
	Ordinary shares
	Local authority stocks

13   Ms Archer is intending to purchase 8% Treasury Stock 2003-06 with a nominal value of $10,000. The transaction is executed by a broker, who charges commission of 0.8%, at a price of $105.50. Accrued interest is 30 days. What will be the total cost?

A $10,700
B $10,634
C $10,616
D $10,550

Answers to Quick Quiz

1   B   This is a type of investment, not a debt.

2   A3; B1; C2

3   (a)   To take advantage of early settlement discounts
       (b)   To pay suppliers who are pressing for payment

4   B   Interest only paid to the extent funds are required

5   False. Some reasons for building up inventories (coping with seasonal demand, taking advantage of favourable purchase terms) will probably be acceptable to the bank, but generally such build-ups will be temporary. Banks are less likely to grant an increase to support a permanent increase in inventory level.

6   C   This can reduce the investment in foreign receivables, but it does not reduce the risk of bad debts.

7   Safety; profitability

8   Commercial paper

9    $\text{Interest yield} = \dfrac{\text{Coupon rate}}{\text{Market price}} \times 100\%$

10   9%

11   True

12   Preferred shares, 4; Government securities, 1; Company loan stock, 3; Ordinary shares, 5; Local authority stocks, 2.

13   A

	$
Purchase consideration: $10,000 @ $105.50 per $100	10,550
Accrued interest: 30 days at 8% ($10,000 × 0.08 × 30/365)	66
Broker's commission: $10,550 × 0.8%	84
	10,700

Answers to Questions

3.1 Bank overdraft

Although the directors might believe that they are asking the bank to help with financing their current assets, they are really asking for assistance with the purchase of a non-current asset, because the bank lending would leave the total current assets of the company unchanged, but will increase the current liabilities. Consequently, bank borrowing on overdraft to buy a non-current asset would reduce the working capital of Wrong Wreason from $60,000 to $10,000. In contrast, borrowing $50,000 to finance extra current assets would have increased current assets from $120,000 to $170,000, and with current liabilities going from $60,000 to $110,000, total working capital would have remained unchanged at $60,000 and liquidity would arguably still be adequate.

3.2 Investing cash

(a)   Both obviously have made the same amount of profit in the year in question. In absolute terms they are equal.

(b)   However, if we examine more closely, we find that the relative performance of Steve and Andy differs.

	Steve	*Andy*
$\dfrac{\text{Profit}}{\text{Net assets}}$	$\dfrac{\$1,200}{\$4,800} = 25\%$	$\dfrac{\$1,200}{\$3,900} = 30.8\%$

In other words, Andy is making the same amount out of more limited resources. Steve could have easily increased his profit if he had invested his spare cash and earned interest on it.

3.3 Interest yield

$$\text{Interest yield} = \frac{\text{Gross interest}}{\text{Market price}} \times 100\%$$

$$= \frac{9}{134.1742} \times 100\% = 6.71\%$$

3.4 Cost of purchase

	£
Purchase consideration £5,000 @ 111.5064 per £100	5,575.32
Accrued interest: 56 days at 13¾% (£5,000 × 0.1375 × 56/365)	105.48
Broker's commission on consideration 0.8% on £5,575.32	44.60
Total purchase cost	5,725.40

Now try the question from the Exam Question Bank	Number	Level	Marks	Time
	Q3	Examination	20	36 mins

RECEIVABLES AND PAYABLES

The previous chapters have discussed some of the issues of managing cash, and you will have noted the **time lag** between the provision of goods and services and the receipt of cash for them. This time lag, as we have seen, can result in a firm making considerable demands on its bank to finance its working capital. Any increase in the time lag can make it significantly more difficult for a business to pay **its** own debts as they fall due.

This chapter introduces receivables management by considering the policy decisions that a business has to take in relation to **all** receivables.

An important decision in this area is whether to offer **settlement discounts** in return for quicker payment.

The credit controller also has to monitor the ongoing creditworthiness of customers and the **aged receivables listing** is a principal instrument used.

Section 7 deals with ways of limiting or managing the risk from bad debts.

In sections 8 and 9 we look at the need to monitor payables and describe payment methods and procedures. As with receivables, the effect of discounts is important.

topic list	learning outcomes	syllabus references	ability required
1 What is credit control?	E1(e)	E1(ii)	analysis
2 Total credit	E1(e)	E1(ii)	analysis
3 The credit cycle	E1(e)	E1(ii)	analysis
4 Payment terms and settlement discounts	E1(f)	E1(vii)	analysis
5 Maintaining information on receivables	E1(f)	E1(viii)	analysis
6 Collecting debts	E1(f)	E1(ix)	analysis
7 Credit insurance, factoring and invoice discounting	E1(f)	E1(ix)	analysis
8 Managing payables	E1(f)	E1(ix)	analysis
9 Methods of paying suppliers	E1(f)	E1(ii)	analysis

1 What is credit control?

Introduction

Credit control deals with a firm's management of its working capital. **Trade credit** is offered to business customers. **Consumer credit** is offered to household customers.

1.1 Credit

There are two aspects to **credit** we shall consider here.

(a) **Trade credit**

This is credit issued by a business to another business. For example, many invoices state that payment is expected within thirty days of the date of the invoice. In effect this is giving the customer thirty days credit. The customer is effectively borrowing at the supplier's expense.

(b) **Consumer credit**

This is credit offered by businesses to the end-consumer.

(i) Many businesses offer **hire purchase terms**, whereby the consumer takes out a loan to repay the goods purchased. Failure to repay will result in the goods being repossessed.

(ii) In practice, much of the growth in consumer credit has been driven not so much by retailers as by banks. **Credit cards** are largely responsible for the explosive growth in consumer credit.

Credit control issues are closely bound up with a firm's management of liquidity, discussed in earlier chapters. Credit is offered to enhance sales and profitability, but this should not be to the extent that a company becomes illiquid and insolvent.

Credit is also vital in securing orders in certain specified situations.

(a) **Economic conditions** can influence the type and amount of credit offered. In 'boom times, when customers are queuing with orders' (Bass, in *Credit Management Handbook*), new customers can be asked for security, and risk can be minimised. In other times, credit must be used to entice customers in, and so the credit manager's job is to control risk.

(b) **High-risk or marginal customers** require flexible payment arrangements. High risk customers are often profitable, but the risk has to be managed. The customer may require a credit limit of $50,000, on standard terms, but may only deserve $35,000. The supplier might choose instead to offer a $30,000 credit limit, together with a discount policy to encourage early payment.

Just as there is a relationship between offering credit and securing sales, there must also be a suitable working relationship between credit control personnel and sales and marketing staff. This is because, in the words of Bass, 'a sale is not complete until the money is in the bank' and the cost of chasing after slow payers and doubtful debts is considerable.

1.2 A firm's credit policy

A firm should have policies for credit and credit control.

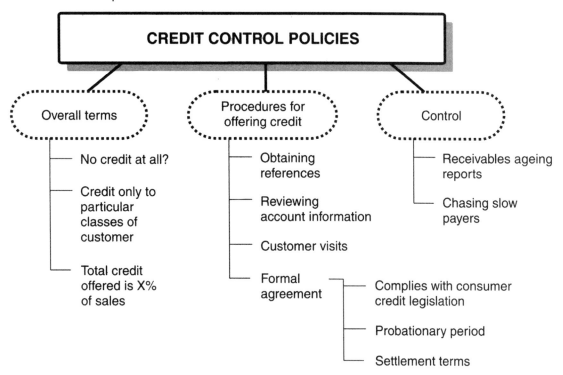

When a new customer applies for credit, their credit status will be assessed in a number of ways:

(a) References. Standard practice is to require a banker's reference and two trade references.
(b) The company's published accounts.
(c) The use of credit reference agencies such as Dun and Bradstreet.

Section summary

Credit control deals with a firm's management of its working capital. **Trade credit** is offered to business customers. **Consumer credit** is offered to household customers.

2 Total credit

Introduction

Total credit can be measured in a variety of ways. Financial analysts use days sales in receivables, but as this is an annualised figure it gives no idea as to the make-up of total receivables.

2.1 The cost of credit

A bank's decision to lend money to a customer is determined by many factors over which the customer has little control. The bank, for example, might only wish to extend so much credit to firms in a particular industry.

Similarly, the firm itself has to maintain a 'global' approach to credit control in the light of the firm's objectives for **profit**, **cash flow**, **asset use** and **reducing interest costs**.

Finding a **total level of credit** which can be offered is a matter of finding the least costly balance between enticing customers, whose use of credit entails considerable costs, and refusing opportunities for profitable sales.

Firstly it helps to see what receivables, which often account for 30% of the total assets of a business, actually represent.

2.2 Measuring total receivables

The **days sales in receivables ratio**, sometimes called **receivables payment period** represents the length of the credit period taken by customers.

$$\frac{\text{Total receivables} \times 365}{\text{Sales in 365 days}} \quad \text{Days sales}$$

For example, in 20X4 X Co made sales of $700,000 and at 31 December 20X4, receivables stood at $90,000. The comparable figures for 20X3 were $600,000 (annual sales) and $70,000 (receivables at 31 December 20X3).

	20X4	*20X3*
Receivables represent	$\dfrac{\$90,000 \times 365}{\$700,000} = 47$ days	$\dfrac{\$70,000 \times 365}{\$600,000} = 43$ days

In 20X4, the company is taking longer to collect its debts.

2.3 Effect on profit of extending credit

The main cost of offering credit is the interest expense. How can we assess the effect on profit?

Let us assume that the Zygo Company sells widgets for $1,000, which enables it to earn a profit, after all other expenses except interest, of $100 (ie a 10% margin).

(a)   Aibee buys a widget for $1,000 on 1 January 20X1, but does not pay until 31 December 20X1. Zygo relies on overdraft finance, which costs it 10% pa. The effect is:

	$
Net profit on sale of widget	100
Overdraft cost $1,000 × 10% pa	(100)
Actual profit after 12 months credit	Nil

In other words, the entire profit margin has been wiped out in 12 months.

(b)   If Aibee had paid after six months, the effect would be:

	$
Net profit	100
Overdraft cost $1,000 × 10% pa × $^{6}/_{12}$ months	(50)
	50

Half the profit has been wiped out. (*Tutorial note.* The interest cost might be worked out in a more complex way to give a more accurate figure.)

(c)   If the cost of borrowing had been 18%, then the profit would have been absorbed before seven months had elapsed. If the net profit were 5% and borrowing costs were 15%, the interest expense would exceed the net profit after four months.

A second general point is the relation of **total credit to bad debts**. Burt Edwards argues that there is a law of 10-to-1: 'Experience in different industries shows that the annual interest expense of borrowings to support overdue debts, ie those in excess of agreed payment terms, is at least ten times the total lost in bad debts'. This is not a 'law', but has been observed to be the case over a variety of UK businesses.

Question 4.1

Cost of credit

Learning outcome E1(e)

Winterson Tools has an average level of receivables of $2m at any time representing 60 days outstanding. (Their terms are thirty days.) The firm borrows money at 10% a year. The managing director is proud of the credit control: 'I only had to write off $10,000 in bad debts last year,' she says proudly. Is she right to be proud?

The level of total credit can therefore have a significant effect on **profitability**. That said, if credit considerations are included in pricing calculations, extending credit can, in fact, increase profitability. If offering credit generates extra sales, then those extra sales will have additional repercussions on:

(a)   The **amount of inventory** maintained in the warehouse, to ensure that the extra demand must be satisfied

(b)   The **amount of money** the company **owes** to its **suppliers** (as it will be increasing its supply of raw materials)

This means an increase in **working capital**. Working capital is an **investment**, just as a non-current asset (eg new machinery) is, albeit of a different kind.

To determine whether it would be profitable to extend the level of total credit, it is necessary to assess the following.

*   The additional sales volume which might result
*   The profitability of the extra sales
*   The extra length of the average debt collection period
*   The required rate of return on the investment in additional receivables

Question 4.2

Increase in credit period

Learning outcome E1(f)

A company is proposing to increase the credit period that it gives to customers from one calendar month to one and a half calendar months in order to raise sales from the present annual figure of $24 million representing 4m units per annum. The price of the product is $6 and it costs $5.40 to make. The increase in the credit period is likely to generate an extra 150,000 unit sales. Is this enough to justify the extra costs given that the company's required rate of return is 20%? Assume no changes to inventory levels, as the company is increasing its operating efficiency. Assume that existing customers will take advantage of the new terms.

Example: total investment in receivables

RB Co is considering a change of credit policy which will result in a slowing down in the average collection period from one to two months. The relaxation in credit standards is expected to produce an increase in sales in each year amounting to 25% of the current sales volume.

Sales price per unit	$10.00
Profit per unit (before interest)	$1.50
Current sales revenue per annum	$2.4 million

The required rate of return on investment is 20%.

Assume that the 25% increase in sales would result in additional inventories of $100,000 and additional payables of $20,000. Advise the company on whether or not it should extend the credit period offered to customers, in the following circumstances.

(a)   If all customers take the longer credit of two months

(b)   If existing customers do not change their payment habits, and only the new customers take a full two months' credit

Solution

The change in credit policy would be justifiable, in the context of this question, if the rate of return on the additional investment in working capital exceeds 20%.

Extra profit
Profit margin $^{\$1.50}/_{\$10}$ =   15%
Increase in sales revenue $2.4m × 25% $0.6 million
Increase in profit (15% × $0.6m) $90,000

The total sales revenue is now $3m ($2.4m + $0.6m)

(a)   *Extra investment, if all customers take two months credit*

	$
Average receivables after the sales increase (2/12 × $3 million)	500,000
Current average receivables (1/12 × $2.4 million)	200,000
Increase in receivables	300,000
Increase in inventories	100,000
	400,000
Increase in payables	(20,000)
Net increase in 'working capital'	380,000

Return on extra investment $\dfrac{\$90,000}{\$380,000}$ = 23.7%

(b)   *Extra investment, if only the new customers take two months credit*

	$
Increase in receivables (2/12 × $0.6 million)	100,000
Increase in inventories	100,000
	200,000
Increase in payables	(20,000)
Net increase in working capital investment	180,000

Return on extra investment $\dfrac{\$90,000}{\$180,000}$ = 50%

In both case (a) and case (b) the new credit policy appears to be worthwhile.

Furthermore, the cost profile of the product can also support extra sales. If the firm has high fixed costs but low variable costs, the extra production and sales could provide a substantial contribution at little extra cost.

Exam skills

You may be required to evaluate whether a proposed change in credit policy is financially justified. This is the procedure you should follow.

2.4 Receivables quality and liquidity

Another objective of any credit control system is to minimise any risks to **cash flow** arising from insolvent customers. The **quality** of receivables has an important impact on a firm's overall liquidity. Receivable quality is determined by their **age** and **risk**.

Some **industries** have a higher level of risk than others, in other words, there is a higher probability that customers will fail to pay. Some markets are riskier than others. Selling goods to a country with possible payment difficulties is riskier than selling them in the home market.

For many customers, delaying payment is the cheapest form of finance available and there has been much publicity recently about the difficulties that delayed payments cause to small businesses. There is no easy answer to this problem.

2.5 Policing total credit

The total amount of credit offered, as well as individual accounts, should be policed to ensure that the senior management policy with regard to the total credit limits is maintained. A **credit utilisation report** can indicate the extent to which total limits are being utilised. An example is given below.

Customer	Limit $'000	Utilisation $'000	%
Alpha	100	90	90
Beta	50	35	70
Gamma	35	21	60
Delta	250	125	50
	435	271	
		62.3%	

This might also contain other information, such as days sales outstanding and so on.

Reviewed in aggregate, this can reveal the following.

- The number of customers who might want more credit
- The extent to which the company is exposed to receivables
- The 'tightness' of the policy
- Credit utilisation in relation to total sales

It is possible to design credit utilisation reports to highlight other trends.

- The degree of exposure to different countries
- The degree of exposure to different industries

Trade receivables analysis as at 31 December

Industry	Current credit utilisation $'000	% of total receivables %	Annual sales $ million	As a % of total sales %
Property	9,480	25.0	146.0	19.2
Construction	7,640	20.2	140.1	18.4
Engineering	4,350	11.5	112.6	14.8
Electricals	4,000	10.6	83.7	11.0
Electricity	2,170	5.7	49.2	6.5
Transport	3,230	8.5	79.9	10.5
Chemicals, plastics	1,860	4.9	43.3	5.7
Motors, aircraft trades	5,170	13.6	105.8	13.9
	37,900	100.0	760.6	100.0

2.6 Analysis

(a)   An industry analysis of credit exposure shows in this case that over 45% of the company's trade receivables (about $17 million) are in the property and construction industries. Management should have a view about this exposure to industry risk.

(b)   The size of the exposure to property and construction could seem excessive, in view of the cyclical nature of these industries, the current economic outlook, and the comparatively slow payment rate from these customers. (These industries account for only 37.6% of annual sales, but 45.2% of trade receivables.) Management might wish to consider whether the company should try to reduce this exposure.

(c)   A decision might also be required about whether the company should be willing to accumulate trade receivables in these sectors, in order to sustain sales, or whether the credit risk would be too high.

2.7 Conclusion

The amount of **total credit** that a business offers is worthy of consideration at the highest management levels. Two issues are:

- The firm's working capital needs and the investment in receivables
- The management responsibility for carrying out the credit control policy

Question 4.3   Inflation

Learning outcome E1(f)

Your company is concerned about the effect of inflation, which (you should suppose) currently stands at 6%, on its credit control policy. Outline the main points to consider, for discussion with your manager.

Section summary

Total credit can be measured in a variety of ways. Financial analysts use days sales in receivables, but as this is an annualised figure it gives no idea as to the make-up of total receivables.

The **total investment in receivables** has to be considered in its impact on the general investment in working capital.

3 The credit cycle

Introduction

The **credit control department** is responsible for those stages in the collection cycle dealing with the offer of credit, and the collection of debts.

3.1 The credit cycle

The credit control function's jobs occupy a number of stages of the **order cycle** (from customer order to invoice despatch) and the **collection cycle** (from invoice despatch to the receipt of cash), which together make up the **credit cycle.** The job of the credit control department can comprise all those activities within the dotted line **in the Collection Cycle diagram**.

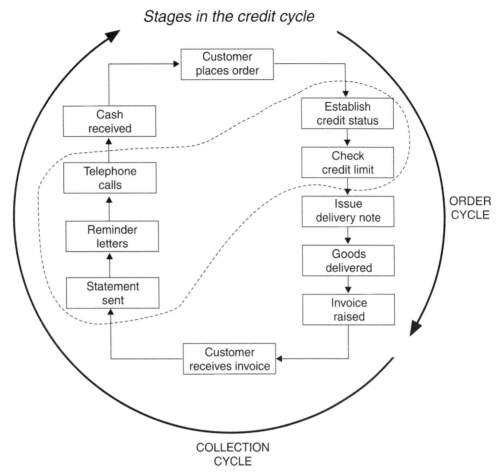

Stages in the credit cycle

(a)   **Establish credit status for new customers or customers who request a credit extension.** This might include references from the customer's bank or from a credit reference agency.

(b)   **Check credit limit**

If the order is fairly routine, and there is no problem with credit status, then credit control staff examine their records or at least the sales ledger records to see if the new order will cause the customer to exceed the credit limit. There are a number of possible responses, as follows.

(i)   **Authorisation**

If the credit demanded is within the credit limit, and there are no reasons to suspect any problems, then the request will be authorised.

(ii)   **Referral**

It is possible that the credit demanded will exceed the limit offered in the agreement.

(1)   The firm can simply **refuse the request for credit**, at the risk of damaging the business relationship. However, credit limits are there for a reason – to protect the business's profitability and liquidity.

(2)   The firm can offer a **revised credit limit**. For example, the customer may be solvent and a regular payee, therefore a low risk. The company might be able to offer a higher credit limit to this customer.

(3)   The firm can **contact the customer**, and request that some of the outstanding debt be paid off before further credit is advanced.

(c)   **Issuing documentation**

Issuing the delivery note, invoicing and so on is not the job of the credit control department, but the credit control department will need to have **access to information** such as invoice details to do its job.

(d)   **Settlement**

The credit control department takes over the collection cycle, although the final payment is ultimately received by the accounts department. Collection involves reviewing overdue debts, and chasing them.

Question 4.4	Credit control and working capital

Learning outcome E1(f)

See if you can explain the likely effects of a company's credit control policy on the control of working capital in general.

Section summary

The **credit control department** is responsible for those stages in the collection cycle dealing with the offer of credit, and the collection of debts.

4   Payment terms and settlement discounts

Introduction

A firm must consider suitable **payment terms** and **payment methods**. **Settlement discounts** can be offered, if cost effective and if they improve liquidity.

4.1 Payment terms

An important aspect of the credit control policy is to devise suitable **payment terms**, covering when should payment be made and how this should be achieved.

(a)   Credit terms have to take into account the **expected profit** on the sale and the seller's cash needs.

(b)   Credit terms also establish when **payment is to be received**, an important matter from the seller's point of view.

TERMS AND CONDITIONS OF SALE
•   Nature of goods to be supplied
•   Price
•   Delivery
•   Date of payment
•   Frequency of payment
•   Discounts

The credit terms the seller offers depend on many factors.

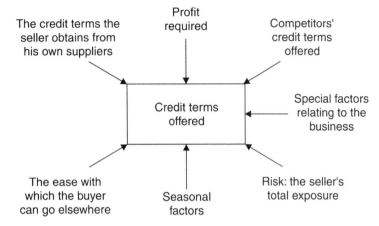

The terms must be simple to understand and easily enforceable. If the seller does not enforce his terms he is creating a precedent.

All sale agreements are **contracts**, as described earlier: credit terms are part of the contract. Although contracts do not have to be in writing, it helps if they are, and these are confirmed by the invoice.

PAYMENT TERMS	
Payment a specified number of days after delivery	Eg Net 10 (10 days)
Weekly credit	All supplies in a week must be paid for by a specified date in the next week
Half monthly credit	All supplies in one half of month must be paid for by a specified date in the next
10th and 25th	Supplies in first half of the month must be paid for by 25th, supplies in second half must be paid for by 10th of next month
Monthly credit	Payment for month's supplies must be paid by specified date in next month; if date 7th might be written Net 7 prox. Some monthly credit called Number MO; 2MO means payment must be in next month but one
Delivery	Certain payment terms geared to delivery • CWO Cash with order • CIA Cash in advance • COD Cash on delivery • CND Cash on next delivery

4.2 Methods of payment

Payment can be accepted in a variety of forms.

- Cash
- BACS
- Cheques
- Banker's draft
- Travellers' cheques or Eurocheques
- Postal orders

- Standing order
- Direct debit
- Credit card
- Debit card
- Bills of exchange, promissory notes
- Internet transfers

4.3 Payment times: settlement discounts   9/10, 5/10

Some firms offer settlement discounts if payment is received early.

(a)   If sensibly priced, they encourage customers to pay earlier, thereby avoiding some of the financing costs arising out of the granting of credit. Thus they can affect **profitability**.

(b)   The seller may be suffering from cash flow problems. If settlement discounts encourage earlier payment, they thus enable a company to **maintain liquidity**. In the short term, liquidity is often more important than profitability.

(c)   Settlement discounts might, conceivably, **affect the volume of demand** if, as part of the overall credit terms offered, they encourage customers to buy.

However discounts can have certain disadvantages.

(a)   If a discount is offered to **one customer**, the company may have to offer it to other customers.
(b)   **Discounts** may be **difficult to withdraw**.
(c)   They establish a **set settlement period**, which might otherwise be lowered in the future.

To consider whether the offer of a discount for early payment is financially worthwhile it is necessary to compare the **cost** of the discount with the **benefit** of a reduced investment in receivables.

Example: settlement discounts

Wingspan currently has sales of $3m, with an average collection period of two months. No discounts are given. The management of the company are undecided as to whether to allow a discount on sales of 2% to settle within one month. The company assumes that all customers would take advantage of the discount. The company can obtain a return of 30% on its investments.

Advise the management whether or not to introduce the discount.

Solution

In this example the offer of a discount is not expected to increase sales demand. The advantage would be in the **reduction of the collection period**, and the resulting saving in the working capital investment required.

Our solution will value receivables at sales value.

(a)   *Change in receivables*

	Receivables valued at sales price $
Current value of receivables (2/12 × $3m)	500,000
New value of receivables (1/12 × $3m)	250,000
Reduction in investment in receivables	250,000

(b)   The cost of reducing receivables is the cost of the discounts, ie

2% × $3 million = $60,000

(c)   The reduction in receivables of $250,000 would cost the company $60,000 per annum. If the company can earn 30% on its investments, the benefit is:

30% × $250,000 = $75,000

The discount policy would be worthwhile, since the benefit of $75,000 exceeds the cost of $60,000.

The percentage cost of an early settlement discount to the company giving it can be estimated by the formula:

LEARN

$$\left(\frac{100}{100-d}\right)^{\frac{365}{t}} - 1$$

Where: d is the discount offered (5% = 5, etc)
         t is the reduction in payment period in days

In the example above, the formula can be applied as follows.

$$\text{Cost of discount} = \left(\frac{100}{100-2}\right)^{\frac{365}{30}} - 1$$

$$= 27.9\%$$

Stages in the calculation:

   100/98 = 1.0204

   365/30 = 12.1666

   1.0204 ^ (or y^x) 12.1666

   = 1.2785

   −1 = 27.85%, say 27.9

Since 27.9% is less than the 30% by which the company judges investments, offering the discount is worthwhile.

Question 4.5   Discount

Learning outcome E1(f)

Gamma grants credit terms of 60 days net to customers, but offers an early settlement discount of 2% for payment within seven days. What is the cost of the discount to Gamma?

Exam skills

Make sure you learn the formula for the percentage cost of an early settlement discount.

As far as an **individual customer** is concerned, the principles are similar. For example, assume Boris has an average $10,000 outstanding, representing two months sales. You offer Boris a 1% settlement discount which would reduce the average amount outstanding to $5,000 (before discounts). You borrow money at 5%. A 1% discount on annual sales of $60,000 would cost you $600. Overdraft interest saved is $250 ($5,000 × 5%) so it is not worth offering the discount.

4.4 Late payment

It has been suggested that businesses should charge interest on overdue debts, however:

(a) **Charging for late payment** might be misconstrued (The supplier might assume that charges for late payment give the customer the authority to pay late.)

(b) A statutory **rate for interest** on overdue debts may not have been established in the country.

(c) Charging for payments relates only to the effect of the late payment on **profitability**, not on liquidity

Question 4.6   Good cash management

Learning outcome E1(a)

Thinking back to topics covered in earlier chapters, explain how good cash management may realise each of the following benefits.

(a) Better control of financial risk
(b) Opportunity for profit
(c) Strengthened statement of financial position
(d) Increased confidence with customers, suppliers, banks and shareholders

Question 4.7   Credit control policy

Learning outcome E1(f)

Your company has been growing rapidly over the last two years and now wishes to introduce a more formal credit control policy. You are asked to give a brief presentation on the factors involved in setting up such a policy.

Section summary

A firm must consider suitable **payment terms** and **payment methods**. **Settlement discounts** can be offered, if cost effective and if they improve liquidity.

5 Maintaining information on receivables

Introduction

For control purposes, **receivables** are generally analysed by age of debt.

5.1 Receivables age analysis   5/10

An **aged receivables listing** will probably look very much like the schedule illustrated below. The analysis splits up the total balance on the account of each customer across different columns according to the dates of the transactions which make up the total balance. Thus, the amount of an invoice which was raised 14 days ago will form part of the figure in the column headed 'up to 30 days', while an invoice which was raised 36 days ago will form part of the figure in the column headed 'up to 60 days'. (In the schedule below, 'up to 60 days' is used as shorthand for 'more than 30 days but less than 60 days'.)

HEATH CO
AGE ANALYSIS OF RECEIVABLES AS AT 31.1.X2

Account number	Customer name	Balance	Up to 30 days	Up to 60 days	Up to 90 days	Over 90 days
B004	Brilliant	804.95	649.90	121.00	0.00	34.05
E008	Easimat	272.10	192.90	72.40	6.80	0.00
H002	Hampstead	1,818.42	0.00	0.00	724.24	1,094.18
M024	Martlesham	284.45	192.21	92.24	0.00	0.00
N030	Nyfen	1,217.54	1,008.24	124.50	0.00	84.80
T002	Todmorden College	914.50	842.00	0.00	72.50	0.00
T004	Tricorn	94.80	0.00	0.00	0.00	94.80
V010	Volux	997.06	413.66	342.15	241.25	0.00
Y020	Yardsley Smith & Co	341.77	321.17	20.60	0.00	0.00
Totals		6,745.59	3,620.08	772.89	1,044.79	1,307.83
Percentage		100%	53.6%	11.5%	15.5%	19.4%

An age analysis of receivables can be prepared manually or, more easily, by computer. In theory this should represent actual invoices outstanding, but there are problems, which we shall discuss later in this chapter, of unmatched or 'unallocated' cash and payments on account.

The age analysis of receivables may be used to help decide what action to take about older debts. Going down each column in turn starting from the column furthest to the right and working across, we can see that there are some rather old debts which ought to be investigated.

A number of **refinements** can be suggested to the aged receivables listing to make it easier to use.

(a)   A report can be printed in which **overdue accounts** are seen first: this highlights attention on these items.

(b)   It can help to aggregate data by **class of customer**.

(c)   There is no reason why this should not apply to individual receivable accounts as below. You could also include the date of the last transaction on the account (eg last invoice, last payment).

Account number	Customer name	Balance	Up to 30 days	Up to 60 days	Up to 90 days	Over 90 days	Sales revenue in last 12 months	Days sales outstanding
B004	Brilliant	804.95	649.90	121.00	0.00	34.05	6,789.00	43

We can see from the age analysis of Heath's receivables given earlier that the relatively high proportion of debts over 90 days (19.4%) is largely due to the debts of Hampstead. Other customers with debts of this age are Brilliant, Nyfen and Tricorn.

Exam alert

The May 2010 exam had a question requiring the preparation of an age analysis of trade receivables and an explanation of its benefits.

Additional ratios which might be useful in management of receivables, in addition to days sales outstanding, are as follows.

(a)   **Overdues as a percentage of total debt.** For example, assume that Heath (Paragraph 1.1) offers credit on 30 day terms. Brilliant's debt could be analysed as:

$$\frac{\$121.00 + \$34.05}{\$804.95} = 19.3\% \text{ overdue.}$$

(b) **If debts are disputed**, it is helpful to see what proportion these are of the total receivables and the total overdue. If, of Heath's total receivables of $6,745.59, an amount of $973.06 related to disputed items, the ratio of disputed debts to total outstanding would be:

$$\frac{\$973.06}{\$6,745.59} = 14.4\%$$

As a percentage of total items *over* 30 days old:

$$\frac{\$973.06}{\$6,745.59 - \$3,620.08} = 31\%$$

An increasing disputes ratio can indicate:

(i)   Invoicing problems
(ii)   Operational problems

5.2 Receivables' ageing and liquidity

Also of interest to the credit controller is the *total* percentage figure calculated at the bottom of each column. In practice the credit controller will be concerned to look at this figure first of all, in order to keep the ageing figures consistent. Why might a credit controller be worried by an increase in the **ageing**? If the credit controller knows the customers are going to pay, should it matter?

Think back to your work on cash forecasting. This is based on the expectation that a company's debts will be paid within, say, 30 days after receipt of goods. In other words revenue booked in Month 1 would be followed up by cash in Month 2. The cash forecast also has an outflow side. Any reduction in the inflow caused by an overall increase in the receivables period affects the company's ability to pay its debts and increases its use of overdraft finance: unauthorised overdrafts carry a hefty fee as well as interest.

5.3 Delays in payments by specific customers

It may be the case that an increase in the overall receivables ageing is caused by the activities of one customer, and there is always the possibility that cut-off dates for producing the report can generate anomalies. (For example, a customer might pay invoices at the end of every calendar month, whereas the receivables ageing analysis might be run every 30 days.)

However, the credit controller should try and avoid situations where a customer starts to delay payment. He or she should review information from:

- Sales staff regarding how the company is doing
- The press for any stories relevant to the company
- Competitors
- The trade 'grapevine'

These can supply early warning signals.

If, however, there is a persistent problem, the credit controller might have to insist on a **refusal of credit**.

(a)   This is likely to be resented by sales staff who will possibly receive less commission as a result of lower sales.

(b)   However, if there is a possibility of default, the loss of a *potential* sale is surely less severe than the failure of *actual* money to arrive.

Section summary

For control purposes, **receivables** are generally analysed by age of debt.

Some customers are **reluctant** to pay. The debt collector should keep a record of every communication. A **staged process** of reminders and demands, culminating in debt collection or legal action, is necessary.

6 Collecting debts   11/10

> ## Introduction
>
> There should be efficiently organised procedures for ensuring that **overdue debts** and **slow payers** are dealt with effectively.

Exam alert

A question might require you to evaluate different methods of debt collection and to recommend the most appropriate method.

6.1 Collecting debts

Collecting debts is a two-stage process.

(a)   Having agreed credit terms with a customer, a business should issue an invoice and expect to receive payment when it is due. **Issuing invoices** and **receiving payments** is the task of sales ledger staff. They should ensure that:

    (i)   The **customer is fully aware** of the terms.
    (ii)   The **invoice is correctly drawn up** and issued promptly.
    (iii)   They are aware of any **potential quirks** in the customer's system.
    (iv)   **Queries** are **resolved quickly**.
    (v)   **Monthly statements** are **issued promptly**.

(b)   If payments become overdue, they should be 'chased'. Procedures for pursuing overdue debts must be established, for example:

    (i)   **Instituting reminders or final demands**

    These should be sent to a named individual, asking for repayment by return of post. A second or third letter may be required, followed by a final demand stating clearly the action that will be taken. The aim is to goad customers into action, perhaps by threatening not to sell any more goods on credit until the debt is cleared.

    (ii)   **Chasing payment by telephone**

    The telephone is of greater nuisance value than a letter, and the greater immediacy can encourage a response. It can however be time-consuming, in particular because of problems in getting through to the right person.

    (iii)   **Making a personal approach**

    Personal visits can be very time-consuming and tend only to be made to important customers who are worth the effort.

    (iv)   **Notifying debt collection section**

    This means not giving further credit to the customer until he has paid the due amounts.

    (v)   **Handing over debt collection to specialist debt collection section**

    Certain, generally larger, organisations may have a section to collect debts under the supervision of the credit manager.

    (vi)   **Instituting legal action to recover the debt**

    Premature legal action may unnecessarily antagonise important customers.

(vii)   **Hiring an external debt collection agency to recover the debt**

This is an expense which must be justified.

6.2 Special cases

6.2.1 'Key account' customers

In most businesses, major **'key account' customers** will receive special treatment in the sales effort, and it is appropriate that special treatment is also given in managing the debts in these cases. In such circumstances, a more personal approach to debt collection is advisable, with the salesman or a debt collection officer (perhaps the credit manager himself) making an approach to the customer to request payment.

6.2.2 Reconciliation and 'on account' payments

A problem you might encounter is a customer who pays a round sum to cover a variety of invoices. The round sum may be a **payment 'on account'**: in other words, the customer might not state which invoices the payment refers to. This might occur because the customer is having liquidity problems. Unallocated payments on account, which have not been agreed, should be investigated.

Section summary

There should be efficiently organised procedures for ensuring that **overdue debts** and **slow payers** are dealt with effectively.

7 Credit insurance, factoring and invoice discounting

Introduction

The earlier **customers** pay the better. **Early payment** can be encouraged by good administration and by **discount policies**. The risk that some **customers** will never pay can be partly guarded against by **insurance**.

7.1 Credit insurance

Companies might be able to obtain **credit insurance (default insurance)** against certain approved debts going bad through a specialist credit insurance firm.

When a company arranges credit insurance, it must submit specific proposals for credit to the insurance company, stating the name of each customer to which it wants to give credit and the amount of credit it wants to give. The insurance company will accept, amend or refuse these proposals, depending on its assessment of each of these customers.

Credit insurance is normally available for only up to about 75% of a company's potential bad debt loss. The remaining 25% of any bad debt costs are borne by the company itself. This is to ensure that the company does not become slack with its credit control.

7.2 Domestic credit insurance

Credit insurance for **domestic** (ie not export) businesses is available from a number of sources.

Insurance companies are prepared to assume for themselves the risk of the debt going bad, and they hope to profit from this. Furthermore, they are less vulnerable, as institutions, to the possibility that debt will ruin their business.

There are several types of credit insurance on offer. These are briefly described below.

7.2.1 'Whole turnover' policies

Whole turnover policies can be used in two ways.

(a) It can **cover** the **firm's entire receivables ledger**, although, normally speaking, the actual amount paid out will rarely be more than 80% of the total loss for any specific claim.

(b) Alternatively, the client **can select** a **proportion of its receivables** and insure these for their entire amount.

In other words, perhaps 80% of each debt is insured; or the entire amount of the debts incurred, say, by perhaps 80% of the customers.

Premiums on a whole turnover policy are usually **1% of the insured sales**.

Question 4.8	Compensation

Learning outcome E1(f)

Gibbony Whey has a whole turnover policy for its debts. The policy is underwritten by Broaken Amis Assurance and is on a whole turnover basis, whereby 80% of the receivables ledger is covered, provided that the total credit offered to customers does not exceed $1m. In the first quarter of 20X4, the company made total sales of $4m: at the end of the quarter receivables for credit sales stood at $1.4m. Gibbony Whey has traded with Sloe Pears: the underwriters approved a credit limit for Sloe Pears of $1,700. At the end of the quarter, Sloe Pears had outstanding debts of $2,100. Sloe Pears turns into a 'bad receivable' when the company's buildings are completely destroyed by a falling asteroid.

Gibbony Whey writes to Broaken Amis claiming for the bad debt. How much will Gibbony Whey be entitled to as compensation?

7.2.2 Annual aggregate excess of loss

Under an **annual aggregate excess of loss policy**, the insurer pays 100% of debts above an agreed limit. This is similar to motor insurers requiring that the first amount (eg $50) of a loss is borne by the insured.

7.2.3 Specific account policies

Insurance can be purchased to cover a **specific customer account** in the event of some contingency. For example, a policy might depend on the customer being formally declared insolvent.

7.3 Factoring 3/11, 5/11

KEY TERM

FACTORING is an arrangement to have debts collected by a factor company, which advances a proportion of the money it is due to collect.

Some businesses might have difficulties in financing the amounts owed by customers. There are two main reasons for this.

(a)   If a business's **sales** are rising **rapidly**, its **total receivables** will **rise quickly too**. Selling more on credit will put a strain on the company's cash flow. The business, although making profits, might find itself in difficulties because it has too many receivables and not enough cash.

(b)   If a business grants **long credit** to its customers, it might run into **cash flow difficulties** for much the same reason. Exporting businesses must often allow long periods of credit to foreign buyers, before eventually receiving payment, and their problem of financing receivables adequately can be a critical one.

Factors are organisations that offer their clients a financing service to overcome these problems. They are prepared to advance cash to the client against the security of the client's receivables. The business will assign its receivables to the factor and will typically ask for an advance of funds against the debts which the factor has purchased, usually up to 80% of the value of the debts.

For example, if a business makes credit sales of $100,000 per month, the factor might be willing to advance up to 80% of the invoice value (here $80,000) in return for a commission charge, and interest will be charged on the amount of funds advanced. The balance of the money will be paid to the business when the customers have paid the factor, or after an agreed period.

This service gives the business immediate cash in place of a debt (which is a promise of cash in the future). If the business needs money to finance operations, borrowing against trade debts is therefore an alternative to asking a bank for an overdraft.

The main aspects of factoring

These are as follows.

(a)   Administration of the client's invoicing, sales accounting and debt collection service.

(b)   Credit protection for the client's debts, whereby the factor takes over the risk of loss from bad debts and so 'insures' the client against such losses. Factoring is often **with recourse**, which means that the client carries the risk of bad debts. However the arrangement can be made **without recourse**, which means that the risk of bad debts has been transferred to the factor.

(c)   Making payments to the client in advance of collecting the debts. This is sometimes referred to as **'factor finance'** because the factor is providing cash to the client against outstanding debts.

The appeal of factor financing to **growing firms** is that factors might advance money when a bank is reluctant to consider granting a larger overdraft. Advances from a factor are therefore particularly useful for companies needing more and more cash to expand their business quickly.

7.4 The advantages of factoring

Benefits of factoring for a business customer

(a)   The business can **pay** its **suppliers promptly**, and so be able to take advantage of any early payment discounts that are available.

(b)   **Optimum inventory levels** can be **maintained**, because the business will have enough cash to pay for the inventories it needs.

(c)   **Growth** can be **financed** through **sales** rather than by injecting fresh external capital.

(d)   The business gets **finance linked** to its **volume of sales**. In contrast, overdraft limits tend to be determined by historical balance sheets.

(e)   The managers of the business do **not** have to **spend their time** on the **problems of slow paying receivables**.

(f)   The business does **not incur** the **costs** of running **its own receivables ledger** department.

An important **disadvantage of factoring** is that customers will be making payments direct to the factor, which is likely to present a **negative picture of the firm**.

Exam alert

The specimen paper contained a five-mark question asking for a discussion of the non-financial factors to consider before making a decision to factor debts. The May 2011 exam contained a five-mark question asking for the advantages and disadvantages of using factoring as a way of managing receivables.

7.5 Invoice discounting

KEY TERM

INVOICE DISCOUNTING is the sale of debts to a third party at a discount, in return for prompt cash. The administration is managed in such a way that the debtor is unaware of the discounter's involvement and continues to pay the supplier. *(CIMA Official Terminology)*

Invoice discounting is related to factoring and many factors will provide an invoice discounting service. For example, if your business had just redecorated the Town Hall it might have sent the Council an invoice for $5,000. This would be an easy invoice to sell on for cash because the Council are very likely to pay. An invoice for $5,000 sent to 'A Cowboy & Co' would not be so easy to sell for immediate cash!

The invoice discounter does **not** take over the administration of the client's sales ledger, and the arrangement is purely for the **advance of cash**. A business should only want to have some invoices discounted when it has a temporary cash shortage.

Confidential invoice discounting is an arrangement whereby a debt is confidentially assigned to the factor, and the client's customer will only become aware of the arrangement if he does not pay his debt to the client.

Question 4.9	Factoring

Learning outcome E1(f)

The Managing Director, the Chief Accountant and the Chief Internal Auditor were meeting to discuss problems over debt collection recently identified in the Forward Company. One point made strongly by the Chief Internal Auditor was that his staff should be involved in much more than the routine verification tasks normally undertaken. It is, therefore, agreed that the internal audit section should look at the problem and consider the possibility of using the services of a factor to take over some, or all, of the work of the receivables credit section.

Required

Outline the advantages and disadvantages of using the services of a factor.

Exam alert

The management of receivables and other elements of working capital gets right down to the day-to-day practicalities of running a business. In questions involving working capital management, you should always consider whether any proposed course of action really makes business sense.

Section summary

The earlier **customers** pay the better. **Early payment** can be encouraged by good administration and by **discount policies**. The risk that some **customers** will never pay can be partly guarded against by **insurance**.

Credit insurance can be obtained against some bad debts. However, the insurers will rarely insure an entire bad debt portfolio - as they are unwilling to bear the entire risk. Also the client's credit control procedures should be of a suitable standard to avoid any unnecessary exposure.

Some companies use **factoring** and **invoice discounting** to help short-term liquidity or to reduce administration costs.

Factoring involves **debt collection** by the **factoring company** which advances a proportion of the monies due. **Invoice discounting** is the sale of debts at a discount in return for cash.

8 Managing payables

Introduction

Effective management of **trade payables** involves seeking satisfactory credit terms from suppliers, getting credit extended during periods of cash shortage, and maintaining good relations with suppliers.

8.1 Trade credit

Trade payables are those suppliers who are owed money for goods and services which they have supplied for the trading activities of the enterprise. For a manufacturing company, trade payables will be raw materials suppliers.

The **management of trade payables** involves:

- Attempting to obtain satisfactory credit from suppliers
- Attempting to extend credit during periods of cash shortage
- Maintaining good relations with regular and important suppliers

Question 4.10	Obtaining credit

Learning outcome E1(f)

What might your firm have to do to obtain credit from a supplier?

Taking credit from suppliers is a normal feature of business. Nearly every company has some trade payables waiting for payment. Trade credit is a source of short-term finance because it helps to keep working capital down. It is usually a cheap source of finance, since suppliers rarely charge interest. However, trade credit *will* have a cost, whenever a company is offered a discount for early payment, but opts instead to take longer credit.

8.1.1 Trade credit and the cost of lost early payment discounts

Trade credit from suppliers is particularly important to small and fast growing firms. The costs of making maximum use of trade credit include:

(a)   The loss of suppliers' goodwill
(b)   The loss of any available cash discounts for the early payment of debts

The cost of lost cash discounts can be estimated by the formula:

LEARN

$$\left(\frac{100}{100-d}\right)^{\frac{365}{t}} - 1$$

where d   is the size of the discount. For a 5% discount, d = 5.

   t   is the reduction in the payment period in days which would be necessary to obtain the early payment discount

Example: trade credit

X has been offered credit terms from its major supplier of 2/10, net 45. That is, a cash discount of 2% will be given if payment is made within ten days of the invoice, and payments must be made within 45 days of the invoice. The company has the choice of paying 98c per $1 on day 10 (to pay before day 10 would be unnecessary), or to invest the 98c for an additional 35 days and eventually pay the supplier $1 per $1. The decision as to whether the discount should be accepted depends on the opportunity cost of investing 98c for 35 days. What should the company do?

Solution

If the company refuses the cash discount, and pays in full after 45 days, the implied cost in interest per annum would be approximately:

$$\left(\frac{100}{100-2}\right)^{\frac{365}{35}} - 1 = 23.5\%$$

Suppose that X can invest cash to obtain an annual return of 25%, and that there is an invoice from the supplier for $1,000. The two alternatives are as follows.

	Refuse discount $	Accept discount $
Payment to supplier	1,000.0	980
Return from investing $980 between day 10 and day 45:		
$980 \times \frac{35}{365} \times 25\%$	(23.5)	
Net cost	976.5	980

It is cheaper to refuse the discount because the investment rate of return on cash retained, in this example, exceeds the saving from the discount.

Although a company may delay payment beyond the final due date, thereby obtaining even longer credit from its suppliers, such a policy would be inadvisable (except where an unexpected short-term cash shortage has arisen). Unacceptable delays in payment will worsen the company's credit rating, and additional credit may become difficult to obtain.

8.2 Other payables

There is usually less scope for flexibility with other types of short-term payables. Things like rent and tax and dividends have to be paid out in full on certain specific dates.

'Management' in such cases is a matter of ensuring that what is due gets paid on time and that the finance is available when needed.

Age analysis of payables

You will be able to appreciate what an age analysis of payables is, having looked at the age analysis of receivables earlier in the last chapter.

Example: age analysis of payables

Here is an age analysis of payables for Heath Co.

HEATH CO AGE ANALYSIS OF TRADE PAYABLES AS AT 31.1.X2						
Account code	Supplier name	Balance	Up to 30 days	Up to 60 days	Up to 90 days	Over 90 days
V001	Vitatechnology	3,284.00	2,140.00	1,144.00	–	–
P002	Prendergast Tubes	1,709.50	1,010.50	699.00	–	–
G072	Gerald Printers	622.64	622.64	–	–	–
P141	Plates of Derby	941.88	510.92	290.75	–	140.21
P142	Plates of Derby	604.22	514.42	–	–	89.80
G048	Greenlands Centre	34.91	–	–	–	34.91
Totals		7,197.15	4,798.48	2,133.75	–	264.92
Percentage		100%	66.7%	29.6%	0.0%	3.7%

Various points of analysis and interpretation could arise from an age analysis of payables.

(a)   Is the company **paying its suppliers earlier** than it needs to?

(b)   Is the company taking **advantage of suppliers' discounts** where this is advantageous?

(c)   Do older amounts represent **disputes**, disagreements or accounting errors that ought to be looked into?

(d)   In the case of Heath Co, is it possible that the fact that there are two accounts for Plates of Derby has led to confusion, perhaps resulting in the older unsettled items?

8.3 The purchasing cycle

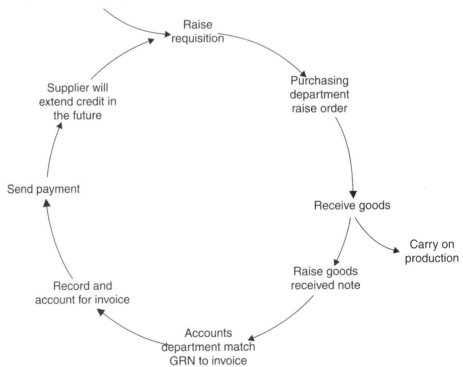

The purchasing business is now the customer, which has its credit status checked, takes delivery of goods and invoice, and pays for the goods or services.

8.4 Payment terms as part of the order

The **payment terms** offered by or agreed with the supplier form part of the contract with the supplier.

8.5 Controls over purchasing

In the same way as controls are maintained over receivables, controls should also be in place over purchase commitments. The **documentation** in the diagram above is an important control. In addition, there should be restrictions on who is allowed to place an order; perhaps only a **centralised purchasing function** should be permitted to order goods. When goods arrive the goods received department should check they **agree to the order** and are of **acceptable quality**. The details of invoices should be **carefully checked**, and the purchasing department should confirm that the goods have been received.

Businesses with several sites should decide whether purchasing should be **centralised** in one location or devolved to each site. A central location may be able to **co-ordinate inventory holdings better, obtain better prices or bulk discounts**, and have access to a **wider range of suppliers**. Local ordering may be more **flexible** to **individual locations'** needs, and local purchasing managers may form **stronger relationships** with **local suppliers**.

Section summary

Effective management of **trade payables** involves seeking satisfactory credit terms from suppliers, getting credit extended during periods of cash shortage, and maintaining good relations with suppliers.

9 Methods of paying suppliers

Introduction

Trade payables are a useful and cheap **source of finance**, but a successful business needs to ensure that it is seen as a good credit risk by its suppliers. Some suppliers must be paid on specific dates. This must be remembered and cash must be available.

We should bear in mind that the methods that a business uses to **make payments** for goods and services, wages and salaries, rent and rates and so on are broadly the same as the methods of **receiving payments**. However, a business is likely to use some methods of payment much more often than others, and the most commonly used are **cheque** and **BACS** (especially for salaries and wages). **Other payment methods** are cash, banker's draft, standing order, direct debit, mail transfer, telegraphic transfer and online payment.

9.1 Payments by cash

Cash payments are used quite often by a business:

(a)   For **small payments** out of petty cash
(b)   For **wages**

Using cash to pay large amounts of money to suppliers ought to be very rare indeed.

(a)   Cash needs to be kept **secure**: it is easily stolen.

(b)   Cash can get **lost in the post**.

(c)   It will be difficult to keep **control over cash** if it is used often for making payments.

(d)   Unless a supplier issues a **receipt**, there will be no evidence that a cash payment has been made. This is bad for record keeping.

9.2 Advantages and disadvantages of paying by cheque

Cheques are widely used in business to pay for supplies and other expenses. It is worth thinking briefly about the advantages and disadvantages of using cheques as a method of payment.

Advantages of cheque payments	Disadvantages of cheque payments
Cheques are **convenient to use** for payments of any amount (provided sufficient money is in the bank, or the organisation has a large enough overdraft facility).	There are **security problems** with keeping cheques safe from theft and misuse (forged signatures), although cheques are certainly more secure than cash as a method of payment.
The cheque **counterfoil** and cheque number can be used to provide a useful method for tracing past payments whenever any queries arise.	Cheques can be a **slow method of payment**, and a supplier might insist on a different method that is more prompt and reliable, such as standing order.
They are commonly used and **widely accepted**.	

9.3 Bank giro credits

Bank giro credits (**credit transfers**) are a means by which payments might be **received** from customers. Bank giro credits can also be used by businesses to **make payments**.

In practice, bank giro credits are rarely used by businesses to pay suppliers, except in cases where the supplier sends an invoice with a detachable preprinted bank giro credit transfer paying-in slip. Suppliers who use their own preprinted bank giro credit transfer forms include the various utility companies.

Bank giro credit transfers are sometimes used by small companies to pay monthly salaries.

9.4 Payments by banker's draft

A supplier might sometimes ask a customer to pay by **banker's draft**. Banker's drafts are not used for small value items, but might be used when a large payment is involved, such as for the purchase of a company car.

9.5 Standing orders

Standing order payments might be used by a business to make regular payments of a fixed amount.

(a)   **Hire purchase (HP) payments** to a hire purchase company (finance house), where an asset has been bought under an HP agreement

(b)   **Rental payments** to the landlord of a building occupied by the business

(c)   Paying **insurance premiums** to an insurance company

9.6 Direct debits

Payments by direct debit **might** be made by some companies for regular bills such as telephone, gas, electricity and water bills. The company being paid by direct debit will inform the payer of the amount and date of each payment in a printed statement.

Question 4.11	Payment methods

Learning outcome E1(f)

Libra has to make the following payments.

(a) $6.29 for office cleaning materials bought from a nearby supermarket.

(b) $231.40 monthly, which represents hire purchase instalments on a new van. The payments are due to Marsh Finance over a period of 36 months.

(c) $534.21 to Southern Electric for the most recent quarter's electricity and standing charge. A bank giro credit form/payment counterfoil is attached to the bill. There is no direct debiting mandate currently in force.

(d) $161.50 monthly for ten months, representing the business rates payable to Clapperton District Council, which operates a direct debiting system.

(e) $186.60 to Renton Hire for a week's hire of a car on company business by the Sales Director. The Sales Director must pay on the spot, and does not wish to use a personal cheque or cash.

(f) $23,425.00 to Selham Motors for a new car to be used by the Finance Director. Selham Motors will not accept one of the company's cheques in payment, since the Finance Director wishes to collect the vehicle immediately upon delivering the payment in person and Selham Motors is concerned that such a cheque might be dishonoured.

Recommend the method of payment which you think would be most appropriate in each case, stating your reasons.

9.7 BACS

When a business uses **Bankers' Automated Clearing Services (BACS)**, it sends information (which will be input into the books of the business) to BACS for processing. Many different businesses use BACS; even small businesses can do so because their bank will help to organise the information for BACS. To give examples, BACS is widely used for monthly salaries by an employer into employees' bank accounts, as already mentioned, and for standing order payments, as well as for payments to suppliers.

9.8 Internet payments

Many organisations now have access to online banking and use this to pay employees and suppliers. Funds can be transferred between accounts with a few clicks. It is very important to prevent unauthorised access to the system and to keep records, such as printouts, of all transactions.

KEY POINT

Don't neglect payables management, as a business can gain cash flow advantages from careful management of payables.

Section summary

Trade payables are a useful and cheap **source of finance,** but a successful business needs to ensure that it is seen as a good credit risk by its suppliers. Some suppliers must be paid on specific dates. This must be remembered and cash must be available.

The most common and convenient methods of payment are by cheque, BACS and **Internet transfer**. Other payment methods are often arranged at the insistence of the supplier, and this explains much of the use of banker's drafts, standing orders and telegraphic transfers.

Chapter Roundup

- ✓ **Credit control** deals with a firm's management of its working capital. **Trade credit** is offered to business customers. **Consumer credit** is offered to household customers.

- ✓ **Total credit** can be measured in a variety of ways. Financial analysts use days sales in receivables, but as this is an annualised figure it gives no idea as to the make-up of total receivables.

- ✓ The **total investment in receivables** has to be considered in its impact on the general investment in working capital.

- ✓ The **credit control department** is responsible for those stages in the collection cycle dealing with the offer of credit, and the collection of debts.

- ✓ A firm must consider suitable **payment terms** and **payment methods**. **Settlement discounts** can be offered, if cost effective and if they improve liquidity.

- ✓ For control purposes, **receivables** are generally analysed by age of debt.

- ✓ Some customers are **reluctant** to pay. The debt collector should keep a record of every communication. A staged process of reminders and demands, culminating in debt collection or legal action, is necessary.

- ✓ There should be efficiently organised procedures for ensuring that **overdue debts** and **slow payers** are dealt with effectively.

- ✓ The earlier customers pay the better. **Early payment** can be encouraged by good administration and by **discount policies**. The risk that some receivables will never pay can be partly guarded against by **insurance**.

- ✓ **Credit insurance** can be obtained against some bad debts. However, the insurers will rarely insure an entire bad debt portfolio - as they are unwilling to bear the entire risk. Also the client's credit control procedures should be of a suitable standard to avoid any unnecessary exposure.

- ✓ Some companies use **factoring** and **invoice discounting** to help short-term liquidity or to reduce administration costs.

- ✓ Factoring involves **debt collection** by the **factoring company** which advances a proportion of the monies due. **Invoice discounting** is the sale of debts at a discount in return for cash.

- ✓ Effective management of **trade payables** involves seeking satisfactory credit terms from suppliers, getting credit extended during periods of cash shortage, and maintaining good relations with suppliers.

- ✓ Trade payables are a useful and cheap **source of finance**, but a successful business needs to ensure that it is seen as a good credit risk by its suppliers. Some suppliers must be paid on specific dates. This must be remembered and cash must be available.

- ✓ The most common and convenient methods of payment are by **cheque**, **BACS** and **internet transfer**. **Other payment methods** are often arranged at the insistence of the supplier, and this explains much of the use of banker's drafts, standing orders and telegraphic transfers.

Quick Quiz

1 Goods and Chattels are considering increasing the period of credit allowed to customers from one calendar month to two months. Annual sales are currently $2.4m, and annual profits are $120,000. It is anticipated that allowing extended credit would increase sales by 20%, while margins would be unchanged. The company's required rate of return is 15%. What is the financial effect of the proposal?

   A   Reduction in profit of $102,000   C   Increase in profit of $102,000
   B   Reduction in profit of $18,000   D   Increase in profit of $18,000

2 The .... cycle and the .... cycle together make up the .... cycle.
   Fill in the blanks, using the following words: credit; collection; order.

3 How can we calculate the number of days sales represented by receivables?

4 What matters should the terms and conditions of sale cover?

5 What is meant by COD?

6 Which of the following would be the last document issued to a customer in the order processing and debt collection cycle?

   A   Statement   C   Advice note
   B   Reminder   D   Invoice

7 List typical column headings that you would expect to see in an aged analysis of receivables.

8 List three types of credit insurance policy.

9 What service involves collecting debts of a business, advancing a proportion of the money it is due to collect?

10 What service involves advancing a proportion of a selection of invoices, without administration of the receivables ledger of the business?

11 Which of the following is likely to be the most effective way of obtaining payment from a difficult customer?

   A   Personal visit   C   Sending a fax reminder
   B   Telephone request   D   Sending an e-mail reminder

12 In what order would a company normally undertake the following actions to collect a debt?

   A   Hiring an external debt collection agency to recover the debt
   B   Notifying the debt collection service
   C   Sending a reminder
   D   Instituting legal action to recover the debt

13 The premium for whole turnover policies is usually ....% of insured sales, and whole turnover policies rarely cover more than ......% of the total loss.

14 Cost of lost cash discount $= \left(\dfrac{100}{100-d} \right)^{\frac{365}{t}} - 1$. What do d and t represent?

15 Avery has been offered a cash discount of 2% by one of its suppliers if it settles its accounts within 10 days. Avery currently takes 60 days credit from the supplier. What is the implied cost in interest per annum to the nearest whole % if Avery decides not to take the discount?

   A   2%   C   16%
   B   12%   D   24%

16 What is the difference between trade credit and consumer credit?

17 Name three ways a company could pay for goods and services.

Answers to Quick Quiz

1	B	Existing receivables	$2.4m ÷ 12	$200,000
		New level of receivables	$2.4m × 1.2 ÷ 6	$480,000
		Increase in receivables		$280,000
		Additional financing cost	$280,000 × 15%	$42,000
		Additional profit	$2.4m × 20% × 5%	$24,000
		Net decrease in profit	$42,000 – $24,000	$18,000

2   The order cycle and the collection cycle together make up the credit cycle.

3   $\dfrac{\text{Total receivables}}{\text{Annual credit sales}} \times 365 = $ Days sales

4   Nature of goods to be supplied, price, delivery, date of payment, frequency of payment (if instalments), discount

5   Cash On Delivery

6   B   The normal sequence is advice note, invoice, statement, reminder.

7   • Account number
    • Customer name
    • Total balance
    • Up to 30 days
    • Up to 60 days
    • Up to 90 days
    • Over 90 days

8   Whole turnover; excess of loss; specific account

9   Factoring

10 Invoice discounting

11 A   Personal visit is the most expensive option, but is the most likely to obtain results. It is therefore recommended in the case of high value receivables.

12 C   Sending a reminder
    B   Notifying the debt collection service
    D   Instituting legal action to recover the debt
    A   Hiring an external debt collection agency to recover the debt

13 The premium for whole turnover policies is usually **1%** of insured sales, and whole turnover policies rarely cover more than **80%** of the total loss.

14 d is the percentage discount given.
    t is the reduction in payment period to obtain this discount (in days)

15 C   In this case:

$$\left(\frac{100}{100-2}\right)^{\frac{365}{50}} - 1 = 15.9\%, \text{ say } 16\%$$

16 Trade credit is offered to business customers whereas consumer credit is offered to household customers.

17 Any of cash, cheque, bank giro credits, banker's draft, standing order, direct debit, BACS, or online payment.

Answers to Questions

4.1 Cost of credit

At the moment, Winterson Tools is paying $10\% \times \$1m$ (ie $^{30}/_{60}$ days $\times \$2m$) = $100,000 in interest caused by customers taking the extra month to pay. The credit control could therefore be much improved.

4.2 Increase in credit period

The existing value of receivables is:

$$\frac{\$24\,m}{12\,months} = \$2m$$

If sales increased by 150,000 units, the value of receivables would be:

$$1\tfrac{1}{2} \times \frac{\$24m + (150,000 \times \$6)}{12\,months} = \$3,112,500.$$

The receivables have to be financed somehow, and the additional $1,112,500 will cost $1,112,500 \times 20\%$ = $222,500 in financing costs.

The profit on the extra sales is: 150,000 units $\times$ ($6 – $5.40) = $90,000

The new credit policy is not worthwhile, mainly because existing customers would also take advantage of it.

4.3 Inflation

Inflation accentuates the importance of credit control, because the cost of the investment in receivables, in real terms, is higher. If a company grants credit of $100,000 for 3 months, and the rate of inflation is 6% per annum, the value in 'today's money' of the eventual receipts in 3 months' time would be about $1\tfrac{1}{2}\%$ less – ie about $1,500 less. If the rate of inflation went up to, say, 12%, the value of the same receipts in 3 months' time would be about $3,000 less. In other words, the cost of granting credit increases as the rate of inflation gets higher. Also, with higher inflation, customers have an increased incentive to pay late.

4.4 Credit control and working capital

Working capital includes inventory, receivables, payables and cash. The effect of credit policy on working capital is that if **more credit** is granted, there will be a **slowdown** in the **inflow of cash** (unless the extension of credit also results in an increase in sales). **Discounts** for **early payment** would also affect cash flows. Similarly, **tightening up on credit** and so granting less credit will result in a **speeding up** of **cash inflows**, provided that there is no reduction in sales as a consequence of the restriction of credit.

The total amount of working capital should be kept under control because the investment in working capital must be financed, and so excessive receivables are unnecessarily costly and would reduce the organisation's return on capital employed.

Credit policy is therefore significant both from the point of view of **liquidity** (cash flow) and the **management of finance** (investment).

4.5 Discount

Gamma is offering customers the option of paying $98 after seven days per $100 invoiced, or payment in full after 60 days.

Using the formula

$$\text{Cost of discount} = \left(\frac{100}{100 - d} \right)^{\frac{365}{t}} - 1$$

$$= \left(\frac{100}{100 - 2} \right)^{\frac{365}{53}} - 1$$

$$= 14.9\%$$

4.6 Good cash management

(a) **Better control of financial risk.** By determining and maintaining the proper level of cash within a company in accordance with the organisation's financial procedures and within defined authorisation limits.

(b) **Opportunity for profit**. By reducing to a minimum the opportunity cost associated with maintaining cash balances in excess of company's operating needs. Earnings (or surpluses) are improved by freeing up surplus cash for investment purposes while reducing interest charged through minimising borrowing.

(c) **Strengthened statement of financial position**. By reducing or eliminating cash balances in excess of target balances and putting surplus cash to work by investing it (eg in the overnight money market); by reducing or eliminating cash borrowing and keeping interest costs as low as possible.

(d) **Increased confidence with customers, suppliers, banks and shareholders**. By having access to funds to disburse to suppliers (creditors), banks (interest, fees and principal payments) and shareholders (dividends) when due. By providing good instructions to customers (receivables) to enable the organisation to convert receipts into usable bank deposits.

4.7 Credit control policy

The factors involved in establishing a credit control policy are as follows.

(a) **A total credit policy** must be **decided**, whereby the organisation decides how much credit it can and should allow to customers in total. Receivables should not be excessive in relation to total sales revenues, and the cost of financing receivables should also be considered. The receivables policy that is established will include maximum periods for payment.

(b) A **credit policy** must be **set** for deciding credit terms for individual customers. This will include establishing a system of credit rating, and procedures for deciding the maximum credit limit and terms for the payment period.

(c) The **purpose of allowing credit** is to **boost sales demand**. Management must consider how 'generous' credit terms should be to encourage sales, whilst at the same time avoiding excessive increases in bad debts, and problems with chasing payment from slow payers.

(d) Granting credit will inevitably mean that **problems will arise with slow payers** and bad debts. Procedures must be established for collecting debts from slow payers and writing off bad debts.

(e) **Discounts** might be **offered** for **early payment of debts**, and a decision should be taken as to how much discount, if any, should be offered to encourage early payment, thereby reducing the volume of receivables.

4.8 Compensation

$1,700 × 80% = $1,360.

Gibbony Whey gave more credit than was underwritten by the insurance company.

4.9 Factoring

The decision to factor the debts should only be taken once a wide ranging assessment of the costs and benefits of so doing has been carried out. This will involve the following steps.

(a) Find out **which organisations** provide debt factoring services. These may include the firm's own bankers, but there might be specialist agencies available who could also do the job.

(b) **Some assessment** of the **services provided** should also be made. Factors take on the responsibility of collecting the client firm's debts. There is a variety of factoring services.

    (i) **With recourse factoring**. This is the most basic service, whereby the bank undertakes to collect the debts and offer an advance, perhaps 80% thereon. The remainder is paid over once the cash has been received from customers. If the debt cannot be collected, the bank can claim back the advance from the client firm.

    (ii) **No recourse factoring**. The bank undertakes to pay the debts, but cannot claim the advance back from the client if the debt does not prove collectable.

    (iii) Some factors are willing to **purchase a number of invoices**, at a **substantial** discount. The factor would not be taking responsibility for the client's overall credit administration. In a way, this is like receiving an advance from a debt collector.

(c) The **costs of the factoring** service can then be assessed. The cost is often calculated as a percentage of the book value of the debts factored, so that if the factor took over $1,000,000 of debt at a factoring cost of 1.5%, then the client would pay a fee of $15,000. Moreover interest might also be charged on the advance, in some cases before the debt was recovered.

(d) This can then be compared with the **costs of doing nothing**. If the choice is between either employing a factor or leaving things as they are, then the costs included in the decision include administration, salaries, interest costs on the overdraft, and other cash flow problems (eg delayed expenditure on purchases owing to bad debts, might mean that the company cannot take advantage of settlement discounts offered).

(e) However, before any final decision is taken, the organisation can try to ensure that factoring is still better value than other choices. These can include:

    (i) The **introduction** of **settlement discounts** as an inducement to pay early might improve the collection period, and hence reduce the outstanding debt

    (ii) The **use** of **credit insurance** in some cases

    (iii) A **stronger credit control policy**

    (iv) Perhaps **appointing more credit control staff** might in the long run be cheaper than factoring if the collection rate increases

There may well be operational or management solutions to this problem. These should be investigated first as customers might not like dealing with a third party.

4.10 Obtaining credit

A firm would have to provide good references, maintain a good payment record, allow the supplier to pay a visit, and generally be *known* to be a successful business and a good credit risk.

4.11 Payment methods

(a)   This is a small business payment which should be paid out of petty **cash** for the sake of convenience.

(b)   A **standing order** is convenient for regular fixed payments. Once the standing order instruction is made, the bank will ensure that all payments are made on the due dates and will stop making payments at the date specified in the instruction. Some finance companies may insist on a standing order being set up, as it is convenient for them to receive instalments regularly without having to issue payment requests or reminders.

(c)   **Pay by cheque at the bank**, accompanied by the bill and completed bank giro credit form. The bank clerk will stamp the bill as evidence that the payment was made. Paying by cheque is safer than paying by cash and is more usual for such a large payment. Handing the cheque over at the bank will be convenient and evidence of payment will be obtained. If the payment is made at a bank other than that at which Libra holds an account, the bank receiving the payment will probably make a small charge for processing it. An alternative method is to send a **crossed cheque by post**, enclosing the payment counterfoil.

(d)   The **direct debit mandate** will allow the Council to debit the amounts due direct from Libra's bank account on the due dates. The mandate will be effective until it is cancelled. The Council must inform Libra in advance of the amounts it will be debiting.

(e)   Payment by **credit card** or **charge card** avoids the need to pay immediately by cash or cheque. The amount paid will appear on the monthly statement for the card used. If the Sales Director's personal card is used, he will claim payment later from the company, which may pay him by cheque or with his monthly salary payment. If a company credit or charge card is used, the company will be responsible for paying the amounts shown on the monthly statement.

(f)   A **banker's draft** cannot be stopped or cancelled once it is issued. Being effectively like a cheque drawn on the bank itself, it is generally accepted as being as good as cash. It is therefore most likely to be accepted by Selham Motors.

Now try these questions from the Exam Question Bank

Number	Level	Marks	Time
Q4	Examination	20	36 mins
Q5	Examination	20	36 mins

MANAGING INVENTORY

 You should be able to apply the **EOQ** model for inventory ordering; it is likely to feature somewhere in every paper. As well as doing the calculations, you need to explain its assumptions and the components of inventory costs.

We also discuss in overview the impact of **lean manufacturing** and **just-in-time** on inventory control and other important aspects of purchasing.

topic list	learning outcomes	syllabus references	ability required
1 Managing inventories	E1(g)	E1(xii)	analysis
2 Purchasing	E1(g)	E1(x)	analysis

1 Managing inventories

Introduction

Business should consider at what level of inventory orders should be made, taking account of demand levels, delivery times and any uncertainties. **Safety inventory** may be held if uncertainties are particularly large.

1.1 Controlling inventory

Almost every company carries inventories of some sort, even if they are only inventories of consumables such as stationery. For a manufacturing business, inventories, in the form of **raw materials**, **work in progress** (goods or projects on which work has been carried out but which are not yet ready for sale) and **finished goods**, may amount to a substantial proportion of the total assets of the business.

Some businesses attempt to control inventories on a scientific basis by balancing the costs of inventory shortages against those of inventory holding.

(a) The **economic order quantity (EOQ) model** can be used to decide the optimum **order size** for inventories which will minimise the costs of ordering inventories plus inventory holding costs.

(b) If **discounts** for **bulk purchases** are **available**, it may be cheaper to buy inventories in **large order sizes** so as to obtain the discounts.

(c) Uncertainty in the demand for inventories and/or the supply lead time may lead a company to **decide to hold buffer inventories** or **safety inventories** (thereby increasing its investment in working capital) in order to reduce or eliminate the risk of running out of inventory

KEY TERM

SAFETY INVENTORY is the quantity of inventories of raw materials, work in progress and finished goods which are carried in excess of the expected usage during the lead time of an activity. The safety inventory reduces the probability of operations having to be suspended due to running out of inventories.

(CIMA Official Terminology)

1.2 Inventory costs

Inventory costs can be conveniently classified into four groups.

(a) **Holding costs** comprise the cost of capital tied up, warehousing and handling costs, deterioration, obsolescence, insurance and pilferage.

(b) **Procuring costs** depend on how the inventory is obtained but will consist of **ordering costs** for goods purchased externally, such as clerical costs, telephone charges and delivery costs.

(c) **Shortage costs** may be:

    (i) The loss of a sale and the contribution which could have been earned from the sale

    (ii) The extra cost of having to buy an emergency supply of inventories at a high price

    (iii) The cost of lost production and sales, where the stock-out (running out of inventory) brings an entire process to a halt

(d) The **cost of the inventory** itself, the supplier's price or the direct cost per unit of production, will also need to be considered when the supplier offers a discount on orders for purchases in bulk.

Businesses need to be aware of rates of **consumption/usage, and lead times**, the time between placing an order with a supplier and the inventory becoming available for use.

Note that inventory demand is sometimes classed as **dependent demand** or **independent demand**. For example, a computer would have an independent demand whereas its accessories such as antivirus software, mouse, monitor and so on, have a dependent demand. We will look at independent demand only.

1.3 Re-order quantities: the basic EOQ model   5/10, 9/10

KEY TERM

ECONOMIC ORDER QUANTITY (EOQ) is the most economic inventory replenishment order size, which minimises the sum of inventory ordering costs and inventory holding costs. EOQ is used in an 'optimising' inventory control system.   *(CIMA Official Terminology)*

Let D =   the usage in units for one year (the demand)

       C_o =   the cost of making one order

       C_h =   the holding cost per unit of inventory for one year } relevant cost only

       Q =   the reorder quantity

Assume that:

(a)   Demand is constant

(b)   The lead time is constant or zero

(c)   Purchase costs per unit are constant (ie no bulk discounts)

LEARN

The **total annual cost** of having inventory is:

Holding costs + **ordering** costs

$$\frac{QC_h}{2} + \frac{C_o D}{Q}$$

The order quantity, Q, which will minimise these total costs is given by the following formula. (You do not need to know how this formula is derived.)

EXAM

Economic Order Quantity EOQ $= \sqrt{\dfrac{2C_o D}{C_h}}$

Where C_o = cost of placing an order

      C_h = cost of holding one unit in inventory for one year

      D = annual demand

Example: economic order quantity

The demand for a commodity is 40,000 units a year, at a steady rate. It costs $20 to place an order, and 40c to hold a unit for a year. Find the order size to minimise inventory costs, the number of orders placed each year, and the length of the inventory cycle.

Solution

$$Q = \sqrt{\frac{2C_o D}{C_h}} = \sqrt{\frac{2 \times 20 \times 40,000}{0.4}} = 2,000 \text{ units. This means that there will be}$$

$\dfrac{40,000}{2,000}$ = 20 orders placed each year, so that the inventory cycle is once every 52 ÷ 20 = 2.6 weeks.

Total costs will be $(20 \times \$20) + \left(\dfrac{2,000}{2} \times 40c\right)$ = $800 a year.

1.4 The effect of discounts

The solution obtained from using the simple EOQ formula may need to be modified if bulk discounts (also called quantity discounts) are available.

To decide mathematically whether it would be worthwhile taking a discount and ordering larger quantities, it is necessary to minimise the total of:

- Total material costs
- Ordering costs
- Inventory holding costs

The total cost will be minimised:

- At the pre-discount EOQ level, so that a discount is not worthwhile, or
- At the minimum order size necessary to earn the discount

Example: bulk discounts

The annual demand for an item of inventory is 45 units. The item costs $200 a unit to purchase, the holding cost for one unit for one year is 15% of the unit cost and ordering costs are $300 an order. The supplier offers a 3% discount for orders of 60 units or more, and a discount of 5% for orders of 90 units or more. What is the cost-minimising order size?

Solution

(a)   The EOQ ignoring discounts is:

$$\sqrt{\frac{2 \times 300 \times 45}{15\% \text{ of } 200}} = 30 \text{ units}$$

	$
Purchases (no discount) 45 × $200	9,000
Holding costs 15 units × $30 (Ch)	450
Ordering costs 1.5 orders × $300	450
Total annual costs	9,900

(b)   With a discount of 3% and an order quantity of 60 units costs are as follows.

	$
Purchases $9,000 × 97%	8,730
Holding costs 30 units × 15% of 97% of $200	873
Ordering costs 0.75 orders × $300	225
Total annual costs	9,828

(c)   With a discount of 5% and an order quantity of 90 units costs are as follows.

	$
Purchases $9,000 × 95%	8,550.0
Holding costs 45 units × 15% of 95% of $200	1,282.5
Ordering costs 0.5 orders × $300	150.0
Total annual costs	9,982.5

The cheapest option is to order 60 units at a time.

Note that the value of C_h varied according to the size of the discount, because C_h was a percentage of the purchase cost. This means that total holding costs are reduced because of a discount. This could easily happen if, for example, most of C_h was the cost of insurance, based on the cost of inventory held.

Question 5.1

Order quantity

Learning outcome E1(g)

A company uses an item of inventory as follows.

Purchase price:	$96 per unit
Annual demand:	4,000 units
Ordering cost:	$300
Annual holding cost:	10% of purchase price
Economic order quantity:	500 units

Should the company order 1,000 units at a time in order to secure an 8% discount?

1.5 Criticisms of the EOQ model

Criticism	Comment
Assumes a constant unit stockholding cost	Costs might have steps or be curvilinear
Assumes a known, constant ordering cost	ABC might help to determine the cost of placing an order
Assumes a constant rate of demand	So that inventory reduces steadily
Assumes zero lead time, ie an order is placed when inventory reaches zero and is received immediately	So that inventory can be assumed to fluctuate evenly between zero and the reorder quantity, Q. Hence average inventory = Q/2

Question 5.2

EOQ

Learning outcome E1(g)

Maurice sells one product for which the annual demand is 50,000 units. Ordering costs are $40 per order, holding costs $0.50 per item per year.

Required

Calculate the economic order quantity

1.6 Uncertainties in demand and lead times: the re-order level system

KEY TERM

RE-ORDER LEVEL = maximum usage × maximum lead time.

It is the measure of inventory at which a replenishment order should be placed. Use of the above formula builds in a measure of safety inventory and minimises the possibility of the organisation running out of inventory.

The EOQ model assumes a level of stability which does not always apply in business.

When the volume of demand is uncertain, or the supply lead time (time taken for the supplier to deliver) is variable, there are problems in deciding what the re-order level should be. By holding a **safety inventory**, a company can reduce the likelihood that inventories run out during the re-order period (due to high demand or a long lead time before the new supply is delivered). The **average annual** cost of such a safety inventory would be:

Quantity of safety inventory (in units) × Inventory holding cost per unit per annum

The diagram below shows how the inventory levels might fluctuate with this system. Points marked 'X' show the re-order level at which a new order is placed. The number of units ordered each time is the EOQ. Actual inventory levels sometimes fall below the safety inventory level, and sometimes the re-supply arrives before inventories have fallen to the safety level, but on average, extra inventory holding amounts to the volume of safety inventory. The size of the safety inventory will depend on whether running out of inventory is allowed.

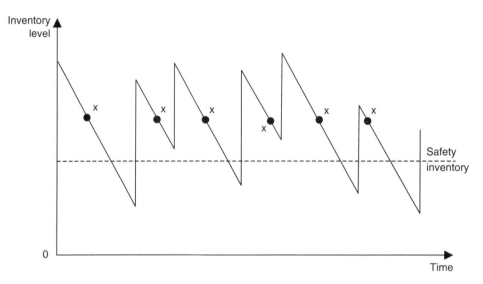

In the modern manufacturing environment running out of inventory can have a disastrous effect on the production process. Nevertheless you may encounter situations where the risk of running out is assumed to be worth taking. In this case the re-order level may not be calculated in the way described above.

1.7 Periodic review

An alternative to the re-order level system is a periodic review system. Using this system, inventory levels are reviewed at fixed intervals, for instance the same day each month. Orders are then put through to top inventory up to pre-set levels.

1.8 Finite number of re-order levels

You may see a question where you are given a list of the re-order levels from which the business will select one. For each **possible re-order level**, and therefore each level of buffer inventory, **calculate**:

- The **costs of holding buffer inventory** per annum
- The **costs of running out of inventory** (Cost of running out of inventory × expected number of times running out per order × number of orders per year)

The expected number of times running out per order reflects the various levels by which demand during the lead time could exceed the re-order level.

Example: possibility of running out of inventory (1)

If re-order level is 4 units, but there was a probability of 0.2 that demand during the lead time would be 5 units, and 0.05 that demand during the lead time would be 6 units, then expected number of times running out = $((5 - 4) \times 0.2) + ((6 - 4) \times 0.05) = 0.3$.

Demand normally distributed

Alternatively you may be told that demand is normally distributed. If this is the case you need to know:

- Average weekly demand
- Standard deviation of demand
- Lead time
- Acceptable risk levels

Re-order level = (Average weekly demand × lead time) + xσ

Where x = number of standard deviations that correspond to the chance the business wishes to have of avoiding running out of inventory

σ = standard deviation of demand

Example: possibility of running out of inventory (2)

Average weekly demand is 200 units, the standard deviation of demand (σ) is 40 units and demand is normally distributed. Lead time for orders is one week. What re-order levels should the business set if it wishes to have

(a)   A 90% chance
(b)   A 95% chance
(c)   A 99% chance

of avoiding running out of inventory. The relevant values from normal distribution tables are respectively:

(a)   1.28
(b)   1.65
(c)   2.33

Solution

Re-order level = (Average weekly demand × lead time) + xσ

(a)   Re-order level   = (200 × 1) + (1.28 × 40)
                         = 251.2 units

(b)   Re-order level   = 200 + (1.65 × 40)
                         = 266 units

(c)   Re-order level   = 200 + (2.33 × 40)
                         = 293.2 units

1.9 Maximum and minimum inventory levels

KEY TERM

MAXIMUM INVENTORY LEVEL = re-order level + re-order quantity – (minimum usage × minimum lead time)

It is the inventory level set for control purposes which actual inventory holding should never exceed.

The maximum level acts as a warning signal to management that inventories are reaching a potentially wasteful level.

KEY TERM

MINIMUM INVENTORY LEVEL or SAFETY INVENTORY = re-order level – (average usage × average lead time)

It is the inventory level set for control purposes below which inventory holding should not fall without being highlighted.

The minimum level acts as a warning to management that inventories are approaching a dangerously low level and that inventory may run out.

KEY TERM

$$\text{Average inventory} = \text{Minimum level} + \frac{\text{re-order quantity}}{2}$$

This formula assumes that inventory levels fluctuate evenly between the minimum (or safety) inventory level and the highest possible inventory level (the amount of inventory immediately after an order is received, safety inventory and reorder quantity).

Section summary

Business should consider at what level of inventory orders should be made, taking account of demand levels, delivery times and any uncertainties. **Safety inventory** may be held if uncertainties are particularly large.

Inventory holding and ordering costs can be minimised using the **economic order quantity** model. If **discounts** are offered for bulk purchases, the higher holding costs should be weighed against the lower ordering and purchasing costs.

2 Purchasing

Introduction

Purchasing may be centralised or decentralised. The optimal mix of quantity, quality, price and delivery arrangements should be sought.

2.1 The purchasing function

Purchases can account for a major part of a company's expenditure, but rarely get subjected to the planning and control constraints that are experienced by other business functions. This comment is not true of all branches of industry and commerce. In high street stores, 'buying' is recognised as one of the most important functions of the business.

The effectiveness of the purchasing function affects profit in three ways.

(a) Effective purchasing ensures the best **value for money** is obtained by the firm.

(b) Effective purchasing assists in **meeting quality targets**. Again this has an impact on a firm's long-term marketing strategy, if quality is an issue.

(c) An effective purchasing strategy minimises the amount of purchased **material held in inventory**.

2.2 The purchasing mix

The purchasing manager has to obtain the best purchasing **quantity**, **quality**, **price**, and **delivery arrangements**. Purchasing may be **centralised** or **decentralised**.

PURCHASING MIX	
Quantity	Size and timing of orders dictated by balance between delays in production caused by insufficient inventory and costs of inventory-holding
Quality	Quality of goods required for the manufacturing process, and the quality of goods acceptable to customers
Price	Short-term trends may influence, but best value over period of time is most important
Delivery	Lead time between placing and delivery of an order and reliability of suppliers' delivery arrangements

2.3 Building supplier relationships

Many companies are seeking to build up **long-term relationships with suppliers**, often offering them advice and help with product development, manufacturing processes and quality. This often leads to a reduction in the number of suppliers a firm deals with. This policy is a means of **ensuring consistency** of bought-in component quality.

2.4 Centralised versus decentralised purchasing

There are advantages to both centralised and decentralised purchasing. Each organisation will make this decision on the basis of their own business and their own business environment.

2.4.1 Advantages of centralised purchasing

- The firm will be buying in larger quantities and so will be able to negotiate more substantial discounts.

- The organisation as a whole should be able to arrange more favourable credit terms than an individual branch.

- Inventory handling functions will be mainly centralised, which should save costs – but some handling will still have to be done at branch level.

- It should be possible to hold lower overall levels of inventory than if inventory was being held at each branch.

- Only one buying department will be needed, which will save costs.

2.4.2 Advantages of decentralised purchasing

- Local branches will be more in control of their production and sales if they have local control of purchasing.

- The purchasing requirements of individual branches may vary. For instance, some lines of inventory may sell better in some areas than others.

- Local branches will be able to form their own relationships with suppliers. There may be more mutual co-operation between a smaller organisation and its supplier than between a large purchasing department and a supplier.

- A local branch can be made more accountable for its own profitability and cash management if it has control of its own purchasing function.

Section summary

Purchasing may be **centralised** or **decentralised**. The optimal mix of **quantity, quality, price** and **delivery arrangements** should be sought.

Chapter Roundup

✓ Businesses should consider at what **level** of inventory orders should be made, taking account of demand levels, delivery times and any uncertainties. **Safety inventory** may be held if uncertainties are particularly large.

✓ Inventory holding and ordering costs can be minimised using the **economic order quantity** model. If **discounts** are offered for bulk purchases, the higher holding costs should be weighed against the lower ordering and purchasing costs.

✓ Purchasing may be **centralised** or **decentralised**. The optimal mix of **quantity**, **quality**, **price** and **delivery arrangements** should be sought.

Quick Quiz

1 The basic EOQ formula for inventories indicates whether bulk discounts should be taken advantage of.

   True ☐

   False ☐

2 What are the elements of the purchasing mix?

3 The Economic Order Quantity can be expressed as follows:

$$\sqrt{\frac{2C_oD}{C_h}}$$

   What does C_h describe in this formula?

   A   The cost of holding one unit of inventory for one year
   B   The cost of placing one order
   C   The cost of a unit of inventory
   D   The customer demand for the item

4 Using the following information:

   Max lead time = 5 days
   Min lead time = 2 days
   Average lead time = 3 days
   Reorder level = 100 units
   Reorder quantity = 150 units
   Maximum usage = 60 units per day
   Average usage = 30 units per day
   Minimum usage = 20 units per day
   Calculate the maximum level of inventory.

5 Calculate the minimum level of inventory, using the information in question 4.

Answers to Quick Quiz

1   False. It may be necessary to modify the formula to take account of bulk discounts.

2   Quantity, quality, price, delivery arrangements.

3   A   The cost of holding one unit of inventory for one year

4   Maximum   = re-order level + re-order quantity – (minimum usage × minimum lead time)
     level of inventory   = 100 + 150 – (20 × 2)
                            = 210 units

5   Minimum   = re-order level – (average usage × average lead time)
     level of inventory   = 100 – (30 × 3)
                            = 10 units

Answers to Questions

5.1 Order quantity

The total annual cost at the economic order quantity of 500 units is as follows.

	$
Purchases 4,000 × $96	384,000
Ordering costs $300 × (4,000/500)	2,400
Holding costs $96 × 10% × (500/2)	2,400
	388,800

The total annual cost at an order quantity of 1,000 units would be as follows.

	$
Purchases $384,000 × 92%	353,280
Ordering costs $300 × (4,000/1,000)	1,200
Holding costs $96 × 92% × 10% × (1,000/2)	4,416
	358,896

The company should order the item 1,000 units at a time, saving $(388,800 – 358,896) = $29,904 a year.

5.2 EOQ

$$\text{EOQ} = \sqrt{\frac{2C_oD}{C_h}}$$

$$= \sqrt{\frac{2 \times 40 \times 50,000}{0.50}}$$

$$= 2,828 \text{ units}$$

COST ACCOUNTING SYSTEMS

Part B

BASIC MANAGEMENT ACCOUNTING TECHNIQUES

 You will have encountered the ideas and principles covered in this chapter in your earlier studies. We revisit these because, although not directly related to any syllabus references, they underpin a lot of what follows in this text, and as knowledge brought forward, are examinable.

First we look at cost behaviour at various levels of output and we examine more closely the two ways used to **split costs** between **fixed** and **variable**. This is an important area which helps you understand the critique that marginal costing may be based on an artificial distinction between fixed and variable costs.

We also revisit the technique of **breakeven** and **cost-volume-profit analysis** and in the last section of this chapter we look at **relevant costing**, the technique required for decision-making situations. We explain how to assess which costs need to be taken into account when a decision is being made and which costs do not.

topic list	learning outcomes	syllabus references	ability required
1 Cost behaviour patterns and levels of activity	Revision	n/a	comprehension
2 Determining the fixed and variable elements of semi-variable costs	Revision	n/a	comprehension
3 CVP and breakeven analysis	Revision	n/a	comprehension
4 The contribution/sales (C/S) ratio and the margin of safety	Revision	n/a	comprehension
5 Profit targets, breakeven charts and profit volume graphs	Revision	n/a	comprehension
6 Relevant costs	Revision	n/a	comprehension
7 Limiting factors	Revision	n/a	comprehension

n/a: not applicable

1 Cost behaviour patterns and levels of activity

Introduction

Cost behaviour describes how costs vary depending on the level of activity undertaken.

1.1 Levels of activity

The level of activity refers to the amount of work done, or the number of events that have occurred. Measures of the level of activity include:

- The volume of production in a period
- The number of items sold
- The value of items sold

- The number of invoices issued
- The number of units of electricity consumed
- The number of purchase orders placed

1.2 Basic principles of cost behaviour and cost behaviour patterns

The basic principle of cost behaviour is that as the level of activity rises, costs will usually rise. The question is to determine, for each item of cost, the relationship between costs and the level of activity.

The level of activity will generally be taken to be the volume of production/output.

1.3 Fixed costs

A **fixed cost** tends to be unaffected by changes in the volume of output. Fixed costs are a **period charge**, relating to a time period; as the period increases, so too will the fixed costs. Examples of fixed costs include the salary of the managing director and factory rent.

1.4 Stepped fixed cost

Consider the depreciation of a machine which may be fixed if production remains below 1,000 units per month. If production exceeds 1,000 units, a second machine may be required, and the cost of depreciation (on two machines) would go up a step. This type of cost is a step cost or a stepped fixed cost.

Examples of step costs may include rent, as accommodation requirements increase with higher output levels, or pay of employees as higher output may require, more employees.

1.5 Variable costs

A **variable cost** is a cost which tends to vary directly with the volume of output. The variable cost **per unit** is the same amount for each unit produced whereas **total** variable cost increases as volume of output increases.

Examples of variable costs may be the cost of raw materials (where there is no discount for bulk purchasing since bulk purchase discounts reduce the unit cost of purchases), sales commission or direct labour costs. The latter are usually classed as a variable cost even though basic wages are often fixed.

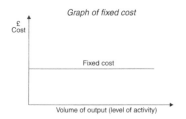

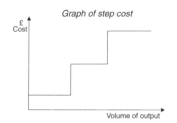

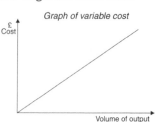

1.6 Non-linear variable costs

Although variable costs are usually assumed to be linear, there are situations where these are **curvilinear**.

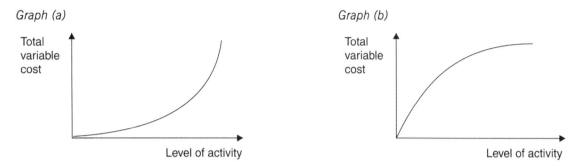

Graph (a)

Graph (b)

Graph (a) becomes steeper as levels of activity increase. Each additional unit of activity is adding more to total variable cost than the previous unit. Graph (b) becomes less steep as levels of activity increase. Each additional unit is adding less to total variable cost than the previous unit.

1.7 Semi-variable costs (or semi-fixed costs or mixed costs)

Semi-variable/semi-fixed or **mixed costs** are costs which are part-fixed and part-variable and which are thus partly affected by a change in the level of activity.

Examples of semi-variable costs may be electricity and gas bills, where there is a basic charge plus a charge per unit of consumption. A sales representative's salary is another example where a basic monthly amount is supplemented by commission on the value of sales made.

The behaviour of a semi-variable cost can be presented graphically as follows.

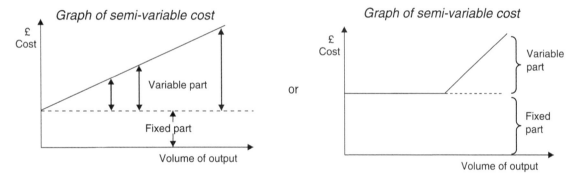

Graph of semi-variable cost

Graph of semi-variable cost

or

1.8 Cost behaviour and total and unit costs

If the variable cost of producing a unit is £5 per unit then it will remain at that cost per unit no matter how many units are produced. However, if the business's fixed costs are £5,000 then the fixed cost **per unit** will **decrease** the **more** units are **produced**. One unit will have fixed costs of £5,000 per unit, but if 2,500 are produced the fixed cost per unit will be £2. If 5,000 are produced the fixed cost per unit will be only £1. Thus as the level of activity increases the total costs **per unit** (fixed cost plus variable cost) will decrease.

In sketch graph form this may be illustrated as follows.

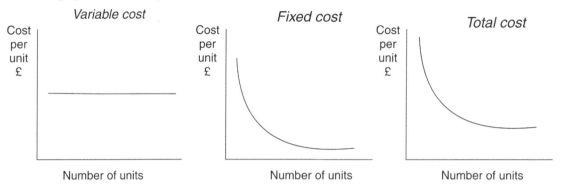

1.9 Assumptions about cost behaviour

It is often possible to assume that, within the normal or relevant range of output, costs are either fixed, variable or semi-variable. Predictions of costs for activity levels which are **outside the relevant range** are unreliable. The other problem is that we usually use data which relates to the past. This may not be representative of what will happen in the future. Managers need to bear this in mind when making decisions.

Question 6a.1   Activity levels

Select the correct words in the following sentence.

The basic principle of cost behaviour is that as the level of activity rises, costs will usually (a) **rise/fall/stay the same**. In general, as activity levels rise, the variable cost per unit will (b) **rise/fall/stay the same**, the fixed cost per unit will (c) **rise/fall/stay the same** and the total cost per unit will (d) **rise/fall/stay the same**.

Question 6a.2   Cost behaviour graphs

Show, by means of a sketch, a separate graph of cost behaviour patterns for each of the listed items of expense. In each case the vertical axis should relate to total cost. Label each horizontal axis clearly.

(a)   Electricity bill: a standing charge for each period plus a charge for each unit of electricity consumed.

(b)   Supervisory labour.

(c)   Production bonus, which is payable when output in a period exceeds 10,000 units. The bonus amounts in total to £20,000 plus £50 per unit for additional output above 10,000 units.

(d)   Sales commission, which amounts to 2% of sales turnover.

(e)   Machine rental costs of a single item of equipment. The rental agreement is that £10 should be paid for every machine hour worked each month, subject to a maximum monthly charge of £480.

Section summary

Costs which are not affected by the level of activity are **fixed costs** or **period costs**.

A **step cost** is a cost which is fixed in nature but only within certain levels of activity.

Variable costs increase or decrease with the level of activity.

Semi-variable/semi-fixed or **mixed costs** are costs which are part-fixed and part-variable and which are thus partly affected by a change in the level of activity.

2 Determining the fixed and variable elements of semi-variable costs

2.1 Analysing semi-variable costs

Introduction

The fixed and variable elements of semi-variable costs can be determined by the **high-low method** or the **scattergraph method**. Make sure that you study the high-low method carefully as it is a very useful technique.

The high-low method and the scattergraph method only give an estimate, and can therefore give differing results from each other. Although you would not actually be required to draw a scattergraph, you may perhaps be required to answer an objective test question about how the technique works, or its advantages and limitations.

2.2 High-low method

(a)   Records of costs in previous periods are reviewed and the two periods with the **highest** and **lowest** volumes of activity selected

(b)   The difference between the total cost of these two periods will be the **variable cost** of the difference in activity levels (since the same fixed cost is included in each total cost).

(c)   The variable cost per unit may be calculated from this (difference in total costs ÷ difference in activity levels), and the **fixed cost** may then be determined by substitution.

Example: the high-low method

The costs of operating the maintenance department of a computer manufacturer, Bread and Butter Ltd, for the last four months have been as follows.

Month	Cost £	Production volume Units
1	110,000	7,000
2	115,000	8,000
3	111,000	7,700
4	97,000	6,000

Required

Calculate the costs that should be expected in month five when output is expected to be 7,500 units. Ignore inflation.

Solution

(a)
	Units		£
High output	8,000	total cost	115,000
Low output	6,000	total cost	97,000
Variable cost of	2,000		18,000

Variable cost per unit £18,000/2,000 = £9

(b)   Substituting in either the high or low volume cost:

	High £		Low £
Total cost	115,000		97,000
Variable costs (8,000 × £9)	72,000	(6,000 × £9)	54,000
Fixed costs	43,000		43,000

(c)   Estimated maintenance costs when output is 7,500 units:

	£
Fixed costs	43,000
Variable costs (7,500 × £9)	67,500
Total costs	110,500

Question 6a.3 _____   High-low method

The Valuation Department of a large firm of surveyors wishes to develop a method of predicting its total costs in a period. The following past costs have been recorded at two activity levels.

	Number of valuations (V)	Total cost (TC)
Period 1	420	82,200
Period 2	515	90,275

Formulate the total cost model for a period.

2.3 Scattergraph method

A scattergraph of costs in previous periods can be prepared (with cost on the vertical axis and volume of output on the horizontal axis). A **line of best fit**, which is a line drawn **by judgement** to pass through the middle of the points, thereby having as many points above the line as below it, can then be drawn and the fixed and variable costs determined.

A scattergraph of the cost and volume data in the example in Paragraph 2.2 is shown below.

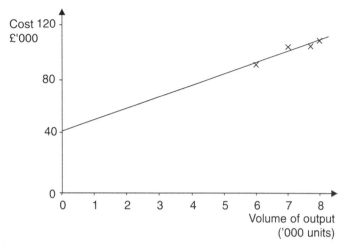

The point where the line cuts the vertical axis (approximately £40,000) is the fixed cost (the cost if there is no output). If we take the value of one of the plotted points which lies close to the line and deduct the fixed cost from the total cost, we can calculate the variable cost per unit.

Total cost for 8,000 units   = £115,000
Variable cost for 8,000 units = £(115,000 − 40,000) = £75,000
Variable cost per unit   = £75,000/8,000 = £9.375

Section summary

The high-low method or the scattergraph method can be used to determine the fixed and variable elements of semi-variable costs.

3 CVP and breakeven analysis

Introduction

Cost-volume-profit (CVP) /breakeven analysis is the study of the interrelationships between costs, volume and profit at various levels of activity. You may get a short question or an objective test question on CVP in your exam as it is assumed knowledge from earlier studies.

3.1 Breakeven point

The management of an organisation usually wishes to know the profit likely to be made if the aimed-for production and sales for the year are achieved. Management may also be interested to know the following.

(a)   The **breakeven** point which is the activity level at which there is neither profit nor loss.
(b)   The **amount** by which actual **sales can fall** below anticipated sales, **without** a **loss** being incurred.

The breakeven point (BEP) can be calculated arithmetically as follows.

$$\text{Breakeven point} = \text{Number of units of sale required to break even} = \frac{\text{Fixed costs}}{\text{Contribution per unit}}$$

Example: breakeven point

Expected sales   10,000 units at £8 = £80,000
Variable cost   £5 per unit
Fixed costs   £21,000

Required

Compute the breakeven point.

Solution

The contribution per unit is £(8 – 5)	=	£3
Contribution required to break even	=	fixed costs = £21,000
Breakeven point (BEP)	=	21,000 ÷ 3
	=	7,000 units
In revenue, BEP	=	(7,000 × £8) = £56,000

Sales above £56,000 will result in profit of £3 per unit of additional sales and sales below £56,000 will mean a loss of £3 per unit for each unit by which sales fall short of 7,000 units. In other words, profit will improve or worsen by the amount of contribution per unit.

	7,000 units £	7,001 units £
Revenue	56,000	56,008
Less variable costs	35,000	35,005
Contribution	21,000	21,003
Less fixed costs	21,000	21,000
Profit	0 (= breakeven)	3

Section summary

$$\text{Breakeven point} = \frac{\text{Fixed costs}}{\text{Contribution per unit}}$$

4 The contribution/sales (C/S) ratio and the margin of safety

Introduction

The C/S ratio (contribution/sales) measures how much contribution is earned from each £1 of sales. An alternative way of calculating the breakeven point to give an answer in terms of sales revenue and using the C/S ratio.

4.1 C/S ratio and breakeven point

LEARN

$$\text{Breakeven point} = \text{Sales revenue required to break even} = \frac{\text{Contribution required to break even}}{\text{C/S ratio}} = \frac{\text{Fixed costs}}{\text{C/S ratio}}$$

Example: C/S ratio

In the example in Paragraph 3.1 the C/S ratio is $\dfrac{£3}{£8}$ = 37.5%

Breakeven is where sales revenue equals $\dfrac{£21,000}{37.5\%}$ = £56,000

At a price of £8 per unit, this represents 7,000 units of sales.

The C/S ratio is a measure of how much contribution is earned from each £1 of sales. The C/S ratio of 37.5% in the above example means that for every £1 of sales, a contribution of 37.5p is earned. Thus, in order to earn a total contribution of £21,000 and if contribution increases by 37.5p per £1 of sales, sales must be:

$$\frac{£1}{37.5p} \times £21,000 = £56,000$$

Question 6a.4   C/S ratio

The C/S ratio of product W is 20%. IB Co, the manufacturer of product W, wishes to make a contribution of £50,000 towards fixed costs. How many units of product W must be sold if the selling price is £10 per unit?

4.2 The margin of safety

The **margin of safety** is the difference in units between the **budgeted sales volume** and the **breakeven sales volume**. It is sometimes expressed as a percentage of the budgeted sales volume. Alternatively the **margin of safety** can be expressed as the difference between the **budgeted sales revenue** and **breakeven sales revenue**, expressed as a percentage of the budgeted sales revenue.

Example: margin of safety

Mal de Mer Ltd makes and sells a product which has a variable cost of £30 and which sells for £40. Budgeted fixed costs are £70,000 and budgeted sales are 8,000 units.

Required

Calculate the breakeven point and the margin of safety.

Solution

(a) Breakeven point $= \dfrac{\text{Total fixed costs}}{\text{Contribution per unit}} = \dfrac{£70,000}{£(40-30)} = 7,000 \text{ units}$

(b) Margin of safety $= 8,000 - 7,000 \text{ units} = 1,000 \text{ units}$

which may be expressed as $\dfrac{1,000 \text{ units}}{8,000 \text{ units}} \times 100 = 12\tfrac{1}{2}\%$ of budget

(c) The margin of safety indicates to management that actual sales can fall short of budget by 1,000 units or 12½% before the breakeven point is reached and no profit at all is made.

Section summary

The **C/S ratio** (or profit/volume **P/V ratio**) is a measure of how much contribution is earned from each £1 of sales.

$$\text{Breakeven point} = \frac{\text{Fixed costs}}{\text{C/S ratio}}$$

Margin of safety = Budgeted sales volume – breakeven sales volume

5 Profit targets, breakeven charts and profit volume graphs

Introduction

This section looks at some more breakeven arithmetic. Remember that at the **breakeven point**, sales revenue equals total costs and there is no profit.

$S = V + F$

where S =   Sales revenue
       V =   Total variable costs
       F =   Total fixed costs

Subtracting V from each side of the equation, we get:

$S - V = F$, that is, **total contribution = fixed costs**

Example: breakeven arithmetic

Butterfingers Ltd makes a product which has a variable cost of £7 per unit.

Required

If fixed costs are £63,000 per annum, calculate the selling price per unit if the company wishes to break even with a sales volume of 12,000 units.

Solution

			£
Contribution required to break even (= Fixed costs)	=	£63,000	
Volume of sales	=	12,000 units	
Required contribution per unit	=	£63,000 ÷ 12,000 =	5.25
Variable cost per unit (V)	=		7.00
Required sales price per unit (S)	=		12.25

5.1 Target profits

A similar formula may be applied where a company wishes to achieve a certain profit during a period. To achieve this profit, sales must cover all costs and leave the required profit.

The **target profit** is achieved when:

$S = V + F + P$

Where S = Sales revenue
     V = Variable costs
     F = Fixed costs
     P = required profit

Subtracting V from each side of the equation, we get:

S − V = F + P, so

Total contribution required = F + P

Example: target profits

Riding Breeches Ltd makes and sells a single product, for which variable costs are as follows.

	£
Direct materials	10
Direct labour	8
Variable production overhead	6
	24

The sales price is £30 per unit, and fixed costs per annum are £68,000. The company wishes to make a profit of £16,000 per annum.

Required

Determine the sales required to achieve this profit.

Solution

Required contribution = fixed costs + profit = £68,000 + £16,000 = £84,000

Required sales can be calculated in one of two ways.

(a) $\dfrac{\text{Required contribution}}{\text{Contribution per unit}} = \dfrac{£84,000}{£(30-24)}$ = 14,000 units, or £420,000 in revenue

(b) $\dfrac{\text{Required contribution}}{\text{C/S ratio}} = \dfrac{£84,000}{20\%*}$ = £420,000 of revenue, or 14,000 units.

* C/S ratio = $\dfrac{£30-£24}{£30} = \dfrac{£6}{£30}$ = 0.2 = 20%.

Question 6a.5

Target profits

Seven League Boots Ltd wishes to sell 14,000 units of its product, which has a variable cost of £15 to make and sell. Fixed costs are £47,000 and the required profit is £23,000.

Required

Calculate the required sales price per unit.

5.2 Decisions to change sales price, sales volume or costs

Altering the selling price, sales volume or variable cost per unit or fixed cost requires slight variations on basic breakeven arithmetic.

Example: profit maximisation

C Ltd has developed a new product which is about to be launched on to the market. The variable cost of selling the product is £12 per unit. The marketing department has estimated that at a sales price of £20, annual demand would be 10,000 units.

However, if the sales price is set above £20, sales demand would fall by 500 units for each 50p increase above £20. Similarly, if the price is set below £20, demand would increase by 500 units for each 50p stepped reduction in price below £20.

Required

Determine the price which would maximise C Ltd's profit in the next year.

Solution

At a price of £20 per unit, the unit contribution would be £(20 – 12) = £8. Each 50p increase (or decrease) in price would raise (or lower) the unit contribution by 50p. The total contribution is calculated at each sales price by multiplying the unit contribution by the expected sales volume.

	Unit price £	Unit contribution £	Sales volume Units	Total contribution £
	20.00	8.00	10,000	80,000
(a) Reduce price				
	19.50	7.50	10,500	78,750
	19.00	7.00	11,000	77,000
(b) Increase price				
	20.50	8.50	9,500	80,750
	21.00	9.00	9,000	81,000
	21.50	9.50	8,500	80,750
	22.00	10.00	8,000	80,000
	22.50	10.50	7,500	78,750

The total contribution would be maximised, and therefore profit maximised, at a sales price of £21 per unit, and sales demand of 9,000 units.

5.3 Breakeven charts

The breakeven point can also be determined graphically using a breakeven chart. This is a chart which shows approximate levels of profit or loss at different sales volume levels within a limited range.

A breakeven chart has the following axes.

- A **horizontal** axis showing the **sales/output** (in value or units)
- A **vertical axis** showing £ for **sales revenues** and **costs**

5.4 Lines on a breakeven chart

The following lines are drawn on the breakeven chart.

(a) The sales line

     (i)   Starts at the origin

     (ii)   Ends at the point signifying expected sales

(b)   The fixed costs line

(i)   Runs parallel to the horizontal axis

(ii)   Meets the vertical axis at a point which represents total fixed costs

(c)   The total costs line

(i)   Starts where the fixed costs line meets the vertical axis

(ii)   Ends at the point which represents anticipated sales on the horizontal axis and total costs of anticipated sales on the vertical axis

The **breakeven point** is the **intersection** of the **sales line** and the **total costs line**.

The distance between the **breakeven point** and the **expected (or budgeted) sales**, in units, indicates the **margin of safety**.

Example: a breakeven chart

The budgeted annual output of a factory is 120,000 units. The fixed overheads amount to £40,000 and the variable costs are 50p per unit. The sales price is £1 per unit.

Required

Construct a breakeven chart showing the current breakeven point and profit earned up to the present maximum capacity.

Solution

We begin by calculating the profit at the budgeted annual output.

	£
Sales (120,000 units)	120,000
Variable costs	60,000
Contribution	60,000
Fixed costs	40,000
Profit	20,000

The breakeven chart is shown on the following page.

The chart is drawn as follows.

(a)   The **vertical axis** represents **money** (costs and revenue) and the **horizontal axis** represents the **level of activity** (production and sales).

(b)   The fixed costs are represented by a **straight line parallel to the horizontal axis** (in our example, at £40,000).

(c)   The **variable costs** are added 'on top of' fixed costs, to give **total costs**. It is assumed that fixed costs are the same in total and variable costs are the same per unit at all levels of output.

The line of costs is therefore a straight line and only two points need to be plotted and joined up. Perhaps the two most convenient points to plot are total costs at zero output, and total costs at the budgeted output and sales.

(i)   At zero output, costs are equal to the amount of fixed costs only, £40,000, since there are no variable costs.

(ii)   At the budgeted output of 120,000 units, costs are £100,000.

	£
Fixed costs	40,000
Variable costs 120,000 × 50p	60,000
Total costs	100,000

(d) The sales line is also drawn by plotting two points and joining them up.

- At zero sales, revenue is nil.

- At the budgeted output and sales of 120,000 units, revenue is £120,000.

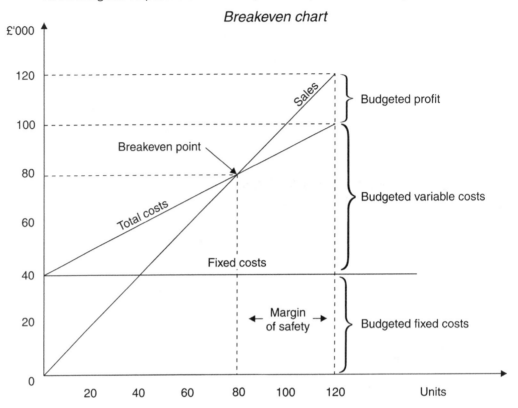

Breakeven chart

5.5 Interpreting the breakeven chart

The breakeven point is where total costs are matched exactly by total revenue. From the chart, you can see that this occurs at output and sales of 80,000 units, when revenue and costs are both £80,000. This breakeven point can be proved mathematically as:

$$\frac{\text{Required contribution (= fixed costs)}}{\text{Contribution per unit}} = \frac{£40,000}{\text{50p per unit}} = 80,000 \text{ units}$$

You can see on the chart that the margin of safety is the difference between the budgeted level of activity and the breakeven level.

5.6 The contribution breakeven chart

The main problem with the traditional breakeven chart is that it is not possible to read contribution directly from the chart.

The contribution breakeven chart remedies this by **drawing the variable cost line instead of the fixed cost line**. A contribution breakeven chart for the example above would include the variable cost line passing through the origin and the total variable cost of £60,000 for 120,000 units. The contribution breakeven chart will look like this.

Contribution breakeven chart

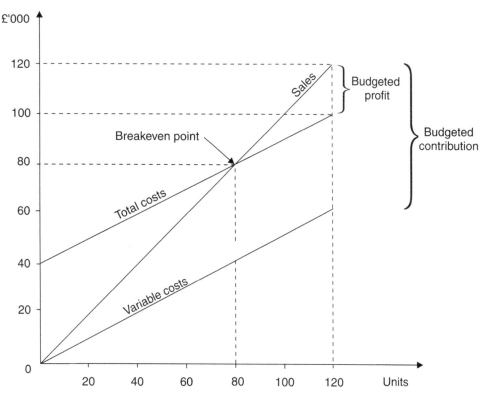

If you look back at the breakeven chart above you will see that the breakeven point is the same, but that the budgeted contribution can now be read more easily from the chart.

5.7 The profit/volume (P/V) chart

The **profit/volume (P/V) chart** is a variation of the breakeven chart which illustrates the relationship of costs and profit to sales, and the margin of safety.

5.8 Construction of a profit/volume chart

A P/V chart is constructed as follows (look at the chart in the example that follows as you read the explanation).

(a)   'P' is on the y axis and actually comprises not only 'profit' but contribution to profit (in monetary value), extending above and below the x axis with a zero point at the intersection of the two axes, and the negative section below the x axis representing fixed costs. This means that at zero production, the firm is incurring a loss equal to the fixed costs.

(b)   'V' is on the x axis and comprises either volume of sales or value of sales (revenue).

(c)   The profit-volume line is a straight line drawn with its starting point (at zero production) at the intercept on the y axis representing the level of fixed costs, and with a gradient of contribution/unit (or the C/S ratio if sales value is used rather than units). The P/V line will cut the x axis at the breakeven point of sales volume. Any point on the P/V line above the x axis represents the profit to the firm (as measured on the vertical axis) for that particular level of sales.

Example: P/V chart

Let us draw a P/V chart for our example in Paragraph 5.4. At sales of 120,000 units, total contribution will be $120,000 \times £(1 - 0.5) = £60,000$ and total profit will be £20,000.

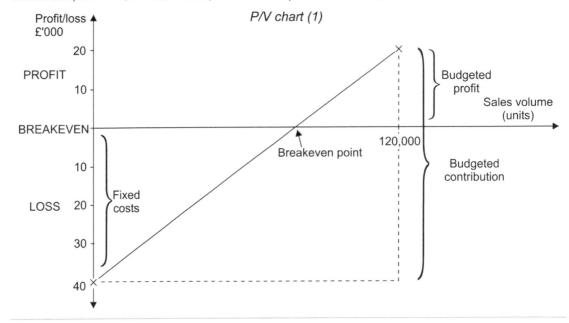

Exam alert

Remember that the examiner can set questions on topics that you covered in your earlier studies, such as P/V charts, even if they are not specifically mentioned in the P1 syllabus.

5.9 The advantage of the P/V chart

(a)   If the budgeted selling price of the product in our example is increased to £1.20, with the result that demand drops to 105,000 units despite additional fixed costs of £10,000 being spent on advertising, we could add a line representing this situation to our P/V chart.

(b)   At sales of 105,000 units, contribution will be $105,000 \times £(1.20 - 0.50) = £73,500$ and total profit will be £23,500 (fixed costs being £50,000).

(c)   The diagram P/V chart (2) shows that if the selling price is increased, the breakeven point occurs at a lower level of sales revenue (71,429 units instead of 80,000 units), although this is not a particularly large decrease when viewed in the context of the projected sales volume. It is also possible to see that for sales above 50,000 units, the profit achieved will be higher (and the loss achieved lower) if the price is £1.20. For sales volumes below 50,000 units the first option will yield lower losses.

(d)   The P/V chart is the clearest way of presenting such information; two conventional breakeven charts on one set of axes would be very confusing.

(e)   Changes in the variable cost per unit or in fixed costs at certain activity levels can also be incorporated easily into a P/V chart. The profit or loss at each point where the cost structure changes should be calculated and plotted on the graph so that the profit/volume line becomes a series of straight lines.

   For example, suppose that at sales levels in excess of 120,000 units the variable cost per unit increases to £0.60 (perhaps because of overtime premiums that are incurred when production exceeds a certain level). At sales of 130,000 units, contribution would therefore be $130,000 \times £(1 - 0.60) = £52,000$ and total profit would be £12,000. (See P/V chart (3).)

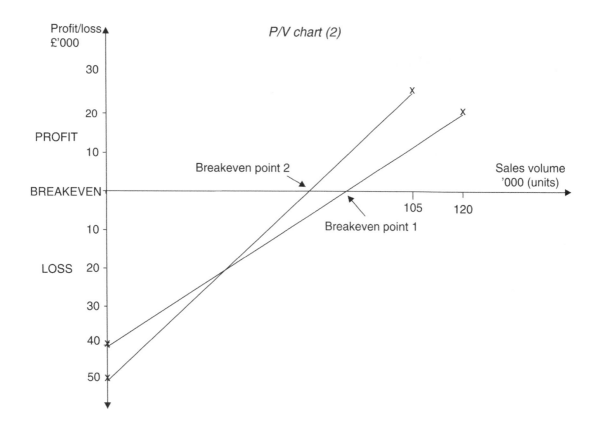

P/V chart (2)

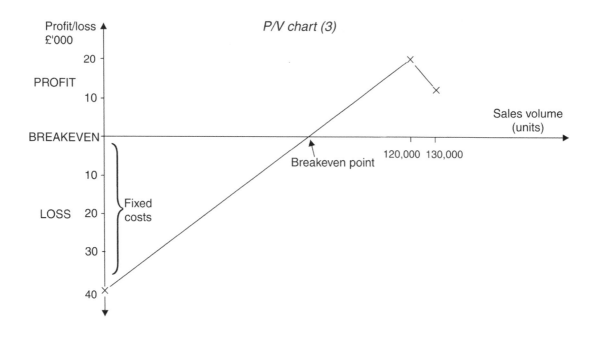

P/V chart (3)

Question 6a.6 Breakeven chart

Match the following labels to (a), (b), (c) and (d) marked on the breakeven chart below.

| Fixed costs | Margin of safety | Budgeted profit | Budgeted variable costs |

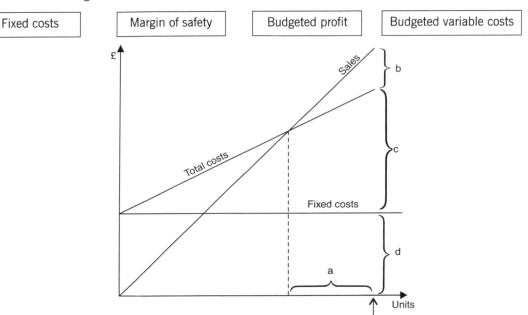

Question 6a.7 G Limited

G Limited manufactures and sells a single product. The profit statement for May is as follows.

	£
Sales value	80,000
Variable cost of sales	48,000
Contribution	32,000
Fixed costs	15,000
Profit	17,000

The management accountant has used the data for May to draw the following profit/volume chart.

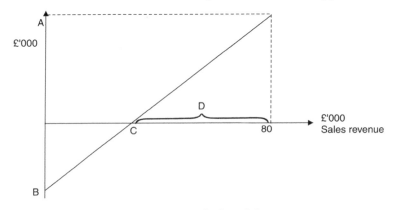

(a)   The monetary values indicated on the chart as A, B and C are:

A   £ [   ]

B   £ [   ]

C   £ [   ]

(b)   The term used to describe the distance D on the chart is [   ]

(c)   For the whole of the current year, G Limited budgets to achieve a sales value of £900,000. Assuming that the unit variable costs and selling price achieved will be the same as that achieved during May, and that fixed costs for the year will be £180,000, the profit for the whole year will be

        £ [   ]

(d)   The annual margin of safety for G Limited's product is [   ] % of budgeted sales.

5.10 Limitations of CVP analysis

- It **can only apply to a single product** or a single mix of a group of products.
- A breakeven chart may be **time-consuming** to prepare.
- It **assumes** fixed costs are constant at all levels of output.
- It **assumes** that **variable costs** are the **same** per unit at all levels of output.
- It **assumes** that **sales prices** are **constant** at all levels of output.
- It assumes **production** and **sales** are the **same** (stock levels are ignored).
- It **ignores** the **uncertainty** in the estimates of fixed costs and variable cost per unit.

5.11 The economist's breakeven chart

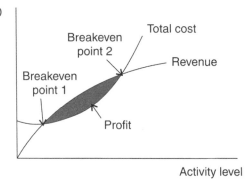

In economics, the lines on the breakeven chart are curved rather than straight. This is because economists assume that costs per unit and revenues per unit are not constant at every level of activity. Note that the total cost line falls initially and then rises again. This is because production is assumed to be more efficient as the number of goods being produced is increased. This is known as **economies of scale**.

Section summary

The **target profit** is achieved when sales revenue equals variable costs plus fixed costs plus profit. Therefore the **total contribution required** for a target profit = **fixed costs + required profit**.

A **contribution breakeven chart** depicts variable costs instead of fixed costs, so that contribution can be read directly from the chart.

The **profit/volume (P/V) chart** is a variation of the breakeven chart which illustrates the relationship of costs and profit to sales, and the margin of safety.

6 Relevant costs

Introduction

Relevant costs are future cash flows arising as a direct consequence of a decision. Relevant costs are:

- Future costs
- Opportunity costs
- Differential costs
- Cash flows
- Incremental costs
- Avoidable costs

6.1 Relevant costs

Decision making should be based on relevant costs.

(a) **Relevant costs are future costs**.

    (i) A decision is about the future; it cannot alter what has been done already. Costs that have been incurred in the past are totally irrelevant to any decision that is being made 'now'. Such costs are **past costs** or **sunk costs**.

    (ii) Costs that have been incurred include not only costs that have already been paid, but also **committed costs** (a future cash flow that will be incurred anyway, regardless of the decision taken now).

(b) **Relevant costs are cash flows**. Only cash flow information is required. This means that costs or charges which do not reflect additional cash spending (such as **depreciation** and **notional costs**) should be **ignored** for the purpose of decision making.

(c) **Relevant costs are incremental costs**. For example, if an employee is expected to have no other work to do during the next week, but will be paid his basic wage (of, say, £100 per week) for attending work and doing nothing, his manager might decide to give him a job which earns the organisation £40. The net gain is £40 and the £100 is irrelevant to the decision because although it is a future cash flow, it will be **incurred anyway** whether the employee is given work or not.

6.2 Relevant costs – other terms

KEY TERM

DIFFERENTIAL COST is 'the difference in total cost between alternatives.'   *(CIMA Official Terminology)*

For example, if decision option A costs £300 and decision option B costs £360, the differential cost is £60.

Example: relevant costs

Suppose for example that there are three options, A, B and C, only one of which can be chosen. The net profit from each would be £80, £100 and £70 respectively.

Since only one option can be selected option B would be chosen because it offers the biggest benefit.

	£
Profit from option B	100
Less opportunity cost (ie the benefit from the most profitable alternative, A)	80
Differential benefit of option B	20

The decision to choose option B would not be taken simply because it offers a profit of £100, but because it offers a differential profit of £20 in excess of the next best alternative.

KEY TERM

AVOIDABLE COST is the 'specific cost of an activity or sector of a business that would be avoided if the activity or sector did not exist.'
(CIMA Official Terminology)

For example a retailing organisation may be considering the closure of one of its shops. **Avoidable costs** would be those that are **saved** by closing the shop, **for example** the **rent** of the shop premises. Costs such as **apportioned head office costs** would **not** be saved by closing the shop, therefore these apportioned costs are not avoidable costs.

KEY TERMS

An OPPORTUNITY COST is 'The value of the benefit sacrificed when one course of action is chosen, in preference to an alternative. The opportunity cost is represented by the foregone potential benefit from the best rejected course of action.'
(CIMA Official Terminology)

A NOTIONAL COST is similar to an opportunity cost. If a business uses its own asset instead of hiring it out to others there is a hidden cost. That is the income lost by not hiring it out. The most common example of a notional cost is rent, where a business owns a property and uses it rather than renting it out. The rental income forgone is the notional cost.

6.3 Sunk costs

A **sunk cost** is a past cost which is not directly relevant in decision making.

6.4 Decision accounting

The principle underlying decision accounting is that **management decisions can only affect the future.** In decision making, managers therefore require information about **future costs and revenues** which would be affected by the decision under review, and they must not be misled by events, costs and revenues in the past, about which they can do nothing.

Therefore **sunk costs**, which have been charged already in a previous accounting period or will be charged in a future accounting period although the expenditure has already been incurred (or the expenditure decision irrevocably taken), are **irrelevant** to **decision making**.

Example: sunk costs

An example of sunk costs is development costs which have already been incurred. Suppose that a company has spent £250,000 in developing a new service for customers, but the marketing department's most recent findings are that the service might not gain customer acceptance and could be a commercial failure. The decision whether or not to abandon the development of the new service would have to be taken, but the £250,000 spent so far should be **ignored** by the **decision makers** because it is a **sunk cost**.

6.5 Fixed and variable costs

Unless you are given an indication to the contrary, you should assume the following.

- Variable costs will be relevant costs.
- Fixed costs are irrelevant to a decision.

This need not be the case, however, and you should analyse variable and fixed cost data carefully. Do not forget that 'fixed' costs may only be fixed in the short term.

6.6 Non-relevant variable costs

There might be occasions when a variable cost is in fact a sunk cost. For example, suppose that a company has some units of raw material in stock. They have been paid for already, and originally cost £2,000. They are now obsolete and are no longer used in regular production, and they have no scrap value. However, they could be used in a special job which the company is trying to decide whether to undertake. The special job is a 'one-off' customer order, and would use up all these materials in stock.

In deciding whether the job should be undertaken, the relevant cost of the materials to the special job is nil. Their original cost of £2,000 is a **sunk cost**, and should be ignored in the decision.

However, if the materials did have a scrap value of, say, £300, then their relevant cost to the job would be the **opportunity cost** of being unable to sell them for scrap, ie £300.

6.7 Attributable fixed costs

There might be occasions when a fixed cost is a relevant cost, and you must be aware of the distinction between 'specific' or 'directly attributable' fixed costs, and general fixed overheads.

(a) **Directly attributable fixed costs** are those costs which, although fixed within a relevant range of activity level are relevant to a decision for either of the following reasons.

   (i) They could **increase** if certain **extra activities** were **undertaken**. For example, it may be necessary to employ an extra supervisor if a particular order is accepted. The extra salary would be an attributable fixed cost.

   (ii) They would **decrease** or be **eliminated entirely** if a decision were taken either to **reduce the scale** of operations or **shut down** entirely.

(b) **General fixed overheads** are those fixed overheads which will be unaffected by decisions to increase or decrease the scale of operations, perhaps because they are an apportioned share of the fixed costs of items which would be completely unaffected by the decisions. An apportioned share of head office charges is an example of general fixed overheads for a local office or department. General fixed overheads are **not relevant in decision making**.

6.8 Absorbed overhead

Absorbed overhead is a **notional** accounting cost and hence should be ignored for decision-making purposes. It is overhead **incurred** which **may** be **relevant** to a decision.

6.9 The relevant cost of materials

The relevant cost of raw materials is generally their **current replacement cost**, *unless* the materials have already been purchased and would not be replaced once used. In this case the relevant cost of using them is the **higher** of the following.

*   Their current resale value
*   The value they would obtain if they were put to an alternative use

If the materials have no resale value and no other possible use, then the relevant cost of using them for the opportunity under consideration would be nil.

You should test your knowledge of the relevant cost of materials by attempting the following question.

Question 6a.8 Relevant cost of materials

O'Reilly Ltd has been approached by a customer who would like a special job to be done for him, and who is willing to pay £22,000 for it. The job would require the following materials.

Material	Total units required	Units already in stock	Book value of units in stock £/unit	Realisable value £/unit	Replacement cost £/unit
A	1,000	0	–	–	6
B	1,000	600	2	2.50	5
C	1,000	700	3	2.50	4
D	200	200	4	6.00	9

Material B is used regularly by O'Reilly Ltd, and if units of B are required for this job, they would need to be replaced to meet other production demand.

Materials C and D are in stock as the result of previous over-buying, and they have a restricted use. No other use could be found for material C, but the units of material D could be used in another job as substitute for 300 units of material E, which currently costs £5 per unit (of which the company has no units in stock at the moment).

Required

Calculate the relevant costs of material for deciding whether or not to accept the contract.

6.10 Qualitative factors

Qualitative factors in decision making are factors which might influence the eventual decisions but which have not been quantified in terms of relevant income or costs. They may stem from two sources.

● Non-financial objectives

● Factors which might be quantifiable in money terms, but which have not been quantified, perhaps because there is insufficient information to make reliable estimates

Example: qualitative factors

Qualitative factors that are relevant to a decision will vary according to the circumstances and nature of the decision. Here are some examples.

Qualitative factor	Comment
Cash availability	There must be sufficient cash to finance any purchases of equipment and build up share capital
Employees	Employee welfare should be considered if work procedures are to be changed
Customers	Changing or removing one product in a range may affect the sales of the rest
Competitors	Some decisions may stimulate a response from rival companies
Suppliers	Some decisions may affect suppliers and their long-term goodwill or even put them out of business
Cost structure changes	Reducing production volume to save on labour costs for example, may reduce the quality of material purchases and hence bulk discounts may be lost.

This is by no means an exhaustive list of the qualitative factors that may be relevant to a decision. However, you should now have an idea of the type of factor that may be worthy of mention, and you should be able to **adapt your understanding** to any situation.

Section summary

Relevant costs are future cash flows arising as a direct consequence of a decision. Relevant costs are:

- Future costs
- Opportunity costs
- Differential costs
- Cash flows
- Incremental costs
- Avoidable costs

A **sunk cost** is a past cost which is not directly relevant in decision making.

The principle underlying decision accounting is that **management decisions can only affect the future.** In decision making, managers therefore require information about **future costs and revenues** which would be affected by the decision under review, and they must not be misled by events, costs and revenues in the past, about which they can do nothing.

Qualitative factors should always be considered alongside the quantitative data in any management accounting situation.

7 Limiting factors

Introduction

A limiting factor is anything that is in scarce supply and therefore limits the activities that a business can carry out.

KEY TERM

A LIMITING FACTOR or KEY FACTOR is 'anything which limits the activity of an entity. An entity seeks to optimise the benefit it obtains from the limiting factor. Examples are a shortage of supply of a resource or a restriction on sales demand at an particular price'. *(CIMA Official Terminology)*

A **limiting factor** could be sales if there is a limit to sales demand but any one of the organisation's resources (labour, materials and so on) may be insufficient to meet the level of production demanded.

It is assumed in limiting factor analysis that management wishes to maximise profit and that profit will be maximised when contribution is maximised (given no change in fixed costs expenditure incurred).

Example: Limiting factor

A company manufactures three products, details of which are as follows.

	Product J $ per unit	Product K $ per unit	Product L $ per unit
Selling price	140	122	134
Direct materials ($2/kg)	22	14	26
Other variable cost	84	72	51
Fixed cost	20	26	40

In a period when direct material is restricted in supply, what is the ranking of the products in terms of the most profitable use of the material?

Solution

1st K, 2nd L, 3rd J.

	Product J	Product K	Product L
	$ per unit	$ per unit	$ per unit
Selling price	140	122	134
Variable cost	106	86	77
Contribution	34	36	57
Kg of material	11	7	13
Contribution per kg	$3.09	$5.14	$4.38
Ranking	3	1	2

Section summary

In a limiting factor situation, contribution will be maximised by earning the biggest possible contribution per unit of limiting factor.

Chapter Roundup

✓ Costs which are not affected by the level of activity are **fixed costs** or **period costs**.

✓ A **step cost** is a cost which is fixed in nature but only within certain levels of activity.

✓ **Variable costs** increase or decrease with the level of activity.

✓ **Semi-variable/semi-fixed** or **mixed costs** are costs which are part-fixed and part-variable and which are thus partly affected by a change in the level of activity.

✓ The high-low method or the scattergraph method can be used to determine the fixed and variable elements of semi-variable costs.

✓ **Breakeven point** $= \dfrac{\text{Fixed costs}}{\text{Contribution per unit}}$.

✓ The **C/S ratio** (or **P/V ratio**) is a measure of how much contribution is earned from each £1 of sales.

✓ **Breakeven point** $= \dfrac{\text{Fixed costs}}{\text{C/S ratio}}$

✓ Margin of safety = Budgeted sales volume − breakeven sales volume.

✓ The **target profit** is achieved when sales revenue equals variable costs plus fixed costs plus profit. Therefore the **total contribution required** for a target profit = **fixed costs + required profit**.

✓ A **contribution breakeven chart** depicts variable costs instead of fixed costs, so that contribution can be read directly from the chart.

✓ The **profit/volume (P/V) chart** is a variation of the breakeven chart which illustrates the relationship of costs and profits to sales and the margin of safety.

✓ **Relevant costs** are future cash flows arising as a direct consequence of a decision. Relevant costs are:

– **Future costs**	– **Differential costs**
– **Cash flows**	– **Avoidable costs**
– **Incremental costs**	– **Opportunity costs**

✓ A **sunk cost** is a past cost which is not directly relevant in decision making.

✓ The principle underlying decision accounting is that **management decisions can only affect the future.** In decision making, managers therefore require information about **future costs and revenues** which would be affected by the decision under review, and they must not be misled by events, costs and revenues in the past, about which they can do nothing.

✓ **Qualitative factors** should always be considered alongside the quantitative data in any management accounting situation.

✓ In a **limiting factor** situation, contribution will be maximised by earning the biggest possible contribution per unit of limiting factor.

Quick Quiz

1 The costs of operating the canteen at 'Eat a lot Company' for the past three months is as follows.

Month	Cost £	Employees
1	72,500	1,250
2	75,000	1,300
3	68,750	1,175

Variable cost (per employee per month) =

Fixed cost per month =

2 Use the following to make up four formulae which can be used to calculate the breakeven point.

Contribution per unit	Contribution required to break even
Contribution per unit	Contribution required to break even
Fixed costs	C/S ratio
Fixed costs	C/S ratio

(a) Breakeven point (sales units) = ┌─────────────────┐

or ┌────────────────────┐

(b) Breakeven point (sales revenue) = ┌─────────────────┐

or ┌────────────────────┐

3 The P/V ratio is a measure of how much profit is earned from each £1 of sales.

True ☐

False ☐

4 Profits are maximised at the breakeven point.

True ☐

False ☐

5 At the breakeven point, total contribution = ...

6 The total contribution required for a **target profit** = ...

7 Give three uses of breakeven charts.

8   Breakeven charts show approximate levels of profit or loss at different sales volume levels within a limited range. Which of the following are true?

   I   The sales line starts at the origin
   II   The fixed costs line runs parallel to the vertical axis
   III   Breakeven charts have a horizontal axis showing the sales/output (in value or units)
   IV   Breakeven charts have a vertical axis showing £ for revenues and costs
   V   The breakeven point is the intersection of the sales line and the fixed cost line

   A   I and II
   B   I and III
   C   I, III and IV
   D   I, III, IV, and V

9   On a breakeven chart, the distance between the breakeven point and the expected (or budgeted) sales, in units, indicates the ....

10   Name six types of relevant costs

11   A sunk cost is:

   A   a cost committed to be spent in the current period
   B   a cost which is irrelevant for decision making
   C   a cost connected with oil exploration in the North Sea
   D   a cost unaffected by fluctuations in the level of activity

12   Select the correct word in the following sentences.

   (a)   For a material item that is regularly used, the relevant cost of using it for a particular order is its **original purchase price/current replacement cost**.

   (b)   For a material item that has already been purchased and would not be replaced once used, the relevant cost of using it for a particular order is the **higher/lower** of its current resale value and its value if put to an alternative use.

Answers to Quick Quiz

1 Variable cost = £50 per employee per month

Fixed costs = £10,000 per month

	Activity No employees	Cost £
High	1,300	75,000
Low	1,175	68,750
	125	6,250

Variable cost per employee = £6,250/125 = £50

For 1,175 employees, total cost = £68,750

Total cost	= variable cost + fixed cost
£68,750	= (1,175 × £50) + fixed cost

∴ Fixed cost = £68,750 – £58,750
= £10,000

2 (a) Breakeven point (sales units) = $\dfrac{\text{Fixed costs}}{\text{Contribution per unit}}$

or $\dfrac{\text{Contribution required to break even}}{\text{Contribution per unit}}$

(b) Breakeven point (sales revenue) = $\dfrac{\text{Fixed costs}}{\text{C/S ratio}}$

or $\dfrac{\text{Contribution required to break even}}{\text{C/S ratio}}$

3 False. The P/V ratio is a measure of how much **contribution** is earned from each £1 of sales.

4 False. At the breakeven point there is no profit.

5 At the breakeven point, total contribution = fixed costs

6 Fixed costs + required profit

7 • To plan the production of a company's products
   • To market a company's products
   • To give a visual display of breakeven arithmetic

8 C The fixed costs line runs parallel to the **horizontal** axis so II is false. The breakeven point is the intersection of the sales line and the total cost line so V is false.

9 Margin of safety

10 (a) Future costs
   (b) Cash flows
   (c) Incremental costs
   (d) Differential costs
   (e) Opportunity costs
   (f) Avoidable costs

11 B A sunk cost is a cost which is irrelevant for decision making.

12 (a) current replacement cost
   (b) higher

Answers to Questions

6a.1 Activity levels

(a)   Rise
(b)   Stay the same
(c)   Fall
(d)   Fall

6a.2 Cost behaviour graphs

(a)

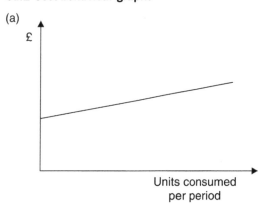

(b)

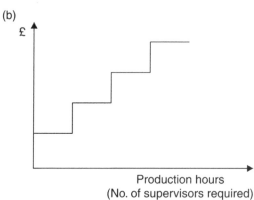

(c)

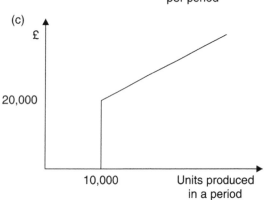

(d)

(e)

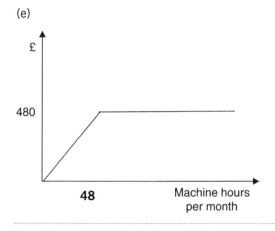

6a.3 High-low method

Although we only have two activity levels in this question we can still apply the high-low method.

	Valuations V	Total cost £
Period 2	515	90,275
Period 1	420	82,200
Change due to variable cost	95	8,075

∴ Variable cost per valuation = £8,075/95 = £85.

Period 2: fixed cost = £90,275 − (515 × £85) = £46,500

The variable cost of £85 per valuation must be added to the fixed cost.

Therefore Total Costs (TC) = Fixed costs + Variable costs = £46,500 + £85V

6a.4 C/S ratio

$$\frac{\text{Required contribution}}{\text{C/S ratio}} = \frac{£50,000}{20\%} = £250,000$$

∴ Number of units = £250,000 ÷ £10 = 25,000.

6a.5 Target profits

Required contribution	= fixed costs plus profit
	= £47,000 + £23,000
	= £70,000
Required sales	= 14,000 units

	£
Required contribution per unit sold (£70,000/14,000)	5
Variable cost per unit	15
Required sales price per unit	20

6a.6 Breakeven chart

Fixed costs (d)
Margin of safety (a)
Budgeted profit (b)
Budgeted variable costs (c)

6a.7 G Limited

(a) A £17,000
B −£15,000
C £37,500
Workings

A: profit achieved from £80,000 sales revenue = £17,000
B: loss at zero sales revenue = fixed costs = −£15,000
C: breakeven point = £37,500 sales revenue (see below)

C/S ratio = 32/80 = 40%

$$\text{Breakeven point} = \frac{\text{fixed costs}}{\text{C/S ratio}} = \frac{£15,000}{0.4} = £37,500 \text{ sales revenue}$$

(b) The term used to describe the distance D on the chart is the margin of safety. (This is the difference between the sales revenue budgeted or achieved, and the revenue required to break even.)

(c) The profit for the whole year will be £180,000.

Workings

Contribution achieved	=	sales revenue × C/S ratio
	=	£900,000 × 0.4
	=	£360,000
Fixed costs		£180,000
∴ Profit for whole year		£180,000

(d) The annual margin of safety for G Limited's product is 50% of budgeted sales.

Workings

$$\text{Annual breakeven point} = \frac{\text{fixed costs}}{\text{C/S ratio}} = \frac{£180,000}{0.4} = £450,000 \text{ sales revenue}$$

Margin of safety = £900,000 – £450,000 = £450,000 sales revenue
                   = 50% of budgeted sales

6a.8 Relevant cost of materials

(a) **Material A** is not yet owned. It would have to be bought in full at the replacement cost of £6 per unit.

(b) **Material B** is used regularly by the company. There are existing stocks (600 units) but if these are used on the contract under review a further 600 units would be bought to replace them. Relevant costs are therefore 1,000 units at the replacement cost of £5 per unit.

(c) 1,000 units of **material C** are needed and 700 are already in stock. If used for the contract, a further 300 units must be bought at £4 each. The existing stocks of 700 will not be replaced. If they are used for the contract, they could not be sold at £2.50 each. The realisable value of these 700 units is an opportunity cost of sales revenue forgone.

(d) The required units of **material D** are already in stock and will not be replaced. There is an opportunity cost of using D in the contract because there are alternative opportunities either to sell the existing stocks for £6 per unit (£1,200 in total) or avoid other purchases (of material E), which would cost 300 × £5 = £1,500. Since substitution for E is more beneficial, £1,500 is the opportunity cost.

(e) **Summary of relevant costs**

	£
Material A (1,000 × £6)	6,000
Material B (1,000 × £5)	5,000
Material C (300 × £4) plus (700 × £2.50)	2,950
Material D	1,500
Total	15,450

ABSORPTION AND MARGINAL COSTING

 The main principles underlying the content of this chapter should be familiar to you from your earlier studies. You should already be able to apply a system of **marginal costing** and understand how it differs from **absorption costing.**

Whereas absorption costing recognises fixed costs (usually fixed production costs) as part of the cost of a unit of output and hence as **product costs**, marginal costing treats all fixed costs as **period costs**.

The emphasis in your *Performance Operations* syllabus is on a comparison between the two systems and their effect on reported profit and inventory valuation, and on their application in different learning environments.

topic list	learning outcomes	syllabus references	ability required
1 The principles of marginal costing	A1(a)	A1(i)	analysis
2 The principles of absorption costing	A1(a)	A1(i)	analysis
3 The effect of marginal costing and absorption costing on reported profit and inventory valuation	A1(a), A1(b)	A1(i)	analysis
4 Marginal costing and absorption costing compared	A1(a), A1(b)	A1(i)	analysis

Knowledge brought forward from earlier studies

Terminology

- **Absorption costing** 'Assigns direct costs, *and* all or part of overhead to cost units using one or more overhead absorption rates'.

- **Marginal cost** is 'Part of the cost of one unit of product or service that would be avoided if the unit were not produced, or that would increase if one extra unit were produced'.

- **Contribution** is 'Sales value less variable cost of sales'. *(CIMA Official Terminology)*

- **Marginal costing** is an alternative method of costing to absorption costing. In marginal costing, only variable costs are charged as a cost of sale and a contribution is calculated which is sales revenue minus the variable cost of sales. Closing inventories of work in progress or finished goods are valued at marginal (variable) production cost. Fixed costs are treated as a period cost, and are charged in full to the income statement in the accounting period in which they are incurred.

1 The principles of marginal costing

Introduction

The marginal costing philosophy is that profit measurement should be based on an analysis of total contribution, that is sales value less the variable cost of sales.

Supporters of marginal costing argue that the valuation of closing inventories should be at variable production cost (direct materials, direct labour, direct expenses (if any) and variable production overhead) because these are the only costs properly attributable to the product.

The principles of marginal costing (also known as variable costing) are as follows.

(a) Period fixed costs are the same for any volume of sales and production (provided that the level of activity is within the 'relevant range'). Therefore, by selling an extra item of product or service the following will happen.

    (i) Revenue will increase by the sales value of the item sold
    (ii) Costs will increase by the variable cost per unit
    (iii) Profit will increase by the amount of contribution earned from the extra item.

(b) Similarly, if the volume of sales falls by one item, the profit will fall by the amount of contribution earned from the item.

(c) Since fixed costs relate to a period of time, and do not change with increases or decreases in sales volume, it is misleading to charge units of sale with a share of fixed costs. Absorption costing is therefore misleading, and it is more appropriate to deduct fixed costs from total contribution for the period to derive a profit figure.

(d) When a unit of product is made, the extra costs incurred in its manufacture are the **variable production costs**. Fixed costs are unaffected, and no extra fixed costs are incurred when output is increased.

Before reviewing marginal costing principles any further, it will be helpful to remind yourself of the basics by looking at a numerical example.

Example: marginal costing

Water and Sons makes a product, the Splash, which has a variable production cost of £6 per unit and a sales price of £10 per unit. At the beginning of September 20X0, there were no opening inventories and production during the month was 20,000 units. Fixed costs for the month were £30,000 for production and £15,000 for administration, sales and distribution. There were no variable marketing costs.

Required

Calculate the contribution and profit for September, using marginal costing principles, if sales were as follows.

(a)   10,000 Splashes
(b)   15,000 Splashes
(c)   20,000 Splashes

Solution

The first stage in the profit calculation must be to identify the variable costs, and then the contribution. Fixed costs are deducted from the total contribution to derive the profit. All closing inventories are valued at marginal production cost (£6 per unit). Production during the month in all three cases is 20,000 units.

	10,000 Splashes		15,000 Splashes		20,000 Splashes	
	£	£	£	£	£	£
Sales (at £10)		100,000		150,000		200,000
Opening inventory	0		0		0	
Variable production cost	120,000		120,000		120,000	
	120,000		120,000		120,000	
Less value of closing inventory (at marginal cost)	60,000		30,000		0	
Variable cost of sales		60,000		90,000		120,000
Contribution		40,000		60,000		80,000
Less fixed costs		45,000		45,000		45,000
Profit/(loss)		(5,000)		15,000		35,000
Profit/(loss) per unit		£(0.50)		£1		£1.75
Contribution per unit		£4		£4		£4

The conclusions which may be drawn from this example are as follows.

(a)   The **profit per unit varies** at differing levels of sales, because the average fixed overhead cost per unit changes with the volume of output and sales.

(b)   The **contribution per unit is constant** at all levels of output and sales. Total contribution, which is the contribution per unit multiplied by the number of units sold, increases in direct proportion to the volume of sales.

(c)   Since the **contribution per unit does not change**, the most effective way of calculating the expected profit at any level of output and sales would be as follows.

(i)   Calculate the total contribution
(ii)   Deduct fixed costs as a period charge in order to find the profit

(d)   In our example the expected profit from the sale of 17,000 Splashes would be as follows.

	£
Total contribution (17,000 × £4)	68,000
Less fixed costs	45,000
Profit	23,000

Section summary

The marginal costing philosophy is that profit measurement should be based on an analysis of total contribution, that is, sales value less the variable cost of sales.

2 The principles of absorption costing

Introduction

With absorption costing, fixed production costs are absorbed into product unit costs using a predetermined overhead absorption rate, based on the normal level of production for the period.

If the actual production is different from the normal level, or actual expenditure on fixed production costs is different from that budgeted, there may be an under or over absorption of fixed production costs for the period. This amount is written off against the absorption costing profit for the period.

The principles of absorption costing are as follows.

(a)   Fixed production costs are an integral part of the production cost of an item and so should be absorbed into product costs.

(b)   Inventories are valued at their full production cost including absorbed fixed production costs.

Exam alert

Over/under absorption could easily be the subject of an objective test question. Make sure you haven't forgotten how to calculate this as it's easy marks.

Example: absorption costing

Using the earlier example of Water and Sons, assume that the normal level of activity is 15,000 Splashes per month and that budgeted fixed production costs were £30,000 for the month.

Required

Prepare profit statements for September, using absorption costing, for the three sales levels given.

Solution

The fixed production cost per unit, based on the normal level of activity, is £30,000/15,000 = £2 per unit.

The full production cost per unit = £6 + £2 = £8 per unit

With production of 20,000 Splashes the fixed overhead will be over-absorbed.

	£
Fixed production costs absorbed (20,000 units × £2)	40,000
Fixed production costs incurred	30,000
Over-absorbed fixed production cost	10,000

	10,000 Splashes		15,000 Splashes		20,000 Splashes	
	£	£	£	£	£	£
Sales		100,000		150,000		200,000
Opening inventory	0		0		0	
Full production costs	160,000		160,000		160,000	
	160,000		160,000		160,000	
Less closing inventory (at full production cost)	80,000		40,000		0	
Full production of sales	80,000		120,000		160,000	
Adjustment for over-absorbed overhead	10,000		10,000		10,000	
Full production costs		70,000		110,000		150,000
Gross profit		30,000		40,000		50,000
Administration, sales and distribution costs		15,000		15,000		15,000
Net profit		15,000		25,000		35,000

Section summary

With absorption costing, fixed production costs are absorbed into product unit costs using a predetermined overhead absorption rate, based on the normal level of production for the period.

Inventories are valued at their full production cost including absorbed fixed production costs.

3 The effect of marginal costing and absorption costing on reported profit and inventory valuation

Introduction

Note that if there are changes in inventories during a period, marginal and absorption costing will report different profit figures.

The results of the last two examples can be compared as follows.

	Sales volume (Splashes)		
	10,000	15,000	20,000
Marginal costing profit/(loss)	£(5,000)	£15,000	£35,000
Absorption costing profit	£15,000	£25,000	£35,000
Increase in inventory units	10,000	5,000	0

In this example the inventory levels increased with the two lower sales volume figures and the reported **profit figure** was **higher with absorption costing** than with marginal costing.

This is because some of the fixed production **overhead** incurred during the period will be **carried forward in closing inventory** (which reduces cost of sales) to be set against sales revenue in the following period instead of being written off in full against profit in the period concerned.

If inventory levels decrease, absorption costing will report the lower profit.

This is because as well as the fixed overhead incurred, fixed production overhead which had been brought forward in opening inventory is released and is included in cost of sales.

In our example the two reported profit figures were the same when sales volume was 20,000 Splashes, ie when production and sales volumes were equal and there was no change in inventory.

It is important to appreciate that the **differences** in reported **profits** occur only in the **short run**, ie in reporting the profit of individual accounting periods.

This is because in the long run, total costs will be the same by either method of accounting. Short term differences are the result of changes in the level of inventory.

3.1 Calculating the difference in reported profit

The difference in the profit reported by the two systems therefore results from the fixed production overhead that is carried forward in inventory in an absorption costing system.

In our example the profit figures can be reconciled as follows.

		Sales volume (Splashes)		
		10,000		15,000
		£		£
Marginal costing profit/(loss)		(5,000)		15,000
Increase in inventory units @ £2 per unit	(10,000 × £2)	20,000	(5,000 × £2)	10,000
Absorption costing profit		15,000		25,000

In both cases the absorption costing profit was higher because the inventory level increased and fixed production overhead was carried forward to next month in the absorption costing valuation.

Exam alert

The calculation of the difference between reported profits and inventory valuation in the two costing systems is a subject that lends itself well to objective testing questions.

Question 6b.1	Marginal versus absorption costing profit

Learning outcome A1(a)

The overhead absorption rate for product X is £10 per machine hour. Each unit of product X requires five machine hours. Opening inventory of product X on 1 January 20X9 was 150 units and closing inventory on 31 December 20X9 it was 100 units. What is the difference in profit between results reported using absorption costing and results reported using marginal costing?

A   The absorption costing profit would be £2,500 less
B   The absorption costing profit would be £2,500 greater
C   The absorption costing profit would be £5,000 less
D   The absorption costing profit would be £5,000 greater

Section summary

If there are changes in inventories during a period, marginal costing and absorption costing systems will report different profit figures.

If inventory levels increase, absorption costing will report a higher profit than marginal costing.

If inventory levels decrease, absorption costing will report the lower profit.

If the opening and closing inventory volumes and values are the same, marginal costing and absorption costing will report the same profit figure.

In the long run, the total reported profit will be the same whether marginal or absorption costing is used.

The difference in reported profit is equal to the change in inventory volume multiplied by the fixed production overhead rate per unit.

4 Marginal costing and absorption costing compared

Introduction

There are arguments in favour of each costing method.

4.1 Arguments in favour of absorption costing

(a) Fixed production costs are incurred in order to make output. It is therefore 'fair' to charge all output with a **share** of these costs.

(b) Closing inventory values, include a share of fixed production overhead, and therefore **follow** the **requirements** of the international accounting standard on **inventory valuation (IAS 2)**.

(c) Absorption costing is consistent with the **accruals concept** as a proportion of the costs of production are carried forward to be matched against future sales.

(d) A problem with calculating the contribution of various products made by an enterprise is that it may **not be clear** whether the **contribution earned** by each product is **enough to cover fixed costs**, whereas by charging fixed overhead to a product it is possible to ascertain whether it is profitable or not. This is particularly important where fixed production overheads are a large proportion of total production costs. Not absorbing production would mean that a large portion of expenditure is not accounted for in unit costs.

4.2 Arguments in favour of marginal costing

(a) It is **simple** to operate.

(b) There are **no apportionments**, which are frequently done on an arbitrary basis, of fixed costs. Many costs, such as the marketing director's salary, are indivisible by nature.

(c) Fixed costs will be the **same regardless of the volume of output**, because they are period costs. It makes sense, therefore, to charge them in full as a cost to the period.

(d) The cost to produce an extra unit is the variable production cost. It is **realistic** to **value closing inventory** items at this directly attributable cost.

(e) **Under or over absorption** of overheads is **avoided**.

(f) Marginal costing provides the **best information for decision making**.

(g) Fixed costs (such as depreciation, rent and salaries) relate to a period of time and should be charged against the **revenues of the period** in which they are incurred.

(h) **Absorption costing** may **encourage over-production** since reported profits can be increased by increasing inventory levels.

Exam alert

Make sure you are completely happy with the pros and cons and calculations for each method.

Example: absorption costing encouraging over-production

To demonstrate the last argument in favour of marginal costing, consider an organisation that produces a product that sells for £60 per unit.

Variable production costs are £35 per unit and the fixed production costs of £30,000 per period are absorbed on the basis of the normal capacity of 5,000 units per period.

Fixed administration, selling and distribution overheads are £19,000 per period. There was no opening inventory for the latest period.

Required

Calculate the profit reported for sales of 5,000 units last period for production volumes of 5,000 units, 6,000 units and 7,000 units, using:

(a)   Absorption costing
(b)   Marginal costing

Solution

Absorption costing

Fixed production cost per unit = £30,000/5,000 = £6 per unit

Full production cost per unit = £35 + £6 = £41 per unit

			Production			
	5,000 units		6,000 units		7,000 units	
	£'000	£'000	£'000	£'000	£'000	£'000
Sales (5,000 units × £60)		300		300		300
Production cost @ £41 per unit	205		246		287	
Less closing inventory	–		41		82	
	205		205		205	
Less over-absorbed fixed production cost	–		6		12	
Total production cost of sales		205		199		193
Gross profit		95		101		107
Administration costs		19		19		19
Net profit		76		82		88

Marginal costing

			Production			
	5,000 units		6,000 units		7,000 units	
	£'000	£'000	£'000	£'000	£'000	£'000
Sales		300		300		300
Variable cost of production @ £35/unit	175		210		245	
Less closing inventory	–		35		70	
Variable production cost of sales		175		175		175
Contribution		125		125		125
Fixed production costs		30		30		30
Administration costs		19		19		19
Net profit		76		76		76

This example demonstrates an important point when considering the impact on profit reporting of marginal and absorption costing methods.

For a given level of sales, marginal costing will report the same level of profit whatever the level of production. In contrast, absorption costing will report higher levels of profit for the same level of sales, if production levels are higher.

Question 6b.2   Shortcomings of absorption costing

Learning outcome A1(a)

A criticism of the use of absorption costing for the internal reporting of profit is that, if a manager's reward is based on the profit for the period, the manager will be encouraged to increase production even if the resulting output cannot be sold. Explain why absorption costing can have this effect.

4.3 Marginal costing – concluding remarks

In spite of the arguments in favour of marginal costing as a decision making tool, **absorption costing** is **widely used** for general accounting purposes and inventory valuation. Fixed production costs should ultimately be charged to cost units in a fair and meaningful way. A central **problem** in cost accounting is to identify the **best method** of attributing these costs.

In later chapters we shall look at new approaches developed to address the weaknesses of both marginal and absorption costing.

Activity based costing (ABC), discussed in Chapter 11, is a form of absorption costing. It is a relatively modern costing approach seeking to address certain weaknesses of traditional absorption costing and identify the most appropriate way of attributing overhead costs to units of production.

Section summary

For a given level of sales, marginal costing will report the same level of profit whatever the level of production. In contrast, absorption costing will report higher levels of profit for the same level of sales, if production levels are higher.

Chapter Roundup

✓   The marginal costing philosophy is that profit measurement should be based on an analysis of total contribution, that is sales value less the variable cost of sales.

✓   With absorption costing, fixed production costs are absorbed into product unit costs using a predetermined overhead absorption rate, based on the normal level of production for the period.

✓   Inventories are valued at their full production cost including absorbed fixed production costs.

✓   If there are changes in inventories during a period, marginal costing and absorption costing systems will report different profit figures.

✓   If inventory levels increase, absorption costing will report a higher profit than marginal costing.

✓   If inventory levels decrease, absorption costing will report the lower profit.

✓   If the opening and closing inventory volumes and values are the same, marginal costing and absorption costing will report the same profit figure.

✓   In the long run, the total reported profit will be the same whether marginal or absorption costing is used.

✓   The difference in reported profit is equal to the change in inventory volume multiplied by the fixed production overhead rate per unit.

✓   For a given level of sales, marginal costing will report the same level of profit whatever the level of production. In contrast, absorption costing will report higher levels of profit for the same level of sales, if production levels are higher.

Quick Quiz

1 Marginal costing and absorption costing are different techniques for assessing profit in a period. If there are changes in inventory during a period, marginal costing and absorption costing give different results for profit obtained.

Which of the following statements are true?

I   If inventory levels increase, marginal costing will report the higher profit.

II   If inventory levels decrease, marginal costing will report the lower profit.

III   If inventory levels decrease, marginal costing will report the higher profit.

IV   If the opening and closing inventory volumes are the same, marginal costing and absorption costing will give the same profit figure.

A   All of the above
B   I, II and IV
C   I and IV
D   III and IV

2 Identify which of the following relate to either

A = Absorption costing   M = Marginal costing

		A or M
(a)	Closing inventories valued at marginal production cost	
(b)	Closing inventories valued at full production cost	
(c)	Cost of sales include some fixed overhead incurred in previous period in opening inventory values	
(d)	Fixed costs are charged in full against profit for the period	

3 Which of the following are arguments in favour of marginal costing?

(a)   Closing inventory is valued in accordance with international accounting standards.
(b)   It is simple to operate.
(c)   There is no under or over absorption of overheads.
(d)   Fixed costs are the same regardless of activity levels.
(e)   The information from this costing method may be used for decision making.

4 When opening inventories were 8,500 litres and closing inventories were 6,750 litres, a firm had a profit of $62,100 using marginal costing.

Assuming that the fixed overhead absorption rate was $3 per litre, what would be the profit using absorption costing?

5 When sales fluctuate but production is constant, absorption costing smoothes out fluctuations in profit.

(delete as appropriate) **True/false**

6 HMF Co produces a single product. The budgeted fixed production overheads for the period are $500,000. The budgeted output for the period is 2,500 units. Opening stock at the start of the period consisted of 900 units and closing stock at the end of the period consisted of 300 units. If absorption costing principles were applied, the profit for the period compared to the marginal costing profit would be:

A $125,000 higher
B $125,000 lower
C $120,000 higher
D $120,000 lower

Answers to Quick Quiz

1   D   If inventory levels increase then absorption costing reports the higher profit. If inventory levels don't move then they will report the same profit figure.

2

		A or M
(a)	Closing inventories valued at marginal production cost	M
(b)	Closing inventories valued at full production cost	A
(c)	Cost of sales include some fixed overhead incurred in previous period in opening inventory values	A
(d)	Fixed costs are charged in full against profit for the period	M

3   (b), (c), (d), (e)

4   Difference in profit = (8,500 – 6,750) × \$3 = \$5,250

Since inventory levels reduced, the absorption costing profit will be lower than the marginal costing profit.

Absorption costing profit = \$62,100 – \$5,250 = \$56,850

5   True. Absorption costing carries fixed production overheads forward in inventory values to be matched against sales as they arise.

6   D

	Units	
Opening stock	900	
Closing stock	300	
Decrease	600	$\times \left(\dfrac{\$500,000}{2,500} \right) = 120,000$ lower

Answers to Questions

6b.1 Marginal versus absorption costing – effect on profit

A

Difference in profit = **change** in inventory levels × fixed overhead absorption per unit = (150 – 100) × £10 × 5 = £2,500 **lower** profit, because inventory levels **decreased**. The correct answer is therefore option A.

The key is the change in the volume of inventory. Inventory levels have **decreased** therefore absorption costing will report a **lower** profit. This eliminates options B and D.

Option C is incorrect because it is based on the closing inventory only (100 units × £10 × 5 hours).

6b.2 Shortcomings of absorption costing

If a manager's reward is based on the profit for the period then the manager will be encouraged to take actions which will increase the reported profit in the short term.

With absorption costing, all production costs are absorbed into product unit costs. Any inventory remaining at the end of the period would include absorbed fixed production costs. The higher production for the period, the greater the amount of fixed production cost that will be carried forward in inventory to be charged against the revenues of future periods. Furthermore, the higher the production level for the period, the lower the full unit cost of production will be because the same amount of fixed production cost will be shared out over a higher number of units.

Thus, the higher the production for the period, the higher the reported profit for the period will be, for a given level of sales, when an absorption costing system is used.

Now try the question from the Exam Question Bank	Number	Level	Marks	Time
	Q6	Introductory	30	54 mins

STANDARD COSTING

 In this chapter we will be looking at **standard costs** and **standard costing.**

Standard costing was covered at Certificate level, but we obviously look at the topic in more depth for your studies of this syllabus.

We begin this chapter by reviewing the **main principles of standard costing** in **Section 1**, as well as looking in some detail at the **way in which standard costs are set** in **Section 2**. **Section 3** then looks at the special case of setting standard costs in a service environment.

Section 4 deals with why costing systems and standard costs must be **reviewed** on a regular basis. **Section 5** provides you with clarification of the **difference between budgets and standards.**

We conclude by addressing some criticisms of standard costing systems in advanced manufacturing environments.

topic list	learning outcomes	syllabus references	ability required
1 The uses of standard costing	A1(e)	A1(x)	comprehension
2 Setting standards for manufacturing	A1(e)	A1(x)	comprehension
3 Setting standards in service industries	A1(e)	A1(x)	comprehension
4 Updating standards	A1(e)	A1(x)	comprehension
5 Budgets and standards compared	A1(e)	A1(x)	comprehension
6 Criticisms of standard costing	A1(e)	A1(iii)	comprehension
7 Economy, efficiency and effectiveness	A1(e)	A1(x)	comprehension

1 The uses of standard costing

Introduction

A **standard** is a **predetermined unit of cost** for inventory valuation, budgeting and control.

1.1 What is a standard cost?

KEY TERM

STANDARD COST is the 'Planned unit cost of a product, component or service.' *(CIMA Official Terminology)*

Standard costs are usually drawn up for a **unit of production** or a unit of service rendered but it is also possible to have a standard cost **per routine task completed**, or a standard cost per £1 of sale. A standard cost per unit of production may include administration, selling and distribution costs, but in many organisations, the assessment of standards is confined to **production costs only**.

1.2 What is standard costing?

KEY TERMS

STANDARD COSTING is a 'Control technique that reports *variances* by comparing actual costs to pre-set standards so facilitating action through *management by exception*.' *(CIMA Official Terminology)*

MANAGEMENT BY EXCEPTION is the 'Practice of focusing on activities which require attention and ignoring those which appear to be conforming to expectations.' *(CIMA Official Terminology)*

A standard cost, when established, is an **average expected unit cost**. Because it is only an average, actual results will **vary** to some extent above and below the average. **Variances** should only be reported where the difference between actual and standard is **significant**.

Standard costing is the **preparation of standard costs** to be used in the following circumstances.

(a)   To assist in setting budgets and evaluating managerial performance.

(b)   To act as a **control device** by establishing standards, highlighting (via **variance analysis**) activities that do not conform to plan and thus alerting management to those areas that may be out of control and in need of corrective action.

(c)   To enable the principle of '**management by exception**' to be practised.

(d)   To **provide a prediction of future costs** to be used in decision-making situations.

(e)   To **value inventories and cost production** for cost accounting purposes. It is an alternative method of valuation to methods like FIFO, LIFO or replacement costing.

(f)   To **motivate staff and management** by the provision of challenging targets.

(g)   To provide guidance on improvement of efficiency and minimisation of waste.

Although the use of standard costs to simplify the keeping of cost accounting records should not be overlooked, we will be **concentrating** on the **control and variance analysis** aspect of standard costing.

1.3 When standard costing is used

Standard costing can be used in a variety of costing situations.

However, the **greatest benefit** from its use can be gained if there is a **degree of repetition** in the production process. It is therefore most suited to **mass production** and **repetitive assembly** work. However, a standard cost can be calculated **per task if there is a similarity of tasks**. In this way standard costing can be used by some **service organisations**.

Section summary

Standard costs are established but the actual results will vary. These variances should only be reported where the difference between actual and standard is significant.

2 Setting standards for manufacturing

Introduction

A **standard cost card** shows full details of the standard cost of each product.

2.1 Setting standard costs

A standard cost implies that a standard or target exists for every single element that contributes to the product. Examples include the types, usage and prices of materials and parts, the grades, rates of pay and times for the labour involved, the production methods, tools and so on.

The standard cost for each part of the product is recorded on a **standard cost card**.

KEY TERM

A STANDARD COST CARD is a 'Document or digital record detailing, for each individual product, the standard inputs required for production as well as the standard selling price. Inputs are normally divided into labour, material and overhead categories, and both price and quantity information is shown for each.'

(CIMA Official Terminology)

An example of a standard cost card is given below.

STANDARD COST CARD
Product: the Splodget, No 12345

	Cost	Requirement	Y	Y
Direct materials				
A	Y2.00 per kg	6 kgs	12.00	
B	Y3.00 per kg	2 kgs	6.00	
	Y4.00 per litre	1 litre	4.00	
Others			2.00	
				24.00
Direct labour				
Grade I	Y4.00 per hour	3 hrs	12.00	
Grade II	Y5.40 per hour	5 hrs	27.00	
				39.00
Variable production overheads	Y1.00 per hour	8 hrs		8.00
Fixed production overheads	Y3.00 per hour	8 hrs		24.00
Standard full cost of production				95.00

Standard costs may be used in **both marginal and absorption costing systems**. The card illustrated has been prepared under an absorption costing system, with selling and administration costs excluded from the standard.

The **responsibility for setting** standard costs should be shared between **managers able to provide the necessary information** about levels of expected efficiency, prices and overhead costs. Standard costs are **usually revised once a year** (to allow for the new overheads budget, inflation in prices, and any changes in expected efficiency of materials usage or of labour). However they may be **revised more frequently if conditions are changing rapidly**.

The standard for each type of cost (labour, material and so on) is made up of a **standard resource price** and a **standard resource usage**.

2.2 Setting standards for materials costs

Direct material prices will be estimated by the purchasing department from their existing knowledge.

- Purchase contracts already agreed
- The forecast movement of prices in the market

- Pricing discussions with regular suppliers
- The availability of bulk purchase discounts

- Quotations and estimates from potential suppliers
- Material quality required

Price inflation can cause difficulties in setting realistic standard prices. Suppose that a material costs £10 per kilogram at the moment, and during the course of the next 12 months, it is expected to go up in price by 20% to £12 per kilogram. **What standard price should be selected?**

- The **current price** of £10 per kilogram
- The **expected price** for the year, say, £11 per kilogram

Either price in would be possible, but neither would be entirely satisfactory.

(a) If the **current price** were used in the standard, the reported price variance would become **adverse** as soon as prices go up, which might be very early in the year. If prices go up gradually rather than in one big jump, it would be difficult to select an appropriate time for revising the standard.

(b) If an **estimated mid-year price** were used, price variances should be **favourable** in the **first half** of the year and **adverse** in the **second half**, again assuming that prices go up gradually. Management could only really check that in any month, the price variance did not become excessively adverse (or favourable) and that the price variance switched from being favourable to adverse around month six or seven and not sooner.

Standard costing for materials is therefore more **difficult in times of inflation but it is still worthwhile**.

(a) **Usage** and **efficiency** variances will still be **meaningful**.

(b) Inflation is **measurable**: there is no reason why its effects cannot be removed from the variances reported.

(c) Standard costs can be **revised**, so long as this is not done too frequently.

2.3 Setting standards for labour rates

Direct labour rates per hour will be set by discussion with the human resources department and by reference to the payroll and to any agreements on pay rises and/or bonuses with trade union representatives of the employees. A separate average hourly rate or weekly wage will be set for each different labour grade/type of employee (even though individual rates of pay may vary according to age and experience).

2.4 Setting standards for material usage and labour efficiency

To estimate the materials required to make each product (material usage) and also the labour hours required (labour efficiency), **technical specifications** must be prepared for each product by production experts (either in the production department or the work study department).

Material usage and labour efficiency standards are known as **performance standards**.

2.5 Types of performance standard

The setting of standards raises the problem of **how demanding** the standard should be. Should the standard represent a perfect performance or an easily attainable performance? The type of performance standard used can have behavioural implications. There are four types of standard.

Type of standard	Description
Ideal	These are based on **perfect operating conditions**: no wastage, no spoilage, no inefficiencies, no idle time, no breakdowns. Variances from ideal standards are useful for pinpointing areas where a close examination may result in large savings in order to maximise efficiency and minimise waste. However ideal standards are likely to have an unfavourable motivational impact because reported variances will always be adverse. Employees will often feel that the goals are unattainable and not work so hard.
Attainable	These are based on the hope that a standard amount of work will be carried out efficiently, machines properly operated or materials properly used. **Some allowance is made for wastage and inefficiencies**. If well-set they provide a useful psychological incentive by giving employees a realistic, but challenging target of efficiency. The consent and co-operation of employees involved in improving the standard are required.
Current	These are based on **current working conditions** (current wastage, current inefficiencies). The disadvantage of current standards is that they do not attempt to improve on current levels of efficiency.
Basic	These are **kept unaltered over a long period of time**, and may be out of date. They are used to show changes in efficiency or performance over a long period of time. Basic standards are perhaps the least useful and least common type of standard in use.

Ideal standards, attainable standards and current standards each have their supporters and it is by **no means clear which of them is preferable**.

Question 7a.1   Performance standards

Learning outcome A1(e)

Which of the following statements is not true?

A   Variances from ideal standards are useful for pinpointing areas where a close examination might result in large cost savings.

B   Basic standards may provide an incentive to greater efficiency even though the standard cannot be achieved.

C   Ideal standards cannot be achieved and so there will always be adverse variances. If the standards are used for budgeting, an allowance will have to be included for these 'inefficiencies'.

D   Current standards or attainable standards are a better basis for budgeting, because they represent the level of productivity which management will wish to plan for.

2.6 Setting standards for variable overheads

Standard variable overhead costs are usually charged to products using a **standard rate per labour hour**.

Where labour hours are to be used as the basis for charging variable overhead costs, the number of standard labour hours for each product will have already been determined when setting the standard labour costs.

Careful analysis of overhead costs will be necessary in order to determine which costs are variable with the selected measure of activity, and which costs are fixed. Examples of overhead costs that might vary with the number of direct labour hours worked include power costs and the cost of lubricating oils. In order to determine the standard variable overhead cost per hour it will be necessary **to prepare forecasts of the hourly expenditure on each cost separately**. These would then be summed to derive the standard total variable production overhead cost per hour.

2.7 Setting standards for fixed overheads

In a **marginal costing** system there is **no need** to determine a **standard unit rate** for **fixed overheads**, since these are not attributed to individual units, but are treated as **period costs** and are charged directly to the income statement.

In an **absorption costing** system the **standard overhead absorption rate** is the **same** as the **predetermined overhead absorption rate**.

The standard overhead absorption rate will depend on the total value of budgeted overheads for the forthcoming period and on the planned activity or production volume for the period.

Production volume will **depend on two factors**.

(a) **Production capacity** (or 'volume capacity') measured perhaps in standard hours of output.

(b) **Efficiency of working**, by labour or machines, allowing for rest time and contingency allowances. This will depend on the type of performance standard to be used (ideal, current, attainable and so on).

Suppose that a department has a workforce of ten employees, each of whom works a 36 hour week to make standard units, and each unit has a standard production time of two hours. The expected efficiency of the workforce is 125%.

(a) **Budgeted capacity**, in direct labour hours, would be $10 \times 36 = 360$ production hours per week.

(b) **Budgeted efficiency** is 125% so that the workforce should take only 1 hour of actual production time to produce 1.25 standard hours of output.

(c) This means in our example that **budgeted output** is 360 production hours $\times$ 125% = 450 standard hours of output per week. At two standard hours per unit, this represents production activity or volume of 225 units of output per week.

Output, **capacity** and **efficiency** are inter-related items, and you should check your understanding of them by attempting the following problem.

| **Question 7a.2** | Linking capacity, efficiency and output |

Learning outcome A1(e)

ABC carries out routine office work in a sales order processing department, and all tasks in the department have been given standard times. There are 40 clerks in the department who work on average 140 hours per month each. The efficiency ratio of the department is 110%.

Required

Calculate the budgeted output in the department.

2.7.1 Capacity levels

When standard absorption costing is used, capacity levels are needed to establish a standard absorption rate for fixed production overhead. Any one of three capacity levels might be used for budgeting.

KEY TERMS

- FULL CAPACITY is 'Output achievable if sales orders, supplies and workforce for example, were all available.'

- PRACTICAL CAPACITY is 'Full capacity less an allowance for known unavoidable volume losses.'

- BUDGETED CAPACITY is 'Standard hours planned for the budget period, taking account of, for example, budgeted sales, workforce and expected efficiency.' CIMA *Official Terminology*

(a) **Full capacity** is the **theoretical** capacity, assuming continuous production without any stoppages due to factors such as machine downtime, supply shortages or labour shortages. Full capacity would be associated with **ideal standards**.

(b) **Practical capacity** acknowledges that **some stoppages are unavoidable**, such as maintenance time for machines, and resetting time between jobs, some machine breakdowns and so on. Practical capacity is below full capacity, and would be associated with **attainable standards**.

(c) **Budgeted capacity** is the capacity (labour hours, machine hours) **needed to produce the budgeted output**, and would be associated with **current standards**, which relate to current conditions but may not be representative of normal practical capacity over a longer period of time.

Idle capacity is defined as the **practical capacity** in a period **less the budgeted capacity** measured in standard hours of output. It represents unused capacity that ought to be available, but which is not needed because the budgeted volume is lower than the practicable volume that could be achieved.

2.8 Setting standards for selling price and margin or contribution

As well as standard costs, standard selling prices and standard margins or contributions can be set. The standard selling price will depend on a number of factors including the following.

- Anticipated market demand
- Competing products and competitors' actions
- Manufacturing costs
- Inflation estimates

The standard sales margin or contribution is the difference between the standard total or variable cost and the standard selling price.

Section summary

A **standard cost card** shows full details of the standard cost of each product.

The standard for each type of cost (labour, material and so on) is made up of a **standard resource price** and a **standard resource usage**.

Performance standards are used to set efficiency targets. There are four types: ideal, attainable, current and basic.

3 Setting standards in service industries

Introduction

It can be difficult to apply standard costing in a service environment because of the difficulty in establishing a measurable cost unit and the heterogeneous nature of most services.

3.1 Difficulties in applying standard costing in service environments

Standard costing was originally used in manufacturing environments and a criticism levelled at standard costing was its **apparent lack of applicability in service industries**.

The application of standard costing in service industries does have its problems.

- It can be **difficult to establish a measurable cost unit** for some services.

- In some service organisations **every cost unit will be different or heterogeneous**. For example each haircut provided in a salon will be different.

- Since the **human influence is so great** in many services it can be difficult to predict and control the quality of the output and the resources used in its production.

To overcome these problems and enable the application of standard costing for planning and control in service industries it is therefore necessary to do the following.

- **Establish a measurable cost unit**. This is relatively easy in some service organisations. For example in your earlier studies you will have learned about cost units for transport companies, such as a passenger-mile or a tonne-mile, or for hotels, such as a guest-night. (You might recall that these are referred to as **composite cost units**).

- **Attempt to reduce the heterogeneity of services**. If every service provided to the customer is the same as the last then it will be possible to set a standard cost for the service and use this to maximise efficiency and reduce waste.

- **Reduce the element of human influence**. This can be achieved by swapping machines for humans wherever possible.

3.2 McDonaldization

McDonaldization is a term coined by George Ritzer in his 1996 book *'The McDonaldization of Society'*. Ritzer analysed the success of the American hamburger chain and noted that the principles of McDonalds's operations are now being applied to many sectors of society.

The application of McDonaldization in service industries is **assisting the use of standard costing for cost planning and control** because it overcomes the problems referred to above.

Ritzer identified four dimensions of McDonaldization.

- **Calculability**. The content of every McDonalds meal is identical and standardised. Every burger should contain a standard amount of meat, every bun is of the same size and all fries are of the same thickness. **The human element is eliminated as far as possible** in the actual production process in order to make the food in a standard time using standard materials. Human initiative is eliminated in actually putting together the meal at the point of sale through the issuing of standard instructions concerning the content of each type of meal ordered. Thus each meal is a **measurable** standard cost unit for which a **standard cost can be established** and the actual cost can be measured for cost control purposes.

- **Control**. Control over the service is achieved in particular by **reducing the human influence**, which can lead to variation in output and quality. Again, machines and technology substitute for humans. Automatic drinks dispensers which measure the exact quantity to be delivered and cash registers which require only one button to be pressed to record the sale of a complete meal are examples of improved control and the reduction of the possibility of human error in the delivery of the service.

- **Efficiency**. Ritzer described efficiency as 'the optimum method of getting from one point to another'. Every McDonalds business is organised to ensure maximum efficiency so that the customer can get exactly what they want as quickly as possible. This **increases customer satisfaction and also increases the company's profitability**.

- **Predictability**. The McDonalds service is the **same in every outlet throughout the world**, whether a meal is purchased in Shanghai or on London. Again this helps with the standardisation of the service and the setting of standard costs throughout the organisation.

Exam alert

Be prepared to think of sensible criticisms of applying McDonaldization to a given business.

| Question 7a.3 | McDonaldization of services |

Learning outcome A1(e)

State three service industries where McDonaldization could be applied to standardise the delivery of services.

3.3 Diagnostic related groups

The use of standard costing to plan and control costs in the **health service** has been assisted by the development of **diagnostic related groups (DRGs)** or **reference groups**.

DRGs provide a **system of classifying patients** according to their diagnosis, age and length of stay. This classification helps to determine the resources that should be used to treat and care for the patient.

The concept of DRGs was originally developed in America in order to calculate a **standard cost for each category of patient**. There are more than 500 different possible DRG classifications and the resulting standard cost can be used for billing purposes by the healthcare insurance industry. This means that the insurance company pays the hospital a **standard rate for each DRG** and the hospital would then need to contain its costs below the payment received.

The use of DRGs **enables the principles of standard costing to be applied in the health service in order to maximise efficiency and minimise waste**.

Section summary

It can be difficult to apply standard costing in a service environment because of the difficulty in establishing a measurable cost unit and the heterogeneous nature of most services.

The four dimensions of McDonaldization are calculability, control, efficiency and predictability.

Diagnostic related groups (DRGs) or reference groups are used in the healthcare industry to group together patients with similar lengths of stay and resource requirements. Standard costs can be established for each DRG which can be used for cost planning and control.

4 Updating standards

Introduction

When an organisation introduces a system of standard costing, it is quite possible that the standards initially set will not be the most accurate reflection of what occurs 'on average'. **Initial standards** may need **substantial revision** in the early period of a standard costing system's life before they are really useful measures for control purposes.

4.1 The need to update standards

The evolution of standards does not stop after a couple of accounting periods. Standards must be **continuously reviewed** to ensure that they **mirror** what is **currently happening** and that they are the **most accurate 'average'**.

Out-of-date standards will produce **variances** that are **illogical bases** for planning, control, decision making or performance evaluation. Current operational performance cannot be compared to out-of-date standards.

'Labour and material usage standards normally are set by the industrial engineering department. Material price normally is considered the responsibility of purchasing. Similarly, the labour rates are set by the personnel department. As the production processes change (improve), past standards become less than realistic, and should be revised. It is the responsibility of departments that originally created the standard to inform the accounting department about the need for revising the standards.'

'But, unfortunately, some managers prefer to keep the old standards because the new improved production process makes their performance look better with old standards.'

(LU Tatikonda, 'Production Managers Need a Course in Cost Accounting', *Management Accounting* (June 1987), published by Institute of Management Accountants, Montvale, N J)

4.2 Improvement of the standard setting process

Standard setting procedures may be refined and extended to enable more accurate standards to be set.

(a) **Work study** methods may be established within the organisation. These enable accurate estimates of labour time to be made.

(b) The introduction of **computerised information systems** provides more reliable standards.

With CADCAM (computer-aided design/computer aided manufacture) systems the planning of manufacturing requirements can be **computerised**, with the useful spin-off that standard costs can also be constructed by computer, thus saving administrative time and expense while providing far more accurate standards.

4.3 Revision of standards

In practice standard costs are usually revised **once a year** to allow for the new overheads budget, inflation in prices and wage rates, and any changes in expected efficiency of material usage, labour or machinery.

Some argue that standards should be revised **as soon as there is any change in the basis upon which they were set.** Clearly, for example, if a standard is based on the cost of a material that is no longer available or the use of equipment which has been replaced, it is meaningless to compare actual performance using the new material and equipment with the old standard.

Coates, Rickwood and Stacey in their book *Management Accounting in Practice* put forward the following reasons why standards might need to be revised.

(a) 'Manufacturing methods are **significantly** changed due to plant layout, machinery alterations, change in product design, use of different materials, etc.

(b) The relationship of normal capacity and actual activity is **significantly** out of balance.

(c) The disparity between the standard and expected performance is **so significant** that the standard as a measurement loses its value.

(d) An existing standard is discovered to be incorrectly set and a **significant** difference exists.'

(JB Coates, CP Rickwood, RJ Stacey, *Management Accounting in Practice,* CIMA)

Frequent changes in standards can cause **problems**.

(a) They may become **ineffective as motivators and measures of performance,** since it may be perceived that target setters are constantly 'moving the goal posts'.

(b) The **administrative effort** may be too time consuming (although the introduction of computer systems renders this objection less forceful).

Coates *et al* concede the following point.

> 'Revisions should be **held to a minimum**, despite the fact that standards may not be precise, in order to provide for relative comparisons between operating periods and/or versus budget.'

The most **suitable approach** would therefore appear to be a policy of revising the standards **whenever changes of a permanent and reasonably long-term nature occur**, but not in response to temporary 'blips' in price or efficiency.

Section summary

In general, standards should be **revised** whenever changes of a permanent or reasonably long-term nature occur.

5 Budgets and standards compared

Introduction

You will recall from your earlier studies that a **budget** is a **quantified monetary plan** for a **future period**, which **managers will try to achieve**. Its major function lies in **communicating plans** and **coordinating activities** within an organisation.

On the other hand, a **standard** is a **carefully predetermined quantity target** which can be **achieved in certain conditions**.

Budgets and standards are **similar** in the following ways.

(a) They both involve looking to the future and **forecasting** what is likely to happen given a certain set of circumstances.

(b) They are both **used for control purposes**. A budget aids control by setting financial targets or limits for a forthcoming period. Actual achievements or expenditures are then compared with the budgets and action is taken to correct any variances where necessary. A standard also achieves control by comparison of actual results against a predetermined target.

As well as being similar, **budgets and standards are interrelated**. For example, a standard unit production cost can act as the basis for a production cost budget. The unit cost is multiplied by the budgeted activity level to arrive at the budgeted expenditure on production costs.

There are, however, **important differences between budgets and standards**.

Budgets	Standards
Gives planned total aggregate costs for a function or cost centre	Shows the unit resource usage for a single task, for example the standard labour hours for a single unit of production
Can be prepared for all functions, even where output cannot be measured	Limited to situations where repetitive actions are performed and output can be measured
Expressed in money terms	Need not be expressed in money terms. For example a standard rate of output does not need a financial value put on it

Section summary

Budgets and standards are very similar and interrelated, but there are important differences between them.

6 Criticisms of standard costing

Introduction

Standard costing is most appropriate in a **stable, standardised** and **repetitive** environment and one of the main objectives of standard costing is to ensure that **processes conform to standards**, that they do not vary and that **variances** are **eliminated**. This may seem **restrictive** and **inhibiting** in the business environment of the early twenty first century.

6.1 Standard costing in the modern business environment

Critics of standard costing have argued that traditional variance analysis has limited applicability in the modern business environment. The modern business environment is characterised by a need to respond to **customer demands** for **immediate availability of products, shortening product life cycles and higher quality standards** and continuous improvement.

6.2 Standard costing and new technology

Standard costing has **traditionally** been associated with **labour-intensive** operations, but can it be **applied to capital-intensive production too?**

(a)   In an environment which includes advanced manufacturing technology (AMT), the **cost of labour** is a **small proportion** of total costs and so labour rate and efficiency variances will have little control value.

(b)   **Fixed costs** represent a **significant** proportion of total costs but there is some **doubt** over the **relevance** of the information provided by **fixed overhead volume variances**.

(c)   **Material usage** variances should be virtually non-existent given the accuracy afforded by machines as opposed to human operators.

(d)   It is quite possible that, with AMT, **variable overheads** are **incurred** in relation to machine time rather than labour time, and standard costs should reflect this where appropriate.

In an AMT environment, **machine efficiency variances** will be of **value**, however, and standards will still be needed for costing, pricing and budgeting purposes.

Question 7a.4	Variance analysis and product quality

Learning outcome A1(e)

AB has been receiving an increasing number of customer complaints about a general weakness in the quality of its products in recent months. The company believes that its future success is dependent on product quality and it is therefore determined to improve it.

Required

Describe the contribution that variance analysis can make towards the aim of improved product quality.

6.3 Other problems with using standard costing in today's environment

(a)   Variance analysis concentrates on only a **narrow range of costs**, and does not give sufficient attention to issues such as quality and customer satisfaction.

(b)   Standard costing places **too much emphasis on direct labour costs**. Direct labour is only a small proportion of costs in the modern manufacturing environment and so this emphasis is not appropriate.

(c) Many of the variances in a standard costing system focus on the control of **short-term variable costs**. In most modern manufacturing environments, the majority of costs, including direct labour costs, tend to be fixed in the short run.

(d) The use of standard costing relies on the existence of **repetitive operations** and relatively **homogeneous** output. Nowadays many organisations are continually forced to respond to customers' changing requirements, with the result that output and operations are not so repetitive.

(e) Standard costing systems were **developed** when the **business environment** was more **stable** and **less prone to change**. The current business environment is more dynamic and it is not possible to assume stable conditions.

(f) Standard costing systems **assume** that **performance to standard is acceptable**. Today's business environment is more focused on continuous improvement.

(g) Most standard costing systems produce **control statements weekly or monthly**. The modern manager needs much more prompt control information in order to function efficiently in a dynamic business environment.

This long list of criticisms of standard costing may lead you to believe that such systems have little use in today's business environment. Standard costing systems can be adapted to remain useful, however.

Question 7a.5	The value of standard costing today

Learning outcome A1(e)

Briefly explain ways in which a standard costing system could be adapted so that it is useful in the modern business environment.

Exam skills

To pass the P1 exam, you must be able to write short punchy paragraphs such as those in question 3.5. This is a skill that you should practise throughout your studying.

6.4 The role in modern business of standards and variances

(a) **Planning**. Even in an environment where the focus is on continual improvement, budgets will still need to be quantified. For example, the planned level of prevention and appraisal costs needs to be determined. Standards, such as returns of a particular product should not exceed one per cent of deliveries during a budget period, can be set.

(b) **Control**. Cost and mix changes from plan will still be relevant in many processing situations.

(c) **Decision making**. Existing standards can be used as the starting point in the construction of a cost for a new product.

(d) **Improvement and change**. Variance trends can be monitored over time.

Section summary

Critics argue that standard costing is most appropriate in a standard, stable and repetitive environment and therefore is of limited usefulness in the modern business environment. However, standard costing can be adapted to remain useful for cost planning and control.

7 Economy, efficiency and effectiveness

Introduction

The three Es (economy, efficiency and effectiveness) are important in any type of business but are generally associated with measuring the performance of public sector organisations.

7.1 Not for profit organisations (NFPOs)

NFPOs include private sector organisations such as charities, churches and much of the public sector. Commercial organisations generally have market competition and the **profit motive** to guide the process of managing resources economically, efficiently and effectively. However, NFPOs cannot by definition be judged by profitability.

7.2 How can performance be measured?

(a) **Economy**. This, fairly obviously means spending money more frugally.

(b) **Efficiency**. This means getting out as much as possible for what goes in. It is a measure of input in relation to output. This measure links economy to effectiveness.

(c) **Effectiveness**. This means getting done, by means of economy and efficiency, what was supposed to be done. This is an output measure and measures what the organisation achieves in relation to its objectives. The key to effectiveness is to find the optimum level of expenditure to achieve a given objective. The problem is that it is difficult to measure effectiveness. For example, locking up young people for petty crime may be effective in the short term but it is expensive. It may be more 'effective' to provide youth recreational facilities to treat the cause of petty crime.

Section summary

Economy, efficiency and effectiveness are associated with measuring the performance of not-for-profit organisations.

Chapter Roundup

- ✓ Standard costs are established but the actual results will vary. These variances should only be reported where the difference between actual and standard is significant.

- ✓ A **standard cost card** shows full details of the standard cost of each product.

- ✓ The standard for each type of cost (labour, material and so on) is made up of a **standard resource price** and a **standard resource usage**.

- ✓ **Performance standards** are used to set efficiency targets. There are four types: ideal, attainable, current and basic.

- ✓ It can be difficult to apply standard costing in a service environment because of the difficulty in establishing a measurable cost unit and the heterogeneous nature of most services.

- ✓ The four dimensions of McDonaldization are calculability, control, efficiency and predictability.

- ✓ Diagnostic related groups (DRGs) or reference groups are used in the healthcare industry to group together patients with similar lengths of stay and resource requirements. Standard costs can be established for each DRG which can be used for cost planning and control.

- ✓ In general, standards should be **revised** whenever changes of a permanent or reasonably long-term nature occur.

- ✓ Budgets and standards are very similar and interrelated, but there are important differences between them.

- ✓ Critics argue that standard costing is most appropriate in a standard, stable and repetitive environment and therefore is of limited usefulness in the modern business environment. However, standard costing can be adapted to remain useful for cost planning and control.

- ✓ Economy, efficiency and effectiveness are associated with measuring the performance of not-for-profit organisations.

Quick Quiz

1   Which one of the following statements is true?

A   Standard costing is not well suited to mass production.

B   Standard costing can never be used by service organisations.

C   Standard costing is most suited to repetitive assembly work.

D   If there is a degree of repetition in the production process, standard costing should not be used.

2   *Match the types of performance standard to the correct descriptions.*

Performance standards	*Descriptions*
(a) Ideal	(1) If well set, can provide a useful psychological incentive
(b) Attainable	(2) Do not attempt to improve on current levels of efficiency
(c) Current	(3) Least common type of standard in use
(d) Basic	(4) Likely to have an unfavourable motivational effect

3   An attainable standard is based on perfect operating conditions. *True or false?*

4   State Ritzer's four dimensions of McDonaldization.

5   Variance control reports should be produced either promptly or accurately. *True or false?*

6   Standards should be amended every time there is a change in price or efficiency. *True or false?*

7   Fill in the gaps using the following words:

standards/budgets/aggregate total/budgets/single task/standards

(a)   Budgets are prepared for .... costs; standards are for a ....

(b)   .... can be prepared for all functions; .... are only suitable for repetitive actions where output can be measured.

(c)   .... are expressed in money terms; .... need not be expressed in money terms.

8   During the month of June, CTF plc produced the following items:

	Units	*Standard minutes per unit*
Item C	7,200	5
Item T	5,970	8
Item F	6,600	11

What was the output in standard hours?

Answers to Quick Quiz

1   C   Standard costing is most appropriate in a stable, standardised and repetitive environment.

2   (a)   4
     (b)   1
     (c)   2
     (d)   3

3   False. An ideal standard is based on perfect operating conditions.

4   Calculability, control, efficiency, predictability

5   False. They should be produced promptly **and** accurately.

6   False. It is probably best to revise standards whenever changes of a permanent or long-term nature occur.

7   (a)   aggregate total
             single task
     (b)   budgets
             standards
     (c)   budgets
             standards

8

	Units	Standard minutes per unit	Standard hours
Item C	7,200	5	600
Item T	5,970	8	796
Item F	6,600	11	1,210
			2,606

Answers to Questions

7a.1 Performance standards

The correct answer is B.

Statement B is describing ideal standards, not basic standards.

7a.2 Linking capacity, efficiency and output

Capacity	=	40 × 140 = 5,600 hours per month
Efficiency	=	110%
Budgeted output	=	5,600 × 110% = 6,160 standard hours of work per month

7a.3 McDonaldization of services

Possible service industries where McDonaldization could be applied include the following.

- Exhaust and tyre fitting centres where a detailed manual dictates the activities of operatives for each standard type of fitting

- Call centres, where a machine provides the caller with numbered options from which to select the desired service and the person that answers is using a standard script

- Laboratory testing of blood samples, where the procedures to be followed by laboratory technicians can be standardised.

7a.4 Variance analysis and product quality

As variance analysis is generally expressed in terms of purely quantitative measures, such as quantity of raw materials used and price per unit of quantity, issues of **quality** would **appear** to be **excluded** from the reporting process. Quality would appear to be an excuse for spending more time, say, or buying more expensive raw materials.

Variance analysis, however, **can** be used to enhance product quality and to keep track of quality control information. This is because variance analysis measures both the **planned use** of **resources** and the **actual use** of **resources** in order to **compare** the two.

Variance analysis can be **adapted** to take account of quality issues as follows.

(a) Variance analysis reports should routinely include **measures such as defect rates**. Although zero defects will be most desirable, such a standard of performance may not be reached at first. However there should be an expected rate of defects: if this is exceeded then management attention is directed to the excess.

(b) The **absolute number of defects** should be measured *and* **their type**. If caused by certain materials and components this can shed light on, say, a favourable materials price variance which might have been caused by substandard materials being purchased more cheaply. Alternatively, if the defects are caused by shoddy assembly work this can shed light on a favourable labour efficiency variance if quality is being sacrificed for speed.

(c) It should also be possible to provide **financial measures for the cost of poor quality**. These can include direct costs such as the wages of inspection and quality control staff, the cost of time in rectifying the defects, and the cost of the materials used in rectification.

(d) Measures could be built into materials price and variance analysis, so that the **materials price variance** as currently reported includes a **factor reflecting the quality of materials purchased**.

7a.5 The value of standard costing today

A standard costing system may be adapted for use in the modern business environment as follows.

(a) **Non-financial measures** can be included within management control reports. Examples include number of defects, percentage of on-time deliveries, and so on.

(b) Even when output is not standardised, it may be possible to identify a number of **standard components and activities** whose costs may be controlled effectively by the setting of standard costs and identification of variances.

(c) The use of computer power enables standards to be **updated rapidly** and more frequently, so that they remain useful for the purposes of control by comparison.

(d) The use of **ideal standards** and **more demanding performance levels** can combine the benefits of **continuous improvement** and standard costing control.

(e) Information, particularly of a non-financial nature, can be **produced more rapidly** with the assistance of **computers**. For example the use of on-line data capture can enable the continuous display of real time information on factors such as hours worked, number of components used and number of defects.

Now try the question from the Exam Question Bank	Number	Level	Marks	Time
	Q7	Examination	5	9 mins

VARIANCE ANALYSIS

 In earlier studies you will have covered the calculation of basic cost and sales variances. Because students often find variance analysis quite difficult (although, really, it isn't) we are going to **go over the basic cost variances** again in detail in **Sections 1 to 5**.

We will be **analysing sales variances in more detail** than you did in earlier studies, and will be looking at the selling price and sales volume variances in **Section 6**. **Section 7** looks at **non-production cost variances**.

This is a **key chapter** in terms of topic **examinability**. Variance calculation and interpretation lends itself well to objective testing or longer calculation-based questions.

In **Chapter 7c** we will build on your revision of the basics in this chapter and cover a number of **additional variance analysis topics**. These include splitting the material usage and labour efficiency variances into mix and yield components and preparing statements to reconcile budgeted profit to actual profit using variances.

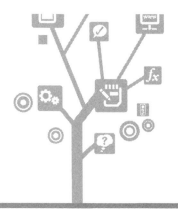

topic list	learning outcomes	syllabus references	ability required
1 Variances	A1(f)	A1(vi)	analysis
2 Direct material cost variances	A1(f)	A1(vi)	analysis
3 Direct labour cost variances	A1(f)	A1(vi)	analysis
4 Variable overhead variances	A1(f)	A1(vi)	analysis
5 Fixed overhead variances	A1(f)	A1(viii)	analysis
6 Sales variances	A1(f)	A1(xi)	analysis
7 Non-production cost variances	A1(f)	A1(vi)	analysis

1 Variances

Introduction

The process by which the total difference between standard and actual results is analysed is known as variance analysis.

KEY TERMS

A VARIANCE is the 'Difference between planned, budgeted, or standard cost and the actual cost incurred. The same comparisons may be made for revenues'.

VARIANCE ANALYSIS is the 'Evaluation of performance by means of variances, whose timely reporting should maximise the opportunity for managerial action.'CIMA *Official Terminology*

When **actual results are better than expected results**, we have a **favourable** variance (F). If, on the other hand, **actual results are worse than expected results**, we have an **adverse** variance (A).

Variances can be divided into three main groups.

- Variable cost variances

    - Direct material
    - Direct labour
    - Variable production overhead

- Fixed production overhead variances

- Sales variances

Section summary

A favourable variance occurs when actual results are better than expected results. An adverse variance occurs when actual results are worse than expected results.

2 Direct material cost variances

Introduction

The direct material total variance is the difference between what the output actually cost and what it should have cost, in terms of material.

KEY TERMS

The DIRECT MATERIAL TOTAL VARIANCE is 'A measurement of the difference between the standard material cost of the output produced and the actual cost incurred'.

The DIRECT MATERIAL PRICE VARIANCE is 'The difference between the actual price paid for purchased materials and their standard cost'.

The DIRECT MATERIAL USAGE VARIANCE 'Measures efficiency in the use of material, by comparing the standard material usage for actual production with actual material used, the difference valued at standard cost.'   *(CIMA Official Terminology)*

The **direct material total variance** can be **divided into two sub-variances**.

(a)   **The direct material price variance**

   This is the difference between what the actual amount of material purchased **should have** cost and what it **did** cost.

(b)   **The direct material usage variance**

This is the difference between the standard quantity of materials that **should have been used** for the number of units **actually produced**, and the **actual quantity** of materials **used**, valued at the standard cost per unit of material. In other words, it is the difference between how much material should have been used and how much material was used, valued at standard cost.

    Example: direct material variances

Product X has a standard direct material cost as follows.

> 10 kilograms of material Y at £10 per kilogram = £100 per unit of X.

During period 4, 1,000 units of X were manufactured, using 11,700 kilograms of material Y which cost £98,600.

Required

Calculate the following variances.

(a)   The direct material total variance
(b)   The direct material price variance
(c)   The direct material usage variance

Solution

(a)   **The direct material total variance**

This is the difference between what 1,000 units should have cost and what they did cost.

	£
1,000 units should have cost (× £100)	100,000
but did cost	98,600
Direct material total variance	1,400 (F)

The variance is favourable because the units cost less than they should have cost.

Now we can break down the direct material total variance into its two constituent parts: the direct material price variance and the direct material usage variance.

(b)   **The direct material price variance**

This is the difference between what 11,700 kgs should have cost and what 11,700 kgs did cost.

	£
11,700 kgs of Y should have cost (× £10)	117,000
but did cost	98,600
Material Y price variance	18,400 (F)

The variance is favourable because the material cost less than it should have.

(c)   **The direct material usage variance**

This is the difference between how many kilograms of Y should have been used to produce 1,000 units of X and how many kilograms were used, valued at the standard cost per kilogram.

1,000 units should have used (× 10 kgs)	10,000 kgs
but did use	11,700 kgs
Usage variance in kgs	1,700 kgs (A)
× standard cost per kilogram	× £10
Usage variance in £	£17,000 (A)

The variance is adverse because more material **was used** than **should have been used**.

(d) **Summary**

	£
Price variance	18,400 (F)
Usage variance	17,000 (A)
Total variance	1,400 (F)

2.1 Materials variances and opening and closing inventory

Suppose that a company uses raw material P in production, and that this raw material has a standard price of $3 per metre. During one month 6,000 metres are bought for $18,600, and 5,000 metres are used in production. At the end of the month, inventory will have been increased by 1,000 metres. In variance analysis, the problem is to decide the **material price variance**. Should it be calculated on the basis of **materials purchased** (6,000 metres) or on the basis of **materials used** (5,000 metres)?

The answer to this problem depends on **how closing inventories** of the raw materials will be **valued**.

(a) If they are valued at **standard cost**, (1,000 units at $3 per unit) the price variance is calculated on material **purchases** in the period.

(b) If they are valued at **actual cost** (FIFO) (1,000 units at $3.10 per unit) the price variance is calculated on materials **used in production** in the period.

A **full standard costing system** is usually in operation and therefore the price variance is usually calculated on **purchases** in the period. The variance on the full 6,000 metres will be written off to the costing income statement, even though only 5,000 metres are included in the cost of production.

There are two main **advantages** in extracting the material price variance at the time of **receipt**.

(a) If variances are extracted at the time of receipt they will be **brought to the attention of managers earlier** than if they are extracted as the material is used. If it is necessary to correct any variances then management action can be more timely.

(b) Since variances are extracted at the time of receipt, **all inventories will be valued at standard price**. This is administratively easier and it means that all issues from inventories can be made at standard price. If inventories are held at actual cost it is necessary to calculate a separate price variance on each batch as it is issued. Since issues are usually made in a number of small batches this can be a time-consuming task, especially with a manual system.

Question 7b.1	Materials price variance

Learning outcome A1(f)

What is the material price variance based on the information in Paragraph 2.1?

A $3,100 (A)
B $600 (A)
C $3,100 (F)
D $600 (F)

Section summary

The direct material total variance is the sum of the direct material price variance and the direct material usage variance.

3 Direct labour cost variances

Introduction

The direct labour total variance is the difference between what the output should have cost and what it did cost, in terms of labour

KEY TERMS

The DIRECT LABOUR TOTAL VARIANCE 'Indicates the difference between the standard direct labour cost of the output which has been produced and the actual direct labour cost incurred'.

The DIRECT LABOUR RATE VARIANCE 'Indicates the actual cost of any change from the standard labour rate of remuneration'.

The DIRECT LABOUR EFFICIENCY VARIANCE 'Indicates the standard labour cost of any change from the standard level of labour efficiency'. *(CIMA Official Terminology)*

The calculation of direct labour variances is very similar to the calculation of direct material variances.

The **direct labour total variance** can be **divided into two sub-variances**.

(a) **The direct labour rate variance**

This is similar to the direct material price variance. It is the difference between the **standard cost** and the **actual cost** for the **actual number of hours paid for**.

In other words, it is the difference between what labour **should have** cost and what it **did cost**.

(b) **The direct labour efficiency variance**

This is similar to the direct material usage variance. It is the difference between the **hours** that **should have been worked** for the number of **units actually produced**, and the **actual** number of **hours worked**, valued at the **standard rate** per hour.

In other words, it is the difference between how many hours should have been worked and how many hours were worked, valued at the standard rate per hour.

Example: direct labour variances

The standard direct labour cost of product X is as follows.

> 2 hours of grade Z labour at £5 per hour = £10 per unit of product X.

During period 4, 1,000 units of product X were made, and the direct labour cost of grade Z labour was £8,900 for 2,300 hours of work.

Required

Calculate the following variances.

(a) The direct labour total variance
(b) The direct labour rate variance
(c) The direct labour efficiency (productivity) variance

Solution

(a) **The direct labour total variance**

This is the difference between what 1,000 units **should have cost** and what they **did** cost.

	£
1,000 units should have cost (× £10)	10,000
but did cost	8,900
Direct labour total variance	1,100 (F)

The variance is favourable because the units cost less than they should have done.

Again we can analyse this total variance into its two constituent parts.

(b) **The direct labour rate variance**

This is the difference between what 2,300 hours should have cost and what 2,300 hours did cost.

	£
2,300 hours of work should have cost (× £5 per hr)	11,500
but did cost	8,900
Direct labour rate variance	2,600 (F)

The variance is favourable because the labour cost less than it should have cost.

(c) **The direct labour efficiency variance**

1,000 units of X should have taken (× 2 hrs)	2,000 hrs
but did take	2,300 hrs
Efficiency variance in hours	300 hrs (A)
× standard rate per hour	×£5
Efficiency variance in £	£1,500 (A)

The variance is adverse because more hours were worked than should have been worked.

(d) **Summary**

	£
Rate variance	2,600 (F)
Efficiency variance	1,500 (A)
Total variance	1,100 (F)

3.1 Idle time variance

Idle time occurs when no actual work is done but the workforce still has to be paid for the time at work. The idle time variance is (hours paid – hours worked) × standard direct labour rate per hour.

A company may operate a costing system in which **any** idle time is **recorded**. Idle time may be caused by machine breakdowns or not having work to give to employees, perhaps because of bottlenecks in production or a shortage of orders from customers. Time paid for without any work being done is unproductive and therefore inefficient. In variance analysis, **idle time is usually an adverse efficiency variance**. If, however, idle time is built into the cost budget, it could be a favourable variance.

KEY TERM

The DIRECT LABOUR IDLE TIME VARIANCE '...occurs when the hours paid exceed the hours worked and there is an extra cost caused by this idle time.' *(CIMA Official Terminology)*

When idle time is recorded separately, it is helpful to provide control information which identifies the cost of idle time separately, and in variance analysis, there will be an idle time variance **as a separate part of the total labour efficiency variance**. The remaining **efficiency variance** will then relate only to the productivity of the labour force during the **hours spent actively working**.

Example: labour variances with idle time

Refer to the standard cost data in the previous example called direct labour variances. During period 5, 1,500 units of product X were made and the cost of grade Z labour was £17,500 for 3,080 hours. During the period, however, there as a shortage of customer orders and 100 hours were recorded as idle time.

Required

Calculate the following variances.

(a)   The direct labour total variance
(b)   The direct labour rate variance
(c)   The idle time variance
(d)   The direct labour efficiency variance

Solution

(a)   **The direct labour total variance**

	£
1,500 units of product X should have cost (× £10)	15,000
but did cost	17,500
Direct labour total variance	2,500 (A)

Actual cost is greater than standard cost. The variance is therefore adverse.

(b)   **The direct labour rate variance**

The rate variance is a comparison of what the hours paid should have cost and what they did cost.

	£
3,080 hours of grade Z labour should have cost (× £5)	15,400
but did cost	17,500
Direct labour rate variance	2,100 (A)

Actual cost is greater than standard cost. The variance is therefore adverse.

(c)   **The idle time variance**

The idle time variance is the hours of idle time, valued at the standard rate per hour.

Idle time variance = 100 hours (A) × £5 = £500 (A)

It is an **adverse** variance because it was not built into the cost budget.

(d)   **The direct labour efficiency variance**

The efficiency variance considers the hours **actively worked** (the difference between hours paid for and idle time hours). In our example, there were (3,080 – 100) = 2,980 hours when the labour force was not idle. The variance is calculated by taking the amount of output produced (1,500 units of product X) and comparing the time it should have taken to make them, with the actual time spent **actively** making them (2,980 hours). Once again, the variance in hours is valued at the standard rate per labour hour.

1,500 units of product X should take (× 2 hrs)	3,000 hrs
but did take (3,080 – 100)	2,980 hrs
Direct labour efficiency variance in hours	20 hrs (F)
× standard rate per hour	× £5
Direct labour efficiency variance in £	£100 (F)

(e)   **Summary**

	£
	£
Direct labour rate variance	2,100 (A)
Idle time variance	500 (A)
Direct labour efficiency variance	100 (F)
Direct labour total variance	2,500 (A)

KEY POINTS

- Remember that, if idle time is recorded, the actual hours used in the **efficiency variance** calculation are the **hours worked and not the hours paid for**.

- If there is a budgeted level of idle time and the actual level is less than the budgeted level, the idle time variance will be favourable.

- Some organisations might experience 'expected' or 'normal' idle time at less busy periods, perhaps because demand is seasonal or irregular (but they wish to maintain and pay a constant number of workers). In such circumstances, the standard labour rate may include an allowance for the cost of the expected idle time. Only the impact of unexpected/abnormal idle time would be included in the idle time variance.

Question 7b.2   Labour variances

Learning outcome A1(f)

Growler Ltd is planning to make 100,000 units per period of product AA. Each unit of AA should require 2 hours to produce, with labour being paid £11 per hour. Attainable work hours are less than clock hours, so 250,000 hours have been budgeted in the period.

Actual data for the period was:

Units produced	120,000
Direct labour cost	£3,200,000
Clock hours	280,000

Required

Calculate the following variances.

(a)   Labour rate variance
(b)   Labour efficiency variance
(c)   Idle time variance

Question 7b.3   Idle time and efficiency variances

Learning outcome A1(f)

There is seasonal demand for CH Ltd's product N. Average idle time during control period 11 is expected to be 10% of hours paid. An allowance for this idle time is included in the standard labour rate, which is €15.30 before the allowance. Standard (productive) time per unit is six labour hours.

During control period 11, 1,800 units of N were manufactured, 13,500 hours were paid for and 12,420 hours actually worked.

What are the idle time and labour efficiency variances?

	Idle time	Labour efficiency
A	€4,590 (F)	€27,540 (A)
B	€4,590 (A)	€27,540 (F)
C	€4,131 (A)	€24,786 (A)
D	€4,131 (F)	€24,786 (F)

Section summary

The direct labour total variance is the sum of the direct labour rate variance and the direct labour efficiency variance.

The idle time variance is the number of hours of idle time valued at the standard rate per hour. Idle time variance = (hours paid − hours worked) × standard direct labour rate per hour

4 Variable overhead variances

Introduction

The variable overhead total variance is the difference between what the output should have cost and what it did cost, in terms of variable overheads. You should be able to follow the same pattern for calculating the variances as you did for the material and labour variances.

Suppose that the variable production overhead cost of product X is as follows.

2 hours at £1.50 = £3 per unit

During period 6, 400 units of product X were made. The labour force worked 820 hours, of which 60 hours were recorded as idle time. The variable overhead cost was £1,230.

Calculate the following variances.

(a)   The variable overhead total variance
(b)   The variable overhead expenditure variance
(c)   The variable overhead efficiency variance

Since this example **relates to variable production costs**, the total variance is **based on actual units of production**. (If the overhead had been a **variable selling cost**, the variance would be **based on sales volumes**.)

	£
400 units of product X should cost (× £3)	1,200
but did cost	1,230
Variable production overhead total variance	30 (A)

In many variance reporting systems, the variance analysis goes no further, and expenditure and efficiency variances are not calculated. However, the adverse variance of £30 may be explained as the **sum of two factors**.

(a)   The hourly rate of spending on variable overheads was higher than it should have been, that is there is an **expenditure variance**.

(b)   The labour force worked inefficiently, and took longer to make the output than it should have done. This means that spending on variable overhead was higher than it should have been, in other words there is an **efficiency (productivity) variance**. The variable overhead efficiency variance is exactly the same, in hours, as the direct labour efficiency variance, and occurs for the same reasons.

It is usually assumed that **variable overheads are incurred during active working hours**, but are not incurred during idle time (for example the machines are not running, therefore power is not being consumed, and no indirect materials are being used). This means in our example that although the labour force was paid for 820 hours, they were actively working for only 760 of those hours and so variable overhead spending occurred during 760 hours.

(a) **The variable overhead expenditure variance**

This is the **difference between the amount of variable overhead that should have been incurred in the actual hours actively worked, and the actual amount of variable overhead incurred.**

	£
760 hours of variable overhead should cost (× £1.50)	1,140
but did cost	1,230
Variable overhead expenditure variance	90 (A)

(b) **The variable overhead efficiency variance**

if you already know the direct **labour efficiency variance**, the variable overhead efficiency variance is **exactly the same in hours**, but **priced at the variable overhead rate per hour**. In our example, the efficiency variance would be as follows.

400 units of product X should take (× 2 hrs)	800 hrs
but did take (active hours)	760 hrs
Variable overhead efficiency variance in hours	40 hrs (F)
× standard rate per hour	× £1.50
Variable overhead efficiency variance in £	£60 (F)

(c) **Summary**

	£
Variable overhead expenditure variance	90 (A)
Variable overhead efficiency variance	60 (F)
Variable overhead total variance	30 (A)

Exam skills

Learn the following.

Material price, labour rate or variable overhead expenditure variance		Material usage or labour/variable overhead efficiency variance	
Actual kgs or hrs should have cost	X	X units should have used/taken (kg/hrs)	X
But did cost	X	But did use/take	X
	X̄ A/F		X̄
		× std rate per kg/hr	× X
			X̄ A/F

Section summary

Variances	What they measure
Price (material) Rate (labour) Expenditure (variable overhead)	Measure the difference between what should have been paid for the actual quantity of materials/ labour hours/variable overheads and what was paid
Usage (material) Efficiency (labour and variable overhead)	Measure the difference between what the quantities of material used or hours taken should have been and what was actually used or taken. These differences are converted into monetary values by multiplying by the standard price

5 Fixed overhead variances

Introduction

Fixed overhead variances are the same as material and labour variances in that they **measure the difference between what the output should have cost and what it did cost**. There is a fundamental difference underlying their calculation, however.

Fixed costs do not vary with changes in output (provided output remains within the relevant range). This is a statement of fact since it describes the way in which fixed costs behave. The **budgeted or planned level of fixed costs should therefore be the same whatever the level of output**. So if an organisation budgets fixed costs to be £5,000 for budgeted output of 100 units, the expected fixed costs if actual output is 120 units should still be £5,000.

Contrast this with standard material and labour costs, which vary according to the actual level of output (because they are variable costs).

In this sense there is no equivalent to a usage or efficiency variance when dealing with fixed overheads.

5.1 Fixed overhead variances and marginal costing

If the **actual fixed cost differs** from the **planned fixed cost**, the only reason can be that **expenditure** was **higher or lower than planned**.

The **fixed overhead expenditure variance** is therefore the **difference between planned expenditure and actual expenditure**. This is the only fixed overhead variance which occurs if marginal costing is being used.

5.2 Fixed overhead variances and absorption costing

The calculation of fixed overhead variances is slightly more complicated when absorption costing is used.

The fixed overhead total variance in an absorption costing system may be broken down into two parts as usual.

- An **expenditure variance**
- A **volume variance**

In an absorption costing system, **fixed overhead variances** are an attempt to **explain the reasons for any under- or over-absorbed overhead.**

Remember that the absorption rate is calculated as budgeted fixed overhead ÷ budgeted level of activity.

Generally the level of activity used in the overhead absorption rate will be units of production or hours of activity. More often than not, if just one product is being produced, the level of activity is in terms of units produced.

You should remember from your earlier studies that if either the budgeted overhead expenditure or the budgeted activity level or both are incorrect then we will have under- or over-absorbed overhead.

5.3 Expenditure variance

The fixed overhead **expenditure variance** measures the under or over absorption caused by the **actual overhead expenditure being different from budget**.

5.4 Volume variance

The fixed overhead **volume variance** measures the under or over absorption caused by the **actual production level being different to the budgeted production level** used in calculating the absorption rate.

KEY POINT

The volume variance applies to fixed overhead costs only and not to variable overheads.

(a) **Variable overheads** incurred **change** with the **volume of activity**. If the budget is to work for 300 hours and variable overheads are incurred and absorbed at a rate of £6 per hour, the variable overhead budget will be £1,800. If only 200 hours are actually worked, the variable overhead absorbed will be £1,200 and the expected expenditure will also be £1,200, so that there will be no under or over absorption of overhead because of volume changes.

(b) **Fixed overheads** are **different** because the level of **expenditure does not change** as the number of hours worked varies. If the budget is to work for 300 hours and fixed overheads are budgeted to be £2,400, the fixed overhead absorption rate will be £8 per hour. If actual hours worked are only 200 hours, the fixed overhead absorbed will be £1,600, but expected expenditure will be unchanged at £2,400. There is an under absorption of £800 because of the volume variance of 100 hours shortfall multiplied by the absorption rate of £8 per hour.

5.5 How to calculate the variances

KEY TERMS

FIXED OVERHEAD TOTAL VARIANCE is the difference between fixed overhead incurred and fixed overhead absorbed (the under- or over-absorbed fixed overhead).

FIXED OVERHEAD EXPENDITURE VARIANCE is the difference between the overhead that should have been incurred and that which was incurred. It is calculated as the difference between the budgeted fixed overhead expenditure and actual fixed overhead expenditure.

FIXED OVERHEAD VOLUME VARIANCE is a measure of the over or under absorption of fixed overhead costs caused by actual production volume differing from that budgeted. It is calculated as the difference between actual and budgeted production/volume multiplied by the standard absorption rate per *unit*.

You should now be ready to work through an example to demonstrate all of the fixed overhead variances.

Example: fixed overhead variances

Suppose that a company budgets to produce 1,000 units of product E during August. The expected time to produce a unit of E is five hours, and the budgeted fixed overhead is £20,000. The standard fixed overhead cost per unit of product E will therefore be 5 hours at £4 per hour (= £20 per unit). Actual fixed overhead expenditure in August turns out to be £20,450. The labour force manages to produce 1,100 units of product E in 5,400 hours of work.

Required

Calculate the fixed overhead total variance and its sub-variances.

Solution

(a) **Fixed overhead total variance**

	£
Fixed overhead incurred	20,450
Fixed overhead absorbed (1,100 units × £20 per unit)	22,000
Fixed overhead total variance (= under-/over-absorbed overhead)	1,550 (F)

The variance is favourable because more overheads were absorbed than budgeted.

(b) **Fixed overhead expenditure variance**

	£
Budgeted fixed overhead expenditure	20,000
Actual fixed overhead expenditure	20,450
Fixed overhead expenditure variance	450 (A)

The variance is adverse because expenditure was greater than budgeted.

(c) **Fixed overhead volume variance**

The production volume achieved was greater than expected. The fixed overhead volume variance measures the difference at the standard rate.

	£
Actual production at standard rate (1,100 × £20 per unit)	22,000
Budgeted production at standard rate (1,000 × £20 per unit)	20,000
Fixed overhead volume variance	2,000 (F)

The variance is favourable because output was greater than expected.

Question 7b.4
Fixed overhead variances

Learning outcome A1(f)

In an absorption costing system the fixed overhead total variance can be analysed into the fixed overhead expenditure variance and the fixed overhead volume variance.

Explain briefly the meaning of each of these three variances in an absorption costing system.

Question 7b.5
Variance calculations

Learning outcome A1(f)

Brian produces and sells one product only, the Blob, and the standard cost for one unit is as follows.

	£
Direct material A - 10 kilograms at £20 per kg	200
Direct wages - 5 hours at £6 per hour	30
Fixed overhead	50
Total standard cost	280

The fixed overhead included in the standard cost is based on an expected monthly output of 900 units.

During April the actual results were as follows.

Production	800 units
Material A	7,800 kg used, costing £159,900
Direct wages	4,200 hours worked for £24,150
Fixed overhead	£47,000

Required

(a)   Calculate material price and usage variances.
(b)   Calculate labour rate and efficiency variances.
(c)   Calculate fixed overhead expenditure and volume variances.

Section summary

The only fixed overhead variance which occurs in a marginal costing system is the fixed overhead expenditure variance.

In an absorption costing system, the fixed overhead total variance is the sum of the fixed overhead expenditure variance and the fixed overhead volume variance.

6   Sales variances

Introduction

The **selling** (or **sales**) **price variance** is the difference between what revenue should have been for the quantity sold and the actual revenue.

6.1 Selling price or sales price variance

KEY TERM

The SALES PRICE VARIANCE is the 'Change in revenue caused by the actual selling price differing from that budgeted.'   CIMA *Official Terminology*

Suppose that the standard selling price of product X is £15. Actual sales in year 3 were 2,000 units at £15.30 per unit. The selling price variance is calculated as follows.

	£
Sales revenue from 2,000 units should have been (× £15)	30,000
but was (× £15.30)	30,600
Selling price variance	600 (F)

The variance is favourable because the price was higher than expected.

6.2 Sales volume variance

The sales volume variance in units is calculated as the difference between the **actual units sold** and the **budgeted quantity**. This variance in units can be valued in one of three ways.

(a)   At the **standard gross profit margin per unit**. This is the **sales volume profit variance** and it measures the change in profit (in an absorption costing system) caused by the sales volume differing from budget.

(b)   At the **standard contribution per unit**. This is the **sales volume contribution variance** and it measures the change in profit (in a marginal costing system) caused by the sales volume differing from budget.

(c) At the **standard revenue per unit**. This is the **sales volume revenue variance** and it measures the change in sales revenue caused by sales volume differing from that budgeted.

Suppose that a company budgets to sell 8,000 units of product J for $12 per unit. The standard variable cost per unit is $4 and the standard full cost is $7 per unit. Actual sales were 7,700 units, at $12.50 per unit.

The sales volume variance in units is 300 units adverse (8,000 units budgeted – 7,700 units sold). The variance is **adverse** because actual sales volume was less than budgeted. The sales volume variance in units can be evaluated in the three ways described above.

(a)	Sales volume profit variance	= 300 units × standard gross profit margin per unit
		= 300 units × $(12 – 7)
		= $1,500 (A)
(b)	Sales volume contribution variance	= 300 units × standard contribution per unit
		= 300 units × $(12 – 4)
		= $2,400 (A)
(c)	Sales volume revenue variance	= 300 units × standard revenue per unit
		= 300 units × $12
		= $3,600 (A)

Note that the sales volume profit variance (in an absorption costing system) and the sales volume contribution variance (in a marginal costing system) can be derived from the sales volume revenue variance, if the profit mark-up percentage and the contribution to sales (C/S) ratio respectively are known.

In our example the profit mark-up percentage is 41.67% ($5/$12) and the C/S ratio is 66.67% ($8/$12).

Therefore the sales volume profit variance and the sales volume contribution variance, derived from the sales volume revenue variance, are as follows.

Sales volume profit variance = $3,600 (A) × 41.67% = $1,500 (A), as above

Sales volume contribution variance = $3,600 (A) × 66.67% = $2,400 (A), as above

Question 7b.6	Sales variance

Learning outcome A1(f)

Jasper has the following budget and actual figures for year 4.

	Budget	Actual
Sales units	600	620
Selling price per unit	€30	€29

Standard full cost of production = €28 per unit. Standard variable cost of production = €19 per unit

Calculate the following sales variances

(a) Selling price variance
(b) Sales volume profit variance
(c) Sales volume contribution variance
(d) Sales volume revenue variance

6.3 The significance of sales variances

The possible **interdependence** between sales price and sales volume variances should be obvious to you. A **reduction** in the sales **price** might **stimulate** bigger sales **demand**, so that an adverse sales price variance might be counterbalanced by a favourable sales volume variance. Similarly, a price rise would give a favourable price variance, but possibly at the cost of a fall in demand and an adverse sales volume variance.

It is therefore important in analysing an unfavourable sales variance that the overall consequence should be considered, that is, has there been a counterbalancing favourable variance as a direct result of the unfavourable one?

Question 7b.7	Sales variances for professional services

Learning outcome A1(f)

A management consultancy has an IT division which operates a standard absorption costing system. Details from the latest period are as follows.

Standard charge per hour of client services	£180
Standard absorption cost per hour of client service provided	£110
Budgeted hours to be charged to clients per period	780
Actual hours charged to clients during period	730
Actual amount billed to clients during period	£139,800

Calculate the following variances for the period.

(a)   The selling price variance
(b)   The sales volume profit variance

Section summary

The selling (or sales) price variance is the difference between what revenue should have been for the quantity sold and the actual revenue.

The sales volume variance in units is the difference between the actual units sold and the budgeted quantity. This variance in units can be valued in one of three ways: in terms of standard revenue, standard gross margin or standard contribution margin.

7   Non-production cost variances

Introduction

Non-production costs, such as administration and selling/distribution costs, must **also** be **monitored** and **controlled**.

Some selling/distribution costs may **vary with units sold**, and variances for such costs can be calculated in much the **same way as variable production overhead variances**.

Simple **expenditure variances** may be all that is required for monitoring and controlling **most non-production costs**, however, such as administration.

Section summary

Most **non-production cost variances** can be monitored and controlled using simple expenditure variances.

Chapter Roundup

✓ A favourable variance occurs when actual results are better than expected results. An adverse variance occurs when actual results are worse than expected results.

✓ The direct material total variance is the sum of the direct material price variance and the direct material usage variance.

✓ The direct labour total variance is the sum of the direct labour rate variance and the direct labour efficiency variance.

✓ The **idle time variance** is the number of hours of idle time valued at the standard rate per hour.

Idle time variance = (hours paid − hours worked) × standard direct labour rate per hour

✓

Variances	What they measure
Price (material) Rate (labour) Expenditure (variable overhead)	Measure the difference between what should have been paid for the actual quantity of materials/ labour hours/variable overheads and what was paid
Usage (material) Efficiency (labour and variable overhead)	Measure the difference between what the quantities of material used or hours taken should have been and what was actually used or taken. These differences are converted into monetary values by multiplying by the standard price

✓ The only fixed overhead variance which occurs in a marginal costing system is the fixed overhead expenditure variance.

✓ In an absorption costing system, the fixed overhead total variance is the sum of the fixed overhead expenditure variance and the fixed overhead volume variance.

✓ The **selling** (or **sales**) **price variance** is the difference between what revenue should have been for the quantity sold and the actual revenue.

✓ The sales volume variance in units is the difference between the actual units sold and the budgeted quantity. This variance in units can be valued in one of three ways: in terms of standard revenue, standard gross margin or standard contribution margin.

✓ Most **non-production cost variances** can be monitored and controlled using simple expenditure variances.

Quick Quiz

1   An adverse variance occurs when actual results are the same as expected results. *True or false?*

2   *Choose the appropriate words from those highlighted.*

If material price variances are extracted **at the time of receipt/as the material is used**, they will be brought to the attention of managers earlier than if they are extracted **at the time of receipt/as the material is used**.

And if variances are extracted **at the time of receipt/as material is used**, all inventories will be valued at **standard price/actual price**, which is administratively easier.

3   *Match up the variances and the methods of calculation.*

Variances

Variable overhead total variance
Variable overhead expenditure variance
Variable overhead efficiency variance

Methods of calculation

(a)   The difference between the amount of variable overhead that should have been incurred in the actual hours worked, and the actual amount of variable overhead incurred.

(b)   The labour efficiency variance in hours valued at the standard variable overhead rate per hour.

(c)   The difference between budgeted variable overhead expenditure and actual overhead expenditure.

(d)   The difference between what actual production should have cost in terms of variable overhead, and what it did cost.

(e)   The difference between the labour hours that should have been worked for the actual level of output, and the labour hours actually paid, valued at the standard variable overhead rate per hour.

4   Which of the following statements about the fixed production overhead volume variance is true?

A   It is the same in a standard marginal costing system as in a standard absorption costing system.
B   It does not exist in a standard absorption costing system.
C   It does not exist in a standard marginal costing system.
D   It is the difference between budgeted overhead expenditure and actual overhead expenditure.

5   *Fill in the blank.*

Sales volume profit variance = (actual sales volume – budgeted sales volume) × ....

6   Which of the following is not a suitable basis for valuing the sales volume variance?

A   Selling price
B   Contribution
C   Absorption rate
D   Profit

7   HMF plc uses standard absorption costing. In June the following information was recorded.

	Budget	Actual
Output and sales (units)	17,400	16,400
Selling price per unit	£25	£30
Variable cost per unit	£15	£15
Total fixed overheads	$42,500	$45,800

The sales price variance for June was:

A $87,000 favourable
B $82,000 favourable
C $82,000 adverse
D $131,200 adverse

Answers to Quick Quiz

1   False. It occurs when actual results are worse than expected results.

2   at the time of receipt
     as the material is used
     at the time of receipt
     standard price

3   Total variance (d)
     Expenditure variance (a)
     Efficiency variance (b)

4   C. This variance does not exist in a standard marginal costing system.

5   Standard profit per unit

6   C   All others are specifically mentioned in the syllabus

7   B

	£
Sales revenue from 16,400 units should have been (× £25)	410,000
but was (× £30)	492,000
Selling price variance	82,000 (F)

Answers to Questions

7b.1 Materials price variance

The correct answer is B.

The price variance would be calculated as follows.

	$
6,000 metres of material P purchased should cost (× $3)	18,000
but did cost	18,600
Price variance	600 (A)

7b.2 Labour variances

The information means that clock hours have to be multiplied by 200,000/250,000 (80%) in order to arrive at a realistic efficiency variance.

(a) **Labour rate variance**

	£'000
280,000 hours should have cost (× £11)	3,080
but did cost	3,200
Labour rate variance	120 (A)

(b) **Labour efficiency variance**

120,000 units should have taken (× 2 hours)	240,000 hrs
but did take (280,000 × 80%)	224,000 hrs
Variance in hours	16,000 hrs (F)
× standard rate per hour	× £11
Labour efficiency variance	£176,000 (F)

(c) **Idle time variance**

280,000 × 20%	56,000 hrs
	× £11
	£616,000 (A)

7b.3 Idle time and efficiency variances

The correct answer is A.

The basic standard rate per hour must be increased to allow for idle time. The revised standard hourly rate is €15.30/0.9 or €17

Variances are now calculated at this revised rate.

Idle time should have been (10% × 13,500 hours paid)	1,350 hrs
but was (13,500 – 12,420)	1,080 hrs
	270 hrs (F)
× standard rate per hour worked	× €17
Idle time variance	£4,590 (F)

Efficiency variance

1,800 units should have taken (× 6 hrs)	10,800 hrs
but did take	12,420 hrs
	1,620 hrs (A)
× standard rate per hour worked	× €17
Efficiency variance	€27,540 (A)

Options C and D have been evaluated at the original standard rate of €15.30.

7b.4 Fixed overhead variances

Fixed overhead total variance

The fixed overhead total variance in an absorption costing system evaluates the **amount of under- or over-absorbed** fixed production **overhead** for the period. If the overhead is **over-absorbed** then the fixed overhead total variance will be **favourable**. If the overhead is **under-absorbed** then the variance will be **adverse**.

The other two variances sum to the fixed overhead total variance and they attempt to evaluate the reason why the fixed production overhead was under or over absorbed.

Fixed overhead expenditure variance

The expenditure variance is the **under or over absorption caused by** the **expenditure** on overheads **being different from that budgeted**. The variance is calculated as the difference between the budgeted expenditure for the period and the actual expenditure. If the **actual expenditure exceeds** the **budgeted** expenditure then this potentially leads to under absorption and the variance is **adverse**. If the actual expenditure is lower than budgeted then over absorption could result and the variance is favourable.

Fixed overhead volume variance

The volume variance is the **under or over absorption caused by** the **volume of activity being different from that budgeted**. The variance is calculated as the difference between budgeted and actual activity, multiplied by the standard overhead absorption rate per unit of activity. If the **actual activity** is **lower than budgeted** then this could lead to under absorption and the variance is **adverse**. If the actual activity is higher than budgeted the potential over absorption means that the variance is favourable.

7b.5 Variance calculations

(a) **Material price variance**

	£
7,800 kgs should have cost (× £20)	156,000
but did cost	159,900
Price variance	3,900 (A)

Material usage variance

800 units should have used (× 10 kgs)	8,000 kgs
but did use	7,800 kgs
Usage variance in kgs	200 kgs (F)
× standard cost per kilogram	× £20
Usage variance in £	£4,000 (F)

(b) **Labour rate variance**

	£
4,200 hours should have cost (× £6)	25,200
but did cost	24,150
Rate variance	1,050 (F)

Labour efficiency variance

800 units should have taken (× 5 hrs)	4,000 hrs
but did take	4,200 hrs
Efficiency variance in hours	200 hrs (A)
× standard rate per hour	× £6
Labour efficiency variance in £	£1,200 (A)

(c)   **Fixed overhead expenditure variance**

	£
Budgeted expenditure (£50 × 900)	45,000
Actual expenditure	47,000
Expenditure variance	2,000 (A)

Fixed overhead volume variance

	£
Budgeted production at standard rate (900 × £50)	45,000
Actual production at standard rate (800 × £50)	40,000
Volume variance	5,000 (A)

7b.6 Sales variance

(a)

	£
Sales revenue for 620 units should have been (× £30)	18,600
but was (× £29)	17,980
Selling price variance	620 (A)

(b)

Budgeted sales volume	600 units
Actual sales volume	620 units
Sales volume variance in units	20 units (F)

Sales volume profit variance = 20 units × €(30 – 28) = €40 (F)

(c)   Sales volume contribution variance = 20 units × €(30 – 19) = €220(F)

(d)   Sales volume revenue variance = 20 units × €30 = €600(F)

In this question you were asked to calculate both the **sales volume profit** variance and the **sales volume contribution** variance to give you some practice. However, the two variances would **never** be found together in the **same system in a real situation**. Either a **marginal** costing system is used, in which case the sales volume **contribution** variance is calculated, or an **absorption** costing system is used, in which case a sales volume **profit** variance is calculated.

7b.7 Sales variances for professional services

		£
(a)		
	Sales revenue for 730 hours should have been (x £180)	131,400
	but was	139,800
	Selling price variance	8,400 (F)
(b)	Budgeted sales volume	780 hours
	Actual sales volume	730 hours
	Sales volume variance in units	50 hours
	× standard profit per unit (£(180 − 110))	× £70
	Sales volume profit variance	£3,500 (A)

Now try the question from the Exam Question Bank

Number	Level	Marks	Time
Q8	Examination	30	54 mins

INTERPRETATION OF VARIANCES

The **calculation of variances** in itself **does little to help management**. Managers need to know whether or not a variance should be investigated, why the variance might have occurred, what it means and whether its occurrence is linked to any other reported variance. Sections 1 to 4 will explain how this is done.

In **Section 1** we will look at the issues that need to be considered before management decide **whether they need to look into the occurrence of a variance** more closely.

Section 2 looks at the **models** which can be used to determine whether or not a variance is worthy of investigation. You may need to think back to your *Business Maths* studies at Fundamentals level here!

Joint variances, which arise when both price and quantity of inputs differ from standards, are covered briefly in **Section 3**. Such variances are of particular relevance when allocating responsibility for the occurrence of variances.

Section 4 looks at **why variances might occur** and at the meaning of fixed overhead variances.

Benchmarking, in **Section 6**, is another comparison exercise, involving comparison against best available performance, whether that be inside or outside the organisation.

topic list	learning outcomes	syllabus references	ability required
1 To investigate or not to investigate?	A1(f), (g)	A1(xii)	analysis
2 Variance investigation models	A1(f), (g)	A1(xii)	analysis
3 Joint variances: the controllability principle	A1(f), (g)	A1(xii)	analysis
4 Interpreting variances	A1(f), (g)	A1(xii)	analysis
5 Benchmarking	A1(g)	A1(xiii)	application

1   To investigate or not to investigate?

Introduction

Before management decide whether or not to investigate a particular variance, there are a number of factors which should be considered.

Materiality

Small variations in a single period are bound to occur and **are unlikely to be significant**. Obtaining an 'explanation' is likely to be time-consuming and irritating for the manager concerned. The explanation will often be 'chance', which is not, in any case, particularly helpful. For such variations further investigation is not worthwhile.

Controllability

Controllability must also influence the decision whether to investigate further. If there is a general worldwide price increase in the price of an important raw material there is **nothing that can be done internally** to control the effect of this. If a central decision is made to award all employees a 10% increase in salary, staff costs in division A will increase by this amount and the variance is not controllable by division A's manager. Uncontrollable variances call for a **change in the plan**, not an investigation into the past.

Variance trend

If, say, an efficiency **variance** is £1,000 adverse in month 1, the obvious conclusion is that the process is **out of control** and that corrective action must be taken. This may be correct, but what if the same variance is £1,000 adverse every month? The **trend** indicates that the process is **in control** and the standard has been wrongly set. Suppose, though, that the same variance is consistently £1,000 adverse for each of the first six months of the year but that production has steadily fallen from 100 units in month 1 to 65 units by month 6. The variance trend in absolute terms is constant, but relative to the number of units produced, efficiency has got steadily worse.

Cost

The likely cost of an investigation needs to be weighed against the cost to the organisation of allowing the variance to continue in future periods.

Interrelationship of variances

Generally speaking, individual variances should not be looked at in isolation. One variance might be inter-related with another, and much of it might have occurred only because the other, inter-related, variance occurred too. When two variances are **interdependent (interrelated) one** will usually be **adverse** and the other **one favourable**. Here are some examples.

Interrelated variances	Explanation
Materials price and usage	If cheaper materials are purchased in order to obtain a favourable price variance, materials wastage might be higher and an adverse usage variance will occur. If the cheaper material is more difficult to handle, there might be an adverse labour efficiency variance too.
	If more expensive material is purchased, however, the price variance will be adverse but the usage variance might be favourable.

Interrelated variances	Explanation
Labour rate and efficiency	If employees in a workforce are paid higher rates for experience and skill, using a highly skilled team might lead to an adverse rate variance and possibly a favourable efficiency variance. In contrast, a favourable rate variance might indicate a larger-than-expected proportion of inexperienced workers which could result in an adverse labour efficiency variance, and perhaps poor materials handling and high rates of rejects and hence an adverse materials usage variance.
Selling price and sales volume	We looked at this in Chapter 7b.
Materials mix and yield variance (calculations of these variances are covered in the next chapter)	If the mix is cheaper than standard, there may be a resulting lower yield, so that a favourable mix variance might be offset by an adverse yield variance. Alternatively, a mix which is cheaper than standard might have no effect on yield, but the end product might be of sub-standard quality. Sales volumes might then be affected, or sales prices might have to be reduced to sell off the output that customers are not willing to buy at the normal price.

Because management accountants analyse total variances into component elements, ie materials price and usage, labour rate, idle time, efficiency, and so on, they should not lose sight of the overall 'integrated' picture of events, and any interdependence between variances should be reported whenever it is suspected to have occurred.

Question 7c.1

Interdependence between variances

Learning outcome A1(f)

There is likely to be interdependence between an adverse labour rate variance and

A   a favourable materials usage variance
B   an adverse fixed overhead expenditure variance
C   an adverse selling price variance
D   none of the above

Exam skills

'Interpretation of variances: interrelationship, significance' is a specific syllabus topic. You could be required to perform calculations *and* to analyse and **explain** your results.

The **efficiency variance** reported in any control period, whether for materials or labour and overhead, will **depend on the efficiency level in the standard cost**.

The performance standard used

(a)   If an **ideal standard** is used, **variances** will always be **adverse**.

(b)   If an **attainable standard** is used, or a **current** standard, we should expect **small variances around the standard** from one period to the next, which may not necessarily be significant.

(c)   Management might set a **target** standard **above the current** standard but **below the ideal** standard of efficiency. In such a situation, there will probably be adverse efficiency variances, though not as high as if ideal standards were used. However, if there is **support from the workforce** in trying to improve efficiency levels to the new standard, management would hope to see the **adverse**

efficiency variances gradually diminish period by period, until the workforce eventually achieves 100% efficiency at the target standard level.

It is therefore necessary to make a judgement about what an adverse or favourable efficiency variance signifies, in relation to the 'toughness' of the standard set. **Trends** in efficiency variances, that is gradual improvements or deteriorations in efficiency, should be monitored, because these might be more informative than the variance in a single control period.

1.1 Management signals from variance trend information

Variance analysis is a means of assessing performance, but it is only a method of signalling to management areas of possible weakness where control action might be necessary. It does not provide a ready-made diagnosis of faults, nor does it provide management with a ready-made indication of what action needs to be taken. It merely **highlights items for possible investigation**.

Signals that may be extracted from variance trend information

(a) Materials price variances may be favourable for a few months, then shift to adverse variances for the next few months and so on. This could indicate that prices are **seasonal** and perhaps inventory could be built up in cheap seasons.

(b) Regular, perhaps fairly slight, increases in adverse price variances usually indicate the workings of general **inflation**. If desired, allowance could be made for general inflation when flexing the budget.

(c) Rapid large increases in adverse price variances may suggest a sudden **scarcity** of a resource. It may soon be necessary to seek out cheaper substitutes.

Question 7c.2	Trends in variances

Learning outcome A1(f)

A production department has experienced an improving trend in reported labour efficiency variances but a worsening trend in machine running expenses. Suggest possible reasons for these trends and comment on the management action that may be necessary.

1.1.1 Percentage variance charts

A trend in variances is often easier to appreciate when the variances are presented as percentages. These percentages become even easier to interpret and understand when presented graphically.

Example: percentage variance charts

The standard cost of a material is £15 per kg and the standard usage for one unit of product B is 10 kgs. In the first six months of the year actual usage and costs and associated variances have been as follows.

	Output Units	Usage Kgs	Cost £	Price variances £	Usage variances £
January	30	300	4,800	300 (A)	–
February	40	425	6,800	425 (A)	375 (A)
March	35	385	6,160	385 (A)	525 (A)
April	42	465	6,975	–	675 (A)
May	38	420	6,300	–	600 (A)
June	40	435	6,525	–	525 (A)

Required

(a)   Calculate the price and usage variances in percentage terms (based on standard cost or usage).

(b)   Comment on the trend as revealed by the absolute and percentage variances.

(c)   Present a percentage variance chart of the data.

Solution

(a)

	Price variances %		Usage variances %	
January	$6^2/_3$ (A)	(300/4,500 × 100%)*	0	
February	$6^2/_3$ (A)	(425/6,375 × 100%)	6.25 (A)	(25/400 × 100%)**
March	$6^2/_3$ (A)	(385/5,775 × 100%)	10.00 (A)	(35/350 × 100%)
April	–		10.70 (A)	(45/420 × 100%)
May	–		10.50 (A)	(40/380 × 100%)
June	–		8.75 (A)	(35/400 × 100%)

* Price variance ÷ what actual usage should have cost × 100%

** (Actual usage – what should have been used) ÷ what should have been used × 100%

(b)   The absolute price variances indicate that suppliers were charging more than had been anticipated but the price charged appears to be **fluctuating**. The percentage measures show that there was a **temporary blip** of a constant amount in the first quarter of the year. Perhaps a bulk discount was not being claimed, and **corrective action** was taken in April.

There is less to choose between the two approaches for the usage variance. The process seems to have gone out of control in February but corrective action appears to be bringing it back under control. Both absolute and percentage measures show this, but the percentage measures more clearly indicate that the control action is working (compare June and April).

(c)

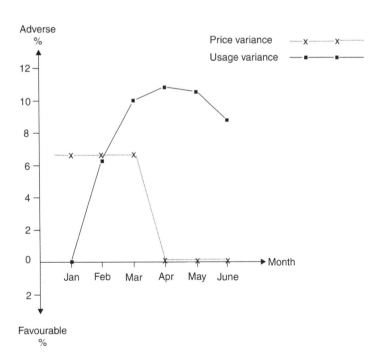

Exam skills

You may be asked to sketch a percentage variance chart in the exam.

Question 7c.3

Learning outcome A1(f)

What conclusion could you reach from the following percentage variance chart?

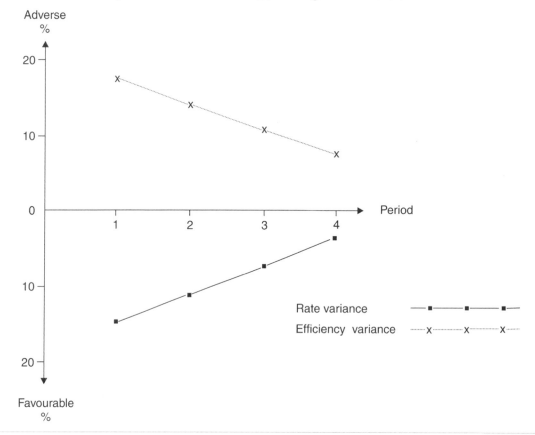

KEY POINT

A variance may represent a small percentage of the standard value but involve significant amounts of money. Both percentages and absolute values should therefore be considered when analysing variances.

1.2 Why might actual and standard performance differ?

Here are some common reasons.

Reason	Comment
Measurement errors	Scales may be misread. Pilfering or wastage may go unrecorded.
Out of date standards	Price standards may become out of date during periods of high inflation. Standards may also become out of date due to technological development.
Efficient or inefficient operations	Spoilage, idle time, better quality material or more highly skilled labour may all affect efficiency of operations.
Random or chance fluctuations	A standard is an average figure. Individual measurements are likely to deviate from the standard.

Section summary

Before investigating variances management should bear in mind materiality, controllability, variance trend, cost, interrelationships and performance standards.

The **efficiency variance** reported in any control period, whether for materials or labour and overhead, will **depend on the efficiency level in the standard cost**.

Individual variances should not be looked at in isolation since one variance might be **interrelated** with another, and much of the variance might have occurred only because the other, interrelated variance occurred too.

Actual and standard performance might differ because of measurement errors, out of date standards, efficient or inefficient operations and/or random or chance fluctuations.

2 Variance investigation models

Introduction

Variance investigation models involve the **rule-of-thumb** model, the **statistical significance model** and **statistical control charts**.

2.1 Rule-of-thumb model

This involves **deciding a limit** and if the size of a **variance is within the limit**, it should be considered **immaterial**. Only if it exceeds the limit is it considered materially significant, and worthy of investigation.

In practice many managers believe that this approach to deciding which variances to investigate is perfectly adequate. However, it has a number of **drawbacks**.

(a)   Should variances be investigated if they exceed 10% of standard? Or 5%? Or 15%?

(b)   Should a different fixed percentage be applied to favourable and unfavourable variances?

(c)   Suppose that the fixed percentage is, say, 10% and an important category of expenditure has in the past been very closely controlled so that adverse variances have never exceeded, say, 2% of standard. Now if adverse variances suddenly shoot up to, say, **8% or 9%** of standard, there might well be **serious excess expenditures incurred that ought to be controlled**, but with the fixed percentage limit at 10%, the variances would not be 'flagged' for investigation.

(d)   **Unimportant categories** of low-cost expenditures might be loosely controlled, with variances commonly exceeding 10% in both a favourable and adverse direction. These would be regularly - and **unnecessarily - flagged for investigation**.

(e)   Where actual expenditures have **normal and expected wide fluctuations** from period to period, but the 'standard' is a fixed expenditure amount, variances will be **flagged for investigation unnecessarily often**.

(f)   There is **no attempt to consider the costs and potential benefits of investigating variances** (except insofar as the pre-set percentage is of 'material significance').

(g)   The **past history of variances in previous periods is ignored**. For example, if the pre-set percentage limit is set at 10% and an item of expenditure has regularly exceeded the standard by, say, 6% per month for a number of months in a row, in all probability there is a situation that ought to warrant control action. Using the pre-set percentage rule, however, the variance would never be flagged for investigation in spite of the cumulative adverse variances.

Some of the difficulties can be overcome by **varying the pre-set percentage from account to account** (for example 5% for direct labour efficiency, 2% for rent and rates, 10% for sales representatives' expenditure, 15% for postage costs, 5% for direct materials price, 3% for direct materials usage and so on). On the other hand, some difficulties, if they are significant, can only be overcome with a different cost-variance investigation model.

2.2 Statistical significance model

The normal distribution and standard deviation were covered in CIMA C3 Fundamentals of Business Maths. You may need to read through your old notes if you have forgotten the concepts.

Historical data are used to **calculate** both a standard as **an expected average** and the **expected standard deviation** around this average when the process is under control. An **in-control process** (process being material usage, fixed overhead expenditure and so on) is one in which any resulting **variance is simply due to random fluctuations** around the expected outcome. An **out-of-control process**, on the other hand, is one in which **corrective action can be taken to remedy any variance**.

By assuming that variances that occur are normally distributed around this average, a **variance will be investigated if it is *more* than a distance from the expected average that the estimated normal distribution suggests is likely if the process is in control**. (Note that such a variance would be deemed significant.)

(a) A 95% or 0.05 significance level rule would state that variances should be investigated if they exceed 1.96 standard deviations from the standard.

(b) A 99% or 0.01 significance level rule would state that variances should be investigated if they exceed 2.58 standard deviations from the standard. This is less stringent than a 0.05 significance level rule.

(c) For simplicity, 1.96 and 2.58 standard deviations can be rounded up to 2 and 3 standard deviations respectively.

For example, data could be collected and analysed to reveal the following pattern.

Mean weight per batch	450 kg
Standard deviation	50 kg

Assume that a 0.05 significance level rule is in use for investigating variances, and that the weights conform to a normal distribution.

Suppose that in June, one sample batch weighed 600kg. 95% of outcomes will be within +/–1.96 standard deviations of the mean. So 95% of outcomes will be in the range 450 +/– (1.96 × 50), that is 352kg to 548kg. The actual weight of this batch was 600kg, so this batch falls outside the 95% limit and the variance should be investigated.

Question 7c.4	Investigating variances

Learning outcomes A1(f), (g)

Data has been collected and analysed and reveals that travel costs per month are Y25,000, with a standard deviation of Y2,000. A 0.01 significance rule is in use. Actual travel expenses are Y28,750. Should the resulting variance be investigated?

The statistical significance rule has two principal **advantages** over the rule of thumb approach.

(a)   **Important costs** that normally vary by only a small amount from standard will be **signalled for investigation if variances increase significantly**.

(b)   Costs that **usually fluctuate by large amounts will not be signalled** for investigation unless variances are extremely large.

The main **disadvantage** of the statistical significance rule is the problem of assessing standard deviations in expenditure.

2.3 Statistical control charts

By marking variances and control limits on a control chart, **investigation** is signalled not only when a particular **variance exceeds the control limit** (since it would be non-random and worth investigating) but also when the **trend of variances shows a progressively worsening movement** in actual results (even though the variance in any single control period has not yet overstepped the control limit).

The $\bar{x}$ **control chart** is based on the principle of the statistical significance model. For each cost item, a chart is kept of monthly variances and **tolerance limits are set at 1, 2 or 3 standard deviations**.

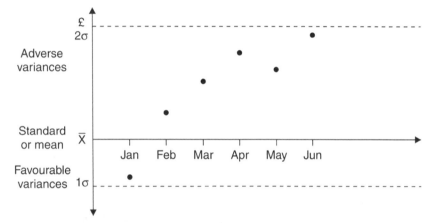

In this example, variances do not exceed the tolerance limits in any month, but the chart shows a worsening of variances over time, and so management might decide that an investigation is warranted, perhaps when it exceeds an inner warning limit.

Using a **cusum chart, the cumulative sum of variances** over a long period of time **is plotted**. If the variances are not significant, these 'sums' will simply fluctuate in a random way above and below the average to give a total or cumulative sum of zero. But if significant variances occur, the cumulative sum will start to develop a positive or negative drift, and when it exceeds a set tolerance limit, the situation must be investigated.

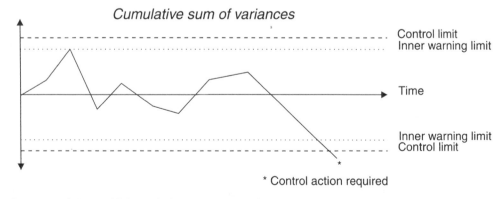

Cumulative sum of variances

* Control action required

The **advantage** of the multiple period approach over the single period approach is that **trends are detectable earlier**, and control action would be introduced sooner than might have been the case if only current-period variances were investigated.

Section summary

Variance investigation models involve the **rule-of-thumb** model, the **statistical significance model** and **statistical control charts**.

3 Joint variances: the controllability principle

Introduction

A **joint** or **composite variance** should be reported to each of the managers jointly responsible for it.

Suppose that a company makes a standard product, which uses six kilograms of material at £2 per kilogram. If actual output during a period is 100 units, which uses 640 kilograms at a cost of £2.30 per kilogram, the variances would be calculated as follows.

		£
640 kilograms should cost (× £2)		1,280
but did cost (× £2.30)		1,472
Price variance		192 (A)

100 units should use (× 6 kgs)		600 kg
but did use		640 kg
Usage variance in kgs		40 kg (A)
× standard cost per kg		× £2
Usage variance in £		£80 (A)

The **usage variance** would probably be **reported to the production manager**, and the **price variance** to the **purchasing manager**. Each would be held responsible for 'controlling' their respective variance item.

This traditional method of reporting fails to show that some of the price variance could have been avoided by the production manager. If the usage of materials had not been adverse, there would have been no need to buy the extra 40 kilograms of material, and the savings would have been 40 kg × £2.30 = £92. The purchasing manager could also have avoided the variance, of course, by buying all the materials at £2 per kilogram. This means that the **excess purchase price of the excess usage of materials could have been avoided by either the purchasing manager or the production manager**.

The name sometimes given to this **adverse price of adverse usage* is a joint or composite variance**, and it may be shown in a diagram as follows.

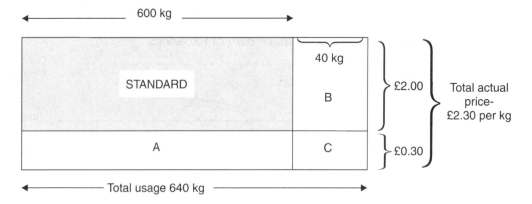

(* A **composite variance could also apply to labour rate and labour efficiency variances**.)

(a)   The traditional price variance is A + C (£192 (A)).

(b)   The traditional usage variance is B (£80(A)).

(c)   However, the composite variance, C, is £0.30 per kg × 40 kg (A) = £12 (A), and so we might
        argue that the composite variance should be reported to each of the managers jointly responsible
        for it.

This is an application of the **controllability principle** in variance reporting. The principle is that managers
should only be held responsible for costs over which they can exercise control.

KEY TERM

A JOINT VARIANCE is 'A variance which is caused by both the prices and quantities of inputs differing from
the specifications in the original standard'.

(CIMA Official Terminology)

Section summary

A **joint** or **composite variance** should be reported to each of the managers jointly responsible for it.

4   Interpreting variances

4.1 Material price variances

Introduction

An **adverse** price variance would suggest that the **managers responsible for buying decisions have paid
too much for the materials**, and should be more careful in future. There are **reasons** why a large adverse
or favourable price variance might occur, however, which are **outside the buying management's control**.

Reason	Comment
Inflation	This was discussed in Chapter 7a.
Seasonal variations in prices	If material prices fluctuate seasonally, the standard price might be an average price for the year as a whole, on the assumption that it is impractical to buy a whole year's supply in the cheap season and store it until needed. In such a situation, price variances should be favourable for purchases in the cheap season and adverse for purchases in the more expensive season.
Rush orders	If buying managers are asked to make an order for immediate delivery, they might have to forgo a bulk purchase discount, or pay more for the quick supply lead time. The responsibility for the resulting adverse price variance should therefore belong to whoever made the rush order necessary in the first place.

Price variances should be **reported in the period when the purchases are made**, not when the materials
are issued from stores and used. This is mainly because control information about price variances ought
to be made available as soon as possible after the buying decision which gave rise to the variance, that is
when the materials are bought.

4.2 Materials usage variances

A materials usage variance indicates that the quantity of materials consumed was larger or smaller than
standard. It could indicate that materials **wastage** was higher or lower than it should have been or that
the quantity of **rejects** was above or below standard. Wastage costs money, and should be kept to a
minimum. The size of a materials usage variance, however, just like the size of a labour efficiency
variance, **depends on the standard rate of usage** (or efficiency) and **whether the standard was attainable
or ideal**.

In certain circumstances it could be worthwhile carrying out further analysis into mix and yield variances. These variances are covered in the next chapter.

4.3 Labour rate variances

It might be tempting to think that the rate variance is something that operational managers can do little about, since rates of pay will be agreed at a senior level. A rate variance might, however, be due to **unexpected overtime working** (with overtime paid at a premium rate) or **productivity bonuses** added on to basic rates. To some extent, these should be **controllable by operational managers.**

4.4 Labour efficiency variances

The labour efficiency variance indicates that the actual production time needed to do the work was longer or less than expected. **Inefficiency costs money**: after all, if it takes three hours to make a unit of product instead of two hours, the unit cost of production will be higher and the profit from selling the unit will be less.

A standard time for labour to produce an item of work will normally take into account **contingency allowances** for down time and rest periods. Whether or not there is an allowance for these factors will depend on the type of **performance standard** used (ideal, attainable and so on). In a production industry based on batch production or jobbing work, the standard time will include an allowance for setting up times and clearing up times for each batch or job finished.

An **adverse** labour efficiency variance might indicate **poor labour productivity** in a period, for which a **badly-motivated** workforce or **weak supervision** might be to blame, but other causes of a variance might be as follows.

- Excessively **high down times**, due to a serious machine break down, or a bottleneck in production which left many of the workforce idle and waiting for work

- **Shorter batch runs** than expected, which increase the amount of setting up time and cleaning up time between batches, when no physical output is being produced

4.5 Overhead variances

Variances are supposed to provide management with **control information**. For example, an adverse material price variance of £100 tells management that the material used cost £100 more than it should have cost. But what about information provided by overhead variances? What control information can managers get from the fact that there is an adverse fixed overhead volume variance of £450? The information is not nearly so clear or understandable as that provided by labour and material variances, is it? But why is this?

4.5.1 Fixed overhead volume variance

Unlike expenditure variances or variable cost efficiency variances, the fixed overhead volume variance is **not a true reflection of the extra or lower cash spending** by an organisation as a result of the variance occurring. This is because the **variance** is **valued** in terms of **overhead absorption rates**. The estimates used in the calculation of these rates are often quite **arbitrary** but it is these absorption rates which determine the value assigned to the **overhead volume variance**.

Together with the expenditure variance, the **fixed overhead volume variance** shows the **under- or over-absorbed fixed overhead**. Under/over absorption is simply a **book balancing exercise**, however, which occurs as a result of the cost ascertainment process of absorption costing, and the level of under-/over-absorbed overhead depends on the **accuracy** of the **original estimates** used in calculating the absorption rates. The level of under/over absorption is **not control information**, it is simply a figure used to balance the books.

Perhaps the overhead volume variance would be more useful, however, if the losses or gains in output were valued in terms of **contribution** rather than in terms of absorption rates (which have arbitrary elements and were designed for quite a different purpose). The existence of a fixed overhead volume variance can therefore be important; it is only the **monetary value** given to the variance that **can be misleading** to managers.

4.5.2 Variable overhead efficiency variance

This arises because labour is either **more** or **less efficient than standard**. Variable production overheads tend to be incurred in **direct proportion** to **production hours** worked, and so if the workforce spends too much time on a job, it will incur not only more labour cost than it should, but also more variable overhead cost too.

4.5.3 Expenditure variances

The **fixed overhead expenditure variance** probably provides the **most useful** management information as the size of the variance can be said to be **controllable**.

(a)　It does have its limitations, however. It is made up of a price component and a usage component. It can therefore vary if there are changes in charges (for example salary increases) or if quantities change (for example if more staff are taken on).

(b)　For such variances to have any practical value as a control measure, the variances for each **cost centre** need to be calculated, and reported to the **managers responsible**. Within each overhead cost centre, the manager should be able to analyse the total variance into indirect **materials** cost variances, indirect **labour** cost variances and excess or favourable spending on other items, such as depreciation, postage and so on.

4.6 Selling price variance

This is perhaps the variance with the **most obvious meaning**. A selling price variance indicates by how much actual selling prices of products or services have exceeded or been less than standard.

Selling price variances will be **common**. Many companies sell their products to customers at a discount, with the size of the discount depending on the size of the order or who the customer is. (For example, regular customers might be given a minimum discount on their purchases, regardless of order quantity). The standard selling price might ignore discounts altogether, or it might have an allowance for the average expected discount. In either event, the actual sales prices and standard sales prices will usually differ.

4.7 Sales volume variance

A sales volume variance will result in **higher-than-expected sales revenue if it is favourable, but there will be an off-setting increase in the cost of sales**. Similarly, an adverse sales volume variance will result in lower-than-expected sales revenue, but there will be an offsetting reduction in the cost of sales.

The **net effect** of a sales volume variance is an **increase or reduction in profitability**, which is valued in terms of **profit margin** when a standard **absorption costing system** is in use and in terms of **contribution** margin, when a standard **marginal costing system** is in use.

4.8 Summary

Variance	Favourable	Adverse
Material price	Unforeseen discounts received Greater care in purchasing Change in material standard	Price increase Careless purchasing Change in material standard
Material usage	Material used of higher quality than standard More efficient use of material Errors in allocating material to jobs	Defective material Excessive waste or theft Stricter quality control Errors in allocating material to jobs
Labour rate	Use of workers at a rate of pay lower than standard	Wage rate increase
Idle time	Idle time was build into budget to allow for bad weather, say, but none occurred	Machine breakdown, illness or injury to worker
Labour efficiency	Output produced more quickly than expected because of worker motivation, better quality materials etc Errors in allocating time to jobs	Lost time in excess of standard Output lower than standard set because of lack of training, sub-standard materials etc Errors in allocating time to jobs
Fixed overhead expenditure	Savings in costs incurred More economical use of services	Increase in cost of services used Excessive use of services Change in type of service used

Overhead expenditure variances ought to be traced to the individual cost centres where the variances occurred.

Fixed overhead volume	Production or level of activity greater than budgeted	Production or level of activity less than budgeted

Question 7c.5

Reasons for variances

Learning outcome A1(f)

M absorbs fixed production overhead at a predetermined rate based on budgeted output. Extracts from the variance analysis for April are as follows.

Fixed production overhead expenditure variance £6,000 (F)
Fixed production overhead volume variance £1,000 (A)

Consider the following statements concerning production in April.

Statement

1   The fixed production overhead was over-absorbed by £5,000
2   Production output was higher than budget
3   Production overhead expenditure was £6,000 lower than budgeted

Which of these statements are consistent with the reported variances?

A   Statements 1 only
B   Statements 2 and 3 only
C   Statements 1 and 3 only
D   Statements 1, 2 and 3 only

| Question 7c.6 | Standard costing and inflation |

Learning outcome A1(f)

Jot down ideas for answering the following questions.

(a) Explain the problems concerning control of operations that a manufacturing company can be expected to experience in using a standard costing system during periods of rapid inflation.

(b) Suggest three methods by which the company could try to overcome the problems to which you have referred in answer to (a) above, indicating the shortcomings of each method.

Section summary

An adverse material price variance may be partly due to inflation and therefore not wholly within the buying management's control.

5 Benchmarking

Introduction

We have seen how standard costing achieves control by the comparison of actual results with a pre-determined standard.

Benchmarking is another type of comparison exercise through which an organisation attempts to improve performance. The idea is to seek the best available performance against which the organisation can monitor its own performance.

KEY TERM

CIMA's *Official Terminology* defines BENCHMARKING as 'The establishment, through data gathering, of targets and comparators, that permit relative levels of performance (and particularly areas of underperformance) to be identified. Adoption of identified best practices should improve performance.'

CIMA lists four types of benchmarking.

Type	Description
Internal benchmarking	A method of comparing one operating unit or function with another within the same organisation
Functional benchmarking	Internal functions are compared with those of the best external practitioners of those functions, regardless of the industry they are in (also known as operational or generic benchmarking)
Competitive benchmarking	Information is gathered about direct competitors, through techniques such as reverse engineering*
Strategic benchmarking	A type of competitive benchmarking aimed at strategic action and organisational change

* **Reverse engineering**: buying a competitor's product and dismantling it, in order to understand its content and configuration

From this list you can see that a benchmarking exercise **does not necessarily have to involve the comparison of operations with those of a competitor**. Indeed, it might be difficult to persuade a direct competitor to part with any information which is useful for comparison purposes. **Functional** benchmarking, for example, **does not always involve direct competitors**. For instance a railway company may be identified as the 'best' in terms of on-board catering, and an airline company that operates on different routes could seek opportunities to improve by sharing information and comparing their own catering operations with those of the railway company.

5.1 Obtaining information

Financial information about competitors is **easier** to acquire than non-financial information. Information about **products** can be obtained from **reverse engineering**, **product literature**, **media comment** and **trade associations**. Information about **processes** (how an organisation deals with customers or suppliers) is more **difficult** to find.

Such information can be obtained from **group companies** or possibly **non-competing organisations in the same industry** (such as the train and airline companies mentioned above).

5.2 Why use benchmarking?

5.2.1 For setting standards

Benchmarking allows **attainable standards** to be established following the examination of both **external and internal information**. If these standards are **regularly reviewed** in the light of information gained through benchmarking exercises, they can become part of a programme of **continuous improvement** by becoming increasingly demanding.

5.2.2 Other reasons

(a)   Its **flexibility** means that it can be used in both the public and private sector and by people at different levels of responsibility.

(b)   Cross comparisons (as opposed to comparisons with similar organisations) are more likely to expose radically **different ways of doing things**.

(c)   It is an **effective method** of **implementing change**, people being involved in identifying and seeking out different ways of doing things in their own areas.

(d)   It identifies the **processes** to improve.

(e)   It helps with **cost reduction**.

(f)   It improves the **effectiveness** of **operations**.

(g)   It delivers services to a **defined standard**.

(h)   It provides a **focus** on **planning**.

(i)   It can provide early **warning** of **competitive disadvantage**.

(j)   It should lead to a greater incidence of **team working** and **cross-functional learning**.

Benchmarking works, it is claimed, for the following reasons.

(a)   The **comparisons** are **carried out** by the **managers** who have to live with any changes implemented as a result of the exercise.

(b)   Benchmarking focuses on improvement in key areas and sets targets which are challenging but 'achievable'. What is *really* achievable can be discovered by examining what others have achieved. Managers are therefore able to accept that they are not being asked to perform miracles.

Care must be taken, however, to ensure that benchmarking exercises are comparing like with like. For example, different accounting policies may produce different results for different businesses. It might be unfair to suggest that one business is more efficient than the other because of a particular figure in a benchmarking report.

| Question 7c.7 | Benchmarking |

Learning outcome A1(g)

We've looked at the advantages of benchmarking. Can you think of any disadvantages?

Section summary

Benchmarking is an attempt to identify best practices and to achieve improved performance by comparison of operations.

Chapter Roundup

✓ Before investigating variances management should bear in mind **materiality**, **controllability**, **variance trend**, **cost**, **interrelationships** and **performance standards**.

✓ The **efficiency variance** reported in any control period, whether for materials or labour and overhead, will **depend on the efficiency level in the standard cost**.

✓ Individual variances should not be looked at in isolation since one variance might be **interrelated** with another, and much of the variance might have occurred only because the other, interrelated variance occurred too.

✓ **Actual and standard performance might differ** because of measurement errors, out of date standards, efficient or inefficient operations and/or random or chance fluctuations.

✓ **Variance investigation models** involve the **rule-of-thumb** model, the **statistical significance model** and **statistical control charts**.

✓ A **joint** or **composite variance** should be reported to each of the managers jointly responsible for it.

✓ An adverse material price variance may be partly due to inflation and therefore not wholly within the buying management's control.

✓ **Benchmarking** is an attempt to identify best practices and to achieve improved performance by comparison of operations.

Quick Quiz

1   Favourable variances are never worthy of investigation because they result in profit increases. *True or false?*

2   Which of the following is not a reason why actual and standard performance might differ?

 A Measurement errors
 B Realistic standards
 C Efficient or inefficient operations
 D Random or chance fluctuations

3   *Choose the correct words from those highlighted.*

 A **cusum/cumus** chart plots **individual/the cumulative sum of** variances **over a period of time/on a one-off basis**.

4   The following variances were reported for period 1.

 Direct labour rate   £2,800 adverse
 Direct labour efficiency   £1,350 favourable

 Which of the following statements are consistent with these variances?

 A Direct labour achieved levels of efficiency which were higher than standard, and were accordingly paid bonuses at higher rates than standard

 B The original standard labour rate was unrealistically low because it failed to take account of rapid wage inflation

 C The production manager elected to use more skilled labour at a higher hourly rate of pay than budgeted

5   If ideal standards are used, reported efficiency variances will tend to be favourable. *True or false?*

6   *Match the type of benchmarking to the descriptions.*

 Type of benchmarking

 Internal; functional; competitive; strategic

 Descriptions

 (a) Information is gathered about direct competitors

 (b) Internal functions are compared with those of the best external practitioners of those functions, regardless of the industry they are in

 (c) One operating unit or function is compared with another within the same industry

 (d) A type of competitive benchmarking aimed at strategic action and organisational change

7   The joint variance based on the excess labour rate over the standard rate and the excess number of hours worked over standard is the responsibility of the production manager. *True or false?*

8   Data has been collected and reveals that labour times for a batch of product C have a mean standard labour time of 48 hours. Assume that the times conform to a normal distribution and that the standard deviation is 4 hours. The company policy is to investigate variances that fall outside the range that includes 95% of outcomes. In June, one batch took 57 hours.

 Should this be investigated?

Answers to Quick Quiz

1   False. Variances are interrelated so one favourable variance could be the cause of a more significant adverse variance. This may result in a profit decrease.

2   B. Out of date standards would cause a difference.

3   A cusum chart plots the cumulative sum of variances over a period of time.

4   All of the statements are consistent with the reported variances.

5   False. They will tend to be adverse.

6   Internal benchmarking   (c)
    Functional benchmarking   (b)
    Competitive benchmarking (a)
    Strategic benchmarking   (d)

7   True – although it is also the responsibility of the manager responsible for labour rates.

8   95% of the outcomes will be within +/–1.96 standard deviations of the mean. So 95% of outcomes will be in the range 48 +/– (1.96 × 4), that is 40.16 hours to 55.84 hours. The actual number of hours was 57, so this batch falls outside the 95% limit and should be investigated.

Answers to Questions

7c.1 Interdependence between variances

The correct answer is A.

A higher paid and hence more skilled workforce could use materials most efficiently.

7c.2 Trends in variances

Gradually improving labour efficiency variances may signal that the **employees** were **inexperienced** at first and that the standard time was set based upon measures taken in the early stages of production. However the employees are now **increasing in speed as they learn the task** and the efficiency variances are improving as a result.

Alternatively the improving trend could indicate the success of a recently introduced **productivity bonus scheme** which has not been incorporated into the standard cost.

In either case opportunities should be sought to encourage the trend and the standard cost should be **revised** if it is to **remain useful** for control purposes.

Another reason, which may be connected with the increased machine running expense, is that employees are operating the machine at a higher speed than expected in the standard, thus **improving the rate of output** and the labour efficiency variance, but increasing the machine running expenses. Management will need to investigate the overall effect of these changes on total costs and on the product quality.

The worsening trend in machine running expenses may be the result of operating the machines at a faster speed than standard, thus **increasing the power costs**. Another possible cause is that the **equipment may be deteriorating** and will soon need repair or even replacement. Management will need to investigate whether repair or replacement of the machine is necessary.

7c.3 Percentage variance chart

These variances could be **interrelated**. As the rate has increased (reducing favourable percentage rate variance), the efficiency has tended more closer to standard levels (reducing percentage adverse efficiency variance).

Since both variances are tending towards a zero percentage it may not be necessary to undertake detailed investigation at this stage.

(Such conclusions may not have been immediately apparent from absolute figures.)

7c.4 Investigating variances

Variance

	Y
Travel costs should have been	25,000
But were	28,750
	3,750 (A)

Number of standard deviations = 3,750/2,000 = 1.875

At a 99% significance level rule, variances should be investigated if they exceed 2.58 standard deviations from the standard. Therefore this variance would not be investigated.

7c.5 Reasons for variances

The correct answer is C.

Statement 1 is correct because over-absorbed fixed overhead is represented by a favourable total overhead variance.

If the production output was higher than budget, the volume variance would be favourable. Statement 2 is incorrect.

The expenditure variance is favourable therefore actual overhead expenditure was lower than budgeted.

Statement 3 is correct.

7c.6 Standard costing and inflation

(a)　(i)　Inflation should be budgeted for in standard prices. But **how** can the rate of inflation and the timing of inflationary increases be accurately **estimated**? Who decides **how much inflationary 'allowance'** should be added to each manager's expenditure budget?

　　(ii)　How can actual expenditure be judged against a **realistic 'standard' price level**. Ideally, there would be an external price index (for example, one published by the Office for National Statistics) but even external price indices are not reliable guides to the prices an organisation ought to be paying.

　　(iii)　The existence of inflation tends to **eliminate the practical value of price variances** as a pointer to controlling spending.

　　(iv)　Inflation affects operations more directly. Usually costs go up before an organisation can put up the prices of its own products to customers. Inflation therefore tends to **put pressure on a company's cash flows**.

　　(v)　To provide useful and accurately-valued variances (accurate efficiency variances as well as reliable price variances) the **standard costs ought to be revised frequently**. This would be an administrative burden on the organisation.

　　(vi)　If the organisation uses standard costs for pricing or inventory valuation, frequent revisions of the standard would be necessary to keep prices ahead of costs or inventories sensibly valued.

(b)　To overcome the problems, we could suggest the following.

　(i)　**Frequent revision** of the standard costs. **Problem** - the administrative burden.

　(ii)　**Incorporating estimates** of the rate of inflation and the timing of inflation into budget expenditure allowances and standard costs. **Problem** - accurate forecasting.

　(iii)　Constructing **internal indices** of material prices to measure what actual price levels should have been. **Problem** - the administrative burden of constructing and maintaining the index.

　(iv)　A **determined effort** by management to **keep costs down**, and resist unnecessary spending. Cost control can minimise the damaging effects of price inflation. **Problem** - obtaining the cooperation of all management and employees in cost control efforts.

7c.7 Benchmarking

- Difficulties in deciding which activities to benchmark
- Identifying the 'best in class' for each activity
- Persuading other organisations to share information
- Successful practices in one organisation may not transfer successfully to another
- The danger of drawing incorrect conclusions from inappropriate comparisons

FURTHER VARIANCE ANALYSIS

 Chapter 7c should have **refreshed your memory** on the basics of standard costing and those variances which you should have covered in your earlier studies.

We begin this chapter by looking at how we can reconcile between **budgeted profit** and **actual profit**, using the range of variances we covered in Chapter 7b to draw up an **operating statement**.

Section 2 considers the impact on variance analysis of using **marginal costing**, which we covered at various points in the last chapter but will consolidate here.

Section 3 is about what we call the '**backwards** approach' to variance analysis. Basically, this means that you are provided with the variances and have to calculate standard and actual data.

The chapter then moves on to more advanced variance analysis. When a product requires **two or more materials** in its make-up the materials usage variance can be split into a **materials mix variance** and a **materials yield variance**. Likewise, labour efficiency variances can be split into a **labour mix variance** and a **labour yield variance**. Don't be put off by these new terms. The **basic principle of variance calculation** covered in the previous chapter **still applies**: an actual result is compared with an original standard result.

topic list	learning outcomes	syllabus references	ability required
1 Operating statements	A1(d)	A1(vi)(viii)	application
2 Variances in a standard marginal costing system	A1(f)	A1(vi)(viii)	analysis
3 Working backwards approach to variance analysis	A1(f)	A1(vi)	analysis
4 Materials mix and yield variances	A1(f)	A1(vii)	analysis
5 Labour mix and yield variances	A1(f)	A1(vii)	analysis
6 Sales mix and quantity variances	A1(f)	A1(xi)	analysis
7 Planning and operational variances	A1(f)	A1(ix)	analysis

1 Operating statements

Introduction

So far, we have considered how variances are calculated without considering how they combine to **reconcile the difference between budgeted profit and actual profit** during a period. This reconciliation is usually presented as a report to senior management at the end of each control period. The report is called an **operating statement** or statement of variances.

KEY TERM

An OPERATING STATEMENT is a report for management, normally prepared on a regular basis showing actual costs and revenues, usually comparing actual with budget and showing variances.

An extensive example will now be introduced, both to revise the variance calculations from Chapter 7b, and also to show how to combine them into an operating statement.

Example: variances and operating statements

Sydney manufactures one product, and the entire product is sold as soon as it is produced. There are no opening or closing inventories and work in progress is negligible. The company operates a standard absorption costing system and analysis of variances is made every month. The standard cost card for the product, a boomerang, is as follows.

STANDARD COST CARD – BOOMERANG

		£
Direct materials	0.5 kgs at £4 per kg	2.00
Direct wages	2 hours at £2.00 per hour	4.00
Variable overheads	2 hours at £0.30 per hour	0.60
Fixed overhead	2 hours at £3.70 per hour	7.40
Standard cost		14.00
Standard profit		6.00
Standing selling price		20.00

Selling and administration expenses are not included in the standard cost, and are deducted from profit as a period charge.

Budgeted output for the month of June year 7 was 5,100 units. Actual results for June year 7 were as follows.

Production of 4,850 units was sold for £95,600.
Materials consumed in production amounted to 2,300 kgs at a total cost of £9,800.
Labour hours paid for amounted to 8,500 hours at a cost of £16,800.
Actual operating hours amounted to 8,000 hours.
Variable overheads amounted to £2,600.
Fixed overheads amounted to £42,300.
Selling and administration expenses amounted to £18,000.

Required

Calculate all variances and prepare an operating statement for the month ended 30 June year 7.

Solution

(a)

	£
2,300 kg of material should cost(× £4)	9,200
but did cost	9,800
Material price variance	600 (A)

(b)

4,850 boomerangs should use (× 0.5 kgs)	2,425 kg
but did use	2,300 kg
Material usage variance in kgs	125 kg (F)
× standard cost per kg	× £4
Material usage variance in £	£ 500 (F)

(c)

	£
8,500 hours of labour should cost (× £2)	17,000
but did cost	16,800
Labour rate variance	200 (F)

(d)

4,850 boomerangs should take (× 2 hrs)	9,700 hrs
but did take (active hours)	8,000 hrs
Labour efficiency variance in hours	1,700 hrs (F)
× standard cost per hour	× £2
Labour efficiency variance in £	£3,400 (F)

(e) Idle time variance 500 hours (A) × £2   £1,000 (A)

(f)

	£
8,000 hours incurring variable o/hd expenditure should cost	
(× £0.30)	2,400
but did cost	2,600
Variable overhead expenditure variance	200 (A)

(g) Variable overhead efficiency variance in hours is the same as the labour efficiency variance:

1,700 hours (F) × £0.30 per hour   £510 (F)

(h)

	£
Budgeted fixed overhead (5,100 units × 2 hrs × £3.70)	37,740
Actual fixed overhead	42,300
Fixed overhead expenditure variance	4,560 (A)

(i)

	£
Actual production at standard rate (4,850 units × £7.40)	35,890
Budgeted production at standard rate (5,100 units × £7.40)	37,740
Fixed overhead volume variance	1,850 (A)

(j)

Revenue from 4,850 boomerangs should be (× £20)	97,000
but was	95,600
Selling price variance	1,400 (A)

(k) In order to reconcile the budget and actual profit the sales volume variance in units must be valued at the standard profit per unit.

Budgeted sales volume	5,100 units
Actual sales volume	4,850 units
Sales volume variance in units	250 units (A)
× standard profit per unit	× £6
Sales volume profit variance in £	£1,500 (A)

There are several ways in which an operating statement may be presented. Perhaps the most common format is one which reconciles budgeted profit to actual profit. In this example, **sales and administration costs will be introduced at the end of the statement**, so that we shall **begin with 'budgeted profit before sales and administration costs'**.

Sales variances are reported first, and the **total of the budgeted profit and the two sales variances** results in a figure for **'actual sales minus the standard cost of sales'**. The **cost variances** are then reported, and an **actual profit** (before sales and administration costs) calculated. **Sales and administration costs** are then **deducted** to reach the **actual profit**.

SYDNEY – OPERATING STATEMENT JUNE YEAR 7

	£	£	£
Budgeted profit before sales and administration costs (5,100 × £6)			30,600
Sales volume profit variance			1,500 (A)
Budgeted profit from actual sales			29,100
Selling price variance			1,400 (A)
Actual sales minus the standard cost of sales			27,700
Cost variances	(F)	(A)	
	£	£	
Material price		600	
Material usage	500		
Labour rate	200		
Labour efficiency	3,400		
Labour idle time		1,000	
Variable overhead expenditure		200	
Variable overhead efficiency	510		
Fixed overhead expenditure		4,560	
Fixed overhead volume		1,850	
	4,610	8,210	3,600 (A)
Actual profit before sales and admin costs			24,100
Sales and administration costs			18,000
Actual profit, June year 7			6,100

Check		£	£
Sales			95,600
Materials		9,800	
Labour		16,800	
Variable overhead		2,600	
Fixed overhead		42,300	
Sales and administration		18,000	
			89,500
Actual profit			6,100

Exam alert

Operating statements lend themselves well to the longer Section C questions.

Section summary

An **operating statement/statement of variances** is a report, usually to senior management, at the end of a control period, reconciling budgeted profit for the period to actual profit.

2 Variances in a standard marginal costing system

Introduction

At various stages in Chapter 7b we looked at the ways in which variances in a marginal costing system differ from those in an absorption costing system. In this section we will summarise these differences and look at how an operating statement would appear in a marginal costing system.

2.1 How marginal costing variances differ from absorption costing variances

If an organisation uses **standard marginal costing** instead of standard absorption costing, there will be two differences in the way the variances are calculated.

(a)   In marginal costing, fixed costs are not absorbed into product costs and so there are no fixed cost variances to explain any under or over absorption of overheads. There will, therefore, be **no fixed overhead volume variance**. There will be a fixed overhead expenditure variance which is calculated in exactly the same way as for absorption costing systems.

(b)   The **sales volume variance in units** will be valued at **standard contribution margin** (sales price per unit minus variable costs of sale per unit). It will be called the **sales volume contribution variance.**

KEY TERM

The SALES VOLUME CONTRIBUTION VARIANCE is a 'Measure of the effect on contribution of not achieving the budgeted volume of sales.'   *(CIMA Official Terminology)*

Question 8.1   Impact of costing system on variances

Learning outcome A1(d)

What is the monetary difference between absorption costing and marginal costing sales volume variances?

A   Variance in units × selling price per unit
B   Variance in units × contribution per unit
C   Variance in units × fixed overhead absorption rate per unit
D   Sales volume × fixed overhead absorption rate per unit

2.2 Preparing a marginal costing operating statement

Returning once again to the example of Sydney, the variances in a system of standard marginal costing would be as follows.

(a)   There is no fixed overhead volume variance.

(b)   The standard contribution per unit of boomerang is £(20 – 6.60) = £13.40 and so the sales volume contribution variance of 250 units (A) is valued at (× £13.40) = £3,350 (A).

The other variances are unchanged. However, this operating statement differs from an absorption costing operating statement in the following ways.

(a) It **begins with the budgeted contribution** (£30,600 + budgeted fixed production costs £37,740 = £68,340) or 5,100 units × £13.40 per unit.

(b) The subtotal before the analysis of cost variances is **actual sales** (£95,600) **less the standard variable cost of sales (**4,850 × £6.60) = £63,590.

(c) **Actual contribution** is highlighted in the statement.

(d) Budgeted fixed production overhead is adjusted by the fixed overhead expenditure variance to show the **actual fixed production overhead expenditure**.

Therefore a **marginal costing** operating statement might look like this.

SYDNEY – OPERATING STATEMENT JUNE YEAR 7

	£	£	£
Budgeted contribution			68,340
Sales volume contribution variance			3,350 (A)
Budgeted contribution from actual sales			64,990
Selling price variance			1,400 (A)
Actual sales minus the standard variable cost of sales			63,590
Variable cost variances	(F)	(A)	
	£	£	
Material price		600	
Material usage	500		
Labour rate	200		
Labour efficiency	3,400		
Labour idle time		1,000	
Variable overhead expenditure		200	
Variable overhead efficiency	510		
	4,610	1,800	
			2,810 (F)
Actual contribution			66,400
Budgeted fixed production overhead		37,740	
Expenditure variance		4,560(A)	
Less: Actual fixed production overhead			(42,300)
Actual profit before sales and administration costs			24,100
Less: Sales and administration costs			(18,000)
Actual profit			6,100

Notice that the actual profit is the same as the profit calculated by standard absorption costing because there were no changes in inventory levels. Absorption costing and marginal costing do not normally produce an identical profit figure.

Question 8.2
Operating statement

Learning outcome A1(d)

MilBri, a manufacturing firm, operates a standard marginal costing system. It makes a single product, LI, using a single raw material AN.

Standard costs relating to LI have been calculated as follows.

Standard cost schedule - LI

	Per unit
	£
Direct material, AN, 100 kg at £5 per kg	500
Direct labour, 10 hours at £8 per hour	80
Variable production overhead, 10 hours at £2 per hour	20
	600

The standard selling price of a LI is £900 and MilBri produce 1,020 units a month. Budgeted fixed production overheads are £40,000 per month.

During December, 1,000 units of LI were produced and sold. Relevant details of this production are as follows.

Direct material AN

90,000 kgs costing £720,000 were bought and used.

Direct labour

8,200 hours were worked during the month and total wages were £63,000.

Variable production overhead

The actual cost for the month was £25,000.

Fixed production overhead

The actual expenditure for the month was £41,400

Each LI was sold for £975.

Required

Calculate the following for the month of December and present the results in an operating statement which reconciles the budgeted contribution with the actual gross profit for the month.

(a)   Variable production cost variance
(b)   Direct labour cost variance, analysed into rate and efficiency variances
(c)   Direct material cost variance, analysed into price and usage variances
(d)   Variable production overhead variance, analysed into expenditure and efficiency variances
(e)   Selling price variance
(f)   Sales volume contribution variance
(g)   Fixed production overhead expenditure variance

2.3 The inventory adjustment

If **actual sales and production volumes** are **different**, there will be a **closing inventory** value in the actual profit calculation. If these inventories are **valued at actual cost** rather than standard cost, an **inventory adjustment** must be made in **the operating statement**.

Inventory adjustment = difference between inventory at standard cost and inventory at actual cost,
                    where inventory at actual cost = ((units in closing inventory ÷ production
                    volume) × total of actual production costs)

This **difference** is simply **added to the bottom of the operating statement**.

	£	£
Actual profit, with inventory at standard cost		X
Inventory adjustment		
inventory at standard cost	X	
inventory at actual cost	X	
		X
Actual profit, with inventory at actual cost		X

KEY POINT

An inventory adjustment is **only needed if inventory is valued at actual cost** (either marginal or total absorption) in the actual income statement.

Section summary

In a **standard marginal costing system**, there will no fixed overhead volume variance and the sales volume variance will be valued at standard contribution margin, not standard profit margin.

3 Working backwards approach to variance analysis

Introduction

Examination questions usually provide you with data about actual results and you have to calculate variances. One way in which your understanding of the topic can be tested, however, is to provide information about variances from which you have to '**work backwards**' to determine the actual results.

Example: working backwards

The standard cost card for the trough, one of the products made by Pig, is as follows.

	£
Direct material 16 kgs × £6 per kg	96
Direct labour 6 hours × £12 per hour	72
Fixed production overhead 6 hours × £14 per hour	84
	252

Pig reported the following variances in control period 13 in relation to the trough.

Direct material price: £18,840 favourable   Fixed production overhead expenditure: £14,192 adverse
Direct material usage: £480 adverse   Fixed production overhead volume: £11,592 favourable
Direct labour rate: £10,598 adverse
Direct labour efficiency: £8,478 favourable

Actual fixed production overhead cost £200,000 and direct wages, £171,320. Pig paid £5.50 for each kg of direct material. There were no opening or closing inventories of the material.

Required

Calculate the following.

(a)   Budgeted output   (d)   Average actual wage rate per hour
(b)   Actual output   (e)   Actual number of kilograms purchased and used
(c)   Actual hours worked

Solution

(a)   Let budgeted output = q

     Fixed production overhead expenditure variance = budgeted overhead – actual overhead
                                                   = £(84q – 200,000) = £14,192 (A)

     Therefore   84q –   200,000 = –14,192
                    84q   = –14,192 + 200,000
                       q   =   185,808 ÷ 84

     Therefore q   =   2,212 units*

(b)

	£
Total direct wages cost	171,320
Adjust for variances:	
labour rate	(10,598)
labour efficiency	8,478
Standard direct wages cost	169,200

     ∴ Actual output   = Total standard cost ÷ unit standard cost
                        = £169,200 ÷ £72 = 2,350 units

(c)

	£
Total direct wages cost	171,320.0
Less rate variance	(10,598.0)
Standard rate for actual hours	160,722.0
÷ standard rate per hour	÷ £12.0
Actual hours worked	13,393.5 hrs

(d)   Average actual wage rate per hour = actual wages/actual hours = £171,320/13,393.5 = £12.79 per hour.

(e)   Number of kgs purchased and used = x

	£
x kgs should have cost (× £6)	6.0x
but did cost (× £5.50)	5.5x
Direct material price variance	0.5x

$$\therefore \quad £0.5x = £18,840$$
$$\therefore \quad x = 37,680 \text{ kgs}$$

---

* Alternative approach to find budgeted output

	£
Budgeted expenditure (budgeted output × overhead absorption per unit) £84/unit	
Actual expenditure given	200,000
Variance	14,192 (A)

∴ Budgeted expenditure = £200,000 – £14,192 = £185,808

$$\therefore \text{ Budgeted output } = \frac{£185,808}{£84} = 2,212 \text{ units}$$

Question 8.3 Working backwards

Learning outcome A1(f)

The standard material content of one unit of product A is 10kgs of material X which should cost £10 per kilogram. In June, 5,750 units of product A were produced and there was an adverse material usage variance of £1,500.

The quantity of material X used in June was

A   56,000 kg
B   57,350 kg
C   57,650 kg
D   59,000 kg

Section summary

Exam questions might provide you with information about variances from which you have to 'work backwards' to determine the actual results.

4 Materials mix and yield variances

Introduction

When a product requires two or more raw materials in its make-up, it is often possible to sub-analyse the materials usage variance into materials mix and materials yield variances.

Adding a greater proportion of one material (therefore a smaller proportion of a different material) might make the materials mix cheaper or more expensive.

For example the standard mix of materials for a product might consist of the following.

	£
($^2/_3$) 2 kg of material A at £1.00 per kg	2.00
($^1/_3$) 1 kg of material B at £0.50 per kg	0.50
	2.50

It may be possible to change the mix so that one kilogram of material A is used and two kilograms of material B. The new mix would be cheaper.

	£
($^1/_3$) 1 kg of material A	1
($^2/_3$) 2 kg of material B	1
	2

By changing the proportions in the mix, the efficiency of the combined material usage may change. In our example, in making the proportions of A and B cheaper, at 1:2, the product may now require more than three kilograms of input for its manufacture, and the new materials requirement per unit of product might be 3.6 kilograms.

	£
($^1/_3$) 1.2 kg of material A at £1.00 per kg	1.20
($^2/_3$) 2.4 kg of material B at £0.50 per kg	1.20
	2.40

In establishing a materials usage standard, management may therefore have to **balance** the **cost** of a particular **mix** of materials **with** the **efficiency of the yield** of the mix.

Once the standard has been established it may be possible to exercise control over the materials used in production by calculating and reviewing mix and yield variances.

KEY TERMS

'If different materials can be substituted, the [DIRECT MATERIAL] MIX VARIANCE measures the cost of any variation from the standard mix.'

The DIRECT MATERIAL YIELD VARIANCE 'Measures the effect on cost of any difference between the actual material usage and that justified by the output produced.' *(CIMA Official Terminology)*

4.1 Calculating the variances

The mix variance for each material input is based on the following.

(a) The change in the material's weighting within the overall mix

(b) Whether the material's unit standard cost is greater or less than the standard weighted average cost of all material inputs.

A **yield variance** is calculated as the **difference between the standard output from what was actually input**, and the **actual output**, valued at the standard cost per unit of output.

4.2 When to calculate mix and yield variances

Mix and yield variances have no meaning, and should never be calculated, unless they are a guide to control action. They are **only appropriate in the following situations**.

(a)   Where **proportions of materials in a mix are changeable and controllable**. If the materials in a mix are in different units, say kilograms and litres, they are obviously completely different and so cannot be substituted for each other.

(b)   Where the **usage variance of individual materials is of limited value because of the variability of the mix**, and a combined yield variance for all the materials together is more helpful for control.

It would be **totally inappropriate** to calculate a mix **variance where the materials in the 'mix' are discrete items**. A chair, for example, might consist of wood, covering material, stuffing and glue. These materials are separate components, and it would not be possible to think in terms of controlling the proportions of each material in the final product. The usage of each material must be controlled separately.

Example: materials usage, mix and yield variances

A company manufactures a chemical, Dynamite, using two compounds Flash and Bang. The standard materials usage and cost of one unit of Dynamite are as follows.

		£
Flash	5 kg at £2 per kg	10
Bang	10 kg at £3 per kg	30
	15 kg	40

In a particular period, 80 units of Dynamite were produced from 500 kg of Flash and 730 kg of Bang.

Required

Calculate the materials usage, mix and yield variances.

Solution

(a)   **Usage variance**

	Flash	Bang
80 units of Dynamite should have used	400 kgs	800 kgs
but did use	500 kgs	730 kgs
Usage variance in kgs	100 kgs (A)	70 kgs (F)
× standard cost per kg	× £2	× £3
Usage variance in £	£200 (A)	£210 (F)
Total usage variance		£10 (F)

The total usage variance can be analysed into mix and yield variances.

(b)   **Mix variance**

Actual input = (500 + 730) kgs = 1,230 kgs

Standard mix of actual input

Flash 5/15 = 1/3	∴1/3 × 1,230 kgs =	410 kgs
Bang 10/15 = 2/3	∴2/3 × 1,230 kgs =	820 kgs
		1,230 kgs

	'Should' mix Actual quantity Standard mix	'Did' mix Actual quantity Actual mix	Difference	Standard price	Variance
Flash	410kg	500kg	90kg (A)	£2	£180 (A)
Bang	820kg	730kg	90kg (F)	£3	£270 (F)
	1,230kg	1,230kg	–		£90 (F)

The **total difference** or mix variance in **kgs** must **always** be **zero** as the mix variance measures the change in the relative proportions of the actual total input. The variance is calculated by comparing the expected mix of the total actual input with the actual mix of the total actual input: the difference between the two totals is zero.

The favourable total variance is due to the greater use in the mix of the cheaper material, Flash. However, this cheaper mix may have an adverse effect on the yield which is obtained from the mix, as we shall now see.

(c)   **Yield variance**

Each unit of output (Dynamite) requires

	5 kg	of Flash, costing	£10
	10 kg	of Bang, costing	£30
	15 kg		£40

Actual input

1,230 kg should have yielded (÷ 15 kg)	82 units of Dynamite
but did yield	80 units of Dynamite
Yield variance in units	2 units (A)
× standard cost per unit of output	× £40
Yield variance in £	£80 (A)

The adverse yield variance is due to the output from the input being less than standard.

The mix variance and yield variance together add up to the usage variance, which is favourable, because the adverse yield from the mix did not negate the price savings which were made by using proportionately more of the cheaper material.

KEY POINT

CIMA recommends two approaches to valuing mix variances. **Either or both may be tested**, because both methods are on your syllabus. The one above (valuing the individual mix variances in units at the **individual standard prices**) is the easier of the two and so, if given a choice, we recommend that it is the approach you use. The second approach is shown below.

4.3 Mix variances: Alternative approach

This approach uses a **weighted average price** to value the individual mix variances in units.

The standard weighted average price of the input materials is £40/15kg = £2.67 per kg.

	'Should' mix Actual quantity Standard mix	'Did' mix Actual quantity Actual mix	Difference*	£ (W1)	Variance**
Flash	410kg	500kg	90kg more	× £0.67 less	£60 (F)
Bang	820kg	730kg	90kg less	× £0.33 more	£30 (F)
	1,230kg	1,230kg			

Workings

Flash

Difference between weighted average price and standard price	= £(2.67 − 2)
	= £0.67 less than average

Bang

Difference between weighted average price and standard price	= £(2.67 − 3)
	= £0.33 more than average

* Here we calculate a **difference in units** (more or less than standard) rather than a variance.

** **To determine whether a mix variance is (A) or (F) using the weighted average method see below.**

	Variance
Input more than standard of a material **costing more** than average	(A)
Input more than standard of a material **costing less** than average	(F)
Input less than standard of a material **costing more** than average	(F)
Input less than standard of a material **costing less** than average	(A)

In this example:

More Flash than standard was input, and Flash **costs** less than the average price, so the variance is **favourable**.

Less Bang than standard was input, and Bang **costs more** than the average price, so the variance is **favourable**.

Question 8.4   Mix and yield variances

Learning outcome A1(f)

The standard materials cost per unit of product D456 is as follows.

	£
Material X 3 kg at £2.00 per kg	6
Material Y 5 kg at £3.60 per kg	18
8̲ kg	2̲4̲

During period 2, 2,000 kg of material X costing £4,100 and 2,400 kg of material Y costing £9,600 were used to produce 500 units of D456.

Required

Calculate price, mix and yield variances.

Question 8.5   Limitations of mix and yield variances

Learning outcome A1(f)

Explain briefly the limitations of the calculation of materials mix and yield variances.

Summary

- Both methods are based on individual mix **variances in units** calculated as the **difference between actual input and the standard mix of actual input**.

- The **total mix variance in units** is **zero** using **both methods**.

- The **first method values** the individual mix variances in units at the **individual standard prices**.

- The **second method values** the individual mix variances in units at the **difference between the weighted average price and the standard price**.

- The **total mix variance** in £ is the **same** under both methods.

4.4 Deviations from standardised mix

In an exam question under an old syllabus, candidates were given the percentage deviations for standardised mix and the data used to calculate those deviations. They then had to calculate deviations for a third month and comment on the usefulness of such analysis for operational control.

The question stated that the deviations were shown in weight and were from the standard mix for the quantity input expressed as a percentage of the standardised weight for each ingredient. This sounds complicated but is actually referring to the individual mix variances in units (think about it!). And because source data for the figures shown was provided, candidates could check their understanding of the method of calculation.

Try the question below, to see whether you could have coped with the exam question.

| Question 8.6 | Deviations from standardised mix |

Learning outcome A1(f)

Standard mix for one litre of product J

0.4 litres of ingredient O
0.2 litres of ingredient H
0.5 litres of ingredient N

Actual usage in control period 2

Ingredient O	420 litres
Ingredient H	180 litres
Ingredient N	550 litres
Actual output	1,000 litres

Calculate the percentage deviation from the standardised mix using the method of calculation described above.

Section summary

When two or more types of material are mixed together to produce a product it is possible to carry out further analysis on the usage variance. The **mix variance** explains how much of the usage variance was caused by a change in the relative proportions of the materials used. The **yield variance** shows how much of the usage variance was caused by using more or less material than the standard allowance.

The purpose of a mix variance is to provide management with information to help in controlling the proportion of each item actually used. If it is not possible for managers to exercise control over the actual mix of material then there is little to be gained by calculating mix variances.

5 Labour mix and yield variances

Introduction

If more than one type of labour is used in a product, the labour efficiency variance can be analysed further into a **labour mix (team composition) variance** and a **labour yield (team productivity or output) variance**.

KEY TERMS

'Where substitutions between the grades of labour used to operate a process are possible, the [DIRECT LABOUR] MIX VARIANCE measures the cost of any variation from the standard mix'.

The DIRECT LABOUR YIELD VARIANCE 'Measures the effect on cost of any difference between the actual labour hours worked and the hours justified by output produced.' *(CIMA Official Terminology)*

The labour mix variance is also known as the **team composition variance**, the labour yield variance as the **labour output variance** or **team productivity variance**.

The calculations are the same as those required for materials mix and yield variances.

KEY POINT

Don't confuse labour efficiency with labour yield variances. Remember that the labour efficiency variance is the total of the labour mix and labour yield variances.

Example: labour mix variances

Two grades of labour work together in teams to produce product X. The standard composition of each team is five grade A employees paid at £6 per hour and three grade B employees paid at £4 per hour. Output is measured in standard hours and expected output is 95 standard hours for 100 hours worked in total. During the last period, 2,280 standard hours of output were produced using 1,500 hours of grade A labour (costing £9,750) and 852 hours of grade B labour (costing £2,982).

Required

Calculate all possible labour variances.

Solution

Initial working

Calculation of **standard rate per hour of output**

Labour grade

			£
A	5.00	hours × £6 =	30
B	3.00	hours × £4 =	12
	8.00	hours	42
Less 5%	0.40	hours	
	7.60	hours	

∴ Standard rate per hour of output = £42/7.6 = £5.5263 per standard hour

Direct labour total variance

	£
2,280 standard hours of output should have cost (× £5.5263)	12,600
but did cost	12,732
Direct labour total variance	132 (A)

Direct labour rate variance

		A £		B £
Actual hours worked should have cost	(1,500 × £6)	9,000	(852 × £4)	3,408
but did cost		9,750		2,982
Direct labour rate variance		750 (A)		426 (F)
Total direct labour rate variance			£324 (A)	

Direct labour efficiency variance

		A		B
2,280 standard hours of output				
should take an input of	(2,280 ÷ 0.95 × ⁵/₈)	1,500 hrs	(2,280 ÷ 0.95 × ³/₈)	900 hrs
but did take		1,500 hrs		852 hrs
Efficiency variance in hours		–		48 hrs (F)
× standard rate per hour		× £6		× £4
		–		£192 (F)

The **labour efficiency variance** can be analysed further into the **team composition** variance (the **labour mix** variance) and the **team productivity** variance (the **labour yield** variance).

Team composition (labour mix) variance

Again there are two approaches to valuing the variance.

Approach 1

Total actual hours = 1,500 + 852 = 2,352 hours

Standard mix of actual input

		Hrs
A	5/8 × 2,352 =	1,470
B	3/8 × 2,352 =	882
		2,352

	'Should' mix Actual hrs Standard mix	'Did' mix Actual hrs Actual mix	Difference	× Standard price	Variance
A	1,470 hrs	1,500 hrs	30 hrs (A)	× £6	£180 (A)
B	882 hrs	852 hrs	30 hrs (F)	× £4	£120 (F)
	2,352 hrs	2,352 hrs	–		£60 (A)

Approach 2

The standard weighted rate per hour of labour is £42/8 = £5.25 per hour.

	'Should' mix Actual hrs Standard mix	'Did' mix Actual hrs Actual mix	Difference	£ (W1)	Variance
X	1,470 hrs	1,500 hrs	30 hrs more	× £0.75 more	£22.50 (A)
Y	882 hrs	852 hrs	30 hrs less	× £1.25 less	£37.50 (A)
	2,352 hrs	2,352 hrs	–		£60.00 (A)

Workings

	X	Y
Difference between w/av price and std price	£(5.25 – 6) = £0.75 more	£(5.25 – 4) = £1.25 less

Team productivity (labour yield) variance

2,352 hours of work should have produced (× 0.95)	2,234.4 std hrs
but did produce	2,280.0 std hrs
Team productivity variance in hrs	45.6 std hrs (F)
× std rate per std hr	× £5.5263
Team productivity variance in £	£252 (F)

Question 8.7

Learning outcome A1(f)

A firm has established the following standard composition of a team of its staff performing the year end audit of a medium-sized company.

	Standard hours to perform audit	Rate per hour $	Standard labour cost of audit $
Audit manager	30	450	13,500
Junior auditors	120	170	20,400
Audit clerks	50	50	2,500
	200		36,400

A year end audit has just been completed for company X and the hours recorded in respect of each grade of staff are as follows.

	Actual hours to perform audit
Audit manager	27
Junior auditors	125
Audit clerks	58
	210

Required

Calculate the following labour variances for the company X audit.

(a) The labour efficiency variance
(b) The labour yield variance
(c) The labour mix variance, using the weighted average valuation basis

---

Variance tree diagram

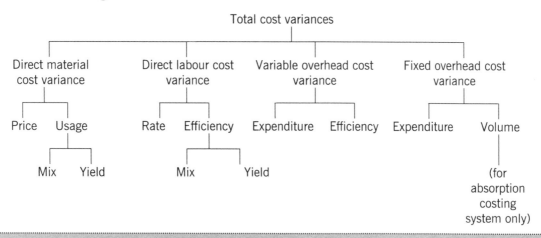

Section summary

If more than one type of labour is used in a product, the labour efficiency variance can be analysed further into a **labour mix (team composition) variance** and a **labour yield (team productivity or output) variance.**

6 Sales mix and quantity variances

5/11

Introduction

The sales volume profit variance can be analysed further into a sales mix variance and a sales quantity variance.

6.1 Sales volume variance

You learned how to calculate the sales volume variance in Chapter 7b. It measures the increase or decrease in the standard profit or contribution as a result of the sales volume being higher or lower than budgeted. It is calculated as the difference between actual sales units and budgeted sales units, multiplied by the standard profit per unit.

6.2 Sales mix and quantity variances

If a company **sells more than one product**, it is possible to analyse the overall sales volume variance into a sales mix variance and a sales quantity variance.

The SALES MIX VARIANCE occurs when the proportions of the various products sold are different from those in the budget.

The SALES QUANTITY VARIANCE shows the difference in contribution/profit because of a change in sales volume from the budgeted volume of sales.

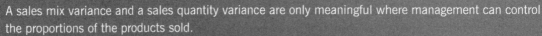

A sales mix variance and a sales quantity variance are only meaningful where management can control the proportions of the products sold.

In particular, sales mix variances are only of use if there is some kind of link between the products in question.

- Complementary products, such as pancake mix and lemon juice
- Substitute products, such as branded and 'own-label' goods
- Same products, different sizes
- Products produced within a limiting factor environment

6.3 The units method of calculation

The sales mix variance is calculated as the difference between the actual quantity sold in the standard mix and the actual quantity sold in the actual mix, valued at standard margin per unit. The sales quantity variance is calculated as the difference between the actual sales volume in the budgeted proportions and the budgeted sales volumes, multiplied by the standard margin.

Example: sales mix and quantity variances

Just Desserts Limited makes and sells two products, Bland Fete and Gotters Dew. The budgeted sales and profit are as follows.

	Sales Units	Revenue £	Costs £	Profit £	Profit per unit £
Bland Fete	400	8,000	6,000	2,000	5
Gotters Dew	300	12,000	11,100	900	3
				2,900	

Actual sales were 280 units of Bland Fete and 630 units of Gotters Dew. The company management is able to control the relative sales of each product through the allocation of sales effort, advertising and sales promotion expenses.

Required

Calculate the sales volume profit variance, the sales mix variance and the sales quantity variance.

Solution

(a)

	Bland Fete	Gotters Dew
Budgeted sales	400 units	300 units
Actual sales	280 units	630 units
Sales volume variance in units	120 units (A)	330 units (F)
× standard margin per unit	× £5	× £3
Sales volume variance in £	£600 (A)	£990 (F)
Total **sales volume variance**	£390 (F)	

The favourable sales volume variance indicates that a potential increase in profit was achieved as a result of the change in sales volume compared with budgeted volume. Now we will see how to analyse this favourable variance into its mix and quantity elements.

(b)   When we look at the mix of sales in this example it is apparent that a bigger proportion than budgeted of the less profitable Gotters Dew has been sold, therefore the **sales mix variance** will be adverse. The method for calculating the variance is as follows.

(i)   Take the **actual total of sales** and **convert** this total into a **standard or budgeted mix**, on the assumption that sales should have been in the budgeted proportions or mix.

(ii)   The difference between actual sales and 'standard mix' sales for each product is then converted into a variance by multiplying by the standard margin.

		Units
Total quantity sold (280 + 630)		910
Budgeted mix for actual sales:	4/7 Bland Fete	520
	3/7 Gotters Dew	390
		910

	'Should' mix Actual quantity Standard mix	'Did' mix Actual quantity Actual mix	Difference	× Standard margin	Variance
Bland Fete	520 units	280 units	240 (A)	× £5	£1,200 (A)
Gotters Dew	390 units	630 units	240 (F)	× £3	£720 (F)
	910 units	910 units	–		£480 (A)

The profit would have been £480 higher if the 910 units had been sold in the budgeted mix of 4:3.

(c)   The **sales quantity variance** is calculated as follows.

	Actual sales Standard mix	Standard sales Standard mix	Difference in units	× Standard profit	Variance
Bland Fete	520 units	400 units	120 units (F)	× £5	£600 (F)
Gotters Dew	390 units	300 units	90 units (F)	× £3	£270 (F)
	910 units	700 units	210 units		£870 (F)

Summary

	£
Sales mix variance	480 (A)
Sales quantity variance	870 (F)
Sales volume profit variance	390 (F)

If an organisation uses **standard marginal costing** instead of standard absorption costing then standard **contribution** rather than standard **profit margin** is used in the calculations.

Exam skills

Try not to confuse the sales volume profit variance with the sales quantity profit variance.

Section summary

The sales volume profit variance can be analysed further into a sales mix variance and a sales quantity variance.

7 Planning and operational variances

Introduction

To date in your studies, we have been looking at variances which are calculated using what we will call the **conventional approach** to variance analysis, whereby an **actual cost** is **compared** with an **original standard cost**. In this section of the chapter we will be examining **planning** and **operational variances**. They are not really alternatives to the conventional approach, they merely provide a much **more detailed analysis**.

KEY TERMS

A PLANNING VARIANCE (or REVISION VARIANCE) compares an original standard with a revised standard that should or would have been used if planners had known in advance what was going to happen.

An OPERATIONAL VARIANCE (or OPERATING VARIANCE) compares an actual result with the revised standard.

EX ANTE means original budget/standard. EX POST means revised budget/standard.

Planning and operational variances are based on the principle that variances ought to be reported by taking as the **main starting point**, not the original standard, but a **standard** which can be seen, in hindsight, to be the **optimum** that should have been **achievable**.

This idea is that the monetary value of variances ought to be a realistic reflection of what the causes of the variances have cost the organisation. In other words they should show the cash (and profit) gained or lost as a consequence of operating results being different to what should have been achieved. Variances can be valued in this way by **comparing actual results with a realistic standard or budget**. Such variances are called **operational variances**.

Planning variances arise because the **original standard and revised more realistic standards are different** and have nothing to do with operational performance. In most cases, it is unlikely that anything could be done about planning variances: they are **not controllable by operational managers but by senior management**.

In other words the **cause of a total variance** might be one or both of the following.

- Adverse or favourable operational performance (**operational variance**)
- Inaccurate planning, or faulty standards (**planning variance**)

KEY TERMS

The CIMA *Official Terminology* defines an OPERATIONAL VARIANCE as 'Classification of variances in which non-standard performance is defined as being that which differs from an *ex post* standard. Operational variances can relate to any element of the standard product specification.'

The CIMA *Official Terminology* defines PLANNING VARIANCES as 'Classification of variances caused by *ex ante* budget allowances being changed to an *ex post* basis. Also known as revision variances.'

7.1 Calculating total planning and operational variances

We will begin by looking at how to split a total cost variance into its planning and operational components.

Example: total cost planning and operational variances

At the beginning of 20X0, WB set a standard marginal cost for its major product of £25 (5kg x £5) per unit. The standard cost is recalculated once each year. Actual production costs during August 20X0 were £304,000, when 8,000 units were made.

With the benefit of hindsight, the management of WB realises that a more realistic standard cost for current conditions would be £40 (4kg x £10) per unit. The planned standard cost of £25 is unrealistically low.

Required

Calculate the planning and operational variances.

Solution

With the benefit of hindsight, the **realistic standard should have been £40**. The variance caused by favourable or adverse **operating** performance should be calculated by comparing actual results against this realistic standard.

	£
Revised std cost for revised std kg for actual output (£10 x 4kg x 8,000)	320,000
Actual cost	304,000
Total **operational** variance	16,000 (F)

The variance is favourable because the actual cost was lower than would have been expected using the revised basis. (You can still think of this in terms of 'should have cost' but 'did cost' in your mind to help you decide whether it's adverse or favourable.)

The **planning** variance reveals the extent to which the original standard was at fault.

		£
Revised std cost for revised kg for actual output	£10 × 4kg ×8,000	320,000
Original std cost for original kg for actual output	£5 × 5kg ×8,000	200,000
Planning variance		120,000 (A)

It is an adverse variance because the original standard was too optimistic, overestimating the expected profits by understating the standard cost. More simply, it is adverse because the revised cost is much higher than the original cost.

	£
Planning variance	120,000 (A)
Operational variance	16,000 (F)
Total	104,000 (A)

If **traditional variance analysis** had been used, the total cost variance would have been the same, but **all the 'blame' would appear to lie on actual results** and operating inefficiencies (rather than some being due to faulty planning).

	£
Standard cost of 8,000 units (× £25)	200,000
Actual cost of 8,000 units	304,000
Total cost variance	104,000 (A)

Question 8.8

Total planning and operational variances

Learning outcome A1(f)

Suppose a budget is prepared which includes a raw materials cost per unit of product of £2 (2 kg of copper at £1 per kg). Due to a rise in world prices for copper during the year, the average market price of copper rose to £1.50 per kg. During the year, 1,000 units were produced at a cost of £3,250 for 2,200 kg of copper.

The planning and operational variances are

	Operational variance	*Planning variance*
A	£250 (A)	£1,000 (A)
B	£250 (A)	£1,100 (A)
C	£250 (F)	£1,000 (F)
D	£250 (A)	£1,000 (F)

7.2 Operational price and usage variances

So far we have only considered planning and operational variances in total, without carrying out the usual two-way split. In question 6.8 above, for instance, we identified a total operational variance for materials of £250 without considering whether this operational variance could be split between a usage variance and a price variance.

This is not a problem so long as you retain your grasp of knowledge you already possess. You know that a **price** variance measures the difference between the actual amount of money paid and the amount of money that should have been paid for that quantity of materials (or whatever). Thus, in our example:

	£
Revised std price of actual purchases (£1.50 × 2,200 kg)	3,300
Actual price of actual purchases (2,200 kg)	3,250
Operational price variance	50 (F)

The variance is favourable because the materials were purchased more cheaply than would have been expected.

Similarly, a **usage** variance measures the difference between the actual physical quantity of materials used or hours taken and the quantities that should have been used or taken for the actual volume of production. Those physical differences are then converted into money values by applying the appropriate standard cost.

In our example we are calculating **operational variances**, so we are not interested in planning errors. This means that the **appropriate standard cost is the revised standard cost** of £1.50.

Actual output should have used	2,000 kgs
but did use	2,200 kgs
Operational usage variance in kgs	200 kgs (A)
× revised standard cost per kg	× £1.50
Operational usage variance in £	£300 (A)

The two variances of course reconcile to the total variance as previously calculated.

	£
Operational price variance	50 (F)
Operational usage variance	(300) (A)
Total operational variance	250 (A)

7.3 Operational variances for labour and overheads

Precisely the same argument applies to the calculation of operational variances for labour and overheads, and the examples already given should be sufficient to enable you to do the question below.

Question 8.9	Planning and operational variances

Learning outcome A1(f)

A new product requires three hours of labour per unit at a standard rate of £6 per hour. In a particular month the budget is to produce 500 units. Actual results were as follows.

Hours worked	1,700
Production	540 units
Wages cost	£10,500

Within minutes of production starting it was realised that the job was extremely messy and the labour force could therefore claim an extra 25p per hour in 'dirty money'.

Required

What are the planning and operational variances?

	Planning	Operational rate	Operational efficiency
A	£405 (F)	£125 (F)	£500 (A)
B	£405 (A)	£125 (F)	£500 (A)
C	£405 (F)	£300 (A)	£500 (F)
D	£405 (A)	£300 (F)	£480 (A)

7.4 Planning sub-variances

So far we have looked at the total planning variances. Now we'll look at how to calculate specific planning variances.

The labour **rate**/material **price variance** shows the effect of a change in the standard rate or price and is calculated as follows:

	£
The original standard cost for the revised standard hours/kgs etc for actual output was	X
The revised standard cost for the revised hours/kgs etc for actual output is	X
Planning labour rate/material price variance	X

The labour **efficiency**/material **usage** planning variance shows the effect of a change in the standard hours or usage of material per unit and is calculated as follows:

	£
The original standard hours/kgs etc for actual output was	X
The revised standard hours/kgs etc for actual output is	X
Labour efficiency/material usage planning variance in hours/kgs etc	X
× standard rate per hour/standard cost per kg etc	× £ X
Labour efficiency/material usage planning variance in £	X

Example: planning rate variance

Bean Ltd operates a standard absorption costing system. The following information is available for product P:

Budgeted production	3,000 units
Direct material cost: 10kg × £2.05	£20.50 per unit

Actual results for the quarter were:

Production	3,200 units	
Direct material (purchased and used): 15,000 kg	£72,000

In retrospect, it is realised that the standard cost for material should have been £2.50 per kg during the period.

Required

Calculate the material price planning variance

Solution

	£
Original std cost for the revised std hours for actual output (£2.05 × 10 kg × 3,200)	65,600
Revised std cost for the revised std hours for actual output (£2.50 × 10 kg × 3,200)	80,000
Material price planning variance	14,400 (A)

7.5 Two planning errors

In the example above there was only one planning error which was the error in the standard cost. It is also possible to make a mistake with the number of standard hours. There would then be two planning errors. The following example includes two planning errors.

Example: two planning errors

A company estimates that the standard direct labour cost for a product should be £20 (4 hours × £5 per hour). Actual production of 1,000 units took 6,200 hours at a cost of £23,800. In retrospect, it is realised that the standard cost should have been 6 hours × £6 per hour = £36 per unit.

Required

Calculate the planning and operational variances.

Solution

(a) **Operational variances**

(i)

1,000 units should take (× 6 hours)	6,000 hrs
but did take	6,200 hrs
Efficiency variance in hours	200 hrs (A)
× revised standard cost per hour	× £6 (A)
Efficiency variance in £	£1,200 (A)

(ii)

	£
Revised std price of actual hrs paid (£6 × 6,200)	37,200
Actual price of actual hours paid	23,800
Rate variance	13,400 (F)

(iii) *Check*

	£
Revised std cost for revised std hrs (£36 × 1,000 units)	36,000
Actual costs	23,800
Total operational variance (1200 (A) + 13,400 (F))	12,200 (F)

(b) **Planning variance**

	£
Revised std cost for revised std hrs for actual o/put (£6 × 6 hr × 1,000)	36,000
Original std cost for orig std hrs for actual o/put (£5 × 4 hrs × 1,000)	20,000
Total planning variance	16,000 (A)

Planning rate variance

	£
Original std cost for revised std hrs for actual output (£5 × 6 hours × 1,000)	30,000
Revised standard cost for revised std hrs for actual output (£6 × 6 hours × 1,000)	36,000
Planning rate variance	6,000 (A)

Planning efficiency variance

The original standard hours for actual output were (4 hours × 1000)	4,000
The revised standard hours for actual output are (6 hours × 1000)	6,000
Labour efficiency planning variance in hours	2,000 (A)
× original standard rate per hour	× £5
Labour efficiency planning variance in £	10,000 (A)

Question 8.10   Planning variances and sub-variances

Learning outcome A1(f)

The standard materials cost of a product is 3 kg × £1.50 per kg = £4.50. Actual production of 10,000 units used 28,000 kg at a cost of £50,000. In retrospect it was realised that the standard materials cost should have been 2.5 kg per unit at a cost of £1.80 per kg (so that the *total* cost per unit was correct).

Required

Calculate the planning and operational variances in as much detail as possible.

Exam alert

The specimen paper contained a 6-mark question in Section C asking for a calculation of the planning variance and the operational rate and efficiency variances. They came up again in the September 2010 exam.

7.6 Planning and operational sales variances

Our final calculations in this chapter deal with planning and operational sales variances.

Example: planning and operational sales variances

Dimsek budgeted to make and sell 400 units of its product, the role, in the four-week period no 8, as follows.

	£
Budgeted sales (100 units per week)	40,000
Variable costs (400 units × £60)	24,000
Contribution	16,000
Fixed costs	10,000
Profit	6,000

At the beginning of the second week, production came to a halt because inventories of raw materials ran out, and a new supply was not received until the beginning of week 3. As a consequence, the company lost one week's production and sales. Actual results in period 8 were as follows.

	£
Sales (320 units)	32,000
Variable costs (320 units × £60)	19,200
Contribution	12,800
Fixed costs	10,000
Actual profit	2,800

In retrospect, it is decided that the optimum budget, given the loss of production facilities in the third week, would have been to sell only 300 units in the period.

Required

Calculate appropriate planning and operational variances.

Solution

The **planning** variance **compares the revised budget** with the **original budget**.

Revised sales volume, given materials shortage	300 units
Original budgeted sales volume	400 units
Planning variance in units of sales	100 units(A)
× standard contribution per unit	× £40
Planning variance in £	£4,000 (A)

Arguably, **running out of raw materials is an operational error** and so the loss of sales volume and contribution from the materials shortage is an opportunity cost that could have been avoided with better purchasing arrangements. The operational variances are variances calculated in the usual way, except that actual results are compared with the revised standard or budget. There is a sales volume contribution variance which is an **operational variance**, as follows.

Actual sales volume	320 units
Revised sales volume	300 units
Operational sales volume variance in units	20 units (F)
(possibly due to production efficiency or marketing efficiency)	
× standard contribution per unit	× £40
	£800 (F)

These variances can be used as **control information** to reconcile budgeted and actual profit.

	£	£
Operating statement, period 8		
Budgeted profit		6,000
Planning variance	4,000 (A)	
Operational variance – sales volume contribution	800 (F)	
		3,200 (A)
Actual profit in period 8		2,800

You will have noticed that in this example sales volume variances were **valued at contribution forgone**, and there were no fixed cost volume variances. This is because contribution forgone, in terms of lost revenue or extra expenditure incurred, is the nearest equivalent to **opportunity cost** which is readily available to management accountants (who assume linearity of costs and revenues within a relevant range of activity).

Question 8.11

Sales planning and operational variances

Learning outcome A1(f)

KSO budgeted to sell 10,000 units of a new product during 20X0. The budgeted sales price was £10 per unit, and the variable cost £3 per unit.

Although actual sales in 20X0 were 10,000 units and variable costs of sales were £30,000, sales revenue was only £5 per unit. With the benefit of hindsight, it is realised that the budgeted sales price of £10 was hopelessly optimistic, and a price of £4.50 per unit would have been much more realistic.

Required

Calculate planning and operational variances.

7.7 The value of planning and operational variances

Advantages of a system of planning and operational variances

(a)   The analysis highlights those variances which are **controllable** and those which are **non-controllable**.

(b)   **Managers' acceptance** of the use of variances for performance measurement, and their **motivation**, is likely to increase if they know they will not be held responsible for poor planning and faulty standard setting.

(c)   The **planning and standard-setting processes** should improve; standards should be more accurate, relevant and appropriate.

(d)   Operational variances will provide a 'fairer' reflection of actual performance.

The limitations of planning and operational variances, which must be overcome if they are to be applied in practice.

(a)   It is difficult to **decide in hindsight** what the **realistic standard** should have been.

(b)   It may become **too easy to justify all the variances as being due to bad planning**, so no operational variances will be highlighted.

(c)   Establishing realistic revised standards and analysing the total variance into planning and operational variances can be a **time consuming** task, even if a spreadsheet package is devised.

(d)   Even though the intention is to provide more meaningful information, **managers may be resistant** to the very idea of variances and refuse to see the virtues of the approach. Careful presentation and explanation will be required until managers are used to the concepts.

7.8 Management reports involving planning and operational variances

The format of a management report that includes planning and operational variances should be tailored to the information requirements of the managers who receive it.

From the **point of view of senior management** reviewing performance as a whole, a layout that identifies **all of the planning variances together**, and then **all of the operational variances** may be most illuminating. The difference due to planning is the responsibility of the planners, and the remainder of the difference is due to functional managers.

One possible layout is shown below.

OPERATING STATEMENT PERIOD 1

	£	£
Original budget contribution		X
Planning variances		
Material usage	X	
Material price	X	
Labour efficiency	X	
Labour idle time	X	
Labour rate	X	
Selling price	X	
		X
Revised budget contribution		X
Sales volume contribution variance		X
Revised standard contribution from sales achieved		X
Operational variances	X	
Selling price	X	
Material usage	X	
Material price	X	
Labour efficiency	X	
Labour rate	X	
Variable overhead expenditure	X	
Variable overhead efficiency	X	
		X
Actual contribution		X
Less: fixed costs budget	X	
expenditure variance	X	
		X
Actual margin		X

Exam alert

All of the topics covered in this chapter are **likely question topics**. Variance calculations could be examined in any section of the paper. In addition to variance calculations, you could be asked to draw up an operating statement using variances and to discuss and analyse the results covered in both this chapter and Chapters 7b and 7c.

Section summary

A planning and operational variance attempts to **divide a total variance** (which has been calculated conventionally) into a group of **variances** which have arisen because of **inaccurate planning or faulty standards (planning variances)** and a group of **variances** which have been caused by **adverse or favourable operational performance (operational variances)**.

Chapter Roundup

✓ An **operating statement/statement of variances** is a report, usually to senior management, at the end of a control period, reconciling budgeted profit for the period to actual profit.

✓ In a **standard marginal costing system**, there will no fixed overhead volume variance and the sales volume variance will be valued at standard contribution margin, not standard profit margin.

✓ Exam questions might provide you with information about variances from which you have to work backwards to determine the actual results.

✓ When two or more types of material are mixed together to produce a product it is possible to carry out further analysis on the usage variance. The **mix variance** explains how much of the usage variance was caused by a change in the relative proportions of the materials used. The **yield variance** shows how much of the usage variance was caused by using more or less material than the standard allowance.

✓ The purpose of a mix variance is to provide management with information to help in controlling the proportion of each item actually used. If it is not possible for managers to exercise control over the actual mix of material then there is little to be gained by calculating mix variances.

✓ If more than one type of labour is used in a product, the labour efficiency variance can be analysed further into a **labour mix (team composition) variance** and a **labour yield (team productivity or output) variance**.

✓ The sales volume profit variance can be analysed further into a sales mix variance and a sales quantity variance.

✓ A planning and operational variance attempts to **divide a total variance** (which has been calculated conventionally) into a group of **variances** which have arisen because of **inaccurate planning or faulty standards (planning variances)** and a group of **variances** which have been caused by **adverse or favourable operational performance (operational variances)**.

Quick Quiz

1   *Put the following items in the correct order so as to provide a reconciliation between budgeted
     contribution and actual profit.*

     Actual sales and admin costs
     Actual fixed production overhead
     Variable cost variances
     Sales variances
     Fixed production overhead expenditure variance
     Actual contribution
     Actual profit
     Budgeted fixed production overhead
     Actual sales minus the standard variable cost of sales
     Budgeted contribution
     Actual profit before sales and admin costs

2   Which of the following statements about the materials mix variance is true?

     A   It should only be calculated if the proportions in the mix are controllable.
     B   In quantity, it is always the same as the usage variance.
     C   In quantity, it is always zero whatever method of calculation is used
     D   It can only be calculated for a maximum of three materials in the mix.

3   *Fill in the blanks.*

     Materials .... variance = materials mix variance + materials .... variance.

4   The labour mix variance is sometimes known as the team mix variance and the labour yield variance is
     sometimes known as the team yield variance. True or false?

5   The material cost for an actual production level of 510 units was £32,130. There was a material price
     variance of £1,020 (A) and the standard price per kg was £6.10. How many kgs of material were used?

     A   5,100 kgs
     B   5,434 kgs
     C   5,267 kgs
     D   Impossible to tell from the information provided

6   In an operational and planning approach to variance analysis, which standards are used to calculate the
     operational variances?

     Ex ante standards   ☐

     Ex post standards   ☐

7   Chocos Ltd uses a standard absorption costing system. The following information is available from the
     standard cost card.

Production budget	3,000 units	Actual production	3,200 units
Direct material per unit	8kg	Direct material purchased and used 10,000kg	£57,500
Direct material cost per kg	£5.50		

     With the benefit of hindsight, the management of Chocos Ltd realises that a more realistic standard cost
     for current conditions would be £5.90.

     Calculate the material price planning variance.

Answers to Quick Quiz

1

	£	£
Budgeted contribution		X
Sales variances		X
Actual sales minus standard variable cost of sales		X
Variable cost variances		X
Actual contribution		X
Budgeted fixed production overhead	X	
Fixed production overhead expenditure variance	X	
Actual fixed production overhead		X
Actual profit before sales and admin costs		X
Actual sales and admin costs		X
Actual profit		X

2   A It should only be calculated if the proportions in the mix are controllable.

3   Materials usage variance = materials mix variance + materials yield variance.

4   False. They are sometimes known as the team composition variance and the team productivity variance.

5   A

Total actual material cost	£32,130
Price variance	£(1,020)
Standard price for actual usage	£31,110
÷ standard cost per kg	÷ £6.10
Actual kgs used	5,100

6   Ex post standards

7

	£
Original standard cost for revised standard kg for actual output	
(£5.50 × 8kg × 3,200)	140,800
Revised standard cost for revised standard kg for actual output	
(£5.90 × 8kg × 3,200)	151,040
Material price planning variance	10,240 (A)

Answers to Questions

8.1 Impact of costing system on variances

The correct answer is C.

8.2 Operating statement

(a) This is simply a **'total'** variance.

	£
1,000 units should have cost (× £600)	600,000
but did cost (see working)	808,000
Variable production cost variance	208,000 (A)

(b) **Direct labour cost variances**

	£
8,200 hours should cost (× £8)	65,600
but did cost	63,000
Direct labour rate variance	2,600 (F)

1,000 units should take (× 10 hours)	10,000 hrs
but did take	8,200 hrs
Direct labour efficiency variance in hrs	1,800 hrs (F)
× standard rate per hour	× £8
Direct labour efficiency variance in £	£14,400 (F)

Summary

	£
Rate	2,600 (F)
Efficiency	14,400 (F)
Total	17,000 (F)

(c) **Direct material cost variances**

	£
90,000 kg should cost (× £5)	450,000
but did cost	720,000
Direct material price variance	270,000 (A)

1,000 units should use (× 100 kg)	100,000 kg
but did use	90,000 kg
Direct material usage variance in kgs	10,000 kg (F)
× standard cost per kg	× £5
Direct material usage variance in £	£50,000 (F)

Summary

	£
Price	270,000 (A)
Usage	50,000 (F)
Total	220,000 (A)

(d) **Variable production overhead variances**

	£
8,200 hours incurring o/hd should cost (× £2)	16,400
but did cost	25,000
Variable production overhead expenditure variance	8,600 (A)

	£
Efficiency variance in hrs (from (b))	1,800 hrs (F)
× standard rate per hour	× £2
Variable production overhead efficiency variance	£3,600 (F)

Summary

	£
Expenditure	8,600 (A)
Efficiency	3,600 (F)
Total	5,000 (A)

(e) **Selling price variance**

	£
Revenue from 1,000 units should have been (× £900)	900,000
but was (× £975)	975,000
Selling price variance	75,000 (F)

(f) **Sales volume contribution variance**

Budgeted sales	1,020 units
Actual sales	1,000 units
Sales volume variance in units	20 units (A)
× standard contribution margin (£(900 – 600))	× £300
Sales volume contribution variance in £	£6,000 (A)

(g) **Fixed production overhead expenditure variance**

	£
Budgeted expenditure	40,000
Actual expenditure	41,400
Fixed production overhead expenditure variance	1,400 (A)

Workings

	£
Direct material	720,000
Total wages	63,000
Variable production overhead	25,000
	808,000

MilBri – OPERATING STATEMENT FOR DECEMBER

	(F) £	(A) £	£
Budgeted contribution (1,020 × £(900 – 600))			306,000
Sales volume contribution variance			6,000 (A)
Budgeted contribution from actual sales			300,000
Selling price variance			75,000 (F)
Actual sales minus the standard variable cost of sales			375,000
Variable cost variances	(F)	(A)	
Material price		270,000	
Material usage	50,000		
Labour rate	2,600		
Labour efficiency	14,400		
Variable overhead expenditure		8,600	
Variable overhead efficiency	3,600		
	70,600	278,600	208,000 (A)
Actual contribution			167,000
Budgeted fixed production overhead		40,000	
Expenditure variance		1,400 (A)	
Actual fixed production overhead			41,400
Actual gross profit			125,600

Check on actual gross profit:

	£	£
Sales revenue (£975 × 1,000)		975,000
Material cost	720,000	
Labour cost	63,000	
Variable production overhead cost	25,000	
Fixed production overhead cost	41,400	
Actual gross profit		849,400
		125,600

8.3 Working backwards

The correct answer is C.

Let the quantity of material X used = Y

5750 units should have used (× 10kgs)	57,500 kgs
but did use	Y kgs
Usage variance in kgs	(Y – 57,500) kgs
× standard price per kg	× £10
Usage variance in £	£1,500 (A)

∴ $10(Y – 57,500) = 1,500$ $Y – 57,500 = 150$ ∴ $Y = 57,650$ kgs

> **Alternative approach**
>
> $$\text{Usage variance in kgs} = \frac{\text{Usage variance £}}{\text{Std price}} = \frac{£1,500}{£10}(A) = 150\text{kg (A)}$$
>
> ∴ Quantity of X actually used 57,500 + 150 = 57,650 kgs

8.4 Mix and yield variances

	£
Price variances	
2,000 kg of X should cost (× £2)	4,000
but did cost	4,100
Material X price variance	100 (A)
2,400 kg of Y should cost (× £3.60)	8,640
but did cost	9,600
Material Y price variance	960 (A)

First approach for mix variances

Total quantity used (2,000 + 2,400) kgs = 4,400 kgs
Standard mix for actual use = $^3/_8$ X (1,650 kgs) + $^5/_8$ Y (2,750 kgs) = 4,400 kgs

	'Should' mix Actual quantity Standard mix	'Did' mix Actual quantity Actual mix	Difference	× Standard price	Variance
X	1,650kg	2,000kg	350kg (A)	× £2	£700 (A)
Y	2,750kg	2,400kg	350kg (F)	× £3.60	£1,260 (F)
	4,400kg	4,400kg	–		£560 (F)

Alternative approach for mix variances

The alternative method will produce the same total mix variance, but a different split between the mix variance for each material.

The standard weighted average price of the input materials is £24/8 kg = £3 per kg.

	'Should' mix Actual quantity Standard mix	'Did' mix Actual quantity Actual mix	Difference	£ (W1)	Variance
X	1,650kg	2,000kg	350kg more	× £1 less	£350 (F)
Y	2,750kg	2,400kg	350kg less	× £0.60 more	£210 (F)
	4,400kg	4,400kg	–		£560 (F)

Workings

	X	Y
Difference between w/av price and std price	£(3 – 2) = £1 less	£(3 – 3.60) = £0.60 more

Yield variance

Each unit of D456 requires	3 kg	of X, costing	£6
	5 kg	of Y, costing	£18
	8 kg		£24

4,400 kg should have yielded (÷ 8 kg)	550 units
but did yield	500 units
Yield variance in units	50 units (A)
× standard material cost per unit of output	× £24
Yield variance in £	£1,200 (A)

8.5 Limitations of mix and yield variances

Some limitations of the calculation of material mix and yield variances are as follows.

(a)   A **change in the mix** of materials used will almost certainly have an **impact upon the yield**, but this will not be isolated from other causes of the yield variance, such as substandard materials quality.

(b)   If a **favourable mix variance can be established**, without adverse effects upon yield or output quality, the **standard mix is obsolete**.

(c)   Changes in actual unit costs of some ingredients may make a change in mix economically viable. An attempt **to optimise the price variance** may therefore result in an **adverse mix variance**.

(d)   **Changes to the proportions of the input materials** are **assumed** to have **no impact on product quality**.

8.6 Deviations from standardised mix

Quantity input = (420 + 180 + 550) = 1,150 litres

Standard mix for the quantity input

The standardised mix for the quantity input is the calculation we carry out to determine the individual mix variances in units. You can check you have done it correctly by ensuring that the sum of the individual components equals total quantity input.

	Standardised mix for quantity input	Litres
O	1,150 × (0.4/1.1) =	418.18
H	1,150 × (0.2/1.1) =	209.09
N	1,150 × (0.5/1.1) =	522.73
		1,150.00

Deviations – absolute

These are simply the differences between the actual input and the standard input calculated above.

	Actual input Litres	Standard mix for actual input(see above) Litres	Deviation (or difference) Litres
O	420	418.18	1.82 (A)
H	180	209.09	29.09 (F)
N	550	522.73	27.27 (A)
	1,150	1,150.00	–

Deviations as a %

O	(1.82/418.18) × 100% = 0.435%
H	(29.09/209.09) × 100% = 13.913%
N	(27.27/522.73) × 100% = 5.217%

8.7 Labour mix variances

(a) **Labour efficiency variance**

	Audit manager	Junior auditors	Audit clerks	Total $
Audit should take	30 hrs	120 hrs	50 hrs	
but did take	27 hrs	125 hrs	58 hrs	
Efficiency variance in hours	3 hrs (F)	5 hrs (A)	8 hrs (A)	
× standard rate per hour	× $450	× $170	× $50	
	$1,350 (F)	$850 (A)	$400 (A)	$100 (F)

(b) **Labour yield variance**

Standard weighted average labour rate per hour $= \dfrac{\$36,400}{200} = \$182$

Audit should have taken	200 hrs
but did take	210 hrs
Labour yield variance in hours	10 hours (A)
× standard rate per hour	× $182
Labour yield variance	$1,820 (A)

(c) **Labour mix variance**

	Should mix Actual hrs Std mix	Did mix Actual hrs Actual mix	Difference	$	Variance $
Audit manager	31.5	27	4.5 less	× $268 more	1,206 (F)
Junior auditor	126.0	125	1.0 less	× $12 less	12 (A)
Audit clerks	52.5	58	5.5 more	× $132 less	726 (F)
	210.0	210	–		1,920 (F)

8.8 Total planning and operational variances

The correct answer is A.

Operational variance

	£
Revised std cost for revised std kg for actual output (£1.50 × 2kg × 1,000)	3,000
Actual cost for 1,000 units	3,250
Total operational variance	250 (A)

Planning variance

	£
Revised std cost for revised std kg for actual output (£1.50 × 2 kg × 1000)	3,000
Original std cost for original std kg for actual output(£1 × 2 kg × 1,000)	2,000
Total planning variance	1,000 (A)

8.9 Planning and operational variances

The correct answer is B.

Keep calm and calculate the *total* variance in the normal way to begin with. Then you will understand what it is that you have to analyse. Next follow through the workings shown above, substituting the figures in the exercise for those in the example.

Total labour variance	£
540 units should have cost (× 3 hrs × £6)	9,720
but did cost	10,500
	780 (A)

Planning variance	£
Revised std cost for revised std hrs for actual output (£6.25 × 3 hrs × 540)	10,125
Original std cost for original std hrs for actual output (£6 × 3 hrs × 540)	9,720
	405 (A)

Operational rate variance	£
Revised std cost of actual hrs paid (£6.25 × 1,700)	10,625
Actual cost of actual hrs paid	10,500
	125 (F)

Operational efficiency variance	
540 units should have taken (× 3 hrs)	1,620 hrs
but did take	1,700 hrs
Operational efficiency variance in hours	80 hrs (A)
× revised standard rate per hour	× £6.25
Operational efficiency variance in £	£500 (A)

8.10 Planning variances and sub-variances

As always, calculate the *total* materials variance first, to give you a point of reference. Then follow through the workings above.

Total materials variance	£
10,000 units should have cost (× £4.50)	45,000
but did cost	50,000
	5,000 (A)
Operational price variance	
Revised std price of actual purchases (£1.80 × 28,000)	50,400
Actual price of actual purchases	50,000
	400 (F)
Operational usage variance	
10,000 units should use (× 2.5 kgs)	25,000 kgs
but did use	28,000 kgs
Variance in kgs	3,000 kgs (A)
× standard rate per kg	× 1.80
	£5,400 (A)

Planning variance

	£
Original std cost for revised std kg for actual output (£1.50 × 2.5kg × 10,000)	37,500
Revised std cost for revised std kg for actual output (£1.80 × 2.5kg × 10,000)	45,000
Planning rate variance	7,500 (A)

	£
The original standard kg for actual output (10,000 × 3kg)	30,000
The revised standard kg for actual output (10,000 × 2.5kg)	25,000
Efficiency planning variance in kg	5,000 (F)
× standard rate per kg	× £1.50
Planning efficient variance	7,500 (F)

Total planning variance

	£
Revised std cost for revised std kg for actual output (£1.80 × 2.5kg × 10,000)	45,000
Original std cost for original std kg for actual output(£1.50 × 3kg × 10,000)	45,000
Total planning variance	–

(Note that total planning variance = planning rate variance + planning efficiency variance.)

8.11 Sales planning and operational variances

The only variances are selling price variances.

Planning (selling price) variance

	£
Original budget (10,000 × £10.00)	100,000
Revised budget (10,000 × £4.50)	45,000
Planning variance	55,000 (A)

The original variance was too optimistic and so the planning variance is an adverse variance.

Operational (selling price) variance

	£
Actual sales (10,000 × £5)	50,000
Revised sales (10,000 × £4.50)	45,000
Operational (selling price) variance	5,000 (F)

The total difference between budgeted and actual profit of £50,000 (A) is therefore analysed as follows.

	£
Operational variance (selling price)	5,000 (F)
Planning variance	55,000 (A)
	50,000 (A)

Now try these questions from the Exam Question Bank

Number	Level	Marks	Time
Q9	Examination	20	36 mins
Q10	Introductory	30	54 mins
Q11	Examination	30	54 mins
Q12	Examination	20	36 mins

THE MODERN BUSINESS ENVIRONMENT

In recent years there have been **significant changes in the business environment** in which both manufacturing and service organisations operate.

We look at these **changes** in some detail in **Section 1**.

Organisations have therefore adopted new **management approaches (Sections 6 and 7)**, have changed their **manufacturing systems (Sections 3 to 5 and 8)** and

have invested in **new technology (Section 2)**. It is these changes that we will be looking at in this chapter.

These changes do mean that **traditional management accounting methods may no longer be appropriate** and in the chapters which follow we look at **alternative systems of management accounting** that have been developed and which are claimed to be more suitable for the modern business environment.

topic list	learning outcomes	syllabus references	ability required
1 The changing business environment	A1(h)	A1(xiv)	comprehension
2 Advanced manufacturing technology (AMT)	A1(h), A2(a)	A2(i)	comprehension
3 Production management strategies	A1(h), A2(a)	A1(xiv), A2(i)	comprehension
4 Just-in-time (JIT) systems	A1(h)	A1(xiv)	comprehension
5 Synchronous manufacturing	A1(h)	A1(xiv)	comprehension
6 Total quality management (TQM)	A1(h)	A1(xiv)	comprehension
7 Costs of quality and cost of quality reports	A1(h)	A1(xiv)	comprehension
8 World class manufacturing (WCM)	A1(h)	A1(xiv)	comprehension

1 The changing business environment

Introduction

Before the 1970s, barriers of communication and **geographical distance** limited the extent to which overseas organisations could compete in domestic markets. Cost increases could often be passed on to customers and so there were **few efforts to maximise efficiency and improve management practices**, or to reduce costs. **During the 1970s**, however, **overseas competitors** gained access to domestic markets by **establishing global networks for acquiring raw materials and distributing high-quality, low-priced goods**. To succeed, organisations had to compete against the best companies in the world.

1.1 The changing competitive environment for service organisations

Prior to the 1980s, many service organisations (such as the utilities, the financial services and airlines industries) were either **government-owned monopolies** or were **protected by a highly-regulated, non-competitive environment**. **Improvements in quality and efficiency** of operations or levels of profitability were not expected, and costs increases were often covered by increasing service prices. Cost systems to measure costs and profitability of individual services were not deemed necessary.

The competitive environment for service organisations changed radically in the **1980s**, however, following **privatisation** of government-owned monopolies and **deregulation**. The resulting intense competition and increasing product range has led to the **requirement for cost management and management accounting information systems** which allow service organisations to assess the costs and profitability of services, customers and markets.

1.2 Changing product life cycles

Today's **competitive environment**, along with high levels of **technological innovation** and **increasingly discriminating and sophisticated customer demands**, constantly **threaten a product's life cycle**.

KEY TERM

PRODUCT LIFE CYCLE is the 'Period which begins with the initial product specification and ends with the withdrawal from the market of both the product and its support. It is characterised by defined stages including research, development, introduction, maturity, decline and abandonment.'

(CIMA Official Terminology)

Organisations can no longer rely on years of high demand for products and so, to compete effectively, they need to continually **redesign their products** and to **shorten the time it takes to get them to the market place**.

In many organisations today, **up to 90% of a product's life cycle cost is determined by decisions made** early within the cycle, **at the design stage. Management accounting systems that monitor spending and commitment to spend during the early stages of a product's life cycle** are therefore becoming **increasingly important**.

1.3 Changing customer requirements

Successful organisations in today's competitive environment make **customer satisfaction** their **priority** and concentrate on the following **key success factors**.

Key success factor	Detail
Cost efficiency	Not wasting money
Quality	Focusing on total quality management (TQM), covered in Section 6
Time	Providing a speedier response to customer requests, ensuring 100% on-time delivery and reducing the time taken to develop and bring new products to market
Innovation	Developing a steady stream of innovative new products and having the flexibility to respond to customer requirements

They are also taking on board **new management approaches**.

Approach	Detail
Continuous improvement	A facet of TQM, being a continuous search to reduce costs, eliminate waste and improve the quality and performance of activities that increase customer satisfaction or value
Employee empowerment	Providing employees with the information to enable them to make continuous improvements without authorisation from superiors
Total value-chain analysis	Ensuring that all the factors which add value to an organisation's products - the value chain of research and development, design, production, marketing, distribution and customer service - are coordinated within the overall organisational framework

1.4 Changing manufacturing systems

Traditionally, manufacturing industries have fallen into a few broad groups according to the **nature of the production process** and **materials flow**.

Type of production	Description
Jobbing industries	Industries in which **items are produced individually**, often for a specific customer order, as a 'job'. Such a business requires versatile equipment and highly skilled workers to give it the flexibility to turn its hand to a variety of jobs. The jobbing factory is typically laid out on a **functional** basis with, say, a milling department, a cutting department, finishing, assembly and so on.
Batch processing	Involves the manufacture of **standard goods in batches**. 'Batch production is often carried out using **functional** layouts but with a greater number of more **specialised machines**. With a functional layout batches move by different and complex routes through various specialised departments travelling over much of the factory floor before they are completed.' (Drury, *Management and Cost Accounting*)
Mass or flow production	Involves the **continuous production of standard items** from a sequence of continuous or repetitive operations. This sort of production often uses a **product-based** layout whereby product A moves from a milling machine to a cutting machine to a paint-spraying machine, product B moves from a sawing machine to a milling machine to an oven and then to finishing and so on.
	The point is that there is no separate 'milling department' or 'assembly department' to which all products must be sent to await their turn on the machines: each product has its own dedicated machine.

In recent years, however, a new type of manufacturing system known as **group technology** (or **repetitive manufacturing**) has emerged. The system involves a **flexible or cellular arrangement of machines** which **manufacture groups of products having similar manufacturing requirements.** By grouping together facilities required to produce similar products, some of the **benefits associated with flow production systems** (lower throughput times, easier scheduling, reduced set-up times and reduced work in progress) are possible to achieve. Moreover, the increase in **customer demand for product diversity can be satisfied** by such a manufacturing system.

1.4.1 Dedicated cell layout

The modern development in this sphere is to merge the flexibility of the functional layout with the speed and productivity of the product layout. **Cellular** manufacturing involves a **U-shaped flow** along which are arranged a number of different machines that are used to make products with similar machining requirements.

The machines are operated by workers who are **multi-skilled** (can operate each machine within the cell rather than being limited to one operation such as 'lathe-operator', 'grinder', or whatever) and are able to perform routine preventative maintenance on the cell machines. The aim is to facilitate **just-in-time** production (see Section 4) and obtain the associated improvements in **quality** and reductions in **costs**.

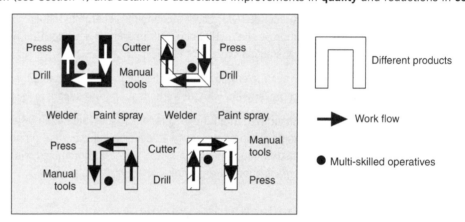

In January 1994 the *Financial Times* carried a good example of this approach in an article about the Paddy Hopkirk car accessory factory in Bedfordshire.

One morning the factory was just an untidy sprawl of production lines surrounded by piles of crates holding semi-finished components. Two days later, when the workforce came to work (after Christmas), the machines has been brought together in tightly grouped 'cells'. The piles of components had disappeared, and the newly cleared floor space was neatly marked with colour-coded lines mapping out the flow of materials.

Overnight there were dramatic differences. In the first full day, productivity on some lines increased by up to 30%, the space needed for some processes had been halved, and work in progress had been cut considerably. The improved layout had allowed some jobs to be combined, freeing up operators for development elsewhere in the factory.

Section summary

Changes to the **competitive environment, product life cycles** and **customer requirements** have had a significant impact on the modern business environment.

Different approaches for **organising a manufacturing process** include **jobbing industries, batch processing** and **mass production**.

To compete effectively organisations need to **continually redesign their products** and to **shorten the time it takes to get them to the market place. Manufacturing processes** must therefore be **sufficiently flexible** both to accommodate new product design rapidly and to satisfy the demand for greater product diversity.

2 Advanced manufacturing technology (AMT)

Introduction

Advanced manufacturing technology (AMT) is a general expression encompassing computer-aided design (CAD), computer aided manufacturing (CAM), flexible manufacturing systems (FMS) and a wide array of innovative computer equipment.

2.1 Computer-aided design (CAD)

Computer-aided design allows new products to be designed (and old ones modified) on a computer screen.

(a)   The effects of **changing product specifications** (for example to test stress and find weaknesses or to optimise usage of materials) can be explored.

(b)   **Designs can be assessed in terms of cost and simplicity**. A simple design is likely to produce a more reliable product and a simple product is easier to manufacture, thereby reducing the possibility of production errors. Quality and cost reduction can therefore be incorporated into a product at the design stage.

(c)   **Databases can be used** to match part requirements of the new design with existing product parts, thereby allowing a reduction in product parts required and a minimisation of inventories.

2.2 Computer-aided manufacturing (CAM)

Computer-aided manufacturing refers to the control of the physical production process by computers.

Feature	Detail
Robots	Typically comprise computer controlled arms and attachments that can perform tasks like welding, bolting parts together and moving them about.
Computer numerically controlled (CNC) machines	Programmable machine tools for punching holes, cutting and so on. Manufacturing configurations and set-up instructions are stored on computer programs and so can be changed almost immediately via a keyboard. Flexibility and a reduction in set-up times are thus major advantages of CAM. Moreover, computers can repeat the same operation in an identical manner time and time again, without tiring or error, unlike human operators, with obvious advantages for both quality control and production control.
Automated guided vehicles (AGV)	Used for materials handling, often in place of the traditional conveyor belt approach.

The **ultimate aim** of CAM is a **set-up time of zero**. Although this may not be achievable (in the near future at least), CAM has provided, and still is providing, the **possibility** of economic **production in smaller and smaller batch sizes** with the result that the production schedule is becoming more and more driven by customer requirements.

2.3 Flexible manufacturing systems (FMS)

KEY TERM

A FLEXIBLE MANUFACTURING SYSTEM (FMS) is an 'Integrated, computer-controlled production system which is capable of producing any of a range of parts, and of switching quickly and economically between them.'
(CIMA Official Terminology)

A flexible manufacturing system (FMS) is a **highly-automated manufacturing system**, which is computer controlled and capable of producing a broad 'family' of parts in a flexible manner. **It is characterised by**

small batch production, the ability to change quickly from one job to another and very fast response times, so that output can be produced quickly in response to specific orders that come in.

The sophistication of flexible manufacturing systems varies from one system to another, but **features** can include the following.

- A **JIT system** (discussed later in this chapter)

- Full **computer-integrated manufacturing (CIM)** (the integration of many or all of the elements of AMT into one coherent system) or perhaps just **islands of automation (IAs)** (a series of automated sub-systems within the factory)

- **Computerised materials handling systems (MHS)**

- **Automated storage and retrieval systems (ASRS)** for raw materials and parts

2.4 Electronic data interchange (EDI)

It is not simply within the manufacturing functions of an organisation that technology has made an impact. Electronic data interchange facilitates communication between an organisation and its customers and suppliers by the electronic transfer of information.

Section summary

Advanced manufacturing technology (AMT) is a general expression encompassing **computer-aided design (CAD), computer-aided manufacturing (CAM), flexible manufacturing systems (FMS)** and a wide array of innovative computer equipment.

3 Production management strategies

Introduction

In Section 1 we looked at the various methods of organising the production process. In this section and the next we shall look at **various production management strategies** and **resource planning systems** that are used to **manage the production process**.

3.1 Traditional approach

The traditional approach to **determining materials requirements** is **to monitor the level of inventories** constantly so that once they fall to a preset level they can be reordered. The problem with this approach is that **relationships between different inventory lines** are **ignored** whereas, in reality, the demand for a particular item of inventory is interdependent on the assemblies and subassemblies of which it forms a part. The computer techniques we will look at below overcome this problem by integrating interrelationships into the inventory ordering process.

3.2 Material requirements planning (MRP)

KEY TERM

MATERIAL REQUIREMENTS PLANNING **(MRP)** is a 'System that converts a production schedule into a listing of the materials and components required to meet that schedule, so that adequate stock levels are maintained and items are available when needed.' *(CIMA Official Terminology)*

MRP is a computerised information, planning and control system that can be used in a traditional manufacturing environment as well as with AMT. MRP uses information from a master production schedule which details **how many** finished goods items are needed, **and when**, and works back from this to determine the **requirements for parts and materials** in the earlier stages of the production process. MRP systems are chiefly used in a batch manufacturing environment.

3.3 The aims of MRP

- Minimising inventory levels
- Avoiding the high costs of rush orders
- Minimum disruption to production

MRP is therefore concerned with **maximising efficiency in the timing of orders for raw materials or parts that are placed with external suppliers** and **efficient scheduling of the manufacturing and assembly of the end product**.

3.4 Manufacturing resource planning (MRP II)   5/10

KEY TERM

MANUFACTURING RESOURCE PLANNING (MRPII) is 'An expansion of material requirements planning (MRP) to give a broader approach than MRP to the planning and scheduling of resources, embracing areas such as finance, logistics, engineering and marketing'.   *(CIMA Official Terminology)*

MRP evolved into MRP II. MRP II **plans production jobs and also calculates resource needs such as labour and machine hours**. It therefore attempts to integrate materials requirement planning, factory capacity planning, shopfloor control, management accounting, purchasing and even marketing into a **single complete (and computerised) manufacturing control system**. Most MRP II systems are a collection of computer programs that permit the sharing of information with and between departments in an organisation.

MRP II is used by many companies for manufacturing planning, but with the advent of JIT manufacturing (see Section 4) it has been **criticised** as a planning system.

> 'The primary criticism of the MRP II approach is that **by modelling the reality of manufacturing plant, it builds in all the bad habits**. It takes account of long leadtimes, shopfloor queues, large batch sizes, scrap and quality problems. Instead of accommodating these things, it should be driving towards their elimination. Poor productivity is built into MRPII and planned into the production process.'

> (Brian Maskell, *Management Accounting,* January 1989 (with BPP's emphasis))

Many world class manufacturers in Japan have therefore taken an alternative approach to dealing with complex production scheduling and purchasing by attempting to simplify their production processes.

Even so, MRP II has advantages as a system for planning and controlling manufacturing systems, especially when JIT methods are unsuitable.

3.5 Enterprise resource planning (ERP)

KEY TERM

ENTERPRISE RESOURCE PLANNING (ERP) SYSTEMS are accounting-orientated information systems for identifying and planning the enterprise-wide resources needed to take, make, distribute and account for customer orders.   *(S Shankarnarayanan* 'ERP Systems - Using IT to gain competitive advantage')

Exam alert

Make sure that you learn what all of these acronyms (FMS, EDI, MRP, ERP and so on) mean as their definitions could easily be examined in Section A or Section B of your exam.

LEARNING MEDIA

The *Official CIMA Terminology* definition is 'A software system is designed to support and automate the business processes of medium and large enterprises. ERP systems are accounting orientated information systems which aid in identifying and planning the enterprise wide resources needed to resource, make, account for and deliver customer orders. Initially developed from MRPII systems, ERP tends to incorporate a number of software developments such as the use of relational databases, object-oriented programming and open system portability...'.

ERP has been described as an **umbrella term** for **integrated business software systems** that power a corporate information structure, thus helping companies to control their inventory, purchasing, manufacturing, finance and personnel operations.

Originally, ERP systems were simple **extensions** of **MRP II** systems, but their **scope has now widened**. They allow an organisation to **automate** and **integrate** most of its business processes, share common data and practices across the whole enterprise and produce and access information in a real-time environment. ERP may also incorporate transactions with an organisation's suppliers.

They help large national and multinational companies in particular to manage **geographically dispersed and complex operations**. For example, an organisation's UK sales office may be responsible for marketing, selling and servicing a product assembled in the US using parts manufactured in France and Hong Kong. ERP enables the organisation to understand and manage the demand placed on the plant in France.

3.6 Customer relationship management (CRM) systems

Customer relationship management (CRM) systems, which contain information about customers and customer requirements, are often integrated with ERP systems and use websites and e-commerce facilities. Within such a system, a customer's order may automatically schedule the required production facilities and order the appropriate components.

3.7 Supply chain management (SCM) systems

Supply chain management (SCM) systems aim to integrate the flow of information between the various companies on a supply chain. If a customer places an order with A, the SCM system will automatically schedule the production and delivery of components from B (A's supplier). Obviously, to operate successfully, participating organisations must have confidence in each other's operations and be willing to swap information.

3.8 Lean manufacturing

However, 'For the past decade, organizations have spent billions of dollars and countless worker-hours installing huge integrated software packages known as enterprise resource planning (ERP) applications. Now many manufacturing companies are realizing that the infrastructure they spent years creating is deficient on their plant floor. The ERP systems of the 1990s have become a liability for many manufacturers because they perpetuate some of the legendary material requirements planning (MRP) problems such as complex bills of materials, inefficient work-flows and unnecessary data collection. A new manufacturing model has emerged that's taking the place of the traditional MRP model. It's called Lean, Flow or Demand-Pull.

Lean manufacturing, a concept with roots in the production processes of Toyota, aims at improving efficiency, eliminating product backlogs and synchronizing production to customer demand rather than a long-term (often incorrect) forecast.'

> 'Does ERP fit in a LEAN world?', M Bradford, A Mayfield and C Tonney, *Strategic Finance*, May 2001

The point to note is that the **Lean approach** is focused on a **production plan based on actual demand** rather than production being based on a plan which it is hoped demand will follow.

3.9 Optimised production technology (OPT)

One further innovation deserves a brief mention. (Bear in mind though that a new TLA (Three-Letter Acronym) seems to gain favour every few months.) OPT also requires detailed information about inventory levels, product structures, routings, set-up times and operation times for each procedure of each product but it *also* **seeks to optimise the use of bottleneck resources**.

> 'The OPT philosophy contends that the **primary goal of manufacturing is to make money**. Three important criteria are identified to evaluate progress towards achieving this goal. These are throughput, inventory and operating expenses. The goal is to **maximise throughput** while simultaneously **maintaining or decreasing inventory and operating expenses**.
>
> The OPT approach determines what prevents throughput [of products through the production process] from being higher by **distinguishing between bottleneck and non-bottleneck resources**. A bottleneck might be a machine whose capacity limits the throughput of the whole production process. The aim is to identify bottlenecks and remove them or, if this is not possible, ensure that they are fully utilised at all times. Non-bottleneck resources should be scheduled and operated based on constraints within the system, and should not be used to produce more than the bottlenecks can absorb.
>
> With the OPT approach, it is vitally important to schedule all non-bottleneck resources within the manufacturing system based on the constraints of the system (ie the bottlenecks). For example, if only 70% of the output of a non-bottleneck resource can be absorbed by the following bottleneck resource then 30% of the utilisation of the non-bottleneck is simply concerned with increasing inventory. It can therefore be argued that by operating at the 70% level, the non-bottleneck resource is achieving 100% efficiency.'
>
> (Drury, *Management and Cost Accounting (with BPP's emphasis)*)

| Question 9.1 | MRP and ERP |

Learning outcome A2(a)

Explain how MRP and ERP systems can assist the management accountant in preparing budgets, maintaining standard costing systems and presenting variances to management.

Section summary

The **production management strategies** linked to AMT are materials requirement planning (MRPI), manufacturing resource planning (MRPII), enterprise resource planning (ERP), optimised production technology (OPT) and just-in-time (JIT).

4 Just-in-time (JIT) systems

Introduction

'Traditional' responses to the problems of improving manufacturing capacity and reducing unit costs of production might be described as follows.

- Longer production runs
- Economic batch quantities
- Reduced time on preventive maintenance, to keep production flowing
- Fewer products in the product range
- More overtime

In general terms, longer production runs and large batch sizes should mean less disruption, better capacity utilisation and lower unit costs.

Just-in-time systems challenge such 'traditional' views of manufacture.

KEY TERM

JUST-IN-TIME (JIT) is a 'System whose objective is to produce or to procure products or components as they are required by a customer or for use, rather than for stock. A JIT system is a *pull* system, which responds to demand, in contrast to a *push* system, in which stocks act as buffers between the different elements of the system, such as purchasing, production and sales.'

JUST-IN-TIME PRODUCTION is a 'Production system which is driven by demand for finished products whereby each component on a production line is produced only when needed for the next stage.'

JUST-IN-TIME PURCHASING is a 'Purchasing system in which material purchases are contracted so that the receipt and usage of material, to the maximum extent possible, coincide.'   *(CIMA Official Terminology)*

Although described as a technique in the *Official Terminology*, JIT is more of a **philosophy or approach to management** since it encompasses a **commitment to continuous improvement** and the **search for excellence** in the design and operation of the production management system.

JIT has the following **essential elements**.

Element	Detail
JIT purchasing	Parts and raw materials should be purchased as near as possible to the time they are needed, using small frequent deliveries against bulk contracts.
Close relationship with suppliers	In a JIT environment, the responsibility for the quality of goods lies with the supplier. A long-term commitment between supplier and customer should therefore be established. The supplier is guaranteed a demand for products because of being the sole supplier and the supplier can plan to meet the customer's production schedules. If an organisation has confidence that suppliers will deliver material of 100% quality, on time, so that there will be no rejects, returns and hence no consequent production delays, usage of materials can be matched with delivery of materials and inventories can be kept at near zero levels. Suppliers are also chosen because of their close proximity to an organisation's plant.
Uniform loading	All parts of the productive process should be operated at a speed which matches the rate at which the final product is demanded by the customer. Production runs will therefore be shorter and there will be smaller inventories of finished goods because output is being matched more closely to demand (and so storage costs will be reduced).
Set-up time reduction	Machinery set-ups are non-value-added activities (see below) which should be reduced or even eliminated.
Machine cells	Machines or workers should be grouped by product or component instead of by the type of work performed. The non-value-added activity of materials movement between operations is therefore minimised by eliminating space between work stations. Products can flow from machine to machine without having to wait for the next stage of processing or returning to stores. Lead times and work in progress are thus reduced.
Quality	Production management should seek to eliminate scrap and defective units during production, and to avoid the need for reworking of units since this stops the flow of production and leads to late deliveries to customers. Product quality and production quality are important 'drivers' in a JIT system.

Element	Detail
Pull system (*Kanban*)	A *Kanban*, or signal, is used to ensure that products/ components are only produced when needed by the next process. Nothing is produced in anticipation of need, to then remain in inventory, consuming resources.
Preventative maintenance	Production systems must be reliable and prompt, without unforeseen delays and breakdowns. Machinery must be kept fully maintained, and so preventative maintenance is an important aspect of production.
Employee involvement	Workers within each machine cell should be trained to operate each machine within that cell and to be able to perform routine preventative maintenance on the cell machines (ie to be multiskilled and flexible).

Question 9.2	JIT system

Learning outcome A1(h)

A company is considering changing to a JIT system. Which of the following changes in their working practices are likely to be necessary?

I   More frequent revision of stock control levels and of the economic order quantity
II   Increase in the number of raw material suppliers in order to guarantee supply
III   Selection of suppliers close to the company's manufacturing facility
IV   Increased focus on the accurate forecasting of customer demand
V   Increased quality control activity

A   I and II
B   III, IV and V
C   II, III, IV and V
D   All of them

4.1 Value added

JIT aims to eliminate all **non-value-added costs**. Value is only added while a product is actually being processed. Whilst it is being inspected for quality, moving from one part of the factory to another, waiting for further processing and held in store, value is not being added. Non value-added activities (or **diversionary** activities) should therefore be eliminated.

KEY TERM

'A VALUE-ADDED cost is incurred for an activity that cannot be eliminated without the customer's perceiving a deterioration in the performance, function, or other quality of a product. The cost of a picture tube in a television set is value-added.

The costs of those activities that can be eliminated without the customer's perceiving deterioration in the performance, function, or other quality of a product are non-value-added. The costs of handling the materials of a television set through successive stages of an assembly line may be non-value-added. Improvements in plant layout that reduce handling costs may be achieved without affecting the performance, function, or other quality of the television set.'   *(Horngren)*

Question 9.3

Value-added activity

Learning outcome A1(h)

Which of the following is a value-added activity?

A   Setting up a machine so that it drills holes of a certain size
B   Repairing faulty production work
C   Painting a car, if the organisation manufactures cars
D   Storing materials

CASE STUDY

The following extract from an article in the *Financial Times* illustrates how 'just-in-time' some manufacturing processes can be. The emphasis is BPP's.

'Just-in-time manufacturing is down to a fine art at *Nissan Motor Manufacturing (UK)*. **Stockholding of some components is just ten minutes** - and the holding of all parts bought in Europe is less than a day.

Nissan has moved beyond just-in-time to **synchronous supply** for some components, which means manufacturers deliver these components directly to the production line minutes before they are needed.

These manufacturers do not even receive an order to make a component until the car for which it is intended has started along the final assembly line. Seat manufacturer *Ikeda Hoover*, for example, has about 45 minutes to build seats to specification and deliver them to the assembly line a mile away. It delivers 12 sets of seats every 20 minutes and they are mounted in the right order on an overhead conveyor ready for fitting to the right car.

Nissan has **close relationships with this dozen or so suppliers** and deals exclusively with them in their component areas. It involves them and even their own suppliers in discussions about future needs and other issues. These companies have generally established their own manufacturing units close to the Nissan plant.

Other parts from further afield are collected from manufacturers by *Nissan* several times at fixed times. This is more efficient than having each supplier making individual haulage arrangements.'

4.2 Problems associated with JIT

JIT should not be seen as a panacea for all the endemic problems associated with Western manufacturing. It might not even be appropriate in all circumstances.

(a)   It is **not** always **easy** to **predict** patterns of **demand**.

(b)   JIT makes the organisation far more vulnerable to **disruptions** in the supply chain.

(c)   JIT, originated by Toyota, was designed at a time when all of Toyota's manufacturing was done within a 50 km **radius** of its headquarters. Wide geographical spread, however, makes this difficult.

CASE STUDY

JIT and supply chains

The flight ban which affected much of Europe after the volcanic eruption in Iceland in April 2010 threatened to force worldwide car production to grind to a halt, as manufacturers were unable to source key electronic components.

The flight disruption highlighted the car industry's dependence on complex, worldwide supply chains that need multiple modes of transport to deliver goods and components just in time, to where they are needed.

Among the carmakers, BMW and Nissan said they planned to suspend some production because of disruption to supplies. Audi said it might have to cancel shifts because of missing parts.

Although all three mainly use suppliers based near their factories and use road and sea for most deliveries, they depend on air freight for a small number of high-value electronic components. Nissan UK, for example, said it might have to halt production of its Cube, Murano SUV and Rogue crossover models because it lacked supplies of a critical sensor made in Ireland.

Some commentators have questioned whether this disruption will make companies re-examine their arrangements for sourcing goods. Companies have become more vulnerable to disruption since moving to just-in-time production methods, where hardly any inventory of products is held.

Adapted from article 'Pressure grows on supply chains'

Financial Times, 21 April, 2010

| **Question 9.4** | JIT |

Learning outcome A1(h)

Batch sizes within a JIT manufacturing environment may well be smaller than those associated with traditional manufacturing systems.

What costs might be associated with this feature of JIT?

1   Increased set-up costs

2   Opportunity cost of lost production capacity as machinery and the workforce reorganise for a different product

3   Additional materials handling costs

4   Increased administrative costs

A   None of the above
B   1, 2, 3 and 4
C   1 only
D   2 and 3 only

4.3 Modern versus traditional inventory control systems

There is no reason for the newer approaches to supersede the old entirely. A restaurant, for example, might find it preferable to use the traditional economic order quantity approach for staple non-perishable food items, but adopt JIT for perishable and 'exotic' items. In a hospital a stock-out could, quite literally, be fatal, and JIT would be quite unsuitable.

4.4 Standard costing and JIT

Some commentators have argued that **traditional variance analysis is unhelpful and potentially misleading** in the modern organisation, and can make managers focus their attention on the wrong issues. Here are just two examples.

(a)   **Efficiency variance**. Traditional variance analysis emphasises that adverse efficiency variances should be avoided, which means that managers should try to prevent idle time and keep up production. In an environment where the focus is on improving continuously, JIT should be used. In these circumstances, manufacturing to eliminate idle time could result in the production of unwanted products that must be held in store and might eventually be scrapped. Efficiency variances could focus management attention on the wrong problems.

(b) **Materials price variance**. In a JIT environment the key issues in materials purchasing are supplier reliability, materials quality, and delivery in small order quantities. Purchasing managers should not be shopping around every month looking for the cheapest price. Many JIT systems depend on long-term contractual links with suppliers, which means that material price variances are not relevant for management control purposes.

Section summary

JIT aims for zero inventory and perfect quality and operates by demand-pull. It consists of **JIT purchasing** and **JIT production** and results in lower investment requirements, space savings, greater customer satisfaction and increased flexibility.

5 Synchronous manufacturing

Introduction

Synchronous manufacturing requires managers to **focus on areas of operations which offer the greatest possibilities for global improvements** (such as at a bottleneck resource) rather than improving the process everywhere in the system, which is the JIT philosophy.

KEY TERM

SYNCHRONOUS MANUFACTURING is a manufacturing philosophy which aims to ensure that all operations within an organisation are performed for the common good of the organisation and that nothing is done unless it improves the bottom line.

Proponents of synchronous manufacturing **regard JIT as unfocused**. They claim that it fails to identify capacity restraints in advance but waits until a problem occurs, which disrupts the entire processing system. Synchronous manufacturing, on the other hand, attempts to **detect problems before they happen** so that the production process and hence throughput are unaffected. According to advocates of synchronous manufacturing, **JIT** fails to focus effectively on bottleneck resources, with the result that **throughput may not be optimal**.

Synchronous manufacturing aims to **develop a production schedule that takes account of the constraints within the processing system**. This involves a detailed analysis of the plant's capabilities and the manufacturing environment with the aim of identifying the system's constraints. Time buffers are then built into the system at strategic points throughout the plant so as to avoid disruption and to ensure that the planned production schedule is met.

Section summary

Synchronous manufacturing aims to ensure that all operations within an organisation are performed for the common good of the organisation.

6 Total quality management (TQM)

Introduction

Quality means 'the **degree of excellence of a thing**' - how well made it is, or how well performed if it is a service, how well it serves its purpose, and how it measures up against its rivals. These criteria imply two things.

- That quality is something that requires care on the part of the provider.
- That **quality** is largely subjective - it is in the eye of the beholder, the **customer**.

6.1 The management of quality

The **management** of quality is the process of:

(a) Establishing **standards of quality** for a product or service

(b) Establishing **procedures or production methods** which ought to ensure that these required standards of quality are met in a suitably high proportion of cases

(c) **Monitoring** actual quality

(d) Taking **control action** when actual quality falls below standard

Take the postal service as an example. The postal service might establish a standard that 90% of first class letters will be delivered on the day after they are posted, and 99% will be delivered within two days of posting.

(a) Procedures would have to be established for ensuring that these standards could be met (attending to such matters as frequency of collections, automated letter sorting, frequency of deliveries and number of staff employed).

(b) Actual performance could be monitored, perhaps by taking samples from time to time of letters that are posted and delivered.

(c) If the quality standard is not being achieved, management should take control action (employ more postal workers or advertise the use of postcodes again).

Quality management becomes **total (Total Quality Management (TQM)) when it is applied to everything a business does**.

KEY TERM

TOTAL QUALITY MANAGEMENT (TQM) is an 'Integrated and comprehensive system of planning and controlling all business functions so that products or services are produced which meet or exceed customer expectations. TQM is a philosophy of business behaviour, embracing principles such as employee involvement, continuous improvement at all levels and customer focus, as well as being a collection of related techniques aimed at improving quality such as full documentation of activities, clear goal setting and performance measurement from the customer perspective.' CIMA *Official Terminology*

Exam skills

As you learn the mechanics of these new management approaches, try not to view each one in isolation. For example, a question may require you to give reasons why the adoption of TQM is important in a JIT environment.

6.2 Get it right, first time

One of the basic principles of TQM is that the **cost of preventing mistakes is less than the cost of correcting them** once they occur. The aim should therefore be **to get things right first time**. Every mistake, delay and misunderstanding, directly costs an organisation money through **wasted time and effort**, including time taken in pacifying customers. The **lost potential for future sales because of poor customer service must also be taken into account**.

6.3 Continuous improvement

A second basic principle of TQM is dissatisfaction with the *status quo*: the belief that it is **always possible to improve** and so the aim should be to **'get it more right next time'**.

6.4 Quality assurance procedures

Because TQM embraces every activity of a business, quality assurance procedures **cannot be confined to the production process** but must also cover the work of sales, distribution and administration departments, the efforts of external suppliers, and the reaction of external customers.

Area	Procedure
Quality assurance of goods inwards	Suppliers' quality assurance schemes are being used increasingly. This is where the supplier guarantees the quality of goods supplied.
Inspection of output	The aim of carrying out inspection samples is to satisfy management that quality control in production is being maintained.
Monitoring customer reaction	Customer complaints should be monitored. Some companies survey customers on a regular basis
Employees and quality	To ensure that employees have a positive attitude towards quality • Responsibility for quality checking could be given to the worker himself • Inter-group competition to meet and beat quality standards could be introduced

Problems can therefore be overcome by **changing people's attitudes** rather than teaching them new tricks. The key issue is to instil **understanding of, and commitment to, working practices that lead to quality**.

CASE STUDY

As part of its TQM programme *BICC Cables* reorganised its factory from its traditional process-based operation into a dedicated product layout. It then launched two separate but related training and development activities, teamwork training and JIT training.

'To implement (JIT) working it was decided to use a firm of consultants in the first manufacturing cell to ensure a comprehensively structured introduction, with our own people working alongside them, and then to implement JIT in the other three cells ourselves.

We decided to create a **game** to convey JIT principles, and all employees in the first cell participated in it. This was followed by a series of **training/information sessions**, during which the importance of bottleneck management and inventory control was emphasised.

Employees rapidly gained an understanding of JIT and learnt the basic lessons that lots of work in progress was not necessary for the factory to be productive and that people did not always have to be busy to be effective. As in the game, we installed '**Kanbans**' on the shopfloor to limit and control the flow of inventory. When the Kanban is full, it acts as a signal to the previous process not to transfer any more work and, if required, to stop the previous process.

This was a difficult idea to take on. In effect we went **against traditional practice** by asking people to stop processes even though there was work to be done and to make themselves available for other work. This focuses attention on where effort needs to be applied to get products dispatched.

This cycle of training and implementation was repeated in the remaining three cells until the complete factory unit was operating along the JIT lines. The use of Kanbans has significantly reduced work in progress, and space has been released which has been used to accommodate new machines.'

6.5 Empowerment

Workers themselves are frequently the best source of information about how (or how not) to improve quality. **Empowerment** therefore has two key aspects.

(a)   Allowing workers to have the **freedom to decide how to do** the necessary work, using the skills they possess and acquiring new skills as necessary to be an effective team member.

(b)   Making workers **responsible** for achieving production targets and for quality control.

It is important to **question the value of these developments**, however.

> 'Do employees and management really find 'empowerment' to be liberating? Empirical studies suggest that 'empowerment' often amounts to the delegation of additional duties to employees. Limits have to be placed on what employees can do, so empowerment is often associated with rules, bureaucracy and form-filling. That apart, many employees find most satisfaction from outside work activities and are quite happy to confine themselves to doing what they are told while at work. The proponents of TQM are often very work-centred people themselves and tend to judge others by their own standards.
>
> Do teams contribute to organisational effectiveness? Just calling a group of people who work in the same office 'a team' does not make it a team. A team requires a high level of co-operation and consensus. Many competitive and motivated people find working in a team environment to be uncongenial. It means that every time you want to do anything you have to communicate with and seek approval from fellow team members. In practice, this is likely to involve bureaucracy and form-filling.
>
> ... it can be argued that TQM merely moves empowerment from management to employees. It has been argued that the latter cannot be expected to succeed where the former have failed.'

'Quality Streak', Bob Scarlett, *CIMA Insider,* September 2001

6.6 Design for quality

A TQM environment aims to get it right first time, and this means that **quality, not faults, must be designed into the organisation's products and operations from the outset**.

Quality control happens at various stages in the process of designing a product or service.

(a) At the **product design stage**, quality control means trying to design a product or service so that its specifications provide a suitable balance between price and quality (of sales and delivery, as well as manufacture) which will make the product or service competitive.

(b) **Production engineering** is the **process of designing the methods for making a product** (or service) **to the design specification**. It sets out to make production methods as efficient as possible, and to avoid the manufacture of sub-standard items.

(c) **Information systems** should be designed to get the required information to the right person at the right time; **distribution systems** should be designed to get the right item to the right person at the right time; and so on.

6.7 Quality control and inspection

A distinction should be made between **quality control** and **inspection**.

(a) **Quality control** involves setting controls for the process of manufacture or service delivery. It is a aimed at **preventing the manufacture of defective items** or the provision of defective services.

(b) **Inspection** is a technique of **identifying when defective items are being produced at an unacceptable level.** Inspection is usually carried out at three main points.

    (i) Receiving inspection – for raw materials and purchased components
    (ii) Floor or process inspection for WIP
    (iii) Final inspection or testing for finished goods

Question 9.5

Learning outcome A1(h)

Read the following extract from an article in the *Financial Times* in April 1993, and then list the features and methods of a quality information system that *Lloyds Bank* might have devised to collect information on the impact of the 'service challenge' described here.

'If you telephone a branch of *Lloyds Bank* and it rings five times before there is a reply; if the person who answers does not introduce him or herself by name during the conversation; if you are standing in a queue with more people in it than the number of tills, then something is wrong.'

'If any of these things happen then the branch is breaching standards of customer service set by the bank since last July ... the "service challenge" was launched in the bank's 1,888 branches last summer after being tested in 55 branches in 1990 ...'

'*Lloyds* already has evidence of the impact. Customers were more satisfied with pilot branches in 1991 than with others.'

Exam skills

Your syllabus emphasises the need for you to know about the possible impacts of methods such as TQM on performance measurement.

Examples such as the monitoring of quality at Lloyds Bank above might help you to give a practical emphasis to your answer.

6.8 Standard costing and TQM

Standard costing concentrates on **quantity** and ignores other factors contributing to an organisation's effectiveness. In a **total quality** environment, however, quantity is not an issue, **quality** is. Effectiveness in such an environment therefore centres on high quality output (produced as a result of high quality input); the cost of failing to achieve the required level of effectiveness is not measured in variances, but in terms of the **internal and external failure costs** which would not be identified by traditional standard costing analysis.

Standard costing might measure, say, **labour efficiency** in terms of individual tasks and the level of **output**. In a **total quality environment**, labour is most likely to be viewed as a number of **multi-task teams** who are responsible for completion of a part of the production process. The effectiveness of such a team is more appropriately measured in terms of **re-working** required, **returns** from customers, **defects** identified in subsequent stages of production and so on.

In a **TQM** environment there are likely to be **minimal rate variances** if the workforce are paid a guaranteed weekly wage. Fixed price contracts, with suppliers guaranteeing levels of quality, are often a feature, especially if a JIT system is also in place, and so there are likely to be **few, if any, material price and usage variances**.

So **can standard costing and TQM exist together?** Or do we need to **SCRAP** standard costing in a TQM environment?

Standard costing v TQM	
Scrap	Standard costs often incorporate a planned level of scrap in material standards. This is at odds with the TQM aim of 'zero defects' and there is no motivation to 'get it right first time'.
Continual improvements	Continual improvements should alter quantities of inputs, prices and so on, whereas standard costing is best used in a stable, standardised, repetitive environment.

Standard costing v TQM	
Responsibility	Standard costing systems make individual managers responsible for the variances relating to their part of the organisation's activities. A TQM programme, on the other hand, aims to make all personnel aware of, and responsible for, the importance of supplying the customer with a quality product.
Attainable standards	Attainable standards, which make some allowance for wastage and inefficiencies, are commonly set. The use of such standards conflicts with the elimination of waste which is a vital ingredient of a TQM programme.
Predetermined standards	Predetermined standards conflict with the TQM philosophy of continual improvement.

Now go back to question 7a.4 'Variance analysis and product quality' in Chapter 7a to remind yourself how variance analysis can help towards improving product quality.

Section summary

In the context of **Total Quality Management** 'quality' means getting it right first time, and improving continuously.

7 Costs of quality and cost of quality reports

Introduction

Cost of quality reports highlight the total cost to an organisation of producing products or services that do not conform with quality requirements. Four categories of cost should be reported: prevention costs, appraisal costs, internal failure costs and external failure costs.

7.1 Costs of quality

When we talk about quality-related costs you should remember that a concern for **good quality saves money**; it is **poor quality that costs money**.

KEY TERMS

The COST OF QUALITY is the 'Difference between the actual cost of producing, selling and supporting, products or services and the equivalent costs if there were no failures during production or usage.'

The cost of quality can be analysed into:

COST OF CONFORMANCE – 'Costs of achieving specified quality standards'

- COST OF PREVENTION – 'Costs incurred prior to or during production in order to prevent substandard or defective products or services from being produced'

- COST OF APPRAISAL – 'Costs incurred in order to ensure that outputs produced meet required quality standards'

(CIMA Official Terminology)

COST OF NON-CONFORMANCE is 'The cost of failure to deliver the required standard of quality.'

- COST OF INTERNAL FAILURE – 'Costs arising from inadequate quality which are identified before the transfer of ownership from supplier to purchaser'

- COST OF EXTERNAL FAILURE – 'Costs arising from inadequate quality discovered after the transfer of ownership from supplier to purchaser.'

(CIMA Official Terminology)

Quality-related cost	Example
Prevention costs	Quality engineering
	Design/development of quality control/inspection equipment
	Maintenance of quality control/inspection equipment
	Administration of quality control
	Training in quality control
Appraisal costs	Acceptance testing
	Inspection of goods inwards
	Inspection costs of in-house processing
	Performance testing
Internal failure costs	Failure analysis
	Re-inspection costs
	Losses from failure of purchased items
	Losses due to lower selling prices for sub-quality goods
	Costs of reviewing product specifications after failures
External failure costs	Administration of customer complaints section
	Costs of customer service section
	Product liability costs
	Cost of repairing products returned from customers
	Cost of replacing items due to sub-standard products/marketing errors

The **cost of conformance** is a **discretionary** cost which is incurred with the intention of **eliminating the costs of internal and external failure**. The **cost of non-conformance**, on the other hand, can **only be reduced by increasing the cost of conformance**. The **optimal investment in conformance costs** is when **total costs of quality reach a minimum** (which may be below 100% quality conformance). This is illustrated in the following diagram.

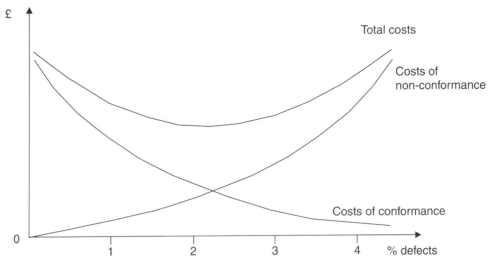

To achieve **0% defects, costs of conformance must be high**. As a **greater proportion of defects are accepted**, however, these costs can be **reduced**. At a level of **0% defects, costs of non-conformance** should be **nil** but these will **increase** as the **accepted level of defects rises**. There should therefore be an **acceptable level of defects** at which the **total costs of quality are at a minimum**.

7.2 Cost of quality reports

Shown below is a typical cost of quality report. **Some figures** in the report, such as the contribution forgone due to sales lost because of poor quality, may have to be **estimated,** but it is better to include an estimate rather than omit the category from the report.

The report has the following **uses.**

(a) By expressing each cost category as a percentage of sales revenue, **comparisons** can be made with previous periods, divisions within the group or other organisations, thereby highlighting problem areas. A comparison of the proportion of external failure costs to sales revenue with the figures for other organisations, for example, can provide some idea of the level of customer satisfaction.

(b) It can be used to make senior management aware of **how much is being spent** on quality-related costs.

(c) It can provide an indication of **how total quality costs could be reduced by a more sensible division of costs between the four categories.** For example, an increase in spending on prevention costs should reduce the costs of internal and external failure and hence reduce total spending.

COST OF QUALITY REPORT
YEAR ENDING 31 DECEMBER 20X0

	£'000	£'000	Cost as % of annual turnover (£10 million)
Prevention costs			
Design of quality control equipment	80		
Quality control training	80		
		160	1.6
Appraisal costs			
Inspection of goods inwards	90		
Inspection of WIP	100		
		190	1.9
Internal failure costs			
Scrap	150		
Rework	200		
		350	3.5
External failure costs			
Returns	500		
Contribution forgone on lost sales	400		
Handling customer complaints	100		
		1,000	10.0
		1,700	17.0

Although cost of quality reports provide a useful summary of the costs, effort and progress of quality, **non-financial quality measures** may be more appropriate for **lower levels of management**. Here are some examples of such measures.

- Number of customer complaints
- Number of warranty claims
- Number of defective units delivered to customers as a percentage of total units delivered

Section summary

Quality costs can be analysed into **prevention, appraisal, internal failure and external failure** costs and should be detailed in a **cost of quality report**.

8   World class manufacturing (WCM)

Introduction

World class manufacturing (WCM) is a term which was coined in the mid-1980s to **describe the fundamental changes taking place in manufacturing companies** we have been examining. WCM is a very broad term.

KEY TERM

'WORLD CLASS MANUFACTURING (WCM) describes the manufacture of high-quality products reaching customers quickly (or the delivery of a prompt and quality service) at a low cost to provide high performance and customer satisfaction.'

Peter J Clarke ('The old and the new in management accounting',
Management Accounting, June 1995)

The *Official Terminology*'s definition of WORLD CLASS MANUFACTURING is a 'Position of international manufacturing excellence, achieved by developing a culture based on factors such as continuous improvement, problem prevention, zero defect tolerance, customer-driven JIT-based production and total quality management.'

In essence, however, WCM can be taken to have four key elements.

Key element	Description
A new approach to product quality	Instead of a policy of trying to detect defects or poor quality in production as and when they occur, WCM sets out to identify the root causes of poor quality, eliminate them, and achieve zero defects, that is 100% quality, thereby incorporating the principles of TQM.
Just-in-time manufacturing	See Section 4
Managing people	WCM aims to utilise the skills and abilities of the work force to the full. Employees are given training in a variety of skills, so that they can switch from one task to another. They are also given more responsibility for production scheduling and quality. A team approach is encouraged, with strong trust between management and workers.
Flexible approach to customer requirements	The WCM policy is to develop close relationships with customers in order to know what their requirements are, supply them on time, with short delivery lead times and change the product mix quickly and develop new products or modify existing products as customer needs change.

A WCM manufacturer will have a clear **manufacturing strategy** aimed at issues such as quality and reliability, short lead times (the time from start to finish of production), flexibility and customer satisfaction. But to compete, the world class manufacturer must appreciate that it is **not just in manufacturing that he must excel**. A **clear understanding** of the relationship between all of the factors which add value to an organisation's products (the **value chain**) is vital.

8.1 The value chain

The value chain is made up of the following.

- Research and development
- Design
- Production
- Marketing

- Distribution
- Customer service
- Customers

It **starts externally** with suppliers, links them to the internal functions of R&D, design, production, marketing, distribution and customer service, and **ends externally** with suppliers.

To improve quality, reduce costs and increase innovation, the manufacturer must ensure that the **functions within the value chain are coordinated** within the overall organisational framework.

Section summary

World class manufacturing (WCM) aims for high quality, fast production, and the flexibility to respond to customer needs.

Chapter Roundup

✓ Changes to the **competitive environment**, **product life cycles** and **customer requirements** have had a significant impact on the modern business environment.

✓ Different approaches for **organising a manufacturing process** include **jobbing industries, batch processing** and **mass production**.

✓ To compete effectively organisations need to continually redesign their products and to shorten the time it takes to get them to the market place. Manufacturing processes must therefore be sufficiently flexible both to accommodate new product design rapidly and to satisfy the demand for greater product diversity.

✓ **Advanced manufacturing technology (AMT)** is a general expression encompassing **computer-aided design (CAD), computer-aided manufacturing (CAM), flexible manufacturing systems (FMS)** and a wide array of innovative computer equipment.

✓ The **production management strategies** linked to AMT are materials requirement planning (MRPI), manufacturing resource planning (MRPII), enterprise resource planning (ERP), optimised production technology (OPT) and just-in-time (JIT).

✓ **JIT** aims for zero inventory and perfect quality and operates by demand-pull. It consists of **JIT purchasing** and **JIT production** and results in lower investment requirements, space savings, greater customer satisfaction and increased flexibility.

✓ **Synchronous manufacturing** aims to ensure that all operations within an organisation are performed for the common good of the organisation.

✓ In the context of **Total Quality Management** 'quality' means getting it right first time, and improving continuously.

✓ **Quality costs** can be analysed into **prevention, appraisal, internal failure** and **external failure** costs and should be detailed in a **cost of quality report.**

✓ **World class manufacturing (WCM)** aims for high quality, fast production, and the flexibility to respond to customer needs.

Quick Quiz

1   Match the type of production with one of the descriptions (1) to (4).

Jobbing industries   (1)   Merges the flexibility of the functional layout with the speed and productivity of the product layout

Batch processing   (2)   Uses a product-based layout

Mass/flow production   (3)   Factory is typically laid out on a functional basis

Cellular manufacturing   (4)   Uses functional layout but with a high number of specialised machines

2   Choose the correct words from those highlighted.

Materials requirement planning/manufacturing requirement planning/materials resource planning/manufacturing resource planning is concerned with maximising efficiency in the timing of orders for raw materials or parts that are placed with external suppliers and efficient scheduling of the manufacturing and assembly of the end product.

3   Fill in the blanks in this list of the nine essential elements of JIT.

(a)   JIT ....
(b)   Close relationships with ....
(c)   Uniform ....
(d)   Set-up time ....
(e)   .... cells
(f)   ....
(g)   .... (Kanban)
(h)   .... maintenance
(i)   .... involvement

4   The cost of inspecting a product for quality is a value-added cost. True or false?

5   Which of the following is/are correct?

(a)   Cost of conformance = cost of prevention + cost of internal failure
(b)   Cost of conformance = cost of internal failure + cost of external failure
(c)   Cost of non-conformance = cost of internal failure + cost of external failure
(d)   Cost of conformance = cost of appraisal + cost of prevention
(e)   Cost of non-conformance = cost of prevention + cost of appraisal
(f)   Cost of non-conformance = cost of appraisal + cost of external failure

6   Match the cost to the correct cost category.

Costs

(a)   Administration of quality control
(b)   Product liability costs
(c)   Acceptance testing
(d)   Losses due to lower selling prices for sub-quality goods

Cost categories

•   Prevention costs   •   Internal failure costs
•   Appraisal costs   •   External failure costs

7   What is an FMS?

A   Fast manufacturing system   C   Flexible materials system
B   Flexible manufacturing system   D   Fixed manufacturing sequence

8   Proponents of synchronous manufacturing are also supporters of JIT. True or false?

9   *Choose the correct words from those highlighted.*

     Quality control/inspection is aimed at preventing the manufacture of defective items.

10   What are the four key elements of WCM?

11   Which of the following is not a feature of JIT?

A	Pull system	C	Employee involvement
B	Zero inventory	D	Increased lead times

Answers to Quick Quiz

1   Jobbing industries   - description (3)
     Batch processing   - description (4)
     Mass/flow production   - description (2)
     Cellular manufacturing   - description (1)

2   Materials requirement planning

3   (a) JIT purchasing
     (b) Close relationships with suppliers
     (c) Uniform loading
     (d) Set-up time reduction
     (e) Machine cells
     (f) Quality
     (g) Pull system (Kanban)
     (h) Preventative maintenance
     (i) Employee involvement

4   False

5   (c) and (d) are correct.

6   (a) Prevention costs
     (b) External failure costs
     (c) Appraisal costs
     (d) Internal failure costs

7   B   Flexible manufacturing system.

8   False. They regard JIT as unfocussed.

9   Quality control

10   A new approach to product quality
     JIT manufacturing
     Managing people
     Flexible approach to customer requirements

11   D   JIT features machine cells which help products flow from machine to machine without having to
          wait for the next stage of processing or returning to store. Lead times and WIP are therefore
          reduced.

Answers to Questions

9.1 MRP and ERP

MRP and ERP systems are production management strategies that are primarily designed to plan enterprise-wide resources. They can assist the management accountant in a variety of ways as follows.

- MRP systems use a **master production schedule** to derive **details** of the **parts** and **materials** required at various stages of the production process. The management accountant can use this information as a basis for completing the **production cost budget** and the underlying budgets (materials cost budget, labour cost budget and so on) for the forthcoming period

- The detailed scheduling of manufacturing and assembly requirements will **facilitate preparation** of **budgets** such as the **materials purchases budget** and this in turn will provide an input to the **cash budget**

- ERP systems plan enterprise-wide resources. For example even the marketing and personnel functions are integrated so that the management accountant can **identify** the **cash** and other **resources** that will be required by the **various business functions** and the **timing** of those requirements

- The detailed schedule of resources required for each product provides the management accountant with the basis for calculating the **product standard cost** and keeping it **up to date** if there are any changes to resource specifications

- An ERP system produces information on resource consumption in a **real-time environment**, thus enabling **early comparison** with the standard resources according to the detailed schedule and hence **rapid feedback** of **variance information** to management

9.2 JIT system

The correct answer is B.

Revision of stock controls levels would not be necessary because the control level system would be abandoned completely. Parts and raw materials would be purchased in small frequent deliveries against bulk contracts. Therefore statement I is not correct.

II is not correct because the number of suppliers would be reduced in a JIT environment. There may be a long-term commitment to a single supplier.

III is correct. Suppliers may be chosen because of their close proximity so that they can respond quickly to changes in the company's demands.

IV is correct. Accurate forecasting of demand reduces the need for inventories.

V is correct. Production management will aim to eliminate the occurrence of rejects and defective materials since these situations stop the flow of production.

9.3 Value-added activity

The correct answer is C.

The other activities are non-value-adding activities.

9.4 JIT

The correct answer is B.

9.5 Quality

A wide variety of answers is possible. The article goes on to explain how the bank is actually going about monitoring the impact of the initiative.

(a)   It has devised a 100 point scale showing average satisfaction with branch service.

(b)   It conducts a 'first impressions' survey of all new customers.

(c)   There is also a general survey carried out every six months which seeks the views of a weighted sample of 350 customers per branch.

(d)   A survey company telephones each branch anonymously twice a month to test how staff respond to enquiries about products.

(e)   A quarter of each branch's staff answer a monthly questionnaire about the bank's products to test their knowledge.

(f)   Groups of employees working in teams in branches are allowed to set their own additional standards. This is to encourage participation.

(g)   Branches that underperform are more closely watched by 24 managers who monitor the initiative.

Now try these questions from the Exam Question Bank	**Number**	**Level**	**Marks**	**Time**
	Q13	Examination	5	9 mins
	Q14	Examination	5	9 mins

MODERN COSTING TECHNIQUES –
THROUGHPUT AND BACKFLUSH ACCOUNTING

 Having looked at recent developments in manufacturing and business practice, you will now go on to learn about costing systems and performance monitoring systems that have been developed to **suit modern practices.**

The theory of constraints (TOC) provides the basis for the development of throughput accounting (TA) (Sections 1 and 2). As a production system (TOC) and an accounting and performance monitoring system (TA), they are ideally suited to the modern manufacturing environment in which production is an immediate response to customer demand. The aim is to maximise the net return on sales. They can also be used in service industries where bottleneck processes can be identified and alleviated.

Backflush accounting (Section 3) is an accounting system that has been specifically designed for use with JIT systems. It cannot be used unless inventory levels are minimal. Its main advantage is the simplification it brings.

topic list	learning outcomes	syllabus references	ability required
1 The theory of constraints (TOC)	A1(a), (h)	A1(xiv)	analysis
2 Throughput accounting	A1(a)	A1(i)	analysis
3 Backflush accounting	A1(h)	A1(xiv)	comprehension

1 The theory of constraints (TOC)

Introduction

Theory of constraints is a set of concepts developed in the USA which aim to identify the binding constraints in a production system and which strive for evenness of production flow so that the organisation works as effectively as possible. No inventories should be held, except prior to the binding constraint.

Its key financial concept is to **turn materials into sales as quickly as possible**, thereby maximising throughput and the net cash generated from sales. This is to be achieved by striving for **balance in production processes**, and so **evenness of production flow** is an important aim.

KEY TERM

THEORY OF CONSTRAINTS (TOC) is a 'Procedure based on identifying bottlenecks (constraints), maximising their use, subordinating other facilities to the demand of the bottleneck facilities, alleviating bottlenecks and re-evaluating the whole system.'

A CONSTRAINT (or BOTTLENECK RESOURCE) is an 'Activity, resource or policy that limits the ability to achieve an objective.

(CIMA Official Terminology)

1.1 Managing constraints

One process will inevitably act as a bottleneck (or limiting factor) and constrain throughput. This is known as a **binding constraint** in TOC terminology.

In order to manage constraints effectively, **Goldratt** has proposed a **five-step process** of ongoing improvement. The process operated as a **continuous loop**.

Identify the **binding constraint**/bottleneck

Exploit

The highest possible output must be achieved from the binding constraint. This output must never be delayed and as such a buffer inventory should be held immediately before the constraint.

Subordinate

Operations prior to the binding constraint should operate at the same speed as it so that WIP does not build up.

Elevate the system bottleneck. Steps should be taken to increase resources or improve its efficiency.

Return to Step 1

The removal of one bottleneck will create another elsewhere in the system.

KEY TERMS

THROUGHPUT CONTRIBUTION = **sales revenue – direct material cost**

CONVERSION COST (in TOC) = **all operating costs except direct material cost** (ie all costs except totally variable costs)

INVESTMENT COST = **inventory, equipment, building costs and so on**

1.2 Throughput contribution

The aim of TOC is to maximise throughput contribution while keeping conversion and investment costs to a minimum. If a strategy for increasing throughput contribution is being considered it will therefore only be accepted if conversion and investment costs increase by a lower amount than contribution.

KEY POINT

It is important to realise that TOC is not an accounting system but a production system.

Section summary

Theory of constraints is a set of concepts developed in the USA which aim to identify the binding constraints in a production system and which strive for evenness of production flow so that the organisation works as effectively as possible. No inventories should be held, except prior to the binding constraint.

Goldratt's five steps for dealing with a bottleneck activity are:

Step 1: Identify   Step 4: Elevate
Step 2: Exploit   Step 5: Return to step 1
Step 3: Subordinate

2 Throughput accounting

Introduction

Throughput accounting is the accounting system developed in the UK, based on the theory of constraints and JIT. It measures the throughput contribution per factory hour. It is very similar to marginal costing but can be used to make longer-term decisions about production equipment/capacity.

The concept of throughput accounting has been developed from TOC as an **alternative system of cost and management accounting in a JIT environment**.

KEY TERM

'THROUGHPUT ACCOUNTING (TA) is an approach to accounting which is largely in sympathy with the JIT philosophy. In essence, TA assumes that a manager has a given set of resources available. These comprise existing buildings, capital equipment and labour force. Using these resources, purchased materials and parts must be processed to generate sales revenue. Given this scenario the most appropriate financial objective to set for doing this is the maximisation of throughput (Goldratt and Cox, 1984) which is defined as: sales revenue *less* direct material cost.'

(Tanaka, Yoshikawa, Innes and Mitchell, *Contemporary Cost Management*)

The *Official Terminology*'s definition of THROUGHPUT ACCOUNTING (TA) is 'Variable cost accounting presentation based on the definition of throughput (sales minus material and component costs).'

TA is different from all other management accounting systems because of what it **emphasises**.

- Firstly **throughput**
- Secondly inventory minimisation
- Thirdly cost control

TA is based on three concepts.

2.1 Concept 1

In the short run, most costs in the factory (with the exception of materials costs) are fixed. Because TA differentiates between fixed and variable costs it is often compared with marginal costing and **some people argue that there is no difference between marginal costing and throughput accounting.** For this reason TA is sometimes referred to as super variable costing and indeed there are some similarities in the assumptions underlying the two methods. However, on marginal costing direct labour costs are usually assumed to be variable costs. Years ago this assumption was true, but employees are not usually paid piece rate today and they are not laid off for part of the year when there is no work, and so labour cost is not truly variable. If this is accepted the two techniques are identical in some respects, but **marginal costing is generally thought of as being purely a short-term decision-making technique** while **TA, or at least TOC, was conceived with the aim of changing manufacturing strategy to achieve evenness of flow. It is therefore much more than a short-term decision technique.**

Because **TA combines all conversion costs** together and does not attempt to examine them in detail it is particularly **suited to use with activity based costing (ABC),** which examines the behaviour of these costs and assumes them to be variable in the long run. We will examine ABC in detail in the next chapter.

2.2 Concept 2

In a JIT environment, all inventory is a 'bad thing' and the **ideal inventory level is zero.** Products should not be made unless there is a customer waiting for them. This means **unavoidable idle capacity must be accepted in some operations,** but not for the operation that is the bottleneck of the moment. There is one exception to the zero inventory policy, being that a buffer inventory should be held prior to the bottleneck process.

2.3 Concept 3

Profitability is determined by the rate at which 'money comes in at the door' (that is, sales are made) and, in a JIT environment, this depends on how quickly goods can be produced to satisfy customer orders. Since the goal of a profit-orientated organisation is to make money, inventory must be sold for that goal to be achieved.

The buffer inventory and any other work in progress or finished goods inventory should be **valued at material cost only** until the output is eventually sold, so that **no value will be added and no profit earned until the sale takes place.** Producing output just to add to work in progress or finished goods inventory creates no profit, and so should not be encouraged.

Question 10.1	Throughput vs conventional cost accounting

Learning outcome A1(a)

Throughput accounting versus conventional cost accounting

How are the concepts of throughput accounting a direct contrast to the fundamental principles of conventional cost accounting?

Exam skills

Be prepared for a question such as 'compare and contrast marginal and throughput accounting'.

2.4 Bottleneck resources

The aim of **modern manufacturing** approaches is to match production resources with the demand for them. This implies that there are **no constraints, termed bottleneck resources** in TA, within an organisation. The throughput philosophy entails the **identification** and **elimination** of these bottleneck resources. Where they **cannot be eliminated production must be limited to the capacity of the bottleneck resource in order to avoid the build-up of work in progress.** If a rearrangement of existing resources or buying-in resources does not alleviate the bottleneck, investment in new equipment may be necessary. The **elimination of one bottleneck is likely to lead to the creation of another** at a previously satisfactory location, however. The **management of bottlenecks** therefore becomes a **primary concern** of the manager seeking to increase throughput.

(a)   There is nothing to be gained by measuring and encouraging the efficiency of machines that do not govern the overall flow of work.

(b)   Likewise, there is little point in measuring the efficiency of production staff working on non-bottleneck processes.

(c)   Bonuses paid to encourage faster working on non-bottleneck processes are wasted and could lead to increased storage costs and more faulty goods.

Other factors that might limit throughput other than a lack of production resources (bottlenecks)

(a)   The existence of an non-competitive selling price.

(b)   The need to deliver on time to particular customers, which may disrupt normal production flow.

(c)   The lack of product quality and reliability, which may cause large amounts of rework or an unnecessary increase in production volume.

(d)   Unreliable material suppliers, which will lead to poor quality products that require rework.

2.5 Identifying the bottleneck resource

It may not always be obvious which is the bottleneck resource and a process of trial and error for a few periods can be an expensive and inefficient way of attempting to identify it.

If the resource constraint is machine capacity, it is possible to identify the constrained machine through the calculation of **machine utilisation rates**.

Example: machine utilisation rates

A company produces three products using three different machines. The following data is available for the latest period.

	Product L Hours per unit	Product M Hours per unit	Product N Hours per unit
Machine hours required:			
Mixing machine	2	5	3
Cutting machine	3	4	2
Finishing machine	1	2	2
Sales demand	2,700 units	1,200 units	2,500 units

Maximum capacity is as follows.

	Hours available
Mixing machine	22,000
Cutting machine	15,400
Finishing machine	7,300

Required

(a)   Calculate the machine utilisation rate for each machine

(b)   Identify which of the machines is the bottleneck resource

Solution

(a)   Number of machine hours required to fulfil sales demand.

	Product L Hours	Product M Hours	Product N Hours	Total Hours
Mixing machine	5,400	6,000	7,500	18,900
Cutting machine	8,100	4,800	5,000	17,000
Finishing machine	2,700	2,400	5,000	10,100

$$\text{Machine utilisation rate} = \frac{\text{machine hours required to meet sales demand}}{\text{machine hours available}}$$

	Mixing machine	Cutting machine	Finishing machine
Machine utilisation rate	$\dfrac{18,900}{22,000}$	$\dfrac{17,900}{15,400}$	$\dfrac{10,100}{7,300}$
	= 85.9%	= 116.2%	= 138.3%

(b)   Capacity on the finishing machine is the bottleneck resource. The machine utilisation rate is higher than 100 per cent and it is the largest of the three rates.

2.6 Throughput measures

2.6.1 Return per time period

In a throughput accounting environment, the overall **focus of attention** is the **rate at which the organisation can generate profits**. To monitor this, the return on the throughput through the bottleneck resource is monitored using:

$$\textbf{Return per time period} = \frac{\text{sales revenue} - \text{material costs}}{\text{time period}}$$

This measure shows the **value added** by an organisation during a particular time period. Time plays a crucial role in the measure, so **managers** are strongly **encouraged to remove bottlenecks that might cause production delays**.

2.6.2 Return per time period on bottleneck resource

In throughput accounting, the limiting factor is the bottleneck. The return per time period measure can be adapted and used for **ranking products to optimise production** in the **short term**.

$$\textbf{Product return per minute} = \frac{\text{sales price} - \text{material costs}}{\text{minutes on key/bottleneck resource}}$$

Ranking products on the basis of throughput contribution per minute (or hour) on the bottleneck resource is **similar in concept to maximising contribution per unit of limiting factor**. Such product rankings are for **short-term production scheduling only**. In throughput accounting, bottlenecks should be eliminated and so rankings may change quickly. Customer demand can, of course, cause the bottleneck to change at short notice too.

Rankings by TA product return and by contribution per unit of limiting factor may be different. Which one leads to profit maximisation? The correct approach depends on the variability or otherwise of labour and variable overheads, which in turn depends on the time horizon of the decision. Both are short-term profit maximisation techniques and given that labour is nowadays likely to be fixed in the short term, it could be argued that TA provides the more correct solution. An analysis of variable overheads would be needed to determine their variability.

KEY POINT

Bear in mind that the huge majority of organisations cannot produce and market products based on short-term profit considerations alone. Strategic-level issues such as market developments, product developments and stage reached in the product life cycle must also be taken into account.

2.6.3 TA ratio

Products can also be ranked according to the **throughput accounting ratio (TA ratio).**

$$\text{TA ratio} = \frac{\text{throughput contribution or value added per time period}}{\text{conversion cost per time period}}$$

$$= \frac{(\text{sales} - \text{material costs}) \text{ per time period}}{(\text{labour} + \text{overhead}) \text{ per time period}}$$

This measure has the **advantage** of **including the costs involved in running the factory. The higher the ratio, the more profitable the company**.

A profitable product should have a ratio greater than one. If a product's ratio is less than one the organisation is losing money every time that product is produced.

Here's an example. Note the figures are in £ per hour.

	Product A £ per hour	Product B £ per hour
Sales price	100	150
Material cost	(40)	(50)
Throughput	60	100
Conversion cost	(50)	(50)
Profit	10	50
TA ratio	$\frac{60}{50} = 1.2$	$\frac{100}{50} = 2.0$

Profit will be maximised by manufacturing as much of product B as possible.

Question 10.2	Product return per factory hour and TA ratio

Learning outcome A1(a)

Each unit of product B requires 4 machine hours. Machine time is the bottleneck resource, there being 650 machine hours available per week.

B is sold for £120 per unit and has a direct material cost of £35 per unit. Total factory costs are £13,000 per week.

Required

Calculate the return per factory hour and the TA ratio for product B.

If conversion cost cannot be directly allocated to products (because it is not a unit-level manufacturing cost), the TA ratio cannot be calculated and products have to be ranked in terms of throughput contribution per hour or minute of bottleneck resource.

2.6.4 Effectiveness measures and cost control

Traditional efficiency measures such as standard costing variances and labour ratios are **unsuitable** in a TA environment because traditional efficiency should not be encouraged (as the **labour force should not produce just for inventory**).

Effectiveness is a **more important** issue. The **current effectiveness ratio** compares current levels of effectiveness with the standard.

$$\text{Current effectiveness ratio} = \frac{\text{standard minutes of throughput achieved}}{\text{minutes available}}$$

Question 10.3	Variances and throughput accounting

Learning outcome A1(a)

Briefly explain whether or not an adverse labour rate variance caused by overtime worked at the bottleneck is a good or bad thing in a throughput accounting environment.

2.7 Is it good or bad?

TA is seen by some as **too short term**, as all costs other than direct material are regarded as fixed. This is not true. But it does **concentrate on direct material costs** and does nothing for the control of other costs. These characteristics make throughput accounting a **good complement for activity based costing (ABC)**, as ABC focuses on labour and overhead costs. We will cover ABC in detail in the next chapter.

TA attempts to maximise throughput whereas traditional systems attempt to maximise profit. By attempting to maximise throughput an organisation could be producing in excess of the profit-maximising output.

2.8 Where TA helps direct attention

- Bottlenecks
- Key elements in making profits
- Inventory reduction

- Reducing the response time to customer demand
- Evenness of production flow
- Overall effectiveness and efficiency

(a) An article in *Management Accounting* in April 1992 describes a case study of Garrett Automotive that adopted TA with the particular aim of managing and alleviating bottlenecks in the production process and moving towards 'evenness of flow'. When the project started one particular manufacturing area had three machines with the following outputs:

Machine A 30 units per hour
Machine B 18 units per hour
Machine C 80 units per hour

The production system was certainly not in balance.

As a result of the initial analysis, machine D was moved to assist B and this increased capacity at this point to 21 units per hour. Then machine E was purchased very cheaply and this increased output at B to 26 units per hour. (Machine E paid for itself in just five weeks.) Machine C was due for replacement shortly afterwards and it was replaced with a new and cheaper machine that produced just 26 units per hour. These three changes raised output from 2,025 units to 2,700 units per week and greatly increased profit.

Changing the production process brought considerable financial benefits and changed the reporting emphasis to the critical need to adhere to production schedules and to 'first-time capability' (getting it right first time). The monthly management report was reduced from more than forty pages to five pages and it was made available if requested to all employees. It forced management accounting staff to get back to understanding what is actually happening on the shop floor and to be inventive about performance measures.

(b)   An article in the *Harvard Business Review* September-October 1996 cites the instance of Pratt & Whitney the jet engine manufacturer, which had ten computer controlled grinding machines that were used to shape cast blades. The machines cost $80M and were technical marvels, grinding a blade in just three minutes. They were fed and unloaded by robots but it took eight hours to change the machines so that they could grind a different sort of blade. In addition each blade had to be encased in a special metal alloy to prevent it fracturing during grinding and this was difficult to remove after the process. Twenty two members of staff were required to maintain the complicated computerised control system. As a result of all this, each blade took ten days to pass through the grinding department.

After studies, eight simple grinding machines that did not require the blades to be encased in metal were purchased to replace the computer controlled machines. The time it took to change from grinding one type of blade to the next took just 100 seconds with these machines and it only took the labour of one full-time and one part-time member of staff to feed and control the machines. Processing time increased from three minutes to 75 minutes, however, but this was not a major disadvantage. The factory space required was halved and the time for a blade to pass through the grinding department fell from ten days to 75 minutes.

Example: throughput accounting

Corrie produces three products, X, Y and Z. The capacity of Corrie's plant is restricted by process alpha. Process alpha is expected to be operational for eight hours per day and can produce 1,200 units of X per hour, 1,500 units of Y per hour, and 600 units of Z per hour.

Selling prices and material costs for each product are as follows.

Product	Selling price $ per unit	Material cost $ per unit	Throughput contribution $ per unit
X	150	70	80
Y	120	40	80
Z	300	100	200

Conversion costs are $720,000 per day.

Requirements

(a)   Calculate the profit per day if daily output achieved is 6,000 units of X, 4,500 units of Y and 1,200 units of Z.

(b)   Determine the efficiency of the bottleneck process given the output in (a).

(c)   Calculate the TA ratio for each product.

(d)   In the absence of demand restrictions for the three products, advise Corrie's management on the optimal production plan.

Solution

(a) Profit per day = throughput contribution – conversion cost
                     = [($80 × 6,000) + ($80 × 4,500) + ($200 × 1,200)] – $720,000
                     = $360,000

(b)

Product	Minutes in alpha per unit	Minutes in alpha per day
X	60/1,200 = 0.05	6,000 × 0.05 = 300
Y	60/1,500 = 0.04	4,500 × 0.04 = 180
Z	60/600 = 0.10	1,200 × 0.10 = 120
		600

Total hours = 600 minutes ÷ 60 = 10 hours

Hours available = 8, hours produced = 10, ∴ Efficiency = 125%

(c) TA ratio = throughput contribution per factory hour/conversion cost per factory hour

Conversion cost per factory hour = $720,000/8 = $90,000

Product	Throughput contribution per factory hour	Cost per factory hour	TA ratio
X	$80 × (60 ÷ 0.05 mins) = $96,000	$90,000	1.07
Y	$80 × (60 ÷ 0.04 mins) = $120,000	$90,000	1.33
Z	$200 × (60 ÷ 0.10 mins) = $120,000	$90,000	1.33

(d) An attempt should be made to remove the restriction on output caused by process alpha's capacity. This will probably result in another bottleneck emerging elsewhere. The extra capacity required to remove the restriction could be obtained by working overtime, making process improvements or product specification changes. Until the volume of throughput can be increased, output should be concentrated upon products Y and Z (greatest TA ratios), unless there are good marketing reasons for continuing the current production mix.

Question 10.4   Binding constraints and TA ratio

Learning outcome A1(a)

A company's binding constraint is the capacity of machine M. The throughput accounting (TA) ratio for product P on machine M is 1.4.

Explain how the TA ratio is calculated and state FOUR actions that management could consider to improve the TA ratio for product P.

2.9 Throughput accounting in service and retail industries

Sales staff have always preferred to use a marginal costing approach so that they can use their discretion on discounts, and **retail organisations** have traditionally thought in terms of sales revenue less the bought in price of goods. The throughput accounting approach is therefore **nothing new** to them.

Throughput accounting can be used very effectively in **support departments and service industries** to **highlight and remove bottlenecks**. For example, if there is a delay in processing a potential customer's application, business can be lost or the potential customer may decide not to proceed. Sometimes credit rating checks are too detailed, slowing the whole procedure unnecessarily and delaying acceptance from say 24 hours to eight days.

A similar problem could occur in hospitals where work that could be done by nurses has to be carried out by doctors. Not only does this increase the cost of the work but it may well cause a bottleneck by tying up a doctor's time unnecessarily.

| **Question 10.5** | Product costing versus TA |

Learning outcome A1(a)

Here are some statements about traditional product costing. Provide the equivalent statements about throughput accounting.

Statement 1: Inventory is valued in the financial statements at full production cost.
Statement 2: Labour, material and variable overheads are treated as variable costs.
Statement 3: A process is deemed efficient if labour and machine time are fully utilised.
Statement 4: Value is added when a unit of product is produced.

Section summary

Throughput accounting is the accounting system developed in the UK, based on the theory of constraints and JIT. It measures the throughput contribution per factory hour. It is very similar to marginal costing but can be used to make longer-term decisions about production equipment/capacity.

3 Backflush accounting

9/10

Introduction

Backflush accounting is a method of accounting that can be used with JIT production systems. It saves a considerable amount of time as it avoids having to make a number of accounting entries that are required by a traditional system.

Backflush accounting is the name given to the method of keeping cost accounts employed if **backflush costing** is used. The two terms are almost interchangeable.

Traditional costing systems use **sequential tracking** (also known as **synchronous tracking**) to track costs sequentially as products pass from raw materials to work in progress, to finished goods and finally to sales. In other words, material costs are charged to WIP when materials are issued to production, direct labour and overhead costs are charged in a similar way as the cost is incurred or very soon after.

If a production system such as **JIT** is used, sequentially tracking means that **all entries are made at almost the same moment** and so a different accounting system can be used. In **backflush costing/accounting, costs are calculated and charged when the product is sold, or when it is transferred to the finished goods store**.

KEY TERM

BACKFLUSH COSTING is 'A method of costing, associated with a JIT production system, which applies cost to the output of a process. Costs do not mirror the flow of products through the production process, but are attached to the output produced (finished goods inventory and cost of sales), on the assumption that such backflushed costs are a realistic measure of the actual costs incurred.' CIMA *Official Terminology*

The CIMA definition above omits the fact that **budgeted or standard costs are used to work backwards to 'flush' out manufacturing costs** for the units produced. (Hence the rather unattractive name for the system!) The application of **standard costs** to finished goods units, or to units sold, is used in order to **calculate cost of goods sold**, thereby **simplifying** the costing system and creating **savings in**

administrative effort. In a true backflush accounting system, records of materials used and work in progress are not required as material cost can be calculated from either finished goods or goods sold.

Backflush costing runs **counter to the principle enshrined in IAS 2**, and the staple of cost accounting for decades, that inventory and WIP should be accounted for by calculating cost and net realisable value of 'specific individual items of inventory'. The substantial **reduction in inventories that is a feature of JIT** means that **inventory valuation is less relevant,** however, and therefore the **costing system** can be **simplified** to a considerable extent. In the 1980s, Johnson & Kaplan in fact wrote that **management rarely requires a value to be placed on inventory for internal management purposes,** the **value only being required for external reporting**.

Backflush costing is therefore **appropriate** for organisations trying to keep **inventories to the very minimum**. In such circumstances, the **recording** of every little increase in inventory value, as each nut and bolt is added, is simply an expensive and **non-value-added activity** that should be **eliminated**.

Example: working backwards from output

To take a **very simplified example**, if backflush costing is used, the management accountant might extract the following information from the monthly accounting transaction records and production records.

Orders completed and despatched in July	196 units
Orders prepared in advance 1 July	3 units
Orders prepared in advance 31 July	2 units
Scrapped items	5 units
Conversion costs in the month	£250,000
Material costs in the month	£475,000

This is enough to place a value on inventories and production as follows.

	Units		£
B/f	(3)	Conversion costs	250,000
Despatched	196	Material costs	475,000
Scrapped	5	Total costs	725,000
C/f	2		
Units produced	200		

Cost per unit is £725,000 divided by 200 units = £3,625

In this case a single process account could be drawn up as follows.

	Dr (£)	Cr (£)
Inventory b/fwd (3 × £3,625)	10,875	
Materials	475,000	
Conversion costs	250,000	
To finished goods (196 × £3,625)		710,500
Losses etc written off to income statement (5 × £3,625)		18,125
Inventory c/fwd (2 × £3,625)		7,250
	735,875	735,875

3.1 Arguments of traditional management accountants

(a) The figure for **losses** here is **inaccurate**. They would say that in reality the faulty goods would have been scrapped when only partially complete and it is wrong to value them at the same cost as a fully finished good unit.

(b) Using this approach, the figure for inventories b/fwd and c/fwd will not tie up with the accounts for last month and next month, because the material and conversion costs may be different.

3.2 Reply of modern management accountants

(a)   **Losses** represent only about 2% of total cost and are **not material**. In any case putting a value to them is less **important** than **improving the quality of production procedures** (on the basis of **TQM** practices and non-financial production information) to ensure that they do not occur again.

(b)   **Finished good inventories represent between 1% and 2% of total cost and are immaterial.** Slight discrepancies in valuation methods of b/fwds and c/fwds will amount to a **fraction** of a percentage, and can be written off in the month as a small **variance**.

(c)   Even with computers the **cost of tracing units** every step of the way through production – with 'normal' and 'abnormal' losses, equivalent units and numerous process accounts – **is simply not worth it, in terms of the benefit derived** from the information it provides.

3.3 Variants of backflush costing

(a)   **Trigger points determine when the entries are made in the accounting system**. There will be either one or two trigger points that trigger entries in the accounts.

    (i)   When materials are purchased/received

    (ii)   When goods are completed or when they are sold

        In a **true JIT system** where no inventories are held the **first trigger**, when raw materials are purchased, is **unnecessary**.

(b)   Actual conversion costs are recorded as incurred, just as in conventional recording systems. Conversion costs are applied to products at the second trigger point based on a standard cost. It is assumed that any conversion costs not applied to products are carried forward and disposed of at the period end.

(c)   **Direct labour** is included as an **indirect cost in conversion cost with overheads**. (Production is only required when there is demand for it in a JIT system, and so production labour will be paid regardless of the level of activity.)

(d)   All indirect costs are treated as a fixed period expense.

Example: accounting entries at different trigger points

The transactions for period 8 20X1 for Clive are as follows.

Purchase of raw materials	£24,990
Conversion costs incurred	£20,220
Finished goods produced (used in methods 2 & 3 only)	4,900 units
Sales	4,850 units

There are no opening inventories of raw materials, WIP or finished goods. The standard cost per unit is made up of £5.10 for materials and £4.20 for conversion costs.

Solution

For 1 trigger point – when goods are sold (method 1)

This is the simplest method of backflush costing. There is only one **trigger point** and that is **when the entry to the cost of goods sold account is required** when the goods are sold. (This method assumes that units are sold as soon as they are produced.)

			£	£
(a)	DEBIT	Conversion costs control	20,220	
	CREDIT	Expense payables		20,220
		Being the actual conversion costs incurred		

			£	£
(b)	DEBIT	Cost of goods sold (4,850 × £9.30)	45,105	
	CREDIT	Payables (4,850 × £5.10)		24,735
	CREDIT	Conversion costs allocated (4,850 × £4.20)		20,370

Being the standard cost of goods sold

(c)	DEBIT	Conversion costs allocated	20,370	
	CREDIT	Cost of goods sold		150
	CREDIT	Conversion costs control		20,220

Being the under or over allocation of conversion costs

Solution

For 1 trigger point – when goods are completed (method 2)

This is very similar to the solution above but in this instance the **trigger** is the completion of a unit and its **movement into finished goods store**. The accounting entries are as follows.

			£	£
(a)	DEBIT	Conversion costs control	20,220	
	CREDIT	Expense payables		20,220

Being the actual conversion costs incurred

(b)	DEBIT	Finished goods inventory (4,900 × £9.30)	45,570	
	CREDIT	Payables (4,900 × £5.10)		24,990
	CREDIT	Conversion costs allocated (4,900 × £4.20)		20,580

Being the standard cost of goods produced

(c)	DEBIT	Cost of goods sold (4,850 × £9.30)	45,105	
	CREDIT	Finished goods inventory		45,105

Being the standard cost of goods sold

(d)	DEBIT	Conversion costs allocated	20,580	
	CREDIT	Cost of goods sold		360
	CREDIT	Conversion costs control		20,220

Being the under or over allocation of conversion costs

The end of period finished goods inventory balance is £465 (50 × £9.30).

Question 10.6
Backflush accounting

Learning outcome A1(h)

RM uses backflush accounting in conjunction with JIT. The system does not include a raw material inventory control account. During control period 7, 300 units were produced and sold and conversation costs of £7,000 incurred. The standard unit cost is £55, which includes material of £25.

What is the debit balance on the cost of goods sold account at the end of control period 7.

A   £16,500
B   £14,500
C   £23,500
D   £18,500

Solution

For 2 trigger points – (method 3)

There are two **trigger points**, the **first** when **materials and components are received** and the **other** at the **point of transfer to finished goods**.

			£	£
(a)	DEBIT	Raw materials	24,990	
	CREDIT	Payables		24,990
	Being the purchase of raw materials on credit			
(b)	DEBIT	Conversion costs control	20,220	
	CREDIT	Expense payables		20,220
	Being the actual conversion costs incurred			
(c)	DEBIT	Finished goods inventory (4,900 × £9.30)	45,570	
	CREDIT	Raw materials		24,990
	CREDIT	Conversion costs allocated		20,580
	Being the standard cost of goods produced			
(d)	DEBIT	Cost of goods sold (4,850 × £9.30)	45,105	
	CREDIT	Finished goods inventory		45,105
	Being the standard cost of goods sold			
(e)	DEBIT	Conversion costs allocated	20,580	
	CREDIT	Cost of goods sold		360
	CREDIT	Conversion costs control		20,220
	Being the under or over allocation of conversion costs			

Note that the **WIP account is eliminated** using all methods. In a JIT system the vast majority of manufacturing costs will form part of the cost of sales and will not be deferred in closing inventory values. In such a situation the amount of work involved in tracking costs through WIP, cost of sales and finished goods is unlikely to be justified. This considerably **reduces the volume of transactions recorded** in the internal accounting system.

The successful operation of backflush costing rests upon **predictable levels of efficiency** and **stable material prices and usage**. In other words there should be **insignificant cost variances**.

3.4 Possible problems with backflush costing

(a)   **It is only appropriate for JIT operations** where production and sales volumes are approximately equal.

(b)   Some people claim that it **should not be used for external reporting** purposes. If, however, **inventories are low** or are practically **unchanged** from one accounting period to the next, operating income and inventory valuations derived from backflush accounting will **not be materially different from the results using conventional systems**. Hence, in such circumstances, backflush accounting is acceptable for external financial reporting.

(c)   It is vital that adequate production controls exist so that cost control during the production process is maintained.

3.5 Advantages of backflush costing

(a)   It is much **simpler**, as there is no separate accounting for WIP.

(b)   Even the **finished goods** account is **unnecessary**, as we demonstrated in the first example above.

(c)   The number of **accounting entries should be greatly reduced**, as are the supporting vouchers, documents and so on.

(d)   The system should **discourage** managers from **producing simply for inventory** since working on material does not add value until the final product is completed or sold.

Question 10.7	Backflush accounting and behavioural issues

Learning outcome A1(h)

How might backflush accounting, with goods being sold as the one trigger point, be said to manipulate employees to behave in a certain way?

Exam alert

Backflush accounting lends itself particularly well to objective testing questions but of course it could be tested in any one of the three sections.

Section summary

Backflush accounting is a method of accounting that can be used with JIT production systems. It saves a considerable amount of time as it avoids having to make a number of accounting entries that are required by a traditional system.

Chapter Roundup

✓   **Theory of constraints** is a set of concepts developed in the USA which aim to identify the binding constraints in a production system and which strive for evenness of production flow so that the organisation works as effectively as possible. No inventories should be held, except prior to the binding constraint.

✓   Goldratt's five steps for dealing with a bottleneck activity are:

Step 1: Identify	Step 4: Elevate
Step 2: Exploit	Step 5: Return to step 1
Step 3: Subordinate	

✓   **Throughput accounting** is the accounting system developed in the UK, based on the theory of constraints and JIT. It measures the throughput contribution per factory hour., It is very similar to marginal costing but can be used to make longer-term decisions about production equipment/capacity.

✓   **Backflush accounting** is a method of accounting that can be used with JIT production systems. It saves a considerable amount of time as it avoids having to make a number of accounting entries that are required by a traditional system.

Quick Quiz

1   Fill in the blanks in the statements below, using the words in the box. Some words may be used twice.

    (a)   The theory of constraints is an approach to production management which aims to maximise (1)............. less (2)........ and (3)........... It focuses on factors such as (4)................ which act as (5).....................

    (b)   Throughput contribution = (6)............. minus (7) ....

    (c)   TA ratio = (8) .... per factory hour ÷ (9) ....per factory hour

• variable overhead costs
• bottlenecks
• material costs
• sales revenue
• throughput contribution
• constraints
• conversion cost

2   CH Ltd operates a throughput accounting system. Product B sells for £27.99, has a material cost of £7.52 and a conversion cost of £1.91. The product spends 27 minutes on the bottleneck resource. What is the return per factory hour for product B?

    A   £45.49
    B   £20.47
    C   £26.08
    D   £57.96

3   Throughput accounting policy is to hold zero inventories throughout all operations

    True/false (delete as appropriate)

4   Choose the correct words from those highlighted.

    (a)   Backflush accounting is a cost accounting system which focuses on the (1) **input/output** of an organisation and then works (2) **forwards/backwards** to allocate costs between cost of goods sold and inventory.

    (b)   The point at which a physical activity causes an entry in the accounts which flushes out cost in a backflush system is known as the (3) **trigger point/bottleneck**.

5   Which of the following is not an advantage of backflush accounting?

    A   Backflushed costs are a realistic measure of actual costs incurred
    B   There is no subjective dividing of apportioned overheads
    C   The system may discourage managers from producing inventory
    D   It is appropriate for all types of operations

Answers to Quick Quiz

1   1   sales revenue
     2   material costs
     3   variable overhead costs
     4   bottlenecks
     5   constraints
     6   sales revenue
     7   material costs
     8   throughput contribution
     9   conversion cost

2   A   Return per hour = (sales – material cost) per hour on bottleneck resource

∴ Return per 27 minutes = £(27.99 – 7.52) = £20.47

∴ Return per hour = £20.47 $\times \dfrac{60}{27}$ = £45.49

3   False. A buffer inventory should be held prior to the bottleneck process.

4   (1)   output
     (2)   backwards
     (3)   trigger point

5   D   It is only appropriate for JIT operations where production and sales volumes are approximately equal.

Answers to Questions

10.1 Throughput accounting vs conventional cost accounting

Conventional cost accounting	Throughput accounting
Inventory is an asset.	Inventory is *not* an asset. It is a result of unsynchronised manufacturing and is a barrier to making profit.
Costs can be classified either as direct or indirect.	Such classifications are no longer useful.
Product profitability can be determined by deducting a product cost from selling price.	Profitability is determined by the rate at which money is earned.
Profit is a function of costs.	Profit is a function of throughput as well as costs.

10.2 Product return per factory hour and TA ratio

Return per factory hour = £(120 – 35)/4 = £21.25
TA ratio = £21.25/£20* = 1.0625
*Cost per factory hour = £13,000/650 = £20

10.3 Variances and throughput accounting

In a **traditional** management accounting environment, **adverse** variances would be considered **bad** because they **reduce accounting profit** below the standard expected for the activity achieved.

In a **throughput** accounting environment the **focus is on maximising throughput contribution** while keeping conversion and investment costs to the minimum level possible.

Therefore, in a throughput environment the increased cost of overtime working would be a good thing and would increase reported profits providing the extra labour cost incurred was less than the throughput contribution added.

10.4 Binding constraints and TA ratio

The throughput accounting (TA) ratio is calculated as follows.

$$\text{TA ratio} = \frac{\text{throughput per time period}}{\text{conversion cost per time period}} = \frac{(\text{sales} - \text{material costs}) \text{ per time period}}{\text{conversion cost per time period}}$$

Actions that could be considered to improve the TA ratio are as follows.

1   Increase the selling price of product P. This will increase the throughput per time period.

2   Reduce the material cost per unit of product P. This will also increase the throughput per time period.

3   Reduce the total expenditure on conversion costs. This would reduce the conversion cost per time period.

4   Change the working practices on machine M to increase the number of hours of capacity available. This should be achieved without extra conversion cost being incurred, perhaps by altering the method of setting up the machine, to improve productivity. This action would reduce the conversion cost per time period.

10.5 Product costing versus TA

1   Inventory is valued at material cost only (ie variable cost).
2   Only direct material is treated as a variable cost.
3   Effectiveness is measured in terms of schedule adherence and meeting delivery dates.
4   Value is added when an item is sold.

10.6 Backflush accounting

The correct answer is B.

	£
Conversion cost allocated to cost of goods sold a/c = 300 × (£55 – 25)	9,000
Conversion cost incurred	7,000
Difference set against cost of goods sold a/c	2,000
Standard charge to cost of goods sold a/c (300 × £55)	16,500
Charge to cost of goods sold a/c	14,500

Option A is the standard charge. **Option C** is the sum of conversion cost incurred and the standard charge. **Option D** results from adding the difference instead of deducting it.

10.7 Backflush accounting and behavioural issues

Employees have to concentrate on making sales because cost of sales is the trigger, and so nothing gets recorded until a sale is made.

Unlike in traditional systems, when management can increase profit by producing for finished goods inventory, there is no benefit in producing for inventory.

Now try these questions from the Exam Question Bank

Number	Level	Marks	Time
Q15	Examination	5	9 mins
Q16	Introductory	10	18 mins

MODERN COSTING TECHNIQUES – ACTIVITY BASED COSTING

 In this chapter we look at a third costing system that has been developed to suit modern practices: **activity based costing**.

Basically, activity based costing (ABC) is the **modern alternative to traditional absorption costing**.

Exam questions (both objective test questions and long questions) could ask you to **calculate activity-based**

costs, and we show you how to do this in **Section 3**. Or you could get a **discursive question** on the topic, the material for which you will find in the remaining sections of this chapter.

Note that activity based costing is also on the CIMA P2 syllabus.

topic list	learning outcomes	syllabus references	ability required
1 The reasons for the development of ABC	A1(c)	A1(ii)	analysis
2 Outline of an ABC system	A1(c)	A1(ii)	analysis
3 Absorption costing versus ABC	A1(c)	A1(ii)	analysis
4 Marginal costing versus ABC	A1(c)	A1(ii)	analysis
5 Introducing an ABC system	A1(c)	A1(ii)	analysis
6 Merits and criticisms of ABC	A1(c)	A1(ii)	analysis

1 The reasons for the development of ABC

Introduction

The traditional cost accumulation system of **absorption costing** was developed in a time when most organisations produced only a **narrow range of products** and when **overhead costs were only a very small fraction of total costs**. Direct labour and direct material costs accounted for the largest proportion of the costs. Errors made in attributing overheads to products were not too significant.

Nowadays, however, with the advent of **advanced manufacturing technology (AMT)**, **overheads** are likely to be far **more important** and in fact direct labour may account for as little as five per cent of a product's cost. It therefore now appears difficult to justify the use of direct labour or direct material as the basis for absorbing overheads or to believe that errors made in attributing overheads will not be significant.

Many resources are used in **non-volume related support activities**, (which have increased due to AMT) such as setting-up, production scheduling, inspection and data processing. These support activities assist the efficient manufacture of a wide range of products (necessary if businesses are to compete effectively) and are **not, in general, affected by changes in production volume**. They tend to **vary in the long term according to the range and complexity** of the products manufactured rather than the volume of output.

The wider the range and the more complex the products, the more support services will be required. Consider, for example, factory X which produces 10,000 units of one product, the Alpha, and factory Y which produces 1,000 units each of ten slightly different versions of the Alpha. Support activity costs in the factory Y are likely to be a lot higher than in factory X but the factories produce an identical number of units. For example, factory X will only need to set-up once whereas Factory Y will have to set-up the production run at least ten times for the ten different products. Factory Y will therefore incur more set-up costs for the same volume of production.

Section summary

Traditional costing systems, which assume that all products consume all resources in proportion to their production volumes, tend to **allocate too great a proportion of overheads to high volume products** (which cause relatively little diversity and hence use fewer support services) and **too small a proportion of overheads to low volume products** (which cause greater diversity and therefore use more support services). **Activity based costing (ABC) attempts to overcome this problem**.

2 Outline of an ABC system   9/10, 11/10, 3/11

Introduction

The **major ideas** behind activity based costing are as follows.

(a)   **Activities cause costs**. Activities include ordering, materials handling, machining, assembly, production scheduling and despatching.

(b)   Producing products creates demand for the activities.

(c)   Costs are assigned to a product on the basis of the product's consumption of the activities.

2.1 The definition of ABC

KEY TERM

ACTIVITY BASED COSTING (ABC) is an 'Approach to the costing and monitoring of activities which involves tracing resource consumption and costing final outputs. Resources are assigned to activities and activities to cost objects based on consumption estimates. The latter utilise cost drivers to attach activity costs to outputs.'

(CIMA Official Terminology)

2.2 The operation of an ABC system

An ABC system operates as follows.

Identify an organisation's major activities.

Identify the **factors which determine the size of the costs of an activity/cause the costs of an activity**. These are known as **cost drivers.**

KEY TERM

A COST DRIVER is a 'Factor influencing the level of cost. Often used in the context of ABC to denote the factor which links activity resource consumption to product outputs, for example the number of purchase orders would be a cost driver for procurement cost.'

(CIMA Official Terminology)

Look at the following examples.

Costs	Possible cost driver
Ordering costs	Number of orders
Materials handling costs	Number of production runs
Production scheduling costs	Number of production runs
Despatching costs	Number of despatches

For those **costs that vary with production levels in the short term**, ABC uses **volume-related cost drivers** such as labour or machine hours. The cost of oil used as a lubricant on the machines would therefore be added to products on the basis of the number of machine hours, since oil would have to be used for each hour the machine ran.

Collect the costs associated with each cost driver into what are known as cost pools.

KEY TERM

A COST POOL is 'Grouping of costs relating to a particular activity in an activity-based costing system.'

(CIMA Official Terminology)

Charge the costs of each cost pool to products on the basis of their usage of the activity (measured by the number of the activity's cost driver a product generates) using a cost driver rate (total costs in cost pool/number of cost drivers).

Question 11.1	Cost drivers

Learning outcome A1(c)

Which of the following definitions best describes a cost driver?

A   Any activity which causes an increase in costs

B   A collection of costs associated with a particular activity

C   A cost that varies with production levels

D   Any factor which causes a change in the cost of an activity

2.3 Transactions analysis

When using ABC, for costs that vary with production levels in the short term, the cost driver will be volume related (labour or machine hours). Overheads that vary with some other activity (and not volume of production) should be traced to products using transaction-based cost drivers such as production runs or number of orders received. One way of classifying these transactions is **logistical, balancing, quality** and **change**.

ABC recognises that factors other than volume can explain the level of overhead. Miller and Vollman ('The Hidden Factory', *Harvard Business Review*, 1985) provided a useful system for analysing the different types of transactions which cause overheads to be incurred.

Types of transaction	Detail
Logistical transactions	Those activities concerned with organising the flow of resources throughout the manufacturing process.
Balancing transactions	Those activities which ensure that demand for and supply of resources are matched.
Quality transactions	Those activities which relate to ensuring that production is at the required level of quality.
Change transactions	Those activities associated with ensuring that customers' requirements (delivery date, changed design and so on) are met.

Note that the primary driver of these transactions is not usually production volume. For example, the level of change transactions might be determined by the number of customers and the number of different product types, rather than by production volume.

Such an analysis provides a better understanding of long-term cost behaviour and allows for the costs associated with particular transactions to be assigned to only those products causing the transactions.

Section summary

An alternative to the traditional method of accounting for costs - absorption costing - is **activity based costing (ABC)**. ABC involves the identification of the factors (**cost drivers**) which cause the costs of an organisation's major activities. Support overheads are charged to products on the basis of their usage of an activity.

Transactions which cause overheads to be incurred can be classified as logical, balancing, quality and change transactions.

3   Absorption costing versus ABC

Introduction

Although ABC has obvious merits, a number of criticisms have been raised.

The following example illustrates the point that traditional cost accounting techniques result in a misleading and inequitable division of costs between low-volume and high-volume products, and that ABC can provide a more meaningful allocation of costs.

Example: activity based costing

Suppose that Cooplan manufactures four products, W, X, Y and Z. Output and cost data for the period just ended are as follows.

	Output units	Number of production runs in the period	Material cost per unit £	Direct labour hours per unit	Machine hours per unit
W	10	2	20	1	1
X	10	2	80	3	3
Y	100	5	20	1	1
Z	100	5	80	3	3
		14			

Direct labour cost per hour £5

	£
Overhead costs	
Short run variable costs	3,080
Set-up costs	10,920
Expediting and scheduling costs	9,100
Materials handling costs	7,700
	30,800

Required

Prepare unit costs for each product using conventional costing and ABC.

Solution

Using a **conventional absorption costing approach** and an absorption rate for overheads based on either direct labour hours or machine hours, the product costs would be as follows.

	W £	X £	Y £	Z £	Total £
Direct material	200	800	2,000	8,000	
Direct labour	50	150	500	1,500	
Overheads *	700	2,100	7,000	21,000	
	950	3,050	9,500	30,500	44,000
Units produced	10	10	100	100	
Cost per unit	£95	£305	£95	£305	

* £30,800 ÷ 440 hours = £70 per direct labour or machine hour.

Using **activity based costing** and assuming that the number of production runs is the cost driver for set-up costs, expediting and scheduling costs and materials handling costs and that machine hours are the cost driver for short-run variable costs, unit costs would be as follows.

	W £	X £	Y £	Z £	Total £
Direct material	200	800	2,000	8,000	
Direct labour	50	150	500	1,500	
Short-run variable overheads (W1)	70	210	700	2,100	
Set-up costs (W2)	1,560	1,560	3,900	3,900	
Expediting, scheduling costs (W3)	1,300	1,300	3,250	3,250	
Materials handling costs (W4)	1,100	1,100	2,750	2,750	
	4,280	5,120	13,100	21,500	44,000

	W	*X*	*Y*	*Z*	*Total*
Units produced	10	10	100	100	
Cost per unit	£428	£512	£131	£215	

Workings

1	£3,080 ÷ 440 machine hours =	£7 per machine hour
2	£10,920 ÷ 14 production runs =	£780 per run
3	£9,100 ÷ 14 production runs =	£650 per run
4	£7,700 ÷ 14 production runs =	£550 per run

Summary

Product	Conventional costing Unit cost £	ABC Unit cost £	Difference per unit £	Difference in total £
W	95	428	+ 333	+3,330
X	305	512	+ 207	+2,070
Y	95	131	+ 36	+3,600
Z	305	215	− 90	−9,000

The figures suggest that the **traditional volume-based absorption costing system is flawed**.

(a)　It underallocates overhead costs to low-volume products (here, W and X) and over-allocates overheads to higher-volume products (here Z in particular).

(b)　It underallocates overhead costs to smaller-sized products (here W and Y with just one hour of work needed per unit) and over allocates overheads to larger products (here X and particularly Z).

3.1 ABC versus traditional costing methods

Both traditional absorption costing and ABC systems adopt the two stage allocation process.

3.1.1 Allocation of overheads

ABC establishes **separate cost pools for support activities** such as despatching. As the costs of these activities are assigned directly to products through cost driver rates, **reapportionment of service department costs is avoided**.

3.1.2 Absorption of overheads

The principal difference between the two systems is the way in which overheads are absorbed into products.

(a)　**Absorption costing** most commonly uses two **absorption bases** (labour hours and/or machine hours) to charge overheads to products.

(b)　**ABC** uses **many cost drivers** as absorption bases (number of orders, number of despatches and so on).

Absorption rates under **ABC** should therefore be **more closely linked to the causes of overhead costs**.

3.2 Cost drivers

The **principal idea** of ABC is to **focus attention on what causes costs to increase, ie the cost drivers**.

(a)　Those **costs that do vary with production volume**, such as power costs, should be traced to products using production **volume-related cost drivers** as appropriate, such as direct labour hours or direct machine hours. Such costs tend to be **short-term variable overheads** such as power costs.

Overheads which do not **vary** with output but **with some other activity** should be traced to products using **transaction-based cost drivers**, such as number of production runs and number of orders received. Such costs tend to be **long-term variable overheads** (overheads that traditional accounting would classify as fixed).

(b) Traditional costing systems allow overheads to be related to products in rather more arbitrary ways producing, it is claimed, less accurate product costs.

Question 11.2   ABC versus traditional costing

Learning outcome A1(c)

A company manufactures two products, L and M, using the same equipment and similar processes. An extract of the production data for these products in one period is shown below.

	L	*M*
Quantity produced (units)	5,000	7,000
Direct labour hours per unit	1	2
Machine hours per unit	3	1
Set-ups in the period	10	40
Orders handled in the period	15	60

	$
Overhead costs	
Relating to machine activity	220,000
Relating to production run set-ups	20,000
Relating to handling of orders	45,000
	285,000

Required

Calculate the production overheads to be absorbed by one unit of each of the products using the following costing methods.

(a) A traditional absorption costing approach using a direct labour hour rate to absorb overheads
(b) An activity based costing approach, using suitable cost drivers to trace overheads to products

Section summary

Although ABC has obvious merits, a number of criticisms have been raised.

Exam skills

Note that the syllabus specifically mentions ABC compared with traditional methods and its relative advantages and disadvantages. Make sure that you understand the differences between the costing methods and the pros and cons.

4 Marginal costing versus ABC

Introduction

Some commentators argue that only marginal costing provides suitable information for decision making but this is not true. Marginal costing provides a crude method of differentiating between different types of cost behaviour by splitting costs into their variable and fixed elements. However, such an analysis can be used only for **short-term decisions** and usually even these have longer-term implications which ought to be considered.

The problem with marginal costing is that it analyses cost behaviour patterns according to the volume of production. However, although certain costs may be fixed in relation to the volume of production, they **may in fact be variable in relation to some other cost driver.** A failure to allocate such costs to individual products could result in incorrect decisions concerning the future management of the products.

The advantage of ABC is that **it spreads costs across products according to a number of different bases.** For example an ABC analysis may show that one particular activity which is carried out primarily for one or two products is expensive. A correct allocation of the costs of this activity may reveal that these particular products are not profitable. If these costs are fixed in relation to the volume of production then they would be treated as **period costs** in a marginal costing system and **written off against the marginal costing contribution for the period.**

The marginal costing system would therefore make no attempt to allocate these 'fixed' costs to individual products and a false impression would be given of the long run average cost of the products.

Thus, marginal costing may provide incorrect decision making information, **particularly in a situation where 'fixed' costs are vary large compared with 'variable' costs.**

Section summary

The main criticism of marginal costing decision making information is that marginal costing analyses cost behaviour patterns according to the volume of production. However, although certain costs may be fixed in relation to the volume of production, they **may in fact be variable in relation to some other cost driver.**

5 Introducing an ABC system

5.1 When should ABC be introduced?

Introduction

ABC should only be introduced if the **additional information** it provides will **result in action that will increase** the organisation's overall **profitability**. This is most likely to **occur** in situations such as the following, when the **ABC analysis differs significantly from the traditional absorption costing analysis.**

- Production overheads are high in relation to direct costs, especially direct labour.
- Overhead resource consumption is not just driven by production volume.
- There is wide variety in the product range.
- The overhead resource input varies significantly across the product range.

5.2 Analysis of activities

ABC attempts to **relate the incidence of costs to the level of activities undertaken**. A **hierarchy of activities** has been suggested.

KEY TERM

The HIERARCHY OF ACTIVITIES is a 'Classification of activities by level of organisation, for example unit, batch, product sustaining and facility sustaining.'   *(CIMA Official Terminology)*

Type of activities	Costs are dependent on	Examples
Product level	Volume of production	Machine power
Batch level	Number of batches	Set-up costs
Product sustaining	Existence of a product group/line	Product management
Facility sustaining	Organisation simply being in business	Rent and rates

KEY TERMS

CIMA *Official Terminology* provides definitions for two of these classifications.

PRODUCT-SUSTAINING ACTIVITIES are 'Activities undertaken to develop or sustain a product (or service). Product sustaining costs are linked to the number of products or services not to the number of units produced.'

FACILITY-SUSTAINING ACTIVITIES are 'Activities undertaken to support the organisation as a whole, and which cannot be logically linked to individual units of output.'

The difference between a unit product cost determined using traditional absorption costing and one determined using ABC will depend on the proportion of overhead cost which falls into each of the categories above.

(a)   If most overheads are related to unit level and facility level activities, the costs will be similar.

(b)   If the overheads tend to be associated with batch or product level activities they will be significantly different.

Consider the following example.

Example: batch-level activities

XYZ produces a number of products including product D and product E and produces 500 units of each of products D and E every period at a rate of ten of each every hour. The overhead cost is £500,000 and a total of 40,000 direct labour hours are worked on all products. A traditional overhead absorption rate would be £12.50 per direct labour hour and the overhead cost per product would be £1.25.

Production of D requires five production runs per period, while production of E requires 20. An investigation has revealed that the overhead costs relate mainly to 'batch-level' activities associated with setting-up machinery and handling materials for production runs.

There are 1,000 production runs per period and so overheads could be attributed to XYZ's products at a rate of £500 per run.

- Overhead cost per D = (£500 × 5 runs)/500 = £5
- Overhead cost per E = (£500 × 20 runs)/500 = £20

These overhead costs are activity based and recognise that overhead costs are incurred due to batch level activities. The fact that E has to be made in frequent small batches, perhaps because it is perishable, means that it uses more resources than D. This is recognised by the ABC overhead costs, not the traditional absorption costing overhead costs.

KEY POINT

As we noted in Chapter 9, in the **modern manufacturing environment**, production often takes place in short, discontinuous production runs and a high proportion of product costs are incurred at the design stage. An increasing proportion of **overhead costs** are therefore **incurred at batch or product level**.

Such an analysis of costs gives management an **indication of the decision level at which costs can be influenced**. For example, a decision to reduce production costs will not simply depend on making a general reduction in output volumes: production may need to be organised to reduce **batch** volumes; a **process** may need to be modified or eliminated; **product lines** may need to be merged or cut out; **facility** capacity may need to be altered.

5.3 ABC in service and retail organisations

ABC was **first introduced in manufacturing organisations** but it can equally well be used in **other types of organisation**. For example, the management of the Post Office in the USA uses ABC. They analysed the activities associated with cash processing as follows.

Activities	Examples	Possible cost driver
Unit level	Accept cash	Number of transactions
	Processing of cash by bank	Number of transactions
Batch level	'Close out' and supervisor review of clerk	Number of 'close outs'
	Deposits	Number of deposits
	Review and transfer of funds	Number of accounts
Product level	Maintenance charges for bank accounts	Number of accounts
	Reconciling bank accounts	Number of accounts

Question 11.3   ABC and retail organisations

Learning outcome A1(c)

List five activities that might be identified in a retail organisation and state one possible cost driver for each of the activities you have identified.

Section summary

ABC should only be introduced if the additional information it provides will result in action that will increase the organisation's overall profitability.

ABC identifies four levels of activities: product level, batch level, product sustaining level and facility sustaining level.

6 Merits and criticisms of ABC

Introduction

ABC has a range of uses and has many advantages over more traditional costing methods. However, the system does have its critics and it is not used as a panacea for all costing problems.

6.1 Merits of ABC

As you will have discovered when you attempted the question above, there is nothing difficult about ABC. Once the necessary information has been obtained it is similar to traditional absorption costing. This simplicity is part of its appeal. Further merits of ABC are as follows.

(a) The **complexity of manufacturing has increased**, with wider product ranges, shorter product life cycles and more complex production processes. **ABC recognises this complexity with its multiple cost drivers.**

(b) In a more competitive environment, companies must be able to assess product profitability realistically. **ABC facilitates a good understanding of what drives overhead costs.**

(c) In modern manufacturing systems, overhead functions include a lot of non-factory-floor activities such as product design, quality control, production planning and customer services. **ABC is concerned with all overhead costs** and so it takes management accounting beyond its 'traditional' factory floor boundaries.

(d) By controlling the incidence of the cost driver, the level of the **cost** can be **controlled**.

(e) The costs of activities not included in the costs of the products an organisation makes or the services it provides can be considered to be **not contributing to the value of the product/service**. The following questions can then be asked.

    (i) What is the purpose of this activity?

    (ii) How does the organisation benefit from this activity?

    (iii) Could the number of staff involved in the activity be reduced?

(f) ABC can help with **cost management**. For example, suppose there is a fall in the number of orders placed by a purchasing department. This fall would not impact on the amount of overhead absorbed in a traditional absorption costing system as the cost of ordering would be part of the general overhead absorption rate (assuming no direct link between the overhead absorption basis of, say, direct labour hours, and the number of orders placed). The reduction in the workload of the purchasing department might therefore go unnoticed and the same level of resources would continue to be provided, despite the drop in number of orders. In an ABC system, however, this drop would be immediately apparent because the cost driver rate would be applied to fewer orders.

(g) Many costs are driven by customers (delivery costs, discounts, after-sales service and so on), but traditional absorption costing systems do not account for this. Organisations may be trading with certain customers at a loss but may not realise it because costs are not analysed in a way that reveals the true situation. ABC can be **used in conjunction with customer profitability analysis (CPA)** to determine more accurately the profit earned by servicing particular customers.

KEY TERM

CUSTOMER PROFITABILITY ANALYSIS (CPA) is 'Analysis of the revenue streams and service costs associated with specific customers or customer groups.' *(CIMA Official Terminology)*

(h) Many **service businesses** have characteristics similar to those required for the successful application of ABC.

    (i) A highly **competitive** market

    (ii) **Diversity** of products, processes and customers

    (iii) **Significant overhead costs** not easily assigned to individual 'products'

    (iv) Demands placed on overhead resources by individual 'products' and customers, which are not proportional to volume

        If ABC were to be used in a hotel, for example, attempts could be made to identify the activities required to support each guest by category and the cost drivers of these activities. The cost of a one-night stay midweek by a businessman could then be distinguished from the cost of a one-night stay by a teenager at the weekend. Such information could prove invaluable for **CPA.**

6.2 Criticisms of ABC

It has been suggested by critics that **activity based costing has some serious flaws.**

(a) Some measure of (arbitrary) cost apportionment may still be required at the cost pooling stage for items like rent, rates and building depreciation.

(b) Can a single cost driver explain the cost behaviour of all items in its associated pool?

(c) On the other hand, the number of cost pools and cost drivers cannot be excessive otherwise an ABC system would be too complex and too expensive.

(d) Unless costs are caused by an activity that is measurable in quantitative terms and which can be related to production output, cost drivers will not be usable. What drives the cost of the annual external audit, for example?

(e) ABC is sometimes introduced because it is fashionable, not because it will be used by management to provide meaningful product costs or extra information. If management is not going to use ABC information, an absorption costing system may be simpler to operate.

(f) The costs of ABC may outweigh the benefits.

6.3 Other uses of ABC

The information provided by analysing activities can support the management functions of planning, control and decision making, provided it is used carefully and with full appreciation of its implications.

6.3.1 Planning

Before an ABC system can be implemented, management must analyse the organisation's activities, determine the extent of their occurrence and establish the relationships between activities, products/services and their cost.

The **information database** produced from such an exercise can then be **used as a basis for forward planning and budgeting**. For example, once an organisation has set its budgeted production level, the database can be used to determine the number of times that activities will need to be carried out, thereby establishing necessary departmental staffing and machine levels. Financial budgets can then be drawn up by multiplying the budgeted activity levels by cost per activity.

This activity-based approach may not produce the final budget figures but it can **provide the basis for different possible planning scenarios**.

6.3.2 Control

The information database also provides an **insight into the way in which costs are structured and incurred in service and support departments**. Traditionally it has been difficult to control the costs of such departments because of the lack of relationship between departmental output levels and departmental cost. With ABC, however, it is possible to **control or manage the costs by managing the activities which underlie them** by monitoring a number of key performance measures.

6.3.3 Decision making

Many of ABC's supporters claim that it can assist with decision making in a number of ways.

*   Provides accurate and reliable cost information
*   Establishes a long-run product cost
*   Provides data which can be used to evaluate different ways of delivering business.

It is therefore particularly suited to the following types of decision.

*   Pricing
*   Promoting or discontinuing products or parts of the business
*   Redesigning products and developing new products or new ways to do business

Note, however, that an ABC cost is **not a true cost**, it is **simply a long run average cost** because some costs such as depreciation are still arbitrarily allocated to products. An ABC cost is therefore **not a relevant cost** for all decisions. For example, even if a **product/service ceases** altogether, **some costs** allocated to that product/service using an activity based approach (such as building occupancy costs or depreciation) would **not disappear** just because the product/service had disappeared. Management would need to bear this in mind when making product deletion decisions.

6.4 Activity-based management (ABM)

Although the terms are sometimes used interchangeably, ABM is a broader concept than ABC, being likely to incorporate ABC and activity based budgeting (ABB) which will be covered in a later chapter.

KEY TERMS

ACTIVITY-BASED MANAGEMENT (ABM)

OPTIMAL ABM 'Actions, based on activity driver analysis, that increase efficiency, lower costs and/or improve asset utilisation.'

STRATEGIC ABM 'Actions, based on activity-based cost analysis, that claim to change the demand for activities so as to improve profitability.'   *(CIMA Official Terminology)*

Section summary

ABC has a range of uses and has many advantages over more traditional costing methods. However, the system does have its critics and it is not used as a panacea for all costing problems.

Chapter Roundup

✓   Traditional costing systems, which assume that all products consume all resources in proportion to their production volumes, tend to allocate too great a proportion of overheads to high volume products (which cause relatively little diversity and hence use fewer support services) and too small a proportion of overheads to low volume products (which cause greater diversity and therefore use more support services). Activity based costing (ABC) attempts to overcome this problem.

✓   An alternative to the traditional method of accounting for costs - absorption costing - is activity based costing (ABC). ABC involves the identification of the factors (cost drivers) which cause the costs of an organisation's major activities. Support overheads are charged to products on the basis of their usage of an activity.

Transactions which cause overheads to be incurred can be classified as logical, balancing, quality and change transactions.

✓   Although ABC has obvious merits, a number of criticisms have been raised.

✓   The main criticism of marginal costing decision making information is that marginal costing analyses cost behaviour patterns according to the volume of production. However, although certain costs may be fixed in relation to the volume of production, they **may in fact be variable in relation to some other cost driver.**

✓   ABC should only be introduced if the additional information it provides will result in action that will increase the organisation's overall profitability.

ABC identifies four levels of activities: product level, batch level, product sustaining level and facility sustaining level.

✓   ABC has a range of uses and has many advantages over more traditional costing methods. However, the system does have its critics and it is not used as a panacea for all costing problems.

Quick Quiz

1   Choose the correct words from those highlighted.

Traditional costing systems tend to allocate **too great/too small** a proportion of overheads to high volume products and **too great/too small** a proportion of overheads to low volume products.

2   Fill in the blanks.

The major ideas behind ABC are as follows.

(a)   Activities cause ....
(b)   Producing products creates demand for the ....
(c)   Costs are assigned to a product on the basis of the product's consumption of the ....

3   Match the most appropriate cost driver to each cost.

Costs		*Cost driver*
(a)	Set-up costs	Number of machine hours
(b)	Short-run variable costs	Number of production runs
(c)	Materials handling and despatch	Number of orders executed

4   ABC recognises the complexity of modern manufacturing by the use of multiple cost pools. True or false?

5   The use of direct labour hours or direct machine hours to trace costs to products occurs with the use of absorption costing but not with the use of ABC. True or false?

6 · · · · ABC is not a system that is suitable for use by service organisations. True or false?

7 · · · · Activity based management is a system of management which uses activity based cost information to achieve which three of the following?

Improve asset utilisation
Reduce costs
Customer profitability analysis
Simplify pricing decisions

Answers to Quick Quiz

1 · · · · Too great
· · · · · · Too small

2 · · · · (a) · · · · Costs
· · · · · · (b) · · · · Activities
· · · · · · (c) · · · · Activities

3 · · · · (a) · · · · Number of production runs
· · · · · · (b) · · · · Number of machine hours
· · · · · · (c) · · · · Number of orders executed

4 · · · · False. Complexity is recognised by the use of multiple cost drivers.

5 · · · · False. The use of volume-related cost drivers should be used for costs that do vary with production volume.

6 · · · · False. It is highly suitable.

7 · · · · ABM is used to achieve customer profitability analysis, improve asset utilisation and reduce costs. Pricing decisions are not aims of an ABC system.

Answers to Questions

11.1 Cost drivers

The correct answer is D.

11.2 ABC versus traditional costing

(a) **Traditional absorption costing approach**

	Direct labour hours
Product L = 5,000 units × 1 hour	5,000
Product M = 7,000 units × 2 hours	14,000
	19,000

$$\therefore \text{Overhead absorption rate} = \frac{\$285,000}{19,000}$$

$$= \quad \$15 \text{ per hour}$$

Overhead absorbed would be as follows.

Product L	1 hour × $15	=	$15 per unit
Product M	2 hours × $15	=	$30 per unit

(b) **ABC approach**

		Machine hours
Product L	= 5,000 units × 3 hours	15,000
Product M	= 7,000 units × 1 hour	7,000
		22,000

Using ABC the overhead costs are absorbed according to the **cost drivers**.

	$	
Machine-hour driven costs	220,000 ÷ 22,000 m/c hours	= $10 per m/c hour
Set-up driven costs	20,000 ÷ 50 set-ups	= $400 per set-up
Order driven costs	45,000 ÷ 75 orders	= $600 per order

Overhead costs are therefore as follows.

		Product L £		*Product M* £
Machine-driven costs	(15,000 hrs × $10)	150,000	(7,000 hrs × $10)	70,000
Set-up costs	(10 × $400)	4,000	(40 × $400)	16,000
Order handling costs	(15 × $600)	9,000	(60 × $600)	36,000
		163,000		122,000
Units produced		5,000		7,000
Overhead cost per unit		$32.60		$17.43

These figures suggest that product M absorbs an unrealistic amount of overhead using a direct labour hour basis. Overhead absorption should be based on the activities which drive the costs, in this case machine hours, the number of production run set-ups and the number of orders handled for each product.

11.3 ABC and retail organisations

Activities	Possible cost driver
Procure goods	Number of orders
Receive goods	Number of orders or pallets
Store goods	Volume of goods
Pick goods	Number of packs
Handle returnables/recyclables	Volume of goods

Now try these questions from the Exam Question Bank

Number	Level	Marks	Time
Q17	Examination	30	54 mins
Q18	Examination	5	9 mins
Q19	Examination	5	9 mins

ENVIRONMENTAL COSTING

Environmental issues are becoming increasingly important in the business world. Firms have become responsible for the environmental impacts of their operations and therefore they are now more aware of problems such as carbon emissions.

The growth of environmental legislation and regulations has also affected business operations and reporting.

In section 1 we look at why environmental costs are important to the management accountant. Then in section 2 we look at the external environmental impacts of business activity and ways to save energy and costs. Section 3 looks at the different types of internal environmental costs and section 4 looks at environmental costing and environmental management systems. Section 5 looks at how ABC can be adapted for use within environmental costing.

topic list	learning outcomes	syllabus references	ability required
1 The importance of environmental costs	A3(a)	A3(i)	application
2 Environmental footprints	A3(a)	A3(i)	application
3 Types of cost	A3(a)	A3(i)	application
4 Environmental cost accounting	A3(a)	A3(i)	application
5 Environmental costing using ABC	A3(a)	A3(i)	application

1   The importance of environmental costs

Introduction

Awareness of environmental costs is a relatively recent development. Business activities in general were formerly regarded as problems for the environmental movement but the two are now increasingly complementary. Environmental costs, like any other costs, need to be considered with regard to planning, control and decision making. The main difference between environmental costs and other costs is that they may be more difficult to identify and to quantify. For example businesses may suffer a loss of reputation if problems arise.

1.1 Why are environmental costs important to the management accountant?

There are, of course, ethical reasons why environmental costs are important to the management accountant. For example, using energy generates carbon dioxide emissions and these contribute to climate change and threaten the future of our planet. Management accountants, however, should also consider environmental costs for the following reasons.

(a)   Identifying environmental costs associated with individual products, services or processes helps with correct product or service **pricing**. **Correct pricing** helps to **increase profitability**.

(b)   Poor environmental behaviour can result in **fines**, increased liability to **environmental taxes** and **damage** to the business's **reputation**.

(c)   Recording environmental costs is important as some may require **regulatory compliance**. Most western countries now have laws to cover land-use planning, smoke emissions, water pollution and destruction of animals and natural habitats.

(d)   Saving energy generally leads to cost savings.

Environmental accounting is a subset of social accounting. Social accounting is a method of reporting whereby a business analyses the impact it has on society and the environment. Environmental accounting involves preparation, presentation and communication of information about a business's interaction with the natural environment. It is a legal requirement in some countries such as Denmark and Australia.

1.2 Significance of environmental effects

Is there a problem and how serious is it?

CASE STUDY

The World Wildlife Fund warned in a report published in October 2006 that current global consumption levels could result in a large scale ecosystem collapse by the middle of the twenty-first century. It warned that if demand continued at the current rate, two planets' worth of resources would be needed to meet the consumption demand by 2050. The loss in biodiversity (ie the amount of plant and animal life in the world) is the result of resources being consumed faster than the planet can replace them.

Section summary

There is increasing awareness about businesses' relationship with the natural environment. Businesses may suffer **significant costs** and a **loss of reputation** if problems arise.

2 Environmental footprints

Introduction

Much business activity takes place at some cost to the environment. This type of cost is sometimes referred to as the environmental footprint. This section looks at these costs and how they can be minimised in the business environment. Reducing the environmental footprint can save business costs and increase profits.

KEY TERM

ENVIRONMENTAL FOOTPRINT is the impact that a business's activities have upon the environment including its resource environment and pollution emissions.

2.1 Key external environmental impacts

At an individual firm or business level environmental impact can be measured in terms of environmental costs in various areas. Much business activity takes place at some cost to the environment. A 1998 IFAC (International Federation of Accountants) report identified several examples of impacts on the environment:

- Depletion of natural resources
- Noise and aesthetic impacts
- Residual air and water emissions
- Long-term waste disposal (exacerbated by excessive product packaging)
- Uncompensated health effects
- Change in the local quality of life (through for example the impact of tourism)

2.2 Carbon

The first world summit on the environment was convened in Stockholm in 1972, at which time world leaders declared the intention of having regular assessments of **global environmental issues**. In 1987, the Intergovernmental Panel on Climate Change was formed by the United Nations Environmental Programme (UNEP) together with the World Meteorological Organisation (WMO).

In 1992 the UN general assembly proposed a treaty now known as the United Nations Framework Convention on Climate Change (UNFCCC), which was subsequently accepted and signed by more than 150 nations represented at the second summit which was held in 1992 in Rio de Janeiro.

Countries ratifying the convention agreed:

(a)   To develop programs to slow climate change
(b)   To share technology and cooperate to reduce greenhouse gas emissions
(c)   To develop a greenhouse gas inventory listing national sources and carbon sinks

At the summit, it was also agreed that the responsibility falls upon the **developed nations** to lead the fight against **climate change**, as they are largely responsible for the current concentrations of **greenhouse gases (GHG)** in the atmosphere. The original target for emission reductions that was generally accepted in 1992 was that the developed nations should, at a minimum, seek to return to 1990 levels of emissions by the year 2000. Additionally, developed nations should provide financial and technological aid and assistance to the developing nations to produce inventories and work toward more **efficient energy use**.

In December 1997 the countries which met in Rio in 1992 re-convened in Kyoto to develop a set of legally binding agreements on the reduction of greenhouse gas emissions. The objective of the **Kyoto Protocol** is to **reduce greenhouse gas** concentrations in the atmosphere to a level which would prevent dangerous man-made impacts on the climate system.

The Kyoto Protocol was adopted for use in December 1997, and came into force in February 2005. By March 2010, 190 countries had ratified the Protocol, although the US has so far refused to do so. During the period 2008-2012 industrialised countries have to reduce their GHG emissions by on average 5% below their 1990 levels. For EU-15 the reduction target is 8%.

2.2.1 The EU gas emissions allowance scheme

As part of their policy towards implementation of the Kyoto Protocol, the EU **set the total amount of CO_2** emissions to be produced in the EU as a whole to **no more than 2.2 billion tonnes per annum**. This total amount was then **allocated to member states** based primarily on the historical emission of CO_2. Each member state was therefore allocated a European Union Allowance to emit CO_2 for a specific compliance period.

2.2.2 The EU Emissions Trading Scheme

The European Union Emissions Trading Scheme (ETS) commenced on 1 January 2005, creating the world's first multi-country emissions trading system and the largest scheme ever implemented. The EU ETS runs in two phases: 2005-2007 (Phase I) and 2008-2012 (Phase II, coinciding with the first commitment period of the Kyoto Protocol).

The **EU allowance** given to a company **represents their target** or 'cap' for a compliance period. If at the end of the period their total **emissions** during the period are **below their cap** then they have **allowances to sell**; if not, they must **purchase allowances** from companies which have exceeded their emissions reductions targets.

Thus the underlying commodity being traded are EU allowances (EUAs) as issued under the EU ETS. One EUA equals one tonne of CO_2 (right-to-emit). These allowances are traded on a special exchange, the **ECX.**

Emissions trading is using a **market-based mechanism** for **environment protection**. The rationale behind emission trading is to ensure that the required **overall emission** reductions take place where the cost of the reduction is lowest, thus lowering the overall costs of combating climate change. It does not impose a particular type of technology or set rigid limitations on how much can be emitted.

This approach also provides an **incentive** for economies to **reduce their greenhouse gas emissions**, because doing so has an **economic benefit** through the **sale of carbon credits** to countries who have failed to reach their targets. (The market for buying and selling carbon credits has become known as the **carbon market**.)

2.3 Energy

Businesses can **reduce** the amount of **energy** they use which **reduces carbon emissions**, saves money and **increases profits**.

'Energy is one of the largest controllable costs in most organisations, because there is usually considerable scope for reducing consumption in buildings.'

http://www.carbontrust.co.uk/energy/startsaving/top_tips.htm

Energy consumption can be reduced in the following ways.

Vehicles	These should be regularly maintained as inefficiencies increase energy use and therefore increase costs.
Energy bills	Monitoring and understanding energy bills can help businesses to work out how to save costs.

Heating	Increasing the temperature by one degree can increase costs by 8% so it is important to think twice before increasing the thermostat. Space should be left around radiators to maximise their efficiency and therefore reduce costs. Rooms which are not being used should not be heated. All heating equipment should be maintained to ensure maximum efficiency.
Lighting	Lights should be switched off in rooms and corridors that are not being used. Lighting systems should be maintained to ensure maximum efficiency and therefore reduce costs.
Windows	When heating or air conditioning is on, windows should be kept shut to save energy. Windows should also be kept clean as this increases the natural daylight reducing the need for lights.
Other equipment	Photocopiers and printers, for example, produce heat. These should not be kept near cooling systems as more energy will be needed to counteract the heat from the photocopiers. Equipment should be turned off when it is not in use.

2.4 Water usage

Water usage links closely to energy usage because saving water saves energy. Businesses should try to save water wherever they can and this will save costs. Obvious ways of reducing water wastage include fixeingdripping taps and dealing quickly with burst water pipes. Other savings can be made depending on the industry of the business and significant cost savings can be made by commissioning a water audit.

CASE STUDY

A water cost reduction specialist surveyed HM Prison Service Parkhurst in the Isle of Wight. They detected unaccounted water losses which were found to be leaks and wastage. The leakage detection and repair cost less than £8,000 and the savings amounted to £42,888 per annum.

www.h2obuildingservices.co.uk

CASE STUDY

The British Airports Authority (BAA) has developed a sustainable development programme with a number of aspects:

*   **Carbon emissions** – Climate change is a concern for all businesses. BAA is one of the UK's major energy users and air travel is a source of greenhouse gas emissions. It is BAA's objective to reduce its CO_2 emissions from energy use by 30% by 2020 compared to 1990 levels, despite expected passenger numbers growing by 130% during that time.

*   **Bio-diversity** – BAA's programme has been developed in consultation with stakeholders including DEFRA, English Nature and Earthwatch. All BAA airports have a local biodiversity strategy and biodiversity action plans in place.

*   **Car sharing** – BAA has introduced car share schemes for its employees and employees of companies based at its airports.

*   **Environmental awareness** – BAA has promoted environmental awareness by having training days focused on the workplace and the home. Recycling targets have been set for the new Terminal 5 at London's Heathrow Airport. By working in partnership with suppliers for the new Terminal 5, BAA was able to reuse of recycle more than 97% of the construction waste from the Terminal 5 site.

www.baa.com

Section summary

Business activity has an impact on the environment known as the environmental footprint. Saving energy reduces carbon emissions (and therefore the footprint) and saves costs.

BPP
LEARNING MEDIA

3 Types of cost

Introduction

The IFAC's 1998 report also listed a large number of costs that the business might suffer internally.

3.1 Direct or indirect environmental costs

- Waste management
- Remediation costs or expenses
- Compliance costs
- Environmental certification and labelling
- Environmentally driven research and development

- Legal costs and fines
- Permit fees
- Record keeping and reporting
- Environmental training

3.2 Contingent or intangible environmental costs

- Uncertain future remediation or compensation costs
- Risk posed by future regulatory changes
- Sustainability of raw material inputs

- Product quality
- Employee health and safety
- Public/customer perception

3.3 Environmental failure costs

Costs are also sometimes categorised into **environmental internal failure costs** and **environmental external failure costs**.

Environmental internal failure costs are the costs of activities that must be undertaken when contaminants and waste have been **created** by a business but **not released into the environment**. Examples include maintaining pollution equipment and recycling scrap.

Environmental external failure costs are the costs which arise when a business releases harmful waste into the environment. A business can harm its reputation by doing this. Examples include cleaning up oil spills or decontaminating land.

Exam alert

The specimen exam contained a 5-mark question asking for an explanation of environmental internal failure costs and environmental external failure costs.

Clearly, failing to take sufficient account of environmental effects can have a significant impact on the business's accounts as well as the outside world.

Section summary

A business may suffer direct and indirect environmental costs such as legal costs and fines. It may also suffer contingent or intangible environmental costs such as employee health and safety.

4 Environmental cost accounting

Introduction

Businesses need to monitor and manage the impact of environmental issues. This means keeping up to date with emerging environmental issues and changes in industry best practice.

4.1 What is environmental cost accounting?

In CIMA's book *'Environmental Cost Accounting: An introduction and practical guide'* by Rupert Howe, environmental accounting is defined as the following.

'The generation analysis and use of monetarised environmentally-related information in order to improve corporate environmental and economic performance.'

Rupert Howe suggests that **businesses should pay for external environmental costs** which contribute to environmental problems such as climate change. This would change the prices of goods and services and their profitability. The profits reported in the financial accounts will not be **environmentally sustainable** unless the external environmental costs are included.

According to Rupert Howe, sustainable profits are

'profits (or loss) that would remain at the end of an accounting period after provision has been made, or expenditure incurred, to restore or avoid the most significant external environmental impacts resulting from the company's activities and operations'.

4.2 How to estimate sustainable profits

Environmental costing is a relatively new concept but several leading companies are using a consistent methodology.

 Set boundaries. The environmental costs must be controllable in some way, otherwise there is nothing that the business can do to reduce the effects.

 Establish targets. The Royal Commission on Environmental Pollution produced a report in June 2000 which suggested reducing carbon dioxide emissions by 60% by 2050. Marks and Spencer aims to be 'carbon neutral' by 2012.

 Identify impacts. Every business will be different but many will produce emissions associated with energy used in the office, company cars and distribution.

 Valuation. This is what the business needs to spend to avoid the impacts of environmental damage or to restore damage done, using real or market prices.

4.2.1 Valuation

Valuation is now becoming slightly easier. For example, energy emissions can be avoided by using electricity generated from **renewable energy sources such as wind or solar power**. The valuation would be any premium which would be payable for switching to renewable sources.

Another way of valuing carbon dioxide emissions is to use the price charged by an emissions **offsetting** company such as Climate Care (currently £8.81 per tonne). Climate Care can reduce the carbon emissions in the air on the business's behalf thereby offsetting the effect of the carbon emissions.

4.3 Environmental management systems

4.3.1 ISO 14000

ISO 14000 was first published in 1996 and based on earlier quality management standards. It provides a general framework on which a number of specific standards have been based (the ISO family of standards). ISO 14001 prescribes that an environmental management system must comprise:

- An **environmental policy statement**
- An assessment of environmental aspects and legal and voluntary obligations
- A management system
- Internal audits and reports to senior management
- A public declaration that ISO 14001 is being complied with

Critics of ISO 14000 claim that its emphasis on management systems rather than performance is misplaced, and that it does not include rigorous verification and disclosure requirements.

4.3.2 Management systems

In *Accounting for the Environment* Gray and Bebbington listed the functions that environmental management systems should cover.

Environmental review and policy development	A first review of environmental impacts of materials, issues and products and of business issues arising, also the development of a tailored in-house policy or measures to ensure adherence to external standards
Objectives and target development	As with all business objectives and targets, it is preferable that those set be unambiguous and achievable. Targets should be quantified within a specified time period eg reducing carbon dioxide emissions by X% within a specified time period
Life-cycle assessment	This aims to identify all interactions between a product and its environment during its lifetime, including energy and material usage and environmental releases. • Raw materials used have to be traced back to the biosphere and the company recognise impact on habitat, gas balance, the energy used in the extraction and transportation and the energy used to produce the means of extraction • For intermediate stages, emissions, discharges and co-products • At the consumer purchase stage, the impact of manufacture and disposal of packaging, transport to shops and ultimately impacts of consumers using and disposing of the product
Establishment and maintenance of environmental management systems	Key features of environmental management systems (as with other management systems) including information systems, budgeting, forecasting and management accounting systems, structure of responsibilities, establishment of an environmentally-friendly culture, considering impact on human resource issues such as education and performance appraisal
Regulatory compliance	Making sure that current legal requirements are being fulfilled and keeping up-to-date with practical implications of likely changes in legislation
Environmental impact assessment	A regular review of interactions with the environment, the degree of impact and also the impact of forthcoming major investments
Eco-label applications	Eco-labelling allows organisations to identify publicly products and services that meet the highest environmental standards. To be awarded an eco-label requires the product to be the result of a reliable quality management system
Waste minimisation	Whether waste can be minimised (or better still eliminated), possibility of recycling or selling waste

Pollution prevention programmes	Deciding what to target
Research, development and investment in cleaner technologies	How to bring desirable features into product development, bearing in mind product development may take several years, and opinion and legal requirements may change during that period. Desirable features may include minimum resource usage, waste, emissions, packaging and transport, recycling, disassembly and longer product life
Environmental performance and issues reporting	Consideration of the benefits and costs of reporting, how to report and what to include (policies, plans, financial data, activities undertaken, sustainability)

Note that environmental costing can be incorporated into the management system as mentioned above but some issues may still be covered in a dedicated annual **environmental report**. The report may contain performance indicators which can be compared from year to year or against industry benchmarks.

Question 12.1	Environmental cost control systems

Learning outcomes A3(a)

How do the main elements of control systems for environmental management systems differ from control systems in other areas?

Section summary

Environmental cost accounting initially involves establishing the impacts of business activity on the environment. The impacts must then be valued on the basis of what it would cost to avoid them or to restore any damage. These costs are deducted from the main annual report to obtain an environmentally sustainable profit figure.

5 Environmental costing using ABC

Introduction

The problem with traditional management accounting systems is that they fail to analyse environmental costs. Costs such as water, energy and waste become hidden within production overheads. One possible solution is to incorporate environmental costing into the activity based system.

5.1 Cost drivers

Using an activity based system, **environmental costs** become **cost drivers**. To decide on the environmental cost drivers, the production processes involved in making a product or providing a service need to be carefully analysed. The **levels** of environmental **hazards** and **costs** need to be **established**. This may mean installing **tracking systems** to track environmental waste.

5.2 Life cycle costing

Environmental costs should be considered right **from** the **design stage** of a new product right up to the **end-of-life costs** such as decommissioning and removal. This is particularly important in some countries where businesses are held responsible for costs associated with the end of the life of the product. The consideration of future disposal or remediation costs at the design stage may influence the design of the product itself, saving on future costs.

The consideration of all the costs throughout the product's life is known as the **life cycle costing approach**.

5.2.1 Benefits of life cycle approach

- Costs become more visible
- Potential future costs (such as disposal costs) may be prevented or reduced before they occur

5.3 Allocation of environmental costs

When allocating environmental costs it is important to consider the following.

- Volume of emissions or waste
- How toxic the emissions or waste are
- The relative costs of treating different types of emissions

Section summary

Using an activity based system, environmental costs become cost drivers.

Chapter Roundup

✓ There is increasing awareness about businesses' relationship with the natural environment. Businesses may suffer **significant costs** and a **loss of reputation** if problems arise.

✓ Business activity has an impact on the environment known as the environmental footprint. Saving energy reduces carbon emissions (and therefore the footprint) and saves costs.

✓ A business may suffer direct and indirect environmental costs such as legal costs and fines. It may also suffer contingent or intangible environmental costs such as employee health and safety.

✓ Environmental cost accounting initially involves establishing the impacts of business activity on the environment. The impacts must then be valued on the basis of what it would cost to avoid them or to restore any damage. These costs are deducted from the main annual report to obtain an environmentally sustainable profit figure.

✓ Using an activity based system, environmental costs become cost drivers.

Quick Quiz

1   Fill in the blank.

     .... is the impact that a business's activities have upon the environment including its resource environment and pollution emissions.

2   What are the main elements of an environmental management system per ISO 14001?

3   Which of the following is an example of an environmental external failure cost?

     A   Maintaining pollution equipment
     B   Decontaminating land
     C   Recycling scrap
     D   Record keeping

4   What are the four steps that can be used to estimate sustainable profits?

5   Identify four reasons why environmental costs are important to management accountants.

Answers to Quick Quiz

1   Environmental footprint

2
- An environmental policy
- An assessment of environmental aspects and legal and voluntary obligations
- A management system
- Internal audits and reports to senior management
- A public declaration that ISO 14001 is being complied with

3   B   Decontaminating land

4   Step 1   Set boundaries
         Step 2   Establish targets
         Step 3   Identify impacts
         Step 4   Valuation

5   (a)   Environmental costing can help to produce more accurate product or service pricing leading to increased profitability.
         (b)   Poor environmental behaviour can result in fines and damage to reputation.
         (c)   Recording environmental costs is important as some may require regulatory compliance.
         (d)   Saving energy generally leads to cost savings.

Answers to Questions

12.1 Environmental cost control systems

As we have seen in this section, they don't. Environmental management systems are a good illustration of how control systems work in practice.

Now try the question from the Exam Question Bank	Number	Level	Marks	Time
	Q20	Examination	5	9

FORECASTING AND BUDGETING TECHNIQUES

Part C

356

BUDGETING

This chapter begins a new topic, **budgeting**.

You may recognise much of this chapter from your earlier studies. You have already covered most of the topics in this chapter at a basic level and so we have included a couple of deemed knowledge boxes on the most straightforward areas.

The chapter begins by explaining the **reasons for operating a budgetary planning and control system** (**Section 1**), explains some of the **key terms** associated with budgeting and reminds you of the steps in the preparation of a master budget (**Section 2**).

You should have already covered budget preparation in earlier studies (including the preparation of cash budgets) but we will look at some more complex examples in **Sections 4 and 5**. Cash budgets link closely with Part E of this Study Text on managing short-term finance.

Section 6 explains how the budgeting process does not stop once the master budget has been prepared but is a **constant task** of the management accountant.

We review a number of **alternative approaches to budgeting** in **Section 7**.

Our study of budgeting continues in Chapter 14 with a look at forecasting.

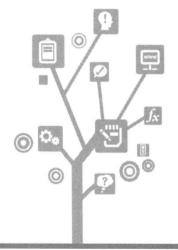

topic list	learning outcomes	syllabus references	ability required
1 Budgetary planning and control systems	B1(a),(b)	B1(ii)	comprehension
2 The preparation of budgets	B1(a)	B1(ii)	comprehension
3 The sales budget	B3(a)	B3(i)	application
4 Production and related budgets	B3(a)	B3(i)	application
5 Cash budgets and the master budget	B3(a)	B3(i)	application
6 Monitoring procedures	B1(a)	B1(ii)	comprehension
7 Alternative approaches to budgeting	B3(b)	B3(ii)	application

1   Budgetary planning and control systems

Introduction

A **budget** is a quantified plan of action for a forthcoming accounting period. A **budget** is a plan of what the organisation is aiming to achieve and what it has set as a target whereas a **forecast** is an estimate of what is likely to occur in the future

KEY TERM

The BUDGET is the 'Quantitative expression of a plan for a defined period of time. It may include planned sales volumes and revenues; resource quantities, costs and expenses; assets, liabilities and cashflows.'

(CIMA Official Terminology)

The **objectives of budget preparation** are shown in the table below. Sometimes these objectives can **conflict with one another**. For example, **planning can conflict with motivation**. Targets set in the planning process must be **challenging but fair**, otherwise individuals will become dissatisfied. Integration may also conflict with evaluation. For example, the **goals of the organisation** as a whole may not coincide with the **personal aspirations of individual managers**. Managers may therefore build '**slack**' into their expenditure estimates in order to increase the chances of receiving a bonus for achieving targets. Motivation and evaluation may also cause conflict. For example, managers might resent control information which is used in evaluation as they may see it as part of a system of trying to find fault in their work. This is more likely when budgets are imposed on managers without their consultation.

Objective	Comment
Planning	Compelling manages to plan is probably the most important feature of a budgetary planning and control system. Planning forces management to look ahead, to set out detailed plans for achieving the targets for each department, operation and (ideally) each manager and to anticipate problems. It thus prevents management from relying on ad hoc or uncoordinated planning which may be detrimental to the performance of the organisation. It also helps managers to foresee potential threats or opportunities, so that they may take action now to avoid or minimise the effect of the threats and to take full advantage of the opportunities.
Responsibility	Objectives are set for the organisation as a whole, and for individual departments and operations within the organisation. Quantified expressions of these objectives are then drawn up as targets to be achieved within the timescale of the budget plan. Budgetary planning and control systems require that managers of budget centres are made responsible for the achievement of budget targets for the operations under their personal control.
Integration and co-ordination	The activities of different departments or sub-units of the organisation need to be coordinated to ensure maximum integration of effort towards common goals. This concept of coordination implies, for example, that the purchasing department should base its budget on production requirements and that the production budget should in turn be based on sales expectations. Although straightforward in concept, coordination is remarkably difficult to achieve, and there is often 'sub-optimality' and conflict between departmental plans in the budget so that the efforts of each department are not fully integrated into a combined plan to achieve the company's best targets. Communication is important here to ensure that each person affected by the plans is aware of what they are supposed to be doing.
Motivation	The interest and commitment of employees can be retained via a system of feedback of actual results, which lets them know how well or badly they are performing. The identification of controllable reasons for departures from budget with managers responsible provides an incentive for improving future performance.

Objective	Comment
Evaluation and control	As well as providing a yardstick for control by comparison, the monitoring of actual results compared with the budget can provide a basis for evaluating the performance of the budget holder. As a result of this evaluation the manager might be rewarded, perhaps with a financial bonus or promotion. Alternatively the evaluation process might highlight the need for more investment in staff development and training.

Section summary

The **objectives** of a budgetary planning and control system are as follows.

P – Planning
R – Responsibility
I – Integration and co-ordination
M – Motivation
E – Evaluation and control

2 The preparation of budgets

Introduction

Having seen why organisations prepare budgets, we will now turn our attention to the mechanics of budget preparation. We will begin by defining and explaining a number of terms.

2.1 Planning

KEY TERM

PLANNING is described in the *Official Terminology* as the 'Establishment of objectives, and the formulation, evaluation and selection of the policies, strategies, tactics and action required to achieve them. Planning comprises long-term/strategic planning, and short-term operational planning. The latter is usually for a period of up to one year.'

The overall planning process therefore covers both the long and short term.

Type of planning	Detail
Strategic/corporate /long-range planning	Covers periods longer than one year and involves 'The formulation, evaluation and selection of strategies for the purpose of preparing a long-term plan of action to attain objectives'. CIMA *Official Terminology*
Budgetary/short-term tactical planning	Involves preparing detailed plans, which generally cover one year, for an organisation's functions, activities and departments. Works within the framework set by the strategic plans and converts those strategic plans into action.
Operation planning	Planning on a very short-term or day-to-day basis and is concerned with planning how an organisation's resources will be used. Works within the framework set by the budgetary plans and converts the budgetary plans into action.

2.1.1 The value of long-term planning

A **budgetary planning and control system** operating in **isolation** without any form of long-term planning as a framework is **unlikely to produce maximum potential benefits** for an organisation.

(a)   Without stated long-term objectives, managers do not know what they should be trying to achieve and so there are no criteria against which to assess possible courses of action.

(b)   Without long-term planning, budgets may simply be based on a sales forecast. Performance can therefore only be judged in terms of previous years' results, no analysis of the organisation's potential having been carried out.

(c)   Many business decisions need to be taken on a long-term basis. For instance, new products cannot simply be introduced when sales of existing products begin to decline. Likewise, capital equipment cannot necessarily be purchased and installed in the short term if production volumes start to increase.

(d)   With long-term planning, limiting factors (other than sales) which might arise can possibly be anticipated, and avoided or overcome.

2.2 The budget period

KEY TERM

The BUDGET PERIOD is the 'Period for which a budget is prepared and used, which may then be sub-divided into control periods.'   *(CIMA Official Terminology)*

Except for capital expenditure budgets, the budget period is commonly the accounting year (sub-divided into 12 or 13 control periods).

2.3 The budget manual

KEY TERM

The BUDGET MANUAL is a collection of instructions governing the responsibilities of persons and the procedures, forms and records relating to the preparation and use of budgetary data.

Likely contents of a budget manual	Examples
An explanation of the objectives of the budgetary process	• The purpose of budgetary planning and control • The objectives of the various stages of the budgetary process • The importance of budgets in the long-term planning and administration of the enterprise
Organisational structures	• An organisation chart • A list of individuals holding budget responsibilities
Principal budgets	• An outline of each • The relationship between them
Administrative details of budget preparation	• Membership and terms of reference of the budget committee • The sequence in which budgets are to be prepared • A timetable
Procedural matters	• Specimen forms and instructions for their completion • Specimen reports • Account codes (or a chart of accounts) • The name of the budget officer to whom enquiries must be sent

2.4 The responsibility for preparing budgets

The initial responsibility for preparing the budget will normally be with the managers (and their subordinates) who will be carrying out the budget, selling goods or services and authorising expenditure. However, the budget is normally set as part of a longer process, involving the authorisation of set targets by senior management and the negotiation process with the budget holders. Depending on the size of the organisation there may be a large number of **budget centres** and a separate **budget holder** would be responsible for setting and achieving the budget for the centre.

Examples of the functional budgets that would be prepared and **the managers responsible for their preparation** are as follows.

(a) The **sales manager** should draft the **sales budget** and **selling overhead** cost centre budgets.

(b) The **purchasing manager** should draft the material purchases budget.

(c) The **production manager** should draft the **direct production** cost budgets.

(d) Various **cost centre managers** should prepare the individual production, administration and distribution cost centre budgets for their own cost centre.

(e) The **cost accountant** will **analyse** the budgeted overheads to determine the overhead absorption rates for the next budget period.

2.5 Budget committee

The **coordination** and **administration** of budgets is usually the responsibility of a **budget committee** (with the managing director as chairman).

(a) The budget committee is assisted by a **budget officer** who is usually an accountant. Every part of the organisation should be represented on the committee, so there should be a representative from sales, production, marketing and so on.

(b) **Functions of the budget committee**

(i) **Coordination** of the preparation of budgets, which includes the issue of the budget manual

(ii) **Issuing of timetables** for the preparation of functional budgets

(iii) **Allocation of responsibilities** for the preparation of functional budgets

(iv) **Provision of information** to assist in the preparation of budgets

(v) **Communication of final budgets** to the appropriate managers

(vi) **Comparison** of actual results with budget and the investigation of variances

(vii) **Continuous assessment** of the budgeting and planning process, in order to improve the planning and control function

2.6 Budget preparation

Let us now look at the steps involved in the preparation of a budget. The procedures will differ from organisation to organisation, but the step-by-step approach described in this chapter is indicative of the steps followed by many organisations. The preparation of a budget may take weeks or months, and the budget committee may meet several times before the functional budgets are co-ordinated and the master budget is finally agreed.

KEY TERM

The CIMA *Official Terminology* defines a DEPARTMENTAL/FUNCTIONAL BUDGET as 'A budget of income and/or expenditure applicable to a particular function.

A function may refer to a department or a process. Functional budgets frequently include:

- Production cost budget (based on a forecast of production and plant utilisation)
- Marketing cost budget, sales budget
- Personnel budget
- Purchasing budget
- Research and development budget'

2.7 The principal budget factor

The first task in the budgetary process is to identify the **principal budget factor**. This is also known as the **key** budget factor or **limiting** budget factor.

KEY TERM

The PRINCIPAL BUDGET FACTOR is the factor which limits the activities of an organisation.

Likely principal budget factors

(a) The **principal budget factor** is usually **sales demand**: a company is usually restricted from making and selling more of its products because there would be no sales demand for the increased output at a price which would be acceptable/profitable to the company.

(b) Other possible factors

    (i)   Machine capacity
    (ii)   Distribution and selling resources
    (iii) The availability of key raw materials
    (iv) The availability of cash.

Once this factor is defined then the remainder of the budgets can be prepared. For example, if sales are the principal budget factor then the production manager can only prepare his budget after the sales budget is complete.

Management may not know what the limiting budget factor is until a draft budget has been attempted. The first draft budget will therefore usually begin with the preparation of a draft sales budget.

Knowledge brought forward from earlier studies

Steps in the preparation of a budget

 Identification of **principal/key/limiting budget factor**

 Preparation of a **sales budget,** assuming that sales is the principal budget factor (in units and in sales value for each product, based on a sales forecast)

 Preparation of a **finished goods inventory budget** (to determine the planned change in finished goods inventory levels)

 Preparation of a **production budget** (calculated as sales + closing inventory – opening inventory)

 Preparation of **budgets for production resources**

    • Materials usage
    • Machine usage
    • Labour

 Preparation of a **raw materials inventory budget** (to determine the planned change in raw materials inventory levels)

 Preparation of a **raw materials purchases budget** (calculated as usage + inventory – opening inventory)

 Preparation of **overhead cost budgets** (such as production, administration, selling and distribution and R&D)

Calculation of **overhead absorption rates** (if absorption costing is used)

 Preparation of a **cash budget** (and others as required, **capital expenditure** and **working capital** budgets)

 Preparation of a **master budget** (budgeted income statement and budgeted statement of financial position)

Remember that it is **unlikely** that the execution of the **above steps** will be **problem-free** as data from one budget becomes an input in the preparation of another budget. For example, the materials purchases budget will probably be used in preparing the payables budget. The payables budget will then become an input to the cash budget, and so on. The budgets must therefore be **reviewed in relation to one another**. Such a review may indicate that some budgets are out of balance with others and need modifying so that they will be compatible with other conditions, constraints and plans. The budget officer must identify such inconsistencies and bring them to the attention of the manager concerned.

Alternatively, there may have been a **change in one of the organisational policies**, such as a change in selling prices, which will need to be **incorporated into the budget**. The revision of one budget may lead to the revision of all budgets. This process must continue until all budgets are acceptable and co-ordinated with each other.

If such changes are made manually, the process can be very time consuming and costly. Computer **spreadsheets** can help immensely.

Question 13.1
Budgets

Learning outcome B3(a)

A company that manufactures and sells a range of products, with sales potential limited by market share, is considering introducing a system of budgeting.

Required

(a) List (in order of preparation) the functional budgets that need to be prepared.

(b) State which budgets will comprise the master budget.

(c) Consider how the work outlined in (a) and (b) can be coordinated in order for the budgeting process to be successful.

Section summary

The **budget committee** is the coordinating body in the preparation and administration of budgets.

The **principal budget factor** should be identified at the beginning of the budgetary process, and the budget for this is prepared before all the others.

3 The sales budget

Introduction

We have already established that, for many organisations, the principal budget factor is sales volume. The sales budget is therefore **often the primary budget** from which the majority of the other budgets are derived.

Before the sales budget can be prepared a sales forecast has to be made. A **forecast** is an estimate of what is likely to occur in the future. A budget, in contrast, is a plan of what the organisation is aiming to achieve and what it has set as a target. We will be looking at forecasting techniques in detail in the next chapter.

On the basis of the sales forecast and the production capacity of the organisation, a sales budget will be prepared. This may be subdivided, possible subdivisions being by product, by sales area, by management responsibility and so on.

Once the sales budget has been agreed, related budgets can be prepared.

Section summary

For many organisations, the principal budget factor is sales volume.

4 Production and related budgets   5/10

Introduction

If the principal budget factor was production capacity then the production budget would be the first to be prepared. To assess whether production is the principal budget factor, the **production capacity available** must be determined, taking account of a number of factors.

- **Available labour**, including idle time, overtime and standard output rates per hour

- **Availability of raw materials** including allowances for losses during production

- **Maximum machine hours available**, including expected idle time and expected output rates per machine hour

It is, however, normally sales volume that is the constraint and therefore the production budget is usually prepared after the sales budget and the finished goods inventory budget.

The production budget will show the quantities and costs for each product and product group and will tie in with the sales and inventory budgets. This co-ordinating process is likely to show any shortfalls or excesses in capacity at various times over the budget period.

If there is likely to be a **shortfall** then consideration should be given to how this can be avoided. Possible **options** include the following.

- Overtime working
- Subcontracting
- Machine hire
- New sources of raw materials

A significant shortfall means that production capacity is, in fact, the limiting factor.

If **capacity exceeds sales volume** for a length of time then consideration should be given to **product diversification**, a **reduction in selling price** (if demand is price elastic) and so on.

Once the production budget has been finalised, the labour, materials and machine budgets can be drawn up. These budgets will be based on budgeted activity levels, planned inventory positions and projected labour and material costs.

Example: the production budget and direct labour budget

Landy manufactures two products, A and B, and is preparing its budget for 20X3. Both products are made by the same grade of labour, grade Q. The company currently holds 800 units of A and 1,200 units of B in inventory, but 250 of these units of B have just been discovered to have deteriorated in quality, and must therefore be scrapped. Budgeted sales of A are 3,000 units and of B 4,000 units, provided that the company maintains finished goods inventories at a level equal to three months' sales.

Grade Q labour was originally expected to produce one unit of A in two hours and one unit of B in three hours, at an hourly rate of £2.50 per hour. In discussions with trade union negotiators, however, it has been agreed that the hourly wage rate should be raised by 50p per hour, provided that the times to produce A and B are reduced by 20%.

Required

Prepare the production budget and direct labour budget for 20X3.

Solution

The expected time to produce a unit of A will now be 80% of 2 hours = 1.6 hours, and the time for a unit of B will be 2.4 hours. The hourly wage rate will be £3, so that the direct labour cost will be £4.80 for A and £7.20 for B (thus achieving a saving for the company of 20p per unit of A produced and 30p per unit of B).

(a) **Production budget**

		Product A			*Product B*	
		Units	Units		Units	Units
Budgeted sales			3,000			4,000
Closing inventories	(^{3}/12 of 3,000)	750		($^3/_{12}$ of 4,000)	1,000	
Opening inventories (minus inventories scrapped)		800			950	
(Decrease)/increase in inventories			(50)			50
Production			2,950			4,050

(b) **Direct labour budget**

	Grade Q	*Cost*
	Hours	£
2,950 units of product A	4,720	14,160
4,050 units of product B	9,720	29,160
Total	14,440	43,320

It is assumed that there will be no idle time among grade Q labour which, if it existed, would have to be paid for at the rate of £3 per hour.

Exam skills

You are unlikely to get straightforward budget preparation questions at this level given that the topic is initially covered at an earlier level but the syllabus does require you to understand the construction of budgets.

4.1 The standard hour

KEY TERM

A STANDARD HOUR or standard minute is the 'Amount of work achievable at standard efficiency levels in an hour or minute.'

(CIMA Official Terminology)

This is a useful concept in budgeting for labour requirements. For example, budgeted **output of different products or jobs** in a period could be converted into standard hours of production, and a labour budget constructed accordingly.

Standard hours are particularly useful when management wants to monitor the production levels of a variety of dissimilar units. For example product A may take five hours to produce and product B, seven hours. If four units of each product are produced, instead of saying that total output is eight units, we could state the production level as $(4 \times 5) + (4 \times 7)$ standard hours = 48 standard hours.

Example: direct labour budget based on standard hours

Truro manufactures a single product, Q, with a single grade of labour. Its sales budget and finished goods inventory budget for period 3 are as follows.

Sales	700 units
Opening inventories, finished goods	50 units
Closing inventories, finished goods	70 units

The goods are inspected only when production work is completed, and it is budgeted that 10% of finished work will be scrapped.

The standard direct labour hour content of product Q is three hours. The budgeted productivity ratio for direct labour is only 80% (which means that labour is only working at 80% efficiency).

The company employs 18 direct operatives, who are expected to average 144 working hours each in period 3.

Required

(a)   Prepare a production budget.

(b)   Prepare a direct labour budget.

(c)   Comment on the problem that your direct labour budget reveals, and suggest how this problem might be overcome.

Solution

(a)   **Production budget**

	Units
Sales	700
Add closing inventory	70
	770
Less opening inventory	50
Production required of 'good' output	720

Wastage rate 10%

Total production required $720 \times \dfrac{100^*}{90} = 800$ units

(* Note that the required adjustment is 100/90, not 110/100, since the waste is assumed to be 10% of total production, not 10% of good production.)

(b)   Now we can prepare the **direct labour budget**.

Standard hours per unit	3
Total standard hours required = 800 units × 3 hours	2,400 hours
Productivity ratio	80%

Actual hours required $2,400 \times \dfrac{100}{80} = 3,000$ hours

(c)   If we look at the **direct labour budget** against the information provided, we can identify the problem.

	Hours
Budgeted hours available (18 operatives × 144 hours)	2,592
Actual hours required	3,000
Shortfall in labour hours	408

The (draft) budget indicates that there will not be enough direct labour hours to meet the production requirements.

Overcoming insufficient labour hours

(i)   **Reduce the closing inventory** requirement below 70 units. This would reduce the number of production units required.

(ii)   Persuade the workforce to do some **overtime** working.

(iii)   Perhaps **recruit** more direct labour if long-term prospects are for higher production volumes.

(iv)   **Improve** the **productivity** ratio, and so reduce the number of hours required to produce the output.

(v)   If possible, **reduce** the **wastage** rate below 10%.

Example: the material purchases budget

Tremor manufactures two products, S and T, which use the same raw materials, D and E. One unit of S uses 3 litres of D and 4 kilograms of E. One unit of T uses 5 litres of D and 2 kilograms of E. A litre of D is expected to cost Y3 and a kilogram of E Y7.

Budgeted sales for 20X2 are 8,000 units of S and 6,000 units of T; finished goods in inventory at 1 January 20X2 are 1,500 units of S and 300 units of T, and the company plans to hold inventories of 600 units of each product at 31 December 20X2.

Inventories of raw material are 6,000 litres of D and 2,800 kilograms of E at 1 January, and the company plans to hold 5,000 litres and 3,500 kilograms respectively at 31 December 20X2.

The warehouse and stores managers have suggested that a provision should be made for damages and deterioration of items held in store, as follows.

Product S :   loss of 50 units
Product T :   loss of 100 units
Material D :   loss of 500 litres
Material E :   loss of 200 kilograms

Required

Prepare a material purchases budget for the year 20X2.

Solution

To calculate material purchase requirements, it is first of all necessary to calculate the budgeted production volumes and material usage requirements.

	Product S		Product T	
	Units	Units	Units	Units
Sales		8,000		6,000
Provision for losses		50		100
Closing inventory	600		600	
Opening inventory	1,500		300	
(Decrease)/increase in inventory		(900)		300
Production budget		7,150		6,400

	Material D		Material E	
	Litres	Litres	Kg	Kg
Usage requirements				
To produce 7,150 units of S		21,450		28,600
To produce 6,400 units of T		32,000		12,800
Usage budget		53,450		41,400
Provision for losses		500		200
		53,950		41,600
Closing inventory	5,000		3,500	
Opening inventory	6,000		2,800	
(Decrease)/increase in inventory		(1,000)		700
Material purchases budget		52,950		42,300

	Material D	Material E	
	Material D	Material E	
Cost per unit	Y3 per litre	Y7 per kg	
Cost of material purchases	Y158,850	Y296,100	
Total purchases cost		Y454,950	

Question 13.2   Material purchases budget

Learning outcome B3(a)

J purchases a basic commodity and then refines it for resale. Budgeted sales of the refined product are as follows.

	April	May	June
Sales in kg	9,000	8,000	7,000

- The basic raw material costs £3 per kg.

- Material losses are 10% of finished output.

- The target month-end raw material inventory level is 5,000 kg plus 25% of the raw material required for next month's budgeted production.

- The target month-end inventory level for finished goods is 6,000 kg plus 25% of next month's budgeted sales.

What are the budgeted raw material purchases for April?

A	8,500 kg	C	9,444.25 kg
B	9,350 kg	D	9,831.25 kg

4.2 Non-production overheads

In the modern business environment, an increasing proportion of overheads are not directly related to the volume of production, such as administration overheads and research and development costs.

4.3 Key decisions in the budgeting process for non-production overheads

It is important to decide

(a) Which fixed costs are committed (will be incurred no matter what) and which fixed costs will depend on management decisions.

(b) What factors will influence the level of variable costs. Administration costs for example may be partly governed by the number of orders received.

Section summary

To assess whether production is the principal budget factor, the production capacity available must be determined.

5 Cash budgets and the master budget

Introduction

Cash budgets show the expected receipts and payments during a budget period and are a vital management planning and control tool.

KEY TERM

A CASH BUDGET is a 'Detailed budget of estimated cash inflows and outflows incorporating both revenue and capital items.'
(CIMA Official Terminology)

5.1 The usefulness of cash budgets

The cash budget is one of the most important planning tools that an organisation can use. It shows the **cash effect of all plans made within the budgetary process** and hence its preparation can lead to a **modification of budgets** if it shows that there are insufficient cash resources to finance the planned operations.

It can also give management an indication of **potential problems** that could arise and allows them the opportunity to take action to avoid such problems. A cash budget can show **four positions**. Management will need to take appropriate action depending on the potential position.

Cash position	Appropriate management action
Short-term surplus	• Pay suppliers early to obtain discount • Attempt to increase sales by increasing receivables and inventories • Make short-term investments
Short-term deficit	• Increase payables • Reduce receivables • Arrange an overdraft

Cash position	Appropriate management action
Long-term surplus	• Make long-term investments • Expand • Diversify • Replace/update non-current assets
Long-term deficit	• Raise long-term finance (such as via issue of share capital) • Consider shutdown/disinvestment opportunities

Exam alert

A cash budgeting question in an examination could ask you to recommend appropriate action for management to take once you have prepared the cash budget. Ensure your advice takes account both of whether there is a surplus or deficit and whether the position is long or short term.

5.2 What to include in a cash budget

A cash budget is prepared to show the expected receipts of cash and payments of cash during a budget period.

Sources of cash receipts

- Cash sales
- Payments by customers for credit sales
- The sale of property, plant and equipment
- The issue of new shares or loan inventory and less formalised loans
- The receipt of interest and dividends from investments outside the business

Remember that bad debts will **never be received in cash** and doubtful debts may not be received so you have to adjust if necessary for such items.

Although all the **receipts** above would affect a cash budget they would **not all appear in the income statement**.

(a) The issue of new shares or loan inventory would appear in the statement of financial position.

(b) The cash received from an asset affects the statement of financial position, and the profit or loss on the sale of an asset, which appears in the income statement, is not the cash received but the difference between cash received and the written down value of the asset at the time of sale.

Reasons for paying cash

- Purchase of inventories
- Payroll costs or other expenses
- Purchase of capital items
- Payment of interest, dividends or taxation

Not all payments are **income statement items**. The purchase of property, plant and equipment and the payment of VAT affect the statement of financial position. Some costs in the income statement such as profit or loss on sale of non-current assets or depreciation are not cash items but are costs derived from accounting conventions.

In addition, the **timing** of cash receipts and payments **may not coincide** with the recording of income statement transactions. For example, a dividend might be declared in the results for year 6 and shown in the income statement for that year, but paid in cash in year 7.

Cash budgets are most effective if they are treated as **rolling budgets**. We looked at this in Chapter 2.

Steps in the preparation of a cash budget

- Set up a proforma cash budget.

	Month 1 £	Month 2 £	Month 3 £
Cash receipts: Receipts from customers	X	X	X
Loan etc	X	X	X
	X̄	X̄	X̄
Cash payments: Payments to suppliers	X	X	X
Wages etc	X	X	X
	X̄	X̄	X̄
Opening balance	X	X	X
Net cash flow (receipts – payments)	X	X	X
Closing balance	X̳	X̳	X̳

- Enter the figures that can be entered straightaway (receipts or payments that you are told occur in a specific month)

- Sort out cash receipts from customers.

    - Establish budgeted sales month by month.

    - Establish the length of credit period taken by customers, using the following formula:

    $$\text{Receivables collection period (no of days credit)} = \frac{\text{Average (or year-end) receivables}}{\text{Total credit sales in period}} \times \text{no of days in period}$$

    - Hence determine when budgeted sales revenue will be received as cash (by considering cash receipts from customers, ignoring any provision for doubtful debts).

    - Establish when opening receivables will pay.

- Establish when any other cash income will be received.

- Sort out cash payments to suppliers.

    - Establish production quantities and materials usage quantities each month.

    - Establish materials inventory changes and hence the quantity and cost of materials purchases each month.

    - Establish the length of credit period taken from suppliers, using the following formula:

    $$\text{Payables payment period (no of days credit)} = \frac{\text{Average (or year-end) payables}}{\text{Total purchases on credit in period}} \times \text{no of days in period}$$

    - Hence calculate when cash payments to suppliers will be made and when the amount due to opening payables will be paid.

- Establish when any other cash payments (excluding non-cash items such as depreciation) will be made.

Exam alert

The May 2011 exam contained a section C question which required the preparation of a flexed budget and a discussion of the benefits of a flexible budget. This is on the CIMA C1 syllabus and so is deemed to be knowledge brought forward. Don't underestimate the importance of your earlier studies.

Example: income statement and cash budget

Penny operates a retail business. Purchases are sold at cost plus $33^1/_3\%$.

(a)

	Budgeted sales in month £	Labour cost in month £	Expenses incurred in month £
January	40,000	3,000	4,000
February	60,000	3,000	6,000
March	160,000	5,000	7,000
April	120,000	4,000	7,000

(b)   It is management policy to have sufficient inventory in hand at the end of each month to meet half of next month's sales demand.

(c)   Suppliers for materials and expenses are paid in the month after the purchases are made/expenses incurred. Labour is paid in full by the end of each month. Labour costs and expenses are treated as period costs in the income statement.

(d)   Expenses include a monthly depreciation charge of £2,000.

(e)   (i)   75% of sales are for cash.
      (ii)   25% of sales are on one month's credit.

(f)   The company will buy equipment costing £18,000 for cash in February and will pay a dividend of £20,000 in March. The opening cash balance at 1 February is £1,000.

Required

(a)   Prepare a cash budget for February and March.
(b)   Prepare an income statement for February and March.

Solution

(a)   CASH BUDGET

	February £	March £
Receipts		
Receipts from sales	55,000 (W1)	135,000 (W2)
Payments		
Trade payables	37,500 (W3)	82,500 (W3)
Expense payables	2,000 (W4)	4,000 (W4)
Labour	3,000	5,000
Equipment purchase	18,000	–
Dividend	–	20,000
Total payments	60,500	111,500
Receipts less payments	(5,500)	23,500
Opening cash balance b/f	1,000	(4,500)*
Closing cash balance c/f	(4,500)*	19,000

Workings

1   **Receipts in February**

	£
75% of Feb sales (75% × £60,000)	45,000
25% of Jan sales (25% × £40,000)	10,000
	55,000

2   **Receipts in March**

	£
75% of Mar sales (75% × £160,000)	120,000
25% of Feb sales (25% × £60,000)	15,000
	135,000

3   **Purchases**

	January		February	
		£		£
For Jan sales	(50% of £30,000)	15,000		
For Feb sales	(50% of £45,000)	22,500	(50% of £45,000)	22,500
For Mar sales		–	(50% of £120,000)	60,000
		37,500		82,500

These purchases are paid for in February and March.

4   **Expenses**

Cash expenses in January (£4,000 – £2,000) and February (£6,000 – £2,000) are paid in February and March respectively. Depreciation is not a cash item.

(b)   INCOME STATEMENT

	February		March	
	£	£	£	£
Sales		60,000		160,000
Cost of purchases (75%)		45,000		120,000
Gross profit		15,000		40,000
Less: Labour	3,000		5,000	
Expenses	6,000		7,000	
		9,000		12,000
Net profit		6,000		28,000

KEY POINT

(a)   The asterisks show that the cash balance at the end of February is carried forward as the opening cash balance for March.

(b)   The fact that profits are made in February and March **disguises** the fact that there is a **cash shortfall** at the end of February.

(c)   Steps should be taken either to ensure that an **overdraft facility** is available for the cash shortage at the end of February, or to **defer certain payments** so that the overdraft is avoided.

(d)   Some payments must be made on due dates (payroll, taxation and so on) but it is possible that other payments can be delayed, depending on the requirements of the business and/or the goodwill of suppliers.

5.3 A comparison of profit and cash flows

Look at the example above. Had you noticed that the total profit of £34,000 differs from the total receipts less total payments (£18,000). Profit and cash flows during a period need not be the same amount and, in fact, are actually more likely to be different.

(a)   **Sales** and **cost of sales** are recognised in an **income statement** as soon as they are **made/incurred**. The **cash budget** does not show figures for sales and cost of sales but is concerned with **cash actually received** from customers and **paid** to suppliers.

(b) An **income statement** may include **accrued** amounts for rates, insurance and other expenses. In the **cash budget** such amounts will appear in full in the **period in which they are paid**. There is no attempt to apportion payments to the period to which they relate.

(c) Similarly an **income statement** may show a charge for **depreciation**. This is not a cash expense and will never appear in a cash budget. The **cash budget** will show **purchase of a non-current asset** as a payment in the **period when the asset is paid for**, and may also show the proceeds on disposal of a non-current asset as a receipt of cash. No attempt is made to allocate the purchase cost over the life of the asset.

Question 13.3	Cash budgets (receipts)

Learning outcome B3(a)

X will begin trading on 1 January 20X3. The following sales revenue is budgeted for January to March 20X3.

January	February	March
€13,000	€17,000	€10,000

Five per cent of sales will be for cash. The remainder will be credit sales. A discount of 5% will be offered on all cash sales. The payment pattern for credit sales is expected to be as follows.

Invoices paid in the month after sale	75%
Invoices paid in the second month after sale	23%
Bad debts	2%

Invoices are issued on the last day of each month.

The amount budgeted to be received from customers in March 20X3 is

A   €15,428
B   €15,577.50
C   €15,928
D   €16,065.50

5.4 The role of the master budget

KEY TERM

The MASTER BUDGET 'Consolidates all subsidiary budgets and is normally comprised of the budgeted profit and loss account, balance sheet and cash flow statement.' *(CIMA Official Terminology)*

It is this master budget which is **submitted** to senior managers or directors for their approval. If the master budget is **approved** as an acceptable plan for the forthcoming budget period then it acts as an **instruction and authorisation** to budget managers, to allow them to take action to achieve their budgets.

If the master budget is not approved as an acceptable plan then it will be returned to the budget committee for amendment. The **amended** master budget will then be reviewed again by senior management. Thus, budgeting is an **iterative process** and it may be necessary to perform many iterations before an acceptable, workable budget is adopted and approved.

Section summary

Cash budgets show the expected receipts and payments during a budget period and are a vital management planning and control tool.

The **master budget** is a summary of the functional (subsidiary) budgets and cash budget and includes a budgeted income statement and a budgeted statement of financial position.

6 Monitoring procedures

Introduction

The budgeting process does not end for the forthcoming year once the budget period has begun: budgeting should be seen as a **continuous and dynamic process.**

The budgeting process does not stop once the budgets have been agreed. **Actual results should be compared on a regular basis with the budgeted results.** The frequency with which such comparisons are made depends very much on the organisation's circumstances and the sophistication of its control systems but it should occur at least **monthly**. Management should receive a report detailing the differences and should investigate the reasons for the differences. If the **differences** are **within the control** of management, **corrective action** should be taken to bring the reasons for the difference under control and to ensure that such inefficiencies do not occur in the future.

The differences may have occurred, however, because the budget was **unrealistic** to begin with or because the actual conditions did not reflect those anticipated (or could have possibly been anticipated). This would therefore **invalidate** the remainder of the budget.

Because the original budget was unrealistic or because of changes in anticipated conditions, the budget committee may need to reappraise the organisation's future plans and may need to adjust the budget to take account of such changes. The **revised budget** then represents a revised statement of formal operating plans for the remaining portion of the budget period.

Section summary

The budgeting process does not end for the forthcoming year once the budget period has begun: budgeting should be seen as a **continuous and dynamic process.**

7 Alternative approaches to budgeting

Introduction

This section looks at incremental budgeting, zero based budgeting, programme planning and activity based budgeting.

7.1 Incremental budgeting

The **traditional approach** to budgeting is to **base next year's budget on the current year's results plus an extra amount for estimated growth or inflation next year.** This approach is known as **incremental budgeting** since it is concerned mainly with the increments in costs and revenues which will occur in the coming period.

Question 13.4	Incremental budgeting I

Learning outcome B3(b)

CP produces two products, X and Y. In the year ended 30 April 20X1 it produced 4,520 X and 11,750 Y and incurred costs of £1,217,200.

The costs incurred are such that 60% are variable. 70% of these variable costs vary with the number of X produced, with the remainder varying with the output of Y.

The budget for the three months to 31 October 20X1 is being prepared using an incremental approach based on the following.

- All costs will be 5% higher than the average paid in the year ended 30 April 20X1

- Efficiency levels will be unchanged

- Expected output

  X   1,210 units
  Y   3,950 units

What is the budgeted cost for the output of X (to the nearest £100) for the three months ending 31 October 20X1?

A   £100
B   £127,800
C   £536,800
D   £134,200

Incremental budgeting is a reasonable procedure if current operations are as effective, efficient and economical as they can be. It is also appropriate for budgeting for costs such as staff salaries, which may be estimated on the basis of current salaries plus an increment for inflation and are hence administratively fairly easy to prepare.

Question 13.5   Incremental budgeting 2

Learning outcome B3(b)

Explain what is meant by incremental budgeting and discuss its suitability for budgeting for rent costs and for advertising expenditure.

In general, however, it is an **inefficient form of budgeting** as it **encourages slack** and **wasteful spending** to creep into budgets. Past inefficiencies are perpetuated because cost levels are rarely subjected to close scrutiny.

To ensure that inefficiencies are not concealed, however, alternative approaches to budgeting have been developed. One such approach is **zero based budgeting (ZBB)**.

7.2 Zero based budgeting   9/10, 11/10, 3/11

7.2.1 The principles of ZBB

ZBB rejects the assumption inherent in incremental budgeting that this year's activities will continue at the same level or volume next year, and that next year's budget can be based on this year's costs plus an extra amount, perhaps for expansion and inflation.

KEY TERM

ZERO BASED BUDGETING is a method of budgeting which requires each cost element to be specifically justified, as though the activities to which the budget relates were being undertaken for the first time. Without approval the budget allowance is zero.

In reality, however, managers do not have to budget from zero, but can **start from their current level of expenditure and work downwards**, asking what would happen if any particular aspect of current expenditure and current operations were removed from the budget. In this way, every aspect of the budget is examined in terms of its cost and the benefits it provides and the selection of better alternatives is encouraged.

7.2.2 Implementing ZBB

The implementation of ZBB involves a number of steps but of greater importance is the **development of a questioning attitude** by all those involved in the budgetary process. Existing practices and expenditures must be challenged and searching questions asked.

- Does the activity need to be carried out?
- What would be the consequences if the activity were not carried out?
- Is the current level of provision adequate?
- Are there alternative ways of providing the function?
- How much should the activity cost?
- Is the expenditure worth the benefits achieved?

The three steps of ZBB

 STEP 1 Define decision packages, comprehensive descriptions of specific organisational activities (decision units) which management can use to evaluate the activities and rank them in order of priority against other activities. There are two types.

    (a)   **Mutually exclusive packages** contain alternative methods of getting the same job done. The best option among the packages must be selected by comparing costs and benefits and the other packages are then discarded.

    (b)   **Incremental packages** divide one aspect of an activity into different levels of effort. The 'base' package will describe the minimum amount of work that must be done to carry out the activity and the other packages describe what additional work could be done, at what cost and for what benefits.

 STEP 2 **Evaluate and rank each activity (decision package)** on the basis of its benefit to the organisation. This can be a lengthy process. Minimum work requirements (those that are essential to get a job done) will be given high priority and so too will work which meets legal obligations. In the accounting department these would be minimum requirements to operate the payroll, payables ledger and receivables ledger systems, and to maintain and publish a satisfactory set of accounts.

 STEP 3 **Allocate resources** in the budget according to the funds available and the evaluation and ranking of the competing packages.

 Example: Step 1

Suppose that a cost centre manager is preparing a budget for maintenance costs. He might first consider two mutually exclusive packages. Package A might be to keep a maintenance team of two men per shift for two shifts each day at a cost of £60,000 per annum, whereas package B might be to obtain a maintenance service from an outside contractor at a cost of £50,000. A cost-benefit analysis will be conducted because the quicker repairs obtainable from an in-house maintenance service might justify its extra cost. If we now suppose that package A is preferred, the budget analysis must be completed by describing the incremental variations in this chosen alternative.

- The **'base' package** would describe the minimum requirement for the maintenance work. This might be to pay for one man per shift for two shifts each day at a cost of £30,000.

- **Incremental package 1** might be to pay for two men on the early shift and one man on the late shift, at a cost of £45,000. The extra cost of £15,000 would need to be justified, for example by savings in lost production time, or by more efficient machinery.

- **Incremental package 2** might be the original preference, for two men on each shift at a cost of £60,000. The cost-benefit analysis would compare its advantages, if any, over incremental package 1; and so on.

Question 13.6   ZBB

Learning outcome B3(b)

What might the base package and incremental packages for a personnel department cover?

	Base	Incremental
A	Recruitment	Training
B	Dismissal	Recruitment
C	Training	Pension administration
D	Pension administration	Recruitment

7.2.3 The advantages and limitations of ZBB

Advantages of ZBB

- It is possible to identify and **remove inefficient or obsolete operations.**
- It forces employees to **avoid wasteful expenditure**.
- It can **increase motivation**.
- It responds to changes in the business environment.
- ZBB documentation provides an in-depth appraisal of an organisation's operations.
- It **challenges the status quo**.
- In summary, ZBB should result in a **more efficient allocation of resources**.

The major **disadvantage** of ZBB is the **volume of extra paperwork** created. The assumptions about costs and benefits in each package must be continually updated and new packages developed as soon as new activities emerge. The following problems might also occur.

(a) **Short-term benefits** might be **emphasised** to the detriment of long-term benefits.

(b) It may give the impression **that all decisions have to be made in the budget**. Management must be able to meet unforeseen opportunities and threats at all times, however, and must not feel restricted from carrying out new ideas simply because they were not approved by a decision package, cost benefit analysis and the ranking process.

(c) It may be a **call for management skills** both in constructing decision packages and in the ranking process **which the organisation does not possess**. Managers may therefore have to be trained in ZBB techniques.

(d) The organisation's information systems may not be capable of providing suitable information.

(e) **The ranking process can be difficult**. Managers face three common problems.

    (i) A large number of packages may have to be ranked.

    (ii) It can be difficult to rank packages which appear to be equally vital, for legal or operational reasons.

    (iii) It is difficult to rank activities which have qualitative rather than quantitative benefits – such as spending on staff welfare and working conditions.

In summary, perhaps the **most serious drawback to ZBB is that it requires a lot of management time and paperwork**. One way of obtaining the benefits of ZBB but of overcoming the drawbacks is to apply it selectively on a rolling basis throughout the organisation. This year finance, next year marketing, the year after personnel and so on. In this way all activities will be thoroughly scrutinised over a period of time.

Question 13.7	Base and incremental packages

Learning outcome B3(b)

What might the base and incremental packages cover in your department if your organisation used ZBB?

7.2.4 Using ZBB

ZBB is not particularly suitable for direct manufacturing costs, which are usually budgeted using standard costing, work study and other management planning and control techniques. ZBB is best applied to **support expenses,** that is expenditure incurred in departments which exist to support the essential production function. These support areas include marketing, finance, quality control, personnel, data processing, sales and distribution. In many organisations, these expenses make up a large proportion of the total expenditure. These activities are less easily quantifiable by conventional methods and are more **discretionary** in nature. We return to the problem of budgeting for discretionary costs later in this section.

ZBB can also be successfully applied to **service industries** and **not-for-profit organisations** such as local and central government, educational establishments, hospitals and so on, and in any organisation where alternative levels of provision for each activity are possible and costs and benefits are separately identifiable.

Question 13.8	Using ZBB

Learning outcome B3(b)

You work for a large multinational company which manufactures weedkillers. It has been decided to introduce zero base budgeting (ZBB) in place of the more traditional incremental budgeting. The manager of the research and development department has never heard of ZBB.

Required

Write a report to the manager of the research and development department which explains how ZBB may assist in planning and controlling discretionary costs

7.3 Programme planning and budgeting systems

A programme planning and budgeting system (PPBS) sets a budget in terms of **programmes** (groups of activities with common objectives). By focusing on objectives, the budget is therefore **orientated towards the ultimate output of the organisation**. This contrasts with the traditional approach to budgeting, which focuses on inputs (such as material and labour).

Such an approach is therefore particularly useful for **public sector** and **not-for-profit** organisations, such as government departments, schools, hospitals and charities, to ensure that expenditure is **focused** on programmes and activities that generate the most **beneficial results**. This is of particular value at a time when there is increasing public demand for **accountability** by such organisations: donors to charities have recently expressed concern over the high proportion of donations used to pay administrative expenses. PPBS allows people (taxpayers and donors) to see where their money is going and how it has been spent.

Disadvantages of using traditional budgeting for public sector and not-for-profit organisations

(a)   Activities often span several years but the emphasis is on annual figures.

(b)   It is difficult to incorporate into a budget report planned or actual achievements (number of sufferers helped, level of education and so on) as these achievements tend to be non-financial in nature.

(c)   Costs relating to a particular objective are spread across a number of cost categories. For example, the costs relating to an objective of a police force to protect people and property from traffic hazards might be allocated to a variety of traditional cost categories – personnel, transport, administration, training and so on. It would be impossible to tell how much was spent, or authorised, to achieve that objective.

(d)   There is no evidence as to how effectively or efficiently resources are being used.

PPBS would overcome these problems as the emphasis would be on objectives and the best use of resources to achieve effectiveness over the medium to long term.

PPBS approach

 Review long-term objectives (such as, for a police force, protect persons and property and deal with offenders).

 Set out the programmes of activities needed to achieve the objectives (such as police patrol on foot, police patrol in vehicles and so on).

 Evaluate the alternative programmes in terms of costs and benefits and select the most appropriate programmes.

 Analyse the programmes selected, finding out (for example) what would happen to the level of achievement of objectives if resources allocated to a particular programme were reduced by, say, 10%.

7.4 Discretionary costs

KEY TERM

A DISCRETIONARY (or MANAGED or POLICY) COST is 'A cost whose amount within a time period is determined by a decision taken by the appropriate budget holder. Marketing, research and training are generally regarded as discretionary costs.' CIMA *Official Terminology*

7.4.1 Budgeting for discretionary costs

It is much easier to set budgets for **engineered costs** (costs for which there is a **demonstrable relationship between the input** to a process and the **output** of that process) than for **discretionary costs** (costs for which there is **no clear relationship between the input and output of a process**, often because the **output is difficult to measure**, in terms of quantity and/or quality). It is obviously easier to budget for direct material costs (engineered cost) than for the cost of the accounts department (discretionary cost).

Budgeting for discretionary costs can be made **easier** by **converting them into engineered costs**.

*   Develop suitable output measures
*   Understand how input impacts on output

For example, by analysing the work undertaken to process an invoice for payment, an **average time** for dealing with an invoice can be established and the relationship between the number of invoices processed and the resources required to do this ascertained.

The analysis required for **activity based costing** will also add to an understanding of the relationship between the inputs and outputs of a process.

If a discretionary cost cannot be converted into an engineered cost, ZBB or PPBS will be needed.

7.4.2 Control of discretionary costs

Discretionary costs **cannot be controlled on the basis of outputs** because of the difficulty in specifying outputs in financial terms. In order to set minimum standards of performance, some measure of output is needed, however. An accounts department may be required to pay invoices within two weeks of receipt, for example.

Inputs can be **controlled**, however, if the **budget** acts as a device to ensure financial resources allocated to the activity are not exceeded.

7.5 Activity-based budgeting   5/10

KEY TERM

ACTIVITY-BASED BUDGETING is a 'Method of budgeting based on an activity framework and utilising cost driver data in the budget-setting and variance feedback processes.'   *(CIMA Official Terminology)*

At its **simplest**, activity based budgeting (ABB) is merely the **use of costs determined using** ABC **as a basis for preparing budgets**.

A budget for an activity is therefore based on the budgeted number of the activity's cost driver × the appropriate cost driver rate. For example, if an organisation expects to place 500 orders and the rate per order is £100, the budgeted cost of the ordering activity will be 500 × £100 = £50,000.

Implementing ABC leads to the realisation that the **business as a whole** needs to be **managed** with far more reference to the behaviour of activities and cost drivers identified.

(a)   **Traditional budgeting may make managers 'responsible' for activities which are driven by factors beyond their control**: the cost of setting-up new personnel records and of induction training would traditionally be the responsibility of the personnel manager even though such costs are driven by the number of new employees required by managers other than the personnel manager.

(b)   The **budgets for costs not directly related to production** are often traditionally set using an **incremental approach** because of the difficulty of linking the activity driving the cost to production level. But this assumes that all of the cost is unaffected by any form of activity level, which is often not the case in reality. Some of the costs of the purchasing department, for example, will be fixed (such as premises costs) but some will relate to the number of orders placed or the volume of production, say. Surely the budget for the purchasing department should take some account of the expected number of orders?

More **formally**, therefore, ABB involves **defining the activities** that underlie the financial figures in each function and using the level of activity to decide **how much resource should be allocated,** how well it is being **managed** and to explain **variances** from budget.

Claimed results of using ABB

(a)   Different activity levels will provide a foundation for the base package and incremental packages of ZBB.

(b)   The organisation's overall strategy and any actual or likely changes in that strategy will be taken into account because ABB attempts to manage the business as the sum of its interrelated parts.

(c)   Critical success factors (an activity in which a business must perform well if it is to succeed) will be identified and key metrics devised to monitor progress towards them.

(d)   The focus is on the whole of an activity, not just its separate parts, and so there is more likelihood of getting it right first time. For example, what is the use of being able to produce goods in time for their despatch date if the budget provides insufficient resources for the distribution manager who has to deliver them.

(e)   Traditional accounting tends to focus on the nature of the costs being incurred (the input side) and traditional budgeting tends to mirror this. ABB emphasises the activities that are being achieved (the outputs).

Exam alert

The May 2010 exam asked for the benefits of introducing an activity-based budgeting system.

Section summary

- The principle behind **zero based budgeting** is that the budget for each cost centre should be prepared from 'scratch' or zero. Every item of expenditure must be justified to be included in the budget for the forthcoming period.

- There is a three-step approach to ZBB.
    - Define decision packages
    - Evaluate and rank packages
    - Allocate resources

- ZBB is particularly useful for budgeting for discretionary costs.

- **PPBS** is particularly useful for public sector and non-profit-seeking organisations.

- **Activity-based budgeting** is a 'Method of budgeting based on an activity framework and utilising cost driver data in the budget-setting and variance feedback processes.' *CIMA Official Terminology*

Chapter Roundup

✓ The **objectives** of a budgetary planning and control system are as follows.
  - P – Planning
  - R – Responsibility
  - I – Integration and co-ordination
  - M – Motivation
  - E – Evaluation and control

✓ The **budget committee** is the coordinating body in the preparation and administration of budgets.

✓ The **principal budget factor** should be identified at the beginning of the budgetary process, and the budget for this is prepared before all the others.

✓ For many organisations, the **principal budget factor** is sales volume.

✓ To assess whether production is the principal budget factor, the production capacity available must be determined.

✓ **Cash budgets** show the expected receipts and payments during a budget period and are a vital management planning and control tool.

✓ The **master budget** is a summary of the functional (subsidiary) budgets and cash budget and includes a budgeted income statement and a budgeted statement of financial position.

✓ The budgeting process does not end for the forthcoming year once the budget period has begun: budgeting should be seen as a **continuous and dynamic process.**

✓ The principle behind **zero based budgeting** is that the budget for each cost centre should be prepared from 'scratch' or zero. Every item of expenditure must be justified to be included in the budget for the forthcoming period.

✓ There is a three-step approach to ZBB.
  - Define decision packages
  - Evaluate and rank packages
  - Allocate resources

✓ ZBB is particularly useful for budgeting for discretionary costs.

✓ **PPBS** is particularly useful for public sector and non-profit-seeking organisations.

✓ Activity based budgeting is a 'Method of budgeting based on an activity framework and utilising cost driver data in the budget-setting and variance feedback processes'. *(CIMA Official Terminology).*

Quick Quiz

1   Which of the following is not an objective of a system of budgetary planning and control?

    A   To establish a system of control
    B   To coordinate activities
    C   To compel planning
    D   To motivate employees to maintain current performance levels

2   Sales is always the principal budget factor and so it is always the first budget to be prepared. *True or false?*

3   *Choose the appropriate words from those highlighted.*

A **forecast/budget** is an **estimate/guarantee** of what is **likely to occur in the future/has happened in the past.**

A **forecast/budget** is a **quantified plan/unquantified plan/guess** of what the organisation is aiming to **achieve/spend**.

4   *Fill in the blanks.*

When preparing a production budget, the quantity to be produced is equal to sales ....
opening inventory .... closing inventory.

5   Which of the following should be included in a cash budget?

	Include	Do not include
Funds from the issue of share capital		
Revaluation of a non-current asset		
Receipt of dividends from outside the business		
Depreciation of production machinery		
Bad debts written off		
Repayment of a bank loan		

6   What are the three components of the master budget?

    1   ....
    2   ....
    3   ....

Answers to Quick Quiz

1   D. The objective is to motivate employees to *improve* their performance.

2   False. The budget for the principal budget factor must be prepared first, but sales is not always the principal budget factor.

3   A forecast is an estimate of what is likely to occur in the future.

    A budget is a quantified plan of what the organisation is aiming to achieve.

4   When preparing a production budget, the quantity to be produced is equal to sales minus opening inventory plus closing inventory.

5

	Include	Do not include
Funds from the issue of share capital	✓	
Revaluation of a non-current asset		✓
Receipt of dividends from outside the business	✓	
Depreciation of production machinery		✓
Bad debts written off		✓
Repayment of a bank loan	✓	

6   Budgeted cash flow, budgeted income statement and budgeted statement of financial position.

 Answers to Questions

13.1 Budgets

(a)   The **sequence of budget preparation** will be roughly as follows.

(i)   Sales budget. (The market share limits demand and so sales is the principal budget factor. All other activities will depend upon this forecast.)

(ii)   Finished goods inventory budget (in units)

(iii)   Production budget (in units)

(iv)   Production resources budgets (materials, machine hours, labour)

(v)   Overhead budgets for production, administration, selling and distribution, research and development and so on

Other budgets required will be the capital expenditure budget, the working capital budget (receivables and payables) and, very importantly, the cash budget.

(b)   The **master budget** is the summary of all the functional budgets. It often includes a summary income statement and statement of financial position.

(c)   Procedures for preparing budgets can be contained in a **budget manual** which shows which budgets must be prepared when and by whom, what each functional budget should contain and detailed directions on how to prepare budgets including, for example, expected price increases, rates of interest, rates of depreciation and so on.

The formulation of budgets can be coordinated by a **budget committee** comprising the senior executives of the departments responsible for carrying out the budgets: sales, production, purchasing, personnel and so on.

The budgeting process may also be assisted by the use of a **spreadsheet/computer budgeting package**.

13.2 Material purchases budget

The correct answer is B.

	March kg	April kg	May kg
Required finished inventory:			
Base inventory	6,000	6,000	6,000
+ 25% of next month's sales	2,250	2,000	1,750
= Required inventory	8,250	8,000	7,750
Sales for month		9,000	8,000
		17,000	15,750
Less: opening inventory		8,250	8,000
Required finished production		8,750	7,750
+ 10% losses = raw material required		9,625	8,525

	March	April	May
	kg	kg	kg
Required material inventory:			
Base inventory	5,000.00	5,000.00	
+ 25% of material for next month's production	2,406.25	2,131.25	
= Required closing material inventory	7,406.25	7,131.25	
Production requirements		9,625.00	
		16,756.25	
Less: opening inventory		7,406.25	
Required material purchases		9,350.00	

13.3 Cash budgets (receipts)

The correct answer is A.

	Received in March
	€
Cash sales (5% × €10,000) × 95%	475.00
February sales (€17,000 × 95%) × 75%	12,112.50
January sales (€13,000 × 95%) × 23%	2,840.50
	15,428.00

13.4 Incremental budgeting 1

The correct answer is D.

Proportion of actual annual costs related to X = £1,217,200 × 0.6 × 0.7 = £511,224

Proportion applicable to three-month period = £511,224/4 = £127,806

Inflated cost = £127,806 × 1.05 = £134,196

Option A is the budgeted cost per X. If you selected option B you forgot to inflate the cost. If you selected **option C**, you forgot to reduce the annual cost to a quarterly cost.

13.5 Incremental budgeting 2

Incremental budgeting is a method of setting budgets whereby **the latest period's budget is used as a base for preparing the budget for the forthcoming period.** Adjustments are made for any expected changes, for example changes in staffing levels or in the level of activity.

Incremental budgeting may be appropriate for budgeting for rent because the rent cost for the forthcoming period may be **estimated on the basis of the current rent plus an increment for the annual rent increase.**

Incremental budgeting might not be appropriate for budgeting for advertising expenditure because such expenditure is not so easily quantifiable and is more discretionary in nature. Using incremental budgeting for advertising expenditure could allow **slack (unnecessary expenditure)** and wasteful spending to creep into the budget. Simply adding an increment to the current year's budget **does not force managers to question whether the current level of expenditure is necessary.** Furthermore there will be a tendency for the relevant manager to **ensure that the current budget is spent**, in case the allowance is removed for the forthcoming year, if it is not spent this year.

13.6 ZBB

The correct answer is A.

The base package might cover the recruitment and dismissal of staff. Incremental packages might cover training, pension administration, trade union liaison, staff welfare and so on.

13.8 Using ZBB

REPORT

To:	R&D manager
From:	Management accountant Date: 01.01.X6
Subject:	Zero based budgeting

Discretionary cost is 'expenditure whose value is a matter of policy', that is, it is not vital to the continued existence of an organisation in the way that, say, raw materials are to a manufacturing business. ZBB was developed originally to help management with the difficult task of allocating resources in precisely such areas. Research and development is a frequently cited example; others are advertising and training.

Within a research and development department ZBB will establish priorities by ranking the projects that are planned and in progress. Project managers will be forced to consider the benefit obtainable from their work in relation to the costs involved. The result may be an overall increase in R&D expenditure, but only if it is justified.

It is worth mentioning that when R&D costs are subsequently being monitored, care is needed in interpreting variances. A favourable expenditure variance may not be a good thing: it may mean that not enough is being spent on R&D activity.

Now try the question from the Exam Question Bank	Number	Level	Marks	Time
	Q21	Examination	5	9 mins

PREPARING FORECASTS

In Chapter 13 we saw how to prepare budgets but we have not yet looked at where the figures which go into the budgets come from. To produce a budget calls for the **preparation of forecasts of costs and revenues**. Various quantitative techniques can assist with these '**number-crunching' aspects of budgeting**. This chapter aims to provide an understanding of those techniques. Note that the techniques will be described within their budgetary context.

We will be covering **two principal forecasting techniques** in this chapter, **regression analysis** and **time series analysis**.

Regression analysis can be applied to costs and revenues while time series analysis is generally applied to revenue.

Multiple choice or objective test questions on forecasting techniques are **likely**. **Longer questions** could **involve both regression analysis and time series analysis**. For example, you might have to apply seasonal variations to a trend determined using regression analysis.

Much of this chapter will be **revision** from your earlier studies in business mathematics, but work through all of the material slowly and carefully to ensure that you have a thorough knowledge of quantitative forecasting techniques.

topic list	learning outcomes	syllabus references	ability required
1 Forecasting using historical data	B2(a), (b)	B2(i), (ii)	application
2 Linear regression analysis	B2(a), (b)	B2(i), (ii)	application
3 Scatter diagrams and correlation	B2(a), (b)	B2(i), (ii)	application
4 Sales forecasting	B2(a), (b)	B2(i), (ii)	application
5 Regression and forecasting	B2(a), (b)	B2(i), (ii)	application
6 The components of time series	B2(a), (b)	B2(i), (ii)	application
7 Finding the trend	B2(a), (b)	B2(i), (ii)	application
8 Finding the seasonal variations	B2(a), (b)	B2(i), (ii)	application
9 Time series analysis and forecasting	B2(a), (b)	B2(i), (ii)	application
10 Using spreadsheet packages to build business models	B2(b)	B2(i), (ii)	application
11 Forecasting problems	B2(a)	B2(i), (ii)	application

1 Forecasting using historical data

Introduction

Numerous techniques have been developed for using past costs as the basis for forecasting future values. These techniques range from simple arithmetic and visual methods to advanced computer-based statistical systems. With all these, there is the **presumption that the past will provide guidance to the future**.

Before using any extrapolation techniques, **past data** must therefore be critically examined to **assess their appropriateness for the intended purpose**. The following checks should be made.

(a) The **time period** should be long enough to include any periodically paid costs but short enough to ensure that averaging of variations in the level of activity has not occurred.

(b) The **data** should be examined to ensure that any non-activity level factors affecting costs were roughly the same in the past as those forecast for the future. Such factors might include changes in technology, changes in efficiency, changes in production methods, changes in resource costs, strikes, weather conditions and so on. Changes to the past data are frequently necessary.

(c) The **methods of data collection** and the accounting policies used should not introduce bias. Examples might include depreciation policies and the treatment of by-products.

(d) Appropriate choices of **dependent** and **independent variables** must be made.

The two forecasting methods which follow (the scatter diagram method and linear regression analysis) are based on the assumption that a **linear relationship** links levels of cost and levels of activity.

Knowledge brought forward from earlier studies

Linear relationships

- A **linear relationship** can be expressed in the form of an equation which has the general form
  $Y = a + bX$

  where Y   is the **dependent** variable, depending for its value on the value of X

       X   is the **independent** variable, whose value helps to determine the corresponding value of y

       a   is a **constant**, a fixed amount

       b   is a constant, being the **coefficient of X** (that is, the number by which the value of X should be multiplied to derive the value of Y)

- If there is a linear relationship between total costs and level of activity, Y = total costs, X = level of activity, a = fixed cost (the cost when there is no activity level) and b = variable cost per unit.

- The graph of a linear equation is a **straight line** and is determined by two things, the **gradient** (or slope) of the straight line and the point at which the straight line crosses the Y axis (the **intercept**).

  - Gradient = b in the equation $Y = a + bX = (Y_2 - Y_1)/(X_2 - X_1)$ where (X_1, Y_1), (X_2, Y_2) are two points on the straight line

  - Intercept = a in the equation $Y = a + bX$

1.1 The high-low method

An important technique that you have already covered when analysing linear cost behaviour patterns is the **high-low method**. Have a go at the following question to ensure that you remember how to use it. Some of the cost and revenue behaviour patterns are quite complicated so you will need to prepare careful workings.

Question 14.1 _____ Analysing cost behaviour and making

Learning outcome B2(b)

The manager of a nail salon is using the results of two recent periods to forecast the revenues and costs for a forthcoming period. The results for the two periods to be used as a basis for forecasting are as follows.

	Period 1		Period 2	
Activity				
Number of manicures	240		305	
Number of pedicures	180		246	
	£	£	£	£
Revenue		9,780		11,574.00
Materials	756		991.80	
Staff salaries	5,100		6,862.00	
Utilities	712		856.10	
Laundry	466		570.80	
Rent	430		430.00	
Other	375		375.00	
		7,839		10,085.70
Profit		1,941		1,488.30

The manager has ascertained the following information.

1 Revenue for period 4 is expected to be £6,095 for manicures and £4,125 for pedicures.

2 The variable element of all costs varies in direct proportion to the total number of manicures and pedicures.

3 All staff are paid a fixed salary, plus a bonus for each customer. The fixed element of staff salary costs increases by £1,500 per period once total activity reaches 450 manicures and pedicures because of the need to employ temporary staff.

4 The variable element of laundry costs is expected to increase by 50% in period 4.

5 Forecast activity for period 4 is as follows.

- 265 manicures
- 165 pedicures

Required

Prepare a forecast profit statement for period 4.

Section summary

- A number of quantitative methods may be used by the management accountant to obtain information for inclusion in budgets.

- Before using any technique based on past data, the past data must be assessed for appropriateness for the intended purpose. There is no point in using a 'sophisticated' technique with unreliable data.

2 Linear regression analysis

Introduction

You will have learned simple linear regression analysis in your earlier studies. However, as **regression** is specifically mentioned in the Paper P1 syllabus we will start from basics in this Text.

Linear regression analysis, also known as the **'least squares technique'**, is a **statistical method** of estimating costs using historical data from a number of previous accounting periods. The analysis is used to derive a **line of best fit which has the general form**

Y = a + bX where

Y, the dependent variable = total cost
X, the independent variable = the level of activity
a, the intercept of the line on the Y axis = the fixed cost
b, the gradient of the line = the variable cost per unit of activity.

Historical data is collected from previous periods and adjusted to a common price level to remove inflationary differences. This provides a number of readings for activity levels (X) and their associated costs (Y). Then, by substituting these readings into the formulae below for a and b, estimates of the fixed cost and variable cost per unit are provided.

LEARN

If $Y = a + bX$, $b = \dfrac{n\Sigma XY - \Sigma X \Sigma Y}{n\Sigma X^2 - (\Sigma X)^2}$ and $a = \overline{Y} - b\overline{X}$

where $\overline{X}, \overline{Y}$ are the average values of X and Y and n is the number of pairs of data for X and Y.

An example will help to illustrate this technique.

Example: least squares method

The transport department of Norwest Council operates a large fleet of vehicles. These vehicles are used by the various departments of the Council. Each month a statement is prepared for the transport department comparing actual results with budget. One of the items in the transport department's monthly statement is the cost of vehicle maintenance. This maintenance is carried out by the employees of the department. To facilitate control, the transport manager has asked that future statements should show vehicle maintenance costs analysed into fixed and variable costs.

Data from the six months from January to June year 2 inclusive are given below.

Year 2	Vehicle maintenance cost £	Vehicle running hours
January	13,600	2,100
February	15,800	2,800
March	14,500	2,200
April	16,200	3,000
May	14,900	2,600
June	15,000	2,500

Required

Analyse the vehicle maintenance costs into fixed and variable costs, based on the data given, utilising the least squares method.

Solution

If $Y = a + bX$, where Y represents costs and X represents running hours (since costs depend on running hours) then $b = (n\Sigma XY - \Sigma X\Sigma Y)/(n\Sigma X^2 - (\Sigma X)^2)$, when n is the number of pairs of data, which is 6 in this problem.

X	Y	XY	X^2
'000 hrs	£'000		
2.1	13.6	28.56	4.41
2.8	15.8	44.24	7.84
2.2	14.5	31.90	4.84
3.0	16.2	48.60	9.00
2.6	14.9	38.74	6.76
2.5	15.0	37.50	6.25
15.2	90.0	229.54	39.10

Variable cost per hour, b = $(6(229.54) - (15.2)(90.00))/(6(39.1) - (15.2)^2)$
= $(1,377.24 - 1,368)/(234.6 - 231.04) = 9.24/3.56 = £2.60$

Fixed costs (in £'000), a = $\bar{Y} - b\bar{X}$ = $(\Sigma Y/n) - (b\Sigma X/n) = (90/6) - (2.6(15.2)/6) = 8.41$ approx, say £8,400

Question 14.2

Regression analysis

Learning outcome B2(b)

You are given the following data for output at a factory and costs of production over the past five months.

Month	Output	Costs
	'000 units	£'000
	X	y
1	20	82
2	16	70
3	24	90
4	22	85
5	18	73

Required

(a)   Calculate an equation to determine the expected cost level for any given output volume.
(b)   Prepare a budget for total costs if output is 22,000 units.

2.1 The conditions suited to the use of linear regression analysis

Conditions which should apply if linear regression analysis is to be used to estimate costs

(a)   A **linear cost function should be assumed**. This assumption can be tested by measures of reliability, such as the correlation coefficient and the coefficient of determination (which ought to be reasonably close to 1). We will be looking at these concepts later in the chapter.

(b)   When calculating a line of best fit, there will be a range of values for X. In the question above, the line $Y = 28 + 2.6X$ was predicted from data with output values ranging from $X = 16$ to $X = 24$. Depending on the degree of correlation between X and Y, we might safely use the estimated line of best fit to forecast values for Y, provided that the value of X remains within the range 16 to 24. We would be on less safe ground if we used the equation to predict a value for Y when $X = 10$, or 30, or any other value outside the range 16 to 24, because we would **have to assume that costs behave in the same way outside the range of x values used to establish the line in the first place.**

INTERPOLATION means using a line of best fit to predict a value within the two extreme points of the observed range.

EXTRAPOLATION means using a line of best fit to predict a value outside the two extreme points.

(c) The **historical data** for cost and output should be **adjusted to a common price level** (to overcome cost differences caused by inflation) and the historical data should also be **representative of current technology, current efficiency levels and current operations** (products made).

(d) As far as possible, **historical data should be accurately recorded** so that variable costs are properly matched against the items produced or sold, and fixed costs are properly matched against the time period to which they relate. For example, if a factory rental is £120,000 per annum, and if data is gathered monthly, these costs should be charged £10,000 to each month instead of £120,000 in full to a single month.

(e) Management should either be **confident that conditions** which have existed in the past **will continue into the future or amend the estimates** of cost produced by the linear regression analysis to **allow for expected changes** in the future.

(f) As with any forecasting process, the **amount of data available is very important**. Even if correlation is high, if we have fewer than about ten pairs of data, we must regard any forecast as being somewhat unreliable.

(g) It must be assumed that the value of one variable, Y, can be predicted or estimated from the value of one other variable, X.

Question 14.3
Limitations of regression analysis

Learning outcomes B2(a), (b)

The relationship between total operating cost and quantity produced (in a manufacturing company) is given by the linear regression model $TC = 5,000 + 500Q$, where TC = total operating cost (in £) per annum and Q = quantity produced per annum (kg).

Explain five reservations that you might have about relying on the above model for budgetary planning purposes.

Exam alert

In an exam you could be given a regression equation which you need to use to determine the expected or standard cost for an actual level of activity. By comparing this standard cost with an actual cost provided you can then establish a total cost variance.

Section summary

Linear regression analysis (least squares technique) involves determining a **line of best fit**.

3   Scatter diagrams and correlation

3.1 The scatter diagram method of forecasting

Introduction

Scatter diagrams can be used to estimate the fixed and variable components of costs.

By this method of cost estimation, cost and activity data are plotted on a graph. A **'line of best fit'** is then drawn. This line should be drawn through the middle of the plotted points as closely as possible so that the distance of points above the line are equal to distances below the line. Where necessary costs should be adjusted to the same indexed price level to allow for inflation.

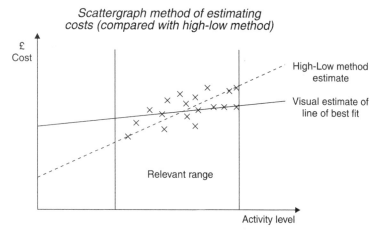

Scattergraph method of estimating costs (compared with high-low method)

The fixed cost is the intercept of the line of best fit on the vertical axis. Suppose the fixed cost is £500 and that one of the plotted points (which is very close to the line or actually on it) represents output of 100 units and total cost of £550. The variable cost of 100 units is therefore calculated as £(550 − 500) = £50 and so the variable cost per unit is £0.50. The equation of the line of best fit is therefore *approximately* Y = 500 + 0.5X.

If the company to which this data relate wanted to forecast total costs when output is 90 units, a forecast based on the equation would be 500 + (0.5 × 90) = £545. Alternatively the **forecast could be read directly from the graph using the line of best fit.**

The disadvantage of the scatter diagram method is that the cost line is drawn by visual judgement and so is a **subjective approximation**. The subjectivity is very clear from the diagram, which demonstrates how **different** our estimates of fixed and variable costs would be if we used the **high-low method** of cost analysis.

3.2 Correlation

Correlation describes the extent to which the values of two variables are related. Two variables might be **perfectly** correlated, **partly** correlated or **uncorrelated**. The correlation may be **positive** or **negative**. The degree of correlation between two variables can be measured using the **Pearsonian coefficient of correlation, r**. The **coefficient of determination** indicates the variations in the dependent variable that can be explained by variations in the independent variable.

KEY POINT

Although your Paper P1 syllabus does not specifically mention correlation, it does include regression analysis. The successful application of linear regression models depends on X and Y being closely linearly related. Therefore an understanding of correlation is essential to the ability to discuss the quality or reliability of a forecast prepared using regression techniques.

KEY TERM

CORRELATION is the degree to which change in one variable is related to change in another - in other words, the interdependence between variables.

3.3 Degrees of correlation

Two variables might be **perfectly correlated**, **partly correlated**, **uncorrelated** or subject to **non-linear correlation**.

Perfect correlation

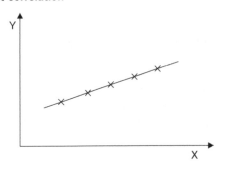 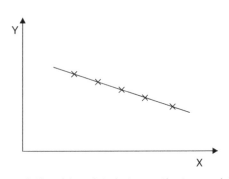

All the pairs of values lie on a straight line. An **exact linear relationship** exists between the two variables.

Partial correlation

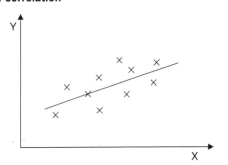 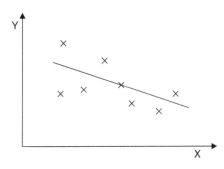

In the left hand diagram, although there is no exact relationship, **low values of X tend to be associated with low values of Y, and high values of X with high values of Y.**

In the right hand diagram, there is no exact relationship, but **low values of X tend to be associated with high values of Y and vice versa.**

No correlation   **Non-linear or curvilinear correlation**

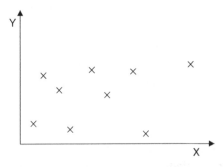 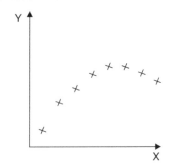

In the left hand diagram, the values of these two variables are not correlated with each other.

In the right hand diagram, there is a relationship between X and Y since the points are on an obvious curve but it is not a linear relationship.

3.3.1 Positive and negative correlation

Correlation, whether perfect or partial, can be **positive** or **negative**.

KEY TERMS

POSITIVE CORRELATION is the type of correlation where low values of one variable are associated with low values of the other, and high values of one variable are associated with high values of the other.

NEGATIVE CORRELATION is the type of correlation where low values of one variable are associated with high values of the other, and high values of one variable with low values of the other.

3.4 Measures of correlation

3.4.1 The coefficient of correlation, r

The **degree of correlation between two variables** can be measured using the **Pearsonian coefficient of correlation** (also called the **product moment correlation coefficient**).

r has a value between –1 (perfect negative correlation) and +1 (perfect positive correlation). If r = 0 then the variables are uncorrelated.

LEARN

The **coefficient of correlation**, r, is calculated as follows.

$$r = \frac{n\Sigma XY - \Sigma X \Sigma Y}{\sqrt{[n\Sigma X^2 - (\Sigma X)^2][n\Sigma Y^2 - (\Sigma Y)^2]}}$$

Look back at the example in Paragraph 2 called least squares method. Suppose that we wanted to know the correlation between vehicle maintenance costs and vehicle running hours. We can use a lot of the calculation in Paragraph 2 to determine r.

$$r = \frac{6(229.54) - (15.2)(90.0)}{\sqrt{[6(39.1) - (15.2)^2][6\Sigma Y^2 - (90.0)^2]}}$$

$$= \frac{1,377.24 - 1,368}{\sqrt{[(234.6 - 231.04)(6\Sigma Y^2 - 8,100)]}}$$

All we need to calculate is ΣY^2.

							Total
Y (£'000)	13.60	15.80	14.50	16.20	14.90	15.00	90.00
Y^2	184.96	249.64	210.25	262.44	222.01	225.00	1,354.30

$$r = \frac{9.24}{\sqrt{(3.56)(6 \times (1,354.30) - 8,100)}} = 0.96$$

A **fairly high degree of positive correlation** between X (vehicle running hours) and Y (vehicle maintenance cost) is indicated here **because r is quite close to +1.**

3.4.2 The coefficient of determination, r^2

KEY TERM

The COEFFICIENT OF DETERMINATION is a measure of the proportion of the change in the value of one variable that can be explained by variations in the value of the other variable.

In our example, $r^2 = (0.96)^2 = 0.9216$, and so 92% of variation in the value of Y (cost) can be explained by a linear relationship with X (running hours). This leaves only 8% of variations in y to be predicted from other factors. It is therefore **likely that vehicle** running hours could be used with a high degree of confidence to predict costs during a period.

3.5 Correlation and causation

If two variables are well correlated this may be due to pure chance or there may be a reason for it. The **larger the number of pairs of data**, the **less likely it is that the correlation is due to chance**, though that possibility should never be ignored.

If there is a reason, it may not be causal. Monthly net income is well correlated with monthly credit to a person's bank account, for the logical (rather than causal) reason that for most people the one equals the other. **Even if there is a causal explanation** for a correlation, it **does not follow that variations in the value of one variable cause variations in the value of the other.** Sales of ice cream and of sunglasses are well correlated, not because of a direct causal link but because the weather influences both variables.

Having said this, it is of course possible that where two variables are correlated, there is a direct causal link to be found.

3.6 The interactions of r^2 and r with linear regression

The successful application of linear regression models depends on X and Y being closely linearly related. r measures the strength of the linear relationship between two variables but **what numerical value of r is suggestive of sufficient linearity in data to allow one to proceed with linear regression?** The lower the value of r, the less chance of forecasts made using linear regression being adequate.

If there is a perfect linear relationship between the two variables (r = ±1), we can predict y from any given value of X with great confidence. If correlation is high (for example r = 0.9), the actual values will all be quite close to the regression line and so predictions should not be far out. If correlation is below about 0.7, predictions will only give a very rough guide to the likely value of Y.

If r = 0.75, say, you may feel that the linear relationship between the two variables is fairly strong. But $r^2 = 56.25\%$ indicates that only just over half of the variations in the dependent variable can be explained by a linear relationship with the independent variable. The low figure could be because a non-linear relationship is a better model for the data or because extraneous factors need to be considered. It is a **common rule of thumb that $r^2 \geq 80\%$ indicates that linear regression may be applied for the purpose of forecasting.**

Section summary

Scatter diagrams can be used to estimate the fixed and variable components of costs.

4 Sales forecasting

Introduction

The sales budget is frequently the first budget prepared since **sales is usually the principal budget factor**, but before the sales budget can be prepared a sales forecast has to be made.

Sales forecasting is complex *and* difficult and involves the consideration of a number of factors including the following.

- Past sales patterns
- The economic environment
- Results of market research
- Anticipated advertising during the budget period
- Competition
- Changing consumer taste

- New legislation
- Pricing policies and discounts offered
- Legislation
- Environmental factors
- Distribution and quality of sales outlets and personnel

As well as bearing in mind those factors, management can use a number of forecasting methods, often combining them to reduce the level of uncertainty.

Method	Detail
Sales personnel	They can be asked to provide estimates.
Market research	Especially relevant for new products or services.

Method	Detail
Mathematical models	Set up so that repetitive computer simulations can be run which permit managers to review the results that would be obtained in various circumstances.
Mathematical techniques	See later in this chapter.

Section summary

Sales forecasting techniques include asking sales personnel, market research, and using mathematical models and techniques.

5 Regression and forecasting

Introduction

The same regression techniques as those considered earlier in the chapter can be used to **calculate a regression line (a trend line) for a time series**. A time series is simply a series of figures or values recorded over time (such as total annual costs for the last ten years). The determination of a trend line is particularly useful in forecasting. (We will be looking at time series and trend lines in more detail in the next section.)

The years (or days or months) become the X variables in the regression formulae by numbering them from 1 upwards.

Example: regression and forecasting

Sales of product B over the seven year period from year 1 to year 7 were as follows.

Year	Year 1	Year 2	Year 3	Year 4	Year 5	Year 6	Year 7
Sales of B ('000 units)	22	25	24	26	29	28	30

There is high correlation between time and the volume of sales.

Required

Calculate the trend line of sales, and forecast sales in year 8 and year 9.

Solution

Workings

Year	X	Y	XY	X^2
1	1	22	22	1
2	2	25	50	4
3	3	24	72	9
4	4	26	104	16
5	5	29	145	25
6	6	28	168	36
7	7	30	210	49
	$\Sigma X = \underline{\underline{28}}$	$\Sigma Y = \underline{\underline{184}}$	$\Sigma XY = \underline{\underline{771}}$	$\Sigma X^2 = \underline{\underline{140}}$

n = 7

Where Y   = a + bX
      b   = ((7 × 771) − (28 × 184))/((7 × 140) − (28 × 28)) = 245/196 = 1.25
      a   = (184/7) − ((1.25 × 28)/7) = 21.2857, say 21.3
      Y   = 21.3 + 1.25X where X = 1 in year 1, X = 2 in year 2 and so on.

Using this trend line, predicted sales in year 8 (X = 8) would be 21.3 + 1.25 × 8 = 31.3 = 31,300 units.

Similarly, for year 9 (X = 9) predicted sales would be 21.3 + 1.25 × 9 = 32.55 = 32,550 units.

Section summary

When **regression analysis** is used for **forecasting sales**, the years (or days or months) become the x variables in the regression formulae by numbering them from 1 upwards.

6 The components of time series

Introduction

A **time series** records a series of figures or values over time. A time series has four components: a **trend**, **seasonal variations**, **cyclical variations** and **random variations**.

KEY TERM

A TIME SERIES is a series of figures or values recorded over time.

Examples of time series

- Output at a factory each day for the last month
- Monthly sales over the last two years
- The Retail Prices Index each month for the last ten years

A graph of a time series is called a **historigram**.

(Note the 'ri'; this is not the same as a histogram.) For example, consider the following time series.

Year	Year 0	Year 1	Year 2	Year 3	Year 4	Year 5	Year 6
Sales (£'000)	20	21	24	23	27	30	28

The historigram is as follows.

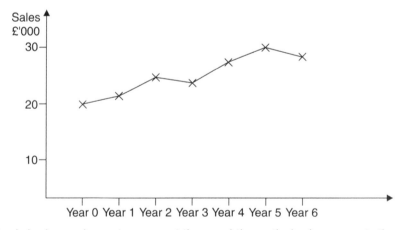

The horizontal axis is always chosen to represent time, and the vertical axis represents the values of the data recorded.

Components of a time series

- A **trend**

- **Seasonal variations** or fluctuations

- Cycles, or **cyclical variations**

- Non-recurring, **random variations**, caused by unforeseen circumstances such as a change in government, a war, technological change or a fire

6.1 The trend

KEY TERM

The TREND is the underlying long-term movement over time in values of data recorded.

In the following examples of time series, there are three types of trend.

Year	Output per labour hour Units	Cost per unit £	Number of employees
4	30	1.00	100
5	24	1.08	103
6	26	1.20	96
7	22	1.15	102
8	21	1.18	103
9	17	1.25	98
	(A)	**(B)**	**(C)**

(a) In time series **(A)** there is a **downward trend** in the output per labour hour. Output per labour hour did not fall every year, because it went up between year 5 and year 6, but the long-term movement is clearly a downward one.

(b) In time series **(B)** there is an **upward trend** in the cost per unit. Although unit costs went down in year 7 from a higher level in year 6, the basic movement over time is one of rising costs.

(c) In time series **(C)** there is **no clear movement** up or down, and the number of employees remained fairly constant. The trend is therefore a static, or level one.

6.2 Seasonal variations

KEY TERM

SEASONAL VARIATIONS are short-term fluctuations in recorded values, due to different circumstances which affect results at different times of the year, on different days of the week, at different times of day, or whatever.

Here are two examples of seasonal variations.

(a) Sales of ice cream will be higher in summer than in winter.

(b) The telephone network may be heavily used at certain times of the day (such as mid-morning and mid-afternoon) and much less used at other times (such as in the middle of the night).

Seasonal is a term which may appear to refer to the seasons of the year, but its meaning in time series analysis is somewhat broader, as the examples given above show.

Example: a trend and seasonal variations

The number of customers served by a company of travel agents over the past four years is shown in the following historigram.

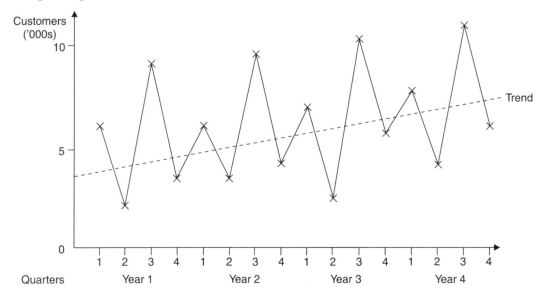

In this example, there would appear to be large seasonal fluctuations in demand, but there is also a basic upward trend.

6.3 Cyclical variations

Cyclical variations are **medium-term changes in results caused by circumstances which repeat in cycles**. In business, cyclical variations are commonly associated with economic cycles, successive booms and slumps in the economy. Economic cycles may last a few years. Cyclical variations are longer term than seasonal variations.

6.4 Summarising the components

In practice a time series could incorporate all of the four features we have been looking at and, to make reasonably accurate forecasts, the four features often have to be isolated. We can begin the process of isolating each feature by summarising the components of a time series as follows.

The **actual time series, TS = T + SV + C + R**

where **TS** = the actual time series   **C** = the cyclical component
      T = the trend series   **R** = the random component
     SV = the seasonal component

Though you should be aware of the cyclical component, it is unlikely that you will be expected to carry out any calculation connected with isolating it. The mathematical model which we will use, the **additive model**, therefore excludes any reference to C and is **TS = T + SV + R**.

KEY TERM

The ADDITIVE MODEL expresses a time series as TS = T + SV + R.

Section summary

A **time series** records a series of figures or values over time. A time series has four components: a **trend**, **seasonal variations**, **cyclical variations** and **random variations**.

7 Finding the trend

Introduction

This section looks at how to find the trend in a time series.

Look at these monthly sales figures.

Year 6	August	September	October	November	December
Sales (£'000)	0.02	0.04	0.04	3.20	14.60

It looks as though the business is expanding rapidly and so it is, in a way. But when you know that the business is a Christmas card manufacturer, then you see immediately that the January sales will no doubt slump right back down again.

It is obvious that the business will do better in the Christmas season than at any other time; that is the seasonal variation. Using the monthly figures, how can we tell whether or not the business is doing well overall – whether there is a rising sales trend over time other than the short-term rise over Christmas?

One possibility is to compare figures with the equivalent figures of a year ago. However, many things can happen over a year to make such a comparison misleading for example, new products might now be manufactured and prices will probably have changed.

In fact, there are a number of ways of overcoming this problem of distinguishing trend from seasonal variations. One such method is called **moving averages**. This method attempts to **remove seasonal (or cyclical) variations from a time series by a process of averaging so as to leave a set of figures representing the trend**.

A **moving average** is an average of the results of a fixed number of periods. Since it is an average of several time periods, it is **related to the mid-point of the overall period**.

Example: moving averages

Year	Sales Units	Year	Sales Units
0	390	4	470
1	380	5	440
2	460	6	500
3	450		

Required

Take a moving average of the annual sales over a period of three years.

Solution

(a) Average sales in the three year period year 0 – year 2 were (390 + 380 + 460)/3 = 1,230/3 = 410. This average relates to the middle year of the period, year 1.

(b) Similarly, average sales in the three year period year 1 – year 3 were (380 + 460 + 450)/3 = 1,290/3 = 430. This average relates to the middle year of the period, year 2.

(c)   The average sales can also be found for the periods year 2 - year 4, year 3 - year 5 and year 4 - year 6, to give the following.

Year	Sales	Moving total of 3 years sales	Moving average of 3 years sales (÷ 3)
0	390		
1	380	1,230	410
2	460	1,290	430
3	450	1,380	460
4	470	1,360	453
5	440	1,410	470
6	500		

Note the following points

(i)   The moving average series has five figures relating to years 1 to 5. The original series had seven figures for years 0 to 6.

(ii)   There is an upward trend in sales, which is more noticeable from the series of moving averages than from the original series of actual sales each year.

The above example averaged over a three-year period. Over what period should a moving average be taken? The answer to this question is that the **moving average which is most appropriate will depend on the circumstances and the nature of the time series**.

(a)   A moving average which takes an average of the results in many time periods will represent results over a longer term than a moving average of two or three periods.

(b)   On the other hand, with a moving average of results in many time periods, the last figure in the series will be out of date by several periods. In our example, the most recent average related to year 5. With a moving average of five years' results, the final figure in the series would relate to year 4.

(c)   When there is a known cycle over which seasonal variations occur, such as all the days in the week or all the seasons in the year, the most suitable moving average would be one which covers one full cycle.

7.1 Moving averages of an even number of results

In the previous example, **moving averages were taken of the results in an *odd* number of time periods**, and the **average then related to the mid-point of the overall period**.

If a **moving average** were taken of results in an **even number of time periods**, the basic technique would be the same, but the mid-point of the overall period would not relate to a single period. For example, suppose an average were taken of the following four results.

Spring	120	
Summer	90	
Autumn	180	average 115
Winter	70	

The average would relate to the mid-point of the period, between summer and autumn.

The trend line average figures need to relate to a particular time period; otherwise, seasonal variations cannot be calculated. To overcome this difficulty, we take a **moving average of the moving average**. An example will illustrate this technique.

Example: moving averages over an even number of periods

Calculate a moving average trend line of the following results of Linden.

Year	Quarter	Volume of sales '000 units
5	1	600
	2	840
	3	420
	4	720
6	1	640
	2	860
	3	420
	4	740

Solution

A moving average of four will be used, since the volume of sales would appear to depend on the season of the year, and each year has four quarterly results. The moving average of four does not relate to any specific period of time; therefore a second moving average of two will be calculated on the first moving averages.

Year	Quarter	Actual volume of sales '000 units (A)	Moving total of 4 quarters' sales '000 units (B)	Moving average of 4 quarters' sales '000 units (B ÷ 4)	Mid-point of 2 moving averages Trend line '000 units (C)
5	1	600			
	2	840			
	3	420	2,580	645.0	650.00
	4	720	2,620	655.0	657.50
6	1	640	2,640	660.0	660.00
	2	860	2,640	660.0	662.50
	3	420	2,660	665.0	
	4	740			

By taking a mid point (a moving average of two) of the original moving averages, we can relate the results to specific quarters (from the third quarter of year 5 to the second quarter of year 6).

Question 14.4   Trend figures

Learning outcomes B2(a), (b)

Actual sales volumes during years 3 and 4 were as follows.

Year	Quarter	Actual sales volume '000 units
3	1	47
	2	59
	3	92
	4	140
4	1	35
	2	49
	3	89
	4	120

What trend figures can be calculated from the information above? (Choose A, B, C or D from the following.)

Year	Quarter	A	B	C	D
3	2	338	–	–	84.50
	3	326	83.000	84.50	81.50
	4	316	80.250	81.50	79.00
4	1	313	78.625	79.00	78.25
	2	293	75.750	78.25	73.25
	3	–	–	73.25	–

Section summary

Trend values can be distinguished from seasonal variations by a process of **moving averages**.

8 Finding the seasonal variations

Introduction

Once a trend has been established we can find the seasonal variations. As we saw earlier, the additive model for time series analysis is $TS = T + SV + R$. We can therefore write $TS - T = SV + R$. In other words, if we deduct the trend series from the actual series, we will be left with the seasonal and residual components of the time series. If we assume that the random component is relatively small, and hence negligible, the **seasonal component can be found as SV = TS – T**, the de-trended series.

The actual and trend sales for Linden (as calculated in the previous example) are set out below. The **difference between the actual results for any one quarter (TS) and the trend figure for that quarter (T)** will be the seasonal variation for that quarter.

Year	Quarter	Actual	Trend	Seasonal variation
5	1	600		
	2	840		
	3	420	650.00	–230.00
	4	720	657.50	62.50
6	1	640	660.00	–20.00
	2	860	662.50	197.50
	3	420		
	4	740		

Suppose that seasonal variations for the third and fourth quarters of year 6 and the first and second quarters of year 7 are –248.75, 62.50, –13.75 and 212.50 respectively. The variation between the actual result for a particular quarter and the trend line average is not the same from year to year, but an **average of these variations can be taken**.

Year	Q_1	Q_2	Q_3	Q_4
5			–230.00	62.50
6	–20.00	197.50	–248.75	62.50
7	–13.75	212.50		
Total	–33.75	410.00	–478.75	125.00
Average (÷ 2)	–16.875	205.00	–239.375	62.50

Variations around the basic trend line should cancel each other out, and add up to zero. At the moment, they do not. We therefore **spread the total of the variations (11.25) across the four quarters (11.25 ÷ 4) so that the final total of the variations sum to zero.**

	Q_1	Q_2	Q_3	Q_4	Total
Estimated quarterly variations	– 16.8750	205.0000	–239.3750	62.5000	11.250
Adjustment to reduce variations to 0	–2.8125	–2.8125	–2.8125	–2.8125	–11.250
Final estimates of quarterly variations	–19.6875	202.1875	–242.1875	59.6875	0

These might be rounded as follows Q_1: –20, Q_2: 202, Q_3:-242, Q_4: 60,   Total: 0

8.1 Seasonal variations using the proportional model

The method of estimating the seasonal variations in the above example was to use the differences between the trend and actual data. This model **assumes that the components of the series are independent** of each other, so that an increasing trend does not affect the seasonal variations and make them increase as well, for example.

The alternative is to use the **proportional model** whereby each actual figure is expressed as a proportion of the trend. Sometimes this method is called the **multiplicative model.**

KEY TERM

The PROPORTIONAL (MULTIPLICATIVE) MODEL summarises a time series as TS = T × SV × R (or TS = T*SV*R).

The **trend component** will be the **same whichever model is used** but the values of the **seasonal and random components** will **vary according to the model being applied.**

The example in section 7.1 can be reworked on this alternative basis. The trend is calculated in exactly the same way as before but we need a different approach for the seasonal variations. The proportional model is TS = T × SV × R and, just as we calculated SV = TS – T for the additive model (Example in 7.1) we can calculate **SV = TS/T** for the proportional model.

Year	Quarter	Actual (TS)	Trend (T)	Seasonal percentage (TS/T)
5	1	600		
	2	840		
	3	420	650.00	0.646
	4	720	657.50	1.095
6	1	640	660.00	0.970
	2	860	662.50	1.298
	3	420		
	4	740		

Suppose that seasonal variations for the next four quarters are 0.628, 1.092, 0.980 and 1.309 respectively. The summary of the seasonal variations expressed in proportional terms is therefore as follows.

Year	Q_1 %	Q_2 %	Q_3 %	Q_4 %
5			0.646	1.095
6	0.970	1.298	0.628	1.092
7	0.980	1.309		
Total	1.950	2.607	1.274	2.187
Average	0.975	1.3035	0.637	1.0935

Instead of summing to zero, as with the additive approach, the **averages should sum (in this case) to 4.0, 1.0 for each of the four quarters.** They actually sum to 4.009 so 0.00225 has to be deducted from each one.

	Q_1	Q_2	Q_3	Q_4
Average	0.97500	1.30350	0.63700	1.09350
Adjustment	–0.00225	–0.00225	–0.00225	–0.00225
Final estimate	0.97275	1.30125	0.63475	1.09125
Rounded	0.97	1.30	0.64	1.09

Note that the **proportional model is better than the additive model when the trend is increasing or decreasing over time**. In such circumstances, seasonal variations are likely to be increasing or decreasing too. The additive model simply adds absolute and unchanging seasonal variations to the trend figures whereas the proportional model, by multiplying increasing or decreasing trend values by a constant seasonal variation factor, takes account of changing seasonal variations.

Section summary

Seasonal variations can be estimated using the additive model or the proportional (multiplicative) model.

9 Time series analysis and forecasting

Introduction

By extrapolating a trend and then adjusting for seasonal variations, forecasts of future values can be made.

Making forecasts of future values

Find a trend line using moving averages or using linear regression analysis (see Section 5).

Use the trend line to forecast future trend line values.

Adjust these values by the average seasonal variation applicable to the future period, to determine the forecast for that period. With the additive model, add (or subtract for negative variations) the variation. With the multiplicative model, multiply the trend value by the variation proportion.

Extending a trend line outside the range of known data, in this case forecasting the future from a trend line based on historical data, is known as **extrapolation**.

Example: forecasting

The sales (in £'000) of swimwear by a large department store for each period of three months and trend values found using moving averages are as follows.

Quarter	Year 4		Year 5		Year 6		Year 7	
	Actual £'000	Trend £'000	Actual £'000	Trend £'000	Actual £'000	Trend £'000	Actual £'000	Trend £'000
First			8		20	40	40	57
Second			30	30	50	45	62	
Third			60	31	80	50	92	
Fourth	24		20	35	40	54		

Using the additive model, seasonal variations have been determined as follows.

Quarter 1	Quarter 2	Quarter 3	Quarter 4
–£18,250	+£2,750	+£29,750	–£14,250

Required

Predict sales for the last quarter of year 7 and the first quarter of year 8, stating any assumptions.

Solution

We might guess that the trend line is rising steadily, by (57 – 40)/4 = 4.25 per quarter in the period 1st quarter year 6 to 1st quarter year 7 (57 being the prediction in 1st quarter year 7 and 40 the prediction in 1st quarter year 6). Since the trend may be levelling off a little, a quarterly increase of +4 in the trend will be assumed.

		Trend	Seasonal variation	Forecast
1st quarter	Year 7	57		
4th quarter	Year 7 (+ (3 × 4))	69	–14.25	54.75
1st quarter	Year 8 (+ (4 × 4))	73	–18.25	54.75

Rounding to the nearest thousand pounds, the forecast sales are £55,000 for each of the two quarters.

Note that you could actually plot the trend line figures on a graph, extrapolate the trend line into the future and read off forecasts from the graph using the extrapolated trend line.

If we had been using the proportional model, with an average variation for (for example) quarter 4 of 0.8, our prediction for the fourth quarter of year 7 would have been 69 × 0.8 = 55.2, say £55,000.

Question 14.5

Regression analysis and seasonal variations

Learning outcome B2(b)

The trend in a company's sales figures can be described by the linear regression equation Y = 780 + 4X, where X is the month number (with January year 3 as month 0) and Y is sales in thousands of pounds. The average seasonal variation for March is 106%.

The forecast sales for March year 5 (to the nearest £'000) are

A   £890,000
B   £933,000
C   £937,000
D   £941,000

Exam alert

The specimen paper contained a 5-mark question asking for a calculation based on a regression analysis equation.

Section summary

Forecasts can be made by calculating a **trend line** (using moving averages or linear regression), using the trend line to forecast future trend line values, and adjusting these values by the **average seasonal variation** applicable to the future period.

10   Using spreadsheet packages to build business models

Introduction

Spreadsheet packages can be used to build business models to assist the forecasting and planning process.

KEY TERM

A SPREADSHEET is 'The term commonly used to describe many of the modelling packages available for microcomputers, being loosely derived from the likeness to a "spreadsheet of paper" divided into rows and columns.'

(CIMA Official Terminology)

It is a type of general purpose software package with **many business applications**, not just accounting ones. It **can be used to build a model**, in which data is presented in **cells** at the intersection of these **rows and columns**. It is up to the model builder to determine what data or information should be presented in the spreadsheet, how it should be presented and how the data should be manipulated by the spreadsheet program. The most widely used spreadsheet packages are Lotus 1-2-3 and Excel.

The idea behind a spreadsheet is that the model builder should **construct a model as follows**.

(a)   Identify what data goes into each row and column and by **inserting text** (for example, column headings and row identifications).

(b)   **Specify how the numerical data in the model should be derived**. Numerical data might be derived using one of the following methods.

     (i)   **Insertion into the model via keyboard input**.

     (ii)   **Calculation from other data in the model** by means of a formula specified within the model itself. The model builder must insert these formulae into the spreadsheet model when it is first constructed.

     (iii)   **Retrieval from data on a disk file** from another computer application program or module.

10.1 The advantages of spreadsheets

The uses of spreadsheets are really only limited by your imagination, and by the number of rows and columns in the spreadsheet, but some of the more **common accounting applications** are listed below.

- Statements of financial position
- Cash flow analysis/forecasting
- General ledger
- Inventory records
- Job cost estimates
- Market share analysis and planning

- Profit projections
- Profit statements
- Project budgeting and control
- Sales projections and records
- Tax estimation

The great value of spreadsheets derives from their **simple format** of rows, columns and worksheets of data, and the ability of the data **users to have direct access themselves** to their spreadsheet model via their own PC. For example, an accountant can construct a cash flow model with a spreadsheet package on the PC on their desk: they can **create** the model, **input** the data, **manipulate** the data and **read or print the output** direct. They will also have fairly **instant access** to the model whenever it is needed, in just the time it takes to load the model into the PC. Spreadsheets therefore bring computer modelling within the everyday reach of data users.

10.2 The disadvantages of spreadsheets

Spreadsheets have disadvantages if they are not properly used.

(a)   A **minor error in the design** of a model at any point can **affect the validity of data** throughout the spreadsheet. Such errors can be very difficult to trace.

(b)   Even if it is properly designed in the first place, it is very **easy to corrupt** a model by accidentally changing a cell or inputting data in the wrong place.

(c)   It is possible to **become over-dependent on them**, so that simple one-off tasks that can be done in seconds with a pen and paper are done on a spreadsheet instead.

(d)   The possibility for experimentation with data is so great that it is possible to **lose sight of the original intention** of the spreadsheet.

(e)   Spreadsheets **cannot take account of qualitative factors** since they are invariably difficult to quantify. Decisions should not be made on the basis of quantitative information alone.

Spreadsheets are a **tool in planning and decision making** with the user making the decision.

In 'Spreadsheets and databases as budgeting tools' (CIMA *Student*, July 1999), Bob Scarlett expanded on the limitations of spreadsheets for budgeting. (The emphasis is BPP's.)

'The process of creating a budget in a large organisation is a **complex** operation. Each area in the organisation needs to prepare a plan and these plans need to be **collated and consolidated**. The system must then accommodate **adjustments** on a **top-down** and **bottom-up** basis. A budgeting operation based on spreadsheets has the following **problems**:

- It is **inflexible** and **error prone**. A large number of spreadsheets can be linked and consolidated but this process presents many difficulties. Calculations are complex and mistakes are easily made. Random 'what if' analyses across centres may become very difficult to carry out.

- It is a **single-user tool in a multi-user environment**. A large number of spreadsheet users are involved using similar templates over periods of weeks. This involves massive duplication of effort and gives rise to risks relating to loss of data integrity and consistency of structure.

- It **lacks 'functionality'**. There are many users in the budget management process ranging from cost centre managers to the chief financial officer. All require ready access to the system in order to input data to it and draw information from it. The budget controller must be able to track revisions. Spreadsheet based systems are notorious for complexity – and they can be anything but easy to use.

Spreadsheet-based budgeting systems may be perfectly adequate for the small and simple operation. However, the limitations of such systems may become increasingly apparent as larger and more complex operations are considered.'

Section summary

Spreadsheet packages can be used to build business models to assist the forecasting and planning process.

---

11   Forecasting problems

Introduction

All forecasts are subject to error, but the likely errors vary from case to case.

- The **further into the future** the forecast is for, the **more unreliable** it is likely to be.
- The **less data** available on which to base the forecast, the **less reliable** the forecast.
- The **pattern** of trend and seasonal variations **may not continue** in the future.
- **Random variations** may upset the pattern of trend and seasonal variation.

There are a number of changes that also may make it difficult to forecast future events.

Type of change	Examples
Political and economic changes	Changes in interest rates, exchange rates or inflation can mean that future sales and costs are difficult to forecast.
Environmental changes	The opening of high-speed rail links might have a considerable impact on some companies' markets.
Technological changes	These may mean that the past is not a reliable indication of likely future events. For example new faster machinery may make it difficult to use current output levels as the basis for forecasting future production output.
Technological advances	Advanced manufacturing technology is changing the cost structure of many firms. Direct labour costs are reducing in significance and fixed manufacturing costs are increasing. This causes forecasting difficulties because of the resulting changes in cost behaviour patterns, breakeven points and so on.
Social changes	Alterations in taste, fashion and the social acceptability of products can cause forecasting difficulties.

Section summary

Certain changes may make it difficult to forecast future events. These include political and economic changes, environmental changes, technological changes and social changes.

Chapter Roundup

✓ A number of quantitative methods may be used by the management accountant to obtain information for inclusion in budgets.

✓ Before using any technique based on past data, the past data must be assessed for appropriateness for the intended purpose. There is no point in using a 'sophisticated' technique with unreliable data.

✓ **Linear regression analysis** (least squares technique) involves determining a **line of best fit.**

✓ **Scatter diagrams** can be used to estimate the fixed and variable components of costs.

✓ **Sales forecasting** techniques include asking sales personnel, market research, and using mathematical models and techniques.

✓ When **regression analysis** is used for **forecasting sales**, the years (or days or months) become the x variables in the regression formulae by numbering them from 1 upwards.

✓ A **time series** records a series of figures or values over time. A time series has four components: a **trend**, **seasonal variations**, **cyclical variations** and **random variations**.

✓ **Trend** values can be distinguished from seasonal variations by a process of **moving averages**.

✓ **Seasonal variations** can be estimated using the **additive** model or the **proportional** (**multiplicative**) model.

✓ **Forecasts** can be made by calculating a **trend line** (using moving averages or linear regression), using the trend line to forecast future trend line values, and adjusting these values by the **average seasonal variation** applicable to the future period.

✓ **Spreadsheet packages** can be used to build business models to assist the forecasting and planning process.

✓ Certain changes may make it difficult to forecast future events. These include political and economic changes, environmental changes, technological changes and social changes.

Quick Quiz

1   In the equation $Y = a + bX$, which is the dependent variable?

A   Y   C   b
B   a   D   X

2   *Fill in the missing words.*

Extrapolation involves using a .... of best .... to predict a value .... the two extreme points of the observed range.

3   Between sales of suntan cream and sales of cold drinks, one would expect (assuming spending money to be unlimited)

A   positive, but spurious, correlation   C   positive correlation indicating direct causation
B   negative, but spurious, correlation   D   negative correlation indicating direct causation

4   Which of the following statements is/are true of the coefficient of determination?

		True	False
(a)	It is the square of the Pearsonian coefficient of correlation		
(b)	It can never quite equal 1		
(c)	If it is high, this proves that variations in one variable cause variations in the other		

5   *Choose the appropriate words from those highlighted.*

When using **regression analysis/analytical regression** for forecasting, the X variables are the **years (or days or months)/the level of sales (or costs)**.

6   What are the four components of a time series?

A   Trend, seasonal variations, cyclical variations, relative variations
B   Trend, systematic variations, cyclical variations, relative variations
C   Trend, systematic variations, seasonal variations, random variations
D   Trend, seasonal variations, cyclical variations, random variations

7   The multiplicative model expresses a time series as $TS = T + SV + R$. *True or false?*

8   A time series for weeks 1 to 12 has been analysed into a trend and seasonal variations, using the additive model. The trend value is $84 + 0.7w$, where w is the week number. The actual value for week 9 is 88.7. What is the seasonal variation for week 9?

A   90.3
B   −1.6
C   1.6
D   6.3

9   *List six factors to consider when forecasting sales.*

1   ....
2   ....
3   ....
4   ....
5   ....
6   ....

10 Complete the following table.

Year	Quarter	Actual volume of sales Units	Moving total of 4 quarters' sales Units	Moving average of 4 quarters' sales Units	Trend
3	1	1,350			
	2	1,210			
	3	1,080			
	4	1,250			
4	1	1,400			
	2	1,260			
	3	1,110			
	4	1,320			

11 The further into the future the forecast is for, the more reliable it is likely to be. *True or false?*

12 The time series for sales in 20X7 at Teatime Ltd is 930. The trend for 20X7 is 400 and the random component is zero. Calculate the seasonal variation (assume additive model).

Answers to Quick Quiz

1   A

2   Line; fit; outside.

3   A. When cold drinks sell well, so will suntan cream. Neither sales level causes the other; both are caused by the weather.

4   Statement (a) is true. The coefficient of determination is r^2
     Statement (b) is false. r can reach 1 or –1, so r^2 can reach 1
     Statement (c) is false. Correlation does not prove a causal link

5   regression analysis, years (or days or months)

6   D

7   False. The multiplicative model expresses a time series as $TS = T \times SV \times R$

8   B. For week 9, the trend value is $84 + (0.7 \times 9) = 90.3$. The seasonal variation is actual – trend = $88.7 – 90.3 = –1.6$, indicating that the value for week 9 is below what one might expect from the trend.

9   Here are some examples.

- Past sales patterns
- The economic environment
- Results of market research
- Anticipated advertising during the budget period
- Competition

- New legislation
- Environmental factors
- Pricing policies and discounts offered
- Distribution and quality of sales outlets and personnel

10

Year	Quarter	Actual volume of sales Units	Moving total of 4 quarters' sales Units	Moving average of 4 quarters' sales Units	Trend
3	1	1,350			
	2	1,210			
	3	1,080	4,890	1,222.5	1,228.75
	4	1,250	4,940	1,235.0	1,241.25
4	1	1,400	4,990	1,247.5	1,251.25
	2	1,260	5,020	1,255.0	1,263.75
	3	1,110	5,090	1,272.5	
	4	1,320			

11   False. It is likely to be more unreliable.

12   Time series = trend + seasonal variation + random component

     930 =   400 + SV
     SV   =   930 – 400 = 530
     SV   =   530

Answers to Questions

14.1 Analysing cost behaviour and making projections

Forecast profit statement for period 4

	£	£
Revenue		10,220
Materials (W1)	774	
Staff salaries (W2)	5,120	
Utilities (W3)	723	
Laundry (W4)	646	
Rent	430	
Other	375	
		8,068
Profit		2,152

Workings

1 **Material costs**

Period 1	£756/420	= £1.80 per unit
Period 2	£991.80/551	= £1.80 per unit

This is a wholly variable cost

Forecast for period 4 = £1.80 × (265 + 165) = £774

2 **Staff salaries**

To use the high-low method it will be necessary to eliminate the effect of the step in fixed costs that occurs at the 450 total activity level.

	Units		£
High activity	551	(£6,862 – £1,500)	5,362
Low activity	420		5,100
	131		262

Variable cost per unit $\qquad$ = £262/131 = £2 (the staff bonus)

Substitute in low activity:

Fixed cost $\qquad$ = £5,100 – (420 × £2) = £4,260
Forecast for 430 total units in period 4 $\quad$ = £4,260 + (430 × £2) = £5,120

3 **Utilities**

	Units	£
High activity	551	856.10
Low activity	420	712.00
	131	144.10

Variable cost per unit $\quad$ = £144.10/131 = £1.10

Substitute in low activity:

Fixed cost $\qquad$ = £712 – (420 × £1.10) = £250
Forecast for period 4 $\quad$ = £250 + (430 × £1.10) = £723

4   **Laundry**

	Units	£
High activity	551	570.80
Low activity	420	466.00
	131	104.80

Variable cost per unit   = £104.80/131 = £0.80

Substitute on low activity:

Fixed cost   = £466 – (420 × £0.80) = £130
Forecast for period 4   = £130 + (430 × £0.80 × 1.5) = £646

14.2 Regression analysis

(a)   *Workings*

X	Y	XY	X^2
20	82	1,640	400
16	70	1,120	256
24	90	2,160	576
22	85	1,870	484
18	73	1,314	324
ΣX = 100	ΣY = 400	ΣXY = 8,104	ΣX^2 = 2,040

n   =   5 (There are five pairs of data for x and y values)
b   = $(n\Sigma XY - \Sigma X \Sigma Y)/(n\Sigma X^2 - (\Sigma X)^2)$ = ((5 × 8,104) – (100 × 400))/ ((5 × 2,040) – 100^2)
     =   (40,520 – 40,000)/(10,200 – 10,000) = 520/200 = 2.6
a   = $\overline{Y} - b\overline{X}$ = (400/5) – (2.6 × (100/5)) = 28
Y   =   28 + 2.6X

where Y = total cost, in thousands of pounds and X = output, in thousands of units.

(b)   If the output is 22,000 units, we would expect costs to be 28+ 2.6 × 22 = 85.2 = £85,200.

14.3 Limitations of regression analysis

(a)   The reliability of the model is unknown if we do not know the correlation coefficient. A low correlation would suggest that the model may be unreliable.

(b)   The model is probably valid only over a certain range of quantity produced. Outside this range, the relationship between the two variables may be very different.

(c)   The model is based on past data, and assumes that what has happened in the past will happen in the future.

(d)   The model assumes that a linear relationship exists between the quantity produced per annum and the total operating costs per annum. It is possible that a non-linear relationship may exist.

(e)   The fixed costs of £5,000 per annum may be misleading if they include an element of allocated costs.

14.4 Trend figures

The correct answer is B.

Year	Quarter	Actual sales	Moving total of 4 quarters' sales	Moving average	Mid-point Trend
		'000 units	'000 units	'000 units	'000 units
3	1	47			
	2	59			
			338	84.5	
	3	92			83.000
			326	81.5	
	4	140			80.250
			316	79.0	
4	1	35			78.625
			313	78.25	
	2	49			75.750
			293	73.25	
	3	89			
	4	120			

14.5 Regression analysis and seasonal variations

The correct answer is C.

$X = 26$

Forecast $= 1.06 \times [780 + (4 \times 26)] = 937.04 = £937,040$ or about £937,000.

Now try these questions from the Exam Question Bank	**Number**	**Level**	**Marks**	**Time**
	Q22	Examination	15	27 mins
	Q23	Examination	5	9 mins

PROJECT APPRAISAL

Part D

INVESTMENT DECISION MAKING

In the next four chapters we will be examining the appraisal of **projects** which involve the **outlay of capital**.

Capital expenditure differs from day to day revenue expenditure for two reasons.

- **Capital expenditure** often involves a **bigger outlay of money**.

- The **benefits** from capital expenditure are likely to **accrue over a long period of time**. Therefore the benefits cannot all be set against costs in the current year's income statement.

For these reasons any proposed capital expenditure project should be **properly appraised**, and found to be worthwhile, before the decision is taken to go ahead with the expenditure.

We begin the chapter with an overview of the **investment decision-making process** in **Sections 1 and 2** before moving on to examine two capital investment appraisal techniques, the straightforward **payback method** (**Section 3**) and the slightly more involved **accounting rate of return method** (**Section 4**).

In Chapter 16 we look at methods of investment appraisal based on discounted cash flow techniques.

topic list	learning outcomes	syllabus references	ability required
1 The process of investment decision making	C1(a)	C1(i)	comprehension
2 Post audit	C1(a)	C1(i)	comprehension
3 The payback method	C2(a), (b)	C2(i), (ii)	evaluation
4 The accounting rate of return method	C2(a), (b)	C2(i), (ii)	evaluation

1 The process of investment decision making

1.1 Creation of capital budgets

Introduction

The capital budget will normally be **prepared to cover a longer period than sales, production and resource budgets**, say from three to five years, although it should be **broken down** into periods matching those of other budgets. It should indicate the expenditure required to cover **capital projects already underway** and those it is **anticipated will start** in the three to five year period (say) of the capital budget.

The budget should therefore be based on the current production budget, future expected levels of production and the long-term development of the organisation, and industry, as a whole.

Budget limits or constraints might be imposed internally (**soft capital rationing**) or externally (**hard capital rationing**).

The **administration of** the capital budget is usually separate from that of the other budgets. Overall responsibility for **authorisation and monitoring** of capital expenditure is, in most large organisations, the **responsibility of a committee**.

1.2 The investment decision-making process

We have seen in the introduction to this chapter that capital expenditure often involves the outlay of **large sums of money**, and that any expected **benefits may take a number of years to accrue**. For these reasons it is vital that capital expenditure is subject to a rigorous process of appraisal and control.

A typical **model for investment decision making** has a number of distinct stages.

- Origination of proposals
- Project screening
- Analysis and acceptance
- Monitoring and review

We will look at these stages in more detail below.

1.3 Origination of proposals

Investment opportunities **do not just appear** out of thin air. They **must be created**.

An organisation must set up a **mechanism that scans the environment for potential opportunities and gives an early warning of future problems**. A technological change that might result in a drop in sales might be picked up by this scanning process, and steps should be taken immediately to respond to such a threat.

Ideas for investment might come from those working in technical positions. A factory manager, for example, could be well placed to identify ways in which expanded capacity or new machinery could increase output or the efficiency of the manufacturing process. Innovative ideas, such as new product lines, are more likely to come from those in higher levels of management, given their strategic view of the organisation's direction and their knowledge of the competitive environment.

The overriding feature of any **proposal** is that it should be **consistent with the organisation's overall strategy to achieve its objectives**.

1.4 Project screening

Each proposal must be subject to detailed screening. So that a **qualitative evaluation** of a proposal can be made, a number of key questions such as those below might be asked before any financial analysis is undertaken. Only if the project passes this initial screening will more detailed financial analysis begin.

(a)   What is the **purpose** of the project?
(b)   Does it **'fit'** with the organisation's long-term objectives?
(c)   Is it a **mandatory** investment, for example to conform with safety legislation?
(d)   What **resources** are required and are they available, eg money, capacity, labour?
(e)   Do we have the necessary management **expertise** to guide the project to completion?
(f)   Does the project expose the organisation to **unnecessary risk**?
(g)   How **long** will the project last and what factors are **key** to its **success**?
(h)   Have all possible **alternatives** been considered?

1.5 Analysis and acceptance

The analysis stage can be broken down into a number of steps.

 Complete and submit standard format financial information as a formal investment proposal.

 Classify the project by type (to separate projects into those that require more or less rigorous financial appraisal, and those that must achieve a greater or lesser rate of return in order to be deemed acceptable).

 Carry out financial analysis of the project. We look at this in more detail in Section 1.5.1.

 Compare the outcome of the financial analysis to predetermined acceptance criteria.

 Consider the project in the light of the capital budget for the current and future operating periods.

 Make the **decision (go/no go)**. This is considered in more detail below.

 Monitor the progress of the project (covered below).

1.5.1 Financial analysis

The financial analysis will involve the **application of the organisation's preferred investment appraisal techniques**. We will be studying these techniques in detail in this chapter and the next. In many projects some of the financial implications will be extremely difficult to quantify, but every effort must be made to do so, in order to have a formal basis for planning and controlling the project.

Here are examples of the type of question that will be addressed at this stage.

(a)   What cash flows/profits will arise from the project and when?
(b)   Has inflation been considered in the determination of the cash flows?
(c)   What are the results of the financial appraisal?
(d)   Has any allowance been made for risk, and if so, what was the outcome?

Some types of project, for example a marketing investment decision, may give rise to cash inflows and **returns which are so intangible and difficult to quantify that a full financial appraisal may not be possible**. In this case more weight may be given to a consideration of the qualitative issues.

1.5.2 Qualitative issues

Financial analysis of capital projects is obviously vital because of the amount of money involved and the length of time for which it is tied up. A consideration of qualitative issues is also relevant to the decision, however (ie factors which are difficult or impossible to quantify). We have already seen that qualitative issues would be considered in the **initial screening stage**, for example in reviewing the project's 'fit' with the organisation's overall objectives and whether it is a mandatory investment. There is a very wide range of other qualitative issues that may be relevant to a particular project.

(a)   What are the implications of not undertaking the investment, eg adverse effect on staff morale, loss of market share?

(b)   Will acceptance of this project lead to the need for further investment activity in future?

(c)   What will be the effect on the company's image?

(d)   Will the organisation be more flexible as a result of the investment, and better able to respond to market and technology changes?

1.5.3 Go/no go decision

Go/no go decisions on projects may be **made at different levels within the organisational hierarchy**, depending on three factors.

(a)   The type of investment
(b)   Its perceived riskiness
(c)   The amount of expenditure required

For example, a divisional manager may be authorised to make decisions up to $25,000, an area manager up to $150,000 and a group manager up to $300,000, with board approval for greater amounts.

Once the go/no go (or **accept/reject**) decision has been made, the organisation is committed to the project, and the decision maker must accept that the project's success or failure reflects on his or her ability to make sound decisions.

1.6 Monitoring the progress of the project

During the project's progress, **project controls** should be applied to ensure the following.

- Capital spending does not exceed the amount authorised.
- The implementation of the project is not delayed.
- The anticipated benefits are eventually obtained.

The first two items are probably easier to control than the third, because the controls can normally be applied soon after the capital expenditure has been authorised, whereas monitoring the benefits will span a longer period of time.

1.6.1 Controls over excess spending

There are a number of controls which organisations can implement to ensure that capital spending does not exceed the amount authorised.

(a)   The authority to make capital expenditure decisions must be formally assigned.

(b)   Capital expenditure decisions should be documented and approval of the project should specify the manager authorised to carry out the expenditure, the amount of expenditure authorised and the period of time in which the expenditure should take place.

(c)   Some overspending above the amount authorised – say 5% or 10% – might be allowed. If the required expenditure exceeds the amount authorised by more than this amount, a fresh submission for reauthorisation of the project should be required.

(d)   There should be a total capital budget, and the authorisation of any capital expenditure which would take total spending above the budget should be referred to, for example, board level for approval.

1.6.2 Control over delays

If there is a delay in carrying out the project and the capital expenditure has not taken place before the stated deadline is reached, the project should be **resubmitted for fresh authorisation**. The proposer should be asked to **explain the reasons for the delay**.

1.6.3 Control over the anticipated benefits

Further control can be exercised over capital projects by ensuring that the anticipated benefits do actually materialise, the benefits are as big as anticipated and running costs do not exceed expectation.

A **difficulty** with control measurements of capital projects is that most **projects are 'unique' with no standard or yardstick to judge them against** other than their own appraisal data. Therefore if actual costs were to exceed the estimated costs, it might be impossible to tell just how much of the variance is due to bad estimating and how much is due to inefficiencies and poor cost control.

In the same way, if benefits are below expectation, is this because the original estimates were optimistic, or because management has been inefficient and failed to get the benefits they should have done?

Many capital projects such as the purchase of replacement assets and marketing investment decisions **do not have clearly identifiable costs and benefits**. The incremental benefits and costs of such schemes can be estimated, but it would need a very sophisticated management accounting system to be able to identify and measure the actual benefits and many of the costs. Even so, some degree of monitoring and control can still be exercised by means of a **post-completion appraisal** or audit review.

Section summary

A typical **model for investment decision making** has a number of distinct stages.

- Origination of proposals
- Project screening
- Analysis and acceptance
- Monitoring and review

During the project's progress, **project controls** should be applied to ensure the following.

- Capital spending does not exceed the amount authorised.
- The implementation of the project is not delayed.
- The anticipated benefits are eventually obtained.

2   Post audit

Introduction

The post completion audit is a **forward-looking** rather than a backward-looking technique. It seeks to **identify general lessons** to be learned from a project.

KEY TERM

A POST-COMPLETION AUDIT (PCA) is 'An objective independent assessment of the success of a capital project in relation to plan. Covers the whole life of the project and provides feedback to managers to aid the implementation and control of future projects.'   (CIMA *Official Terminology*)

2.1 Why perform a post-completion appraisal (PCA) or audit?   5/11

(a)   The **threat** of the PCA will **motivate managers** to work to achieve the promised benefits from the project.

(b)   If the audit takes place before the project life ends, and if it finds that the benefits have been less than expected because of management inefficiency, steps can be taken to **improve efficiency**. Alternatively, it will **highlight those projects which should be discontinued**.

(c)   It can help to **identify** managers who have been **good performers** and those who have been poor performers.

(d)   It might identify weaknesses in the forecasting and estimating techniques used to evaluate projects, and so should help to **improve** the discipline and quality of **forecasting** for future investment decisions.

(e)   Areas where improvements can be made in methods which should help to achieve **better results in general from capital investments** might be revealed.

(f)   The **original estimates may be more realistic** if managers are aware that they will be monitored, but post-completion audits **should not be unfairly critical**.

2.2 Which projects should be audited?

A reasonable **guideline** might be to **audit all projects above a certain size, and a random selection of smaller projects**.

A PCA does not need to focus on all aspects of an investment, but should **concentrate on those aspects which have been identified as particularly sensitive or critical to the success of a project**. The most important thing to remember is that post-completion audits are time-consuming and costly and so **careful consideration should be given to the cost-benefit trade-off** arising from the post-completion audit results.

2.3 When should projects be audited?

If the audit is carried out too soon, the information may not be complete. On the other hand, if the audit is too late then management action will be delayed and the usefulness of the information is greatly reduced.

There is no correct answer to the question of when to audit, although research suggests that in practice most companies perform the PCA **approximately one year after the completion of the project**.

2.4 Who performs a PCA?

Because it can be very difficult to evaluate an investment decision completely objectively, it is generally appropriate to **separate responsibility** for the **investment decision** from that for the **PCA**. Line management involved in the investment decision should therefore not carry out the PCA. To avoid conflicts of interest, **outside experts** could even be used.

2.5 Problems with PCA

(a)   There are many **uncontrollable factors** which are outside management control in long-term investments, such as environmental changes.

(b)   It **may not be possible** to **identify separately the costs and benefits** of any particular project.

(c)   PCA can be a **costly** and **time-consuming** exercise, although 'contrary to what is often thought, conducting a PCA does not appear to be an expensive business' reported Brantjes, von Eije, Eusman and Prins in *Management Accounting* ('Post-completion auditing with Heineken) in April 1999.

(d)   Applied punitively, post-completion audit exercises may lead to **managers becoming over cautious** and unnecessarily **risk averse**.

(e)   The **strategic effects** of a capital investment project **may take years** to materialise and it may in fact **never be possible** to identify or quantify them effectively.

Despite the growth in popularity of post-completion audits, you should bear in mind the possible **alternative** control processes.

(a)   **Teams** could manage a project from beginning to end, control being used **before** the project is started and **during** its life, rather than at the end of its life.

(b)   **More time could be spent choosing projects** rather than checking completed projects.

CASE STUDY

A 1999 *Management Accounting* article looked at post completion auditing at Heineken and how it was applied to a project to replace a 20-year old bottling line. The following table shows the planned objectives of the investment and the actual situation at the time a PCA was carried out on the investment. This should give you an idea of the type of objectives that can be monitored with a PCA.

Objectives	Plan	Actual
Efficiency	Increase from 65% to 80%	No increase yet
Staff savings	From 13 to 7 per shift	Achieved
Forklift savings	1 vehicle less	1 and possibly 2 vehicles less
Savings on overhaul of old bottling line	1.3 million guilders of savings	Savings achieved, but as a result of reusing part of the old bottling line another 1.8 million guilders was spent in additional overhaul costs
Savings on maintenance	Savings of 0.4 million guilders annually	Savings estimated at 0.3 million guilders annually
Quality	50% reduction in damage	Achieved
Working conditions	Level of noise Accessibility Safety Attainability	All much improved, but not quantified

Section summary

A **post audit** cannot reverse the decision to incur the capital expenditure, because the expenditure has already taken place, but it does have a certain control value.

3 The payback method

Introduction

Now that we have discussed all the stages involved in the capital budgeting process, we will return to study in detail the stage that many managers consider to be the most important: the financial appraisal. We will begin with what is probably the most straightforward appraisal technique: the payback method.

KEY TERM

PAYBACK is 'The time required for the cash inflows from a capital investment project to equal the cash outflows'.   (CIMA *Official Terminology*)

When **deciding between two or more competing projects**, the usual decision is to **accept the one with the shortest payback**.

Payback is often used as a **'first screening method'**. By this, we mean that when a capital investment project is being subjected to financial appraisal, the first question to ask is: 'How long will it take to pay back its cost?' The organisation might have a target payback, and so it would reject a capital project unless its payback period were less than a certain number of years.

However, a project should not be evaluated on the basis of payback alone. Payback should be a *first* screening process, and if a project gets through the payback test, it ought **then to be evaluated with a more sophisticated project appraisal technique**.

You should note that when payback is calculated, we take **profits before depreciation**, because we are trying to estimate the *cash* returns from a project and profit before depreciation is likely to be a **rough approximation of cash flows**.

3.1 Why is payback alone an inadequate project appraisal technique?

Look at the figures below for two mutually exclusive projects (this means that only one of them can be undertaken).

	Project P	Project Q
Capital cost of asset	$60,000	$60,000
Profits before depreciation		
Year 1	$20,000	$50,000
Year 2	$30,000	$20,000
Year 3	$40,000	$5,000
Year 4	$50,000	$5,000
Year 5	$60,000	$5,000

Project P pays back in year 3 (about one quarter of the way through year 3). Project Q pays back half way through year 2. **Using payback alone** to judge projects, **project Q would be preferred. But the returns from project P over its life are much higher than the returns from project Q**. Project P will earn total profits before depreciation of $200,000 on an investment of $60,000, whereas Project Q will earn total profits before depreciation of only $85,000 on an investment of $60,000.

Question 15.1	Payback

Learning outcome C2(a)

An asset costing $120,000 is to be depreciated over ten years to a nil residual value. Profits after depreciation for the first five years are as follows.

Year	$
1	12,000
2	17,000
3	28,000
4	37,000
5	8,000

How long is the payback period to the nearest month?

A   3 years 7 months
B   3 years 6 months
C   3 years
D   The project does not payback in five years

3.2 Disadvantages of the payback method

There are a number of serious drawbacks to the payback method.

(a)   It **ignores the timing of cash flows** within the payback period, the cash flows after the end of the payback period and therefore the total project return.

(b)   It **ignores the time value of money** (a concept incorporated into more sophisticated appraisal methods). This means that it does not take account of the fact that $1 today is worth more than $1 in one year's time. An investor who has $1 today can either consume it immediately or alternatively can invest it at the prevailing interest rate, say 10%, to get a return of $1.10 in a year's time.

There are also other disadvantages.

(a)   The method is unable to distinguish between projects with the same payback period.

(b)   The choice of any cut-off payback period by an organisation is arbitrary.

(c)   It may lead to excessive investment in short-term projects.

(d)   It takes account of the risk of the timing of cash flows but does not take account of the variability of those cash flows.

3.3 Advantages of the payback method

The use of the payback method does have advantages, especially as an initial screening device.

(a)   Long payback means **capital is tied up**
(b)   Focus on early payback can **enhance liquidity**
(c)   **Investment risk is increased** if payback is longer
(d)   **Shorter-term forecasts** are likely to be **more reliable**
(e)   The calculation is **quick** and **simple**
(f)   Payback is an **easily understood** concept

Section summary

The **payback method** looks at how long it takes for a project's net cash inflows to equal the initial investment.

4   The accounting rate of return method

Introduction

The accounting rate of return (ARR) method (also called the return on capital employed (ROCE) method or the return on investment (ROI) method) of appraising a project is to estimate the accounting rate of return that the project should yield. If it exceeds a target rate of return, the project will be undertaken.

KEY TERM

The CIMA *Official Terminology* definition is $\dfrac{\text{Average annual profit from investment} \times 100}{\text{Average investment}}$

Unfortunately there are several different definitions of ARR.

$$ARR = \frac{\text{Estimated total profits}}{\text{Estimated initial investment}} \times 100\% \quad OR$$

$$ARR = \frac{\text{Estimated average profits}}{\text{Estimated initial investment}} \times 100\%$$

KEY POINT

There are arguments in favour of each of these definitions. The most important point is, however, that the **method selected should be used consistently**. For **examination** purposes we recommend the **first definition** (CIMA's definition) unless the question clearly indicates that some other one is to be used.

Note that this is the only appraisal method that we will be studying that **uses profit** instead of cash flow. If you are not provided with a figure for profit, **assume that net cash inflow minus depreciation equals profit**.

Example: the accounting rate of return

A company has a target accounting rate of return of 20% (using the CIMA definition above), and is now considering the following project.

Capital cost of asset	$80,000
Estimated life	4 years
Estimated profit before depreciation	
Year 1	$20,000
Year 2	$25,000
Year 3	$35,000
Year 4	$25,000

The capital asset would be depreciated by 25% of its cost each year, and will have no residual value.

Required

Assess whether the project should be undertaken.

Solution

The annual profits after depreciation, and the mid-year net book value of the asset, would be as follows.

Year	Profit after depreciation $	Mid-year net book value $	ARR in the year %
1	0	70,000	0
2	5,000	50,000	10
3	15,000	30,000	50
4	5,000	10,000	50

As the table shows, the ARR is low in the early stages of the project, partly because of low profits in Year 1 but mainly because the NBV of the asset is much higher early on in its life. The project does not achieve the target ARR of 20% in its first two years, but exceeds it in years 3 and 4. Should it be undertaken?

When the **ARR from a project varies from year to year**, it makes sense to **take an overall or 'average' view of the project's return**. In this case, we should look at the return over the four-year period.

	$
Total profit before depreciation over four years	105,000
Total profit after depreciation over four years	25,000
Average annual profit after depreciation	6,250
Original cost of investment	80,000
Average net book value over the four year period ((80,000 + 0)/2)	40,000

The project would not be undertaken because its ARR is 6,250/40,000 = 15.625% and so it would fail to yield the target return of 20%.

4.1 The ARR and the comparison of mutually exclusive projects

The ARR method of capital investment appraisal can also be used to compare two or more projects which are mutually exclusive. The project with the highest ARR would be selected (provided that the expected ARR is higher than the company's target ARR).

| Question 15.2 | The ARR and mutually exclusive projects |

Learning outcome C2(a)

Arrow wants to buy a new item of equipment. Two models of equipment are available, one with a slightly higher capacity and greater reliability than the other. The expected costs and profits of each item are as follows.

	Equipment item X	Equipment item Y
Capital cost	$80,000	$150,000
Life	5 years	5 years
Profits before depreciation	$	$
Year 1	50,000	50,000
Year 2	50,000	50,000
Year 3	30,000	60,000
Year 4	20,000	60,000
Year 5	10,000	60,000
Disposal value	0	0

ARR is measured as the average annual profit after depreciation, divided by the average net book value of the asset.

Equipment item Y should be selected if the company's target ARR is 30%. *True or false?*

4.2 The drawbacks and advantages to the ARR method of project appraisal

The ARR method has the serious **drawback** that it **does not take account of the timing of the profits from a project**. Whenever capital is invested in a project, money is tied up until the project begins to earn profits which pay back the investment. Money tied up in one project cannot be invested anywhere else until the profits come in. Management should be aware of the benefits of early repayments from an investment, which will provide the money for other investments.

There are a number of other disadvantages.

(a)   It is **based on accounting profits** which are **subject to a number of different accounting treatments**

(b)   It is a **relative measure** rather than an absolute measure and hence **takes no account of the size of the investment**

(c)   **It takes no account of the length of the project**

(d)   Like the payback method, it **ignores the time value of money**

There are, however, **advantages** to the ARR method.

(a)   It is quick and **simple** to calculate

(b)   It involves a **familiar concept** of a percentage return

(c)   Accounting profits can be **easily calculated from financial statements**

(d)   It **looks at the entire project life**

(e)   Managers and investors are accustomed to thinking in terms of profit, and so an appraisal method which **employs profit** may therefore be more **easily understood**

Question 15.3

Payback and ARR

Learning outcomes C2(a), C2(b)

A company is considering two capital expenditure proposals. Both proposals are for similar products and both are expected to operate for four years. Only one proposal can be accepted.

The following information is available.

	Profit/(loss) after depreciation	
	Proposal A	Proposal B
	$	$
Initial investment	46,000	46,000
Year 1	6,500	4,500
Year 2	3,500	2,500
Year 3	13,500	4,500
Year 4	(1,500)	14,500
Estimated scrap value at the end of year 4	4,000	4,000

Depreciation is charged on the straight line basis.

Required

(a)   Calculate the following for both proposals.

(i)   The payback period to one decimal place

(ii)   The return on capital employed on **initial investment**, to one decimal place

(b)   Give two advantages for each of the methods of appraisal used in (a) above.

Section summary

The accounting rate of return has several different definitions but the CIMA Official Terminology definition is $\dfrac{\text{Average annual profit from investment} \times 100\%}{\text{Average investment}}$

Exam skills

Make sure you are happy with the payback method and the ARR as they could earn you easy marks in an exam. There was an ARR calculation required in Section C of the specimen paper.

Chapter Roundup

✓ A typical model for investment decision making has a number of distinct stages.

- Origination of proposals
- Project screening
- Analysis and acceptance
- Monitoring and review

During the project's progress, project controls should be applied to ensure the following.

- Capital spending does not exceed the amount authorised.
- The implementation of the project is not delayed.
- The anticipated benefits are eventually obtained.

✓ A **post audit** cannot reverse the decision to incur the capital expenditure, because the expenditure has already taken place, but it does have a certain control value.

✓ The **payback method** looks at how long it takes for a project's net cash inflows to equal the initial investment.

✓ The accounting rate of return has several different definitions but the CIMA Official Terminology definition is $\dfrac{\text{Average annual profit from investment} \times 100\%}{\text{Average investment}}$

Quick Quiz

1 Fill in the blanks in these statements about the advantages of the payback method.

(a) Focus on early payback can enhance ....
(b) Investment risk is .... if payback is longer.
(c) .... –term forecasts are likely to be more reliable.

2 The accounting rate of return method of investment appraisal uses accounting profits before depreciation charges. *True or false?*

3 Which of the following statements about post-completion audit is correct?

A Size should not be used as a guide as to which projects should be audited.

B Managers should perceive that every capital expenditure project has a chance of being the subject of a detailed audit.

C All capital expenditure projects should be audited.

D In general, projects should be audited approximately one week after completion.

4 *Choose the correct words from those highlighted.*

(a) The imposition of internal capital budget constraints is known as **hard/soft** capital rationing
(b) **Hard/soft** capital rationing occurs when external capital budget limits are set.

5 *Fill in the blank.*

The average net book value of an asset is calculated as ....

6 Applied punitively, PCA exercises may lead to managers becoming risk seekers. *True or false?*

7 *Fill in the blanks.*

The recommended definition of ARR is: $\dfrac{\text{.........................}}{\text{.........................}} \times 100\%$

Answers to Quick Quiz

1   (a)   liquidity   (b)   increased   (c)   shorter

2   False. It uses accounting profits after depreciation.

3   B. This should improve the overall capital expenditure decision-making process.

4   (a)   soft   (b)   hard

5   (Capital cost + disposal value)/2

6   False. They are likely to become unnecessarily risk averse.

7   $\dfrac{\text{Average annual profit from investment}}{\text{Average investment}} \times 100\%$

Answers to Questions

15.1 Payback

The correct answer is A.

Profits before depreciation should be used.

Year	Profit after depreciation $'000	Depreciation $'000	Profit before depreciation $'000	Cumulative profit $'000
1	12	12	24	24
2	17	12	29	53
3	28	12	40	93
4	37	12	49	142
5	8	12	20	

$$\therefore \text{Payback period} = 3 \text{ years} + \left(\frac{(120-93)}{(142-93)} \times 12 \text{ months} \right)$$

$$= 3 \text{ years } 7 \text{ months}$$

15.2 The ARR and mutually exclusive projects

The correct answer is that X should be selected and so the statement is false.

	Item X $	Item Y $
Total profit over life of equipment		
Before depreciation	160,000	280,000
After depreciation	80,000	130,000
Average annual profit after depreciation	16,000	26,000
Average investment = (capital cost + disposal value)/2	40,000	75,000
ARR	40%	34.7%

Both projects would earn a return in excess of 30%, but since **item X would earn a bigger ARR, it would be preferred to item Y**, even though the profits from Y would be higher by an average of $10,000 a year.

15.3 Payback and ARR

(a)   Depreciation must first be **added** back to the **annual profit figures**, to arrive at the annual cash flows.

$$\text{Depreciation} = \frac{\text{Initial investment } \$46,000 - \text{scrap value } \$4,000}{4 \text{ years}}$$

$$= \$10,500 \text{ pa}$$

Adding $10,500 per annum to the profit figures produces the cash flows for each proposal.

	Proposal A		Proposal B	
	Annual	Cumulative	Annual	Cumulative
Year	cash flow	cash flow	cash flow	cash flow
	$	$	$	$
0	(46,000)	(46,000)	(46,000)	(46,000)
1	17,000	(29,000)	15,000	(31,000)
2	14,000	(15,000)	13,000	(18,000)
3	24,000	9,000	15,000	(3,000)
4	9,000	18,000	25,000	22,000
4	4,000	22,000	4,000	26,000

(i)   *Proposal A*   *Proposal B*

$$\text{Payback period} = 2 + \left(\frac{15,000}{24,000} \times 1 \text{ year}\right) \qquad \text{Payback period} = 3 + \left(\frac{3,000}{25,000} \times 1 \text{ year}\right)$$

$$= 2.6 \text{ years} \qquad\qquad\qquad = 3.1 \text{ years}$$

(ii)   The return on capital employed (ROCE) is calculated using the accounting profits given in the question.

Proposal A	Average profit	= $(6,500 + 3,500 + 13,500 − 1,500)/4
		= $22,000/4 = $5,500
	ROCE	= $\dfrac{\$5,500}{\$46,000} \times 100\% = 12.0\%$

Proposal B	Average profit	= $(4,500 + 2,500 + 4,500 + 14,500)/4
		= $26,000/4 = $6,500
	ROCE	= $\dfrac{\$6,500}{\$46,000} \times 100\% = 14.1\%$

(b)   Two advantages of each of the methods of appraisal can be selected from the following.

Payback period

(i)   It is simple to calculate.
(ii)   It preserves liquidity by preferring early cash flows.
(iii)   It uses cash flows instead of more arbitrary accounting profits.
(iv)   It reduces risk by preferring early cash flows.

Return on capital employed

(i)   It uses readily available **accounting profits**.
(ii)   It is **understood** by **non-financial managers**.
(iii)   It is a measure used by **external analysts** which should be monitored by the company.

Now try these questions from the Exam Question Bank

Number	Level	Marks	Time
Q24	Examination	10	18 mins
Q25	Examination	10	18 mins

DCF TECHNIQUES OF INVESTMENT APPRAISAL

Having considered two relatively straightforward investment appraisal techniques in Chapter 15, we are now going to turn our attention to methods based on discounted cashflow (DCF) techniques.

You will have encountered discounting at an introductory level in your earlier studies but we go over the basics again to begin with.

Sections 1, 2 and 4 look at the calculations required when using the DCF techniques of net present value

(NPV), internal rate of return (IRR) and discounted payback. **Sections 3 and 5** cover issues that could be examined in discursive questions.

This chapter is where you learn the groundwork for more sophisticated analysis. This is therefore one of the **key chapters** in this Text.

In Chapters 17 and 18 we look at further aspects of investment appraisal, in particular sensitivity analysis and accounting for inflation and taxation.

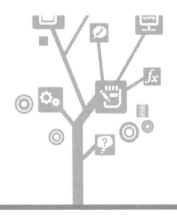

topic list	learning outcomes	syllabus references	ability required
1 The net present value method	C2(a), (b)	C1(iv), C2(i), (ii)	evaluation
2 The internal rate of return method	C2(a), (b)	C2(i), (ii)	evaluation
3 NPV and IRR compared	C2(b)	C2(ii)	analysis
4 Discounted payback	C2(a), (b)	C2(i), (ii)	evaluation
5 DCF: additional points	C1(b), (e)	C2(ii)	comprehension

1 The net present value method 5/11, 3/11, 11/10, 9/10, 5/10

1.1 Discounting

Introduction

Compounding means that, as interest is earned, it is added to the original investment and starts to earn interest itself. Discounting is the reverse of compounding. These concepts were covered in CIMA C3 Fundamentals of Business Maths, so should not be completely new to you.

Suppose that a company has $10,000 to invest, and wants to earn a return of 10% (compound interest) on its investments. This means that if the $10,000 could be invested at 10%, the value of the investment with interest would build up as follows.

(a) After 1 year $10,000 × (1.10) = $11,000
(b) After 2 years $10,000 × (1.10)^2 = $12,100
(c) After 3 years $10,000 × (1.10)^3 = $13,310

and so on.

This is **compounding**. The formula for the future value of an investment plus accumulated interest after n time periods is $V = X(1 + r)^n$

where V   is the future value of the investment with interest

X   is the initial or 'present' value of the investment

r   is the compound rate of return per time period, expressed as a proportion (so 10% = 0.10, 5% = 0.05 and so on)

n is the number of time periods.

Discounting starts with the future value (a sum of money receivable or payable at a future date), and converts the future value to a **present value**, which is the cash equivalent now of the future value.

For example, if a company expects to earn a (compound) rate of return of 10% on its investments, how much would it need to invest now to have the following investments?

(a) $11,000 after 1 year
(b) $12,100 after 2 years
(c) $13,310 after 3 years

The answer is $10,000 in each case, and we can calculate it by discounting.

The **discounting formula** to calculate the present value (X) of a future sum of money (V) at the end of n time periods is $X = V/(1+r)^n$.

(a) After 1 year, $11,000 × 1/1.10 = $10,000
(b) After 2 years, $12,100 × 1/1.10^2 = $10,000
(c) After 3 years, $13,310 × 1/1.10^3 = $10,000

KEY TERM

PRESENT VALUE is 'The cash equivalent now of a sum of money receivable or payable at a future date'.
(CIMA *Official Terminology*)

The **timing of cash flows is taken into account by discounting them**. The effect of discounting is to **give a bigger value per $1 for cash flows that occur earlier**: $1 earned after one year will be worth more than $1 earned after two years, which in turn will be worth more than $1 earned after five years, and so on.

Question 16.1

Present value calculation

Learning outcome C2(a)

Spender expects the cash inflow from an investment to be $40,000 after 2 years and another $30,000 after 3 years. Its target rate of return is 12%.

Required

Fill in the blank in the sentence below.

The present value of these future returns is $.................. .

Question 16.2

Meaning of present value

Learning outcome C2(a)

Look back at the detail of the question above and then fill in the gaps in the paragraph below.

The present value of the future returns, discounted at ......, is .... This means that if Spender can invest now to earn a return of .... on its investments, it would have to invest .... now to earn .... after 2 years plus .... after 3 years.

KEY TERMS

DISCOUNTED CASH FLOW is 'The discounting of the projected net cash flows of a capital project to ascertain its present value. The methods commonly used are:

- yield, or internal rate of return (IRR), in which the calculation determines the return in the form of a percentage;

- net present value (NPV), in which the discount rate is chosen and the present value is expressed as a sum of money;

- discounted payback, in which the discount rate is chosen, and the payback is the number of years required to repay the original investment.'

(CIMA *Official Terminology*)

We will be looking at these methods in the remainder of this chapter.

KEY POINT

DCF looks at the **cash flows** of a project, **not the accounting profits**. Like the payback technique of investment appraisal, DCF is concerned with liquidity, not profitability. Cash flows are considered because they show the costs and benefit of a project when they actually occur. For example, the capital cost of a project will be the original cash outlay, and not the notional cost of depreciation which is used to spread the capital cost over the asset's life in the financial accounts.

1.2 The net present value (NPV) method

KEY TERM

NET PRESENT VALUE (NPV) is 'The difference between the sum of the projected discounted cash inflows and outflows attributable to a capital investment or other long-term project'. (CIMA *Official Terminology*)

The NPV method therefore **compares the present value of all the cash inflows** from a project **with the present value of all the cash outflows** from a project. The **NPV** is thus calculated as the **PV of cash inflows minus the PV of cash outflows**.

(a) If the **NPV is positive**, it means that the present value of the cash inflows from a project is greater than the present value of the cash outflows. The **project should therefore be undertaken**.

(b) If the **NPV is negative**, it means that the present value of cash outflows is greater than the present value of inflows. The **project should therefore not be undertaken**.

(c)   If the **NPV is exactly zero**, the present value of cash inflows and cash outflows are equal and the **project will be only just worth undertaking**.

Example: NPV

Slogger has a cost of capital of 15% and is considering a capital investment project, where the estimated cash flows are as follows.

Year	Cash flow $
0 (ie now)	(100,000)
1	60,000
2	80,000
3	40,000
4	30,000

Required

Calculate the NPV of the project, and assess whether it should be undertaken.

Solution

Year	Cash flow $	Discount factor 15%	Present value $
0	(100,000)	1.000	(100,000)
1	60,000	$1/(1.15) = 0.870$	52,200
2	80,000	$1/1.15^2 = 0.756$	60,480
3	40,000	$1/1.15^3 = 0.658$	26,320
4	30,000	$1/1.15^4 = 0.572$	17,160
			NPV = 56,160

(*Note*. The **discount factor for any cash flow 'now' (time 0) is always 1**, whatever the cost of capital.)

The **PV of cash inflows exceeds the PV of cash outflows** by $56,160, which means that the project will earn a DCF yield in excess of 15%. It should therefore be **undertaken**.

1.3 Timing of cash flows: conventions used in DCF

Discounting reduces the value of future cash flows to a present value equivalent and so is clearly concerned with the timing of the cash flows. As a general rule, the following guidelines should be applied.

(a)   A cash outlay to be incurred at the beginning of an investment project ('now') occurs in time 0. The present value of $1 now, in time 0, is $1 regardless of the value of the discount rate r. This is common sense. (Note that it is usual to assume that Year 0 is a day, ie the first day of a project. Year 1 is the last day of the first year.)

(b)   A cash flow which occurs during the course of a time period is assumed to occur all at once at the end of the time period (at the end of the year). Receipts of $10,000 during time period 1 are therefore taken to occur at the end of time period 1.

(c)   A cash flow which occurs at the beginning of a time period is taken to occur at the end of the previous time period. Therefore a cash outlay of $5,000 at the beginning of time period 2 is taken to occur at the end of time period 1.

1.4 Discount tables for the PV of $1

The discount factor that we use in discounting is $1/(1+r)^n = (1+r)^{-n}$. Instead of having to calculate this factor every time we can use **tables**. Discount tables for the present value of $1, for different **integer** values of r and n, are **shown in the Appendix at the back of this Study Text** and **will be provided in the exam**. Use these tables to work out your own solution to the following question.

Question 16.3	NPV

Learning outcome C2(a)

LCH manufactures product X which it sells for $5 per unit. Variable costs of production are currently $3 per unit, and fixed costs 50c per unit. A new machine is available which would cost $90,000 but which could be used to make product X for a variable cost of only $2.50 per unit. Fixed costs, however, would increase by $7,500 per annum as a direct result of purchasing the machine. The machine would have an expected life of four years and a resale value after that time of $10,000. Sales of product X are estimated to be 75,000 units per annum. LCH expects to earn at least 12% per annum from its investments.

Required

Choose the appropriate words in the sentence below from those highlighted.

LCH **should purchase/should not purchase** the machine.

Exam alert

Discount tables are provided in the exam, but they cover only integer values of r. If you need to use a discount rate of, say, 10.5%, you would need to use the discounting formula.

1.5 Annuities

KEY TERM

An ANNUITY is a constant cash flow from year to year.

In the previous exercise, the calculations could have been simplified for years 1–3 as follows.

$$30,000 \times 0.893$$
$$+ \quad 30,000 \times 0.797$$
$$+ \quad 30,000 \times 0.712$$
$$= \quad 30,000 \times 2.402$$

Where there is a **constant cash flow from year to year** (in this case $30,000 per annum for years 1–3) it is quicker to calculate the present value by adding together the discount factors for the individual years. These total factors could be described as 'same cash flow per annum' factors, **'cumulative present value' factors** or **'annuity' factors**. They are **shown in the table for cumulative PV of $1 factors which is shown in the Appendix at the back of this Study Text** (2.402, for example, is in the column for 12% per annum and the row for year 3). If you have not used them before, check that you can understand annuity tables by trying this question.

Question 16.4

Learning outcome C2(a)

What is the present value of $2,000 costs incurred each year from years 3–6 when the cost of capital is 5%?

A $6,300
B $6,434
C $6,000
D $4,706

Exam alert

As well as incorporating the use of annuity tables, the example which follows includes **working capital requirements**. Take note of how this is dealt with as such a feature could well be a complicating factor in an exam question.

Example: NPV including use of annuity tables

Elsie is considering the manufacture of a new product which would involve the use of both a new machine (costing $150,000) and an existing machine, which cost $80,000 two years ago and has a current net book value of $60,000. There is sufficient capacity on this machine, which has so far been under-utilised. Annual sales of the product would be 5,000 units, selling at $32 per unit. Unit costs would be as follows.

	$
Direct labour (4 hours at $2 per hour)	8
Direct materials	7
Fixed costs including depreciation	9
	24

The project would have a five-year life, after which the new machine would have a net residual value of $10,000. Because direct labour is continually in short supply, labour resources would have to be diverted from other work which currently earns a contribution of $1.50 per direct labour hour. The fixed overhead absorption rate would be $2.25 per hour ($9 per unit) but actual expenditure on fixed overhead would not alter. Working capital requirements would be $10,000 in the first year, rising to $15,000 in the second year and remaining at this level until the end of the project, when it will all be recovered.

Required

Assess whether the project is worthwhile, given that the company's cost of capital is 20%. Ignore taxation.

Solution

The relevant cash flows are as follows.

Year 0	Purchase of new machine	$150,000

		$
Years 1–5	Contribution from new product (5,000 units × $(32 − 15))	85,000
	Less contribution forgone (5,000 × (4 × $1.50))	30,000
		55,000

The project requires $10,000 of working capital at the start of year 1 and a further $5,000 at the start of year 2. Increases in working capital reduce the net cash flow for the period to which they relate. When the working capital tied up in the project is 'recovered' at the end of the project, it will provide an extra cash inflow (for example customers will eventually pay up).

All other costs, which are past costs, notional accounting costs or costs which would be incurred anyway without the project, are not relevant to the investment decision.

The NPV is calculated as follows.

Year	Equipment $	Working capital $	Contribution $	Net cash flow $	Discount factor 20%	PV of net cash flow $
0	(150,000)	(10,000)		(160,000)	1.000	(160,000)
1		(5,000)		(5,000)	0.833	(4,165)
1–5			55,000	55,000	2.991	164,505
5	10,000	15,000		25,000	0.402	10,050
					NPV =	10,390

The NPV is positive and the project is worthwhile, although there is not much margin for error. Some risk analysis of the project is recommended.

1.6 Annual cash flows in perpetuity

KEY TERM

A PERPETUITY is an annuity that lasts forever.

It can sometimes be useful to calculate the **cumulative present value of $1 per annum** for every year in perpetuity (that is, **forever**).

When the cost of capital is r, the cumulative PV of $1 per annum in perpetuity is **$1/r**. For example, the PV of $1 per annum in perpetuity at a discount rate of 10% would be $1/0.10 = $10.

Similarly, the PV of $1 per annum in perpetuity at a discount rate of 15% would be $1/0.15 = $6.67 and at a discount rate of 20% it would be $1/0.20 = $5.

Question 16.5	Perpetuities

Learning outcome C2(a)

An organisation with a cost of capital of 14% is considering investing in a project costing $500,000 that would yield cash inflows of $100,000 pa in perpetuity.

Required

Choose the appropriate words from those highlighted in the sentence below.

The project **should be/should not be** undertaken.

You might well wonder what is the use of cash flows in perpetuity. This surely is an impractical and nonsensical notion? **Cash flows in perpetuity** do actually have **two practical uses**.

(a)   They are used in the calculation of a company's cost of capital.

(b)   They indicate the maximum value of the cumulative present value factor of $1 per annum. For example, we can say that the maximum present value of $1 pa for any period of time at a discount rate of 10% is $1/0.1 = $10. The longer the period of time under review, and the more years that are in the project period, the closer the cumulative PV factor of $1 pa will get to $10 at a 10% discount rate.

(i)   The PV factor of $1 pa at 10% for years 1 to 15 is $7.606

(ii)   The PV factor of $1 pa at 10% for years 1 to 20 is $8.514

(iii)   The PV factor of $1 pa at 10% for years 1 to 30 is $9.427

(iv)   The PV factor of $1 pa at 10% for years 1 to 50 is $9.915

As you can see, the cumulative PV gets closer to the limit of $10 as time progresses and the limit has almost been reached by year 50, and even by year 30. Knowing what the limit is might help with project analysis when capital projects extend over a long period of time and certainly it can provide a very useful yardstick and 'ready-reckoner' for managers who must carry out DCF evaluations as a regular part of their job.

In the next chapter we will see a practical example of the application of the present value of an annuity.

1.7 Net terminal value

KEY TERM

NET TERMINAL VALUE (NTV) is the cash surplus remaining at the end of a project after taking account of interest and capital repayments.

The NTV discounted at the cost of capital will give the NPV of the project.

Example: the net terminal value

A project has the following cash flows.

Year	$
0	(5,000)
1	3,000
2	2,600
3	6,200

The project has an NPV of $4,531 at the company's cost of capital of 10% (workings not shown).

Required

Calculate the net terminal value of the project.

Solution

The net terminal value can be determined directly from the NPV, or by calculating the cash surplus at the end of the project.

Assume that the $5,000 for the project is borrowed at an interest rate of 10% and that cash flows from the project are used to repay the loan.

	$
Loan balance outstanding at beginning of project	5,000
Interest in year 1 at 10%	500
Repaid at end of year 1	(3,000)
Balance outstanding at end of year 1	2,500
Interest year 2	250
Repaid year 2	(2,600)
Balance outstanding year 2	150
Interest year 3	15
Repaid year 3	(6,200)
Cash surplus at end of project	6,035

The net terminal value is $6,035.

Check

NPV = $6,035 × 0.751 (discount factor for year 3) = $4,532

Allowing for the rounding errors caused by three-figure discount tables, this is the correct figure for the NPV.

1.8 Assumptions in the NPV model

(a)   Forecasts are assumed to be certain.

(b)   Information is assumed to be freely available and costless.

(c)   The discount rate is a measure of the opportunity cost of funds which ensures wealth maximisation for *all* individuals and companies.

Exam alert

The specimen exam paper required a net present value calculation and a report explaining the strengths and weaknesses of the method.

Question 16.6	Non-standard discount factors

Learning outcome C2(a)

A project has the following forecast cash flows.

Year	$
0	(280,000)
1	149,000
2	128,000
3	84,000
4	70,000

Using two decimal places in all discount factors, what is the net present value of the project at a cost of capital of 16.5%?

A $27,906   B $29,270   C $32,195   D $33,580

Section summary

Discounting starts with the future value (a sum of money receivable or payable at a future date), and converts the future value to a **present value**, which is the cash equivalent now of the future value.

The **discounting formula** to calculate the present value (X) of a future sum of money (V) at the end of n time periods is $X = V/(1+r)^n$.

The **NPV method of project appraisal** is to accept projects with a positive NPV.

An **annuity** is a constant cash flow for a number of years.

A **perpetuity** is a constant cash flow forever.

2 The internal rate of return method   5/11, 3/11, 11/10, 9/10

Introduction

The IRR method of project appraisal is to calculate the exact DCF rate of return which the project is expected to achieve, in other words the rate at which the NPV is zero.

If the expected rate of return (the IRR yield or DCF yield) exceeds a target rate of return, the project would be worth undertaking (ignoring risk and uncertainty factors).

The INTERNAL RATE OF RETURN (IRR) is 'The annual percentage return achieved by a project, at which the sum of the discounted cash inflows over the life of the project is equal to the sum of the discounted cash outflows'.   (CIMA *Official Terminology*)

Without a computer or calculator program, an estimate of the internal rate of return is made using either a graph or using a hit-and-miss technique known as the interpolation method.

2.1 Graphical approach

The easiest way to estimate the IRR of a project is to **find the project's NPV at a number of costs of capital** and **sketch a graph of NPV against discount rate**. You can then use the sketch to estimate the **discount rate at which the NPV is equal to zero (the point where the curve cuts the axis)**.

Example: graphical approach

A project might have the following NPVs at the following discount rates.

Discount rate	NPV
%	$
5	5,300
10	2,900
15	(1,700)
20	(3,200)

This could be sketched on a graph as follows.

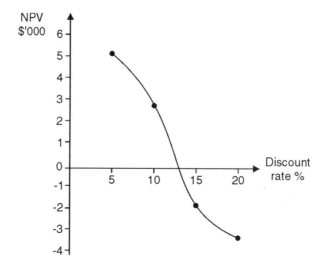

The IRR can be **estimated as 13%.** The NPV should then be **recalculated using this interest rate**. The resulting NPV **should be equal to, or very near, zero. If it is not, additional NPVs at different discount rates should be calculated, the graph resketched and a more accurate IRR determined**.

2.2 Interpolation method

If we were to draw a graph of a 'typical' capital project, with a negative cash flow at the start of the project, and positive net cash flows afterwards up to the end of the project, we could draw a graph of the project's NPV at different costs of capital. It would look like this.

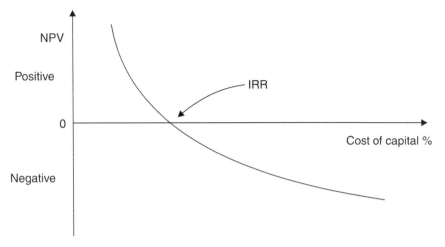

If we determine **a cost of capital where the NPV is slightly positive, and another cost of capital where it is slightly negative**, we can **estimate the IRR – where the NPV is zero – by drawing a straight line between the two points** on the graph that we have calculated.

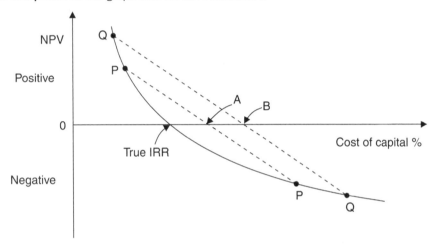

- If we **establish the NPVs at the two points P**, we would estimate the **IRR** to be at **point A**.
- If we **establish the NPVs at the two points Q**, we would estimate the **IRR** to be at **point B**.

The **closer our NPVs are to zero, the closer our estimate will be to the true IRR**.

The **interpolation method assumes that the NPV rises in linear fashion between the two NPVs close to 0**. The real rate of return is therefore assumed to be on a straight line between the two points at which the NPV is calculated.

LEARN

The **IRR interpolation formula** to apply is:

$$IRR = A + \left[\frac{P}{P-N} \times (B-A) \right]\%$$

where A is the (lower) rate of return

B is the (higher) rate of return

P is the NPV at A

N is the NPV at B

Note that N doesn't have to be negative but if it is then we effectively end up adding, in the denominator.

Example: the IRR method and interpolation

A company is trying to decide whether to buy a machine for $80,000 which will save costs of $20,000 per annum for 5 years and which will have a resale value of $10,000 at the end of year 5.

Required

If it is the company's policy to undertake projects only if they are expected to yield a DCF return of 10% or more, ascertain using the IRR method whether this project should be undertaken.

Solution

The first step is to calculate two net present values, both as close as possible to zero, using rates for the cost of capital which are whole numbers. One NPV should be positive and the other negative.

Choosing rates for the cost of capital which will give an NPV close to zero (that is, rates which are close to the actual rate of return) is a hit-and-miss exercise, and several attempts may be needed to find satisfactory rates. **As a rough guide**, try starting at a **return figure which is about two thirds or three quarters of the ARR**.

Annual depreciation would be $(80,000 − 10,000)/5 = $14,000.

The **ARR** would be (20,000 − depreciation of 14,000)/(½ of (80,000 + 10,000)) = 6,000/45,000 = 13.3%

Two thirds of this is 8.9% and so we can start by trying 9%.

Try 9%.	Year	Cash flow	PV factor	PV of cash flow
		$	9%	$
	0	(80,000)	1.000	(80,000)
	1–5	20,000	3.890	77,800
	5	10,000	0.650	6,500
			NPV =	4,300

This is **fairly close to zero**. It is also **positive**, which means that the **real rate of return** is **more than 9%**. We can use 9% as one of our two NPVs close to zero, although for greater accuracy, we should try 10% or even 11% to find an NPV even closer to zero if we can. As a guess, it might be worth trying 12% next, to see what the NPV is.

Try 12%.	Year	Cash flow	PV factor	PV of cash flow
		$	12%	$
	0	(80,000)	1.000	(80,000)
	1–5	20,000	3.605	72,100
	5	10,000	0.567	5,670
			NPV =	(2,230)

This is **fairly close to zero** and **negative**. The **real rate of return** is therefore **greater than 9%** (positive NPV of $4,300) but **less than 12%** (negative NPV of $2,230).

Note. **If the first NPV is positive, choose a higher rate for the next calculation to get a negative NPV. If the first NPV is negative, choose a lower rate for the next calculation.**

So, IRR $= 9 + \left[\dfrac{4,300}{4,300 + 2,230} \times (12 - 9) \right]\% = 10.98\%$, say 11%

If it is company policy to undertake investments which are expected to yield 10% or more, this project would be undertaken.

| **Question 16.7** | IRR |

Learning outcome C2(a)

The project shown below should be accepted if the company requires a minimum return of 17%. *True or false?*

Time		$
0	Investment	(4,000)
1	Receipts	1,200
2	Receipts	1,410
3	Receipts	1,875
4	Receipts	1,150

2.3 The IRR of an annuity

Suppose an investment now of $100,000 will produce inflows of $30,000 each year over the next four years. We know that the IRR is the discount rate which produces an NPV of zero. **At the IRR (rate r) the PV of inflows must therefore equal the PV of outflows**.

∴ $100,000 = PV of $30,000 for years 1 to 4 at rate r
∴ $100,000 = (cumulative PV factor for years 1 to 4 at rate r) × $30,000
∴ $100,000/$30,000 = cumulative PV factor for years 1 to 4 at rate r
∴ 3.333 = cumulative PV factor for years 1 to 4 at rate r

We can now **look in cumulative PV tables along the line for year 4 to find a discount factor which corresponds to 3.333. The corresponding rate is the IRR.** The nearest figure is 3.312 and so the IRR of the project is approximately 8%.

2.4 The IRR of a perpetuity

Suppose an investment of $25,000 will produce annual cash flows in perpetuity of $2,000. Using the **same reasoning** as in Section 2.3:

$25,000 = PV of $2,000 in perpetuity

∴ $25,000 = $2,000/r (where r = IRR)

∴ $r = \dfrac{\$2,000}{\$25,000} = 0.08 = 8\%$

| **Question 16.8** | NPV and IRR |

Learning outcome C2(a)

The VWXYZ Company produces a variety of high-quality garden furniture and associated items, mostly in wood and wrought iron.

There is potential to expand the business. The directors have identified three main options for a four-year plan.

(a)   Expand its flourishing retail outlet to include all products.
(b)   Branch out into mail order.
(c)   Produce greenhouses and conservatories.

These options would require initial expenditure of (a) $75,000, (b) $120,000 or (c) $200,000. The best information on year-end cash flows is as follows.

	Year 1 $'000	Year 2 $'000	Year 3 $'000	Year 4 $'000
(a)	40	50	50	50
(b)	50	60	80	100
(c)	50	100	150	150

Required

(a)   Using the data on expansion plans, evaluate the three investment options using the net present value (NPV) technique, assuming the cost of capital to be 10%, and recommend, with reasons, one option.

(b)   Find the approximate internal rate of return (IRR) of your choice in (a) above.

Section summary

The **IRR method of project appraisal** is to accept projects which have an IRR (the rate at which the NPV is zero) that exceeds a target rate of return. The IRR can be estimated either from a graph or using interpolation.

The IRR interpolation formula to apply is:

$$IRR = A + \left[\frac{P}{P-N} \times (B-A) \right]\%$$

where A is the (lower) rate of return
       B is the (higher) rate of return
       P is the NPV at A
       N is the NPV at B

---

3 NPV and IRR compared

Introduction

Unfortunately there are several disadvantages as well as advantages to the IRR method. Managers should always bear these in mind.

3.1 Advantages of IRR method

(a)   The main advantage is that the information it provides is more **easily understood** by managers, especially non-financial managers. 'The project will be expected to have an initial capital outlay of $100,000, and to earn a yield of 25%. This is in excess of the target yield of 15% for investments' is easier to understand than 'The project will cost $100,000 and have an NPV of $30,000 when discounted at the minimum required rate of 15%'.

(b)   A **discount rate does not have to be specified** before the IRR can be calculated. A hurdle discount rate is simply required to which the IRR can be compared.

3.2 Disadvantages of IRR method

(a) If managers were given information about both **ROCE (or ROI) and IRR**, it might be easy to get their relative **meaning and significance mixed up**.

(b) It **ignores the relative size of investments**. Both projects below have an IRR of 18%.

	Project A $	Project B $
Cost, year 0	350,000	35,000
Annual savings, years 1–6	100,000	10,000

Clearly, project A is bigger (ten times as big) and so more 'profitable' but if the only information on which the projects were judged were to be their IRR of 18%, project B would be made to seem just as beneficial as project A, which is not the case.

(c) **When discount rates are expected to differ over the life of the project, such variations can be incorporated easily into NPV calculations, but not into IRR calculations**. And an **adjustment** can be made to the **discount rate** used in NPV calculations to include an allowance for project **risk**.

(d) There are **problems** with using the IRR **when the project has non-conventional cash flows** (see Section 3.3) or when **deciding between mutually exclusive projects** (see Section 3.4).

'In spite of all the efforts to convince managers that the net present value (NPV) is the 'correct' method of investment appraisal to use, recent research shows that they continue to prefer the internal rate of return (IRR). And, although a number of modified versions of the IRR have been developed, they too have been condemned by some academics even though such modifications are an improvement on the conventional IRR. No single investment appraisal technique will give the right answer in all investment situations, however, and the NPV is no exception. This is reflected again in recent research which shows that companies now use a greater number of financial appraisal techniques than in the past, but with no consensus on the actual combination. This increase in usage has been attributed to the increase in computer software that is now readily available to perform the basic calculations of the various financial appraisal techniques such as payback (PB), accounting rate of return (ARR), IRR, and NPV.'

'The NPV profile – a creative way of looking at the NPV', Frank Lefley and Malcolm Morgan, *Management Accounting,* June 1999

3.3 Non-conventional cash flows

The projects we have considered so far have had **conventional cash flows (an initial cash outflow followed by a series of inflows)** and in such circumstances the NPV and IRR methods give the same accept or reject decision. When flows vary from this they are termed non-conventional. The following project has non-conventional cash flows.

Year	Project X $'000
0	(1,900)
1	4,590
2	(2,735)

Project X above has two IRRs as shown by the diagram which follows.

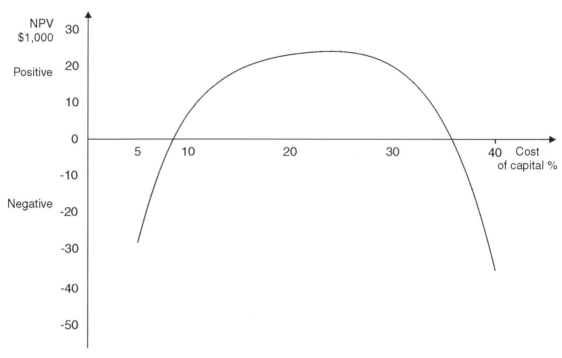

Suppose that the required rate of return on project X is 10% but that the IRR of 7% is used to decide whether to accept or reject the project. The project would be rejected since it appears that it can only yield 7%. The diagram shows, however, that **between rates of 7% and 35% the project should be accepted**. Using the IRR of 35% would produce the correct decision to accept the project. **Lack of knowledge of multiple IRRs** could therefore lead to serious **errors in the decision** of whether to accept or reject a project.

In general, if the sign of the net cash flow changes in successive periods (inflow to outflow or vice versa), it is possible for the calculations to produce **as many IRRs as there are sign changes**.

The use of the **IRR** is therefore **not recommended** in circumstances in which there are **non-conventional cash flow patterns** (unless the decision maker is aware of the existence of multiple IRRs). The NPV method, on the other hand, gives clear, unambiguous results whatever the cash flow pattern.

3.4 Mutually exclusive projects

The IRR and NPV methods give conflicting rankings as to which project should be given priority. Let us suppose that a company with a cost of capital of 16% is considering two mutually exclusive options, option A and option B. The cash flows for each are as follows.

Year		Option A $	Option B $
0	Capital outlay	(10,200)	(35,250)
1	Net cash inflow	6,000	18,000
2	Net cash inflow	5,000	15,000
3	Net cash inflow	3,000	15,000

The NPV of each project is calculated below.

Year	Discount factor	Option A		Option B	
		Cash flow $	Present value $	Cash flow $	Present value $
0	1.000	(10,200)	(10,200)	(35,250)	(35,250)
1	0.862	6,000	5,172	18,000	15,516
2	0.743	5,000	3,715	15,000	11,145
3	0.641	3,000	1,923	15,000	9,615
		NPV =	+ 610	NPV = +	1,026

The **DCF yield (IRR) of option A is 20%, while the yield of option B is only 18%** (workings not shown.)

On a **comparison of NPVs, option B would be preferred**, but on a **comparison of IRRs, option A would be preferred**.

The preference should go to option B. This is because the **differences in the cash flows** between the two options, when discounted at the cost of capital of 16%, show that the present value of the incremental benefits from option B compared with option A exceeds the PV of the incremental costs. This can be re-stated in the following ways.

(a)   The **NPV of the differential cash flows (option B cash flows minus option A cash flows) is positive**, and so it is worth spending the extra capital to get the extra benefits.

(b)   The **IRR of the differential cash flows exceeds the cost of capital 16%,** and so it is worth spending the extra capital to get the extra benefits.

Year	Option A cash flow $	Option B cash flow $	Difference $	Discount factor 16%	Present value of difference $
0	(10,200)	(35,250)	(25,050)	1.000	(25,050)
1	6,000	18,000	12,000	0.862	10,344
2	5,000	15,000	10,000	0.743	7,430
3	3,000	15,000	12,000	0.641	7,692
				NPV of difference	416

The **NPV of the difference**, not surprisingly, **is also the difference between the NPV of option A ($610) and the NPV of option B ($1,026).**

The **IRR of the differential cash flows** (workings not shown) **is approximately 18%.**

It must be stressed that the investment represented by (B − A) is a notional one, but the inflows from this notional project would be enjoyed by the company if project B were accepted and would be lost if project A were accepted.

Mutually exclusive investments do not have to be considered over equal time periods. For example, suppose an organisation has two investment options, one lasting two years and one lasting four years. The two options can be compared and the one with the highest NPV chosen. If, however, the investment is an asset which is required for four years, the organisation will have to re-invest if it chooses the two-year option. In such circumstances the investment options should be compared over a similar period of time. We will be looking at how to do this in the next chapter.

3.5 Reinvestment assumption

An assumption underlying the **NPV method** is that any net cash **inflows generated** during the life of the project will be **reinvested** elsewhere **at the cost of capital** (that is, the discount rate). The **IRR method**, on the other hand, **assumes** these **cash flows** can be **reinvested** elsewhere to earn a **return** equal to the **IRR** of the original project.

In the example in Paragraph 3.4, the **NPV method** assumes that the cash inflows of $6,000, $5,000 and $3,000 for option A will be reinvested at the cost of capital of **16%** whereas the **IRR** method assumes they will be reinvested at **20%**. If the IRR is considerably higher than the cost of capital this is an unlikely assumption. In theory, a firm will have accepted all projects which provide a return in excess of the cost of capital and any other funds which become available can only be reinvested at the cost of capital. (This is the assumption implied in the NPV rule.) If the assumption is not valid the IRR method overestimates the real return.

3.6 Modified internal rate of return (MIRR)

The MIRR overcomes the problem of the **reinvestment assumption** and the fact that **changes in the cost of capital over the life of the project** cannot be incorporated in the IRR method.

Consider a project requiring an initial investment of $24,500, with cash inflows of $15,000 in years 1 and 2 and cash inflows of $3,000 in years 3 and 4. The cost of capital is 10%.

If we calculate the IRR:

Year	Cash flow	Discount factor	Present value	Discount factor	Present value
	$	10%	$	25%	$
0	(24,500)	1.000	(24,500)	1.000	(24,500)
1	15,000	0.909	13,635	0.800	12,000
2	15,000	0.826	12,390	0.640	9,600
3	3,000	0.751	2,253	0.512	1,536
4	3,000	0.683	2,049	0.410	1,230
			5,827		(134)

$$\text{IRR} = 10\% + \left[\frac{5,827}{5,827 + 134} \times (25\% - 10\%)\right] = 24.7\%$$

Remember that the MIRR is calculated on the basis of **investing the inflows** at the **cost of capital**.

The table below shows the **values of the inflows if they were immediately reinvested at 10%**. For example the $15,000 received at the end of year 1 could be reinvested for three years at 10% pa (multiply by $1.1 \times 1.1 \times 1.1 = 1.331$).

Year	Cash inflows	Interest rate multiplier	Amount when reinvested
	$		$
1	15,000	1.331	19,965
2	15,000	1.21	18,150
3	3,000	1.1	3,300
4	3,000	1.0	3,000
			44,415

The total cash outflow in year 0 ($24,500) is compared with the possible inflow at year 4, and the resulting figure of $24,500/44,415 = 0.552$ is the discount factor in year 4. By looking along the year 4 row in present value tables you will see that this gives a return of 16%. This means that the $44,415 received in year 4 is equivalent to $24,500 in year 0 if the discount rate is 16%.

Alternatively, instead of using discount tables, we can calculate the MIRR as follows.

$$\text{Total return} = \frac{44,415}{24,500} = 1.813$$

$$\text{MIRR} = \sqrt[4]{1.813} - 1$$

$$= 1.16 - 1$$

$$= 16\%$$

In theory the MIRR of 16% will be a **better measure** than the IRR of 24.7%.

3.6.1 Advantages of MIRR

MIRR has the advantage of IRR that it assumes the **reinvestment rate** is the **company's cost of capital**. IRR assumes that the reinvestment rate is the IRR itself, which is usually untrue.

In many cases where there is conflict between the NPV and IRR methods, the MIRR will give the same indication as NPV, which is the **correct theoretical method**. This helps when explaining the appraisal of a project to managers, who often find the concept of rate of return easier to understand than that of net present value.

3.6.2 Disadvantages of MIRR

However, MIRR, like all rate of return methods, suffers from the problem that it may lead an investor to reject a project which has a **lower rate of return** but, because of its size, generates a **larger increase in wealth**.

In the same way, a **high-return** project with a **short life** may be preferred over a **lower-return** project with a longer life.

Section summary

When compared with the NPV method, the **IRR method** has a number of **disadvantages**.

- It ignores the relative size of investments.
- There are problems with its use when a project has non-conventional cashflows or when deciding between mutually exclusive projects.
- Discount rates which differ over the life of a project cannot be incorporated into IRR calculations.

The MIRR is calculated on the basis of investing the inflows at the cost of capital.

4 Discounted payback

5/11

Introduction

Payback can be combined with DCF and a **discounted payback period** calculated.

KEY TERM

The DISCOUNTED PAYBACK PERIOD (DPP) is the time it will take before a project's cumulative NPV turns from being negative to being positive.

For example if we have a cost of capital of 10% and a project with the cash flows shown below, we can calculate a discounted payback period.

Year	Cash flow $	Discount factor 10%	Present value $	Cumulative NPV $
0	(100,000)	1.000	(100,000)	(100,000)
1	30,000	0.909	27,270	(72,730)
2	50,000	0.826	41,300	(31,430)
3	40,000	0.751	30,040	(1,390)
4	30,000	0.683	20,490	19,100
5	20,000	0.621	12,420	31,520
		NPV =	31,520	

The DPP is early in year 4.

A company can set a target DPP, and choose not to undertake any projects with a DPP in excess of a certain number of years, say five years.

4.1 Advantages and disadvantages of discounted payback period

The approach has **all the perceived advantages of the payback period** method of investment appraisal: it is easy to understand and calculate, and it provides a focus on liquidity where this is relevant. In addition, however, it **also takes into account the time value of money**. It therefore bridges the gap between the theoretically superior NPV method and the regular payback period method.

However, it does differ from NPV in that the discount rate used is the **unadjusted cost of capital** whereas NPV often uses an **adjusted rate to reflect project risk and uncertainty**.

Because the DPP approach takes the time value of money into consideration, it **produces a longer payback period** than the non-discounted payback approach, and **takes into account more of the project's cash flows**.

Another advantage it has over traditional payback is that it has a **clear accept-or-reject criterion**. Using payback, acceptance of a project depends on an arbitrarily determined cut-off time. Using DPP, a project is acceptable if it pays back within its lifetime.

DPP still shares one disadvantage with the payback period method: **cashflows which occur after the payback period are ignored** (although as the DPP is longer than the payback period, fewer of these are ignored).

4.2 Discounted payback index (DPBI) or profitability index

This is a measure of the number of times a project recovers the initial funds invested, something that is particularly important if funds are scarce.

$$DPBI = \frac{\text{Present value of net cash inflows}}{\text{Initial cash outlay}}$$

The higher the figure, the greater the returns. A DPBI less than 1 indicates that the present value of the net cash inflows is less than the initial cash outlay.

Alternatively the index might be shown as:

$$\frac{\text{PV of project}}{\text{Initial outlay}}$$

This form of the index is known as the **profitability index** and shows the NPV per $1 invested in a project. As we will see in a later chapter, it is particularly useful if investment funds are limited and choices have to be made between different investment options.

4.3 NPV profile

It has been suggested that instead of just relying on the NPV as an absolute figure, a **wider profile** of the capital investment should be provided. This profile should include not only the **NPV**, but **DPB**, **DPBI** and a **marginal growth rate (MGR)**. (The MGR is a measure of the project's rate of net profitability.) This enables management to take into consideration any liquidity restrictions that an organisation may have and allows them to be more flexible in their general approach to capital investment appraisal as they can place different emphasis on different parts of the profile to suit particular situations.

Section summary

The **discounted payback period (DPP)** is the time it will take before a project's cumulative NPV turns from being negative to being positive.

$$\text{Discounted payback index} = \frac{\text{Present value of net cash inflows}}{\text{Initial cash outlay}}$$

5 DCF: additional points

Introduction

One of the principal advantages of the DCF appraisal method is that it takes account of the **time value of money**.

5.1 The time value of money

DCF is a project appraisal technique that is based on the concept of the time value of money, that $1 earned or spent sooner is worth more than $1 earned or spent later. Various reasons could be suggested as to **why a present $1 is worth more than a future $1**.

(a) **Uncertainty.** The business world is full of risk and uncertainty, and although there might be the promise of money to come in the future, it can never be certain that the money will be received until it has actually been paid. This is an important argument, and risk and uncertainty must always be considered in investment appraisal. But this argument does not explain why the discounted cash flow technique should be used to reflect the time value of money.

(b) **Inflation.** Because of inflation it is common sense that $1 now is worth more than $1 in the future. It is important, however, that the problem of inflation should not be confused with the meaning of DCF, and the following points should be noted.

    (i)   If there were no inflation at all, discounted cash flow techniques would still be used for investment appraisal.

    (ii) Inflation, for the moment, has been completely ignored.

    (iii) It is obviously necessary to allow for inflation.

(c) **An individual attaches more weight to current pleasures than to future ones, and would rather have $1 to spend now than $1 in a year's time**. Individuals have the choice of consuming or investing their wealth and so the return from projects must be sufficient to persuade individuals to prefer to invest now. Discounting is a measure of this time preference.

(d) Money is invested now to make profits (more money or wealth) in the future. **Discounted cash flow techniques** can therefore be used to **measure** either of two things.

    (i)   **What alternative uses of the money would earn (NPV method)** (assuming that money can be invested elsewhere at the cost of capital)

    (ii) **What the money is expected to earn (IRR method)**

5.2 Advantages of DCF methods of appraisal

Taking account of the time value of money (by discounting) is one of the principal advantages of the DCF appraisal method. Other advantages include:

(a) The method uses all cash flows relating to the project.
(b) It allows for the timing of the cash flows.
(c) There are universally accepted methods of calculating the NPV and IRR.

5.3 A comparison of the ARR and NPV methods

Managers are often judged on the return on investment (ROI) of their division or business unit. They will only want to **invest in projects that increase divisional ROI** but on occasion such a strategy **may not correspond** with the **decision** that would be arrived at if **NPV** were used to appraise the investment.

For example, suppose that Division M is considering an investment of $200,000 which will provide a net cash inflow (before depreciation) of $78,000 each year for the four years of its life. It is group policy that investments must show a minimum return of 15%.

As the working below shows, using net book value at the start of each year and depreciating on a straight line basis to a nil residual value, in year 1 the ROI would be below the target rate of return of 15%. If management were to take a **short-term view** of the situation, the **investment would be rejected if** using the **ROI** measure. This is despite the fact that the investment's **NPV is positive** and that in **years 2 to 4** the **ROI** is **greater** than the **target** rate of return.

	Years			
	1	2	3	4
	$	$	$	$
NBV of investment at start of year	200,000	150,000	100,000	50,000
Cash flow (before depreciation)	78,000	78,000	78,000	78,000
Less depreciation	(50,000)	(50,000)	(50,000)	(50,000)
Net profit	28,000	28,000	28,000	28,000
ROI	14.00%	18.67%	28.00%	56.00%

Net present value = –$200,000 + ($78,000 × 2.855) = $22,690.

5.4 Future cash flows: relevant costs

KEY POINT

The **cash flows to be considered** in investment appraisal are those which arise as a consequence of the investment decision under evaluation. When comparing two decision options, they are the expected future cash flows that differ between the alternatives.

It therefore follows that any costs incurred **in the past**, or any **committed costs** which will be **incurred regardless** of whether or not an investment is undertaken, are **not relevant cash flows**. They have occurred, or will occur, whatever investment decision is taken.

To a management accountant, it might be apparent that the annual profits from a project can be calculated as the **incremental contribution earned minus any incremental fixed costs** which are cash items of expenditure (that is, ignoring depreciation and so on).

There are, however, other cash flows to consider. These might include the following.

(a) The extra **taxation** that will be payable on extra profits, or the reductions in tax arising from capital allowances or operating losses in any year. We cover this topic in a later chapter.

(b) The **residual value or disposal value of equipment at the end of its life, or its disposal cost.**

(c) **Working capital.** If a company invests $20,000 in working capital and earns cash profits of $50,000, the net cash receipts will be $30,000. Working capital will be released again at the end of a project's life, and so there will be a cash inflow arising out of the eventual realisation into cash of the project's inventory and receivables in the final year of the project.

Finance-related cash flows, on the other hand, are normally **excluded** from DCF project appraisal exercises because the discounting process takes account of the time value of money, that is the opportunity cost of investing the money in the project. The cash inflow from, say, a loan could be included but then the cash outflows of the interest payments and the loan repayment would also have to be included. These flows would all be discounted at the cost of capital (which we assume is the same as the cost of the loan) and they would reduce to a zero net present value. They would therefore have had no **effect on the NPV** and are thus deemed **irrelevant** to the appraisal.

Finance-related cash flows are **only relevant if they incur a different rate of interest from that which is being used as the discount rate**. For example, a company may be offered a loan at a preferential rate below that which it uses for its discount rate and so the inclusion and discounting of the loan's cash flows produces a differential NPV.

5.5 The discount rate

Throughout our study of DCF techniques we have been using the same discount rate across all years of the project under consideration, on the assumption that the cost of capital will remain the same over the life of the project. There are a range of factors that influence the cost of capital, however, including inflation and interest rates, and these can fluctuate widely over fairly short periods of time. An organisation may therefore wish to **use different discount rates at different points over the life of a project** to reflect this. This is **possible if NPV and discounted payback methods of appraisal are being used**, but IRR and ARR methods are based on a single rate.

Another problem is **deciding on the correct rate in the first place**. This is difficult enough in year one of a project's life, but even more problematic five years later, say, because of economic changes and so on.

Section summary

One of the principal advantages of the DCF appraisal method is that it takes account of the **time value of money**.

Chapter Roundup

✓ **Discounting** starts with a future value (a sum of money receivable or payable at a future date), and converts the future value to a **present value**, which is the cash equivalent now of the future value.

✓ The **discounting formula** to calculate the present value (X) of a future sum of money (V) at the end of n time periods is $X = V/(1 + r)^n$.

✓ The **NPV method of project appraisal** is to accept projects with a positive NPV.

✓ An **annuity** is a constant cash flow for a number of years.

✓ A **perpetuity** is a constant cash flow forever.

✓ The **IRR method of project appraisal** is to accept projects which have an IRR (the rate at which the NPV is zero) that exceeds a target rate of return. The IRR can be estimated either from a graph or using interpolation.

✓ The **IRR interpolation formula** is:

$$IRR = A + \left[\frac{P}{P-N} \times (B-A) \right] \%$$

where A is the (lower) rate of return
   B is the (higher) rate of return
   P is the NPV at A
   N is the NPV at B

✓ When compared with the NPV method, the **IRR method** has a number of **disadvantages**.

- It ignores the relative size of investments.

- There are problems with its use when a project has non-conventional cashflows or when deciding between mutually exclusive projects.

- Discount rates which differ over the life of a project cannot be incorporated into IRR calculations.

✓ The MIRR is calculated on the basis of investing the inflows at the cost of capital.

✓ The **discounted payback period (DPP)** is the time it will take before a project's cumulative NPV turns from being negative to being positive.

$$\text{Discounted payback index} = \frac{\text{Present value of net cash inflows}}{\text{Initial cash outlay}}$$

✓ One of the principal advantages of the DCF appraisal method is that it takes account of the **time value of money**.

Quick Quiz

1   In a discounted cash flow exercise, what is the discount factor (to 3 decimal places) for year 4 when the cost of capital is 11.5%?

   A 0.647   B 0.115   C 3.587   D 1.546   E 0.721

2   What is the present value of a cash inflow of $3,000 each year from years 1 – 5, when the required return on investment is 12%?

   A $15,000   B $16,800   C $13,393   D $9,111   E $10,815

3   With a cost of capital of 13%, what is the present value of $2,500 received every year in perpetuity?

   A $2,825   B $17,563   C $2,212   D $28,736   E None of these options

4   For a certain project, the net present value at a discount rate of 15% is $3,670, and at a rate of 18% the net present value is negative at ($1,390). What is the internal rate of return of the project?

   A 15.7%   B 16.5%   C 16.6%   D 17.2%   E None of these options

5   *Tick the correct box to indicate whether or not the following items are included in the cash flows when determining the net present value of a project.*

                                                                                 Included   Not included

   (a)   The disposal value of equipment at the end of its life

   (b)   Depreciation charges for the equipment

   (c)   Research costs incurred prior to the appraisal

   (d)   Interest payments on the loan to finance the investment

6   *At what point on the graph below is the project's IRR?*

   NPV   Point C

   Positive

                                            Point B

                                                  Cost of capital (%)

   Negative   Point A

                                            Point D

   A   Point A   B   Point B   C   Point C   D   Point D

7   *Choose the correct word from those highlighted.*

   When there are non-conventional cashflow patterns, the **IRR/NPV** method is not recommended.

8   *Fill in the blanks.*

   DPBI = $\dfrac{\text{...........................}}{\text{.........................}}$

9   *Fill in the blank in the sentence below.*

   The present value of $1,000 in contribution earned each year from years 1–10, when the required return on investment is 11%, is $................ .

Answers to Quick Quiz

1   A $1/(1 + 0.115)^4 = 0.647$

2   E $3,000 × 3.605 = $10,815

3   E $2,500/0.13 = $19,231

4   D   15% + {(3,670/[3,670 + 1,390]) × 3%} = 17.2%

5   (a)   Included

    (b)   Not included (non-cash)

    (c)   Not included (past cost)

    (d)   Not usually included, unless the loan incurs a different rate of interest from that which is being used as the discount rate

6   B. The IRR is the rate (cost of capital) at which the NPV is zero.

7   IRR

8    $$DPBI = \frac{\text{Sum of net discounted cash inflows}}{\text{Initial cash outlay}}$$

9   The PV of $1,000 earned each year from year 1–10 when the required earning rate of money is 11% is calculated as follows.

    $1,000 × 5.889 = $5,889

Answers to Questions

16.1 Present value calculation

The correct answer is $53,240.

Year	Cash flow $	Discount factor 12%	Present value ($)
2	40,000	$\dfrac{1}{(1.12)^2}=0.797$	31,880
3	30,000	$\dfrac{1}{(1.12)^3}=0.712$	21,360
		Total PV	53,240

16.2 Meaning of present value

The correct answer is: The present value of the future returns, discounted at **12%**, is **$53,240**. This means that if Spender can invest now to earn a return of **12%** on its investments, it would have to invest **$53,240** now to earn **$40,000** after 2 years plus **$30,000** after 3 years.

16.3 NPV

The correct answer is that LCH should purchase the machine.

Savings are 75,000 × ($3 − $2.50) = $37,500 per annum.

Additional costs are $7,500 per annum.

Net cash savings are therefore $30,000 per annum. (Remember, depreciation is not a cash flow and must be ignored as a 'cost'.)

The first step in calculating an NPV is to establish the relevant costs year by year. The relevant cash flows are all future cash flows arising as a direct consequence of the decision should be taken into account.

It is assumed that the machine will be sold for $10,000 at the end of year 4.

Year	Cash flow $	PV factor 12%	PV of cash flow $
0	(90,000)	1.000	(90,000)
1	30,000	0.893	26,790
2	30,000	0.797	23,910
3	30,000	0.712	21,360
4	40,000	0.636	25,440
		NPV =	+7,500

The **NPV is positive** and so the project is expected to **earn more than 12%** per annum and is therefore **acceptable**.

16.4 More complex annuity

The correct answer is B.

The PV of $2,000 in costs each year from years 3–6 when the cost of capital is 5% per annum is calculated as follows.

$$\$2{,}000\times\left[\begin{array}{l}\text{PV of \$1 per annum for years1 - 6 at 5\%} = 5.076\\ \text{Less PV of \$1 per annum for years1 - 2 at 5\%} = \underline{1.859}\\ \text{PV of \$1 per annum for years3 - 6} \qquad = \underline{3.217}\end{array}\right]$$

PV = $2,000 × 3.217 = $6,434

If you chose Option A, you performed the calculation $2,000 x 105% x 3 years. You need to use a discount factor.

If you chose Option C, you simply took the sum of $2,000 paid annually for three years.

If you chose Option D, you deducted the cumulative discount factor for years 1 to 3 instead of the factor for years 1 and 2 from that for years 1 to 6.

16.5 Perpetuities

The correct answer is: The project should be undertaken.

Year	Cash flow $	Discount factor 14%	Present value $
0	(500,000)	1.00	(500,000)
1 – ∞	100,000	1/0.14 = 7.14	714,000
		Net present value	214,000

The NPV is positive and so the project should be undertaken.

16.6 Non-standard discount factors

The correct answer is D.

There are no present value tables for 16.5%, therefore you need to calculate your own discount factors, using discount factor = $1/(1 + r)^n$ where r = cost of capital and n = number of years.

Year		16.5% factor	Cash flow $	Present value $
0		1.00	(280,000)	(280,000)
1	$\dfrac{1}{(1+0.165)}$	0.86	149,000	128,140
2	$\dfrac{1}{(1+0.165)^2}$	0.74	128,000	94,720
3	$\dfrac{1}{(1+0.165)^3}$	0.63	84,000	52,920
4	$\dfrac{1}{(1+0.165)^4}$	0.54	70,000	37,800
			Net present value	33,580

16.7 IRR

The IRR is 15% and so the statement is false.

The total receipts are $5,635 giving a total profit of $1,635 and average profits of $409. The average investment is $2,000. The ARR is $409 ÷ $2,000 = 20%. Two thirds of the ARR is approximately 14%. The initial estimate of the IRR that we shall try is therefore 14%.

		Try 14%		Try 16%	
Time	Cash flow	Discount factor	PV	Discount factor	PV
	$	14%	$	16%	$
0	(4,000)	1.000	(4,000)	1.000	(4,000)
1	1,200	0.877	1,052	0.862	1,034
2	1,410	0.769	1,084	0.743	1,048
3	1,875	0.675	1,266	0.641	1,202
4	1,150	0.592	681	0.552	635
		NPV	83	NPV	(81)

The **IRR must be less than 16%, but higher than 14%.** The NPVs at these two costs of capital will be used to estimate the IRR.

Using the **interpolation formula**

$$IRR = 14\% + \left[\frac{83}{83+81} \times (16\% - 14\%) \right] = 15.01\%$$

The IRR is, in fact, exactly 15%.

The project should be **rejected** as the **IRR is less than the minimum return demanded**.

16.8 NPV and IRR

(a)   **Option A – Expand retail outlet**

Year	Cash flow	Discount factor	NPV
	$'000	10%	$'000
0	(75)	1.000	(75.00)
1	40	0.909	36.36
2	50	0.826	41.30
3	50	0.751	37.55
4	50	0.683	34.15
			74.36

Option B – Mail order

Year	Cash flow	Discount factor	NPV
	$'000	10%	$'000
0	(120)	1.000	(120.00)
1	50	0.909	45.45
2	60	0.826	49.56
3	80	0.751	60.08
4	100	0.683	68.30
			103.39

Option C – Greenhouses and conservatories

Year	Cash flow	Discount factor	NPV
	$'000	10%	$'000
0	(200)	1.000	(200.00)
1	50	0.909	45.45
2	100	0.826	82.60
3	150	0.751	112.65
4	150	0.683	102.45
			143.15

Option C gives the highest net present value and therefore this should be chosen.

(b)   The NPV for option C is quite high relative to the initial investment and the IRR is therefore probably considerably higher than 10%.

Try 30%

Year	Cash flow $'000	Discount factor 30%	NPV $'000
0	(200)	1.000	(200.00)
1	50	0.769	38.45
2	100	0.592	59.20
3	150	0.455	68.25
4	150	0.350	52.50
			18.40

Try 40%

Year	Cash flow $'000	Discount factor 40%	NPV $'000
0	(200)	1.000	(200.0)
1	50	0.714	35.7
2	100	0.510	51.0
3	150	0.364	54.6
4	150	0.260	39.0
			(19.7)

$$\text{IRR} = 30\% + \left[\frac{18.4}{18.4 + 19.7} \times 10\right]\% = 34.83\%$$

Now try these questions from the Exam Question Bank

Number	Level	Marks	Time
Q26	Examination	10	18 mins
Q27	Examination	10	18 mins

TAKING ACCOUNT OF TAXATION AND INFLATION

So far, in considering how to appraise projects, we have ignored inflation and taxation, but in this chapter we look at how to **incorporate their effects into investment appraisal**.

Section 1 looks at inflation and Section 2 looks at tax.

topic list	learning outcomes	syllabus references	ability required
1 Allowing for inflation	C1(c)	C1(ii)	application
2 Allowing for taxation	C1(c)	C1(ii)	application

1 Allowing for inflation

Introduction

As the **inflation rate increases so will the minimum return required by an investor**. For example, you might be happy with a return of 5% in an inflation-free world, but if inflation was running at 15% you would expect a considerably greater yield.

Example: inflation (1)

An organisation is considering investing in a project with the following cash flows.

Time	Actual cash flows $
0	(15,000)
1	9,000
2	8,000
3	7,000

The organisation requires a minimum return of 20% under the present and anticipated conditions. Inflation is currently running at 10% a year, and this rate of inflation is expected to continue indefinitely. Should the organisation go ahead with the project?

Let us first look at the organisation's required rate of return. Suppose that it invested $1,000 for one year on 1 January, then on 31 December it would require a minimum return of $200. With the initial investment of $1,000, the total value of the investment by 31 December must therefore increase to $1,200. During the course of the year the purchasing value of the dollar would fall due to inflation. We can restate the **amount received on 31 December in terms of the purchasing power of the dollar at 1 January** as follows.

Amount received on 31 December in terms of the value of the dollar at 1 January $= \dfrac{\$1,200}{(1.10)^1} = \$1,091$

In terms of the value of the dollar at 1 January, the organisation would make a profit of $91 which represents a rate of return of 9.1% in **'today's money' terms**. This is known as the **real rate of return**. The required rate of 20% is a **money rate of return** (sometimes called a **nominal rate of return**).

(a)   The **money rate** measures the **return in terms of the dollar** which is, of course, **falling in value**.
(b)   The **real rate** measures the return in **constant price level** terms.

The two rates of return and the inflation rate are linked by an equation.

LEARN

$(1 + \text{money rate}) = (1 + \text{real rate}) \times (1 + \text{inflation rate})$

where all the rates are expressed as proportions.

In our example, $(1 + 0.20) = (1 + 0.091) \times (1 + 0.10) = 1.20$

We must decide **which rate** to use for discounting, the **money rate** or the **real rate**. The rule is as follows.

(a)   If the cash flows are expressed in terms of the **actual number of dollars** that will be received or paid on the various future dates, we **use the money rate for discounting**. (Money cash flows should be discounted at a money discount rate.)

(b)   If the cash flows are expressed in terms of the **value of the dollar at time 0 (that is, in constant price level terms), we use the real rate**. (Real cash flows should be discounted at a real discount rate.)

The **cash flows** given in the previous example are expressed **in terms of the actual number of dollars** that will be received or paid at the relevant dates. We should, therefore, **discount** them using the **money rate of return**.

Time	Cash flow $	Discount factor 20%	PV $
0	(15,000)	1.000	(15,000)
1	9,000	0.833	7,497
2	8,000	0.694	5,552
3	7,000	0.579	4,053
			2,102

The project has a positive net present value of $2,102.

The future **cash flows** can be **re-expressed** in terms of the **value of the dollar at time 0** as follows, given inflation at 10% a year.

Time	Actual cash flow $	Cash flow at time 0 price level		$
0	(15,000)			(15,000)
1	9,000	$9,000 \times \dfrac{1}{1.10}$	=	8,182
2	8,000	$8,000 \times \dfrac{1}{(1.10)^2}$	=	6,612
3	7,000	$7,000 \times \dfrac{1}{(1.10)^3}$	=	5,259

The cash flows expressed in terms of the value of the dollar at time 0 can now be **discounted using the real rate** of 9.1%.

Time	Cash flow $	Discount factor 9.1%	PV $
0	(15,000)	1.00	(15,000)
1	8,182	$\dfrac{1}{1.091}$	7,500
2	6,612	$\dfrac{1}{(1.091)^2}$	5,555
3	5,259	$\dfrac{1}{(1.091)^3}$	4,050
		NPV	2,105

The NPV is the same as before (and the present value of the cash flow in each year is the same as before) apart from rounding errors with a net total of $3.

1.1 The advantages and misuses of real values and a real rate of return

Although it is recommended that **companies should discount money values at the money cost of capital**, there are some advantages of using real values discounted at a real cost of capital.

(a)   **When all costs and benefits rise at the same rate of price inflation, real values are the same as current day values**, so that no further adjustments need be made to cash flows before discounting. In contrast, when money values are discounted at the money cost of capital, the prices in future years must be calculated before discounting can begin.

(b)   The government or nationalised industries might prefer to set a real return as a target for investments, as being more suitable to their particular situation than a commercial money rate of return.

1.2 Costs and benefits which inflate at different rates

Not all costs and benefits will rise in line with the general level of inflation. In such cases, we can **apply the money rate** to inflated values to determine a project's NPV.

Example: inflation (2)

RR is considering a project which would cost $5,000 now. The annual benefits, for four years, would be a fixed income (ie not affected by inflation) of $2,500 a year, plus other savings of $500 a year in year 1, rising by 5% each year because of inflation. Running costs will be $1,000 in the first year, but would increase at 10% each year because of inflating labour costs. The general rate of inflation is expected to be 7½% and the organisation's required money rate of return is 16%. Is the project worthwhile? Ignore taxation.

Solution

The cash flows at inflated values are as follows.

Year	Fixed income	Other savings	Running costs	Net cash flow
	$	$	$	$
1	2,500	500	1,000	2,000
2	2,500	525	1,100	1,925
3	2,500	551	1,210	1,841
4	2,500	579	1,331	1,748

The NPV of the project is as follows.

Year	Cash flow	Discount factor	PV
	$	16%	$
0	(5,000)	1.000	(5,000)
1	2,000	0.862	1,724
2	1,925	0.743	1,430
3	1,841	0.641	1,180
4	1,748	0.552	965
			+ 299

The NPV is positive and the project would seem therefore to be worthwhile.

Question 17.1   Investment appraisal and inflation

Learning outcome C1(c)

An investment requires an immediate cash outflow of $120,000. It will have zero residual value at the end of four years. The annual cost inflow will be $40,000. The cost of capital is 10% and the annual inflation rate is 3%.

What is the maximum monetary cost of capital for this project to remain viable (to the nearest %)?

A	16%	C	10%
B	13%	D	7%

Exam skills

Exam questions could be discursive as well as numerical. For example you could be asked to explain what a money rate is or what a real rate is and how they would be used to calculate a NPV.

Section summary

Inflation is a feature of all economies, and it must be accommodated in investment appraisal.

(1 + money rate) = (1 + real rate) × (1 + inflation rate)

where all the rates are expressed as proportions.

Money cash flows should be discounted at a money discount rate.

Real cash flows (ie adjusted for inflation) should be discounted at a real discount rate.

2 Allowing for taxation   5/10

Introduction

Taxation is a major practical consideration for businesses. It is vital to take it into account in making decisions.

Payments of tax, or reductions in the capital of tax that has to be paid, are **relevant cash flows** and so the amounts connected with a project ought to be included in the DCF appraisal.

2.1 Introduction to the calculation of taxation in capital projects

The calculation of taxation in relation to capital projects may seem daunting at first. However, there is a method using simple steps which you could follow. This breaks the calculation down into manageable elements. The method is also summarised at the end of the chapter as an aide memoire.

(a)   Calculate the **total** cost of any new asset.

(b)   Calculate WDA for each year and multiply by the tax rate to give the tax saving.

(c)   Half of tax saving is a benefit in the year in question, half in the following year.

(d)   Calculate a balancing allowance or charge on the sale of the asset

    (i)   If sales price > reducing balance ⇒ balancing charge (increases taxable profit)

    (ii)   If sales price < reducing balance ⇒ balancing allowance (reduces taxable profit)

(e)   Effect of the balancing charge / allowance (which is calculated as amount × tax rate) is felt half in the year in which the asset is sold and half in the following year.

(f)   Include in the appraisal: tax on WDAs and balancing allowance/charge, net cash inflows due to project (ie taxable profits) and tax on these net cash inflows.

2.2 Corporation tax

Under the UK system, corporation tax is **payable** by large companies **quarterly**.

* In the **seventh and tenth months** of the year in which the profit is earned
* In the **first and fourth months** of the following year

This simply means that **half the tax is payable in the year in which the profits are earned** and **half in the following year**.

Example: payment of corporation tax

If a project increases taxable profits by $10,000 in year 2, there will be tax payments of $10,000 × 30% × 50% = $1,500 in both year 2 and in year 3 (assuming a tax rate of 30%). It is these tax payments (that are a direct result of the project) that need to be included in a DCF analysis.

KEY POINT

Note that **net cash flows from a project** should be considered as the **taxable profits** arising from the project (unless an indication is given to the contrary).

2.3 Capital allowances/writing down allowances (WDAs)

Remember that depreciation is a way of charging the cost of plant and machinery against financial accounting profits over a number of periods (thereby reducing profits). Similarly, WDAs or capital allowances are a way of charging the cost of plant and machinery against taxable profits over a number of periods, thereby **reducing taxable profits and hence the tax payable.**

The **reduction in tax payable** (to be included in the DCF analysis) = **amount of WDA × tax rate.**

As half the tax on profit is paid in the year to which the profits relate, and half in the following year, the **benefit of the WDA** is also felt **half in the year to which it relates** and **half in the following year.**

KEY POINT

The rate at which the allowance is given will always be provided in the question, although it is more than likely to be 25% on a reducing balance basis.

Example: WDAs

Suppose an organisation purchases plant costing $80,000. The rate of corporation tax is 30% and WDAs are given on a 25% reducing balance basis. Here are the WDAs and reductions in tax payable for years 1 to 4.

	Reducing balance	Tax saved	Yr 1	Benefit received Yr 2	Yr 3	Yr 4
	$	$	$	$	$	$
Purchase price	80,000					
Yr 1 WDA (25%)	(20,000)	6,000	3,000	3,000		
Value at start year 2	60,000					
Yr 2 WDA (25%)		4,500		2,250	2,250	
	(15,000)					
Value at start year 3	45,000					
Yr 3 WDA (25%)		3,375			1,687	1,688
	(11,250)					
Value at start year 4	33,750					
Yr 4 WDA (25%)	(8,438)	2,531				1,266
Value at start year 5	25,312					

Points to note

(a)   The tax saved is 30% of the WDA.

(b)   Half of the tax saved is a benefit in the year in question, half in the following year.

KEY POINT

You should always make the following assumptions unless told otherwise.

- The organisation in question generates enough profit from other projects to absorb any tax benefits in the year to which they relate.

- Assume the organisation has elected to use **'short life' asset treatment**. This means that the asset is kept separate from the general pool of the organisation's assets provided it is sold within five years of purchase.

You also need to be sure that you **start off with the correct balance** on which to calculate the capital allowances. For example, in addition to the original capital costs of a machine, it may be possible to claim capital allowances on the costs of installation, such as the labour and overhead costs of removing an old machine, levelling the area for the new machine and/or altering part of a building to accommodate the new machine. Remember to **state** your **assumptions** concerning this type of item.

KEY POINT

Assumptions about capital allowances could be simplified in an exam question. For example, you might be told that capital allowances can be claimed at the rate of 25% of cost on a straight line basis (that is, over four years), or a question might refer to 'tax allowable depreciation', so that the capital allowances equal the depreciation charge.

2.4 Balancing allowances and balancing charges

Suppose an organisation sells an item of plant in year 3 at a price which differs from the reducing balance amount **before year 3 WDAs** are included.

(a)   If the **selling price is greater than the reducing balance amount**, the difference between the two is treated as a **taxable profit (balancing charge)**.

(b)   If the **selling price is less than the reducing balance amount**, the difference between the two is treated as a **reduction in tax payable (balancing allowance)**.

'Short-life' asset treatment means any balancing allowance/charge should be dealt with in the year of sale.

Example: balancing allowances/charges

If, in the example above, the plant is sold during year 4 for $20,000, there will be a balancing allowance of $(33,750 − 20,000) = $13,750, being the difference between the reducing balance amount at the end of year 3 / beginning of year 4 and the selling price.

This allowance results in a reduction in tax paid of $13,750 × 30% = $4,125, the benefits of which are received in years 4 and 5.

Here is the full calculation.

	Reducing balance $	Tax saved $	Yr 1 $	Yr 2 $	Yr 3 $	Yr 4 $	Yr 5 $
				Benefits received			
Purchase price	80,000						
Yr 1 WDA (25%)	(20,000)	6,000	3,000	3,000			
	60,000						
Yr 2 WDA (25%)	(15,000)	4,500		2,250	2,250		
	45,000						
Yr 3 WDA (25%)	(11,250)	3,375			1,687	1,688	
	33,750						
Yr 4 sales price	20,000						
Balancing allowance	13,750	4,125				2,062	2,063

If the asset had been sold for $40,000, however, there would be a **balancing charge** of $(40,000 – 33,750) = $6,250, being the difference between the reducing balance amount at the end of year 3 / beginning of year 4 and the selling price.

This charge has to be included in year 4 taxable profits, resulting in an **increase in tax paid** of $6,250 × 30% = $1,875, which must be paid half in year 4 and half in year 5.

Let's now look at how to integrate all of this into a DCF appraisal.

Example: taxation

An organisation is considering whether or not to purchase an item of machinery costing $40,000. It would have a life of four years, after which it would be sold for $5,000. The machinery would create annual cost savings of $14,000.

The machinery would attract writing down allowances of 25% on the reducing balance basis. A balancing allowance or charge would arise on disposal. The rate of corporation tax is 30%. Tax is payable quarterly in the seventh and tenth months of the year in which the profit is earned and in the first and fourth months of the following year. The after-tax cost of capital is 8%.

Should the machinery be purchased?

Solution

WDAs and balancing charges/allowances

We begin by calculating the WDAs and balancing charge /allowance.

Year		Reducing balance $
0	Purchase	40,000
1	WDA	10,000
	Value at start of year 2	30,000
2	WDA	7,500
	Value at start of year 3	22,500
3	WDA	5,625
	Value at start of year 4	16,875
4	Sale	5,000
	Balancing allowance	11,875

Calculate tax savings/payments

Having calculated the allowances each year, the **tax savings** can be computed. The tax savings affect two years, the year for which the allowance is claimed and the following year.

Year of claim	Allowance $	Tax saved $	Yr 1 $	Yr 2 $	Tax saving Yr 3 $	Yr 4 $	Yr 5 $
1	10,000	3,000	1,500	1,500			
2	7,500	2,250		1,125	1,125		
3	5,625	1,688			844	844	
4	11,875	3,562	–	–	–	1,781	1,781
	35,000 *		1,500	2,625	1,969	2,625	1,781

* Net cost $(40,000 – 5,000) = $35,000

These tax savings relate to capital allowances. We must also take the **tax effects of the annual savings** of $14,000 into account.

The savings increase taxable profit (costs are lower) and so extra tax must be paid. Each saving of $14,000 will lead to extra tax of $14,000 × 30% × 50% = $2,100 in the year in question and the same amount in the following year.

Calculate NPV

The **net cash flows and the NPV** are now calculated as follows.

Year	Equipment $	Savings $	Tax on savings $	Tax saved on capital allowances $	Net cash flow $	Discount factor 8%	Present value of cash flow $
0	(40,000)				(40,000)	1.000	(40,000)
1		14,000	(2,100)	1,500	13,400	0.926	12,408
2		14,000	(4,200)	2,625	12,425	0.857	10,648
3		14,000	(4,200)	1,969	11,769	0.794	9,345
4	5,000	14,000	(4,200)	2,625	17,425	0.735	12,807
5			(2,100)	1,781	(319)	0.681	(217)
							4,991

The NPV is positive and so the purchase appears to be worthwhile.

2.5 An alternative and quicker method of calculating tax payments or savings

In the above example, the tax computations could have been combined, as follows.

Year	1 $	2 $	3 $	4 $	5 $
Cost savings	14,000	14,000	14,000	14,000	
Capital allowance	10,000	7,500	5,625	11,875	
Taxable profits	4,000	6,500	8,375	2,125	
Tax (paid)/received at 30%	(1,200)	(1,950)	(2,512)	(638)	
Yr of (payment)/saving	(600)	(600)			
		(975)	(975)		
			(1,256)	(1,256)	
				(319)	(319)
(Payment)/saving	(600)	(1,575)	(2,231)	(1,575)	(319)

The net cash flows would then be as follows.

Year	Equipment $	Savings $	Tax $	Net cash flow $
0	(40,000)			(40,000)
1		14,000	(600)	13,400
2		14,000	(1,575)	12,425
3		14,000	(2,231)	11,769
4	5,000	14,000	(1,575)	17,425
5			(319)	(319)

The net cash flows are exactly the same as calculated previously in Step 3 above.

2.6 Taxation and DCF

The effect of taxation on capital budgeting is theoretically quite simple. Organisations must pay tax, and the effect of undertaking a project will be to increase or decrease tax payments each year. These **incremental tax cash flows should be included in the cash flows** of the project for discounting to arrive at the project's NPV.

When **taxation is ignored** in the DCF calculations, the **discount rate** will reflect the **pre-tax rate of return** required on capital investments. When **taxation is included** in the cash flows, a **post-tax required rate** of return should be used.

Question 17.2

Taxation

Learning outcome C1(c)

An organisation is considering the purchase of an item of equipment, which would earn profits before tax of $25,000 a year. Depreciation charges would be $20,000 a year for six years. Capital allowances would be $30,000 a year for the first four years. Corporation tax is at 30%.

Assume that tax payments occur half in the same year as the profits giving rise to them, half in the following year, and there is no balancing charge or allowance when the machine is scrapped at the end of the sixth year.

Required

Fill in the blanks below.

The net cash inflows of the project after tax in the first six years are:

Year 1 ....   Year 4 ....

Year 2 ....   Year 5 ....

Year 3 ....   Year 6 ....

Question 17.3

Taxation and cash flow

Learning outcome C1(c)

An organisation is considering the purchase of a machine for $150,000. It would be sold after four years for an estimated realisable value of $50,000. By this time capital allowances of $120,000 would have been claimed. The rate of corporation tax is 30%.

The cash flow arising as a result of the tax implications of the sale of the machine at the end of the four years is

A $6,000 inflow
B $6,000 outflow
C $15,000 outflow
D $20,000 outflow

2.7 Sensitivity analysis and taxation

To carry out **sensitivity analysis** when taxation is relevant, **use after-tax cashflows**.

Look back at the example in Section 2.4 called Taxation. Suppose you were required to calculate the sensitivity of the project to changes in the annual cost savings.

To do this you have to calculate (as before) (**NPV of project/PV of annual cost savings**) × 100% but both figures must be **after-tax figures**.

We therefore need to calculate the PV of the savings.

Year	Savings $	Tax on savings $	Net cash flow $	Discount factor 8%	Present value $
1	14,000	(2,100)	11,900	0.926	11,019
2	14,000	(4,200)	9,800	0.857	8,399
3	14,000	(4,200)	9,800	0.794	7,781
4	14,000	(4,200)	9,800	0.735	7,203
		(2,100)	(2,100)	0.681	(1,430)
					32,972

The overall NPV of the project is $4,991 and so the sensitivity is therefore (4,991/32,972) × 100% = 15.14%.

Don't forget that when carrying out sensitivity analysis we need to **consider the cashflows affected by the variables under consideration**. So if you were asked to examine the sensitivity of a project to **price** you would need to calculate the post-tax PV of revenue (as a change in selling price affects revenue and hence revenue is the cashflow affected), whereas sensitivity to **volume** would require the calculation of post-tax contribution (as a change in volume affects revenue and variable costs and hence contribution can be used as the cashflow affected).

2.8 Summary

(a)   Calculate the **total** cost of any new asset.

(b)   Calculate WDA for each year and multiply by the tax rate to give the tax saving. **See example in 2.3 called WDAs.**

(c)   Half of tax saving is a benefit in the year in question, half in the following year. **See example in 2.3 called WDAs.**

(d)   Calculate a balancing allowance or charge on the sale of the asset. **See example in 2.4 called Balancing allowances/charges.**

    (i)   If sales price > reducing balance ⇒ balancing charge (increases taxable profit)

    (ii)   If sales price < reducing balance ⇒ balancing allowance (reduces taxable profit)

(e)   Effect of the balancing charge / allowance (which is calculated as amount × tax rate) is felt half in year in which the asset is sold and half in the following year. **See example in 2.4 called Balancing allowances/charges.**

(f)   Include in the appraisal: tax on WDAs and balancing allowance / charge, net cash inflows due to project (ie taxable profits) and tax on these net cash inflows. **See example in 2.4 called Taxation and section 2.5.**

Question 17.4   Tax effects

Learning outcome C1(c)

Describe the potential major effects of taxation on capital investment decisions.

Exam alert

The May 2010 exam contained a 16 mark question on the calculation of the NPV, taking account of tax.

Section summary

Taxation is a major practical consideration for businesses. It is vital to take it into account in making decisions.

Under the UK system, corporation tax is **payable** by large companies **quarterly**.

- In the **seventh and tenth months** of the year in which the profit is earned
- In the **first and fourth months** of the following year

Capital allowances/WDAs reduce taxable profits and hence tax payable.

If **taxation is ignored** in the project cash flows, the discount rate should be the **pre-tax** cost of capital. When **taxation is included** in the cash flows, the **after tax** cost of capital should be used.

To carry out **sensitivity analysis** when taxation is relevant, **use after-tax cashflows**.

Chapter Roundup

✓   **Inflation** is a feature of all economies, and it must be accommodated in investment appraisal.

✓   (1+ money rate of return) = (1 + real rate of return) × (1 + rate of inflation)

✓   **Money cash flows** should be discounted at a money discount rate.

✓   **Real cash flows** (ie adjusted for inflation) should be discounted at a real discount rate.

✓   **Taxation** is a major practical consideration for businesses. It is vital to take it into account in making decisions.

✓   Under the UK system, corporation tax is **payable** by large companies **quarterly**.

- In the seventh and tenth months of the year in which the profit is earned
- In the first and fourth months of the following year

✓   **Capital allowances/WDAs** reduce taxable profits and hence tax payable.

✓   If **taxation is ignored** in the project cash flows, the discount rate should be the **pre-tax** cost of capital. When **taxation is included** in the cash flows, the **after tax** cost of capital should be used.

✓   To carry out **sensitivity analysis** when taxation is relevant, **use after-tax cashflows**.

Quick Quiz

1 *Fill in the gaps.*

The relationship between the money rate of return, the real rate of return and the rate of inflation is

(1 + ... rate) = (1 + ... rate) x (1 + ... rate).

2 The money cost of capital is 11%. The expected annual rate of inflation is 5%. What is the real cost of capital?

A 16.6%   B 6.0%   C 16.0%   D None of these options

3 A company wants a minimum real return of 3% a year on its investments. Inflation is expected to be 8% a year. What is the company's minimum money cost of capital?

A 4.9%   B 11.24%   C 5%   D 11%

4 A company is appraising an investment that will save electricity costs. Electricity prices are expected to rise at a rate of 15% per annum in future, although the general inflation rate will be 10% per annum. The money cost of capital for the company is 20%. What is the appropriate discount rate to apply to the forecast actual money cash flows for electricity?

A 20.0%   B 22.0%   C 26.5%   D 32.0%

5 *Choose the correct words from those highlighted.*

Capital allowances are used to (1) **increase/reduce** taxable profits, and the consequent reduction in a tax payment should be treated as a (2) **cash saving/cash payment** arising from the acceptance of a project.

Writing down allowances are generally allowed on the cost of (3) **materials and labour/plant and machinery** at the rate of (4) **25%/30%** on a (5) **straight line/reducing balance** basis.

When the plant is eventually sold, the difference between the sales price and the reducing balance amount will be treated as a (6) **taxable profit/tax allowable loss** if the sales price exceeds the reducing balance, and as a (7) **taxable profit/tax allowable loss** if the reducing balance exceeds the sales price.

The cash saving on the capital allowances (or the cash payment for a charge) is calculated by (8) **multiplying/dividing** the allowances (or charge) by (9) the **reducing balance rate/corporation tax rate**.

6 *Fill in the blanks.*

The sensitivity of a project's NPV to changes in volume can be determined using:

(...................../......................) × 100%

Answers to Quick Quiz

1 (1 + money rate) = (1 + real rate) × (1 + inflation rate)

2 D   1.11/1.05 = 1.057. The real cost of capital is 5.7%.

3 B   1.03 × 1.08 = 1.1124. The money cost of capital is 11.24%.

4 A   The money rate of 20% is applied to the money cash flows.

5 (1) reduce   (4) 25%   (7) tax allowable loss
    (2) cash saving   (5) reducing balance   (8) multiplying
    (3) plant and machinery   (6) taxable profit   (9) corporation tax rate

6 (Overall project NPV/PV of contribution) × 100%

Answers to Questions

17.1 Investment appraisal and inflation

The correct answer is A.

The rate required is the IRR (the rate at which the project breaks even).

Let the rate = r

∴ $120,000 = PV of $40,000 for years 1 to 4 at rate r

∴ $120,000 = (cumulative PV factor for years 1 to 4 at rate r) × $40,000

∴ $120,000/$40,000 = cumulative PV factor for years 1 to 4 at rate r

∴ 3.000 = cumulative PV factor for years 1 to 4 at rate r

In cumulative PV tables this corresponds to a rate of approximately 12.5% over 4 years.

∴ The real cost of capital to give an NPV of zero = 12.5%

Substituting in the formula, with X = monetary cost of capital:

$$\frac{(1+X)}{1.03} - 1 = 0.125$$

∴ X = 15.875%

Option B is the real cost of capital. Option C is the current cost of capital. Option D is the difference between the current cost of capital and the rate of inflation.

17.2 Taxation

The correct answer is:

Year 1 $42,750   Year 4 $40,500
Year 2 $40,500   Year 5 $36,000
Year 3 $40,500   Year 6 $31,500

	Years 1–4 $	Years 5–6 $
Profit before tax	25,000	25,000
Add back depreciation	20,000	20,000
Net cash inflow before tax	45,000	45,000
Less capital allowance	30,000	0
	15,000	45,000
Tax at 30%	4,500	13,500

	Yr 1 $	Yr 2 $	Yr 3 $	Yr 4 $	Yr 5 $	Yr 6 $	Yr 7 $
Tax on yr 1 profit	2,250	2,250					
Tax on yr 2 profit		2,250	2,250				
Tax on yr 3 profit			2,250	2,250			
Tax on yr 4 profit				2,250	2,250		
Tax on yr 5 profit					6,750	6,750	
Tax on yr 6 profit						6,750	6,750
	2,250	4,500	4,500	4,500	9,000	13,500	
Net cash inflow before tax	45,000	45,000	45,000	45,000	45,000	45,000	
Net cash inflow after tax	42,750	40,500	40,500	40,500	36,000	31,500	

17.3 Taxation and cash flow

The correct answer is B.

There will be a balancing charge on the sale of the machine of $(50,000 – (150,000 – 120,000)) = $20,000. This will give rise to a tax payment of 30% × $20,000 = $6,000.

If you chose A you got the calculations correct but the direction of the cash flow was wrong.

Option C is 30% taxation on the estimated sales value. The revenue from the actual sale is not taxed directly, but any remaining balancing charge will be taxable.

If you chose option D you forgot to calculate the 30% corporation tax on the balancing charge of $20,000.

17.4 Tax effects

Taxation can affect investment decisions in various ways.

(a)   The existence of taxation will **reduce the returns** and **mitigate the costs** of projects.

(b)   The arrangements for paying tax will determine by how much tax payments are **discounted** in the investment appraisal. It will be significant whether tax is payable in the year profits are earned or in the following year.

(c)   Tax is payable on **taxable profits that relate to the investment**, which are not necessarily the same as the **cash flows**. There may be **timing differences between expenditure being accrued** for accounting and tax purposes, and payment being made.

(d)   Taxation arrangements are complicated by the availability of **capital allowances**, which allow businesses to write off the costs of non-current assets against taxable profit. Businesses need to consider for what types of asset claims can be made and the **timing** of allowances, as this will again affect by how much allowances are discounted. This may determine when an asset is purchased; it may be advantageous to purchase an asset just before the end of a tax year, and thus claim capital allowances a year earlier than would be the case if the asset was purchased early in the new tax year.

(e)   If the effects of taxation are included in the investment appraisal, a **post-tax rate of return** should be used.

Now try the question from the Exam Question Bank	Number	Level	Marks	Time
	Q28	Examination	25	45 mins

FURTHER ASPECTS OF INVESTMENT DECISION MAKING

This chapter builds on the knowledge gained in Chapter 16 and looks at a number of related project appraisal topics.

In **Section 1** we look at **how to choose between mutually exclusive projects with unequal lives**.

In **Section 2** we see how to decide when, and how frequently, an asset should be replaced. **Section 3** considers decisions about project abandonment.

We have seen that the general rule when appraising projects using DCF techniques is to accept all projects with a positive NPV. In **Section 4** we will be looking at the approach to take if there are **insufficient funds** to accept all such projects.

Because project appraisal involves estimating, and taking into account, future cash flows, projects will always be (to varying degrees) **risky** simply because the future is risky. **Sensitivity analysis** (covered in **Section 5**) is one method of assessing the risk associated with a project.

In **Section 6** we look at probability analysis, which will be explained in detail in Chapter 19, but here we consider long-term decision making only.

In **Section 7** we look at some of the non-financial considerations to incorporate into decision support information for management.

topic list	learning outcomes	syllabus references	ability required
1 Mutually exclusive projects with unequal lives	C2(c)	C1(vii)	analysis
2 Asset replacement	C2(c)	C1(vii)	analysis
3 Project abandonment	C1(b)	C1(vii)	application
4 Capital rationing	C2(c)	C1(vii)	analysis
5 Sensitivity analysis	C1(f)	C1(v), D1(ii)	application
6 Probability analysis and long-term decisions	D1(c), (d)	D1(iii), (iv), (v)	analysis
7 Non-financial considerations in long-term decisions	C1(g)	C1(vi)	application

1 Mutually exclusive projects with unequal lives

Introduction

All of the discounted cash flow examples that we have seen so far have involved a choice between projects with equal lives. However if managers are **deciding between projects with different time spans** a direct **comparison of the NPV generated by each project would not be valid**.

For example if an organisation decides to invest in a project with a shorter life it may then have the opportunity to invest in a new project in the future sooner than if a longer term project is accepted. This should be taken into account in the analysis in order to be able to make direct comparisons between projects with unequal lives.

Annualised equivalents are used to enable a comparison to be made between the net present values of projects with different durations. **However, this method cannot be used when inflation is a factor.** Another method, the **lowest common multiple method, is used** instead.

Example: annualised equivalents

An organisation has the opportunity to invest in either project G or project H. The forecast cash flows from the projects are as follows.

		Project G $'000	Project H $'000
Capital cost		(200)	(143)
Cash inflows:	year 1	90	100
	year 2	120	80
	year 3	50	–

The company's cost of capital is 12%. Which project should be accepted?

Solution

Project G

Year	Cash flow $	PV factor 12%	PV of cash flow $
0	(200,000)	1.000	(200,000)
1	90,000	0.893	80,370
2	120,000	0.797	95,640
3	50,000	0.712	35,600
			NPV = 11,610

Project H

Year	Cash flow $	PV factor 12%	PV of cash flow $
0	(143,000)	1.000	(143,000)
1	100,000	0.893	89,300
2	80,000	0.797	63,760
			NPV = 10,060

These NPVs **cannot be compared directly** because they each relate to a different number of years. In order to make a comparison we must convert each NPV to an **annualised equivalent cost**. In other words, we convert the project's NPV into an equivalent annual annuity over its expected life. We do this by using **cumulative discount factors** that you met in the last chapter.

	Project G	Project H
NPV at 12%	$11,610	$10,060
Cumulative 12% discount factor	÷ 2.402	÷ 1.69
Annualised equivalent	$4,833	$5,953

Project H is offering an equivalent annual annuity of $5,953 which is higher than that offered by project G, therefore project H is preferable.

Exam alert

When inflation is a factor, LCM must be used rather than annualised equivalents.

Work through this example carefully bearing in mind the differences between the use of annualised equivalents and LCM.

Example: lowest common multiple (LCM)

Where asset replacement includes inflation you would not be able to use annualised equivalent costs. The correct method is called the lowest common multiple. The key points when using the lowest common multiple method are:

(a)   Calculate cash flows including inflated values for both alternatives
(b)   Use a lowest common multiple to establish a common time period and base asset lives on that

Fred is considering the replacement of a caravan he lets out for hire. He is planning to retire in six years' time and is therefore only concerned with that period of time, but cannot decide whether it is better to replace the caravan every two years or every three years.

The following data have been estimated (all values at today's price levels):

Purchase cost and trade-in values

		$
Cost of a new caravan		20,000
Trade-in value of caravan:	after two years	10,000
	after three years	5,000

Annual costs and revenues

	Per year $
Caravan running cost	10,000
Lettings charged to customers, that is revenue for Fred	20,000

Caravan servicing and repair costs

Caravan servicing and repair costs depend on the age of the caravan. In the following table, year 1 represents the cost in the first year of the caravan ownership; year 2 represents the cost in the second year of ownership, and so on:

	$
Year 1	500
Year 2	2,500
Year 3	4,000

Inflation

New caravan costs and trade in-values are expected to increase by 5% per year. Caravan running costs and lettings are expected to increase by 7% per year. Caravan servicing and repair costs are expected to increase by 10% per year.

Required

Advise Fred on the optimum replacement cycle for his caravan. Use a discount rate of 12% per year. All workings and assumptions should be shown. Ignore taxation.

Solution

In this example you need to consider a six-year time horizon, six being the lowest common multiple of two and three.

Projected cash flows – 2 year trade in

	Year 0 $	Year 1 $	Year 2 $	Year 3 $	Year 4 $	Year 5 $	Year 6 $
Caravan cost (+ 5% pa)	(20,000)		(22,050)		(24,310)		
Trade in value (+ 5% pa)			11,025		12,155		13,401
Annual costs and revenues (net of costs) (+ 7% pa)		10,700	11,449	12,250	13,108	14,026	15,007
Servicing and repair (+ 10% pa)	–	(550)	(3,025)	(666)	(3,660)	(805)	(4,429)
Net cash flow	(20,000)	10,150	(2,601)	11,584	(2,707)	13,221	23,979
Discount at 12%	× 1.000	× 0.893	× 0.797	× 0.712	× 0.636	× 0.567	× 0.507
PV of cash flow	(20,000)	9,064	(2,073)	8,248	(1,722)	7,496	12,157

NPV of cash flow = $13,170

Projected cash flows – 3 year trade in

	Year 0 $	Year 1 $	Year 2 $	Year 3 $	Year 4 $	Year 5 $	Year 6 $
Caravan cost (+ 5% pa)	(20,000)			(23,153)			
Trade in value (+ 5% pa)				5,788			6,700
Annual costs and revenues (net) (+ 7% pa)		10,700	11,449	12,250	13,108	14,026	15,007
Servicing and repair (+ 10% pa)	–	(550)	(3,025)	(5,324)	(732)	(4,026)	(7,086)
Net cash flow	(20,000)	10,150	8,424	(10,439)	12,376	10,000	14,621
Discount at 12%	× 1.000	× 0.893	× 0.797	× 0.712	× 0.636	× 0.567	× 0.507
PV of cash flow	(20,000)	9,064	6,714	(7,433)	7,871	5,670	7,413

NPV of cash flow = $9,299

Assumptions: inflation applies from year 0 to all costs and revenues, which are stated at their values in year 0 in the question.

Based on the NPVs of the two alternative replacement cycles, that with the higher positive NPV is the two-year replacement cycle and so this should be chosen as the optimum replacement cycle.

KEY POINT

Not all mutually exclusive investments need to be considered over the same level of time. It very much depends on what the organisation intends to do once the shorter-life **project ends**. If the organisation has to **invest in similar assets** again at that point, the **projects should be compared over equal time periods**. Investment in manufacturing equipment for a product that will be made for more years than the life of an asset is an example.

If the organisation does **not have to invest in similar assets when the asset's life ends**, however, the approach we have described is not needed. If the investments are alternative advertising campaigns for a short-life product such as a commemorative item, the investments will be one-offs and so can be **compared over different lives**.

Section summary

Annualised equivalents are used to enable a comparison to be made between the net present values of projects with different durations. **However, this method cannot be used when inflation is a factor.** Another method, the **lowest common multiple method, is used** instead.

2 Asset replacement   5/11

Introduction

As well as assisting with decisions between particular assets, DCF techniques combined with annualised equivalents can be used to assess **when** and **how frequently an asset should be replaced**.

2.1 Identical replacement

When an asset is to be replaced by an **'identical' asset**, the problem is to decide the optimum interval between replacements. As the asset gets older, it may cost more to maintain and operate, its residual value will decrease, and it may lose some productivity/operating capability. When an asset is being replaced with an identical asset, the equivalent annual cost method can be used.

Example: replacement of an identical asset

James operates a machine which costs $25,000 to buy and has the following costs and resale values over its four-year life.

	Year 1 $	Year 2 $	Year 3 $	Year 4 $
Running costs (cash expenses)	7,500	10,000	12,500	15,000
Resale value (end of year)	15,000	10,000	7,500	2,500

The organisation's cost of capital is 10%.

Required

Assess how frequently the asset should be replaced.

Solution

To begin, it is necessary to **calculate the present value of costs for each replacement cycle, but over one cycle only**.

Year	Replace every year		Replace every 2 years		Replace every 3 years		Replace every 4 years	
	Cash flow $	PV at 10% $	Cash flow $	PV at 10% $	Cash flow $	PV at 10% $	Cash flow $	PV at 10% $
0	(25,000)	(25,000)	(25,000)	(25,000)	(25,000)	(25,000)	(25,000)	(25,000)
1	7,500*	6,818	(7,500)	(6,818)	(7,500)	(6,818)	(7,500)	(6,818)
2			0*	0	(10,000)	(8,260)	(10,000)	(8,260)
3					(5,000)*	(3,755)	(12,500)	(9,388)
4							(12,500)*	(8,538)
PV of cost over one replacement cycle		(18,182)		(31,818)		(43,833)		(58,004)

* = Resale value – running costs

KEY POINT

- The zeros in the 'Replace every 2 years' column arise from the fact that the running costs in year 2 are $10,000, but if the machine is sold at the end of year 2 James will get $10,000, so the net effect in year 2 is zero.

- In general, in the year in which the machine is replaced, the cash flow is the difference between the running costs in that year and the resale value. In the years leading up to replacement, the cash flow is the running costs for that year.

These **costs are not comparable, because they refer to different time periods, whereas replacement is continuous**. We need to convert each of them to an equivalent annual cost.

The equivalent annual cost is calculated as follows:

$$\frac{\text{The PV of cost over one replacement cycle}}{\text{The cumulative present value factor for the number of years in the cycle}}$$

Given a discount rate of 10%, the equivalent annual cost is as follows.

	Replace every year	Replace every 2 years	Replace every 3 years	Replace every 4 years
PV of cost over one replacement cycle	$18,182	$31,818	$43,833	$58,004
Cumulative PV factor	÷ 0.909	÷ 1.736	÷ 2.487	÷ 3.170
Annualised equivalent cost	$20,002	$18,328	$17,625	$18,298

The **optimum replacement policy** is the one with the **lowest equivalent annual cost**, every three years.

Question 18.1   Asset replacement

Learning outcome C2(c)

An organisation is deciding whether to replace company cars after a three, four or five year cycle. The relevant cash flows are as follows.

	Year	Three-year cycle $	Four-year cycle $	Five-year cycle $
Capital cost	0	(6,000)	(6,000)	(6,000)
Running costs	1	(280)	(280)	(280)
Running costs	2	(1,090)	(1,090)	(1,090)
Running costs	3	(1,120)	(1,120)	(1,120)
Trade in value	3	1,000	–	–
Running costs	4		(1,590)	(1,590)
Trade in value	4		700	–
Running costs	5			(1,260)
Trade in value	5			300
NPV at 15% *		(7,146.6)	(8,313.68)	(9,191.2)

* The workings are not shown, but as an exercise you could check the NPV calculations yourself.

Required

Fill in the blank in the sentence below.

The optimum replacement policy for company cars is every .... years.

2.2 Non-identical replacement

When a machine is to be replaced by a machine of a different type, there is a different replacement problem.

When an asset is being **replaced with a non-identical asset**, the decision is when to replace the asset rather than how frequently. The **present value of an annuity in perpetuity** must be calculated.

Example: non-identical replacement

Suppose that James's machine (in our example in Section 2.1 called Replacement of an identical asset) is a new machine, and will be introduced to replace a non-identical existing machine which is nearing the end of its life and has a maximum remaining life of only three years. James wishes to decide when is the best time to replace the old machine, and estimates of relevant costs have been drawn up as follows.

Year	Resale value of current machine $	Extra expenditure and opportunity costs of keeping the existing machine in operation during the year $
0	8,500	n/a
1	5,000	9,000
2	2,500	12,000
3	0	15,000

Required

Calculate the best time to replace the existing machine.

Solution

The costs of the new machine will be those given in Section 2.1, so that the optimum replacement cycle for the new machine will already have been calculated as three years, with an equivalent annual cost of $17,625 (Solution in Section 2.1 example).

The best time to replace the existing machine will be the option which gives the lowest NPV of cost in perpetuity, for both the existing machine and the machine which eventually replaces it.

We saw in Chapter 16 that the present value of an annuity, $a per annum, in perpetuity is a/r, where r is the cost of capital.

This formula may be used to calculate the PV of cost in perpetuity of the new machine. In our example, PV of cost = $17,625/0.1 = $176,250.

The new machine will have a PV of cost in perpetuity of $176,250 from the start of the year when it is eventually purchased.

The present value relates to the beginning of the year when the first annual cash flow occurs, so that if replacement occurs now, the first annuity is in year 1, and the PV of cost relates to year 0 values. If replacement occurs at the end of year 1 the first annuity is in year 2, and the PV of cost relates to year 1, and so on.

The total cash flows of the replacement decision may now be presented as follows. These cash flows show the **PV of cost in perpetuity of the new machine**, the **running costs of the existing machine**, and the **resale value of the existing machine**, at the **end of year 0, 1, 2 or 3 as appropriate**.

Year	Replace now $	Replace in 1 year $	Replace in 2 years $	Replace in 3 years $
0	(176,250) 8,500	–	–	–
1	–	(176,250) (9,000) 5,000	(9,000)	(9,000)
2	–	–	(176,250) (12,000) 2,500	(12,000)
3	–	–	–	(176,250) (15,000)

The PVs of each replacement option are as follows.

	Year	Cash flow $	Discount factor 10%	Present value $
Replace now	0	(176,250) 8,500 (167,750)	1.000	(167,750)
Replace in one year	1	(176,250) (9,000) 5,000 (180,250)	0.909	(163,847)
Replace in two years	1 2	(9,000) (185,750)	0.909 0.826	(8,181) (153,430) (161,611)
Replace in three years	1 2 3	(9,000) (12,000) (191,250)	0.909 0.826 0.751	(8,181) (9,912) (143,629) (161,722)

The marginally **optimum policy** would be to replace the existing machine in two years' time, because this has the **lowest total PV of cost in perpetuity**.

Section summary

When an asset is being replaced with an identical asset, the equivalent annual cost method can be used.

When an asset is being **replaced with a non-identical asset**, the decision is when to replace the asset rather than how frequently. The **present value of an annuity in perpetuity** must be calculated.

3 Project abandonment

Introduction

Initial project appraisals are based on forecasts of cash inflows and outflows and a decision is made on the basis of these forecasts. These forecasts are subject to uncertainty, however, and the assumptions upon which the original estimates were based become invalid: demand may not be at the level anticipated, costs may have increased due to labour or material shortages and so on.

As part of the **post-completion audit** discussed in Chapter 15, the following factors should therefore be considered at each stage of a project's life.

(a)   The NPV of the cash flows associated with abandoning the project. Many cash flows could be relevant.

  (i)   Redundancy payments
  (ii)   Sale of machinery
  (iii) **Opportunity cost** of tying up funds if there is a more profitable use for them.

(b)   The option with the **highest NPV** (continue or abandon) should be selected.

3.1 Possible abandonment scenarios

3.1.1 Scenario 1

Suppose project B has expected cash flows as shown in the table below.

Year	Expected cash flow $	Discount factor 12%	Present value $
0	(21,000)	1.000	(21,000)
1	9,500	0.893	8,484
2	9,500	0.797	7,572
3	9,500	0.712	6,764
NPV			1,820

The initial investment is in a machine built specifically for the organisation in question, and so it has a low resale value of only $5,000 after it has been purchased. Once the machine is **purchased**, the **expected value of abandoning the project** of $5,000 × 1.000 = $5,000 must therefore be **compared with the expected value of continuing** ($(8,484 + 7,572 + 6,764) = $22,820). The expected benefits from continuing with the project are therefore far greater than those from abandoning it immediately and so the project should continue.

3.1.2 Scenario 2

A decision to abandon a project will usually be made because of revised estimates of costs and revenues likely to be received over the remaining life of the project. These revised estimates might be consistent with the data used to make the initial decision, or they might alter initial estimates.

If the revised estimates are consistent with the original data, project abandonment would have been one of the possible outcomes of the project from the outset.

Suppose the cash flows in the table in scenario 1 were based on the probabilities shown below.

	Year 0		Year 1		Year 2		Year 3	
	$	p	$	p	$	p	$
	(21,000)	0.33 (note)	15,000	0.33	15,000	0.33	15,000
		0.33	9,000	0.33	9,000	0.33	9,000
		0.33	4,500	0.33	4,500	0.33	4,500
EV (expected value)			9,500		9,500		9,500

Note. These probabilities are each 1/3 which is expressed as 0.33 ie recurring. When you calculate the EV, you need to use 1/3 rather than 0.33 to get the correct answer.

At time 0, the expected value of the cash inflows from the project in each of years 1-3 is $9,500. The actual outcome in any of the three years is unknown, however, and there is an equal chance of any of the three possible outcomes occurring each year.

It could be that the **outcome in year 1 will determine the outcomes in years 2 and 3**. For example, an outcome of $9,000 in year 1 could mean that the outcomes in years 2 and 3 will definitely be $9,000 as well. Alternatively outcomes of $15,000 or $4,500 in year 1 may result in the same cash flows in years 2 and 3. In such circumstances, future cash flows are therefore known with certainty at the end of year 1.

If the cash flow in year 1 (and hence in years 2 and 3) is $15,000 or $9,000, the actual overall NPV of the project will be positive ($15,000 × 2.402 – $21,000 = $15,030 and $9,000 × 2.402 – $21,000 = $618). If it is $4,500, however, the actual NPV will be –$10,191 (($4,500 × 2.402) – $21,000)).

Should the project be abandoned? The **information on which to base the decision is now certain** and should be **based on using a risk-free interest rate** rather than the 12% cost of capital. If the risk-free rate were 6%, say, the present value of continuing at the end of year 1 would be:

Year	Cashflow	Discount rate	PV
	$	6%	$
1	4,500	0.943	4,244
2	4,500	0.890	4,005
			8,249

Again we need to compare the expected value of abandoning the project with the expected value of continuing.

The expected benefits of continuing are $8,249 compared to the expected value of abandonment ($5,000 from paragraph 3.1.1). So even if the cash inflow is $4,500 in all three years, the project should **not** be abandoned.

3.1.3 Scenario 3

Now let's suppose that the original sale agreement included a **buy-back clause** which meant that the supplier had to buy back the machine for $13,000 on demand at any time up to and including one year after the sale (ie up to the end of year 1).

Suppose the cash inflow in year 1 was $4,500, which made the inflows in years 2 and 3 $4,500 as well. At the end of year 1 the value of abandonment will therefore be $13,000, the value of continuing with the project $8,249 ($4,500 × 1.833, where 1.833 = discount factors at 6% for years 1 and 2). The project should therefore be abandoned at the end of year 1 if the actual outcome in that year is $4,500. (If the cash flow were $15,000 or $9,000 it would not be abandoned.)

If the **buy-back option is included in the analysis from the outset**, however, the possible **outcomes change** as follows.

Year 0		Year 1		Year 2		Year 3
$	p .	$	p .	$	p .	$
(21,000)	0.33	15,000	0.33	15,000	0.33	15,000
	0.33	9,000	0.33	9,000	0.33	9,000
	0.33	4,500	0.33	0	0.33	0
		13,000				
EV		13,833		8,000		8,000

Note that because we would abandon if cashflows per annum were $4,500, we do not include these flows in years 2 and 3. Also remember that 0.33 is 1/3 rather than 0.33.

Including the abandonment option in the analysis increases the NPV by $(3,425 – 1,820) = $1,605.

Year	Expected cash flow $	Discount factor 12%	Present value $
0	(21,000)	1.000	(21,000)
1	13,833	0.893	12,353
2	8,000	0.797	6,376
3	8,000	0.712	5,696
		NPV	3,425

3.1.4 Scenario 4

During the life of a project, **events** may occur that were **not expected when the decision** was **originally taken** and which have an impact on predicted future cash flows.

For example, a new tax introduced during year 1 may reduce the cash inflows from the project by 40%, which would have the following result on expected cash flows.

Year 0		Year 1		Year 2		Year 3
$	p	$	p .	$	p .	$
(21,000)	0.33	15,000	0.33	9,000	0.33	9,000
	0.33	9,000	0.33	5,400	0.33	5,400
	0.33	4,500	0.33	0	0.33	0
		13,000				
EV		13,833		4,800		4,800

The NPV calculation becomes

Year	Expected cash flow $	Discount factor 12%	Present value $
0	(21,000)	1.000	(21,000)
1	13,833	0.893	12,353
2	4,800	0.797	3,826
3	4,800	0.712	3,418
		NPV	(1,403)

The introduction of the new tax results in a negative NPV for the project which means that it is not worthwhile. The project should therefore be abandoned in year 1.

Example: abandoning projects

When EFG carried out the initial appraisal for project P, it contained the following forecast cash flows.

Year	0	1	2	3	4	5
Cash flow ($'000)	(1,000)	(700)	(400)	900	1,500	1,600

It is now the end of year 0 and the investment is about to be made for year 1. The actual cash outflow for year 0 amounted to $1,300,000 and it seems likely that the required investment in year 1 will be $1,000,000. The estimates of the projected cash flows for years 2 to 5 have not altered.

Another company has offered to take over the project from EFG immediately for a consideration of $1,400,000. If EFG did abandon the project they would be obliged to make redundancy payments of $100,000. EFG's cost of capital is 12%.

Should project P be abandoned?

Solution

The $1,300,000 already spent in year 0 is a sunk cost that is not relevant to the abandonment decision (although the post-completion audit process should investigate the reasons for the overspending, to prevent such an occurrence in future.)

The NPV of the future cash flows associated with continuing the project should be calculated, starting again with a 'new' year 0.

Year X	Cash flow $'000	Discount factor 12%	Present value $'000
0	(1,000)	1.000	(1,000)
1	(400)	0.893	(357)
2	900	0.797	717
3	1,500	0.712	1,068
4	1,600	0.636	1,018
Net present value of the decision to continue			1,446

The present value of abandoning the project   = $1,400,000 – $100,000

= $1,300,000

This is lower than the net present value of the cash flows to be generated by continuing, therefore the project should not be abandoned.

The **decision** to continue with the project in this example relied heavily on **management predictions** that the forecast cash flows for the remainder of the project were still reliable. In view of the errors in their forecasts for the original years 0 and 1 this may seem rather doubtful.

It may be **difficult** for managers who are heavily involved with a project to **admit** that **early problems** are **likely** to continue. For this reason it is important that **abandonment reviews** are carried out **objectively**, preferably overseen by a manager who was not involved in the initial appraisal.

If the reasons for abandonment are caused by **external events**, however (as in scenario 4 above), **resistance** to project termination is likely to be **low**.

3.2 The role of the PCA in project abandonment

If there are problems implementing a project, those involved may try to resolve the situation by changing the original plans and/or incurring additional expenditure to meet the original objective(s).

The appropriateness of these actions will depend on the circumstances, but **all major changes to plans** should be **documented** and formally **approved** by more senior management. **Expected cost overruns** should come to light during routine expenditure monitoring by finance staff, and these should be **formally approved** after a **detailed justification** is provided.

Such controls should ensure that **all major changes** to the character of a project have **senior management approval**, but they do not **ensure** that **project abandonment** is automatically **considered** (although it is unlikely that senior management would not consider this option).

An audit can be carried out on all projects that require **additional funding**, and the funding request can then be viewed in conjunction with the **audit report**, which will focus on costs and revenues and – most importantly – the **future**. This puts the audit team in an ideal position to advise senior management on the **value of continuing** with the project.

Section summary

A decision on whether or not a project should be **abandoned** should be made by selecting the option (continue or abandon) with the higher NPV.

4 Capital rationing

Introduction

If an organisation is in a capital rationing situation it will not be able to enter into all projects with positive NPVs because there is not enough capital for all of the investments.

KEY TERM

CAPITAL RATIONING: a situation in which a company has a limited amount of capital to invest in potential projects, such that the different possible investments need to be compared with one another in order to allocate the capital available most effectively.

SOFT CAPITAL RATIONING is brought about by internal factors; **hard capital rationing** is brought about by external factors.

4.1 Soft and hard capital rationing

Soft capital rationing may arise for one of the following reasons.

(a) Management may be **reluctant** to **issue additional share capital** because of concern that this may lead to **outsiders gaining control** of the business.

(b) Management may be **unwilling** to **issue additional share capital** if it will lead to a **dilution of earnings** per share.

(c) Management may **not want to raise additional debt capital** because they do not wish to be committed to **large fixed interest payments**.

(d) Management may wish to **limit investment** to a level that can be **financed solely from retained earnings**.

(e) **Capital expenditure budgets** may restrict spending.

Hard capital rationing may arise for one of the following reasons.

(a) Raising money through the inventory market may not be possible if **share prices** are **depressed**.

(b) There may be **restrictions** on **bank lending** due to government control.

(c) Lenders may consider an organisation to be **too risky** to be granted further loan facilities.

(d) The **costs** associated with making small **issues** of capital may be too great.

4.2 Capital rationing and DCF

To make a decision in a capital rationing situation we need to make a number of **assumptions**.

(a) Capital rationing occurs in a single period, and capital is freely available at all other times.

(b) If a project is not accepted and undertaken during the period of capital rationing, the opportunity to undertake it is lost. It cannot be postponed until a subsequent period when no capital rationing exists.

(c) There is complete certainty about the outcome of each project, so that the choice between projects is not affected by considerations of risk.

(d)   Projects are divisible, so that it is possible to undertake, say, half of Project X in order to earn half of the net present value (NPV) of the whole project.

4.2.1 Basic approach

The idea is to rank all investment opportunities so that the NPVs can be maximised from the use of the available funds.

Note that ranking **in terms of NPVs** will normally give **incorrect** results since this method leads to the selection of large projects, each of which has a high individual NPV but which have, in total, a lower NPV than a large number of smaller projects with lower individual NPVs.

Ranking is therefore in terms of what is called the **profitability index,** which can be defined as the **ratio of the present value of the project's future cash flows (not including the capital investment) divided by the PV of the total capital outlays**.

This ratio measures the PV of future cash flows per $1 of investment, and so indicates which investments make the best use of the limited resources available.

Suppose that HT is considering four projects, W, X, Y and Z. Relevant details are as follows.

Project	Investment required $	Present value of cash inflows $	NPV $	Profitability index (PI)	Ranking as per NPV	Ranking as per PI
W	(10,000)	11,240	1,240	1.12	3	1
X	(20,000)	20,991	991	1.05	4	4
Y	(30,000)	32,230	2,230	1.07	2	3
Z	(40,000)	43,801	3,801	1.10	1	2

Without capital rationing all four projects would be viable investments. Suppose, however, that only $60,000 was available for capital investment.

Resulting NPV if we select projects in the order of ranking per NPV

Project	Priority	Outlay $	NPV $	
Z	1st	40,000	3,801	
Y (balance)*	2nd	20,000	1,487	(²/₃ of $2,230)
		60,000	5,288	

* Projects are divisible. By spending the balancing $20,000 on project Y, two thirds of the full investment would be made to earn two thirds of the NPV.

Profitability index approach

Project	Priority	Outlay $	NPV $	
W	1st	10,000	1,240	
Z	2nd	40,000	3,801	
Y (balance)	3rd	10,000	743	(¹/₃ of $2,230)
		60,000	5,784	

By choosing projects according to the PI, the resulting NPV if only $60,000 is available is increased by $496.

As we mentioned when discussing the discounted payback index in Chapter 16, the profitability index can be stated as (PV of project/initial outlay).

4.2.2 Problems with the profitability index method

(a)   The approach can **only be used if projects are divisible**. If the projects are not divisible a decision has to be made by examining the absolute NPVs of all possible combinations of complete projects that can be undertaken within the constraints of the capital available. The combination of projects which remains at or under the limit of available capital without any of them being divided, and which maximises the total NPV, should be chosen. We look at this in Section 4.3.

(b)   The selection criterion is fairly simplistic, **taking no account** of the possible **strategic value** of individual investments in the context of the overall objectives of the organisation.

(c)   The method is of **limited use** when projects have **differing cash flow patterns**. These patterns may be important to the company since they will affect the timing and availability of funds. With multi-period capital rationing, it is possible that the project with the highest profitability index is the slowest in generating returns.

(d)   The profitability index **ignores the absolute size** of individual projects. A project with a high index might be very small and therefore only generate a small NPV.

Question 18.2	Capital rationing

Learning outcome C2(c)

Bleak House is experiencing capital rationing in year 0, when only $60,000 of investment finance will be available. No capital rationing is expected in future periods, but none of the three projects under consideration can be postponed. The expected cash flows of the three projects are as follows.

Project	Year 0	Year 1	Year 2	Year 3	Year 4
	$	$	$	$	$
A	(50,000)	(20,000)	20,000	40,000	40,000
B	(28,000)	(50,000)	40,000	40,000	20,000
C	(30,000)	(30,000)	30,000	40,000	10,000

The cost of capital is 10%.

Projects A and B only should be undertaken in year 0, in view of the capital rationing, given that projects are divisible. *True or false?*

KEY POINT

This is the approach to adopt if capital is rationed in a single period. If it is restricted in a number of years, linear programming is needed.

4.3 Indivisible projects and single period capital rationing

Suppose AB has $100,000 to invest and is considering the following indivisible projects.

Project	Initial outlay	Return pa to perpetuity
	$'000	$'000
V	20	4
W	45	7
X	15	3
Y	30	5
Z	50	9

AB's cost of capital is 10%.

Let's look at how to select the best mix of projects.

Calculate the NPV of the projects

Project	Initial outlay $'000	PV of cash flows* $'000	NPV $'000
V	20	40	20
W	45	70	25
X	15	30	15
Y	30	50	20
Z	50	90	40

*PV of a perpetuity = annual cashflow/r

 Consider all possible combinations of projects under the investment limit of $100,000. (Use trial and error in an exam although in real life a modelling tool would probably be used.)

The optimum selection of projects is as follows.

Project	Initial outlay $'000	NPV $'000
V	20	20
Y	30	20
Z	50	40
	100	80
Unused funds	-	
Funds available	100	

The **maximum NPV** available is therefore $80,000.

Section summary

When an organisation has a limited amount of capital to invest in potential projects (**capital rationing**) in a single period, projects should be ranked in terms of the **profitability index**.

---

5 Sensitivity analysis   3/11, 5/10

Introduction

In general risky projects are those whose future cash flows, and hence the project returns, are likely to be variable – the greater the variability, the greater the risk. The problem of **risk is more acute with capital investment decisions** than other decisions because estimates of costs and benefits might be for up to 20 years ahead, and such long-term estimates can at best be approximations. Sensitivity analysis is one method of assessing the risk associated with a project.

5.1 Why are projects risky?

A decision about whether or not to go ahead with a project is based on expectations about the future. Forecasts of cash flows (whether they be inflows or outflows) that are likely to arise following a particular course of action are made. These forecasts are made, however, on the basis of what is expected to happen given the present state of knowledge and the future is, by definition, uncertain. Actual cash flows are almost certain to differ from prior expectations. It is this **uncertainty about a project's future income and costs that gives rise to risk in business generally and investment activity in particular**.

5.2 Using sensitivity analysis

Sensitivity analysis is one method of analysing the risk surrounding a capital expenditure project and enables an assessment to be made of how responsive the project's NPV is to changes in the variables that are used to calculate that NPV.

The NPV could depend on a number of uncertain independent variables.

- Estimated selling price
- Estimated sales volume
- Estimated cost of capital
- Estimated initial cost

- Estimated operating costs
- Estimated benefits
- Estimated length of project

5.3 The margin of error approach to sensitivity analysis

The **margin of error approach to sensitivity analysis** assesses how responsive the project's NPV (or payback period or ARR) is to changes in the variables used to calculate that NPV (or payback period or ARR).

This basic approach involves **calculating the project's NPV under alternative assumptions to determine how sensitive it is to changing conditions, thereby indicating those variables to which the NPV is most sensitive (critical variables)** and the **extent to which those variables may change before the investment decision would change** (ie a **positive NPV becoming a negative NPV**).

Once these critical variables have been identified, management should review them to assess whether or not there is a strong possibility of events occurring which will lead to a change in the investment decision. Management should also pay particular attention to controlling those variables to which the NPV is particularly sensitive, once the decision has been taken to accept the investment.

KEY POINT

The sensitivity of an NPV computation to changes in a variable that affects the cashflows is

$$\frac{\text{NPV of project}}{\text{PV of cashflow affected}} \times 100\%$$

Example: sensitivity analysis

KE, which has a cost of capital of 8%, is considering a project. The 'most likely' cash flows associated with the project are as follows.

	Year	0	1	2
		$'000	$'000	$'000
Initial investment		(7,000)		
Variable costs			(2,000)	(2,000)
Cash inflows (650,000 units at $10 per unit)			6,500	6,500
Net cashflows		(7,000)	4,500	4,500

Required

Measure the sensitivity of the project to changes in variables.

Solution

The PVs of the cash flow are as follows.

Year	Discount factor 8%	PV of initial investment $'000	PV of variable costs $'000	PV of cash inflows $'000	PV of net cash flow $'000
0	1.000	(7,000)			(7,000)
1	0.926		(1,852)	6,019	4,167
2	0.857		(1,714)	5,571	3,857
		(7,000)	(3,566)	11,590	1,024

The project has a positive NPV and would appear to be worthwhile. The **changes in cash flows which would need to occur for the project to only just break even (and hence be on the point of being unacceptable) are as follows**.

(a) **Initial investment**. The initial investment can rise by $1,024,000 before the investment breaks even. The initial investment may therefore increase by (1,024/7,000) × 100% = 14.6%.

(b) **Sales volume**. Sales volume affects the level of variable costs and the level of cash inflows. We know that the PV of cash inflows less the PV of variable costs (ie PV of contribution) will have to fall to $7,000,000 for the NPV to be zero. The PV of contribution can therefore fall by ((1,024/(11,590 – 3,566)) × 100%) = 12.8% before the project breaks even.

(c) **Selling price**. The PV of cash inflows can fall by $1,024,000 before the investment breaks even. On the assumption that sales volumes remain the same, the selling price can therefore fall by ((1,024/11,590) × 100%) = 8.8% before the project just breaks even.

(d) **Variable costs**. The PV of variable costs can rise by $1,024,000 before the investment breaks even. Variable costs may therefore increase by (1,024/3,566) × 100% = 28.7%.

(e) **Cost of capital/IRR**. We need to calculate the IRR of the project. Let us try discount rates of 15% and 20%.

Year	Net cash flow $'000	Discount factor 15%	PV $'000	Discount factor 20%	PV $'000
0	(7,000)	1.000	(7,000)	1.000	(7,000)
1	4,500	0.870	3,915	0.833	3,749
2	4,500	0.756	3,402	0.694	3,123
			NPV = 317		NPV = (128)

IRR = 0.15 +[(317/(317 + 128)) × (0.20 – 0.15)] = 18.56%

The **cost of capital** can therefore increase by 132% before the NPV becomes negative.

Alternatively the **IRR** can fall by (18.56% – 8%)/18.56% = 57% before the project would be rejected on the basis of IRR.

The elements to which the NPV appears to be **most sensitive** are the **selling price** followed by the **sales volume**, and it is therefore important for management to pay particular attention to these factors so that they can be carefully monitored.

Given this information, it might be possible to **re-engineer** the project in some way so as to **alter its risk/return profile**. For example, customers might be prepared to contract for a $9.75 fixed selling price, but guarantee to buy the 650,000 units. Obviously the NPV would drop but a major source of uncertainty affecting project viability would be eliminated.

| **Question 18.3** | Sensitivity analysis |

Learning outcome C1(f)

NU has a cost of capital of 8% and is considering a project with the following 'most-likely' cash flows.

Year	Purchase of plant $	Running costs $	Savings $
0	(7,000)		
1		2,000	6,000
2		2,500	7,000

Required

Fill in the blanks in the sentences below about the sensitivity of the project to changes in the levels of expected costs and savings.

(a)   Plant costs would need to .... by a PV of $........ or ....% for the project to break even.

(b)   Running costs would need to .... by a PV of $.......... or ....% for the project to break even.

(c)   Savings would need to .... by a PV of $..........or............ % for the project to break even.

Alternatively you can **change each variable** affecting the NPV of a project in turn **by a certain percentage** and **recalculate the NPV** to determine whether the project is more vulnerable to changes in some key variables than it is to changes in others.

5.3.1 Sensitivity analysis and payback

This would involve determining by how much profit could change in particular years before the decision to accept/not accept was no longer valid.

For example, suppose project B requires initial capital expenditure of $250,000 and that profits before depreciation from the project are likely to be $80,000 in year one, $100,000 in year 2 and $140,000 in year 3. The payback period is therefore two and a half years. If the target payback is three years project B would be accepted. For project B to be rejected:

(a)   The initial expenditure would have to increase by at least $70,000 (or 28%).
(b)   The profits in year 1 would need to fall by at least $70,000 (or 87.5%).
(c)   The profits in year 2 would need to fall by at least $70,000 (or 70%).
(d)   The profits in year 3 would need to fall by at least $70,000 (or 50%).

The project is therefore most sensitive to changes in the initial capital expenditure and year 3 profits.

5.3.2 Sensitivity analysis and ARR

Suppose CC has a target ARR of 20% and is considering project D.

	$
Total profit before depreciation over five years	120,000
Total profit after depreciation over five years	40,000
Average annual profit after depreciation	8,000
Original cost of investment	64,000
Residual value of investment	nil
Average net book value over the five-year period ((64,000 + 0)/2)	32,000

The project's ARR is ($8,000/$32,000) × 100% = 25% and so it would be acceptable.

For project D to be rejected:

(a) Average annual profit after depreciation would need to fall by at least $1,600 to $6,400 (a fall of 20%).

(b) The original cost of the investment would need to increase by at least $16,000 to $80,000 (an increase of 25%).

(c) The residual value of the investment would need to increase by at least $16,000 to $16,000 (an infinite rise from the original $0).

The project is therefore most sensitive to changes in average annual profit.

5.3.3 Weaknesses of the margin of error approach to sensitivity analysis

(a) The method requires that changes in each key variable are isolated but management is more interested in the combination of the effects of changes in two or more key variables. Looking at factors in isolation is unrealistic since they are often interdependent.

(b) Sensitivity analysis does not examine the probability that any particular variation in costs or revenues might occur.

5.4 Diagrammatic approach to sensitivity analysis

We can use a **graph** either to **show how sensitive a project is to changes in a key variable** or to **compare the sensitivities of two or more projects to changes in a key variable**.

Suppose that an organisation wishes to compare two machines (A and B), both of which produce product X. The machines' initial costs, annual fixed running costs and variable cost of producing one unit of product X are different. Annual demand for product X varies unpredictably between 0 and 10,000 units. The selling price of product X is regulated by government and so is fixed at a certain level, whatever the demand.

The NPV of investments in machines A and B at the highest and lowest demand levels are as follows.

	NPVs	
Demand pa Units	Machine A $'000	Machine B $'000
0	(1)	(4)
10,000	8	11

If we plot these four points we can **see how the NPV changes as demand for product X changes**. Note that the NPV does not change in a linear fashion with changes in other variables but **we can plot straight lines to approximate to the curvilinear behaviour** that would be evident if we calculated the NPV at more demand levels.

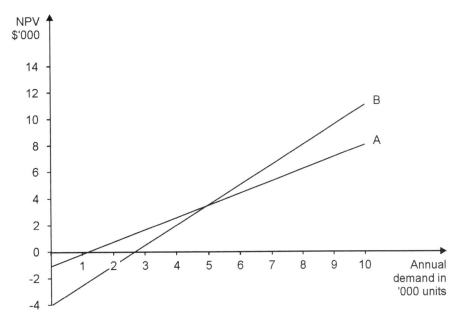

(a)   The two lines cross at demand of 5,000 units so **machine B returns a higher NPV in 50% of the possible outcomes that could arise**.

(b)   On the other hand, machine A crosses the horizontal axis at around 1,100 units. This means that in **approximately 89% of the possible outcomes, machine A would produce a positive NPV**. Contrast this with machine B, where only about 73% of outcomes result in a positive NPV.

(c)   The point at which the **two lines cross** is the point at which the **two machines are equally viable**.

5.5 Sensitivity to changes in discount rate

In all our examples we have assumed, for simplicity, a constant rate of interest. Changes in interest rates can be easily accommodated in NPV and discounted payback calculations but they are not so easily incorporated into IRR or ARR calculations since an IRR or ARR or reflects an average rate of return over a project's life. In **periods of great discount rate volatility** the **NPV method should** therefore **be used**.

In situations of **non-conventional cash flows** a graph can help show the sensitivity of projects to changes in discount rates. Take the following two projects with non-conventional cash flows.

Time	Project Y $'000	Project Z $'000
0	1,920	1,700
1	(4,800)	(4,800)
2	3,000	3,300
NPV @ 10%	$34,800	$62,600

If the projects were **mutually exclusive Project Z would be chosen. If interest rates were not likely to be stable, however, the graph below would illustrate the relative sensitivity of the projects**. (This kind of graph can be sketched by calculating the NPV of the projects at various discount rates but the calculations have not been shown here.)

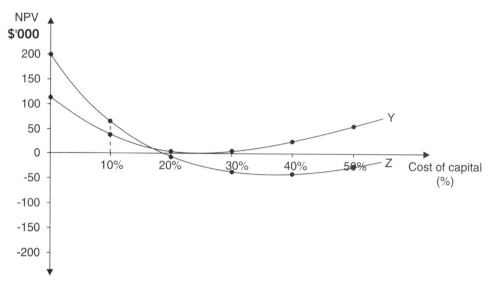

The graph shows that project **Y will remain profitable at any interest rate**, but project **Z would not be worthwhile if interest rates increased beyond about 18%** (unless they then increased to something over 50%). Therefore if one wished to avoid all risk, project Y would be favourable.

5.6 Limitation of sensitivity analysis

One of the **assumptions** commonly made by decision makers in conditions of uncertainty is that the **probability distribution of possible project outcomes is grouped symmetrically around a mean** and **most likely outcome**. The outcomes close to this mean are assumed to be more likely than ones far from it. And many business projects do exhibit this tendency.

The **problem with sensitivity analysis**, however, is that it tends to **focus on ranges** of possible outcomes **without considering the probabilities of different results within those ranges**. It is possible that outcomes at one end of the range are far more likely to occur than outcomes around the central point.

In the scenario illustrated in the graph in Section 5.4, if low levels of demand were more likely than demand in excess of 5,000 units, machine A would be preferred.

Section summary

Sensitivity analysis is one method of analysing the risk surrounding a capital expenditure project and enables an assessment to be made of how responsive the project's NPV is to changes in the variables that are used to calculate that NPV.

The **margin of error approach to sensitivity analysis** assesses how responsive the project's NPV (or payback period or ARR) is to changes in the variables used to calculate that NPV (or payback period or ARR).

6   Probability analysis and long-term decisions

Introduction

Probability distributions of variables in NPV calculations can be drawn up and an **EV of the NPV** calculated.

Before you study this section you might find it useful to read through Section 2 of Chapter 19. Refer to the knowledge brought forward boxes and the simple example in Section 2.2 called Bayes' strategy.

KEY POINT

In the example in Section 5.3 called Sensitivity analysis, attention was drawn to the selling price, which only needed to fall by 8.8% before the project's NPV became negative. A fuller understanding of the impact of the selling price on the attractiveness of the project may therefore be required.

The original NPV was calculated using the 'most likely' selling price, no probability of occurrence having been assigned to this figure. If a **full probability distribution** of selling price were to be drawn up, however, it would indicate the level of confidence that management could have in the original estimate and the probability of other selling prices occurring.

Obviously, it is far more demanding to draw up a full probability distribution than to provide a 'most likely' figure to which no probability has to be attached.

A probability distribution for the selling price could be as follows.

Probability (p)	Price (P) £	pP
0.2	9	1.80
0.5	10	5.00
0.2	11	2.20
0.1	12	1.20
	EV of selling price =	10.20

The **NPV could be recalculated using the EV of the selling price (£10.20) or** alternatively the **NPV could be calculated using each price and then the expected value of the NPVs calculated** (using the probabilities 0.2, 0.5, 0.2 and 0.1).

Such additional information gives management a much greater **awareness** of the financial consequences of the project if **the 'most likely' price proves not to be the actual price**. They are then in a much better position to decide whether or not to proceed with the project. (Don't forget that the outcome of the project depends on the performance of all of the variables, however, not just (for example) the selling price.)

Question 18.4	Probability analysis and long-term decisions

Learning outcomes D1(a), (b), (c)

A company is considering a project involving the outlay of £300,000 which it estimates will generate cash inflows over its two year life at the probabilities shown in the following table.

Cash flows for project

Year 1

Cash flow £	Probability
100,000	0.25
200,000	0.50
300,000	0.25
	1.00

Year 2

If cash flow in Year 1 is: £	there is a probability of:	that the cash flow in Year 2 will be: £
100,000	0.25	Nil
	0.50	100,000
	0.25	200,000
	1.00	
200,000	0.25	100,000
	0.50	200,000
	0.25	300,000
	1.00	

If cash flow in Year 1 is: £	there is a probability of:	that the cash flow in Year 2 will be: £
300,000	0.25	200,000
	0.50	300,000
	0.25	350,000
	1.00	

The company's investment criterion for this type of project is 10% DCF.

Required

Calculate the expected value (EV) of the project's NPV and the probability that the NPV will be negative.

6.1 The standard deviation of the NPV

The disadvantage of using the EV of NPV approach to assess the risk of the project is that the **construction** of the **probability distribution** can become **very complicated**. If we were considering a project over 4 years, each year having five different forecasted cash flows, there would be 625 (5^4) NPVs to calculate. To avoid all of these calculations, an indication of the risk may be obtained by calculating the **standard deviation** of the NPV. We will look at this technique in Chapter 19.

6.2 The expected value of a payback period

An EV of a payback period can be determined using EVs of cashflows for each year of a project.

In the previous question, for example, the EV of the year 1 cashflow is £((100,000 × 0.25) + (200,000 × 0.50) + (300,000 × 0.25)) = £200,000.

The EV of the year 2 cashflows requires the use of the joint probabilities calculated in the answer to the question.

Year 1 cashflow £	Prob	Year 2 cashflow	Prob	Joint prob	EV of Year 2 cashflow*
100,000	0.25	Nil	0.25	0.0625	-
100,000	0.25	100,000	0.50	0.1250	12,500
100,000	0.25	200,000	0.25	0.0625	12,500
200,000	0.50	100,000	0.25	0.1250	12,500
200,000	0.50	200,000	0.50	0.2500	50,000
200,000	0.50	300,000	0.25	0.1250	37,500
300,000	0.25	200,000	0.25	0.0625	12,500
300,000	0.25	300,000	0.50	0.1250	37,500
300,000	0.25	350,000	0.25	0.0625	21,875
					196,875

* Year 2 cashflow × joint probability

We can now calculate the EV of the payback period.

	EV of cashflow £	EV of cumulative cashflow £
Year 0	(300,000)	(300,000)
Year 1	200,000	(100,000)
Year 2	196,875	96,875

∴ EV of payback period = 1 year and ((100,000/196,875) × 12) months
= 1 year 6.1 months

6.3 Problems with expected values and investment decisions

There are the following problems with using expected values in making investment decisions.

- An investment may be **one-off**, and 'expected' NPV may never actually occur.
- **Assigning probabilities** to events is highly **subjective**.
- Expected values **do not evaluate the range** of possible NPV outcomes.

6.4 Use of different cost of money rates

A fairly straightforward way in which organisations can attempt to take account of risk is to use a **higher cost of money rate for higher-risk projects** and a lower rate for lower-risk projects. Higher-risk projects would therefore have to generate larger positive cash flows to be accepted.

Alternatively, **riskier projects can be assessed over a shorter length of time**, so that they have to generate larger positive cashflows than those deemed less risky.

The obvious **disadvantage** of such approaches is that they are **subjective**, because someone must decide what is high risk and what is low risk.

Section summary

Probability distributions of variables in NPV calculations can be drawn up and an **EV of the NPV** calculated.

7 Non-financial considerations in long-term decisions

Introduction

As well as financial considerations, any decision support information provided to management should also incorporate **non-financial considerations**.

Here are some examples.

(a) **Impact on employee morale**. Most investments affect employees' prospects, sometimes for the better, sometimes for the worse. A new cafeteria for employees would have a favourable impact, for example.

(b) **Impact on the community**. This is a particularly important consideration if the investment results in loss of jobs, more jobs or elimination of small businesses.

(c) **Impact on the environment**. The opening of a new mine, the development of products which create environmentally-harmful waste and so on all have an impact on the environment. This can affect an organisation's image and reputation and hence its long-term growth and survival prospects. Some of these environmental effects can also impact directly on project cash flows because organisations have to pay fines, incur legal costs, incur disposal and cleanup costs and so on.

(d) **Ethical issues**. Some investments might be legal but might not be in line with the ethics and code of conduct demanded by various stakeholder groups.

(e) **Learning**. Many investments, particularly those which advance an organisation's technology, provide opportunities for learning. For example, investment in new computerised equipment to revolutionise a production process would enable an organisation to better use highly-technical production methods.

Section summary

Management must also consider the non-financial implications of their decisions.

Chapter Roundup

- ✓ **Annualised equivalents** are used to enable a comparison to be made between the net present values of projects with different durations. However the method cannot be used when inflation is a factor. Another method, the **lowest common multiple** method is used instead.

- ✓ When an asset is **being replaced** with an **identical asset**, the **equivalent annual cost method** can be used.

- ✓ When an asset is being **replaced with a non-identical asset**, the decision is when to replace the asset rather than how frequently. The **present value of an annuity in perpetuity** must be calculated.

- ✓ A decision on whether or not a project should be **abandoned** should be made by selecting the option (continue or abandon) with the higher NPV.

- ✓ When an organisation has a limited amount of capital to invest in potential projects (**capital rationing**) in a single period, projects should be ranked in terms of the **profitability index**.

- ✓ **Sensitivity analysis** is one method of analysing the risk surrounding a capital expenditure project and enables an assessment to be made of how responsive the project's NPV is to changes in the variables that are used to calculate that NPV.

- ✓ The **margin of error approach to sensitivity analysis** assesses how responsive the project's NPV (or payback period or ARR) is to changes in the variables used to calculate that NPV (or payback period or ARR).

- ✓ Probability distributions of variables in NPV calculations can be drawn up and an **EV of the NPV** calculated.

- ✓ Management must also consider the non-financial implications of their decisions.

Quick Quiz

1   The net present value of the costs of operating a machine for the next three years is $10,724 at a cost of capital of 15%. What is the equivalent annual cost of operating the machine?

A $4,697	B $3,575	C $4,111	D $3,109

2   What is the cost of operating the machine detailed in question 1 in perpetuity?

A $31,313	B $71,493	C $23,831	D $12,333

3   Sensitivity analysis allows for uncertainty in project appraisal by assessing the probability of changes in the decision variables. *True or false?*

4   *Fill in the blanks.*

The profitability index used to rank projects in situations where capital is limited is calculated as

.... ÷ ....

5   An organisation's cost of capital is 12%. The IRR of project X is 19.7% and the NPV is $7,900. By how much can the cost of capital increase before the NPV becomes negative?

A   7.7%
B   39.1%
C   19.7%
D   64.2%

6   *Fill in the blanks.*

The sensitivity of a project appraised using DCF to changes in a variable is calculated as:

(................./..................) × 100%.

7   An organisation is deciding whether to replace specialised machinery after a three, four or five year cycle. The NPVs for each cycle are as follows.

	Three-year cycle $	Four-year cycle $	Five-year cycle $
NPV at 10%	(7,150)	(8,300)	(9,190)

Required

Calculate the optimum replacement policy (in years) for the machinery.

Answers to Quick Quiz

1   A $10,724/2.283 = $4,697

2   A $4,697/0.15 = $31,313

3   False. It does not assess the probability of changes in the decision variables.

4   The profitability index used to rank projects in situations where capital is limited is calculated as **the present value of the project's future cash flows** (not including the capital investment) **÷ the present value of the total capital outlay**.

5   D   ((19.7 − 12)/12) × 100% = 64.2%

6   (NPV of project/PV of cashflow affected) × 100%

7   The optimum replacement policy is five years.

	Three-year cycle	Four-year cycle	Five-year cycle
NPV at 10%	$(7,150)	$(8,300)	$(9,190)
Cumulative 10% discount factor	÷ 2.487	÷ 3.170	÷ 3.791
Annualised equivalent cost	$2,875	$2,618	$2,424

The **lowest annualised equivalent cost** results from a five year cycle, therefore the company should replace its machinery every five years.

 # Answers to Questions

18.1 Asset replacement

The correct answer is five years.

	Three-year cycle	Four-year cycle	Five-year cycle
NPV at 15%	$(7,146.6)	$(8,313.68)	$(9,191.2)
Cumulative 15% discount factor	÷ 2.283	÷ 2.855	÷ 3.352
Annualised equivalent cost	$3,130	$2,912	$2,742

The **lowest annualised equivalent cost** results from a five year cycle, therefore the company should replace its cars every five years.

18.2 Capital rationing

The correct answer is that all of projects C and B should be undertaken and part of project A, and so the statement is false.

The ratio of NPV at 10% to outlay in year 0 (the year of capital rationing) is as follows.

Project	Outlay in Year 0 $	PV $	NPV $	Ratio	Ranking
A	50,000	55,700	5,700	1.114	3rd
B	28,000	31,290	3,290	1.118	2nd
C	30,000	34,380	4,380	1.146	1st

The optimal investment policy is as follows.

Ranking	Project	Year 0 outlay $	NPV $
1st	C	30,000	4,380
2nd	B	28,000	3,290
3rd	A (balance)	2,000 (4% of 5,700)	228
NPV from total investment			7,898

18.3 Sensitivity analysis

The correct answer is:

(a)   Plant costs would need to increase by a PV of $560, that is by (560/7,000) × 100% = 8% for the project to break even.

(b)   Running costs would need to increase by a PV of $560, that is by (560/3,995) × 100% = 14% for the project to break even.

(c)   Savings would need to fall by a PV of $560, that is by (560/11,555) × 100% = 4.8% for the project to break even.

The PVs of the cash flows are as follows.

Year	Discount factor 8%	PV of plant cost $	PV of` running costs $	PV of savings $	PV of net cash flow $
0	1.000	(7,000)			(7,000)
1	0.926		(1,852)	5,556	3,704
2	0.857		(2,143)	5,999	3,856
		(7,000)	(3,995)	11,555	560

18.4 Probability analysis and long-term decisions

Calculate expected value of the NPV.

First we need to draw up a probability distribution of the expected cash flows. We begin by calculating the present values of the cash flows.

Year	Cash flow £'000	Discount factor 10%	Present value £'000
1	100	0.909	90.9
1	200	0.909	181.8
1	300	0.909	272.7
2	100	0.826	82.6
2	200	0.826	165.2
2	300	0.826	247.8
2	350	0.826	289.1

Year 1 PV of cash flow £'000 (a)	Probability (b)	Year 2 PV of cash flow £'000 (c)	Probability (d)	Joint probability (b) × (d)	Total PV of cash inflows £'000 (a) + (c)	EV of PV of cash inflows £'000
90.9	0.25	0.0	0.25	0.0625	90.9	5.681
90.9	0.25	82.6	0.50	0.1250	173.5	21.688
90.9	0.25	165.2	0.25	0.0625	256.1	16.006
181.8	0.50	82.6	0.25	0.1250	264.4	33.050
181.8	0.50	165.2	0.50	0.2500	347.0	86.750
181.8	0.50	247.8	0.25	0.1250	429.6	53.700
272.7	0.25	165.2	0.25	0.0625	437.9	27.369
272.7	0.25	247.8	0.50	0.1250	520.5	65.063
272.7	0.25	289.1	0.25	0.0625	561.8	35.113
						344.420

	£
EV of PV of cash inflows	344,420
Less project cost	300,000
EV of NPV	44,420

STEP 2

Measure risk.

Since the EV of the NPV is positive, the project should go ahead unless the risk is unacceptably high. The probability that the project will have a negative NPV is the probability that the total PV of cash inflows is less than £300,000. From the column headed 'Total PV of cash inflows', we can establish that this probability is 0.0625 + 0.125 + 0.0625 + 0.125 = 0.375 or 37.5%. This might be considered an unacceptably high risk.

Now try the question from the Exam Question Bank	Number	Level	Marks	Time
	Q29	Examination	20	36 mins

DEALING WITH UNCERTAINTY IN ANALYSIS

Part E

512

RISK AND UNCERTAINTY IN DECISION MAKING

In Chapter 18 we looked at probability analysis and long-term decision making. In this chapter we look at methods of assessing risk and uncertainty for short-term decision making.

Section 1 contains a general discussion of risk and uncertainty.

Sections 2 to 6 describe the various methods of analysing uncertainty and risk using probability. You need to understand the merits and limitations of these methods for your exam. The uncertainty about the future outcome from taking a decision can sometimes be reduced by obtaining more information first about what is likely to happen. In Section 7 we look at how to **value** that **information** to see if it is worth obtaining it.

Section 8 looks again at a topic we considered in Chapter 18 – **sensitivity analysis. Simulation models**, the topic of Section 9, can be used to deal with decision problems involving a number of uncertain variables.

Learning curve theory (Section 10) is concerned with the reduction in unit labour times (and hence cost) with the repetition of complex, labour intensive activities. This impacts on forecasting future costs.

topic list	learning outcomes	syllabus references	ability required
1 Risk and uncertainty in decision making	D1(a)	D1(i)	analysis
2 Probability analysis and expected values	D1(c), (d)	D1(iii), (iv), (v)	analysis
3 Data tables	D1(c)	D1(iii)	analysis
4 The maximin, maximax and minimax regret bases for decision making	D1(c)	D1(iii), (iv)	analysis
5 Using the standard deviation to measure risk	D1(c)	D1(iii), (iv)	analysis
6 Decision trees	D1(f)	D1(vi)	application
7 The value of information	D1(e)	D1(v)	application
8 Sensitivity analysis	D1(b)	D1(ii)	application
9 Simulation models	D1(b)	D1(ii)	application
10 The learning curve	D1(a)	D1(i)	analysis

1 Risk and uncertainty in decision making

1.1 What are risk and uncertainty?

Introduction

An example of a **risky situation** is one in which we can say that there is a 70% probability that returns from a project will be in excess of $100,000 but a 30% probability that returns will be less than $100,000. If no information can be provided on the returns from the project, we are faced with an **uncertain** situation.

KEY TERMS

RISK involves situations or events which may or may not occur, but whose probability of occurrence can be calculated statistically and the frequency of their occurrence predicted from past records. Thus insurance deals with risk.

UNCERTAIN EVENTS are those whose outcome cannot be predicted with statistical confidence.

1.2 Risk and capital investment decisions

In general, **risky projects** are those which have **future cash flows**, and hence project returns, that are likely to be **variable**. The **greater the variability**, the **greater the risk**.

The problem of **risk is more acute with capital investment decisions** for the following reasons.

(a) **Estimates** of capital expenditure might be for **several years ahead,** such as those for major construction projects. Actual costs may well escalate well above budget as the work progresses.

(b) Estimates of benefits will be for several years ahead, sometimes 10, 15 or 20 years ahead or even longer, and such long-term estimates can at best be approximations.

Exam alert

In everyday usage the terms risk and uncertainty are not clearly distinguished. If you are asked for a definition, do not make the **mistake of believing that the latter** is a more **extreme version of the former**. It is not a question of degree, it is a question of whether or **not sufficient information is available to allow the lack of certainty to be quantified**. As a rule, however, the terms are used interchangeably.

1.3 Risk preference   3/11, 11/10

KEY TERMS

A RISK SEEKER is a decision maker who is interested in the best outcomes no matter how small the chance that they may occur.

A RISK NEUTRAL decision maker is concerned with what will be the most likely outcome.

A RISK AVERSE decision maker acts on the assumption that the worst outcome might occur.

This has clear implications for managers and organisations. A **risk seeking manager** working for an **organisation** that is characteristically **risk averse** is likely to make decisions that are **not congruent with the goals of the organisation**. There may be a role for the management accountant here, who could be instructed to present decision-making information in such a way as to ensure that the manager considers *all* of the possibilities, including the worst.

CASE STUDY

What is an acceptable amount of risk will vary from organisation to organisation. For large public companies it is largely a question of what is acceptable to the shareholders. A 'safe' investment will attract investors who are to some extent risk averse, and so the company will be obliged to follow relatively 'safe' policies. A company that is recognised as being an innovator or a 'growth' inventory in a relatively new market, like *Yahoo!*, will attract investors who are looking for high performance and are prepared to accept some risk in return. Such companies will be expected to make 'bolder' (more risky) decisions.

The risk of an individual strategy should also be considered in the context of the overall 'portfolio' of investment strategies adopted by the company.

(a) If a **strategy is risky**, but its outcome is **not related to the outcome of other strategies**, then adopting that strategy will help the company to **spread its risks**.

(b) If a **strategy is risky**, but is **inversely related** to other adopted strategies (so that if strategy A does well, other adopted strategies will do badly and vice versa) then adopting strategy A would actually **reduce the overall risk of the company's investment portfolio**.

Section summary

People may be **risk seekers**, **risk neutral** or **risk averse**.

In a **risky situation** the **probability** of the outcome can be **quantified**.

In an **uncertain situation** there is not sufficient information for the outcome to be predicted with statistical confidence.

---

2 Probability analysis and expected values   3/11, 5/10

Introduction

Much of this section will be familiar to you from your earlier studies of Business Maths in C3.

2.1 Histograms and probability distributions

2.1.1 Frequency distributions

A **frequency distribution** (or **table**) records the number of times each value of a variable occurs.

2.1.2 Histograms

A frequency distribution can be represented pictorially by means of a **histogram**. As you should remember from your earlier studies, a histogram is a chart that looks like a bar chart except that the bars are joined together. On a histogram, frequencies are represented by the area covered by the bars (not the height of the bars).

2.1.3 Probability distributions

If we convert the frequencies in the following frequency distribution table into proportions, we get a **probability distribution**.

Marks out of 10 (statistics test)	Number of students (Frequency distribution)	Proportion or probability (Probability distribution)
0	0	0.00
1	0	0.00
2	1	0.02 (1/50)
3	2	0.04
4	4	0.08
5	10	0.20
6	15	0.30
7	10	0.20
8	6	0.12
9	2	0.04
10	0	0.00
	50	1.00

KEY TERM

A PROBABILITY DISTRIBUTION is an analysis of the proportion of times each particular value occurs in a set of items.

A **graph of the probability distribution** would be the same as the graph of the frequency distribution (histogram), but with the **vertical axis marked in proportions** rather than in numbers.

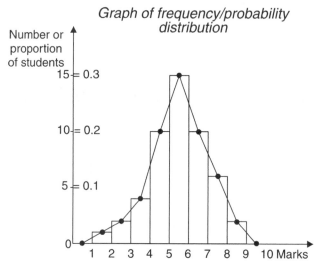

Graph of frequency/probability distribution

(a) The area under the curve in the frequency distribution represents the total number of students whose marks have been recorded, 50 people.

(b) **The area under the curve in a probability distribution is 100%, or 1** (the total of all the probabilities).

2.2 Expected values

Knowledge brought forward from earlier studies

Probability

- **Mutually exclusive outcomes** are outcomes where the occurrence of one of the outcomes excludes the possibility of any of the others happening.

- **Independent events** are events where the outcome of one event in no way affects the outcome of the other events.

- **Dependent** or **conditional** events are events where the outcome of one event depends on the outcome of the others.

- The **addition laws** for two events, A and B, are as follows.

  P(A or B) = P(A) + P(B) when A and B have mutually exclusive outcomes.
  P(A or B) = P(A) + P(B) − P(A and B) when A and B are independent events.

- The **multiplication laws** for two events, A and B, are as follows.

  P(A and B) = 0 when A and B have mutually exclusive outcomes.
  P(A and B) = P(A) P(B) when A and B are independent events.
  P(A and B) = P(A) P(B| A) = P(B) P(A| B) when A and B are dependent/conditional events.

Although the outcome of a decision may not be certain, sometimes probabilities can be assigned to the various possible outcomes from an analysis of previous experience.

Where probabilities are assigned to different outcomes, it is common to evaluate the worth of a decision as the expected value, or weighted average, of these outcomes.

KEY TERM

EXPECTED VALUE is 'The financial forecast of the outcome of a course of action multiplied by the probability of achieving that outcome. The probability is expressed as a value ranging from 0 to 1.'

(CIMA *Official Terminology*)

LEARN

The **expected value** of an opportunity is equal to the sum of the probabilities of an outcome occurring multiplied by the return expected if it does occur:

$$EV = \Sigma\ px$$

where p is the probability of an outcome occurring and x is the value (profit or cost) of that outcome.

If a decision maker is faced with a number of alternative decisions, each with a range of possible outcomes, the optimum decision will be the one which gives the highest **expected value** (EV = Σpx). This is **Bayes' strategy**.

KEY TERM

The choice of the option with the highest EV is known as BAYES' STRATEGY.

Example: Bayes' strategy

Suppose a manager has to choose between mutually exclusive options A and B, and the probability distributions of the profits of both options are as follows.

Option A		Option B	
Probability	Profit $	Probability	Profit $
0.8	5,000	0.1	(2,000)
0.2	6,000	0.2	5,000
		0.6	7,000
		0.1	8,000

The expected value (EV) of profit of each option would be measured as follows.

Probability		Option A Profit $		EV of Profit $	Probability		Option B Profit $		EV of Profit $
0.8	×	5,000	=	4,000	0.1	×	(2,000)	=	(200)
0.2	×	6,000	=	1,200	0.2	×	5,000	=	1,000
		EV	=	5,200	0.6	×	7,000	=	4,200
					0.1	×	8,000	=	800
							EV	=	5,800

In this example, since it offers a higher EV of expected profit, option B would be selected in preference to A, unless further risk analysis is carried out.

Question 19.1 _____ EV calculations

Learning outcomes D1(c)

A manager has to choose between mutually exclusive options A, B, C and D and the probable outcomes of each option are as follows.

Option A		Option B		Option C		Option D	
Probability	*Cost*	*Probability*	*Cost*	*Probability*	*Cost*	*Probability*	*Cost*
	$		$		$		$
0.1	30,000	0.5	21,000	0.29	15,000	0.03	14,000
0.1	60,000	0.5	20,000	0.54	20,000	0.30	17,000
0.1	80,000			0.17	30,000	0.35	21,000
0.7	5,500					0.32	24,000

All options will produce an income of $30,000.

Which option should be chosen?

A   Option A   C   Option C
B   Option B   D   Option D

2.2.1 Limitations of expected values

Referring back to the example in 2.2 called Bayes' strategy, we decided on a preference for B over A on the basis of expected value. Note, however, that A's worst possible outcome is a **profit** of $5,000, whereas B might incur a **loss** of $2,000 (although there is a 70% chance that profits would be $7,000 or more, which would be more than the best profits from option A).

Since the **decision must be made once only** between A and B, the expected value of profit (which is merely a weighted average of all possible outcomes) has severe limitations as a decision rule by which to judge preference as it **ignores the range of outcomes** and their **probabilities**. We consider the concept of **utility** later in this section, which can help overcome this problem.

Expected values are more **valuable** as a guide to decision making where they refer to **outcomes which will occur many times over**.

- The probability that so many customers per day will buy a tin of peaches
- The probability that a call centre will receive so many phone calls per hour

2.3 EVs and elementary risk analysis

Where some analysis of risk is required when probabilities have been assigned to various outcomes, an elementary, but extremely useful, form of risk analysis is a form of the worst possible/most likely/best possible analysis.

Example: elementary risk analysis

Skiver has budgeted the following results for the coming year.

Sales	Probability	EV of Sales
Units		Units
30,000	0.3	9,000
40,000	0.4	16,000
50,000	0.3	15,000
		40,000

The budgeted sales price is $10 per unit, and the expected cost of materials is as follows.

Cost per unit of output $	Probability	EV $
4	0.2	0.8
6	0.6	3.6
8	0.2	1.6
		6.0

Materials are the only variable cost. All other costs are fixed and are budgeted at $100,000.

The **expected value of profit** is $60,000.

	$
Sales (EV 40,000 units) at $10 each	400,000
Variable costs (40,000 × $6)	240,000
Contribution	160,000
Fixed costs	100,000
Profit	60,000

The table below shows the total contribution depending on the level of sales and the material cost per unit.

Contribution table

		Sales units 30,000	40,000	50,000
Material cost per unit	$4 (contribution = $6)	$180,000	$240,000	$300,000
	$6 (contribution = $4)	$120,000	$160,000	$200,000
	$8 (contribution = $2)	$60,000	$80,000	$100,000

Given that fixed costs are $100,000, you can see from the table that Skiver will make a **loss** if material costs are $8 per unit **and** sales are **either** 30,000 pa **or** 40,000 pa. The chance that one **or** other of these events will occur is 14%, as calculated below.

Sales	Probability	Material cost	Probability	Joint probabilities
30,000 units	0.3	$8	0.2	0.06
40,000 units	0.4	$8	0.2	0.08
		Combined probabilities		0.14

However there is also a chance that sales will be 50,000 units and material will cost $4, so that contribution would be $300,000 in total and profits $200,000. This is the **best possible outcome** and it has a 0.3 × 0.2 = 0.06 or 6% probability of occurring.

A **risk averse** decision maker might feel that a 14% chance of making a loss was unacceptable, whereas a **risk seeker** would be attracted by the 6% chance of making $200,000 profit. The **risk neutral** decision maker would need to consider the EV of profit of $60,000.

2.4 EVs and more complex risk analysis

As we have seen, EVs can be used to compare two or more mutually exclusive alternatives: the alternative with the most favourable EV of profit or cost would normally be preferred. However, **alternatives can also be compared** by looking at the **spread of possible outcomes**, and the **probabilities** that they will occur. The technique of drawing up **cumulative probability tables** can be helpful, as the following example shows.

Example: mutually exclusive options and cumulative probability

QRS is reviewing the price that it charges for a major product line. Over the past three years the product has had sales averaging 48,000 units per year at a standard selling price of $5.25. Costs have been rising steadily over the past year and the company is considering raising this price to $5.75 or $6.25. The sales manager has produced the following schedule to assist with the decision.

Price	$5.75	$6.25
Estimates of demand (units)		
Pessimistic estimate (probability 0.25)	35,000	10,000
Most likely estimate (probability 0.60)	40,000	20,000
Optimistic estimate (probability 0.15)	50,000	40,000

Currently the unit cost is estimated at $5.00, analysed as follows.

	$
Direct material	2.50
Direct labour	1.00
Variable overhead	1.00
Fixed overhead	0.50
	5.00

The cost accountant considers that the most likely value for unit variable cost over the next year is $4.90 (probability 0.75) but that it could be as high as $5.20 (probability 0.15) and it might even be as low as $4.75 (probability 0.10). Total fixed costs are currently $24,000 p.a. but it is estimated that the corresponding total for the ensuing year will be $25,000 with a probability of 0.2, $27,000 with a probability of 0.6, $30,000 with a probability of 0.2. (Demand quantities, unit costs and fixed costs can be assumed to be statistically independent.)

Required

Analyse the foregoing information in a way which you consider will assist management with the problem, give your views on the situation and advise on the new selling price. Calculate the expected level of profit that would follow from the selling price that you recommend.

Solution

In this example, there are two mutually exclusive options, a price of $5.75 and a price of $6.25. Sales demand is uncertain, but would vary with price. Unit contribution and total contribution depend on sales price and sales volume, but total fixed costs are common to both options. Clearly, it makes sense to begin looking at EVs of contribution and then to think about fixed costs and profits later.

(a)   A probability table can be set out for each alternative, and an EV calculated, as follows.

Price $5.75

Sales Demand Units	Probability (a)	Variable cost per unit $	Probability (b)	Unit cont'n $	Total cont'n $'000	Joint proba-bility* (a × b)	EV of cont'n $'000
35,000	0.25	5.20	0.15	0.55	19.25	0.0375	0.722
		4.90	0.75	0.85	29.75	0.1875	5.578
		4.75	0.10	1.00	35.00	0.0250	0.875
40,000	0.60	5.20	0.15	0.55	22.00	0.0900	1.980
		4.90	0.75	0.85	34.00	0.4500	15.300
		4.75	0.10	1.00	40.00	0.0600	2.400
50,000	0.15	5.20	0.15	0.55	27.50	0.0225	0.619
		4.90	0.75	0.85	42.50	0.1125	4.781
		4.75	0.10	1.00	50.00	0.0150	0.750
					EV of contribution		33.005

The EV of contribution at a price of $5.75 is $33,005.

* Remember to check that the joint probabilities sum to 1.

Alternative approach

An alternative method of calculating the EV of contribution is as follows.

EV of contribution   =   EV of sales revenue – EV of variable costs

EV of sales revenue =   EV of sales units × selling price
                      =   ((35,000 × 0.25)+ (40,000 × 0.60) + (50,000 × 0.15)) × $5.75

                      =   40,250 × $5.75 = $231,437.50

EV of variable costs =   EV of sales units × EV of unit variable costs

                      =   40,250 × (($5.20 × 0.15) + ($4.90 × 0.75) + ($4.75 × 0.10)) = 40,250 × $4.93 = $198,432.50

∴ EV of contribution = $(231,437.50 – 198,432.50) = $33,005

This method is quicker and simpler, but an extended table of probabilities will help the risk analysis when the two alternative selling prices are compared.

Price $6.25

Sales demand Units	Probability (a)	Variable cost per unit $	Probability (b)	Unit cont'n $	Total cont'n $'000	Joint proba- bility (a × b)	EV of cont'n $'000
10,000	0.25	5.20	0.15	1.05	10.50	0.0375	0.394
		4.90	0.75	1.35	13.50	0.1875	2.531
		4.75	0.10	1.50	15.00	0.0250	0.375
20,000	0.60	5.20	0.15	1.05	21.00	0.0900	1.890
		4.90	0.75	1.35	27.00	0.4500	12.150
		4.75	0.10	1.50	30.00	0.0600	1.800
40,000	0.15	5.20	0.15	1.05	42.00	0.0225	0.945
		4.90	0.75	1.35	54.00	0.1125	6.075
		4.75	0.10	1.50	60.00	0.0150	0.900
						EV of contribution	27.060

The EV of contribution at a price of $6.25 is $27,060.

(b)   The EV of **fixed costs** is $27,200.

Fixed costs $	Probability	EV $
25,000	0.2	5,000
27,000	0.6	16,200
30,000	0.2	6,000
		27,200

(c)   **Conclusion**

On the basis of EVs alone, a price of $5.75 is preferable to a price of $6.25, since it offers an EV of contribution of $33,005 and so an EV of profit of $5,805; whereas a price of $6.25 offers an EV of contribution of only $27,060 and so an EV of loss of $140.

Additional information

A comparison of cumulative probabilities would add to the information for risk analysis. The cumulative probabilities can be used to compare the **likelihood of earning a total contribution of a certain size with each selling price**.

Refer back to the two probability tables above. You should be able to read the probabilities and related total contributions straight from each table.

The table below shows that no matter whether fixed costs are $25,000, $27,000 or $30,000, the **probability of at least breaking even** is much higher with a price of $5.75 than with a price of $6.25. The only reason for favouring a price of $6.25 is that there is a better **probability of earning bigger profits** (a contribution of $50,000 or more), and so although a risk-averse decision maker would choose a price of $5.75, a risk-seeking decision maker might gamble on a price of $6.25.

Probability of total contribution of at least	*Price $5.75*		*Price $6.25*	
$	*Probability*	*Workings*	*Probability*	*Workings*
15,000	1.0000		0.7750	(1 – 0.0375 – 0.1875)
20,000	0.9625	(1 – 0.0375)	0.7500	(0.775 – 0.025)
25,000	0.8725	(0.9625 – 0.09)	0.6600	etc
27,000	0.8725		0.6600	
30,000	0.6625	(0.8725 – 0.1875 – 0.0225)	0.2100	
35,000	0.2125	etc	0.1500	
40,000	0.1875		0.1500	
50,000	0.0150		0.1275	
60,000	0.0000		0.0150	

2.5 The advantages and disadvantages of point estimate probabilities

A **point estimate probability** means an estimate of the **probability of particular outcomes occurring**. In the previous example, there were point estimate probabilities for **variable costs** ($5.20 or $4.90 or $4.75) but in **reality**, the **actual** variable cost per unit **might be any amount**, from below $4.75 to above $5.20. Similarly, point estimate probabilities were given for period fixed costs ($25,000 or $27,000 or $30,000) but in reality, actual fixed costs might be any amount between about $25,000 and $30,000.

This is a disadvantage of using point estimate probabilities: they can be **unrealistic**, and can only be an **approximation** of the risk and uncertainty in estimates of costs or sales demand.

In spite of their possible disadvantages, point estimate probabilities can be very helpful for a decision maker.

(a)   They provide some estimate of risk, which is probably **better than nothing**.

(b)   **If there are enough point estimates** they are likely to be a **reasonably good approximation of** a continuous probability distribution.

(c)   Alternatively, it can be **assumed** that point estimate probabilities **represent a range** of values, so that if we had the probabilities for variable cost per unit, say, of $5.20, $4.90, and $4.75 we could assume that those actually represent probabilities for the ranges, say, $5.05 to $5.30, and $4.82 to $5.04 and $4.70 to $4.81.

Section summary

If a decision maker is faced with a number of alternative decisions, each with a range of possible outcomes, the optimum decision will be the one which gives the highest **expected value** (EV = Σpx). This is **Bayes' strategy**.

The calculation of **joint probabilities** and **cumulative probabilities** adds to the information for risk analysis.

3 Data tables

Introduction

Data tables are often produced using spreadsheet packages and show the effect of changing the values of variables.

A **one-way or one-input data table shows the effect of a range of values of one variable**. For example it might show the effect on profit of a range of selling prices. A **two-way or two-input data table shows the results of combinations of different values of two key variables.** The effect on contribution of combinations of various levels of demand and different selling prices would be shown in a two-way data table.

Any combination of variable values can therefore be changed and the **effects monitored.**

Example: a one-way data table

Suppose a company has production costs which it would expect to be in the region of $5m were it not for the effects of inflation. Economic forecasts for the inflation rate in the coming year range from 2% to 10%. Profit (before inflation is taken into account) is expected to be $475,000.

By using a spreadsheet package and with three or four clicks of the mouse, the data table below is produced. This shows the effects of different levels of inflation on production costs and profit.

		Production costs $'000	Profit $'000
	2%	5,100	375
	3%	5,150	325
Inflation rate	4%	5,200	275
	5%	5,250	225
	6%	5,300	175
	7%	5,350	125
	8%	5,400	75
	9%	5,450	25
	10%	5,500	(25)

So if inflation were to be 7%, the company could expect production costs to be in the region of $5,350,000 and profit to be about $125,000 ($(475,000 − (7% × $5m)).

Example: two-way data table

Suppose now that the company mentioned in the example above, is not sure that its production costs will be $5m. They could be only $4.5m or they could be up to $5.5m.

We therefore need to examine the effects of both a range of rates of inflation and three different production costs on profit, and so we need a two-way data table as shown below.

Two-way data table showing profit for a range of rates of inflation and production costs

		Production costs		
		$4,500,000	$5,000,000	$5,500,000
		$'000	$'000	$'000
	2%	385	375	365
	3%	340	325	310
Inflation rate	4%	295	275	255
	5%	250	225	200
	6%	205	175	145
	7%	160	125	90
	8%	115	75	35
	9%	70	25	(20)
	10%	25	(25)	(75)

So if production costs were $5,500,000 and the rate of inflation was 4%, the profit should be $255,000 ($(475,000 – (4% × $5,500,000)).

3.1 Data tables and probability

If a probability distribution can be applied to either or both of the variables in a data table, a revised table can be prepared to provide improved management information.

Example: data tables and probability

Estimates of levels of demand and unit variable costs, with associated probabilities, for product B are shown below. Unit selling price is fixed at $100.

Levels of demand

Pessimistic	Probability of 0.4	10,000 units
Most likely	Probability of 0.5	12,500 units
Optimistic	Probability of 0.1	13,000 units

Unit variable costs

Optimistic	Probability of 0.3	$20
Most likely	Probability of 0.4	$30
Pessimistic	Probability of 0.3	$35

Required

Produce a two-way data table showing levels of contribution that incorporates information about both the variables and the associated probabilities.

Solution

Table of total contributions

The shaded area on this table shows the possible total contributions and the associated joint probabilities.

Demand			10,000	12,500	13,000
Probability			0.4	0.5	0.1
Unit variable cost	Probability	Unit contribution			
$20	0.3	$80	$800,000	$1,000,000	$1,040,000
			0.12	0.15	0.03
$30	0.4	$70	$700,000	$875,000	$910,000
			0.16	0.20	0.04
$35	0.3	$65	$650,000	$812,500	$845,000
			0.12	0.15	0.03

Section summary

Data tables are often produced using spreadsheet packages and show the effect of changing the values of variables.

4 The maximin, maximax and minimax regret bases for decision making   11/10

Introduction

The **assumption** made so far in this chapter has been that when there is a decision to make, and probabilities of the various outcomes have been estimated, the decision maker should **prefer the option with the highest EV of profit**.

For **once-only decisions**, this choice of option with the best EV does not necessarily make sense. It provides one rational basis for decision making, but it is not the only rational basis.

There are several other ways of making a choice, including the following.

(a)   **Playing safe**, and **choosing the option with the least damaging results if events were to turn out badly**.

(b)   Looking for the **best outcome**, no matter how small the chance that it might occur.

(c)   Looking at the opportunity loss when we choose an option but come to regret it.

(d)   **Balancing the EV of profit against the risk**, measured as the **standard deviation of variations in possible profit around the EV**. We cover this in Section 5.

The 'play it safe' basis for decision making is referred to as the **maximin basis**. This is short for '**maximise the minimum achievable profit**'. (It might also be called '**minimax**' which is short for '**minimise the maximum potential cost or loss**'). Maximin decisions are taken by **risk-averse** decision makers.

A basis for making decisions by looking for the best outcome is known as the **maximax basis**, short for '**maximise the maximum achievable profit**'. (It can also be called the **minimin cost rule** – minimise the minimum costs or losses.) Maximax decisions are taken by **risk-seeking** decision makers.

The 'opportunity loss' basis for decision making is known as **minimax regret**.

Example: maximin decision basis

Suppose that a manager is trying to decide which of three mutually exclusive projects to undertake. Each of the projects could lead to varying net profits which are classified as outcomes I, II and III. The manager has constructed the following **pay-off table or matrix** (a **conditional profit table**).

	Net profit if outcome turns out to be		
Project	I	II	III
A	$50,000	$65,000	$80,000
B	$70,000	$60,000	$75,000
C	$90,000	$80,000	$55,000
Probability	0.2	0.6	0.2

Required

Decide which project should be undertaken.

Solution

If the project with the **highest EV of profit** were chosen, this would be project C.

Outcome	Probability	Project A EV $	Project B EV $	Project C EV $
I	0.2	10,000	14,000	18,000
II	0.6	39,000	36,000	48,000
III	0.2	16,000	15,000	11,000
		65,000	65,000	77,000

However, if the **maximin criterion** were applied the assessment would be as follows.

Project selected	The worst outcome that could happen	Profit $
A	I	50,000
B	II	60,000
C	III	55,000

By **choosing B**, we are **'guaranteed' a profit of at least $60,000**, which is more than we would get from projects A or C if the worst outcome were to occur for them. (We want the maximum of the minimum achievable profits.)

The decision would therefore be to **choose project B**.

The main **weakness** of the maximin basis for decision making is that it **ignores the probabilities** that **various different outcomes might occur**, and so in this respect, it is not as good as the EV basis for decision making.

Example: maximax

Here is a payoff table showing the profits that will be achieved depending upon the action taken (D, E or F) and the circumstances prevailing (I, II or III).

		Profits Actions		
		D	E	F
	I	100	80	60
Circumstances	II	90	120	85
	III	(20)	10	85
Maximum profit		100	120	85

Action E would be chosen if the maximax rule is followed.

Criticisms of this approach would be that it ignores probabilities and that it is over-optimistic.

4.1 Minimax regret

Minimax regret considers the extent to which we might come to regret an action we had chosen.

Regret for any combination of action and circumstances	=	Payoff for **best** action in those circumstances	−	Payoff of the action **actually taken** in those circumstances

An alternative term for regret is **opportunity loss**. We may apply the rule by considering the maximum opportunity loss associated with each course of action and choosing the course which offers the smallest maximum. If we choose an action which turns out not to be the best in the actual circumstances, we have lost an opportunity to make the extra profit we could have made by choosing the best action.

Here are payoff tables for two separate decisions.

			Profits Actions						Costs Actions		
			A	B	C				D	E	F
	I		100	80	60		IV		40	50	60
Circumstances	II		90	120	85	Circumstances	V		70	80	25
	III		−20	10	40		VI		20	30	30
Max profit			100	120	85	Min cost			20	30	25
Difference between best and worst circumstances			120	110	45				50	50	35

(a)   For the first decision, action B (payoff 120) would be chosen using maximax, or C using maximin (payoff 40) and using minimax regret.

(b)   For the second decision, action D would be chosen using maximax, F using maximin and using minimax regret.

Look at the example below. Follow through the solution and make sure you understand how the maximum regret is arrived at.

Example: minimax regret

A manager is trying to decide which of three mutually exclusive projects to undertake. Each of the projects could lead to varying net costs which the manager calls outcomes I, II and III. The following payoff table or matrix has been constructed.

		Outcomes (Net profit)		
		I	II	III
		(Worst)	(Most likely)	(Best)
	A	50	85	130
Project	B	70	75	140
	C	90	100	110

Which project should be undertaken?

Solution

A table of regrets can be compiled, as follows, showing the amount of profit that might be forgone for each project, depending on whether the outcome is I, II or III.

	Outcome			Maximum
	I	II	III	
Project A	40 *	15 ***	10	40
Project B	20 **	25	0	25
Project C	0	0	30	30

* 90 − 50   ** 90 − 70   *** 100 − 85   etc

The **maximum regret** is 40 with project A, 25 with B and 30 with C. The lowest of these three maximum regrets is 25 with B, and so project B would be selected if the minimax regret rule is used.

Section summary

The maximin basis means maximise the minimum achievable profit.

The maximax basis means maximise the maximum achievable profit.

The minimax regret basis means minimise the maximum regrets.

5 Using the standard deviation to measure risk 5/10

Introduction

Risk can be measured by the possible variations of outcomes around the expected value. One useful measure of such variations is the **standard deviation of the expected value**.

LEARN

The standard deviation is $s = \sqrt{\Sigma p(x - \bar{x})^2} = \sqrt{\text{variance}}$

where $\bar{x}$ is the EV of profit
x represents each possible profit
p represents the probability of each possible profit

The decision maker can then **weigh up the EV of each option against the risk** (the standard deviation) that is **associated with it**.

Example: measuring risk

The management of RC is considering which of two mutually exclusive projects to select. Details of each project are as follows.

	Project S			Project T	
Probability	Profit $'000		Probability	Profit $'000	
0.3	150		0.2	(400)	
0.3	200		0.6	300	
0.4	250		0.1	400	
			0.1	800	

Required

Determine which project seems preferable, S or T.

Solution

On the basis of EVs alone, T is marginally preferable to S, by $15,000.

	Project S			Project T	
Probability	Profit $'000	EV $'000	Probability	Profit $'000	EV $'000
0.3	150	45	0.2	(400)	(80)
0.3	200	60	0.6	300	180
0.4	250	100	0.1	400	40
			0.1	800	80
	EV of profit	205		EV of profit	220

Project T is **more risky**, however, offering the prospect of a profit as high as $800,000 but also the possibility of a loss of $400,000.

One measure of this risk is the **standard deviation of the EV of profit**.

(a) **Project S**

Probability p	Profit X $'000	$x - \bar{x}$	$p(x - \bar{x})^2$
0.3	150	−55	907.5*
0.3	200	−5	7.5
0.4	250	45	810.0
		Variance	1,725.0

* $0.3 \times (-55)^2$

Standard deviation $= \sqrt{1,725} = 41.533 = \$41,533$

(b) **Project T**

Probability p	Profit X $'000	$x - \bar{x}$	$p(x - \bar{x})^2$
0.2	(400)	−620	76,880
0.6	300	80	3,840
0.1	400	180	3,240
0.1	800	580	33,640
		Variance	117,600

Standard deviation $= \sqrt{117,600} = 342.929 = \$342,929$

If the management are **risk averse**, they might therefore **prefer project S** because, although it has a smaller EV of profit, the possible profits are subject to less variation.

The **risk associated with project T can be compared with the risk associated with project S** if we calculate the **coefficient of variation** for each project: the **ratio of the standard deviation of each project to its EV**.

	Project S	Project T
Standard deviation	$41,533	$342,929
EV of profit	$205,000	$220,000
Coefficient of variation (standard deviation/EV of profit)	0.20	1.56

Question 19.2	Using the standard deviation to measure risk

Learning outcome D1(c)

Fill in the blank in the sentence below.

On the basis of the information below a 'risk averse' decision maker would choose project ....

Project A		Project B	
Estimated net cash flow $	Probability	Estimated net cash flow $	Probability
		1,000	0.2
2,000	0.3	2,000	0.2
3,000	0.4	3,000	0.2
4,000	0.3	4,000	0.2
		5,000	0.2

Question 19.3   Standard deviation of the net present value

Learning outcome D1(c)

Frame is considering which of two mutually exclusive projects, A or B, to undertake. There is some uncertainty about the running costs with each project, and a probability distribution of the NPV for each project has been estimated, as follows.

Project A		Project B	
NPV $'000	Probability	NPV $'000	Probability
− 20	0.15	+ 5	0.2
+ 10	0.20	+ 15	0.3
+ 20	0.35	+ 20	0.4
+ 40	0.30	+ 25	0.1

Required

Choose the correct words from those highlighted in the sentence below.

The organisation should choose **project A/project B** if management are risk averse.

Section summary

Risk can be measured by the possible variations of outcomes around the expected value. One useful measure of such variations is the **standard deviation of the expected value**.

6 Decision trees   9/10, 5/10

Introduction

A probability problem such as 'what is the probability of throwing a six with one throw of a die?' is fairly straightforward and can be solved using the basic principles of probability.

More complex probability questions, although solvable using the basic principles, require a clear logical approach to ensure that all possible choices and outcomes of a decision are taken into consideration. **Decision trees** are a useful means of interpreting such probability problems.

KEY TERM

A DECISION TREE is 'A pictorial method of showing a sequence of interrelated decisions and their expected outcomes. Decision trees can incorporate both the probabilities of, and values of, expected outcomes, and are used in decision-making.'   (CIMA *Official Terminology*)

Exactly how does the use of a decision tree permit a clear and logical approach?

- All the possible **choices** that can be made are shown as **branches** on the tree.
- All the possible **outcomes** of each choice are shown as **subsidiary branches** on the tree.

6.1 Constructing a decision tree

There are two stages in preparing a decision tree.

- Drawing the tree itself to show all the choices and outcomes
- Putting in the numbers (the probabilities, outcome values and EVs)

Every **decision tree starts** from a **decision point** with the **decision options** that are currently being considered.

(a)   It helps to identify the **decision point**, and any subsequent decision points in the tree, with a symbol. Here, we shall use a **square shape**.

(b)   There should be a **line**, or **branch**, for each **option** or **alternative**.

It is conventional to draw decision trees from left to right, and so a decision tree will start as follows.

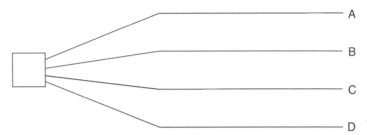

The **square** is the **decision point**, and A, B, C and D represent **four alternatives** from which a choice must be made (such as buy a new machine with cash, hire a machine, continue to use existing machine, raise a loan to buy a machine).

If the outcome from any choice is certain, the branch of the decision tree for that alternative is complete.

If the outcome of a particular choice is uncertain, the various possible outcomes must be shown.

We show the various possible outcomes on a decision tree by inserting an **outcome point** on the **branch** of the tree. Each possible outcome is then shown as a **subsidiary branch**, coming out from the outcome point. The probability of each outcome occurring should be written on to the branch of the tree which represents that outcome.

To distinguish decision points from outcome points, **a circle will be used as the symbol for an outcome point**.

In the example above, there are two choices facing the decision-maker, A and B. The outcome if A is chosen is known with certainty, but if B is chosen, there are two possible outcomes, high sales (0.6 probability) or low sales (0.4 probability).

When several outcomes are possible, it is usually simpler to show two or more stages of outcome points on the decision tree.

 Example: several possible outcomes

A company can choose to launch a new product XYZ or not. If the product is launched, expected sales and expected unit costs might be as follows.

Sales		Unit costs	
Units	Probability	£	Probability
10,000	0.8	6	0.7
15,000	0.2	8	0.3

(a)   The decision tree could be drawn as follows.

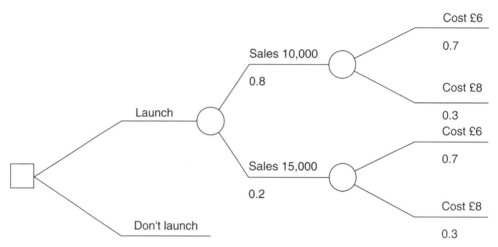

(b)   The layout shown above will usually be easier to use than the alternative way of drawing the tree, which is as follows.

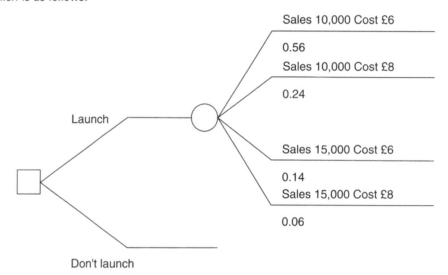

Sometimes, a **decision taken now** will lead to **other decisions to be taken in the future**. When this situation arises, the decision tree can be drawn as a **two-stage tree**, as follows.

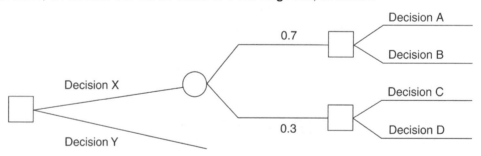

In this tree, either a choice between A and B or else a choice between C and D will be made, depending on the outcome which occurs after choosing X.

The decision tree should be in **chronological order** from **left to right**. When there are two-stage decision trees, the first decision in time should be drawn on the left.

Example: a decision tree

Beethoven has a new wonder product, the vylin, of which it expects great things. At the moment the company has two courses of action open to it, to test market the product or abandon it.

If the company test markets it, the cost will be $100,000 and the market response could be positive or negative with probabilities of 0.60 and 0.40.

If the response is positive the company could either abandon the product or market it full scale.

If it markets the vylin full scale, the outcome might be low, medium or high demand, and the respective net gains/(losses) would be (200), 200 or 1,000 in units of $1,000 (the result could range from a net loss of $200,000 to a gain of $1,000,000). These outcomes have probabilities of 0.20, 0.50 and 0.30 respectively.

If the result of the test marketing is negative and the company goes ahead and markets the product, estimated losses would be $600,000.

If, at any point, the company abandons the product, there would be a net gain of $50,000 from the sale of scrap. All the financial values have been discounted to the present.

Required

(a)   Draw a decision tree.
(b)   Include figures for cost, loss or profit on the appropriate branches of the tree.

Solution

The starting point for the tree is to **establish what decision has to be made now**. What are the options?

(a)   To test market
(b)   To abandon

The outcome of the 'abandon' option is known with certainty. There are two possible outcomes of the option to test market, positive response and negative response.

Depending on the outcome of the test marketing, another decision will then be made, to abandon the product or to go ahead.

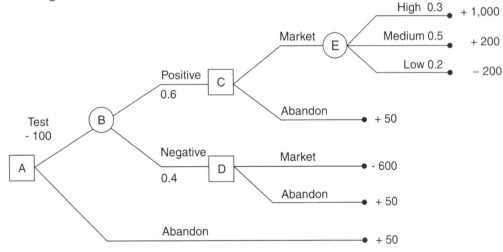

Exam skills

In an examination, remember to draw decision trees (and *all* diagrams) neatly, using a sharp pencil and ruler. Remember also to label decision points and branches as clearly as possible. The specimen paper contained a 5-mark question asking for a decision tree sketch and interpretation and the May 2010 exam did too.

6.2 Evaluating the decision with a decision tree

Rollback analysis evaluates the EV of each decision option. You have to work from right to left and calculate EVs at each outcome point.

The EV of each decision option can be evaluated, using the decision tree to help with keeping the logic on track. The basic rules are as follows.

(a)   We start on the **right hand side** of the tree and **work back** towards the left hand side and the current decision under consideration. This is sometimes known as the **'rollback' technique** or **'rollback analysis'**.

(b)   Working from **right to left**, we calculate the **EV of revenue, cost, contribution or profit** at each outcome point on the tree.

In the above example, the right-hand-most outcome point is point E, and the EV is as follows.

	Profit	Probability	
	x	p	px
	$'000		$'000
High	1,000	0.3	300
Medium	200	0.5	100
Low	(200)	0.2	(40)
		EV	360

This is the EV of the decision to market the product if the test shows positive response. It may help you to write the EV on the decision tree itself, at the appropriate outcome point (point E).

(a)   **At decision point C**, the **choice** is as follows.

(i)   Market, EV = + 360 (the EV at point E)
(ii)   Abandon, value = + 50

The choice would be to market the product, and so the EV at decision point C is +360.

(b)   **At decision point D**, the **choice** is as follows.

(i)   Market, value = – 600
(ii)   Abandon, value = +50

The choice would be to abandon, and so the EV at decision point D is +50.

The second stage decisions have therefore been made. If the original decision is to test market, the company will market the product if the test shows positive customer response, and will abandon the product if the test results are negative.

The evaluation of the decision tree is completed as follows.

(a)   **Calculate the EV at outcome point B.**

        0.6 × 360   (EV at C)
   +   0.4 × 50   (EV at D)
   =   216 + 20 = 236.

(b)   **Compare the options at point A**, which are as follows.

(i)   Test: EV = EV at B minus test marketing cost = 236 – 100 = 136
(ii)   Abandon: Value = 50

The choice would be to test market the product, because it has a **higher EV of profit**.

Question 19.4   Simple decision tree

Learning outcome D1(f)

Consider the following diagram.

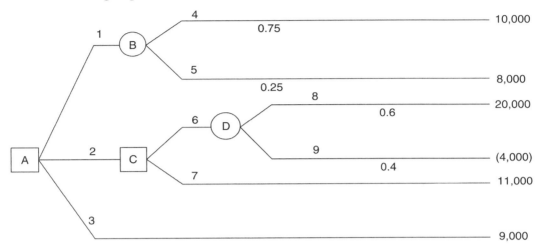

If a decision maker wished to maximise the value of the outcome, which options should be selected?

A   Option 2 and option 7
B   Option 3
C   Option 1 and option 4
D   Option 2, option 6 and option 8

Evaluating decisions by using **decision trees has a number of limitations**.

(a)   The time value of money may not be taken into account.

(b)   Decision trees are not very suitable for use in complex situations.

(c)   The outcome with the highest EV may have the greatest risks attached to it. Managers may be reluctant to take risks which may lead to losses.

(d)   The probabilities associated with different branches of the 'tree' are likely to be estimates, and possibly unreliable or inaccurate.

Section summary

Decision trees are diagrams which illustrate the choices and possible outcomes of a decision.

Rollback analysis evaluates the EV of each decision option. You have to work from right to left and calculate EVs at each outcome point.

7   The value of information

Introduction

The **value of perfect information** is the difference between the EV of profit with perfect information and the EV of profit without perfect information.

KEY TERM

PERFECT INFORMATION removes all doubt and uncertainty from a decision, and enables managers to make decisions with complete confidence that they have selected the optimum course of action.

7.1 The value of perfect information   5/11

If we **do not have perfect information** and we must choose between two or more decision options, we would **select** the decision option which offers the **highest EV** of profit. This option will not be the best decision under all circumstances. There will be some probability that what was really the best option will not have been selected, given the way actual events turn out.

With **perfect information**, the **best decision option will always be selected**. The profits from the decision will depend on the future circumstances which are predicted by the information; nevertheless, the EV of profit with perfect information should be higher than the EV of profit without the information.

The **value of perfect information** is **the difference between these two EVs**.

Example: the value of perfect information

The management of Ivor Ore must choose whether to go ahead with either of two mutually exclusive projects, A and B. The expected profits are as follows.

	Profit if there is strong demand	Profit/(loss) if there is weak demand
Option A	$4,000	$(1,000)
Option B	$1,500	$500
Probability of demand	0.3	0.7

Required

(a) Ascertain what the decision would be, based on expected values, if no information about demand were available.

(b) Calculate the value of perfect information about demand.

Solution

If there were **no information** to help with the decision, the project with the higher EV of profit would be selected.

Probability	Project A		Project B	
	Profit	EV	Profit	EV
	$	$	$	$
0.3	4,000	1,200	1,500	450
0.7	(1,000)	(700)	500	350
		500		800

Project B would be selected.

This is clearly the better option if demand turns out to be weak. However, if demand were to turn out to be strong, project A would be more profitable. There is a 30% chance that this could happen.

Perfect information will indicate for certain whether demand will be weak or strong. If demand is forecast 'weak' project B would be selected. If demand is forecast as 'strong', project A would be selected, and perfect information would improve the profit from $1,500, which would have been earned by selecting B, to $4,000.

Forecast demand	Probability	Project chosen	Profit $	EV of profit $
Weak	0.7	B	500	350
Strong	0.3	A	4,000	1,200
		EV of profit with perfect information		1,550

	$
EV of profit without perfect information (ie if project B is always chosen)	800
EV of profit with perfect information	1,550
Value of perfect information	750

Provided that the information does not cost more than $750 to collect, it would be worth having.

Question 19.5   Decision based on EV of profit

Learning outcome D1(e)

Watt Lovell must decide at what level to market a new product, the urk. The urk can be sold nationally, within a single sales region (where demand is likely to be relatively strong) or within a single area. The decision is complicated by uncertainty about the general strength of consumer demand for the product, and the following conditional profit table has been constructed.

		Demand		
		Weak $	Moderate $	Strong $
Market	nationally (A)	(4,000)	2,000	10,000
	in one region (B)	0	3,500	4,000
	in one area (C)	1,000	1,500	2,000
Probability		0.3	0.5	0.2

Option B should be selected, based on EVs of profit. *True or false?*

Question 19.6   Perfect information

Learning outcome D1(e)

Using the information in your answer to the question above (Decision based on EV of profit), fill in the blank in the sentence below.

The value of information about the state of demand is $.......... .

7.2 Perfect information and decision trees

When the option exists to obtain information, the decision can be shown, like any other decision, in the form of a decision tree, as follows. We will suppose, for illustration, that the cost of obtaining perfect information is $400.

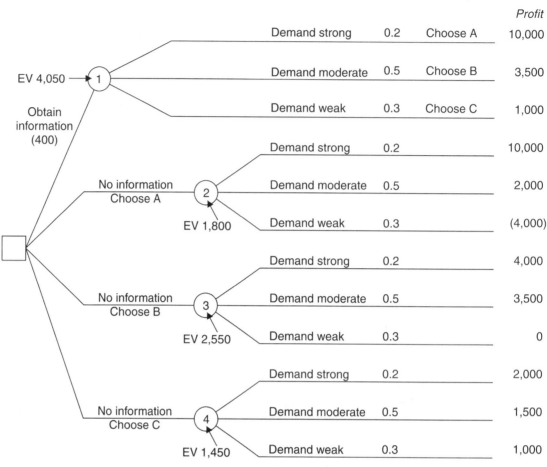

The decision would be to obtain perfect information, since the EV of profit is $4,050 – $400 = $3,650.

Exam skills

You should check carefully that you understand the logic of this decision tree and that you can identify how the EVs at outcome boxes 1, 2, 3 and 4 have been calculated.

Section summary

Perfect information is guaranteed to predict the future with 100% accuracy. **Imperfect information** is better than no information at all but could be wrong in its prediction of the future.

The **value of perfect information** is the difference between the EV of profit with perfect information and the EV of profit without perfect information.

8   Sensitivity analysis

Introduction

We have already encountered sensitivity analysis in relation to NPV analysis. Here we look at it in more general terms.

SENSITIVITY ANALYSIS is 'A modelling and risk assessment procedure in which changes are made to significant variables in order to determine the effect of these changes on the planned outcome. Particular attention is thereafter paid to variables identified as being of special significance.'

(CIMA *Official Terminology*)

Two useful approaches to sensitivity analysis

(a)   Estimate by how much costs and revenues would need to differ from their estimated values before the decision would change

(b)   Estimate whether a decision would change if estimated costs were x% higher than estimated, or estimated revenues y% lower than estimated.

The essence of the approach is therefore to **carry out the calculations with one set of values for the variables** and then **substitute other possible values** for the variables to see **how this affects the overall outcome**.

Example: sensitivity analysis

SS has estimated the following sales and profits for a new product which it may launch on to the market.

	$	$
Sales (2,000 units)		4,000
Variable costs: materials	2,000	
labour	1,000	
		3,000
Contribution		1,000
Less incremental fixed costs		800
Profit		200

Required

Analyse the sensitivity of the project.

Solution

The **margin of safety**   = ((budgeted sales – breakeven sales)/budgeted sales) × 100%

The breakeven point   = fixed costs/contribution per unit
                        = $800/($1,000/2,000 units) = 1,600 units

∴ Margin of safety   = ((2,000 – 1,600)/2,000) × 100% = 20%

If any of the **costs increase by more than $200**, the profit will disappear and there will be a **loss**.

Changes in variables which would result in a loss

- More than ((200/800) × 100%) 25% increase in incremental **fixed costs**
- More than ((200/2,000) × 100%) 10% increase in unit cost of **materials**
- More than ((200/1,000) × 100%) 20% increase in **unit labour costs**
- More than ((200/4,000) × 100%) 5% drop in **unit selling price**

Management would now be able to judge more clearly whether the product is likely to be profitable. The **items to which profitability is most sensitive** in this example are the **selling price** (5%) and **material costs** (10%). Sensitivity analysis can help to **concentrate management attention on the most important forecasts**.

8.1 'What if' analysis

KEY TERM

'WHAT IF' ANALYSIS looks at the results of varying a model's key variables, parameters or estimates.

Sensitivity analysis is a 'what if' technique that examines how a result will change if the original predicted values are not achieved or if an underlying assumption changes.

Once a model has been constructed the consequences of changes or amendments to budget/plan assumptions may be tested by asking **'what if?' questions, a form of sensitivity analysis**. For example, a spreadsheet may be used to develop a cash flow model, such as that shown below.

	A	B	C	D
1		Month 1	Month 2	Month 3
2	Sales	1,000	1,200	1,440
3	Cost of sales	(650)	(780)	(936)
4	Gross profit	350	420	504
5				
6	Receipts:			
7	Current month	600	720	864
8	Previous month	–	400	480
9		–	–	–
10		600	1,120	1,344
11	Payments	(650)	(780)	(936)
12		(50)	340	408
13	Balance b/f	–	(50)	290
14	Balance c/f	(50)	290	698

Typical 'what if?' questions for sensitivity analysis

(a) What if the cost of sales is 68% of sales revenue, not 65%?

(b) What if payment from receivables is received 40% in the month of sale, 50% one month in arrears and 10% two months in arrears, instead of 60% in the month of sale and 40% one month in arrears?

(c) What if sales growth is only 15% per month, instead of 20% per month?

Using the spreadsheet model, the answers to such questions can be obtained simply and quickly, using the editing facility in the program. The information obtained should **provide management with a better understanding of what the cash flow position in the future might be**, and **what factors are critical to ensuring that the cash position remains reasonable**. For example, it might be found that the cost of sales must remain less than 67% of sales value to achieve a satisfactory cash position.

Section summary

Two useful approaches to sensitivity analysis

(a) Estimate by how much costs and revenues would need to differ from their estimated values before the decision would change

(b) Estimate whether a decision would change if estimated costs were x% higher than estimated, or estimated revenues y% lower than estimated.

9 Simulation models

Introduction

One of the chief problems encountered in decision making is the uncertainty of the future. Where only a few factors are involved, probability analysis and expected value calculations can be used to find the most likely outcome of a decision. Often, however, in real life, there are so **many uncertain variables** that this approach does not give a true impression of possible variations in outcome.

To get an idea of what will happen in real life one possibility is to use a **simulation model** in which the **values and the variables are selected at random**. Obviously this is a situation **ideally suited to a computer** (large volume of data, random number generation).

9.1 The Monte Carlo method

The term 'simulation' model is often used to refer to modelling which **makes use of random numbers**. This is the 'Monte Carlo' method of simulation. In the business environment it can, for example, be used to examine inventory, queuing, scheduling and forecasting problems.

Random numbers are allocated to each possible value of the uncertain variable in proportion to the probabilities, so that a probability of 0.1 gets 10% of the total numbers to be assigned. These random numbers are used to assign values to the variables.

Example: simulation and spreadsheets

A supermarket sells a product for which the daily demand varies. An analysis of daily demand over a period of about a year shows the following probability distribution.

Demand per day Units	Probability
35	0.10
36	0.20
37	0.25
38	0.30
39	0.08
40	0.07
	1.00

To develop a simulation model in which one of the variables is daily demand, we would **assign a group of numbers to each value for daily demand**. The **probabilities are stated** to two decimal places, and so there must be **100 random numbers in total**, 00 – 99 (we use 00-99 rather than 1-100 so that we can use **two-digit random numbers.)**

Note that **random numbers are assigned in proportion to the probabilities**, so that a probability of 0.1 gets 10% of the total numbers to be assigned, that is 10 numbers: 0, 1, 2, 3, 4, 5, 6, 7, 8 and 9.

The assignments would therefore be as follows.

Demand per day Units	Probability	Numbers assigned
35	0.10	00 – 09
36	0.20	10 – 29
37	0.25	30 – 54
38	0.30	55 – 84
39	0.08	85 – 92
40	0.07	93 – 99

When the simulation model is run, random numbers will be generated to derive values for daily demand. For example, if the model is used to simulate demand over a ten day period, the **random numbers generated** might be as follows.

19007174604721296802

The model would then **assign values to the demand per** day as follows.

Day	Random number	Demand Units
1	19	36
2	00	35
3	71	38
4	74	38
5	60	38
6	47	37
7	21	36
8	29	36
9	68	38
10	02	35

You might notice that on none of the ten days is the demand 39 or 40 units, because the random numbers generated did not include any value in the range 85 – 99. When a simulation model is used, there must be a long enough run to give a good representation of the system and all its potential variations.

9.2 Uses of simulation

In the supermarket example above, the supermarket would use the information to minimise inventory holding without risking running out of the product. This will reduce costs but avoid lost sales and profit.

A supermarket can also use this technique to estimate queues with predicted length of waiting time determining the number of staff required.

Question 19.7 | Simulation

Learning outcome D1(b)

Gleamy Windows is a company that provides a window cleaning service to offices and shops in a local area. The work force consists of ten workers, but there is a problem with absenteeism and the probability distribution of daily attendance is as follows.

Number at work	Probability
10	0.6
9	0.3
8	0.1

An analysis of past performance has shown that the number of windows that each worker can do in a day is as follows.

Number of windows per worker per day	Probability
120	0.15
125	0.24
130	0.27
135	0.19
140	0.15

The price charged for each window is 50c.

There are two variables, numbers at work and windows cleaned per worker per day.

Required

Complete the table below to show the allocation of groups of numbers to each value for each variable.

Number at work	Probability	Numbers allocated	Windows per worker per day	Probability	Numbers allocated
10	0.6		120	0.15	
9	0.3		125	0.24	
8	0.1		130	0.27	
			135	0.19	
			140	0.15	

Note how the numbers are allocated in the above exercise.

(a)   The **probabilities** for the numbers at work each day are **given to just one decimal place**, and so we can use **numbers in the range 0 – 9** rather than 00 – 99.

(b)   You might find it easiest to allocate number ranges by dealing with the lowest numbers in each range first. In the case of windows per worker per day, the lowest number range starts with 00. We can then add 15, 24, 27 and 19 respectively to get the lowest numbers in the higher ranges.

If we were to run the simulation model in the above exercise over a six-day period to estimate the daily revenue over this period, the **random numbers generated** might be as follows.

*   For the number at work, 971088.
*   For the windows per worker per day, 230998429964.

The **results** from the model would then be as follows.

Day	Random number	Number at work	Random number	Windows per worker per day	Total windows cleaned	Total revenue, at $0.50 per window $
1	9	8	23	125	1,000	500
2	7	9	09	120	1,080	540
3	1	10	98	140	1,400	700
4	0	10	42	130	1,300	650
5	8	9	99	140	1,260	630
6	8	9	64	130	1,170	585

If you have not already done so, **check to see how the figures in the number at work column and windows per worker per day column are derived** and perform the calculations for yourself.

The technique is often used to estimate **queues in shops**, banks, post offices and building societies. The length of waiting time predicted will enable estimates of staff requirements to be made. There are **two uncertainties** in such a scenario, however, as customers do not arrive at a constant rate and some customers require more or less time than the average service time. Two probability distributions and two allocations of random numbers would therefore be required.

Section summary

The **Monte Carlo method of simulation** uses random numbers to recognise that all variables are subject to change.

10 The learning curve

Introduction

Whenever an individual starts a job which is **fairly repetitive** in nature, and provided that the speed of working is not dictated by the speed of machinery (for example a production line), the worker is likely to become **more confident and knowledgeable** about the work as experience is gained, to become **more efficient**, and **to do the work more quickly. Eventually**, however, when the worker has acquired enough experience, there will be nothing more to learn, and so the **learning process will stop**.

Learning curve theory is used to measure how, in some industries and some situations, the incremental cost per unit of output continues to fall for each extra unit produced.

10.1 When does learning curve theory apply?

Labour time should be expected to get shorter, with experience, in the production of items which have any or all of the following features.

(a) **Made largely by labour effort** rather than by a highly mechanised process
(b) **Brand new** or relatively **short-lived** product (the learning process does not continue indefinitely)
(c) **Complex** and **made in small quantities for special orders**

10.2 The learning curve theory

KEY TERM

The LEARNING CURVE is 'The mathematical expression of the commonly observed effect that, as complex and labour-intensive procedures are repeated, unit labour times tend to decrease.' The learning curve models mathematically this reduction in unit production time.   (CIMA *Official Terminology*)

More specifically, the learning curve theory states that the **cumulative average time per unit** produced is assumed to **decrease by a constant percentage every time total output of the product doubles**.

For instance, where an **80% learning effect or rate** occurs, the **cumulative average time required per unit of output is reduced to 80% of the previous cumulative average time when output is doubled**.

KEY POINT

By cumulative average time, we mean the average time per unit for all units produced so far, back to and including the first unit made.

The **doubling of output** is an **important feature** of the learning curve measurement. With a 70% learning curve, the cumulative average time per unit of output will fall to 70% of what it was before, every time output is doubled.

Example: an 80% learning curve

If the first unit of output requires 100 hours and an 80% learning curve applies, the production times would be as follows.

Cumulative number of units produced		Cumulative average time per unit Hours		Total time required Hours	Incremental time taken Total hours		Hours per unit
1		100.0	(× 1)	100.0			
2*	(80%)	80.0	(× 2)	160.0	60.0	÷ 1	60.0
4*	(80%)	64.0	(× 4)	256.0	96.0	÷ 2	48.0
8*	(80%)	51.2	(× 8)	409.6	153.6	÷ 4	38.4

* Output is being doubled each time.

Notice that the incremental time per unit at each output level is much lower than the average time per unit.

10.3 Graph of the learning curve

This learning effect can be shown on a **graph** as a learning curve, either for **unit times (graph (a))** or for **cumulative total times or costs (graph (b))**.

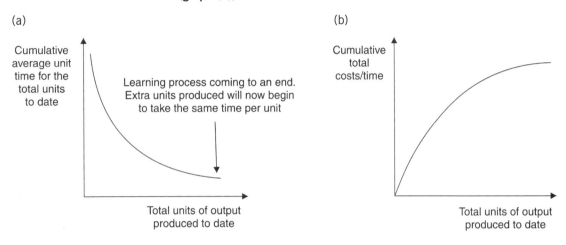

(a)

Cumulative average unit time for the total units to date

Learning process coming to an end. Extra units produced will now begin to take the same time per unit

Total units of output produced to date

(b)

Cumulative total costs/time

Total units of output produced to date

The curve on graph (a) becomes horizontal once a sufficient number of units have been produced. At this point the learning effect is lost and production time should become a constant standard, to which a standard efficiency rate may be applied.

Example: the learning curve effect

Captain Kitts has designed a new type of sailing boat, for which the cost and sales price of the first boat to be produced has been estimated as follows.

	£
Materials	5,000
Labour (800 hrs × £5 per hr)	4,000
Overhead (150% of labour cost)	6,000
	15,000
Profit mark-up (20%)	3,000
Sales price	18,000

It is planned to sell all the yachts at full cost plus 20%. An 80% learning curve is expected to apply to the production work. Only one customer has expressed interest in buying the yacht so far, but he thinks £18,000 is too high a price to pay. He might want to buy two, or even four of the yachts during the next six months.

He has asked the following questions.

(a)   If he paid £18,000 for the first yacht, what price would he have to pay later for a second yacht?

(b)   Could Captain Kitts quote the same unit price for two yachts, if the customer ordered two at the same time?

(c)   If the customer bought two yachts now at one price, what would be the price per unit for a third and fourth yacht, if he ordered them both together later on?

(d) Could Captain Kitts quote a single unit price for the following numbers of yachts if they were all ordered now?

   (i) Four yachts
   (ii) Eight yachts

Assuming there are no other prospective customers for the yacht, how would the questions be answered?

Solution

Number of yachts		Cumulative average time per yacht		Total time for all yachts to date		Incremental time for additional yachts
		Hours		Hours		Hours
1		800.0		800.0		
2	(× 80%)	640.0	(× 2)	1,280.0	(1,280 – 800)	480.0
4	(× 80%)	512.0	(× 4)	2,048.0	(2,048 – 1,280)	768.0
8	(× 80%)	409.6	(× 8)	3,276.8	(3,276.8 – 2,048)	1,228.8

(a) *Separate price for a second yacht*

	£
Materials	5,000
Labour (480 hrs × £5)	2,400
Overhead (150% of labour cost)	3,600
Total cost	11,000
Profit (20%)	2,200
Sales price	13,200

(b) *A single price for the first two yachts*

	£
Materials cost for two yachts	10,000
Labour (1,280 hrs × £5)	6,400
Overhead (150% of labour cost)	9,600
Total cost for two yachts	26,000
Profit (20%)	5,200
Total sales price for two yachts	31,200
Price per yacht (÷ 2)	15,600

(c) *A price for the third and fourth yachts*

	£
Materials cost for two yachts	10,000
Labour (768 hours × £5)	3,840
Overhead (150% of labour cost)	5,760
Total cost	19,600
Profit (20%)	3,920
Total sales price for two yachts	23,520
Price per yacht (÷ 2)	11,760

(d) *A price for the first four yachts together and for the first eight yachts together*

		First four yachts		First eight yachts
		£		£
Materials		20,000		40,000
Labour	(2,048 hrs)	10,240	(3,276.8 hrs)	16,384
Overhead	(150% of labour cost)	15,360	(150% of labour cost)	24,576
Total cost		45,600		80,960
Profit (20%)		9,120		16,192
Total sales price		54,720		97,152
Price per yacht	(÷ 4)	13,680	(÷ 8)	12,144

Learning outcomes: D1(a)

A 90 per cent learning curve applies to the manufacture of product X. If the time taken for the first unit is three hours, what will be the average time per unit for units 5 to 8?

A 1.944 hours   B 2.187 hours   C 7.776 hours   D 17.496 hours

10.4 A formula for the learning curve

LEARN

The formula for the learning curve shown in Section 10.3(a) is $Y_x = aX^b$

where   Y = cumulative average time per unit to produce X units

X = the cumulative number of units

a = the time required to produce the first unit of output

b = the learning coefficient or the index of learning/learning index

By calculating the value of b, using logarithms or a calculator, you can calculate expected labour times for certain work.

10.4.1 Logarithms

We need to take a look at logarithms because they appear in the definition of b, the learning coefficient.

KEY TERM

The LOGARITHM of a number is the power to which ten has to be raised to produce that number.

If you have never learnt how to use logarithms, here is a brief explanation.

The logarithm of a number, x, is the value of x expressed in terms of '10 to the power of'.

$10 = 10^1$ The logarithm of 10 is 1.0
$100 = 10^2$ The logarithm of 100 is 2.0
$1,000 = 10^3$ The logarithm of 1,000 is 3.0

Your **calculator** will provide you with the logarithm of any number, probably using the **button marked log 10^x**. For example, the log of 566 is, using a calculator, 2.7528, which means that $10^{2.7528} = 566$.

Logarithms are useful to us for two principal reasons.

(a)   The logarithm of the product of two numbers is the sum of their logarithms: **log (c × d) = log c + log d**.

(b)   The logarithm of one number (say, f) to the power of another number (say, g), is the second number multiplied by the logarithm of the first: **log (f^g) = g log f**.

Logarithms can therefore be used to derive non-linear functions of the form **y = ax^n**.

If y = ax^n, the logarithm of y and the logarithm of ax^n must be the same and so **log y = log a + nlog x**. **This gives us a linear function similar to y = a + nx**, the only difference being that in place of y we have to use the logarithm of y and in place of x we must use the logarithm of x. **Using simultaneous equations, we can get a value for n and a value for log a**, which we can convert back into a 'normal' figure using antilogarithms (the button probably marked 10^x on your calculator).

For example, suppose the relationship between x and y can be described by the function y = ax^n, and suppose we know that if x = 1,000, y = 80,000 and if x = 750, y = 63,750.

Substitute these values into log y = log a + n log x.

log 80,000 = log a + n log 1,000
4.9031 = log a + 3n
∴ 4.9031 − 3n = log a   (1)

log 63,750 = log a + n log 750
4.8045 = log a + 2.8751n   (2)

Sub (1) into (2).

4.8045 = 4.9031 − 3n + 2.8751n
∴ 0.1249n = 0.0986
∴ n = 0.7894

Sub value of n into (1)

4.9031 − (3 × 0.7894) = log a
2.5349 = log a
∴ 342.69 = a

∴ Our function is **y = 342.69x $^{0.7894}$**

10.4.2 Logarithms and the value of b

When $Y_x = aX^b$ in learning curve theory, the value of **b = log of the learning rate/log of 2**. The learning rate is expressed as a proportion, so that for an 80% learning curve, the learning rate is 0.8, and for a 90% learning curve it is 0.9, and so on.

For an 80% learning curve, b = log 0.8/log 2.

Using the button on your calculator marked log 10^x

$$b = \frac{-0.0969}{0.3010} = -0.322$$

Question 19.9   Learning curve formula

Learning outcomes: D(iv)

The value of b when a 90% learning curve applies is −0.0458. *True or false?*

Example: using the formula

Suppose, for example, that an 80% learning curve applies to production of item ABC. To date (the end of June) 230 units of ABC have been produced. Budgeted production for July is 55 units.

The time taken to produce the very first unit of ABC, in January, was 120 hours.

Required

Calculate the budgeted total labour time for July.

Solution

To solve this problem, we need to calculate three things.

(a)   The cumulative total labour time needed so far to produce 230 units of ABC

(b)   The cumulative total labour time needed to produce 285 units of ABC, that is adding on the extra 55 units for July

(c)   The extra time needed to produce 55 units of ABC in July, as the difference between (b) and (a)

Calculation (a)

$Y_x = aX^b$ and we know that for 230 cumulative units, a = 120 hours (time for first unit), X = 230 (cumulative units) and b = –0.322 (80% learning curve) and so Y = (120) × ($230^{-0.322}$) = 20.83.

So when X = 230 units, the cumulative average time per unit is 20.83 hours.

Calculation (b)

Now we do the same sort of calculation for X = 285.

If X = 285, Y = 120 × (285–0.322) = 19.44

So when X = 285 units, the cumulative average time per unit is 19.44 hours.

Calculation (c)

Cumulative units	Average time per unit	Total time
	Hours	Hours
230	20.83	4,791
285	19.44	5,540
Incremental time for 55 units		749

Average time per unit, between 230 and 285 units = 749/55 = 13.6 hours per unit approx

Instead of the formula you can use the **graphical methodology** (Section 10.3) to determine cumulative average time per unit but you will need considerable drawing skill to obtain an accurate result.

10.5 The practical application of learning curve theory

What costs are affected by the learning curve?

(a)   Direct labour time and costs

(b)   Variable overhead costs, if they vary with direct labour hours worked

(c)   **Materials costs** are usually **unaffected** by learning among the workforce, although it is conceivable that materials handling might improve, and so wastage costs be reduced.

(d)   **Fixed overhead expenditure** should be **unaffected** by the learning curve (although in an organisation that uses absorption costing, if fewer hours are worked in producing a unit of output, and the factory operates at full capacity, the **fixed overheads recovered or absorbed per unit** in the cost of the output **will decline** as more and more units are made).

10.6 The relevance of learning curve effects in management accounting

10.6.1 Situations in which learning curve theory can be used

(a)   To **calculate the marginal (incremental) cost of making extra units** of a product.

(b)   To **quote selling prices for products/services**, where prices are calculated at cost plus a percentage mark-up for profit.

(c)   To **prepare realistic production budgets** and more **efficient production schedules**.

(d)   To **prepare realistic standard costs** for cost control purposes.

10.7 Problems with applying learning curve theory

(a)   The learning curve phenomenon is **not always present**.

(b)   It **assumes stable conditions at work** which will enable learning to take place. This is not always practicable (for example because of labour turnover).

(c)   It must also **assume a certain degree of motivation** amongst employees.

(d)   **Breaks** between repeating production of an item must not be too long, or **workers will 'forget'** and the learning process would have to begin all over again.

(e)   It might be difficult to **obtain enough accurate data** to determine the learning rate.

(f)   **Workers might not agree** to a gradual reduction in production times per unit.

(g)   **Production techniques might change**, or product design alterations might be made, so that it **takes a long time for a 'standard' production method to emerge**, to which a learning effect will apply.

Section summary

Learning curve theory is used to measure how, in some industries and some situations, the incremental cost per unit of output continues to fall for each extra unit produced.

The theory is that the **cumulative average time per unit produced is assumed to fall by a constant percentage every time total output of the product doubles**. Cumulative average time is the average time per unit for all units produced so far, back to and including the first unit made.

The formula for the learning curve is $Y_x = aX^b$, where b, the learning coefficient or learning index, is defined as (log of the learning rate/log of 2).

Chapter Roundup

✓ People may be **risk seekers**, **risk neutral** or **risk averse**.

✓ In a risky situation the probability of the outcome can be quantified. In an uncertain situation there is not sufficient information for the outcome to be predicted with statistical confidence.

✓ If a decision maker is faced with a number of alternative decisions, each with a range of possible outcomes, the optimum decision will be the one which gives the highest **expected value** ($EV = \Sigma px$). This is **Bayes' strategy**.

✓ The calculation of **joint probabilities** and **cumulative probabilities** adds to the information for risk analysis.

✓ **Data tables** are often produced using spreadsheet packages and show the effect of changing the values of variables.

✓ The maximin basis means maximise the minimum achievable profit. The maximax basis means maximise the maximum achievable profit. The minimax regret basis means minimise the maximum regrets.

✓ Risk can be measured by the possible variations of outcomes around the expected value. One useful measure of such variations is the **standard deviation of the expected value**.

✓ **Decision trees** are diagrams which illustrate the choices and possible outcomes of a decision.

✓ **Rollback analysis** evaluates the EV of each decision option. You have to work from right to left and calculate EVs at each outcome point.

✓ **Perfect information** is guaranteed to predict the future with 100% accuracy. **Imperfect information** is better than no information at all but could be wrong in its prediction of the future.

✓ The **value of perfect information** is the difference between the EV of profit with perfect information and the EV of profit without perfect information.

✓ **Two useful approaches to sensitivity analysis**

   • Estimate by how much costs and revenues would need to differ from their estimated values before the decision would change.

   • Estimate whether a decision would change if estimated costs were x% higher than estimated or y% lower than estimated.

✓ The **Monte Carlo method of simulation** uses random numbers to recognise that all variables are subject to change.

✓ **Learning curve theory** is used to measure how, in some industries and some situations, the incremental cost per unit of output continues to fall for each extra unit produced.

✓ The theory is that the **cumulative average time per unit produced is assumed to fall by a constant percentage every time total output of the product doubles**. Cumulative average time is the average time per unit for all units produced so far, back to and including the first unit made.

✓ The formula for the learning curve is $Y_x = aX^b$, where b, the learning coefficient or learning index, is defined as (log of the learning rate/log of 2).

Quick Quiz

1   A particular decision maker is concerned with what will be the most likely outcome of a decision. He
      would be described as

      A   A risk seeker   C   Risk neutral
      B   A risk averse   D   A risk reducer

2   A probability can be expressed as any value from –1 to +1. *True or false?*

3   A manager is trying to decide which of three mutually exclusive projects to undertake. Each of the projects
      could lead to varying net costs which the manager calls outcomes I, II and III. The following payoff table
      or matrix has been constructed.

		I (Worst)	*II (Most likely)*	*III (Best)*
	A	60	70	120
Project	B	85	75	140
	C	100	120	135

      Using the minimax regret decision rule, decide which project should be undertaken?

4   If the decision maker is trying to maximise the figure, what figure would the decision maker choose at
      point B in the diagram below?

      A   40,000   C   13,900
      B   11,800   D   22,000

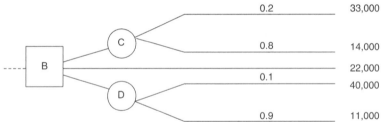

5   Given the probability distribution shown below, assign ranges of numbers in order to run a simulation
      model.

Probability	*Numbers assigned*	*Probability*	*Numbers assigned*
0.132	....	0.083	....
0.410	....	0.060	....
0.315	....		

6   *Fill in the blanks*

      Standard deviation, s $= \sqrt{\text{.................}}$

      where $\bar{x}$ is ...., x represents ...., p represents ....

7   AB can choose from five mutually exclusive projects. The projects will each last for one year only and their net cash inflows will be determined by the prevailing market conditions. The forecast net cash inflows and their associated probabilities are shown below.

Market conditions	Poor	Good	Excellent
Probability	0.20	0.40	0.40
	$'000	$'000	$'000
Project L	550	480	580
Project M	450	500	570
Project N	420	450	480
Project O	370	410	430
Project P	590	580	430

(a)   Based on the expected value of the net cash inflows, which project should be undertaken?

(b)   Calculate the value of perfect information about the state of the market.

8   In the formula for the learning curve, $Y_x = aX^b$, how is the value of b calculated?

A   Log of the learning rate/log of 2

B   Log of 2/learning rate

C   Learning rate × log of 2

D   Log of learning rate/2

Answers to Quick Quiz

1 C Risk reducer is not a term we have covered!

2 False. Should be 0 to 1.

3 A table of regrets can be compiled, as follows, showing the amount of profit that might be forgone for each project, depending on whether the outcome is I, II or III.

	Outcome			Maximum
	I	*II*	*III*	
Project A	40 *	50	20	50
Project B	15 **	45	0	45
Project C	0	0	5	5

* 100 – 60   ** 100 – 85 etc

The **maximum regret** is 50 with project A, 45 with B and 5 with C. The lowest of these three maximum regrets is 5 with C, and so project C would be selected if the minimax regret rule is used.

4 D Choice between $((0.2 \times 33{,}000) + (0.8 \times 14{,}000)) = 17{,}800$ at C, 22,000, and $((0.1 \times 40{,}000) + (0.9 \times 11{,}000)) = 13{,}900$ at D.

5

Probability	*Numbers assigned*	*Probability*	*Numbers assigned*
0.132	000-131	0.083	857-939
0.410	132-541	0.060	940-999
0.315	542-856		

6 Standard deviation, $s = \sqrt{\Sigma p(x - \bar{x})^2}$

where $\bar{x}$ is the EV of profit, x represents each possible profit, p represents the probability of each possible profit

7 (a)

		EV
		$'000
Project L	(550 x 0.20+480 x 0.40+580 x 0.40)	534
Project M	(450 x 0.20+500 x 0.40+570 x 0.40)	518
Project N	(420 x 0.20+450 x 0.40+480 x 0.40)	456
Project O	(370 x 0.20+410 x 0.40+430 x 0.40)	410
Project P	(590 x 0.20+580 x 0.40+430 x 0.40)	522

Project L has the highest EV of expected cash inflows and should therefore be undertaken.

(b)

Market condition	*Probability*	*Project chosen*	*Net cash inflow*	*EV of net cash inflow $'000*
Poor	0.20	P	590	118
Good	0.40	P	580	232
Excellent	0.40	L	580	232
EV of net cash inflows with perfect information				582
EV of net cash inflows without perfect information				534
Value of perfect information				48

8 A. Make sure you can use the log function on your calculator.

Answers to Questions

19.1 EV calculations

The correct answer is C.

A	EV of cost = $20,850	C	EV of cost = $20,250
	EV of profit = $9,150		EV of profit = $9,750
B	EV of cost = $20,500	D	EV of cost = $20,550
	EV of profit = $9,500		EV of profit = $9,450

C has the highest EV of profit.

19.2 Using the standard deviation to measure risk

The correct answer is project A.

The projects have the same EV of net cash flow ($3,000); therefore a risk averse manager would choose the project with the smaller standard deviation of expected profit.

Project A

Cash flow	Probability	EV of cash flow	Cash flow minus EV of cash flow $(x - \bar{x})$	$p(x - \bar{x})^2$
$		$	$	$
2,000	0.3	600	−1,000	300,000
3,000	0.4	1,200	0	0
4,000	0.3	1,200	+1,000	300,000
		EV = 3,000	Variance =	600,000

Standard deviation = $\sqrt{600,000}$ = $775

Project B

Cash flow	Probability	EV of cash flow	Cash flow minus EV of cash flow $(x - \bar{x})$	$p(x - \bar{x})^2$
$		$	$	$
1,000	0.2	200	−2,000	800,000
2,000	0.2	400	−1,000	200,000
3,000	0.2	600	0	0
4,000	0.2	800	+1,000	200,000
5,000	0.2	1,000	+2,000	800,000
		EV = 3,000	Variance =	2,000,000

Standard deviation = $\sqrt{2,000,000}$ = $1,414

19.3 Standard deviation of the net present value

The correct answer is project B.

We can begin by calculating the EV of the NPV for each project.

	Project A			Project B	
NPV $'000	Prob	EV $'000	NPV $'000	Prob	EV $'000
– 20	0.15	(3.0)	5	0.2	1.0
10	0.20	2.0	15	0.3	4.5
20	0.35	7.0	20	0.4	8.0
40	0.30	12.0	25	0.1	2.5
		18.0			16.0

Project A has a higher EV of NPV, but what about the risk of variation in the NPV above or below the EV? This can be measured by the standard deviation of the NPV.

The standard deviation of a project's NPV can be calculated as $\sqrt{\Sigma p(x - \bar{x})^2}$, where $\bar{x}$ is the EV of the NPV.

	Project A, $\bar{x} = 18$				Project B, $\bar{x} = 16$		
x $'000	p	x – $\bar{x}$ $'000	$p(x-\bar{x})^2$	x $'000	p	x – $\bar{x}$ $'000	$p(x-\bar{x})^2$
– 20	0.15	– 38	216.6	5	0.2	– 11	24.2
10	0.20	– 8	12.8	15	0.3	– 1	0.3
20	0.35	+ 2	1.4	20	0.4	+ 4	6.4
40	0.30	+ 22	145.2	25	0.1	+ 9	8.1
			376.0				39.0

	Project A			Project B
Standard deviation	=	√376	Standard deviation	=	√39.0
	=	19.391		=	6.245
	=	$19,391		=	$6,245

Although **Project A has a higher EV of NPV**, it also has a **higher standard deviation of NPV**, and so has **greater risk** associated with it.

Which project should be selected? Clearly it depends on the attitude of the company's management to risk. If management are **risk-averse**, they will opt for the **less risky project B**.

(If management were prepared **to take the risk of a low NPV in the hope of a high NPV** they will opt for **project A**.)

19.4 Simple decision tree

The correct answer is A.

The various outcomes must be evaluated using expected values.

EV at point B: $(0.75 \times 10,000) + (0.25 \times 8,000) = 9,500$
EV at point D: $(0.6 \times 20,000) + (0.4 \times (4,000)) = 10,400$
EV at point C: Choice between 10,400 and 11,000
EV at point A: Choice between B (9,500), C (10,400 or 11,000) and choice 3 (9,000).

If we are trying to maximise the figure, option 2 and then option 7 are chosen to give 11,000.

19.5 Decision based on EV of profit

The correct answer is option B and so the statement is true.

Without perfect information, the option with the highest EV of profit will be chosen.

Probability	Option A (National) Profit $	EV $	Option B (Regional) Profit $	EV $	Option C (Area) Profit $	EV $
0.3	(4,000)	(1,200)	0	0	1,000	300
0.5	2,000	1,000	3,500	1,750	1,500	750
0.2	10,000	2,000	4,000	800	2,000	400
		1,800		2,550		1,450

Marketing regionally (option B) has the highest EV of profit, and would be selected.

19.6 Perfect information

The correct answer is $1,500.

If perfect information about the state of consumer demand were available, option A would be preferred if the forecast demand is strong and option C would be preferred if the forecast demand is weak.

Demand	Probability	Choice	Profit $	EV of profit $
Weak	0.3	C	1,000	300
Moderate	0.5	B	3,500	1,750
Strong	0.2	A	10,000	2,000
EV of profit with perfect information				4,050
EV of profit, selecting option B				2,550
Value of perfect information				1,500

19.7 Simulation

Number at work	Probability	Numbers allocated	Windows per worker per day	Probability	Numbers allocated
10	0.6	0 – 5	120	0.15	00 – 14
9	0.3	6 – 8	125	0.24	15 – 38
8	0.1	9	130	0.27	39 – 65
			135	0.19	66 – 84
			140	0.15	85 – 99

19.8 Learning curves

The correct answer is A.

You should have been able to eliminate options C and D because they are longer times than the three hours taken for the first unit. In fact they are the total time for units 5 to 8 and for units 1 to 8 respectively. Option B is incorrect because it is the average time for units 1 to 8.

Cumulative number of units produced		Cumulative average time per unit Hours	Total time Hours
1		3	
2	(90%)	2.7	
4	(90%)	2.43	9.720
8	(90%)	2.187	17.496
Time taken for units 5 to 8			7.776
Average time per unit (÷ 4)			1.944 hours

19.9 Learning curve formula

The correct answer is –0.152 and so the statement is false.

$b = \log 0.9/\log 2 = -0.0458/0.3010 = -0.152$

You might also be expected to use the formula to calculate expected labour times for some work.

Now try the question from the Exam Question Bank	Number	Level	Marks	Time
	Q30	Examination	25	45 mins

OBJECTIVE TEST
QUESTION AND ANSWER BANK

1   Which of the following statements about standards is/are true?

    I   Can be prepared for all functions, even where output cannot be measured
    II   Must be expressed in money terms
    III   Aids control by setting financial targets or limits for a forthcoming period
    IV   Should be revised every time prices or levels of efficiency change

    A   None of the above   B   All of the above   C   III and IV   D   I, II and IV

(2 marks)

2   JPM has recorded the following data in budget working papers.

Activity	Overhead cost
Labour hours	£
22,000	108,740
24,000	115,080
28,000	127,760
36,000	153,120

In control period 11, 30,600 labour hours were actually worked and the actual overhead cost was £154,952.

What is the total overhead expenditure variance?

    A   £18,950 (A)   B   £57,950 (A)   C   £24,800 (A)   D   £136,002 (A)

(2 marks)

The following information relates to questions 3 and 4.

The standard cost and selling price structure for the single product that is made by CD is as follows.

	£ per unit
Selling price	82
Variable cost	(47)
Fixed production overhead	(29)
	6

The budgeted level of production and sales is 3,200 units per month.

Extract from the actual results for March

Fixed production overhead volume variance	£8,700 favourable
Fixed production overhead expenditure variance	£2,200 adverse

Inventory levels reduced by 200 units during the period.

3   What was the actual expenditure on fixed production overhead during March?

    A   £86,300   B   £90,600   C   £92,800   D   £95,000

(2 marks)

4   What was the actual sales volume during March?

    A   2,900 units   B   3,300 units   C   3,500 units   D   3,700 units

(2 marks)

5   What is budgetary slack?

    A   The difference between the costs built into the budget and the costs actually incurred.
    B   The difference between the minimum necessary costs and the costs actually incurred.
    C   The sum of the minimum necessary costs and the costs built into the budget.
    D   The difference between the flexible budget and the costs actually incurred.   **(2 marks)**

6   Sales of product D during 20X0 (control periods 1 to 13) were noted and the following totals calculated.

$\Sigma X = 91$ $\qquad$ $\Sigma Y = 1,120$ $\qquad$ $\Sigma XY = 9,247$ $\qquad$ $\Sigma X^2 = 819$

There is a high correlation between time and volume of sales. Using a suitable regression line, what is the predicted sales level of product D in control period 4 of 20X1, when a seasonal variation of −13 is relevant?

A   552 $\qquad$ B   158 $\qquad$ C   150 $\qquad$ D   176

7   At the beginning of May 20X3, LB held an inventory of 1,680 units of product C. On 30 April 20X4 the inventory level was 1,120 units. The standard cost of product C is as follows.

	£
Material (15 kgs × £6)	90
Labour (4 hrs × £11)	44
Variable overhead (4 hrs × £20)	80
Fixed overhead (4 hrs × £32)	128
	342

The profit reported in the management accounts for the twelve months ended 30 April 20X4 was £1,219,712. If LB used marginal costing, what profit would have been reported for the period?

A   £1,148,032
B   £1,219,712
C   £1,291,392
D   It cannot be determined from the information provided   **(2 marks)**

8   Which of the following statements about throughput accounting and the theory of constraints (TOC) is/are true?

1   In TOC, a binding constraint is an activity which has a higher capacity than preceding or subsequent activities, thereby limiting throughput.

2   A buffer stock is permissible within TOC.

3   In TOC, throughput contribution = sales revenue – labour cost

4   In throughput accounting, profitability is determined by the rate at which money is earned.

A   All of the above
B   2 and 3
C   3 only
D   2 and 4   **(2 marks)**

9   Y operates a system of backflush costing and has recorded the following transactions for control period 3.

Purchase of raw materials	£54,340
Conversion costs incurred	£67,210
Finished goods produced	286 units
Sales	270 units

There were no opening inventories of raw materials, WIP or finished goods. No variances arose during control period 3.

Assuming that the trigger point for recording costs is when goods are completed, which of the following is the correct double entry to record the standard cost of goods sold

A	DEBIT	Finished goods inventory	£114,750	
	CREDIT	Cost of sales		£114,750
B	DEBIT	Cost of sales	£121,550	
	CREDIT	Finished goods inventory		£121,550
C	DEBIT	Finished goods inventory	£67,210	
	CREDIT	Conversion costs		£67,210
D	DEBIT	Cost of sales	£114,750	
	CREDIT	Finished goods inventory		£114,750

(2 marks)

The following information relates to questions 10 and 11

A firm of financial consultants offers short revision courses on taxation and auditing for professional exams. The firm has budgeted annual overheads totalling £152,625. Until recently the firm had applied overheads on a volume basis, based on the number of course days offered. The firm has no variable costs and the only direct costs are the consultants' own time which they divide equally between the two courses. The firm is considering the possibility of adopting an ABC system and has identified the overhead costs as shown below.

	£
Centre hire	62,500
Enquiries administration	27,125
Brochures	63,000

The following information relates to the past year and is expected to remain the same for the coming year.

Course	No of courses sold	Duration of course	No of enquiries per course	No of brochures printed per course
Auditing	50	2 days	175	300
Taxation	30	3 days	70	200

All courses run with a maximum number of students (30), as it is deemed that beyond this number the learning experience is severely diminished, and the same centre is used for all courses at a standard daily rate. The firm has the human resources to run only one course at any one time.

10   Calculate the overhead cost per course for both auditing and taxation using traditional volume based absorption costing. **(2 marks)**

11   Calculate the overhead cost per course for both auditing and taxation using Activity Based Costing.

(3 marks)

The following information relates to questions 12 and 13

Product B requires 4.5 kg of material per unit. The standard price of the material is €6 per kg. The budgeted production for last month was 750 units. Actual results were as follows.

Material used	2,250 kg
Production	780 units
Material cost	€14,175

Due to worldwide increases in the price of the material used it was realised, after the month had ended, that a more realistic material standard price would have been €6.50 per kg.

12   (a)   Explain what is meant by a planning variance. **(2 marks)**
       (b)   Calculate planning and operational variances for material costs for the month. **(3 marks)**

13   State three possible causes of the operational usage variance you have calculated **(3 marks)**

14   VC is considering investing in a printing machine for a capital cost of $900,000. The machine will have a useful life of four years. Annual running costs will amount to $828,000, including straight line depreciation of $210,000. The estimated disposal value of the machine at the end of year 4 is its net book value.

The printing capacity of the machine will be 6 million copies per annum for each of the first two years, and 5 million copies per annum for the third and fourth years. VC expects to be able to sell whatever the machine produces. Average contribution will be $180 per 1,000 copies.

The payback period for the machine, assuming all cash flows occur evenly, is [   ]

(2 marks)

Data for questions 15 and 16

Mart is launching a new product next year. Forecasts of sales are as follows.

Annual sales	Probability
$'000	
4,000	0.10
4,400	0.15
4,800	0.35
5,200	?
5,600	?

These are predicted to be the only possible outcomes, and the probability of sales of $5.2 million is exactly equal to the probability of sales of $5.6 million. The contribution to sales ratio of the product will be 35%. Fixed costs will be $196,000 per quarter.

15   The expected value of annual profit is [   ]   **(3 marks)**

16   The probability of the product at least breaking even next year is [   ], while the probability of the product earning a profit of at least $900,000 is [   ]   **(3 marks)**

The following information relates to questions 17 and 18

The master budget of PQ reveals the following information,

Statement of financial position extracts

	£'000
Current assets (including inventory 1,950)	3,470
Current liabilities	1,790

Budgeted income statement extracts

	£'000
Revenue	7,550
Profit from operations	1,240
Return on capital employed	24%

17   Calculate the total asset turnover ratio.   **(2 marks)**

18   Calculate the quick or acid test ratio to assess PQ's liquidity.   **(2 marks)**

1   **The correct answer is A.**

I   The use of standards is limited to situations where repetitive actions are performed and output can be measured.

II   Standards need not be expressed in monetary terms.

III   Standards achieve control by comparison of actual results against a predetermined target.

IV   The most suitable approach is probably to revise standards whenever changes of a permanent and reasonably long-term nature occur.

2   **The correct answer is A.**

Determine fixed cost using high-low method

	Hrs	£
Highest activity level	36,000	153,120
Lowest activity level	22,000	108,740
Difference	14,000	44,380

$\therefore$ Variable cost per hour   = £44,380/14,000
                          = £3.17

$\therefore$ Fixed cost (substituting in lowest activity level)

= £(108,740 – (22,000 × £3.17)
= £39,000

Expenditure should have been:	£	£
Fixed	39,000	
Variable (30,600 × £3.17)	97,002	
		136,002
but was		154,952
Variance		18,950 (A)

If you selected option B, you forgot to include the budgeted fixed overhead.

If you selected option C, you performed a pro-rata calculation on the budgeted cost for 36,000 hours to determine the budgeted cost at actual activity level.

Option D is what expenditure should have been.

3   **The correct answer is D.**

	£
Budgeted fixed overhead expenditure (3,200 units × £29)	92,800
Fixed production overhead expenditure variance	2,200 (A)
Actual fixed production overhead expenditure	95,000

If you selected option A, you adjusted the budgeted overhead unnecessarily for the fixed overhead volume variance.

If you selected option B, you had the right idea about adjusting the budgeted overhead for the expenditure variance, but you should have added the variance rather than subtracting it.

If you selected option C, you chose the budgeted fixed overhead expenditure for the month.

4   **The correct answer is D.**

	Units
Budgeted production	3,200
Volume variance in units (£8,700 ÷ £29)	300 (F)
Actual production for March	3,500
Reduction in inventory volume	200
Actual sales for March	3,700

If you selected option A, you subtracted the volume variance in units from the budgeted production. However the volume variance is favourable and so the actual production must be higher than budgeted.

If you selected option B, you subtracted the inventory reduction from the actual production volume. However if inventories reduce, sales volume must be higher than production volume.

Option C is the actual production for March. Since the inventory volume altered, sales must be different from the production volume.

5   **The correct answer is B.**

6   **The correct answer is C.**

During 20X0, there are 13 control periods and so n = 13. The regression line is Y = a + bX.

$$b \;=\; \frac{n\Sigma XY - \Sigma X\Sigma Y}{n\Sigma X^2 - (\Sigma X)^2}$$

$$\;=\; \frac{(13 \times 9{,}247) - (91 \times 1{,}120)}{(13 \times 819) - (91)^2}$$

$$\;=\; 7.731$$

$$a \;=\; \frac{\Sigma Y}{n} - \frac{b\Sigma X}{n}$$

$$\;=\; \frac{1{,}120}{13} - \frac{(7.731 \times 91)}{13}$$

$$\;=\; 32.037$$

Regression line is Y = 32.037 + 7.731X

Control period 4 of 20X1, X = 17

∴ Y = 32.037 + (7.731 × 17) = 163 units

Adjusting by the seasonal variation of –13, predicted sales = 163 – 13 = 150 units

If you chose option A, you mixed up your 'a' and 'b' values and forgot the seasonal adjustment.

If you chose option B, you used X = 18.

If you chose option D, you added the seasonal variation instead of deducting it.

7   **The correct answer is C.**

Inventory levels have fallen so marginal costing reports the higher profit.

	£
Absorption costing profit	1,219,712
+ fixed overhead included in inventory level change	
((1,680 – 1,120) × £128)	71,680
Marginal costing profit	1,291,392

If you chose option A, you deducted the fixed overhead included in the inventory level change. If inventory levels decrease, absorption costing will report the lower profit because as well as the fixed overhead absorbed during the period, fixed overhead which had been carried forward in opening inventory is released and included in cost of sales.

Option B is the absorption costing profit. The marginal costing profit must be different, however, because there has been a change in inventory levels.

8   **The correct answer is D.**

Statement 1 is incorrect because a binding constraint is an activity which has a lower capacity than preceding or subsequent activities

Statement 3 is incorrect because throughput contribution = sales revenue – material cost

9   **The correct answer is D.**

Standard cost per unit = £(54,340 + 67,210)/286 units = £425

If you chose option A you got the double entry the wrong way round. If you chose option B you simply totalled the costs incurred. Option C ignores the material costs.

10 **The correct answer is auditing £1,606.58 per course; taxation £2,409.87 per course.**

	Auditing	Taxation	Total
Number of courses sold	50	30	
Duration of course (days)	2	3	
Number of course days	100	90	190

$$\text{Overhead cost per course day} = \frac{£152,625}{190} = £803.29$$

Overhead cost per course

Auditing   £803.29 × 2 days = £1,606.58

Taxation   £803.29 × 3 days = £2,409.87

11 **The correct answer is auditing £1,995.40 per course; taxation £1,761.85 per course.**

$$\text{Centre hire cost per course day} = \frac{£62,500}{190*} = £328.95$$

* See working in question 10.

$$\text{Enquiries administration cost per enquiry} = \frac{£27,125}{(50 \times 175) + (30 \times 70)} = £2.50$$

$$\text{Brochure cost per brochure printed} = \frac{£63,000}{(50 \times 300) + (30 \times 200)} = £3$$

Overhead costs per course using ABC

		Auditing £ per course		Taxation £ per course
Centre hire at £328.95 per day	(× 2)	657.90	(× 3)	986.85
Enquiries admin at £2.50 per enquiry	(× 175)	437.50	(× 70)	175.00
Brochures at £3 per brochure printed	(× 300)	900.00	(× 200)	600.00
		1,995.40		1,761.85

12 (a)   A planning variance calculates the difference in standard cost arising due to changes from the original standard that are not controllable by operational managers because they are caused by planning errors. In the scenario described a planning variance has arisen because of the worldwide increase in material prices. This is outside the control of operational managers and should therefore be analysed separately from variance related to operational performance.

    (b)   **Planning variance**

	€
Revised standard cost (780 × 4.5kg × €6.50)	22,815
Original standard cost (780 × 4.5kg × €6.00)	21,060
	1,755 (A)

Operational price variance

	€
Actual cost of actual kg used	14,175
Revised standard cost of actual kg (2,250 × €6.50)	14,625
	450 (F)

Operational usage variance

780 units should have used (× 4.5 kg)	3,510 kg
but did use	2,250 kg
Operational usage variance in kg	1,260 kg (F)
× revised standard price per kg	× €6.50
Operational usage variance in €	€8,190 (F)

13   Three possible courses of a favourable operational usage variance are as follows.

(a)   The material was of a higher quality than in the standard therefore wastage was lower than standard.

(b)   The original standard usage per unit was set too low.

(c)   The direct labour were more highly skilled than standard and therefore they used the material more efficiently than standard.

14   **The correct answer is 1.95 years.**

You should always use cash flows to calculate the payback period and so you need to subtract depreciation from running costs.

Cash flow in years 1 and 2

	$
Contribution (6 million x $180 per 1,000)	1,080,000
Cash running costs ($(828,000 – 210,000))	618,000
	462,000

Cash flow in years 3 and 4

	$
Contribution (5 million x $180 per 1,000)	900,000
Cash running costs ($(828,000 – 210,000))	618,000
	282,000

Residual value of the machine = $(900,000 – (4 × 210,000)) = $60,000. This is the estimated disposal value at the end of year 4.

Net cash flows

Year			Cumulative
		$	$
0		(900,000)	(900,000)
1		462,000	(438,000)
2		462,000	24,000
3		282,000	306,000
4	$(282,000 + 60,000)	342,000	648,000

Payback therefore occurs during year 2. Assuming even cash flows throughout the year, interpolation can be used to find the exact period.

Number of years = 1 + (438,000/462,000) = 1.95 years

15   **The correct answer is $931,000.**

We need to know the probabilities of the two highest sales values. Since the sales levels given are predicted to be the only possible outcomes, the sum of the probabilities must be equal to 1. The probabilities of the two highest sales values are therefore (1 – 0.1 – 0.15 – 0.35)/2 = 0.2.

EV of sales = $m(4 × 0.1 + 4.4 × 0.15 + 4.8 × 0.35 + 5.2 × 0.2 + 5.6 × 0.2) = $4.9m

	$
EV of contribution = $4.9m × 35%	1,715,000
Fixed costs ($196,000 × 4)	784,000
EV of annual profit	931,000

16 **The correct answers are 100% and 40%.**

To break even the contribution must be equal to the fixed costs.

Annual contribution required = $784,000

Contribution/sales = 35%

$784,000/sales = 35%

Sales = $2,240,000

The probability of achieving sales of at least $2,240,000 is 100%.

To earn a profit of at least $900,000, contribution required = fixed costs + profit = $784,000 + $900,000 = $1,684,000

Contribution/sales = 35%

$1,684,000/sales = 35%

Required sales = $4,811,429

The probability of achieving sales in excess of this amount is 0.2 + 0.2 = 0.4 = 40%.

17 **The correct answer is 1.5 times**

Profit margin	= (1,240/7,550) × 100% = 16.4%
ROCE	= profit margin × asset turnover
∴ Asset turnover	= ROCE/profit margin
	= 24.0/16.4
	= 1.5 times

18 **The correct answer is 0.8**

Acid test ratio	= (3,470 – 1,950)/1,790
	= 1,520/1,790
	= 0.8

EXAM QUESTION AND ANSWER BANK

What the examiner means

The very important table below has been prepared by CIMA to help you interpret exam questions.

Learning objectives	Verbs used	Definition
1 Knowledge What are you expected to know	• List • State • Define	• Make a list of • Express, fully or clearly, the details of/facts of • Give the exact meaning of
2 Comprehension What you are expected to understand	• Describe • Distinguish • Explain • Identify • Illustrate	• Communicate the key features of • Highlight the differences between • Make clear or intelligible/state the meaning of • Recognise, establish or select after consideration • Use an example to describe or explain something
3 Application How you are expected to apply your knowledge	• Apply • Calculate/ compute • Demonstrate • Prepare • Reconcile • Solve • Tabulate	• Put to practical use • Ascertain or reckon mathematically • Prove with certainty or to exhibit by practical means • Make or get ready for use • Make or prove consistent/compatible • Find an answer to • Arrange in a table
4 Analysis How you are expected to analyse the detail of what you have learned	• Analyse • Categorise • Compare and contrast • Construct • Discuss • Interpret • Prioritise • Produce	• Examine in detail the structure of • Place into a defined class or division • Show the similarities and/or differences between • Build up or compile • Examine in detail by argument • Translate into intelligible or familiar terms • Place in order of priority or sequence for action • Create or bring into existence
5 Evaluation How you are expected to use your learning to evaluate, make decisions or recommendations	• Advise • Evaluate • Recommend	• Counsel, inform or notify • Appraise or assess the value of • Propose a course of action

Guidance in our Practice and Revision Kit focuses on how the verbs are used in questions.

1 GUS

27 mins

Learning outcome E1(b)

GUS is a toy manufacturing company. It manufactures Polly Playtime, the latest doll craze amongst young girls. The company is now at full production of the doll. The final accounts for 20X9 have just been published and are as follows. 20X8's accounts are also shown for comparison purposes.

INCOME STATEMENT YEAR ENDED 31 DECEMBER

	20X9 $'000	20X8 $'000
Sales	30,000	20,000
Cost of sales	20,000	11,000
Gross profit	10,000	9,000
Interest	450	400
Profit before tax	9,550	8,600
Tax	2,000	1,200
Profit for the period	7,550	7,400

Note. Dividends of $2,500,000 were declared in 20X8 and 20X9.

STATEMENT OF FINANCIAL POSITION AS AT 31 DECEMBER

	20X9 $'000	20X9 $'000	20X8 $'000	20X8 $'000
Non-current assets		1,500		1,400
Current assets				
Inventory	7,350		3,000	
Receivables	10,000		6,000	
Cash	2,500	19,850	4,500	13,500
Total assets		21,350		14,900
Equity and liabilities				
Ordinary shares (25c)		5,000		5,000
Retained earnings		8,950		3,900
		13,950		8,900
Non-current liabilities				
8% loan stock		1,200		3,500
Current liabilities				
Overdraft	2,000		–	
Trade payables	4,200		2,500	
		6,200		2,500
Total equity and liabilities		21,350		14,900

(a)   By studying the above accounts and using ratio analysis, identify the main problems facing GUS.

(10 marks)

(b)   Provide possible solutions to the problems identified in (a).

(5 marks)

(This is equivalent to 3 Section B 5 mark questions)

(Total = 15 marks)

2 VX

27 mins

Learning outcome E1(c)

The VX Company has produced the following information from which a cash budget for the first six months of next year is required.

The company makes a single product which sells for $50 and the variable cost of each unit is as follows.

Material	$26
Labour (wages)	$8
Variable overhead	$2

Fixed overheads (excluding depreciation) are budgeted at $5,500 per month payable on the 23rd of each month.

Notes

(a)   Sales units for the last two months of this year.

November	December
1,000	1,200

(b)   Budgeted sales for next year.

January	February	March	April	May	June
1,400	1,600	1,800	2,000	2,200	2,600

(c)   Production quantities for the last two months of this year.

November	December
1,200	1,400

(d)   Budgeted production units for next year.

January	February	March	April	May	June
1,600	2,000	2,400	2,600	2,400	2,200

(e)   Wages are paid in the month when output is produced.

(f)   Variable overhead is paid 50% in the month when the cost is incurred and 50% the following month.

(g)   Suppliers of material are paid two months after the material is used in production.

(h)   Customers are expected to pay at the end of the second month following sale.

(i)   A new machine is scheduled for January costing $34,000, this is to be paid for in February.

(j)   An old machine is to be sold for cash in January for $1,200.

(k)   The company expects to have a cash balance of $35,500 on 1 January.

Required

Prepare a month by month cash budget for the first six months of next year.   **(15 marks)**

(This is equivalent to 3 Section B 5 mark questions)

3 SF

36 mins

Learning outcome E2(b)

SF is a family-owned private company with five main shareholders.

SF has just prepared its cash budget for the year ahead, details of which are shown below. The current overdraft facility is $50,000 and the bank has stated that it would not be willing to increase the facility at present, without a substantial increase in the interest rate charged, due to the lack of assets to offer as security.

The shareholders are concerned by the cash projections, and have sought advice from external consultants.

All figures, $'000

	J	F	M	A	M	J	J	A	S	O	N	D
Collections from customers	55	60	30	10	15	20	20	25	30	40	55	80
Dividend on investment						10						
Total inflows	55	60	30	10	15	30	20	25	30	40	55	80
Payments to suppliers		20		20		25		28		27		25
Wages and salaries	15	15	15	15	15	20	20	15	15	15	15	15
Payments for non-current assets			2		5	10		15				
Dividend payable				25								
Income tax									30			
Other operating expenses	5	5	5	5	7	7	7	7	7	7	8	8
Total outflows	20	40	22	65	27	62	27	65	52	49	23	48
Net in or (out)	35	20	8	(55)	(12)	(32)	(7)	(40)	(22)	(9)	32	32
Bank balance (overdraft)												
Opening	20	55	75	83	28	16	(16)	(23)	(63)	(85)	(94)	(62)
Closing	55	75	83	28	16	(16)	(23)	(63)	(85)	(94)	(62)	(30)

The following additional information relating to the cash budget has been provided by SF.

(i) All sales are on credit. Two months' credit on average is granted to customers.

(ii) Production is scheduled evenly throughout the year. Year-end inventories of finished goods are forecast to be $30,000 higher than at the beginning of the year.

(iii) Purchases of raw materials are made at two-monthly intervals. SF typically takes up to 90 days to pay for goods supplied. Other expenses are paid in the month in which they arise.

(iv) The capital expenditure budget comprises:

Office furniture	March	$2,000
Progress payments on building extensions	May	$5,000
Car	June	$10,000
New equipment	August	$15,000

Required

Assume you are an external consultant employed by SF. Prepare a report for the board:

(a) Advising on the possible actions it might take to improve its budgeted cash flow for the year, and the possible impact of these actions on the company's business **(12 marks)**

(b) Explaining the advantages of borrowing by means of a term loan rather than an overdraft **(5 marks)**

(c) Identifying possible short-term investment opportunities for the cash surpluses identified in the first part of the budget year **(3 marks)**

(Total = 20 marks)

4 Factoring   36 mins

Learning outcome E1(d)

ABC is a small manufacturing company which is suffering cash flow difficulties. The company already utilises its maximum overdraft facility. ABC sells an average of $400,000 of goods per month at invoice value, and customers are allowed 40 days to pay from the date of invoice. Two possible solutions to the company's cash flow problems have been suggested.

- Option 1 The company could factor its trade debts. A factor has been found who would advance ABC 75% of the value of its invoices immediately on receipt of the invoices, at an interest rate of 10% per annum. The factor would also charge a service fee amounting to 2% of the total invoices. As a result of using the factor, ABC would save administration costs estimated at $5,000 per month.

- Option 2 The company could offer a cash discount to customers for prompt payment. It has been suggested that customers could be offered a 2% discount for payments made within ten days of invoicing.

Required

(a) Identify the services that may be provided by factoring organisations.   **(5 marks)**

(b) Calculate the annual net cost (in $) of the proposed factoring agreement.   **(5 marks)**

(c) Calculate the annual cost (in percentage terms) of offering a cash discount to customers.

                                                                                                (5 marks)

(d) Discuss the merits and drawbacks of the two proposals.   **(5 marks)**

                                                                               (Total = 20 marks)

5 Debt collection targets   36 mins

Learning outcome E1(f)

(a) Using an example, describe how you would devise a system of targets for credit control staff to ensure a consistent receivables ageing ratio.

(b) Describe the features of debt factoring, and explain why small, rapidly growing firms might employ a debt factor.

                                                                                       (20 marks)

6 Marginal and absorption costing compared   54 mins

Learning outcome A1(a)

(a)   TLF manufactures a single product, the Claud. The following figures relate to the Claud for a one-year period.

Activity level	50%	100%
Sales and production (units)	400	800
	€	€
Sales	8,000	16,000
Production costs: variable	3,200	6,400
fixed	1,600	1,600
Sales and distribution costs: variable	1,600	3,200
fixed	2,400	2,400

The normal level of activity for the year is 800 units. Fixed costs are incurred evenly throughout the year, and actual fixed costs are the same as budgeted.

There were no inventories of Claud at the beginning of the year.

In the first quarter, 220 units were produced and 160 units sold.

Required

(i)   Calculate the fixed production costs absorbed by Clauds in the first quarter if absorption costing is used.   **(3 marks)**

(ii)   Calculate the under/over recovery of overheads during the quarter.   **(3 marks)**

(iii)   Calculate the profit using absorption costing.   **(6 marks)**

(iv)   Calculate the profit using marginal costing.   **(5 marks)**

(v)   Explain why there is a difference between the answers to (iii) and (iv).   **(3 marks)**

(b)   Explain five arguments in favour of absorption costing.   **(5 marks)**

(c)   Prepare a brief report to the managing director which explains why traditional management accounting systems are now inadequate.   **(5 marks)**

(Total = 30 marks)

7 Setting standard costs   9 mins

Learning outcome A1(e)

Critics of standard costing argue that it is of limited usefulness for cost control in an inflationary environment.

Comment on this statement and explain whether or not you agree with it.   **(5 marks)**

8 DS

54 mins

Learning outcome A1(f)

(a) Describe briefly four purposes of a system of standard costing. **(5 marks)**

(b) Explain the importance of keeping standards meaningful and relevant. **(5 marks)**

(c) DS manufactures a brand of tennis racket, the W, and a brand of squash racket, the B. The budget for October was as follows.

	W	B
Production (units)	4,000	1,500
Direct materials: wood (£0.30 per metre)	7 metres	5 metres
gut (£1.50 per metre)	6 metres	4 metres
Other materials	£0.20	£0.15
Direct labour (£3 per hour)	30 mins	20 mins

Overheads

	£
Variable: power	1,500
maintenance	7,500
	9,000
Fixed: supervision	8,000
heating and lighting	1,200
rent	4,800
depreciation	7,000
	21,000

Variable overheads are assumed to vary with standard hours produced.

Actual results for October were as follows.

Production:	W	3,700 units
	B	1,890 units

			£
Direct materials, bought and used:			
	wood	37,100 metres	11,000
	gut	29,200 metres	44,100
	other materials		1,000
Direct labour		2,200 hours	6,850
Power			1,800
Maintenance			6,900
Supervision			7,940
Heating and lighting			1,320
Rent			4,800
Depreciation			7,000
			92,710

Required

Calculate the cost variances for DS for October. Assume that a standard absorption costing system is in operation. **(20 marks)**

(Total = 30 marks)

9 Wye not

36 mins

Learning outcome A1(f)

Data from the October 20X9 standard cost card of product Wye, the only product of Exe plc, is as follows.

		£
Direct materials	4 kg @ £2.50 per kg	10.00
Direct labour	3 hours @ £6.00 per hour	18.00
Variable overhead	3 hours @ £4.00 per hour	12.00
Fixed overhead		20.00
		60.00
Standard profit		15.00
Standard selling price		75.00

Budgeted fixed overhead cost for October 20X9 was £25,000.

The operating statement for October 20X9, when raw material stock levels remained unchanged, was as follows.

	(A) £	(F) £	£
Budgeted profit			17,250
Sales volume profit variance			750 (A)
			16,500
Selling price variance			5,500 (F)
			22,000
Cost variances:			
Direct materials – price	535		
– usage	375		
Direct labour – rate	410		
– efficiency	1,200		
Variable overhead – expenditure		820	
– efficiency	800		
Fixed overhead – expenditure		1,000	
– volume		1,000	
	3,320	2,820	500 (A)
			21,500

Required

(a) Calculate the following.

(i)	Actual sales units	**(2 marks)**
(ii)	Actual production units	**(2 marks)**
(iii)	Actual selling price per unit	**(2 marks)**
(iv)	Actual material price per kg	**(2 marks)**
(v)	Actual labour hours	**(2 marks)**
(vi)	Actual variable overhead cost	**(2 marks)**
(vii)	Actual fixed overhead cost	**(2 marks)**

(b) Prepare a report addressed to the operations manager which explains the meaning and possible causes of the two most significant variances which occurred in October 20X9. **(6 marks)**

(Total = 20 marks)

10 HP

54 mins

Learning outcome A1(f)

HP manufactures a special floor tile which measures ½m × ¼m × 0.01m. The tiles are manufactured in a process which requires the following standard mix.

Material	Quantity kg	Price £	Amount £
A	40	1.50	60
B	30	1.20	36
C	10	1.40	14
D	20	0.50	10
			120

Each mix should produce 100 square metres of floor tiles of 0.01m thickness. During April, the actual output was 46,400 tiles from the following input.

Material	Quantity kg	Price £	Amount £
A	2,200	1.60	3,520
B	2,000	1.10	2,200
C	500	1.50	750
D	1,400	0.50	700
			7,170

Required

Calculate the following variances for the month of April.

(a) Cost variance for each material

(b) Price variance for each material

(c) Mix variance using the individual valuation basis

(d) Yield variance in total

(e) Suggest possible explanations for the following variances:

    (i) material price and mix variances for material A
    (ii) material price and mix variances for material B

(f) Briefly explain the two situations in which the calculation of mix and yield variances is appropriate

(Total = 30 marks)

11 Wimbrush

54 mins

Learning outcome A1(f)

(a) The management of Wimbrush feel that standard costing and variance analysis have little to offer in the reporting of some of the activities of their firm.

'Although we produce a range of fairly standardised products' states the accountant of Wimbrush, 'prices of many of our raw materials are apt to change suddenly and comparison of actual prices with predetermined, and often unrealistic, standard prices is of little use.

For example, consider the experience over the last accounting period of two of our products, Widgets and Splodgets. To produce a Widget we use 5 kg of X and our plans were based on a cost of X of £3 per kg. Due to market movements the actual price changed and if we had purchased efficiently the cost would have been £4.50 per kg.

Production of Widgets was 2,000 units and usage of X amounted to 10,800 kg at a total cost of £51,840.

A Splodget uses raw material Z but again the price of this can change rapidly. It was thought that Z would cost £30 per tonne but in fact we only paid £25 per tonne and if we had purchased correctly the cost would have been less as it was freely available at only £23 per tonne. It usually takes 1.5 tonnes of Z to produce 1 Splodget but our production of 500 Splodgets used only 700 tonnes of Z.

So you can see that with our particular circumstances the traditional approach to variance analysis is of little use and we don't use it for materials although we do use it for reporting on labour and variable overhead costs.'

Required

(i)   Analyse the material variances for both Widgets and Splodgets, utilising the following.

    (1)   Traditional variance analysis
    (2)   An approach which distinguishes between planning and operational variances

                                                                                (12 marks)

(ii)   Write brief notes which do the following.

    (1)   Explain the approach to variance analysis which distinguishes between planning and operational variances.

    (2)   Indicate the extent to which this approach is useful for firms in general and for Wimbrush Ltd in particular.   **(8 marks)**

(b)   Briefly explain the four dimensions of McDonalization in service industries.   **(5 marks)**

(c)   Discuss the factors to be considered in deciding whether a variance should be investigated.

                                                                                 (5 marks)

                                                                        (Total = 30 marks)

12 M   **36 mins**

Learning outcome A1(f)

(a)   M operates a standard absorption costing system in respect of its only product. The standard cost card of this product for the budget year ending 31 December 20X0 is as follows.

	£	£
Selling price		120.00
Direct material A (5 kgs)	12.50	
Direct material B (10 kgs)	40.00	
Direct wages (3 hours)	18.00	
Variable overhead (3 hours)	9.00	
Fixed overhead* (3 hours)	15.00	
		94.50
Profit/unit		25.50

*Fixed overhead is absorbed on the basis of direct labour hours. Budgeted fixed overhead costs are £180,000 for the year. Cost and activity levels are budgeted to be constant each month.

During January 20X0, when budgeted sales and production were 1,000 units, the following actual results were achieved.

	£
Sales (900 units)	118,800
Production costs (1,050 units)	
Direct material A (5,670 kg)	14,742
Direct material B (10,460 kg)	38,179
Direct wages (3,215 hours)	19,933
Variable overhead	10,288
Fixed overhead	15,432

With the benefit of hindsight you now know that direct labour received a pay increase of 3 per cent which was not allowed for in the standard cost. The original standard is to be used for inventory valuation.

You have also confirmed with the production manager that the nature of the production method is such that direct materials A and B are mixed together to produce the final product.

All materials were purchased and used during January.

Required

Prepare for the production manager a statement that reconciles the budgeted and actual profits for January 20X0 using the following variances.

(i)   Sales volume profit
(ii)   Sales price
(iii)   Direct material price
(iv)   Direct material mix using the average valuation basis
(v)   Direct material yield
(vi)   Direct labour rate, analysed between planning and operating effects
(vii)   Direct labour efficiency
(viii) Variable production overhead expenditure
(ix)   Variable production overhead efficiency
(x)   Fixed production overhead expenditure
(xi)   Fixed production overhead volume

Variances should be calculated so as to provide useful information to the production manager

(Total = 20 marks)

13 Just in time systems   9 mins

Learning outcome A1(h)

State FIVE financial benefits of a Just in Time (JIT) system.   **(5 marks)**

14 Costs of quality   9 mins

Learning outcome A1(h)

A consequence of the introduction of just-in-time manufacturing methods is usually increased quality costs. Briefly describe the four categories of quality costs.   **(5 marks)**

15 Throughput accounting   9 mins

Learning outcome A1(a)

Throughput accounting has been described as 'super variable costing'.

Explain why throughput accounting is sometimes described in this way and identify briefly the differences between throughput accounting and marginal or variable cost accounting.   **(5 marks)**

16 WAQ   18 mins

Learning outcome A1(a)

WAQ produces a single product, X, which passes through three different processes, A, B and C. The throughput per hour of the three processes is 12, 10 and 15 units of X respectively. The company works an 8-hour day, 6 days a week, 48 weeks a year. The selling price of X is £150 per unit and its material cost is £30 per unit. Conversion costs are planned to be £24,000 per week.

Required

(a)   Determine the throughput accounting (TA) ratio per day.

(b)   Calculate how much the company could spend on equipment to improve the throughput of process B if it wished to recover its costs in the following time periods.

        2 years
        12 weeks

(c)   Calculate the revised TA ratio if this money is spent.   **(10 marks)**

17 KH   54 mins

Learning outcome A1(c)

KH is a fairly new company at the leading edge of paint-spraying technology. It has three customers - G, F and R - whose bare metal products are finished by KH.

G's products require 7 coats of paint, F's 6 coats and R's 5 coats. Because the products are different shapes and sizes different quantities of paint are needed. Paint is delivered in batches of various sizes, depending upon the finish required.

Customer	Litres
G	7.6
F	8.6
R	6.3

Production details for each product are budgeted as follows for the coming month.

	G	F	R
Units sprayed	5,400	4,360	3,600
Batches of paint required	27	20	40
Machine attendant time	30 mins	45 mins	75 mins
Cost of paint per unit	£15.20	£11.18	£18.90

Machine attendants are paid £5.30 per hour.

Overhead costs are absorbed on a labour hour basis. The following overheads are anticipated in the coming month.

	£
Paint stirring and quality control	24,081
Electricity	104,700
Filling of spraying machines	64,914

Required

(a) Calculate the unit cost to KH of each sprayed product for the coming month showing each cost element separately.

(b) Given the following additional information calculate the unit cost to KH on an activity based costing approach.

Activity	Cost driver
Paint stirring and quality control	Batches of paint
Electricity	Coats of paint
Filling of spraying machines	Litres of paint

(c) Using the costs calculated for parts (a) and (b) as illustration describe the role in activity based costing of cost drivers. **(20 marks)**

(d) Explain the problems that may cause an organisation to decide not to use, or to abandon use of, activity based techniques. **(10 marks)**

(Total = 30 marks)

18 ABC v traditional absorption costing   9 mins

Learning outcome A1(c)

Explain briefly FOUR situations where a product unit cost calculated using an ABC system is likely to differ significantly from the unit cost for the same product calculated using a traditional absorption costing system based on direct labour hours. **(5 marks)**

19 ABC in the modern environment   9 mins

Learning outcome A1(c)

Explain briefly the reasons why ABC is particularly suitable in a modern business environment and any situations where it is not appropriate. **(5 marks)**

20 Environmentally sustainable profits   9 mins

Learning outcome A3(a)

Briefly explain what is meant by environmentally sustainable profits. **(5 marks)**

21 The purposes of budgeting   9 mins

Learning outcome B1(a)

State why organisations produce budgets. **(5 marks)**

22 PF

27 mins

Learning outcome B2(b)

The manager of PF with responsibility for monitoring sales of product XN30 is convinced that the levels of sales is on a rising trend, but that it is seasonal, with more sales at some times of the year than at others. The manager has gathered the following data about sales in recent years. Trend values are shown in brackets.

Sales (thousands of units of product XN30)

Year	Spring	Summer	Autumn	Winter
20X3			250	340
20X4	186 (281)	343 (285)	263 (289)	357 (293)
20X5	203 (297)	358 (302)	278 (305)	380 (307)
20X6	207 (311)	371 (313)	290 (317)	391 (320)
20X7	222	383		

Required

(a) Show the actual sales level and the trend line on a historigram. **(5 marks)**
(b) Establish seasonal deviations from the trend. **(5 marks)**
(c) Estimate what the level of sales might be in the autumn and winter of 20X7. **(5 marks)**

(Total = 15 marks)

23 Calculating projected costs and revenues

9 mins

Learning outcome B2(a)

Describe briefly how historical data may be assessed for its suitability as the basis for forecasting future costs and revenues. **(5 marks)**

24 PPA

18 mins

Learning outcome: C1(a)

Discuss the advantages and disadvantages of post-project appraisal. **(10 marks)**

25 Payback

18 mins

Learning outcome: C2(a)

Explain the uses, limitations and merits of the payback period method of investment appraisal.

(10 marks)

26 Two projects

18 mins

Learning outcomes: C2(b), C2(c)

A company is considering which of two mutually exclusive projects it should undertake. The finance director thinks that the project with the higher NPV should be chosen whereas the managing director thinks that the one with the higher IRR should be undertaken especially as both projects have the same initial outlay and length of life. The company anticipates a cost of capital of 10% and the net after tax cash flows of the projects are as follows.

		Project X $000	Project Y $000
Year	0	–200	–200
	1	35	218
	2	80	10
	3	90	10
	4	75	4
	5	20	3

Required

(a)   Calculate the NPV and IRR of each project.   **(6 marks)**

(b)   Recommend, with reasons, which project you would undertake (if either).   **(2 marks)**

(c)   Explain the inconsistency in ranking of the two projects in view of the remarks of the directors.
                                                                                                      (2 marks)

                                                                                                      (Total = 10 marks)

27 NPV and IRR   18 mins

Learning outcome: C2(b)

Explain the uses, limitations and merits of the NPV and IRR methods of investment appraisal. **(10 marks)**

28 HP   45 mins

Learning outcome: C1(c)

HP is considering purchasing a new machine to alleviate a bottleneck in its production facilities. At
present it uses an old machine which can process 200 units of product P per hour. HP could replace it
with machine AB, which is product-specific and can produce 500 units an hour. Machine AB costs
$500,000. If it is installed, two members of staff will have to attend a short training course, which will
cost the company a total of $5,000. Removing the old machine and preparing the area for machine AB
will cost $20,000.

The company expects demand for P to be 12,000 units per week for another three years. After this, early
in the fourth year, the new machine would be scrapped and sold for $50,000. The existing machine will
have no scrap value. Each P earns a contribution of $1.40. The company works a 40-hour week for 48
weeks in the year. HP normally expects a payback within two years, and its after-tax cost of capital is 10
per cent per annum. The company pays corporation tax at 30 per cent and receives writing-down
allowances of 25 per cent, reducing balance. Corporation tax is payable quarterly, in the seventh and
tenth months of the year in which the profit is earned, and in the first and fourth months of the following
year.

Required

(a)   Prepare detailed calculations that show whether machine AB should be bought, and advise the
       management of HP as to whether it should proceed with the purchase.

       Make the following assumptions.

       (i)   The company's financial year begins on the same day that the new machines would start
              operating, if purchased.

       (ii)   The company uses discounted cash-flow techniques with annual breaks only.

       (iii) For taxation purposes, HP's management will elect for short-life asset treatment for this
              asset.   **(18 marks)**

(b)   The investment decision in part (a) is a closely defined manufacturing one. Explain how a
       marketing or an IT investment decision might differ in terms of approach and assessment.
                                                                                                      (7 marks)

                                                                                                      (Total = 25 marks)

29 Quarefel plc   **36 mins**

Learning outcomes: C2(a), C1(f), C1(g)

Quarefel plc is considering entering the market for a single product which has an estimated life cycle of three years. The following information has been gathered.

- The total market size is estimated as follows: Year 1: 800,000 units; Year 2: 1,200,000 units; Year 3: 600,000 units.

- Quarefel plc intends to use a flexible manufacturing system which will be able to produce up to 200,000 units per year. The equipment will cost $2,000,000 (payable year 0) and will have an estimated residual value of $400,000 (receivable at the end of year 4).

- An advertising campaign will be implemented by Quarefel plc on the following basis: Year 0: $1,200,000; Year 1: $1,000,000; Year 2: $800,000.

- Quarefel plc has estimated its sales (Q) in '000 units and selling price per unit (P) for each year over the life of the product. This may be expressed in terms of the price/demand function $P = 70 - 0.15Q$.

- The year 1 market share is crucial. Annual sales units for Quarefel plc for years 2 and 3 are expected to increase or decrease from the year 1 level achieved in proportion to the change in the size of the overall market from one year to the next, in so far as the production capacity of Quarefel plc will allow. The prices set by Quarefel plc in each of years 2 and 3 will be set in accordance with the price/demand function estimate detailed above.

- Variable cost is estimated at $25 per product unit.

- Fixed costs directly attributable to the product (other than advertising) are estimated at $600,000 per year for each of years 1 to 3.

- Quarefel plc has an estimated cost of capital of 12% for this type of proposal.

  Ignore taxation and inflation.

Required

(a) Using the above information, calculate the net present value (NPV) and internal rate of return (IRR) of the proposal where a year 1 launch price of $60 per unit is used. (All working calculations must be shown.)   **(12 marks)**

(b) Briefly discuss three non-financial considerations in long-term decision making.   **(5 marks)**

(c) Briefly explain the margin of error approach to sensitivity analysis.   **(3 marks)**

                                     (Total = 20 marks)

30 Elsewhere

45 mins

Learning outcomes: D1(d), (e), (f)

Rubbish Records Ltd are considering the launch of a new pop group, Elsewhere.

If the group is launched without further market research being carried out it is thought that demand for their records and the present value of profit earned from record sales will be as follows.

		Present value of profit
Demand	Probability	$'000
High	0.5	800
Medium	0.2	100
Low	0.3	(300)

It is possible, however, to commission a market research survey which will forecast either a successful or unsuccessful career for Elsewhere. The probability of an unsuccessful career is 0.3.

Probabilities of high, medium or low demand for Elsewhere's records under each of the two market research results are as follows.

	Demand		
	High	Medium	Low
Successful chart career	0.7	0.1	0.2
Unsuccessful chart career	0.1	0.3	0.6

So, for example, if the research indicated an unsuccessful chart career, then the probability of medium demand for the group's records would be 0.3.

The survey would cost $50,000.

Required

(a) Calculate the expected value of profit if Rubbish Records do not commission a market research survey. **(5 marks)**

(b) (i) Draw a decision tree to show the choices facing Rubbish Records. **(10 marks)**

  (ii) Briefly explain whether or not the record company should commission the survey. **(3 marks)**

(c) (i) Determine the maximum the company should pay for the survey. (Often referred to as the value of the imperfect information provided by the survey). **(2 marks)**

  (ii) Establish the disadvantages of using expected values and decision trees as decision-making tools. **(5 marks)**

(Total = 25 marks)

1 GUS

> **Top tips.** This is a good example of *using* ratios to explain what is happening. The ratios alone do not explain anything.

(a) The company has become significantly more reliant on short term liabilities to finance its operations as shown by the following analysis:

	20X9 $'000	20X8 $'000
Total assets	21,350	14,900
Short-term liabilities *	6,200	2,500
Long term funds (equity and debt)	15,150	12,400
	21,350	14,900

* = overdraft + payables

Overtrading

A major reason for this is classic overtrading: sales increased by 50% in one year, but the operating profit margin fell from 9,000/20,000 = 45% in 20X8 to 10,000/30,000 = 33% in 20X9.

Refinancing

However, the effect is **compounded** by the **repayment** of $2.3 million (66%) of the 8% loan stock and replacement with a $2 million bank overdraft and increased trade payable finance.

Liquidity ratios

As a result of overtrading, the company's **current ratio** has deteriorated from 13,500/2,500 = 5.4 in 20X8 to 19,850/6,200 = 3.2 in 20X9. The **quick assets ratio** (or 'acid test') has deteriorated from 10,500/2,500 = 4.2 to 12,500/6,200 = 2.01. However these figures are acceptable and only if they continue to deteriorate is there likely to be a liquidity problem.

Investment in non-current assets

The company has **not maintained an investment in non-current assets** to match its sales growth. Sales/non-current assets has increased from 20,000/1,400 = 14.3 times to 30,000/1,500 = 20 times. This may be putting the quality of production at risk, but may be justified, however, if sales are expected to decline when the doll loses popularity.

Working capital ratios

An investigation of working capital ratios shows that:

(1) **Inventory turnover** has **decreased** from 11,000/3,000 = 3.67 times to 20,000/7,350 = 2.72 times. This indicates that there has been a large investment in inventory.

(2) The **average receivables payment period has increased** from 6,000/20,000 × 365 = 110 days to 10,000/30,000 × 365 = 122 days, indicating a lack of credit control. This has contributed to a weakening of the cash position.

(3) The **payment period to suppliers** (roughly estimated) has **decreased** from 2,500/11,000 × 365 = 83 days to 4,200/20,000 × 365 = 77 days. This result is unexpected, indicating that there has been no increase in delaying payment to suppliers over the year. Suppliers are being paid in a significantly shorter period than the period of credit taken by customers.

Conclusion

In summary, the main problem facing GUS is its increasing overdependence on short term finance, caused in the main by:

(1)   A major investment in inventory to satisfy a rapid increase in sales volumes
(2)   Deteriorating profit margins
(3)   Poor credit control of receivables
(4)   Repayment of loan stock

(b)   **Future sales**

Possible solutions to the above problems depend on **future sales** and **product projections**. If the rapid increase in sales has been a one-product phenomenon, there is little point in over-capitalising by borrowing long term and investing in a major expansion of non-current assets. If, however, sales of this and future products are expected to continue increasing, and further investment is needed, the company's growth should be underpinned by an injection of equity capital and an issue of longer term debt.

Better working capital management

Regardless of the above, various working capital strategies could be improved. **Customers** should be encouraged to **pay more promptly**. This is best done by instituting **proper credit control procedures**. **Longer credit periods** could probably be negotiated with suppliers and quantity discounts should be investigated.

2 VX

> **Top tips.** This is not difficult a difficult question. Set it all out neatly, so that you do not miss anything.

Initial workings

(i)   Sales value

	Nov	Dec	Jan	Feb	Mar	Apr
Sales units	1,000	1,200	1,400	1,600	1,800	2,000
Sales value at $50 ($)	50,000	60,000	70,000	80,000	90,000	100,000

Sales revenue will be received two months after the sale is made.

(ii)   Production costs

	Nov	Dec	Jan	Feb	Mar	Apr	May	June
Production units	1,200	1,400	1,600	2,000	2,400	2,600	2,400	2,200
	$'000	$'000	$'000	$'000	$'000	$'000	$'000	$'000
Wages at $8			12.8	16.0	19.2	20.8	19.2	17.6
Variable o/h at $2	2.4	2.8	3.2	4.0	4.8	5.2	4.8	4.4
50% paid in month	1.2	1.4	1.6	2.0	2.4	2.6	2.4	2.2
50% in following month		1.2	1.4	1.6	2.0	2.4	2.6	2.4
Total payment			3.0	3.6	4.4	5.0	5.0	4.6
Material at $26	31.2	36.4	41.6	52.0	62.4	67.6	62.4	57.2
Payment after two months			31.2	36.4	41.6	52.0	62.4	67.6

CASH BUDGET FOR FIRST SIX MONTHS OF NEXT YEAR

	Jan $'000	Feb $'000	Mar $'000	Apr $'000	May $'000	June $'000
Receipts						
Sales revenue	50.0	60.0	70.0	80.0	90.0	100.0
Sale of old machine	1.2	–	–	–	–	
	51.2	60.0	70.0	80.0	90.0	100.0
Payments						
Wages	12.8	16.0	19.2	20.8	19.2	17.6
Variable overhead	3.0	3.6	4.4	5.0	5.0	4.6
Material	31.2	36.4	41.6	52.0	62.4	67.6
Fixed overhead	5.5	5.5	5.5	5.5	5.5	5.5
New machine		34.0				
	52.5	95.5	70.7	83.3	92.1	95.3
Net cash flow	(1.3)	(35.5)	(0.7)	(3.3)	(2.1)	4.7
Opening cash balance	35.5	34.2	(1.3)	(2.0)	(5.3)	(7.4)
Closing cash balance	34.2	(1.3)	(2.0)	(5.3)	(7.4)	(2.7)

3 SF

> **Top tips**
>
> This question requires you to apply what you have learned in the finance section of the syllabus. Read the information through twice – the situation will become clearer.

To: Board of Directors, SF
From: External consultant
Date: 12 November 20X1
Subject: Cash flow budget

Introduction

The budget shows that the company will experience a **positive cash position** for the first quarter of the year, there being a net inflow of cash during this time as well as no use of the overdraft facility. However, thereafter the position deteriorates, with the company being forecast to exceed its overdraft limit from August to November. By the end of the year, the company's cash reserves will be $50,000 lower than at the start of the period.

Possible remedial actions

1   **Production scheduling**

    Sales show a cyclical movement, with receipts from customers being highest during the winter months. However, production is scheduled evenly throughout the year. If production could be **scheduled to match the pattern of demand**, the cash balance would remain more even throughout the year. Any resulting increase in the overall level of production costs could be quantified and compared with the savings in interest costs to assess the viability of such a proposal.

2   **Defer the income tax payment**

    This might be possible by **agreement with the tax authorities**. The company should consider the relative **costs of the interest** that would be charged if this were done, and the **cost of financing** the payment through some form of debt.

3   **Dividend**

    SF is a private company, and therefore the shareholders could agree to **forgo** or **defer the dividend**. The practicality of this will depend on the personal situation of the five shareholders.

4 **Defer payment for non-current assets**

(a) Presumably the **purchase** of the **office furniture** could be deferred, although the sums involved are relatively insignificant.

(b) The **progress payment** on the **building extension** is likely to be a contractual commitment that cannot be deferred.

(c) The **purchase of the car** could reasonably be **deferred** until the cash position improves. If it is essential to the needs of the business, the company could consider spreading the cost through some form of leasing or hire purchase agreement.

(d) It is not clear why the new **equipment** is being **purchased**. Presumably some form of investment appraisal has been undertaken to establish the financial benefits of the acquisition. However, if it is being purchased in advance of an increase in production then it may be possible to defer it slightly. The company could also look at alternative methods of financing it, as have been suggested in the case of the car.

5 **Realise the investment**

The dividend from this is $10,000, and therefore assuming an interest rate of, say, 5%, it could be worth in the region of $200,000. It is not clear **what form** this takes or for **what purpose** it is being held, but it may be possible to dispose of a part of it without jeopardising the long-term strategic future of the business.

6 **Reduce the inventory holding period**

At present it is forecast that inventories will be $30,000 higher by the end of the year. This represents three months' worth of purchases from suppliers. It is not clear to what extent this increase is predicated upon **increasing sales**, although since the building is being extended it is assumed that there will be some increase in the level of production and sales in the near future. However, the size of the increase seems excessive.

7 **Tighten credit control procedures**

It is not known what level of bad debts is incurred by SF, but even if it is low, **tightening up** the **credit control** and **debt collection procedures** could improve the speed with which money is collected.

8 **Factor the receivables ledger**

The use of a factor to administer the receivables ledger might **reduce the collection period** and **save administration costs**. An **evaluation** of the **relevant costs and benefits** could be undertaken to see whether it is worth pursuing this option.

9 **Reduce the debt collection period**

SF currently allows its customers two months' credit. It is not known how this compares with the industry norms, but it is unlikely to be excessive. However, there may be some scope for **reducing the credit period** for at least some of the customers, and thereby reducing the average for the business as a whole.

10 **Increase the credit period taken**

Since SF already takes 90 days credit, it is unlikely that it will be able to increase this further without **jeopardising** the **relationship** with its suppliers.

11 **Inject additional long-term capital**

The budget assumes that both non-current and working capital will increase by $30,000 during the year, and the directors should therefore consider seeking **additional long term capital** to finance at least the non-current asset acquisitions. Possible sources of capital include:

- Injection of funds from the existing shareholders

- The use of venture capital
- Long-term bank loan, loan stock issue or mortgage

Loans and overdrafts

Companies often have a greater proportion of their debt in the form of overdraft due to the problems of providing sufficient security to lenders. However, a term loan will often be more attractive than an overdraft for the following reasons.

1   Overdraft finance is generally **repayable on demand**. It therefore carries a higher level of financial risk than does a term loan.

2   The bank may become uncomfortable with a growing overdraft and seek to secure scheduled repayment or other **conditions** from the company. This can present a growing firm with cash flow problems.

3   Overdraft finance is generally floating rate, thus exposing the company to **interest rate risk**. Term loans can often be negotiated at a fixed rate thus reducing this element of risk and assisting with cash flow forecasting.

4   Term loans can be negotiated over a timescale that can be related to the company's forecast need for financing, and with a **repayment schedule** that can be tailored to the company's requirements. For example, capital may be repaid in stages or at the end of the period.

5   If the company has a good trading record and/or a good asset base and can therefore offer reasonable security, it may be able to negotiate a **lower interest rate** than would be payable on an overdraft.

Cash surpluses

The company should also consider investing its cash surpluses during the first quarter of the year to earn at least some interest, although this will be restricted by the short periods for which funds are likely to be available. Possible investments include:

- Bank deposits
- Short-term gilts
- Bills of exchange

Conclusions

It can be seen that there are a number of avenues that SF could explore. It appears that the company is fundamentally profitable, given the size of the corporation tax bill, and the fact that were it not for the non-current asset additions and the investment in inventory the cash balance would increase by $10,000 during the year. However, the liquidity issues must be addressed now to avoid exceeding the overdraft limit.

4 Factoring

> **Top tips.** Note that you are asked for the factoring cost in $ and the discount cost in %. You must learn the formula for the cost of a discount.

(a)   A factor normally manages the debts owed to a client on the client's behalf.

Services provided by factoring organisations

(i)   **Administration** of the client's invoicing, sales accounting and debt collection service.

(ii)   **Credit protection** for the client's debts, whereby the factor takes over the risk of loss from bad debts and so 'insures' the client against such losses. The factor may purchase these debts 'without recourse' to the client, which means that if the client's customers do not pay what they owe, the factor will not ask for the money back from the client.

(iii)   **'Factor finance'** may be provided, the factor advancing cash to the client against outstanding debts. The factor may advance up to 85% of approved debts from the date of invoice.

(iv)   A **confidentiality agreement** may be offered to conceal the existence of the arrangement from customers.

(b)   It will be assumed that the factor finance will **not** be **replacing** any **existing credit lines**, and therefore the full interest cost of the agreement will be relevant when determining the cost of factoring.

Annual sales are $400,000 × 12 = $4.8m
Daily sales are $4.8m/365 = $13,151

The annual cost of factoring can now be found:

	$
Interest ($13,151 × 40 days × 75% × 10%)	39,453
Service fee ($4.8m × 2%)	96,000
Total annual charge	135,453
Less internal cost savings ($5,000 × 12)	60,000
Net annual cost	75,453

(c) $\text{Cost} = \left(\dfrac{100}{100-d}\right)^{\frac{365}{t}} - 1$

$t = 40 - 10 = 30$ days

$d = 2\%$

$\text{Cost} = \left(\dfrac{100}{100-2}\right)^{\frac{365}{30}} - 1$

$= 27.9\%$

(d)   **Key issues in the discount option**

(i)   The **proposal is expensive**. The company should be able to get cheaper overdraft finance than this, and longer-term debt may cost even less.

(ii)   The company may need to **offer a discount** in order to make its terms competitive with other firms in the industry.

(iii)   The **level of take-up** among customers is **uncertain**, and will affect the cash flow position.

(iv)   Problems may arise when customers take both the discount and the full forty day credit period. This will **increase administrative costs** in seeking repayment.

Key issues in the factoring option

(i)   The factor may be able to **exercise better credit control** than is possible in a small company.

(ii)   The **amount of finance** that will be received is **much more certain** than for the discounting option as 75% of the value of the invoices will be provided immediately.

(iii)   The **relationship with the customers** may **deteriorate** due partly to the reduction in the level of contact with the company, and partly to the historical view of the factor as the lender of last resort.

Conclusion

The final decision must take into account all the above issues. However, the **most important points** to consider are the ability of each proposal to meet the financing requirements, and the relative costs of the different sources of finance.

5 Debt collection targets

> **Top tips.** Part (a) does require you to come up with some **numbers**. This makes it much easier to construct an example.

(a)   Receivables are assets which it is hoped can be converted into cash, and many companies promote the use of **cash targets** as aids to motivate credit controllers. A cash target is the amount that should be collected in order to arrive at an 'ideal' figure for receivables ageing. For example, assume at the end of November that receivables outstanding of $2m amount to approximately 61 days. This figure is made up as follows.

		$
November	30 days	900,000
October	31 days	1,100,000
		2,000,000

There are no debts older than this.

Sales in December are $700,000, and the target receivables ageing at the end of December is 55 days. The December sales add $700,000 which would mean that if no money were collected total receivables at the end of December would be $2,700,000 or 92 days. Therefore, to reach a target of 55 days receivables outstanding requires that the oldest 37 days receivables (92 − 55) should be collected. These are:

		$
October	31 days	1,100,000
November	6 days $^6/_{30}$ × $900,000	180,000
Cash to be collected		1,280,000

The firm should thus aim to collect $1,280,000. Note the emphasis on collecting the oldest debts. If we simply aggregated the figures for December we would have a target receivables of 55/92 × $2,700,000 = $1,614,130 suggesting a cash recovery of only $1,085,870.

The advantages of highlighting efforts on the oldest debts are that:

(i)   Older debts imply that customers are taking more credit.

(ii)   Staff are not encouraged to ask for *early* payment as a special favour from recent customers.

(iii)   Effort is expended on debts which are proving hard to collect anyway.

(b)   **Factoring** is a service that does not have a concise definition. A factor is defined as 'a doer or transactor of business for another', but a factoring organisation specialises in trade debts, and so manages the receivables of a client (business customer) on the client's behalf. There are the following aspects of factoring.

(i)   Administration of the client's invoicing, sales accounting and debt collection service.

(ii)   Credit protection for the client's debts, whereby the factor takes over the risk of loss from bad debts and so 'insures' the client against such losses. This service is also referred to as 'debt underwriting' or the 'purchase of a client's debts'.

(1)   The **factor might purchase** these **debts 'without recourse'** to the client, which means that, in the event that the client's customers are unable to pay what they owe, the factor will not ask for his money back from the client.

(2)   Not every factoring organisation will purchase approved debts without recourse and **'with recourse' factoring might be provided**, especially in cases where the size of the debt is particularly high, or the factor would not approve the debts for a 'without recourse' agreement.

       (3)   **Credit protection is credit insurance** and so the factoring organisation will want to give its approval to a credit sale before it goes ahead; in other words, the factoring organisation will want to act as a credit controller.

  (iii)   **Making payment** to the **client** in advance of collecting the debts. This might be referred to as 'factor finance' because the factor is providing cash to the client as a prepayment of outstanding debts.

A factoring organisation might be asked by a client to **advance funds** to the client against the **debts** which the factor has purchased, up to 80% of the value of the debts. This service gives the client **immediate cash** in place of a debt (which is a promise of cash in the future). The remainder, less the fees, is received later. If the client needs money to finance operations, borrowing against trade debts is therefore an alternative to asking a bank for an overdraft, although the factor will probably charge higher interest. Whereas a bank overdraft would have shown in the client's balance sheet as a current liability, factor financing does **not show up** in the client's balance sheet at all.

In the client's statement of financial position, the amount of **receivables** would be **reduced** and **cash** would initially **increase** by the same amount (although the cash would be used immediately by the client to buy more inventory, make more sales, and create even more receivables – ie the cash advance from the factor would be to put to operational use). For this reason, advances from a factor are particularly useful for **rapidly-growing companies**, that need more and more cash to expand their business quickly, by purchasing more inventory and allowing more credit sales than they would otherwise be able to do. The appeal of factor financing to growing firms is that factors might advance money when a bank is reluctant to consider granting a larger overdraft.

6 Marginal and absorption costing compared

(a)   (i) $\dfrac{\text{Budgeted fixed production costs}}{\text{Budgeted output (normal level of activity)}} = \dfrac{€1,600}{800 \text{ units}}$

Absorption rate = €2 per unit produced.

During the quarter, the fixed production overhead absorbed was 220 units × €2 = £440.

  (ii)

	€
Actual fixed production overhead	400 (¼ of £1,600)
Absorbed fixed production overhead	440
Over absorption of overhead	40

  (iii)   **Profit for the quarter, absorption costing**

	€	€
Sales (160 × €20)		3,200
Production costs		
Variable (220 × €8)	1,760	
Fixed (absorbed overhead (220 × €2))	440	
Total (220 × €10)	2,200	
Less closing inventories (60 × €10)	600	
Production cost of sales	1,600	
Adjustment for over-absorbed overhead	40	
Total production costs		1,560
Gross profit		1,640
Less: sales and distribution costs		
variable (160 × €4)	640	
fixed (¼ of €2,400)	600	
		1,240
Net profit		400

(iv) **Profit for the quarter, marginal costing**

	€	€
Sales		3,200
Variable production costs	1,760	
Less closing inventories (60 × €8)	480	
Variable production cost of sales	1,280	
Variable sales and distribution costs	640	
Total variable costs of sales		1,920
Total contribution		1,280 -
Less: Fixed production costs incurred	400	
Fixed sales and distribution costs	600	
		1,000
Net profit		280

(v) The difference in profit is due to the different valuations of closing inventory. In absorption costing, the 60 units of closing inventory include absorbed fixed overheads of €120 (60 × €2) , which are therefore costs carried over to the next quarter and not charged against the profit of the current quarter. In marginal costing, all fixed costs incurred in the period are charged against profit.

	€
Absorption costing profit	400
Fixed production costs carried forward in inventory values	120
Marginal costing profit	280

(b) (i) **Fixed production costs** are incurred in order to make output. It therefore seems fair to charge all output with a **share** of these costs.

(ii) The requirements of the international accounting standard on inventory valuation (IAS 2) state that closing inventory values should include a **share** of **fixed production overhead**. Absorption costing **fulfils that requirement**.

(iii) Absorption costing is **consistent** with the **accruals concept** as a proportion of the costs of production are carried forward to be matched against future sales.

(iv) Absorption costing involves charging fixed overheads to a product. This means it is possible to ascertain whether it is profitable or not. The problem with calculating the contribution of various products made by an enterprise is that it may **not be clear** whether the **contribution** earned by each product is **enough to cover fixed costs**.

(v) Absorption costing is particularly useful in pricing decisions in a job or batch costing environment. It ensures that the profit mark up is **sufficient to cover fixed costs**.

(c) **To:** managing director
From: management accountant
Date: 17 July 20X1
Subject: Inadequacy of traditional management accounting

Inadequacy 1

Traditional management accounting grew out of **cost accounting** and hence its roots are in **manufacturing**. For much of the twentieth century, manufacturing operated in a business environment in which the **supplier** was of utmost importance, **competition** was largely **local** and the **speed of technical and social development**, although rapid compared with earlier eras, was far **slower** than at present. This simple operating environment meant that an organisations' managers were able to **anticipate events easily** and **plan with more certainty using minimal external information** than is possible today.

Now however, it is the **customer** who is king and the **competitive environment** constantly threatens a product's life cycle. To compete effectively organisations must therefore be **flexible** enough to cope with changes in customer requirements. Such a focus on customers and competition requires a more **forward-looking** approach, which must be **substantially outward looking** and focus on **external information**, as opposed to the backward-looking and inward-looking approach of traditional management accounting.

Inadequacy 2

The 'management' that traditional management accounting was primarily intended to serve was production management, hence the **traditional emphasis** on accounting for **labour** costs, **materials** costs and **production overheads. Changes in organisations' cost structures** and in the **nature of costs** have affected the relevance of such an emphasis, however, and have led to the use of possibly **misleading information**, especially with regard to **overhead absorption.**

Inadequacy 3

The **internal information** used by management accounting tended to be sourced from accounting systems which were directed towards financial reporting, but the classifications of transactions for reporting purposes **are not necessarily relevant for decision making**.

7 Setting standard costs

> **Top tips**. Be prepared to see both sides of the argument in a question such as this. A good approach is to present a brief discussion which both agrees and disagrees with the statement. However, if the question asks you to state whether or not you agree with the statement then you must ensure that you actually do so.

Price inflation can indeed cause difficulties in setting realistic standard prices.

If **current prices** are used in the standard cost then **reported price variances would become adverse as soon as prices increase**. It would be difficult to tell at any point whether an adverse variance was because of inefficient purchasing or because of unavoidable price rises.

On the other hand, if annual standard costs are set then an **estimated mid-year price** might be used in the standard cost. This would result in **favourable price variances in the first half of the year and adverse variances in the second half**, assuming that prices increase gradually. Again, **control action would be impaired** because it would be difficult to highlight those variances which were controllable and those which were caused by unavoidable price inflation.

I would agree that standard costing can be difficult to apply in inflationary conditions but **this does not mean that its application is not worthwhile**, for the following reasons.

- **Usage and efficiency variances would still be meaningful**

- **It is possible to measure inflation**; there is no reason why its effects cannot be removed from the variances reported to management

- **Standard costs can be revised more frequently** than annually, in order to keep them up to date as a yardstick for current performance.

8 DS

> **Top tips**. Parts (a) and (b) are pure bookwork and should not provide you with too many problems. Although this is a long question which requires a lot of calculations (there are two products, three types of material and two variable overheads) and covers all of the variances we have been looking at in Chapter 7b, it is **not really exam standard**. For a start, the requirement in part (c) is **straightforward** (prepare an operating statement). Secondly, **only basic variances are examined**, a real exam question being likely to incorporate mix and yield or planning and operational variances.
>
> Nevertheless, this is an extremely **good practice question** as it does cover all the basic variances.
>
> The price and usage variance calculations were straightforward, although you may have got stuck trying to calculate a **usage variance for other materials**. This was **impossible** as you were not given standard usage information. You could therefore only calculate an overall cost variance for other materials.
>
> Because you were not provided with a breakdown of the actual hours worked on the individual products, you had to work out the standard time for actual production for each product, add them together and then compare the total with the actual figure provided.
>
> The question did not specify that **variable overheads were incurred in line with labour hours** but, in the absence of further information, you had to make that **assumption**. You could then calculate a total variable overhead cost per standard hour (the sum of (budgeted expenditure/total budgeted labour hours) for each overhead), which could be used in the variable overhead expenditure and efficiency variance calculations.
>
> Again, the question did not provide you with **a fixed overhead absorption rate** so you needed to **calculate** one (using the budgeted hours from the variable overhead calculation). Once you had done this the fixed overhead variances were not difficult to calculate (if you could remember how to calculate them!). Don't worry if you have difficulty in calculating the fixed overhead variances, as their meaning is not as easy to grasp as that of the variable cost variances. Remember you are trying to determine **why the overhead absorbed is not the same as the overhead incurred**.
>
> This might be because there is a **difference between budgeted expenditure and actual expenditure** (expenditure variance) or because there is a **difference between budgeted volume and actual volume** (volume variance).

(a)   **Uses of standard costing**

Standard costing is the preparation of standard costs to be used in a number of circumstances, including the following.

(i)   **To value stocks and cost production for cost accounting purposes**. It is an alternative method of valuation to methods like FIFO and LIFO.

(ii)   **To act as a control device** by establishing standards (expected costs) and **comparing actual costs with the expected costs**, thus highlighting areas of the organisation that may be out of control.

(iii)   **To assist in setting budgets**; standards are the building blocks of periodic budgets.

(iv)   **To motivate staff and management** by the provision of challenging targets.

(b)   **The importance of keeping standards meaningful and relevant**

Standards may be **used as a control device**. If standards which are irrelevant are used, they cannot usefully be used as such a device - they **need to be relevant**. Standards must be determined in a way that is understood by the **employees** whose actual **performance** will be compared with standards, ie they **must be meaningful**. If they are not meaningful, the employees who are being assessed will have no reason to have any faith in the system operating.

Use of out-of-date standards

If **out-of-date** standards are in use, they are not relevant to conditions that are currently operating within a system. Such standards may **encourage slack** and **waste** to be built into the system.

Effect on motivation

Motivation and morale of employees is affected by the control system operating within the workplace. If such a system has been poorly implemented, employees may react adversely. For example, if standards are set which even the most conscientious employee fails to reach, he will be demotivated and may give up working as hard as he can as there 'doesn't seem to be any point'.

Controllability of costs

If standards are to be meaningful and relevant then they should set out to **focus on the controllability of costs**.

(c) **Materials price variance**

	£	£
37,100 metres of wood should cost (× £0.30)	11,130	
but did cost	11,000	
Wood price variance		130 (F)
29,200 metres of gut should cost (× £1.50)	43,800	
but did cost	44,100	
Gut price variance		300 (A)
Wood and gut price variance		170 (A)

Material usage variance

		Wood		*Gut*
3,700 units of W should use	(× 7m)	25,900 m	(× 6 m)	22,200 m
1,890 units of B should use	(× 5m)	9,450 m	(× 4 m)	7,560 m
		35,350 m		29,760 m
Together they did use		37,100 m		29,200 m
Material usage variance in metres		1,750 m(A)		560 m (F)
× standard cost per metre		× £0.30		× £1.50
Material usage variance				
Wood		£525 (A)		
Gut				£840 (F)

Other materials cost variance

	£
3,700 units of W should cost (× £0.20)	740.00
1,890 units of B should cost (× £0.15)	283.50
	1,023.50
Together they did cost	1,000.00
Other materials cost variance	23.50 (F)

Direct labour rate

	£
2,200 hours of labour should cost (× £3)	6,600
but did cost	6,850
Direct labour rate variance	250 (A)

Direct labour efficiency

3,700 units of W should take (× 30 minutes)	1,850 hrs
1,890 units of B should take (× 20 minutes)	630 hrs
	2,480 hrs
Together they did take	2,200 hrs
Efficiency variance in hrs	280 hrs (F)
× standard rate per hour	× £3
Direct labour efficiency variance	£840 (F)

Variable overhead costs

	Hours	Units
Budgeted hours: W	2,000	4,000
B	500	1,500
	2,500	

	£
Power cost per standard hour (£1,500 ÷ 2,500 hrs)	0.60
Maintenance cost per standard hour (£7,500 ÷ 2,500 hrs)	3.00
	3.60

Variable overhead efficiency variance	
= (as labour) 280 hours (F) × £3.60 =	£1,008 (F)

	£	£
Variable overhead cost of 2,200 hours should be (× £3.60)		7,920
but was: power	1,800	
maintenance	6,900	
		8,700
Variable overhead expenditure variance		780 (A)

Fixed overhead

Budgeted fixed costs	£21,000
Budgeted hours (see calculation for variable overheads)	2,500 hrs
Absorption rate per hour	£8.40

Fixed overhead expenditure variance

	Budgeted expenditure £	Actual expenditure £	Expenditure variance £
Supervision	8,000	7,940	60 (F)
Heating and lighting	1,200	1,320	120 (A)
Rent	4,800	4,800	–
Depreciation	7,000	7,000	–
Total	21,000	21,060	60 (A)

Fixed overhead volume variance

	£	£
Actual production at standard rates		
W (3,700 × £8.40 × ½ hr)	15,540	
B (1,890 × £8.40 × ⅓ hr)	5,292	
		20,832
Budgeted production at standard rates		
W (4,000 × £8.40 × ½ hr)	16,800	
B (1,500 × £8.40 × ⅓ hr)	4,200	21,000
		168 (A)

Calculation of unit standard costs

		W £ per unit	B £ per unit
Direct materials:	wood	2.10	1.50
	gut	9.00	6.00
Other materials		0.20	0.15
Direct labour		1.50	1.00
Variable overhead at £3.60 per hour		1.80	1.20
Fixed overhead at £8.40 per hour		4.20	2.80
Total standard cost per unit		18.80	12.65

9 Wye Not

Top tips. In part (b) it is not obvious what is meant by the most 'significant variances'. A small absolute variance can be significant and therefore worthy of management attention if, for example, it recurs on a regular basis. In circumstances such as these, where you feel there may be a different interpretation of the question, you should make an assumption and state it clearly in your answer.

Easy marks. Note that the six marks for part (b) can be earned even if you have made a total mess of part (a). Remember to keep going on each question until you have used up your time allowance.

(a) (i) **Actual sales units** $= \dfrac{\text{Standard profit from actual sales}}{\text{Standard profit per unit}}$

$= \dfrac{£16{,}500}{£15}$

$= \underline{1{,}100 \text{ units}}$

(ii) Production volume in excess of budget $= \dfrac{\text{Fixed overhead volume variance}}{\text{Fixed overhead per unit}}$

$= \dfrac{£1{,}000}{£20}$

$= \underline{50 \text{ units}}$

Budgeted production volume $= \dfrac{\text{Budgeted fixed overhead}}{\text{Fixed overhead per unit}}$

$= \dfrac{£25{,}000}{£20}$

$= \underline{1{,}250 \text{ units}}$

∴**Actual production volume** $= 50 + 1{,}250 = \underline{\underline{1{,}300}} \text{ units}$

(iii)

	£
Standard selling price per unit	75
Selling price variance per unit sold (£5,500 ÷ 1,100)	5
Actual selling price per unit	80

(iv)

	kg
Excess material used above standard (£375 ÷ £2.50)	150
Standard material usage (1,300 units × 4 kg)	5,200
Actual material usage	5,350

Since raw material stock levels remained unchanged, raw material purchases were equal to raw material usage.

$$\text{Material price variance per kg purchased} = \frac{£535}{5,350}$$

$$= £0.10$$

∴ **Actual material price per kg** $= £0.10 + £2.50$

$$= \underline{£2.60}$$

(v)
Excess labour hours above standard (£1,200 ÷ £6)		200
Standard labour hours (1,300 units × 3 hours)		3,900
Actual labour hours		4,100

(vi)
	£
Standard variable overhead for actual hours worked (4,100 × £4)	16,400
Variable overhead expenditure variance	820 (F)
Actual variable overhead cost	15,580

(vii)
	£
Budgeted fixed overhead cost	25,000
Fixed overhead expenditure variance	1,000 (F)
Actual fixed overhead cost	24,000

(b) *Assumption.* The two most **significant** variances for October 20X9 are the **largest** variances, ie the selling price variance and the direct labour efficiency variance.

REPORT

To: Operations manager

From: Management accountant

Subject: Variances for October 20X9   Date: 10 November 20X9

1 Introduction

1.1 This report considers the meaning and possible causes of the two most significant variances which occurred in October 20X9.

2 Selling price variance: meaning

2.1 The **favourable** selling price variance of £5,500 means that the **actual** selling price during October 20X9 was **higher than the standard** selling price.

3 Selling price variance: causes

3.1 There was an unplanned price increase during October 20X9.

3.2 The original standard selling price was set too low.

3.3 Competition in the market was not as fierce as had been expected when the standard selling price was determined, therefore a higher price could be charged.

4 Direct labour efficiency variance: meaning

4.1 The **adverse** labour efficiency variance of £1,200 means that **more** labour hours were **used than the standard allowed** for the output achieved.

5 Direct labour efficiency variance: causes

5.1 Lost time was in excess of the standard allowed.

5.2 Production was slow due to difficulties in processing sub-standard materials.

5.3 The original standard time allowance was set too low.

If I can be of any further assistance please do not hesitate to contact me.

Signed: Management accountant

10 HP

> **Top tips**. This question is complicated by the fact that you are given information in metres and in terms of tiles.
>
> The output of the process is tiles, so the **materials cost variances** must be based on the actual output of **tiles**. You are given information for a standard batch so you therefore need to work out the standard material cost per tile, as shown in the working below.
>
> The price variance is straightforward and based on information provided in the question.
>
> The **mix variance** is simply the **difference between what the mix should have been (for actual output) and what it was**. So the only difficulty is in working out what the mix should have been. To do this you simply apply the standard mix proportions to the total actual usage of material.
>
> Remember that the **individual mix variances in units** should **always total to zero**. This is because the expected mix (the standard mix for actual output) is based on the total quantity actually used and hence the difference between the total expected mix (total actual quantity) and the total actual mix (total actual quantity) is zero.
>
> The **yield variance** has to be worked in terms of **tiles** rather than kgs of material as the variance focuses on output, which is tiles.

Workings

The area of one floor tile is ½ × ¼ = 0.125 sq m. In a standard batch of 100 sq m there will be 800 tiles. The standard cost per tile is therefore as follows.

Material	Quantity kg	Price £	Std cost £
A	0.0500	1.50	0.0750
B	0.0375	1.20	0.0450
C	0.0125	1.40	0.0175
D	0.0250	0.50	0.0125
	0.1250	1.20	0.1500

(a)   **Cost variance**

	A £	B £	C £	D £	Total £
46,400 tiles should cost	3,480	2,088	812	580	6,960
but did cost	3,520	2,200	750	700	7,170
Cost variance	40(A)	112(A)	62(F)	120(A)	210(A)

(b)   **Price variance**

				Price variance	
Material	Quantity kg	Should cost £	Did cost £	Per kg £	Total £
A	2,200	1.50	1.60	0.10 (A)	220 (A)
B	2,000	1.20	1.10	0.10 (F)	200 (F)
C	500	1.40	1.50	0.10 (A)	50 (A)
D	1,400	0.50	0.50	–	–
Total price variance					70 (A)

(c) **Mix variance**

Actual input = (2,200 + 2,000 + 500 + 1,400) kgs = 6,100 kg

Standard mix of actual input

A	40/100 × 6,100 kgs =	2,440 kgs
B	30/100 × 6,100 kgs =	1,830 kgs
C	10/100 × 6,100 kgs =	610 kgs
D	20/100 × 6,100 kgs =	1,220 kgs
		6,100 kgs

Material	Mix should have been kg	But was kg	Variance kg	× std price £	Mix variance £
A	2,440	2,200	240 (F)	1.50	360 (F)
B	1,830	2,000	170 (A)	1.20	204 (A)
C	610	500	110 (F)	1.40	154 (F)
D	1,220	1,400	180 (A)	0.50	90 (A)
	6,100	6,100	–		220 (F)

If you used the alternative valuation method (ie using a weighted average price of £120/100 kg = £1.20 per kg), you would have the following variances: A £72 (F); B £0; C £22 (F); D £126 (F).

(d) **Yield variance**

Each unit of output (800 tiles) requires

40	kg of A, costing	£60
30	kg of B, costing	£36
10	kg of C, costing	£14
20	kg of D, costing	£10
100 kg		£120

6,100 kgs should have yielded (× 800 tiles/100 kgs)	48,800 tiles
but did yield	46,400 tiles
	2,400 tiles (A)
× standard cost per tile	× £0.15
	£360 (A)

(e) (i) The adverse material A price variance shows that it cost more than standard. This could have been because of an out of date standard, price changes by the supplier or perhaps the need to use a more expensive supplier if the original supplier could no longer provided supplies.

The favourable mix variance shows that less was used as input than had been expected. Maybe this is because it was in short supply.

(ii) The favourite material B price variance shows that it cost less than standard. This could have been because of an out of date standard, price changes by the supplier or perhaps a discount.

The adverse mix variance shows that more was used as input than had been expected, maybe because it was cheaper.

It should be noted that any explanation of the mix variances for material A and B cannot really be discussed in isolation from those for material C and material D.

(f) Mix and yield variances have no meaning, and should never be calculated, unless they are a guide to control action. They are **only appropriate in the following situations**.

(i) Where **proportions of materials in a mix are changeable and controllable**. If the materials in a mix are in different units, say kilograms and litres, they are obviously completely different and so cannot be substituted for each other.

(ii) Where the **usage variance of individual materials is of limited value because of the variability of the mix**, and a combined yield variance for all the materials together is more helpful for control

It would be **totally inappropriate** to calculate a mix **variance where the materials in the 'mix' are discrete items**. A chair, for example, might consist of wood, covering material, stuffing and glue. These materials are separate components, and it would not be possible to think in terms of controlling the proportions of each material in the final product. The usage of each material must be controlled separately.

11 Wimbrush

Top tips. Part (a)(i)(1) should have caused you no problems, but you may have found part (a)(i)(2) more difficult.

Operational variances are calculated by **comparing a revised standard with an actual result**, so you cannot work out these variances until you have **established the revised standard**.

Planning variances are calculated by **comparing an original standard with a revised standard** and are based on actual production volumes. If a **revised** standard is **greater** than an **original** standard, the planning variance is **adverse** because the original standard was too optimistic, overstating the profits but understanding the realistic cost.

If you have time in an exam, you could work out 'traditional' variances based on original standards and actual results. As our summary shows, the **sum** of the **operational** variances and the **planning** variance should total the '**traditional**' variance.

If you can answer **part (a)(ii)** successfully then you understand the whole concept of planning and operational variances. Use your answer, if you are happy with it, as a **summary for revision purposes**. If you aren't happy with it maybe you should attempt part (a)(ii) again.

Parts (b) and (c) are good discussion practice questions.

(a) (i) (1) Traditional variance analysis

2,000 Widgets should use (× 5 kg)	10,000 kg
but did use	10,800 kg
Material X usage variance in kgs	800 kg (A)
× standard cost per kg	× £3
Material X usage variance in £	£2,400 (A)

	£
10,800 kg of X should cost (× £3)	32,400
but did cost	51,840
Material X price variance	19,440 (A)

500 Splodgets should use (×1.5 tonnes)	750 tonnes
but did use	700 tonnes
Material Z usage variance in tonnes	50 tonnes (F)
× standard cost per tonne	× £30
Material Z usage variance in £	£1,500 (F)

	£
700 tonnes of Z should cost (× £30)	21,000
but did cost (× £25)	17,500
Material Z price variance	3,500 (F)

Summary	Material X variances £	Material Z variances £	Total £
Price variance	19,440 (A)	3,500 (F)	15,940 (A)
Usage variance	2,400 (A)	1,500 (F)	900 (A)
	21,840 (A)	5,000 (F)	16,840 (A)

(i)   (2)   **Planning and operational variances**

Widgets: the revised standard was 5 kg at £4.50 per kg

	£
10,800 kg of X should have cost (× £4.50)	48,600
but did cost	51,840
Material X price variance (operational variance)	3,240 (A)

	£
Usage variance for X = 800 kg (A) × £4.50 = **(operational variance)**	3,600 (A)

The **planning variance** is calculated as follows.

	£
Original standard (using X) 2,000 units × 5 kg × £3 =	30,000
Revised standard (using X) 2,000 units × 5 kg × £4.50 =	45,000
Planning variance £1.50 (A) per kg, or	15,000 (A)
Splodgets: the revised realistic standard is 1.5 tonnes of Z at £23 =	£34.50

	£
700 tonnes of Z should cost (× £23)	16,100
did cost (× £25)	17,500
Material Z price variance (operational variance)	1,400 (A)

	£
Material Z usage variance = 50 tonnes (F) × £23 = **(operational variance)**	£1,150 (F)

Planning variance	£
Original standard 500 units × 1.5 tonnes × £30 per tonne =	22,500
Revised standard 500 units × 1.5 tonnes × £23 per tonne =	17,250
Total planning variance (£7 per tonne (F)) or	5,250 (F)

Summary	Material X £	Material Z £	Total £
Price variance	3,240 (A)	1,400 (A)	4,640 (A)
Usage variance	3,600 (A)	1,150 (F)	2,450 (A)
Operational variances	6,840 (A)	250 (A)	7,090 (A)
Planning variances	15,000 (A)	5,250 (F)	9,750 (A)
Total variances	21,840 (A)	5,000 (F)	16,840 (A)

(ii)   (1)   The distinction between planning and operational variances is a development of the opportunity cost approach to variance analysis. *Demski* argued that **more helpful and meaningful information will be provided for management control decisions** if variances are reported using an ex-post (revised) standard, that is a **standard which in hindsight should have been used**, when the actual standard used (or the budget) is unrealistic for the conditions which actually prevailed. Thus, when it is realised in retrospect that the planned standard is inaccurate, a more realistic (ex-post) standard should be used to calculate operational variances.

The **final reconciliation between budgeted and actual profit** would then be made as a **planning variance**, which measures the **extent to which the budget targets are at fault** because the original standard used was incorrect. (A planning variance is similar to a budget revision variance.)

(2)   The opportunity cost approach may be useful to companies by indicating more clearly the actual loss sustained by faults which gave rise to the particular variances. There is an attempt to equate variance with the amount of profit or loss sustained, which traditional variances often fail to do. Examples are as follows.

- Traditional absorption costing variances for sales volume and production volume do not show the true effect of the variations from budget on company profitability.

- When a standard is incorrect, traditional variances will mislead managers about the true costs incurred. In the case of Wimbrush the error in the original standard price of material X means that traditional variances would have reported a misleading variance to the purchasing department for price, and a mis-valuation of the usage variance would report the cost of the adverse usage of material X and the favourable usage of Z incorrectly.

Planning and operational variances attempt to **indicate** the following constructively.

- What the real cost of variances should be.

- Which of these variances might have been controllable by better management performance and which were unavoidable.

- The effect on financial targets of a failure to construct realistic standards.

The approach is only different from traditional variance analysis, however, when the revised and original standards are different.

(b)   The four dimensions of McDonaldization are calculability, control, efficiency and predictability.

The application of McDonaldization in service industries is assisting the use of standard costing for cost planning and control.

- **Calculability**. The content of every McDonalds meal is identical and standardised. Every burger should contain a standard amount of meat, every bun is of the same size and all fries are of the same thickness. **The human element is eliminated as far as possible** in the actual production process in order to make the food in a standard time using standard materials. Human initiative is eliminated in actually putting together the meal at the point of sale through the issuing of standard instructions concerning the content of each type of meal ordered. Thus each meal is a **measurable** standard cost unit for which a **standard cost can be established** and the actual cost can be measured for cost control purposes.

- **Control**. Control over the service is achieved in particular by **reducing the human influence**, which can lead to variation in output and quality. Again, machines and technology substitute for humans: automatic drinks dispensers which measure the exact quantity to be delivered and cash registers which require only one button to be pressed to record the sale of a complete meal are examples of improved control and the reduction of the possibility of human error in the delivery of the service.

- **Efficiency**. Ritzer described efficiency as 'the optimum method of getting from one point to another'. Every McDonalds business is organised to ensure maximum efficiency so that the customer can get exactly what they want as quickly as possible. This **increases customer satisfaction and also increases the company's profitability**.

- **Predictability**. The McDonalds service is the **same in every outlet throughout the world**, whether a meal is purchased in Shanghai or on London. Again this helps with the standardisation of the service and the setting of standard costs throughout the organisation.

(c) Before management decide whether or not to investigate the reasons for the occurrence of a particular variance, there are a number of factors which should be considered in assessing the significance of the variance.

Materiality

Because a standard cost is really only an average expected cost, small variations between actual and standard are bound to occur and are unlikely to be significant. Obtaining an 'explanation' of the reasons why they occurred is likely to be time consuming for the manager concerned. For such variations **further investigation is not worthwhile** since such variances are not controllable.

Controllability

This must also influence the decision about whether to investigate. If there is a general worldwide increase in the price of a raw material there is nothing that can be done internally to control the effect of this. If a central decision is made to award all employees a 10% increase in salary, staff costs in division A will increase by this amount and the variance is not controllable by division A's manager. Uncontrollable variances call for a change in the plan.

The type of standard being used

The efficiency variance reported in any control period, whether for materials or labour, will depend on the efficiency level set. If, for example, an ideal standard is used, variances will always be adverse. A similar problem arises if average price levels are used as standards. If inflation exists, favourable price variances are likely to be reported at the beginning of a period, to be offset by adverse price variances later in the period.

Variance trend

Although small variations in a single period are unlikely to be significant, small variations that occur consistently may need more attention. Variance trend is probably more important than a single set of variances for one accounting period. The trend provides an indication of whether the variance is fluctuating within acceptable control limits or becoming out of control.

Individual variances should therefore not be looked at in isolation; variances should be scrutinised for a number of successive periods if their full significance is to be appreciated.

Interdependence between variances

Individual variances should not be looked at in isolation. One variance might be inter-related with another, and much of it might have occurred only because the other variance occurred too. When two variances are interdependent (interrelated) one will usually be adverse and the other one favourable.

Costs of investigation

The costs of an investigation should be weighed against the benefits of correcting the cause of a variance.

12 M

Top tips. You may have put a different interpretation on the question.

- You may have valued the sales volume variance at the revised profit per unit of £24.96 (although the question did say that the original standard should be used for inventory valuation), giving variance of £2,496 (A)

- You may have based the labour rate planning variance on 1,000 units × 3 hours × £0.18, giving a variance of £540 (A)

- You would then have had to make an adjustment for the planning variance left in inventory of (1,050 – 900) units × £0.54 = £81

Workings

(i)

Budgeted sales volume	1,000 units
Actual sales volume	900 units
Variance in units	100 units (A)
× Standard profit per unit	£25.50
Sales volume variance	£2,550 (A)

(ii)

	£
900 units should have sold for (× £120)	108,000
but did sell for	118,800
Sales price variance	10,800 (F)

(iii) *Material A*

	£
5,670 kgs should have cost (× £2.50)	14,175
but did cost	14,742
Material A price variance	567 (A)

Material B

	£
10,460 kgs should have cost (× £4)	41,840
but did cost	38,179
Material B price variance	3,661 (F)

(iv) Standard weighted average cost = standard cost/standard quantity
= £(40 + 12.50)/(5 + 10) kgs
= £3.50 per kg

Actual input = (5,670 + 10,460) kgs = 16,130 kgs

Standard mix of actual input

A = 16,130 × 5/15 = 5,376.67 kgs
B = 16,130 × 10/15 = 10,753.33 kgs
16,130.00

		Actual input Kgs	Standard Mix of actual input Kgs	Difference Kgs	× difference between w. av. price and std price	£	Variance £
	A	5,670	5,376.67	293.33	(£3.50 – £2.50)	1.00	293.33 (F)
	B	10,460	10,753.33	(293.33)	(£3.50 – £4.00)	(0.50)	146.67 (F)
		16,130	16,130.00	–			440.00 (F)

(v) 16,130 kg should have yielded (÷ 15) | 1,075.33 units
        but did yield | 1,050.00 units
Yield variance in units | 25.33
× standard cost per unit of output | × £52.50
Yield variance in £ | £1,330 (A)

(vi) Revised labour rate £6 × 103% = £6.18

	£
Revised standard cost (1,050 units × 3hrs × £6.18)	19,467
Original standard cost (1,050 units × 3hrs × £6)	18,900
	567 (A)

	£
With revised standard, 3,215 hours should have cost (× £6 × 103%)	19,869
but did cost	19,933
Labour rate operating variance	64 (A)

(vii)
1,050 units should have taken (× 3hrs) | 3,150 hrs
but did take | 3,215 hrs
Variance in hrs | 65 hrs (A)
× revised standard rate per hr (× £6 × 103%) | × £6.18
Labour efficiency variance | £402 (A)

(viii)
	£
3,215 hours of variable overhead should have cost (× £3)	9,645
but did cost	10,288
Variable production overhead expenditure variance	643 (A)

(ix)
1,050 units should have taken (× 3hrs) | 3,150 hrs
but did take | 3,215 hrs
Variance in hrs | 65 hrs (A)
× standard rate per hr | × £3
Variable production overhead efficiency variance | £195 (A)

(x)
	£
Budgeted expenditure (£180,000/12)	15,000
Actual expenditure	15,432
Fixed production overhead expenditure variance	432 (A)

(xi)
	£
Actual production at standard rate (1,050 × £15 per unit)	15,750
budgeted production at standard rate (1,000 × £15 per unit)	15,000
Fixed overhead volume variance	750 (F)

PROFIT RECONCILIATION STATEMENT (BUDGET TO ACTUAL) JANUARY 20X0

	£
Budgeted profit (1,000 units × £25.50)	25,500
Planning variances: labour rate	567 (A)
Revised budgeted profit	24,933
Sales volume variance	2,550 (A)
Revised standard profit from sales achieved	22,383

Operating variances	£ (F)	£ (A)	
Sales price	10,800		
Material price – A		567	
– B	3,661		
Material mix – A	293		
– B	147		
Material yield		1,330	
Labour rate		64	
Labour efficiency		402	
Variance production overhead expenditure		643	
Variable production overhead efficiency		195	
Fixed production overhead expenditure		432	
Fixed production overhead volume	750		
	15,651	3,633	12,018 (F)
Actual profit			34,401

We can do a check on the actual profit figure in the reconciliation statement by calculating actual profit based on the figures given in the exam. Closing inventory is to be valued at standard cost.

Note. Only do this if you have time in the exam – perhaps at the very end if you have five minutes to spare.

Check	£	£
Sales		118,800
Costs incurred	98,574	
Closing inventory (150 × £94.50)	(14,175)	
		84,399
Actual profit		34,401

13 Just in time systems

> **Top tips**. We have stated more than the five financial benefits required by the question, so that you can use them for revision practice, if required. In the exam you will be wasting valuable time if you provide more than the required number of benefits.

JIT systems have a number of financial **benefits**.

- Increase in labour productivity due to labour being multiskilled and carrying out preventative maintenance
- Reduction of investment in plant space
- Reduction in costs of storing inventory
- Reduction in risk of inventory obsolescence
- Lower investment in inventory
- Reduction in costs of handling inventory
- Reduction in costs associated with scrap, defective units and reworking
- Higher revenue as a result of reduction in lost sales following failure to meet delivery dates (because of improved quality)
- Reduction in the costs of setting up production runs
- Higher revenues as a result of faster response to customer demands

14 Costs of quality

> **Top tips**. The question asks for a brief description of the four categories of cost. It would not be sufficient to simply list them. It's a good idea to provide an example of each in case your description is a little muddled! Remember the time allowance is about nine minutes so this should give you a rough idea of how much you need to write.

The four categories of cost are prevention costs, appraisal costs, internal failure costs and external failure costs.

Prevention costs

The costs incurred prior to production commencing or during the production process in order to prevent the occurrence of sub-standard output. For example the cost of training quality control personnel.

Appraisal costs

The costs incurred to ascertain whether outputs meet the required quality standards. For example the cost of inspecting goods inwards.

Internal failure costs

The costs incurred as a result of the failure to achieve quality standards before the output is transferred to the customer. For example the cost of re-working output identified as sub-standard.

External failure costs

The costs incurred as a result of sub-standard quality output discovered after the output is transferred to the customer. For example the cost of repairing products returned from customers.

15 Throughput accounting

> **Top tips**. You are asked for a brief identification of the differences between the two systems. A good form of presentation for your answer would be to set out key bullet points, adequately developed in a short paragraph. It is important that your bullet points are not so brief that they do not provide the necessary explanation.

Throughput accounting (TA) **differentiates between fixed and variable costs** in the same way that a system of marginal costing does. However it **goes further** in its analysis of costs to argue that **only a very limited number of costs are actually variable in the short run**. This is the reason for the coining of the term 'super variable costing' to describe TA.

There are a number of differences between TA and marginal or variable cost accounting.

- Both systems distinguish between fixed and variable costs in reporting profit and valuing inventories, but **TA treats only material cost as variable**.

- In a marginal costing system, labour cost would normally be treated as a variable cost to be included in the unit cost in the valuation of inventory. In a TA system **labour cost is treated as a fixed cost** and is combined with all other operating expenses to be written off as a **period cost**.

- Inventory in a marginal costing system is valued at total variable production cost. In a TA system all inventory is valued at material cost only.

- The focus of a marginal costing system is the **provision of information for short term decision making**. TA, or the Theory of Constraints on which it was based, was conceived with the aim of **changing manufacturing strategy to achieve evenness of flow**.

16 WAQ

> **Top tips.** A full question on **throughput accounting** is unlikely, with throughput accounting calculations being more likely to appear in Section A as **MCQs**. These part questions are just the sort of calculations you could be required to do for an MCQ.
>
> In (a) the **throughput accounting ratio** is based on the **process** with the **lowest throughput** per day.
>
> In (b) you need to work out how many **extra units** would be produced over two years, and the extra **contribution** on these units, if the bottleneck were eliminated. This gain should **correspond** to the **possible investment**.

(a)

	Process A	Process B	Process C
Throughput per hour (units)	12	10	15
Throughput per day (units)	96	80	120
Throughput contribution per unit		£120	

$$\text{Throughput accounting ratio} \quad = \frac{£120 \times 80 \text{ units}}{£24,000/6}$$

$$= 2.4$$

(b) (i) Gain if bottleneck at process B is eliminated = 96 – 80 units = 16 units per day.
Gain over two years = 16 units × 6 days × 48 weeks × 2 × £120 = £1,105,920

Therefore £1.1 million could be spent if the cost were to be recovered over two years.

(ii) Gain over 12 weeks = 16 units × 6 days × 12 weeks × £120 = £138,240

Therefore £0.14 million could be spent if the cost were to be recovered over 12 weeks.

(c) **TA ratio** $= \dfrac{96 \text{ units} \times £120}{4,000} = \dfrac{11,250}{4,000} = 2.88$

17 KH

> **Top tips**. The level of calculations required in this question means that it is probably a bit too easy to be classified as exam standard, but nevertheless it provides you with an excellent opportunity to practise calculating product costs using ABC.
>
> The only real difficulty in the ABC calculations is making sure that you use the **correct bases for sharing out the overheads**. Paint stirring and quality control is shared out on the basis of batches, the figures for which are given in the question. An easy mistake to make with **electricity** would be to divide the overhead in the ratio of number of coats of paint but that would not be correct: G's products have substantially more costs overall because more G units are sprayed overall. The cost should therefore be apportioned on the basis of **total coats**. For sharing out the cost of filling of spraying machines you need to work out the total litres of paint used.
>
> Don't forget to make use of your **answers to (a) and (b)** to **illustrate** your answer to (c). Your arguments will carry a lot more weight if you can back them up with examples.

(a)   **Unit cost using absorption costing**

	G £	F £	R £
Paint	15.20	11.18	18.90
Labour (W1)	2.65	3.98	6.63
Stirring and quality control (W2)	1.15	1.73	2.88
Electricity (W2)	5.00	7.50	12.50
Filling of machines (W2)	3.10	4.65	7.75
	27.10	29.04	48.66

(b)   **Unit cost using activity based costing**

	G £	F £	R £
Paint	15.20	11.18	18.90
Labour	2.65	3.98	6.63
Stirring and quality control (W3)	1.38	1.27	3.08
Electricity (W3)	8.94	7.66	6.39
Filling of machines (W3)	4.87	5.52	4.04
	33.04	29.61	39.04

(c)   **Cost drivers** are activities or transactions that are significant determinants of cost, in other words the activities that **cause** costs to occur. Activity based costing acknowledges that some costs vary not with volume of output but with some other cost driver.

The logic of this approach is clearly illustrated by the facts given in the question. If paint delivered is stirred and inspected in batches, then it is the **number of batches** rather than units or labour hours that determine how much stirring and inspection is to be done.

The use of electricity best illustrates the **difference between the two methods** in this example. Under **absorption** costing R's products absorb the **largest** part of the electricity overhead because R's involve more labour time than the other products. Under **activity based** costing R's have the **smallest** share of the electricity overhead, recognising that use of labour time and consumption of electricity are not necessarily related. (Note that R's use more different batches of paint than the other products: the labour time is probably spent adjusting the machinery while it is idle rather than operating it and using electricity.)

The **consequences of adopting activity based costing** are a significant change in the unit cost of R's mainly at the expense of G's. This will have implications for valuing work in progress and also for pricing the service and assessing its overall validity.

Workings

1   *Labour cost per unit*

	G	F	R
Labour hours per unit	0.50	0.75	1.25
Rate per hour	£5.30	£5.30	£5.30
Cost per unit	£2.65	£3.98	£6.63

2   *Overheads - absorption costing*

	G	F	R	Total
Units	5,400	4,360	3,600	13,360
Labour hours/unit	0.5	0.75	1.25	
Total labour hours	2,700	3,270	4,500	10,470

	Total overhead £	Total hours Hrs	Rates per hour £
Paint stirring and quality control	24,081	10,470	2.30
Electricity	104,700	10,470	10.00
Filling of spraying machines	64,914	10,470	6.20

	G £	F £	R £
Stirring @ £2.30 per hour (× 0.5/0.75/1.25)	1.15	1.73	2.88
Electricity @ £10 per hour	5.00	7.50	12.50
Filling @ £6.20 per hour	3.10	4.65	7.75

3　*Overheads - activity based costing*

   (a)　Paint stirring and quality control

	G	F	R	Total
Units	5,400	4,360	3,600	
Batches	27	20	40	87
Share of overhead (27:20:40)	£7,473	£5,536	£11,072	£24,081
Per unit	£1.38	£1.27	£3.08	

   (b)　Electricity

	G	F	R	Total
Coats per unit	7	6	5	
Total coats	37,800	26,160	18,000	81,960
Share of overhead	£48,288	£33,418	£22,994	£104,700
Per unit	£8.94	£7.66	£6.39	

   (c)　Filling

	G	F	R	Total
Litres per unit	7.6	8.6	6.3	
Total litres	41,040	37,496	22,680	101,216
Share of overhead	£26,321	£24,048	£14,545	£64,914
Per unit	£4.87	£5.52	£4.04	

(d)　Despite the many advantages claimed by researchers and writers, there are a number of reasons why an organisation might decide not to use, or even to abandon the use of, activity-based techniques.

   (i)　The implementation of activity-based techniques is a **time-consuming** and **expensive** process. Activities and cost drivers have to be identified, involving data collection, interviews and observation. Management may feel that the possible benefits are outweighed by the associated costs.

   (ii)　The introduction of any new technique will be met with **resistance from those employees** who feel threatened by a change to the status quo or who feel that the current system is more than adequate. Such resistance can be reduced if employees are kept fully informed of the reasons for, and the process of, the techniques' introduction, however.

   (iii)　Any change to the established way of doing things is unlikely to succeed unless the change has a **powerful champion** within the organisation. The champion of any activity-based techniques is likely to be the finance director. If the finance director is not supportive of their introduction or he/she is replaced by another director who is not supportive, their introduction and implementation is likely to fail.

   (iv)　Even if overheads make up a significant proportion of an organisation's costs, if those **overheads cannot be traced easily to products and services** because cost driver identification is difficult (perhaps if the majority of them are administration costs), the introduction of activity-based techniques might not increase the accuracy of product cost information and hence will not be welcomed by management.

   (v)　If the techniques appear to be part of a **policy of overhead cost reduction,** employees may worry about possible redundancies and **resist** their introduction. It is therefore vital that a detailed explanation of the reasoning behind any decision to introduce ABC, ABB, ABM and so on is given to affected members of the workforce.

(vi) An organisation may decide not to use activity-based techniques if it becomes clear that they will not **provide additional information** for management planning and control decisions. If managers are not going to use the techniques to control non-value-added activities, for example, it would be much easier to stick with a simpler absorption costing system.

18 ABC v traditional absorption costing

> **Top tips.** You may have thought of other, equally valid situations in which the product cost would be different. The important thing is to think about the differences between the ways in which the two systems absorb overheads and this will give you the basis for identifying where unit cost differences are likely to occur.

Four situations where the product unit cost is likely to differ significantly are as follows.

1   **Where production overhead costs are high in relation to direct costs, in particular direct labour cost**. If production overheads do not represent a significant proportion of total costs then different methods of allocating overheads to products would not have a significant impact on the resulting total unit cost.

2   **Where the product range is wide and diverse**. If products are all very similar then a different analysis of overheads in unlikely to produce a significant difference in the relative overhead cost allocation.

3   **Where the amount of overhead resources used by products varies across the product range**. Some products may place a much greater burden on certain activities than other products. The traditional labour hour-based overhead absorption is not likely to reflect this different pattern of overhead resource input and the resulting unit cost would be significantly different from the unit cost resulting from an ABC system. The ABC system would reflect the different pattern of resource consumption.

4   **Where direct labour hours are not the primary driver of overhead resource consumption**. Certain overhead costs may be driven by something other than labour hours, such as the number of batches or the number of quality control inspections. If these costs are significant then an ABC analysis will produce a different unit cost from that resulting from a traditional overhead absorption system based on direct labour hours.

19 ABC in the modern environment

> **Top tips.** If the question does not specifically state how many reasons or situations you should explain then, for five marks, you can usually assume that you should make an absolute minimum of five separate points. Try to draw on aspects of the modern environment that you have learned about, for example JIT and throughput. Remember to explain your points reasonably fully, within the time constraint. You cannot expect the examiner to guess what you mean from a few brief words.

Reasons for suitability

(a) Most modern organisations tend to have a high level of overhead costs, especially relating to support services such as maintenance and data processing. ABC, by the use of carefully chosen cost drivers, traces these overheads to product lines in a more logical and less arbitrary manner than traditional absorption costing.

(b) The determination and use of cost drivers helps to measure and improve the efficiency and effectiveness of support departments.

(c) Many costs included in general overheads can actually be traced to specific JIT lines and/or product lines using ABC. This improves product costing and cost management because the costs are made the responsibility of the line manager.

(d) ABC forces the organisation to ask such searching questions as 'What causes the demand for the activity?', 'What does the department achieve?', 'Does it add value?' and so on.

(e) ABC systems may encourage reductions in throughput time and inventory and improvements in quality.

Unsuitable situations

(a) A number of businesses have recently been split into several small autonomous sections. In this situation there may be no need for a sophisticated costing system such as ABC because staff should be aware of cost behaviour.

(b) ABC can work against modern manufacturing methods such as JIT. JIT seeks to reduce set-up time so that very small batches can be made economically.

(c) The aim of set-up time reduction is to allow more set-ups, not just to reduce set-up costs. The use of a cost driver based on the number of set-ups will therefore work against JIT principles as it will tend to encourage larger batches.

20 Environmentally sustainable profits

Sustainability

Sustainability refers to the concept of balancing growth with environmental, social and economic concerns.

External environmental impact

Most business activities have some sort of **external impact** on the environment. The impacts do not necessarily 'cost' the business in the traditional sense of the word cost and so they **do not show up in the accounts** or profits.

For example, a **timber company** would not necessarily account for the damage to the ecosystem and possible **flooding** caused by deforestation.

Internalising costs and changing prices

The idea behind environmentally sustainable profits is that the external impacts and environmental costs **should be included in the accounts**. Industry should **pay for its part** in climate change, poor quality air, contamination of ground water and use of the earth's natural resources. The external environmental costs should be **internalised**.

Internalising costs will impact upon **prices** and costs and the **profitability** of products or services but the profit will be environmentally sustainable.

21 The purposes of budgeting

Organisations prepare budgets for a variety of reasons. These include the following.

- To motivate managers by giving them goals.
- To co-ordinate business activities.
- To help foresee potential problems.
- To formalise business plans and objectives.
- To have a basis on which to make comparisons with actual results.

22 PF

> **Top tips**. This question provides you with valuable practice in determining seasonal variations and forecasting.
>
> We have used the **additive** model and have adjusted the total of the seasonal variations to zero. If you have used the **multiplicative** model you would need to **adjust the totals so that they sum to four**. Given that time series analysis is **not** an **exact** science, you can round the adjusted variations to integer values, but remember to keep the total of the variations to zero.
>
> For part (c) you need to determine the quarterly change in the trend line. Over 11 quarters it increases by 39, which means that the increase per quarter is roughly 3,500. During **20X6** the increase has been **3,000** per quarter, however, so we will use 3,000 as our quarterly increase. Again you do not need to be too accurate.
>
> Make sure that you are aware of the **assumptions** and **limitations** of time series analysis, as this is just the type of issue that you could be called upon to discuss in the exam.

(a)   **Graph of sales**

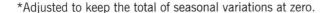

(b)   **Seasonal variations**

	Spring	Summer	Autumn	Winter	Total
20X4	−95	+58	−26	+64	
20X5	−94	+56	−27	+73	
20X6	−104	+58	−27	+71	
	−293	+172	−80	+208	
Average variation	−97.7	+57.3	−26.7	+69.3	+2.2
Adjust to nil	− 0.5	− 0.5	−0.6	− 0.6	−2.2
	−98.2	+56.8	−27.3	+68.7	0.0
Round	−98	+57	−28*	+69	0

*Adjusted to keep the total of seasonal variations at zero.

(c)   The **trend line shows increases in sales of about three thousand per quarter**, and so a forecast of sales will be based on this assumption.

			Trend line	Variation	Forecast
20X6	Winter	Trend line value	320		
20X7	Autumn	Estimate 320 + (3 × 3)	329	–28	301
	Winter	Estimate 320 + (4 × 3)	332	+69	401

The forecasts of sales, based on the calculations and assumptions here, are 301,000 units of product XN30 in autumn 20X7 and 401,000 units of products XN30 in winter 20X7.

23 Calculating projected costs and revenues

> **Top tips**. Criticising the use of historical data for forecasting has always been popular with management accounting examiners! You would be well advised to commit to memory a list of factors to adapt in answer this sort of question.

The following checks should be made on historical data before it can be used as a basis for forecasting future costs and revenues.

(a)   **Conditions that existed in the past should be the same as those expected in the future**. If this is not the case then the data should be **adjusted for any factors that affect the figures other than the level of activity**. For example the effect of any changes in technology, fashion, resource costs, weather conditions and so on should be eliminated from the historical data before it can be used.

(b)   The **time period** of the historical data should be long enough to include any costs that are paid periodically but short enough to ensure that averaging of variations in the level of activity has not occurred.

(c)   The **methods of data collection** used to assemble the historical data should not have introduced bias.

(d)   The **accounting methods** used in the historical data should be the same as those to be used in the future. For example the same inventory valuation policy and the same depreciation policy should be used.

(e)   Appropriate choices should be made of **dependent** and **independent variables**. For example the independent variable must be capable of measurement and it must be possible to forecast it with reasonable accuracy.

24 PPA

> **Top tips**. Although a significant proportion of this answer is simply regurgitation of text book knowledge, this *was* part of an old syllabus question and was worth 10 marks. Questions on this topic could well centre on such an appraisal's advantages and disadvantages.

What is post project appraisal and audit?

Post project appraisal and audit (PPAA) involves **measurement of the success of a capital expenditure project** in terms of **the realisation of anticipated benefits**. PPAA should cover the **implementation** of the project from authorisation to commissioning and **its technical and commercial performance** after commissioning. The information provided by the appraisal and audit can also be used by management as **feedback** to help with the implementation and control of future projects.

Advantages of PPAA

PPAA cannot reverse the decision to incur the capital expenditure, because the expenditure has already taken place. It does have **advantages in terms of control**, however.

(a) The threat of a PPAA will **motivate managers** to work to achieve the promised benefits from the project.

(b) If the audit takes place before the project life ends, and if it finds that the benefits have been less than expected because of management inefficiency, steps can be taken to **improve efficiency**. Alternatively, it will **highlight those projects which should be discontinued**.

(c) It can help to **identify** those managers who have been **good performers** and those who have been poor performers.

(d) It might identify weaknesses in the forecasting and estimating techniques used to evaluate projects, and so should help to **improve** the discipline and quality of **forecasting** for future investment decisions.

(e) Areas where improvements can be made in methods which should help to achieve **better results in general from capital investments** might be revealed.

(f) The **original estimates may be more realistic** if managers are aware that they will be monitored, but PPAAs should not be unfairly critical.

Disadvantages of PPAA

There are a number of **problems** with PPAA.

(a) There are many **uncontrollable factors** which are outside management control in long-term decisions, such as environmental changes.

(b) It may **not be possible to identify separately** the costs and benefits of any particular project.

(c) PPAA can be a **costly** and **time-consuming** exercise.

(d) Applied punitively, PPAA may lead to **managers becoming over cautious and unnecessarily risk averse.**

(e) The **strategic effects** of a capital investment project may **take years to materialise** and it may in fact never be possible to identify or quantify them effectively.

25 Payback

> **Top tip**. This is an easy question which you should be able to answer using material in the Study Text. Don't waffle and just put down the main points. Half a page will do for ten marks.

The payback period is the **time taken for the cash inflows from a project** to **equal the cash outflows**. A **maximum payback period may be set** and if the project's payback period exceeds this then it is not acceptable.

The payback method has the **advantage** of being **easily understood** and this may be important to the landowner who might not be a financial specialist. A further advantage is that it **focuses on early cash flows**, thereby **indicating projects likely to improve liquidity positions**. Again this may be important if the management does not wish to tie up cash any longer than necessary.

It is also claimed that the payback method **reduces risk by ignoring longer-term cash flows** occurring further into the future which may be subject to higher risk. The main risk element in a project might stem from the unpredictability of the weather. This risk does not increase in later years and so a shorter payback would not necessarily reduce this risk. There is, of course, a risk that demand could change in the future because of a fashion change or technological change. Use of a shorter payback period would reduce this risk, but it may not be as important as the unpredictability of the weather.

A **disadvantage** of payback is that it **ignores the timing of cash flows** within the payback period, the cash flows after the end of the payback period (which may sometimes be considerable) and therefore the total project return. It also **ignores the time value of money**. Furthermore it is **unable to distinguish between**

projects with the same payback period, the **choice of the payback period is arbitrary**, it may lead to excessive investment in short-term projects and it takes no account of the variability of cash flows. Finally, it **does not distinguish between investments of different sizes**.

26 Two projects

Top tips. This is an easy, very useful question, covering some of the key issues and techniques.

When calculating the **IRR by interpolation**, you should aim to work with a **positive NPV** and a **negative NPV**. If the **NPV** at the cost of capital is **positive**, you need to **use** a **higher** cost of capital for the next calculation so as to produce a **negative** NPV.

If the NPV and IRR rules give **conflicting** results, it is generally accepted that the recommendation of the **NPV rule** should be **followed**.

(a)   **Project X**

Year	Cash flow $'000	Disc factor 10%	PV $	Disc factor 20%	PV $
0	(200)	1.000	(200,000)	1.000	(200,000)
1	35	0.909	31,815	0.833	29,155
2	80	0.826	66,080	0.694	55,520
3	90	0.751	67,590	0.579	52,110
4	75	0.683	51,225	0.482	36,150
5	20	0.621	12,420	0.402	8,040
			29,130		(19,025)

IRR = 10% + [(29,130/(19,025 + 29,130)) × 10]% = 16.05%

NPV at 10% = $29,130

Project Y

Year	Cash flow $'000	Disc factor 10%	PV $	Disc factor 20%	PV $
0	(200)	1.000	(200,000)	1.000	(200,000)
1	218	0.909	198,162	0.833	181,594
2	10	0.826	8,260	0.694	6,940
3	10	0.751	7,510	0.579	5,790
4	4	0.683	2,732	0.482	1,928
5	3	0.621	1,863	0.402	1,206
			18,527		(2,542)

IRR = 10% + [(18,527/(18,527 + 2,542)) × 10]% = 18.8%

NPV at 10% = $18,527

(b)   **Both** projects are **acceptable** because they generate a positive net present value at the company's cost of capital.

The company should **undertake project X**, because it has the **highest forecast net present value**. Although the internal rate of return for Y is greater, the NPV is generally accepted to be the better performance measure for maximising company wealth.

(c)   The **inconsistency** in the ranking of the two projects – ie the conflicting results obtained with IRR and NPV – has **arisen because of the difference in timing of the cash flows** of the two projects. Project X cash flows occur mainly in the middle three years, whereas project Y generates most of its forecast cash flows in the first year, resulting in a higher IRR.

27 NPV and IRR

> **Top tips**. Make sure you get down the key points (those in bold) when you answer a short ten-mark question. You only have eighteen minutes and expect to write round half a page.

(a) **Net present value (NPV)**

This method **takes account of the timing of cash flows and the time value of the money** invested in the project. Future cash flows are discounted back to their present values. These present values are then summed to derive the net present value of the project. If the result is **positive** then the project is **acceptable**. If **two or more projects** are being compared then the **project with the higher NPV should be chosen**.

The major **difficulty** in calculating the NPV is in **determining the most appropriate discount rate** to use. An organisation may have alternative investment opportunities and the discount rate may be the expected return forgone on these investments. This is therefore the opportunity cost of capital. Alternatively an organisation may have raised a loan to cover the project in question, in which case the discount rate may be the interest rate payable on the loan.

A problem with the use of NPV relates to the **difficulty of explaining it** to a (possibly) non-financial manager. The NPV is **preferable to the payback period**, however, since it quantifies the effect of the timing of cash flows and it takes account of the different magnitudes of investments.

(b) **Internal rate of return**

The internal rate of return (IRR) is the **discount rate which produces a zero net present value** when it is applied to a project's cash flows. If the IRR exceeds the cost of capital then the project is acceptable.

The IRR has the **advantage** of being **more easily understood** than the NPV and it does **take account of the time value of money**.

However the IRR may be confused with the accounting return on capital employed and it **ignores the relative size of investments**. Furthermore, when cash flow patterns are non-conventional there **may be several IRRs**. More importantly, the IRR is **inferior to the NPV for ranking mutually exclusive projects** in order of preference.

Lastly, the IRR **assumes that cash flows from a project can be reinvested to earn a return equal to the IRR of the original project**. The organisation may not have this opportunity.

28 HP

> **Top tips.** In part (a) set out your proforma as we have done for the calculation of capital allowances and the tax effect of those allowances. This keeps workings clear. Do separate workings for payback and NPV as both of these are referred to in the question.

(a) **Initial workings**

1 Capital allowances

	$	Tax @30% $	Year 1 $	Year 2 $	Year 3 $	Year 4 $	Year $
Machine cost	520,000						
WDA year 1, 25%	130,000	39,000	19,500	19,500			
	390,000						
WDA year 2, 25%	97,500	29,250		14,625	14,625		
	292,500						
WDA year 3, 25%	73,125	21,938			10,969	10,969	
	219,375						
Sale for scrap, year 4	50,000						
Balancing allowance	169,375	50,813				25,406	25,4◖
Tax payable on contribution (working 2)			(40,320)	(80,640)	(80,640)	(40,320)	
Tax relief on training costs ($5,000 × 30% × 0.5)			750	750			
Total tax recoverable/(payable)			(20,070)	(45,765)	(55,046)	(3,945)	25,4◖

2 Incremental contribution

Demand per week	12,000	units
Demand per hour (12,000/40)	300	units
Current capacity per hour	200	units
Incremental units per hour (300 – 200)	100	units
Contribution per unit	$1.40	
Hours available (40 hours × 48 weeks)	1,920	
Contribution per annum (100 × $1.40 × 1,920)	$268,800	
Tax @ 30%	$80,640	

Cash flows from profit

Year	Acquisition/ disposal $	Contribution (W2) $	Tax (W1) $	Total cash flow $	Discount factor 10%	Present value $
0	(525,000)			(525,000)	1.000	(525,0◖
1		268,800	(20,070)	248,730	0.909	226,0◖
2		268,800	(45,765)	223,035	0.826	184,2◖
3		268,800	(55,046)	213,754	0.751	160,5◖
4	50,000		(3,945)	46,055	0.683	31,4◖
5			25,407	25,407	0.621	15,7◖
Net present value						93,0◖

Payback period

Year	Cash flow	Cumulative cash flow
	$	$
0	(525,000)	(525,000)
1	248,730	(276,270)
2	223,035	(53,235)
Payback period	= 2 years + ($53,235/$213,754)	
	= 2.25 years, or approximately 2 years 3 months	

The net present value (**NPV**) of the project is **positive** at $93,086 and on that basis it is recommended that the **project should go ahead** after consideration is given to the following.

(i)   The company expects a **payback within two years**. In this instance payback is only reached after approximately 2 years and 3 months but this should be over-ridden by the positive NPV.

(ii)   The $50,000 **recoverable value** should be reconsidered in light of the fact that the current machine would be scrapped at a cost of $20,000.

(iii)   Consideration should be given to **alternatives** such as working overtime on the old machine as a way of alleviating the bottleneck, thus eliminating the need for this investment.

(iv)   It is noted that the new machine would be **operating at 60% capacity**. Is there an alternative machine with a capacity matched to our needs of 300 units per hour at a correspondingly lower price? Alternatively, are there actions we could take which would stimulate demand to be closer to our potential 500 unit capacity (assuming there would be no other bottlenecks) which would make this a more attractive investment?

(b)   There are a number of **reasons why investment decision making will be different when the investment involves a marketing or IT project rather than tangible manufacturing equipment**.

(i)   Although most projects will have specific outflows of cash in the investing period, neither IT nor marketing will necessarily give rise to the same sorts of **identifiable and easily measurable cash flows** as manufacturing equipment. In the case of marketing it may be possible to forecast an expected value of additional revenues as an estimate of future cash inflows, but for IT projects there may not be any easily attributable cash inflow.

(ii)   The **estimation of the expected future** life of an IT investment is made difficult by the rapid rate of technological change in this area, and estimating the time that a marketing campaign's impact may be felt is even more problematic.

(iii)   In terms of approach it is often recommended that NPV is used as a way of assessing IT investments. A **high discount factor** should be used to reflect the fact that any identified cash inflows are subject to a high risk of obsolescence.

(iv)   It is possible that a **negative net present value** will be generated from an IT project. The investment decision will be based on management's assessment of whether the negative present value is a price worth paying for the intangible benefits of the system (increased user-friendliness, faster processing and so on).

(v)   For marketing investments the decision-making approach will depend on the **value of marketing spend**.

(1)   For small marketing campaigns it should be adequate merely to consider whether there are sufficient profits available to absorb the cost of the campaign and still leave an acceptable level of reported profit.

(2)   For larger proposed expenditure an expected value of revenue increases should be calculated and compared to the campaign cost. The length of the campaign and its expected impact will often be so short that no discount factor will need to be applied to calculate the net present value of the campaign.

29 Quarefel plc

> **Top tips**. Set out your workings clearly as we have done in part (a) so that the answer is easy to mark. In parts (b) and (c) you will need to write short, clear paragraphs.

(a) **Net present value calculations**

	Year 0 $'000	Year 1 $'000	Year 2 $'000	Year 3 $'000	Year 4 $'000
Cost of equip/residual value	(2,000)	–	–	–	400.0
Advertising	(1,200)	(1,000.00)	(800.0)	–	–
Fixed costs	–	(600.00)	(600.0)	(600.0)	–
Variable costs (W2)	–	(1,666.68)	(2,500.0)	(1,250.0)	–
Sales revenue (W3)	–	4,000.02	5,500.0	3,125.0	–
Net cash flow	(3,200)	733.34	1,600.0	1,275.0	400.0
Discount factor at 12%	× 1.000	× 0.893	× 0.797	× 0.712	× 0.636
Present value	(3,200)	654.87	1,275.2	907.8	254.4

Net present value = – 3,200 + 654.87 + 1,275.2 + 907.8 + 254.4
= –107.73 ie –$107,730

Additional calculations for IRR

Year	Cash flow $'000	Discount factor 10%	PV $'000
0	(3,200.00)	1.000	(3,200.00)
1	733.34	0.909	666.61
2	1,600.00	0.826	1,321.60
3	1,275.00	0.751	957.53
4	400.00	0.683	273.20
			18.94

Using IRR $= a\% + \left[\dfrac{A}{A-B} \times (b-a) \right]\%$

where a and b are interest rates
A = NPV at rate a
B = NPV at rate b

then **IRR** $= 10\% + \left[\dfrac{18.94}{(18.94 + 107.73)} \times 2 \right]\%$

= 10.299%, say **10.3%**

Workings

1   **Year 1**

P = 70 – 0.15Q
P = $60 in year 1
∴60 = 70 – 0.15Q
∴Q = 66,667 units

Year 2

Change in size of overall market from year 1 to year 2 = ((1,200,000 – 800,000)/800,000) × 100% = 50% increase

∴ Q = 66,667 × 150% = 100,000 units

Year 3

Change in size of overall market from year 2 to year 3 = ((600,000 – 1,200,000)/1,200,000) × 100% = 50% decrease

∴Q = 100,000 × 50% = 50,000 units

2 **Variable costs** (using results of working 1)

   Year 1:   66,667 units × $25 = $1,666,675
   Year 2: 100,000 units × $25 = $2,500,000
   Year 3:   50,000 units × $25 = $1,250,000

3 **Year 1**

   Revenue = 66,667 units × $60 = $4,000,020

   Year 2

   P = 70 – (0.15 × 100) = $55
   Revenue = 100,000 units × $55 = $5,500,000

   Year 3

   P = 70 – (0.15 × 50) = $62.50

   Revenue = 50,000 units × $62.50 = $3,125,000

(b) Remember that you only need to discuss three considerations.

   (i)   **Impact on employee morale**. Most investments affect employees' prospects, sometimes for the better, sometimes for the worse. A new cafeteria for employees would have a favourable impact, for example.

   (ii) **Impact on the community**. This is a particularly important consideration if the investment results in loss of jobs, more jobs or elimination of small businesses.

   (iii) **Impact on the environment**. The opening of a new mine, the development of products which create environmentally-harmful waste and so on all have an impact on the environment. This can affect an organisation's image and reputation and hence its long-term growth and survival prospects. Some of these environmental effects can also impact directly on project cash flows because organisations have to pay fines, incur legal costs, incur disposal and cleanup costs and so on.

   (iv) **Ethical issues**. Some investments might be legal but might not be in line with the ethics and code of conduct demanded by various stakeholder groups.

   (v)   **Learning**. Many investments, particularly those which advance an organisation's technology, provide opportunities for learning. For example, investment in new computerised equipment to revolutionise a production process would enable an organisation to better use highly-technical production methods.

(c) The margin of error approach to sensitivity analysis assesses how responsive the project's NPV (or payback period or ARR) is to changes in the variables used to calculate that NPV (or payback period or ARR).

   This basic approach involves calculating the project's NPV under alternative assumptions to determine how sensitive it is to changing conditions, thereby indicating those variables to which the NPV is most sensitive (critical variables). It shows the extent to which those variables may change before the investment decision would change.

30 Elsewhere

Top tips. This question is split into five parts so you have plenty of opportunity to earn marks. Part (a) uses information straight from the table in the question. Part (b) is a lot harder but you will need to practise these decision trees. Refer back to our tips in the chapter for drawing a tree if you have forgotten. Look at how we answered part (c)(i) as a simple equation.

(a)   The expected value of profit is calculated as follows.

Profit $'000	Probability	Expected profit $'000
800	0.5	400
100	0.2	20
(300)	0.3	(90)
		330

(b)   (i)

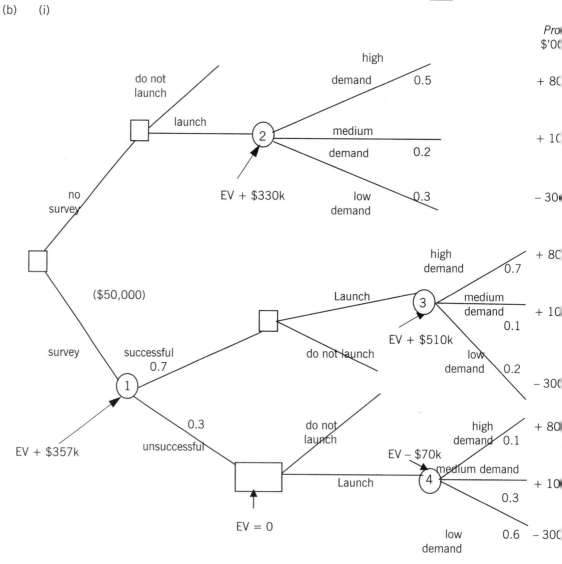

Key: ▢ – decision point   ◯ – outcome point

Expected value of profit

Profit	Probabilities outcome point			EV of profit outcome point		
	2	3	4	2	3	4
$'000				$'000	$'000	$'000
800	0.5	0.7	0.1	400	560	80
100	0.2	0.1	0.3	20	10	30
(300)	0.3	0.2	0.6	(90)	(60)	(180)
				330	510	(70)

(ii) The record company should not commission the survey because the expected value of profit without the survey is $330,000. This is greater than the expected value of profit of $307,000 ($357,000 – $50,000) with the survey.

(c) (i) To find the maximum the company should pay for the survey, solve:

EV (survey) = EV (no survey)
$357K - survey cost = $330K

The maximum that the company should pay for this survey is $27,000.

(ii) Whenever a decision is made when the outcome of the decision is uncertain, there will always be some doubt that the correct decision has been taken. If a decision is based on selecting the option with the highest EV of profit, it can be assumed that in the long run, that is, with enough repetition, the decision so selected will give the highest average profit. But if the decision involves a once-only outcome, there will be a risk that in retrospect, it will be seen that the wrong decision was taken.

A decision tree is a simplified representation of reality, and it may omit some possible decision options, or it may simplify the possible outcomes. For example, in this question, 'success' and 'failure' are two extreme outcomes, whereas a variety of outcomes between success and failure may be possible. The decision tree is therefore likely to be a simplification of reality.

APPENDIX
MATHEMATICAL TABLES

632

PRESENT VALUE TABLE

Present value of £1 ie $(1+r)^{-n}$ where r = interest rate, n = number of periods until payment or receipt.

Periods (n)	Interest rates (r) 1%	2%	3%	4%	5%	6%	7%	8%	9%	10%
1	0.990	0.980	0.971	0.962	0.952	0.943	0.935	0.926	0.917	0.909
2	0.980	0.961	0.943	0.925	0.907	0.890	0.873	0.857	0.842	0.826
3	0.971	0.942	0.915	0.889	0.864	0.840	0.816	0.794	0.772	0.751
4	0.961	0.924	0.888	0.855	0.823	0.792	0.763	0.735	0.708	0.683
5	0.951	0.906	0.863	0.822	0.784	0.747	0.713	0.681	0.650	0.621
6	0.942	0.888	0.837	0.790	0.746	0.705	0.666	0.630	0.596	0.564
7	0.933	0.871	0.813	0.760	0.711	0.665	0.623	0.583	0.547	0.513
8	0.923	0.853	0.789	0.731	0.677	0.627	0.582	0.540	0.502	0.467
9	0.914	0.837	0.766	0.703	0.645	0.592	0.544	0.500	0.460	0.424
10	0.905	0.820	0.744	0.676	0.614	0.558	0.508	0.463	0.422	0.386
11	0.896	0.804	0.722	0.650	0.585	0.527	0.475	0.429	0.388	0.350
12	0.887	0.788	0.701	0.625	0.557	0.497	0.444	0.397	0.356	0.319
13	0.879	0.773	0.681	0.601	0.530	0.469	0.415	0.368	0.326	0.290
14	0.870	0.758	0.661	0.577	0.505	0.442	0.388	0.340	0.299	0.263
15	0.861	0.743	0.642	0.555	0.481	0.417	0.362	0.315	0.275	0.239
16	0.853	0.728	0.623	0.534	0.458	0.394	0.339	0.292	0.252	0.218
17	0.844	0.714	0.605	0.513	0.436	0.371	0.317	0.270	0.231	0.198
18	0.836	0.700	0.587	0.494	0.416	0.350	0.296	0.250	0.212	0.180
19	0.828	0.686	0.570	0.475	0.396	0.331	0.277	0.232	0.194	0.164
20	0.820	0.673	0.554	0.456	0.377	0.312	0.258	0.215	0.178	0.149

Periods (n)	Interest rates (r) 11%	12%	13%	14%	15%	16%	17%	18%	19%	20%
1	0.901	0.893	0.885	0.877	0.870	0.862	0.855	0.847	0.840	0.833
2	0.812	0.797	0.783	0.769	0.756	0.743	0.731	0.718	0.706	0.694
3	0.731	0.712	0.693	0.675	0.658	0.641	0.624	0.609	0.593	0.579
4	0.659	0.636	0.613	0.592	0.572	0.552	0.534	0.516	0.499	0.482
5	0.593	0.567	0.543	0.519	0.497	0.476	0.456	0.437	0.419	0.402
6	0.535	0.507	0.480	0.456	0.432	0.410	0.390	0.370	0.352	0.335
7	0.482	0.452	0.425	0.400	0.376	0.354	0.333	0.314	0.296	0.279
8	0.434	0.404	0.376	0.351	0.327	0.305	0.285	0.266	0.249	0.233
9	0.391	0.361	0.333	0.308	0.284	0.263	0.243	0.225	0.209	0.194
10	0.352	0.322	0.295	0.270	0.247	0.227	0.208	0.191	0.176	0.162
11	0.317	0.287	0.261	0.237	0.215	0.195	0.178	0.162	0.148	0.135
12	0.286	0.257	0.231	0.208	0.187	0.168	0.152	0.137	0.124	0.112
13	0.258	0.229	0.204	0.182	0.163	0.145	0.130	0.116	0.104	0.093
14	0.232	0.205	0.181	0.160	0.141	0.125	0.111	0.099	0.088	0.078
15	0.209	0.183	0.160	0.140	0.123	0.108	0.095	0.084	0.074	0.065
16	0.188	0.163	0.141	0.123	0.107	0.093	0.081	0.071	0.062	0.054
17	0.170	0.146	0.125	0.108	0.093	0.080	0.069	0.060	0.052	0.045
18	0.153	0.130	0.111	0.095	0.081	0.069	0.059	0.051	0.044	0.038
19	0.138	0.116	0.098	0.083	0.070	0.060	0.051	0.043	0.037	0.031
20	0.124	0.104	0.087	0.073	0.061	0.051	0.043	0.037	0.031	0.026

CUMULATIVE PRESENT VALUE TABLE

This table shows the present value of £1 per annum, receivable or payable at the end of each year for n years $\frac{1-(1+r)^{-n}}{r}$.

Periods (n)	Interest rates (r)									
	1%	2%	3%	4%	5%	6%	7%	8%	9%	10%
1	0.990	0.980	0.971	0.962	0.952	0.943	0.935	0.926	0.917	0.909
2	1.970	1.942	1.913	1.886	1.859	1.833	1.808	1.783	1.759	1.736
3	2.941	2.884	2.829	2.775	2.723	2.673	2.624	2.577	2.531	2.487
4	3.902	3.808	3.717	3.630	3.546	3.465	3.387	3.312	3.240	3.170
5	4.853	4.713	4.580	4.452	4.329	4.212	4.100	3.993	3.890	3.791
6	5.795	5.601	5.417	5.242	5.076	4.917	4.767	4.623	4.486	4.355
7	6.728	6.472	6.230	6.002	5.786	5.582	5.389	5.206	5.033	4.868
8	7.652	7.325	7.020	6.733	6.463	6.210	5.971	5.747	5.535	5.335
9	8.566	8.162	7.786	7.435	7.108	6.802	6.515	6.247	5.995	5.759
10	9.471	8.983	8.530	8.111	7.722	7.360	7.024	6.710	6.418	6.145
11	10.368	9.787	9.253	8.760	8.306	7.887	7.499	7.139	6.805	6.495
12	11.255	10.575	9.954	9.385	8.863	8.384	7.943	7.536	7.161	6.814
13	12.134	11.348	10.635	9.986	9.394	8.853	8.358	7.904	7.487	7.103
14	13.004	12.106	11.296	10.563	9.899	9.295	8.745	8.244	7.786	7.367
15	13.865	12.849	11.938	11.118	10.380	9.712	9.108	8.559	8.061	7.606
16	14.718	13.578	12.561	11.652	10.838	10.106	9.447	8.851	8.313	7.824
17	15.562	14.292	13.166	12.166	11.274	10.477	9.763	9.122	8.544	8.022
18	16.398	14.992	13.754	12.659	11.690	10.828	10.059	9.372	8.756	8.201
19	17.226	15.679	14.324	13.134	12.085	11.158	10.336	9.604	8.950	8.365
20	18.046	16.351	14.878	13.590	12.462	11.470	10.594	9.818	9.129	8.514

Periods (n)	Interest rates (r)									
	11%	12%	13%	14%	15%	16%	17%	18%	19%	20%
1	0.901	0.893	0.885	0.877	0.870	0.862	0.855	0.847	0.840	0.833
2	1.713	1.690	1.668	1.647	1.626	1.605	1.585	1.566	1.547	1.528
3	2.444	2.402	2.361	2.322	2.283	2.246	2.210	2.174	2.140	2.106
4	3.102	3.037	2.974	2.914	2.855	2.798	2.743	2.690	2.639	2.589
5	3.696	3.605	3.517	3.433	3.352	3.274	3.199	3.127	3.058	2.991
6	4.231	4.111	3.998	3.889	3.784	3.685	3.589	3.498	3.410	3.326
7	4.712	4.564	4.423	4.288	4.160	4.039	3.922	3.812	3.706	3.605
8	5.146	4.968	4.799	4.639	4.487	4.344	4.207	4.078	3.954	3.837
9	5.537	5.328	5.132	4.946	4.772	4.607	4.451	4.303	4.163	4.031
10	5.889	5.650	5.426	5.216	5.019	4.833	4.659	4.494	4.339	4.192
11	6.207	5.938	5.687	5.453	5.234	5.029	4.836	4.656	4.486	4.327
12	6.492	6.194	5.918	5.660	5.421	5.197	4.988	4.793	4.611	4.439
13	6.750	6.424	6.122	5.842	5.583	5.342	5.118	4.910	4.715	4.533
14	6.982	6.628	6.302	6.002	5.724	5.468	5.229	5.008	4.802	4.611
15	7.191	6.811	6.462	6.142	5.847	5.575	5.324	5.092	4.876	4.675
16	7.379	6.974	6.604	6.265	5.954	5.668	5.405	5.162	4.938	4.730
17	7.549	7.120	6.729	6.373	6.047	5.749	5.475	5.222	4.990	4.775
18	7.702	7.250	6.840	6.467	6.128	5.818	5.534	5.273	5.033	4.812
19	7.839	7.366	6.938	6.550	6.198	5.877	5.584	5.316	5.070	4.843
20	7.963	7.469	7.025	6.623	6.259	5.929	5.628	5.353	5.101	4.870

Probability

$A \cup B$ = A **or** B. $A \cap B$ = A **and** B (overlap). $P(B|A)$ = probability of B, **given** A.

Rules of addition

If A and B are *mutually exclusive*: $P(A \cup B) = P(A) + P(B)$

If A and B are **not** mutually exclusive: $P(A \cup B) = P(A) + P(B) - P(A \cap B)$

Rules of multiplication

If A and B are *independent*: $P(A \cap B) = P(A) * P(B)$

If A and B are **not** independent: $P(A \cap B) = P(A) * P(B|A)$

$E(X) = \Sigma$ (probability * payoff)

Descriptive statistics

Arithmetic mean

$$\bar{x} = \frac{\Sigma x}{n} \quad \text{or} \quad \bar{x} = \frac{\Sigma fx}{\Sigma f} \quad \text{(frequency distribution)}$$

Standard deviation

$$SD = \sqrt{\frac{\Sigma(x - \bar{x})^2}{n}}$$

$$SD = \sqrt{\frac{\Sigma fx^2}{\Sigma f} - \bar{x}^2} \quad \text{(frequency distribution)}$$

Index numbers

Price relative = $100 * P_1 / P_0$

Quantity relative = $100 * Q_1 / Q_0$

Price: $\dfrac{\Sigma W \times P_1 / P_0}{\Sigma W} \times 100$ where W denotes weights

Quantity: $\dfrac{\Sigma W \times Q_1 / Q_0}{\Sigma W} \times 100$ where W denotes weights

Time series

Additive model: Series = Trend + Seasonal + Random
Multiplicative model: Series = Trend * Seasonal * Random

Financial mathematics

Compound Interest (Values and Sums)

Future Value of S, of a sum X, invested for n periods, compounded at r% interest:

$$S = X[1+r]^n$$

Annuity

Present value of an annuity of £1 per annum receivable or payable, for n years, commencing in one year, discounted at r% per annum:

$$PV = \frac{1}{r}\left[1 - \frac{1}{[1+r]^n}\right]$$

Perpetuity

Present value of £1 per annum, payable or receivable in perpetuity, commencing in one year discounted at r% per annum

$$PV = \frac{1}{r}$$

Learning curve

$Y_x = aX^b$

Where Y_x = the cumulative average time per unit to produce X units
           a = the time required to produce the first unit of output
           X = the cumulative number of units
           b = the index of learning

The exponent b is defined as the log of the learning curve improvement rate divided by log 2.

Inventory management

Economic Order Quantity

$$EOQ = \sqrt{\frac{2C_oD}{C_h}}$$

Where C_o = cost of placing an order
           C_h = cost of holding one unit in inventory for one year
           D = annual demand

INDEX

Notes

Review Form – Paper P1 Performance Operations (6/11)

Please help us to ensure that the CIMA learning materials we produce remain as accurate and user-friendly as possible. We cannot promise to answer every submission we receive, but we do promise that it will be read and taken into account when we up-date this Study Text.

Name: _____ Address: _____

_____

_____

How have you used this Study Text? *(Tick one box only)*	**During the past six months do you recall seeing/receiving any of the following?** *(Tick as many boxes as are relevant)*
☐ Home study (book only)	☐ Our advertisement in *Financial Management*
☐ On a course: college _____	☐ Our advertisement in *Pass*
☐ With 'correspondence' package	☐ Our advertisement in *PQ*
☐ Other _____	☐ Our brochure with a letter through the post
	☐ Our website www.bpp.com
Why did you decide to purchase this Study Text? *(Tick one box only)*	**Which (if any) aspects of our advertising do you find useful?** *(Tick as many boxes as are relevant)*
☐ Have used BPP Texts in the past	☐ Prices and publication dates of new editions
☐ Recommendation by friend/colleague	☐ Information on Text content
☐ Recommendation by a lecturer at college	☐ Facility to order books off-the-page
☐ Saw information on BPP website	☐ None of the above
☐ Saw advertising	
☐ Other _____	

Which BPP products have you used?

Text	☑	*Success CD*	☐
Kit	☐	*i-Pass*	☐
Passcards	☐	*Interactive Passcards*	☐

Your ratings, comments and suggestions would be appreciated on the following areas.

	Very useful	Useful	Not useful
Introductory section	☐	☐	☐
Chapter introductions	☐	☐	☐
Key terms	☐	☐	☐
Quality of explanations	☐	☐	☐
Case studies and other examples	☐	☐	☐
Exam skills and alerts	☐	☐	☐
Questions and answers in each chapter	☐	☐	☐
Section summaries and chapter roundups	☐	☐	☐
Quick quizzes	☐	☐	☐
Question Bank	☐	☐	☐
Answer Bank	☐	☐	☐
OT Bank	☐	☐	☐
Index	☐	☐	☐

Overall opinion of this Study Text	Excellent ☐	Good ☐	Adequate ☐	Poor ☐

Do you intend to continue using BPP products?   Yes ☐   No ☐

On the reverse of this page are noted particular areas of the text about which we would welcome your feedback. The BPP Learning Media author of this edition can be e-mailed at: heatherfreer@bpp.com

Please return this form to: Adrian Sims, CIMA Publishing Manager, BPP Learning Media Ltd, FREEPOST, London, W12 8BR

Review Form (continued)

TELL US WHAT YOU THINK

Please note any further comments and suggestions/errors below. For example, was the text accurate, readable, concise, user-friendly and comprehensive?